MONEY,

FINANCIAL INSTITUTIONS, AND THE ECONOMY

Irwin Publications in Economics

Advisory Editor Martin S. Feldstein Harvard University

MONEY,

FINANCIAL INSTITUTIONS, AND THE ECONOMY

Paul A. Meyer
Department of Economics
University of Maryland

1986

IRWIN

Homewood, Illinois 60430

Part of this book was previously published under the title
Monetary Economics and Financial Markets.

ISBN 0-256-03524-5

Library of Congress Catalog Card No. 85–80339

Printed in the United States of America

1 2 3 4 5 6 7 8 9 0 D 3 2 1 0 9 8 7 6

For Brigitte, Chip, and Carl

Preface

The junior-senior level course traditionally called Money and Banking is among the most diversely taught college courses. It ranges from (a) disguised macroeconomics courses for budding theorists to (z) disguised financial management courses for budding loan officers. This book was written for the overwhelming majority of courses somewhere in between these extremes. I have followed the advice of all my English teachers, who always told me to write on those topics and for those people that I know best. I am an economist; I regularly teach Economics 430, Money and Banking; most of my students are business majors. These facts and my English teachers' advice have led to a book that blends economic theory with institutional and historical material in order to help students understand our complex economy.

Part Three is one of the highlights of the book. I believe that this book surpasses nearly every other book in drawing the relationships among regulatory policies and financial structure. Look at the two mini-chapters, Chapter 13–A, "The Case for and against Multiple Bank Regulators," and Chapter 13–B, "Bank Holding Companies and Product Markets." In addition, there are two full chapters, Chapter 14, "Nationwide Branch Banking?" and Chapter 15, "Deposit Insurance and Policies to Prevent Bank Failures." These very topical chapters illustrate that this book is not a 1960s book warmed over. The important regulatory and structural issues change over time. However, the basic economics of regulation remains more or less constant. Our recognition of this fact explains the lead-off chapter to Part Three, namely, "General Reasons for Regulation, with Specific Applications to Banking."

The large size of this book is one obvious consequence of its appeal to diversely taught courses. Less obvious but equally true, the book was designed to permit flexible use. There may be either more monetary theory or institutional material than you care to use, but any "excess" will not impede your getting to the material you want. Numerous chapters can be omitted without loss of continuity, and the chapters can readily be reordered to suit your personal course.

Flexibility begins in Part One. Chapter 2 explains some recent financial innovations and defines money. A logical step after defining money is an analysis of its determinants. Chapters 3 and 4 begin the analysis by explaining the deposit creation process and the money supply multiplier. The analysis of the money supply is not completed, however, until Chapter 17, where we explain the sources of the monetary base. The three money supply chapters are widely separated in order to sustain greater student interest. Instructors who object to the analytical interruption can readily cover the three chapters consecutively. Others can retain the division but place Chapters 3 and 4 after Chapter 11. Introduction of the deposit creation process at an early stage does exemplify the economic viewpoint that banks and other depositories are unique because they create money. More financially oriented courses which stress that depositories are intermediaries can cover Chapters 3 and 4 after the comprehensive coverage of financial institutions, markets, and instruments in Chapters 5 through 11.

Part Two contains several unique features. Chapter 5 discusses direct finance, investment banking, and stock exchanges. These topics are important and interest students. Nevertheless, other money and banking books typically dismiss them. Chapters 6 and 7 on interest rates are distinguished by presentation of the material from the personal finance viewpoint of learning to make a good investment decision. The idea of learning a *theory* in order to *play* the yield curve allows coverage of the term structure in greater depth without loss of students' attention. Coverage of a few topics in depth gives students an appreciation of the complexity of our economic and financial system. Chapter 11 illustrates well our belief that it is not enough to know facts; they must be understood. The numerous features of the Monetary Control Act of 1980, the Garn-St. Germain Act of 1982, and other less comprehensive legislative and regulatory reforms are related to disintermediation and other problems which brought depositories to the brink of bankruptcy.

Chapters 16 through 20, Part Four, concern central banking. In these chapters, as throughout the rest of the book, history and theory are presented as aids to understanding current policy. Even students predisposed against history enjoy Chapter 16 because it is *not* a collection of semi-related musty facts. The analysis of contemporaneous versus lagged reserve accounting in Chapter 18 links ongoing research to current policy issues. Chapter 19 strengthens this sense of the importance of history and theory by using both to explain the two-stage approach to policy and the intermediate target problem. The quotes of Friedman, Modigliani, and Samuelson show that evaluations of the past, not to mention prescriptions for the future, are extremely difficult.

Monetary theory is the subject of Part Five. I do discuss the issues that divide Keynesians and monetarists. For example, see Chapter 27. However, the widely accepted viewpoint that money systematically affects aggregate demand, which in turn affects output in the short run and prices in the long run, implies that Keynesian and neoclassical economics are *complementary* more often than competitive. Both the short-run Keynesian model with output adjustments and the long-run neoclassical model with price adjustments are necessary to understand the response of the economy to monetary policy. In other words, the static Keynesian and neoclassical models are viewed as jointly approximating a complex dynamic theory of economic fluctuations which is beyond the scope of a textbook. The rational expectations approach is presented briefly as a challenge to the traditional viewpoint.

Part Five, more than the other parts, demonstrates that the book accommodates a wide range of students as well as teaching styles. I assume the student took the principles course but by now has forgotten much of it. Given this assumption and the inconvenience of having to thumb through a principles text, most topics are developed pretty much from scratch. For example, Chapter 24 on the basic Keynesian C + I + G = y model is clearly a review chapter. While we may begin at a low level, we methodically reach advanced material. Some chapters in this part have up to three challenging appendixes for the best students. Use of appendixes, footnotes, and sections marked with an asterisk lets other students concentrate on the fundamentals. Placement of appendixes immediately after the end-of-chapter questions or at the end of the book stresses the optional nature of the appendixes.

Domestic and international policy issues are covered in Part Six. I was determined to avoid the all-too-frequent practice of ending a book with unrelated international material dangling worse than a participle. International material was interspersed in earlier chapters. This greatly facilitated the integration of the *three* international chapters with the rest of the book. Chapter 31 on international banking is a clear extension of Chapters 8 and 9, where Eurodollars and changes in bank operations are discussed. IS–LM was used in the theory section. IS–LM reappears when fixed and flexible exchange rates are evaluated in Chapter 33. The final chapter, "Budget Deficits, Monetary Policy, and Exchange Rates," provides a base for lively discussion in the quietest of classrooms.

To cut the book by five chapters, theoretical courses can omit Chapters 8, 9, 16, 17, and 31. Institutional courses can omit Chapters 20, 23, 27, 30, and 33 and, as explained earlier, reorder Chapters 3 and 4. The accompanying *Instructors Manual* offers more detailed suggestions for use of the book. The *Manual* is a real teaching resource. Within its more than *200 pages* are answers to the questions at the end of the chapters, over 1,400 multiple choice and true-false questions, and several problem sets! A computerized test bank also accompanies the book.

Some of the material in the book appeared earlier in my *Monetary Economics and Financial Markets*.

To the Student

To help you in the learning process, the book makes substantial use of italics. My italics or your underlines do pinpoint the important material that should be reviewed. However, they contribute little toward understanding arguments in the first place. The complexity of some material demands careful reading and active learning. Begin each chapter by reading the introductory section up to the first boldfaced head. Then preview the remaining material by reading the end-of-chapter questions, which always precede the optional appendixes, if any. Return to the first head and complete the chapter. Active learning occurs when you now answer the questions. They basically ask *you* to summarize the fundamental issues developed. The questions generally cover the text in sequence. Your search for the answer to, say, question 4 is limited by the location of the answers to questions 3 and 5. The "Summary" section preceding the questions often contains food for further thought but definitely is not comprehensive. A comprehensive summary would defeat the active-learning objective of the questions.

Acknowledgements

I am deeply indebted to a large number of people for their comments and suggestions, which range from the thought-provoking one-liner to a detailed review of the entire manuscript. I especially want to thank Robert Connolly (University of North Carolina, Greensboro), Dannie Harrison

(Murray State University), Thomas Havrilesky (Duke University), James Johannes (University of Wisconsin, Madison), Stephen Miller (University of Connecticut), John Shannon (Suffolk University), and Roger Watson (FDIC). Gail Huh and Paul Wonnacott read parts of the manuscript and as my colleagues helped create a pleasant environment at the University of Maryland. Most of the book was written at home. Pleasant as the environment at Maryland is, I happily and proudly acknowledge that the environment at home is much more pleasant, thanks to my loving wife, Brigitte. Chip and Carl also do a good job.

Paul A. Meyer

Contents

PART FOUR
Central Banking

PART SIX
Domestic and International Policy Issues

(COST PUSH)

APPENDIXES

Introduction

1

The contents of this book reflect the answer to a fundamental question: why study monetary economics and financial institutions? There are many other specialities in economics. Why has "Money and Finance" long been the most popular upper-level economics course? These questions have a double-barreled answer.

a. Money, banks, and other financial variables and institutions can be *controlled by the monetary authorities,* particularly since the passage of the Depository Institutions Deregulation and Monetary Control Act (MCA) of 1980, the 1984 revised reserve requirements, and other recent financial legislation.
b. Money, banks, and other financial variables and institutions significantly *influence the achievement of economic goals.*

Both parts must be shown to be true to justify an entire book on money and finance. Indeed, nothing deserves prolonged discussion unless it "matters" and can be controlled. Why don't we have books on the economics of straight and safety pins? The topic is not sufficiently important. Years ago the sun spot theory of the business cycle was thought to be correct. The theory alleged that sun spots strongly influence the weather, which in turn strongly influences output. While the importance of the weather as a determinant of booms and busts surely has declined with the transformation from agrarian to industrial economies, even in its heyday the sun spot theory was trumpeted in reverential tones but quickly dismissed. Why? Although sun spots were important, no one could control them. The first part of this book largely concerns monetary control, and the second part demonstrates the important effect of money on achieving major economic goals.

Our claim that money matters is not all encompassing in at least two respects. First, money matters, but so do other things. The importance of money does not imply the uselessness of everything else. True: money matters. False: only money matters. Second, money matters, but only in certain areas. The importance of money in achieving certain highly desirable goals does not imply money can cure all our ills. While it is wrong to believe that money is the root of all evil, still money cannot eliminate pollution, discrimination, and other evils. True: money matters. False: only money matters.

Similarly, our claim that money and other financial variables can be controlled by the Federal Reserve, the United States monetary authority, does not imply that *only* the Federal Reserve influences money and finance. We will spend much time showing how you, banks, and the public in general can *potentially* influence the nation's money supply directly. The Federal Reserve's job is to counteract your actions and keep the financial variables on target. The Fed (short for Federal Reserve) will fail in its job if the target is unreasonably small. For example, if the target is a money supply within \$200 of \$550 *billion*, the Fed surely will be wide of the mark. On the other hand, a money supply target within \$200 *billion* of \$550 *billion* would be hit without any difficulty whatsoever. Given this, a few issues in the monetary control area are: (*a*) What policy tools are available to the Fed? (*b*) How can the tools be improved so that the Fed can hit smaller targets? (*c*) What is the size of the minimum target range the Fed must hit before it can claim control? and (*d*) Assuming the Fed cannot control everything, what financial variables should the Fed target and attempt to control in order to achieve its ultimate goals?

Goals of Monetary Policy

We primarily shall analyze the effects of money and finance on three major economic goals. First and foremost, society wants the output of newly produced goods and services to equal productive capacity. In other words, *actual GNP should equal potential GNP*. Goods and services are not produced out of thin air. Labor, capital, and land must be acquired by that mysterious person, the entrepreneur, who transforms the factors of production into goods and services. Labor is by far the most important factor of production as measured by its share of total income. Thus, the high GNP goal more or less has a mirror image—high employment or, equivalently, low unemployment. The goal of high GNP and low unemployment is so obvious that it needs no justification.

Price stability or the lack of inflation is the second goal. All inflations are at least partially unexpected, and all unexpected events misallocate resources and redistribute income. For example, if the exact path of a tornado were certain, tornadoes would cause virtually no damage. No one knowingly builds in the path of a tornado. Unable to predict tornadoes, we observe after the event that construction occurred at the wrong sites, and resources were misallocated. From the viewpoint of resource allocation, unexpected inflation is more devastating than tornadoes. Unexpected inflation also redistributes income because the degree of unexpectedness varies. An event may be predictable to person A, mildly surprising to B, and totally unexpected to C. Those creditors who did not forecast double-digit inflation and lent at a "high" 6 percent rate of interest effectively subsidized debtors. Those who confidently expected double-digit inflation may have purchased durable goods instead of lending at a "low" 6 percent rate of interest. Even if inflation suddenly is forecast correctly by everyone, variations in reaction times misallocate resources and redistribute income. For example, retired people bound by long-term contracts must resign themselves to impoverishment while the wages of young, uncommitted workers are escalated for inflation.

Society not only wants to reach the *current* productive capacity/full-employment GNP (the first goal), but it wants capacity to grow over time. *The third goal is a high rate of growth of output achieved through the expansion of productive capacity.*[1] Generally, capacity expansion occurs when saving increases and investors earn a high rate of return. Higher saving and lower consumption free resources for firms' investment. Growth rates rise when these resources flow to those particular investors who earn the highest rate of return. Note that higher saving does not use *more* resources. Gone are the days when any rapid growth rate, however achieved, is justified. We do not need more commodities if their production denudes the earth. Conservation and pollution abatement regulations, which are relatively recent phenomena, attest to our increasing concern for the environment and our willingness to sacrifice quantity for quality.

Other goals are strongly influenced by money and the financial system. For example, balance of payments equilibrium in a fixed exchange rate system or exchange rate stability in a floating rate system is sometimes listed as another goal of policy. Low interest rates are an independent goal of many citizens and the Treasury. Indeed, during the 1940s, the Federal Reserve gave way to the Treasury and pegged interest rates at extremely low levels, thereby largely sacrificing price stability. Reduction of the government deficit is perhaps the most recent major macroeconomic

---

[1]The growth of actual output can mechanically be attributed to the closure of any gap between current and potential output or to the change of potential output over time. The failure by many journalists and politicians to distinguish between the two sources of growth often causes full employment and growth to be confounded. A high growth rate often is synonymous with getting to full employment, which we already acknowledge is a goal. We make a sharp distinction between the two sources of growth.

goal. To be sure, government deficits are primarily determined by government spending and tax policies, but monetary policy definitely influences the deficit and, in turn, is influenced by it. While we will not ignore these three secondary goals, we emphasize the relationship between money, output, prices, and growth.

The Financial System

As indicated earlier, the first part of this book analyzes the Federal Reserve's tools and monetary control. Of course, such an analysis requires knowledge of the behavior and structure of financial institutions and markets. We must have at least a rough idea how banks operate before evaluating Federal Reserve control. Knowledge of financial institutions also serves a second purpose. *An efficient financial system is virtually indispensable for economic growth.* For example, the economies of large-scale production are realized only because investment bankers sell stocks to thousands of people nationwide. The genius of Thomas Edison and Alexander Graham Bell would have been wasted had they relied exclusively on their own resources to build electric and telephone companies. Channeling funds and resources from savers to investors occurs in financial markets and institutions, of which commercial banks are the largest. The financial system enables savers, who would have earned low rates of return if forced to invest and manage businesses, to transfer resources to investors. Encouraged by the higher return they can earn by lending, savers save more. In a free, capitalistic financial system the investors who acquire the resources generally are those who need the resources and are able to earn the highest rate of return. It is these investors/borrowers who are able to offer the savers/lenders the highest rate of interest. *Our financial system enhances both the amount of saving and investment and the return earned.* While the effects of the financial system on the efficient allocation of resources and growth will be analyzed explicitly quite briefly, the relatively long description of banks and other financial institutions is implicit recognition of the importance of both the growth goal and the role played by financial institutions in its achievement.

By incorporating the growth goal with monetary control issues in the first part of the book, the latter part concentrates primarily on the money, output, and price connection and secondarily on the money, exchange rate, interest rate, and government deficits connection. The effects of money on one goal, assuming the other goal remains constant, are analyzed first. This simplifying assumption is dropped toward the end where we simultaneously determine output and prices. The high output (low unemployment) goal will receive greater attention. While the desirability of price stability should not be played down, this goal gets second billing because the precise effects of inflation on the allocation of resources and distribution of income are not constant over time but depend on tax laws, the source of inflation, and other factors. For example, indexing social security payments certainly has reduced, but not eliminated, the hardship of inflation on the elderly. Oil producers were hurt by the inflation of the late 1960s but benefited handsomely from the late 1970s inflation, for which they were partially to blame. In short, the effects of inflation are not easily generalized.

Reasons for Disagreement about Monetary Relationships

The first part of the book is relatively uncontroversial. There exists substantial agreement about (*a*) the operational methods of the financial system, (*b*) the importance of financial institutions in the transfer of resources and economic growth, and (*c*) the effect of various government policies on money, interest rates, and other financial variables. The disagreements that do exist usually are aired in arcane academic journals or in business publications with a relatively selective audience, for example, *The Wall Street Journal* and *Business Week*. The material in the latter part of the book is much more controversial and widely discussed. The frequent but brief analyses of money, employment, inflation, and the deficit presented in evening news programs and the popular press are heatedly rehashed in beer halls, bowling alleys, and hot tubs. Disagreement appears so widespread that some readers may wonder if they should read this or any other economics book or heed the advice of economic consultants. Given the very real possibility of this wonderment, we should evaluate at least briefly the sources of this disagreement.

Noneconomic Reasons for Monetary Disagreements

Economics is not in a state of total disarray. Much of the apparent disagreement about monetary economics is just that—apparent, and not real. Precisely because money and finance are thought to influence significantly the achievement of important goals, monetary relationships are discussed on TV and in the popular press, as just mentioned. Commercial TV and the press do seek to inform the public. This requires the presentation of some minority opinions. More important, however, the media are owned by profit-seeking business executives who gain from controversy. How do newspaper owners and TV moguls get the public to buy their newspapers and watch their programs? Do they present the tightly reasoned and quite similar statements of three colorless economists? Or do they offer the understandable but incomplete analysis of three economists—one, the former chief Democratic advisor; another, a well-known and colorful conservative Republican; and the third, a slightly outrageous but well-paid professional advocate of lost causes? While my description of the second panel somewhat exaggerates the typical economics panel, the media, from which many get their impressions of the economics profession, rarely present the first type of panel. When three economists express three different opinions, the public may believe that the economics profession, like Gaul, is divided in three. In fact, one economist may represent a full 90 percent of the profession.

A significant proportion of what seems to be monetary and general economic disagreement is, in fact, political disagreement. We can think of the study of economics as learning the functional relationships among policy and nonpolicy variables and the options available. Politics concerns the determination of the desired set of values for the variables and selection of a specific option. In terms of Figure 1–1, which graphs the relationship between two goal variables simply called x and y, the economic problem involves discovery of the position and shape of the curve and the magnitude of its shift in response to policy. The political process selects a point on a given curve. Now, economists are often wont to say, "There is no such thing as a free lunch," and economics is often defined as the science that deals with scarcity. Assuming x and y are either two "goods" (such as apples and oranges) or two "bads" (such as unem-

FIGURE 1–1

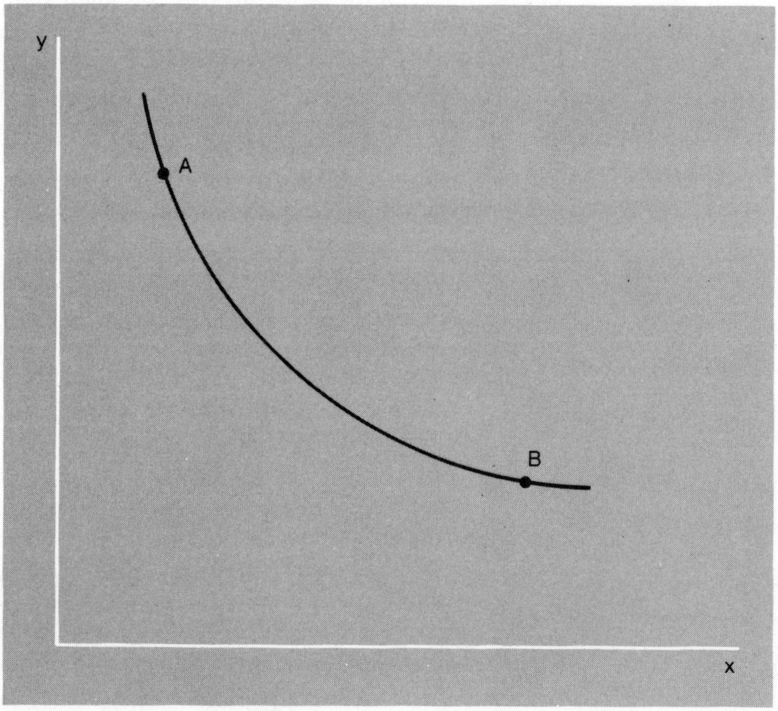

ployment and inflation), the definition of economics and economists' quaint sayings suggest the downward-sloping trade-off curve in Figure 1–1. Particularly when a trade-off exists between such important goals as full employment, price stability, growth, and a balanced government budget, controversy about the specific point selected is not unexpected. *Much of the disagreement among economists occurs when they leave the narrow confines of their discipline and don the hats of good citizen-politicians to help select a point on the curve.*

Toward a Consensus

This being an economics book, let's put aside any further discussion of economic controversies based on noneconomic factors. ''Purely'' economic disagreements also exist. There is no need to preview them now; they will be covered in detail at the appropriate places. Without downplaying current economic controversies, a major theme of this book is the reduction in the magnitude of economic controversies over the past 25 years. This occurred for two reasons. First, statistical studies have convincingly refuted many extreme positions, for example, the extreme fiscalist 1950s viewpoint that monetary policy has no effect on GNP or inflation. Second, there is greater awareness that the short- and long-run impacts of many policies may be quite different, which makes *both* time horizons necessary to understand complete adjustments over time. These two developments have led to a widening and deepening of monetary economics. With more evidence that money matters, analysis of a broader range of financial variables and institutions becomes more important. Monetary economics has widened; it has annexed many topics formerly discussed only in finance courses. Monetary economics is deeper in the sense that traditionally monetary topics must be covered more fully. Both the short- and long-run consequences must be analyzed. Thus, this is a far-ranging and long book. Nevertheless, my apologies for the omissions.

Questions

1. What two conditions must any policy satisfy in order to merit detailed study?
2. State the main goals of monetary policy. Does society have any goals that monetary policy does not influence? What secondary goals does monetary policy influence?
3. A well developed financial system encourages economic growth. Explain.
4. Why are noneconomists likely to overestimate the extent of economic disagreements?

PART ONE

The Measurement and Determinants of Money

2 Functions and definitions of money

> We must have a good definition of Money
> For if we do not, then what have we got,
> But a Quantity Theory of no-one-knows what,
> And this would be almost too true to be funny.
>
> *Kenneth Boulding*[*]

You probably did not realize when you read the last couple of pages how soon we would have to face a purely economic controversy. Economists cannot agree on what money is! Doesn't everyone know that the nickels, dimes, and dollar bills in your pocket are money? True enough, currency is pocket money, but there may be something else. Having taken Principles of Economics, you are aware that all economists additionally consider checking accounts to be money. Agreement ends here, however. Although most economists draw the line at currency and check deposits, some highly respected economists include, as part of the money stock, time and savings deposits at commercial banks and savings and loan associations.[1]

At bottom, the precise items that should be classified as money are arbitrary. Money is not unusual in this respect; the definition of all goods is fundamentally arbitrary. No fundamental truth says that a $5 Federal Reserve note is to be called money and not dinero or Xanadu, and no fundamental truth says that the word *money* is to be reserved exclusively for $5 Federal Reserve notes and some other specified assets. While other courses may simply point out the arbitrariness of defining money and

---

[*] "Ditchley Bank Anthology," *Michigan Business Review*, March 1969, p. 18.

[1] The basic difference between a time and savings deposit is that the former, as the name suggests, has a fixed maturity, which may be automatically renewable, while savings deposits have an indefinite term. Savings deposits usually are evidenced by a small passbook.

quickly proceed to pick a favorite, a serious course in money and finance cannot be so cavalier.

The next section examines different exchange systems since everyone agrees that money is an asset related to exchanges. We discuss some of the difficulties of trading and indicate how societies have reduced transactions costs. This provides a justification for the alternative specific definitions of money since one approach to defining money includes as money those assets that solve, or at least substantially reduce, a particular problem buyers and sellers face. This functional approach to defining money does not yield a unique definition because traders face many problems, and economists cannot agree which problem is the most important. We then present another approach to defining money, the empirical or statistical approach. While this approach again does not yield a single preferred money measure, effective communication does require our choosing a specific definition. The concluding section discusses the advantages of different types of money.

Exchange Systems and the Need for Money

Does money matter? This fundamental question of Money and Banking normally is understood to refer to the possible effects of changes in the quantity of money on certain policy goals. The question is somewhat ambiguous, however. Someone unfamiliar with the economic debate might reasonably think the question centers on the importance of the existence of money. Regardless of the outcome of the debate on the effects of changes in the quantity of money, the existence of money is a prerequisite for the attainment of a high standard of living because (1) exchanges or trades are essential, and (2) money facilitates exchanges. The usefulness of money is not limited to capitalist economies. Despite the hostility toward money displayed by Marx, Lenin, and other Communist leaders, the attempt in the Soviet Union to abolish money and restore a "natural" economy was short lived. Faced with a chaotic situation, the New Economic Policy adopted in 1921 retreated from many favored Communist dogmas, including the abolition of money.

First consider why exchanges are essential in all but the most primitive societies. Individuals soon discover a fundamental principle of economics: *the division of labor and machines in the production process increases output*. Workers and machines that specialize and jointly produce goods are more productive than solitary workers who attempt to produce each and every good. Even the aborigines of Papua-New Guinea, who supposedly are living in the Stone Age, have recognized the advantages of a division of labor, the men hunting and fishing and the women farming and preparing food. The division of labor perhaps has reached its apex in an assembly line, where each worker performs a relatively simple and minor task in the process of producing a complex product. Specialization, however, brings problems as well as advantages. How is the larger potential output from specialization to be distributed? Individuals do not derive satisfaction from the production of goods, but from current and future consumption. Each individual may specialize as a producer, but as a consumer still wants a variety of goods and services. Some exchange system must be devised whereby each individual can enjoy the fruits of the specialization of others.

Even if specialization did not exist because no one enjoyed a comparative advantage in the production of any commodity, trading would occur because of a lack of synchronization between desired consumption and work patterns. Someone anticipating retirement may accumulate a bundle of durable goods for later use. For example, just prior to retirement you may produce a car and house, assuming you are efficient at producing both these goods. However, nondurables and services, by definition, cannot be stored for your retirement. If you want your hair neatly trimmed, you cannot get 120 haircuts now to last you 10 years. During the next decade when you are not working, you trade something to get haircuts. *While there are other reasons for an exchange and distribution system, these two reasons are paramount: (1) specialization occurs in production but not consumption and, (2) desired consumption and work patterns are unsynchronized.* The particular exchange system devised reflects the degree of specialization, technical change, foreign trade, and social cohesiveness. *As economic development progressed, societies successively adopted institutionalized exchange, barter, generalized indirect exchange, and specialized indirect exchange with (common) media of exchange.*

Social cohesiveness is strong enough among many primitive groups that production and consumption of goods and services is determined by some universally accepted schedule. Indian villages of the 19th century, and to some extent until quite recently, had a moderately extensive division of labor. Every needed person—farmer, laborer, servant, blacksmith, barber, Brahmin priest—could be found in the Indian village, and his role and duties were known to all. "Each carried out his duties, providing a portion of the goods and services used by the villagers, and receiving an assortment of goods and services from others. Each was assured his share because each carried out his duties and each had his understood, customary rights to a part of the whole."[2] Nowadays one finds a similar situation within families, "liberated" or not. The mother repairs the family car, the father cooks for the entire family, and the child

---

[2]Walter C. Neale, *Monies in Societies* (San Francisco: Chandler and Sharp, 1976), p. 26.

polishes the family's shoes. There is no need for formal trades. They follow the motto of the Three Musketeers: all for one and one for all.

Other than the family, the number of tradition-bound groups has declined significantly over time. Technological advances have reduced the cost of transportation and increased contact with strangers. As a result, *institutional exchange* became less prevalent. When primitive man encountered a foreign trader for the first time, no customary exchange for his cache of furs had been established. Neither he nor you would give the furs to the trader today and trust him to bring beads and whiskey next week. Customary exchanges were largely replaced by barter, a higgle–haggle exchange of goods *which the parties intend to consume directly.* Each party to a barter exchange believes that the use value of the commodity purchased is greater than the value of the commodity sold.

Barter: An Inefficient Exchange System

Barter has two major disadvantages. First, it requires a "double coincidence of wants." In order to barter, someone has to have what you want and also want what you have. For example, suppose Farmer Brown has milk and wants a pair of shoes. To barter, Farmer Brown must find a thirsty shoemaker. Even in the smallest and most primitive economies, a double coincidence of wants may be so lacking as to prevent consumption of the optimal package, irrespective of the time spent shopping. Table 2–1 shows Tom, Dick, and Harry's preference ordering of food, shoes, and whiskey. For example, Tom is a gourmand teetotaler, preferring food to shoes and abhorring whiskey. Each person owns the item circled in Table 2–1. For example, Tom has shoes, his second choice. How can the commodities be redistributed so that each person has his first choice? The table illustrates a total lack of a double coincidence of wants. Given the preference ordering, barter is impossible. Dick has the food that Tom wants but does not want Tom's shoes. Harry wants Tom's shoes but does not have food to trade. No two individuals would exchange commodities if each had to consume the good acquired. Each would consume what he considers a less desirable commodity.

TABLE 2–1

	Individuals		
	Tom	*Dick*	*Harry*
Preference ordering	Food	Whiskey	Shoes
	(Shoes) ⟷	(Food) ⟷	(Whiskey)
	Whiskey	Shoes	Food

To be sure, preferences may be such that *some* barter exchanges occur. Equally sure, searches by potential barterers for *some* double coincidence of wants will be extremely time-consuming in a large, highly specialized economy with millions of products and people. If barter need not produce the *optimal* consumption package in a three-person, three-product economy, the likelihood of achieving the optimal consumption package in a highly developed economy is virtually nil. While it is impossible to state precisely at what stage in the development process different exchange systems are introduced, as economies become technologically more sophisticated and economic change more frequent, direct barter of goods and services becomes increasingly inconvenient and wasteful of time and effort. Having acquired some information about his trading partner's preferences while searching for a double coincidence of wants, *the typical individual abandoned barter and adopted a system of indirect exchange. That is, undesired commodities are accepted in payment when it is believed that they can be traded for the optimal consumption bundle.* Indirect exchange significantly reduces the time spent on any one transaction, allowing more leisure time, or makes possible consumption of the preferred product by increasing the number of transactions. The arrows in Table 2–1 show a pattern of indirect exchange which enables all three individuals to consume their preferred goods. Although Dick prefers food to shoes, he accepts shoes from Tom in order to acquire whiskey from Harry.

Of course, indirect exchange is not costless. Returning to an earlier example, Farmer Brown exchanges milk for food, whiskey, and other commodities and temporarily postpones consumption in order to have on hand a diverse inventory of tradable commodities. This inventory is a *temporary abode of purchasing power* or store of value; it will be exchanged shortly for the shoes Farmer Brown actually intends to consume. Individuals typically prefer current to future consumption. Nevertheless, the reduced time spent shopping when one has a temporary abode of purchasing power far outweighs the cost of acquiring and maintaining it. *A simple word for the temporary abode of purchasing power surely would be helpful; let's call it money.*

In spite of widely different tastes within a society, the circle of people who accept some commodities for exchange purposes gradually—often over centuries—but inevitably widens. One is hard pressed to explain why a specific commodity becomes generally acceptable. Some generally accepted commodities have religious significance while others are purely ornamental. The important point is that *everyone will maintain an inventory of the generally accepted commodities and virtually all exchanges are made with these commodities. We then have media of exchange or means of payment.* Note well that trading with media of exchange is only a special case of the more general indirect exchange system. Sellers under either system obtain a commodity which they do not intend to consume but plan to trade for other commodities. *Some call the media of exchange money.*

Sales and purchases of commodities are inexorably tied together in a barter economy. A monetary economy separates purchases and sales. *The temporary abodes of purchasing power are the assets people hold between sales and purchases. Media of exchange are those items actually used to make virtually any purchase or sale.* Clearly a medium of exchange is a temporary abode of purchasing power. No one would accept some commodity in exchange for a good or service if the commodity were to evaporate before one's eyes. Individuals will accept an item, which may have no use value, provided they are reasonably certain of being able to pass the item off onto someone else. It does not follow, however, that the media of exchange are the only temporary abodes of purchasing power. *Temporary abodes of purchasing power are broader than the media of exchange.* Anticipating somewhat the current U.S. money definitions in order to make very clear the distinction between these two concepts of money, check deposits are both media of exchange and temporary abodes of purchasing power, while savings deposits are only the latter. You can build up either your check or savings deposits in anticipation of buying a new car; both are temporary abodes of purchasing power. However, the car dealer will accept a check, but not a savings deposit; savings deposits are not a means of payment.

Two views of money—temporary abode of purchasing power and media of exchange—stem from different perspectives on the benefits derived from exchange systems designed to lower the high costs of barter due to a lack of double coincidences of wants. Just as everyone agrees that barter is more costly in terms of time and effort than generalized indirect exchange with temporary abodes of purchasing power, so everyone agrees that specialized indirect exchange with media of exchange is more efficient than generalized exchange. The amount of the temporary abodes of purchasing power necessary for transactions decreases as they become universally accepted media of exchange, and the likelihood of purchases and sales at a moment's notice obviously increases. Some believe that the reduction of transaction costs in going from generalized indirect exchange to media of exchange is small *relative* to the cost reduction achieved when people stop bartering and adopt indirect exchange. These individuals emphasize the temporary abode of purchasing power and play down the media of exchange. Others believe that transaction costs are significantly reduced only when an economy has media of exchange, which are called money.

Barter and the Lack of a Unit of Account

The second major shortcoming of barter is the lack of any common unit to measure and state the values of goods and services. In a barter system where every commodity is exchanged directly for every other good, the value of each commodity would not be stated simply as one quantity but would be stated in as many quantities as there were other commodities. For example, if 1 million commodities existed, the value of *each* would be stated in terms of 999,999 others. One apple is worth two bananas, one half clove of garlic, one onion, and so on. Few individuals or firms could readily keep track of values expressed in so many different ways. Comparison shopping would require such skill and patience that many potentially desirable trading opportunities are ignored.

Since values quite naturally are expressed in terms of the commodities being exchanged, acceptance of media of exchange goes a long way toward solving the second main problem of barter, lack of a common unit to measure and state values. If gold were the only circulating medium, the value of an apple is stated exclusively as so much gold, and not in terms of bananas, garlic, onions, and so forth. Agreement on which commodities are to serve as media of exchange is not sufficient, however, to quickly determine the attractiveness of possible exchanges. There are two reasons for this. First, as our continued use of the term media (plural) of exchange suggests, virtually every society has had several universally accepted commodities. Thus, the price of apples was expressed in terms of gold and a few other commodities. Second, even if there were a single medium, we cannot think of any commodity that naturally comes in a standard quantity and quality. As an example, many primitive tribes expressed values in terms of cattle. The going price for a marriage partner, who typically could be purchased in primitive societies, might be 15 cows. Young people soon discover an additional complication in the already delicate negotiation: just what are cows? Are a sickly calf and a prized bull "cows"? The parents of talented children would have much higher standards for cows.

Societies that attained even moderate economic development used media of exchange which, perhaps coincidentally at first, could be graded quite precisely. Copper, silver, and especially gold are good examples. Metals can be graded precisely but are not naturally found in uniform quantity and quality. Supposing gold were the circulating medium; how much gold does a certain sample contain? The need for a well-defined standard of value not subject to different interpretations fortunately was met. A monetary unit such as a dollar, peso, franc, or pengo was created by stipulating, usually in terms of gold, the content of the unit. The monarch or some highly respected person produced coins, which originally were nothing more than metal slugs with a *Good Housekeeping* seal indirectly certifying metallic content. Rather than stating their metallic content explicitly, coins were denominated in monetary units. For example, prior to 1933 the United States defined the dollar as 23.22 grains of fine (pure) gold, and coins containing 232.20 grains of gold were clearly and simply marked $10. A monetary unit such as the dollar replaced a physical commodity as the standard of value. Merely defining a monetary unit would not have resulted in its use. Prices were quoted in dollars instead of gold only *after* some commodities such as coins were clearly identified as being worth a *fixed* number of dollars. Indeed, one can hardly conceive of a society expressing values in terms of dollars unless something was always worth a dollar.[3] The same principles apply to standards of measurement. The metric standard popular throughout the world would not be used if a certain distance were not always a meter.

With the passage of time, the relationship between the monetary unit and a specific physical commodity typically has become more tenuous. This certainly is true in the United States. Although for some purposes the U.S. government continues to define a dollar in terms of gold, the "official" gold value of the dollar is pure fiction.[4] Nevertheless, the United States has remained on the dollar standard. Why? Because items as diverse as metal slugs, small pieces of paper, and entries on ledger sheets or computer memory banks say that they are worth a fixed number of dollars. Some of the fixed dollar claims are means of payments while others, like savings and loan deposits, are not. Pass a law banning the existence of fixed dollar claims and Americans would abandon the dollar standard. Who would continue to express values in terms of dollar unless something is always worth a dollar? *The unit of account must be anchored by the existence of commodities worth a fixed number of units.*

Justifications for Alternative Definitions of Money: Functional Approach

There are two basic approaches to defining money: (1) the functional or services approach, and (2) the empirical or statistical approach. *The functional approach views money as those assets which were created to reduce the exchange difficulties of a barter economy.* Money is the commodity unavailable in a barter economy which performs a valuable exchange function or service. Commodities fulfilling what specific functions are money? Lack of a double coincidence of wants and unit of account are the two main impediments to transactions in a barter economy. To overcome these impediments society created (1) generally accepted *media of exchange,* also called the means of payment, (2) *temporary abodes of*

---

[3]The British guinea/pound system, which has received more attention than it deserves as it is practiced by only a few West End shops and auction houses, does not contradict the text. Some stores do continue to express prices in terms of guineas although no coin or bill has the word *guinea* printed on its face. However, pound notes circulate, and the guinea was fixed at 1.05 pounds since 1717. Were the guinea to be 1.05 pounds today, 1.23 pounds tomorrow, and 1.15 pounds the day after, the limited practice of quoting prices in guineas would have ended long ago.

[4]Chapter 17 contains a short history of gold policy.

purchasing power or stores of value, *and* (3) *a unit of account* or measuring rod of value.[5] Some commodities serve all three functions and, according to tradition, only these commodities would be called money. However, it is now realized that some commodities perform one or two of the stated functions of money but not all three. Should such commodities be called money? If one is a traditionalist, the answer is no. But a millenium ago conventional wisdom said the sun revolved around the earth, an idea discarded several centuries ago. Most economists who accept the functional approach no longer insist that the commodity called money perform all three functions. Which function of money should be emphasized? An earlier section showed that no advanced economy can operate efficiently without a medium of exchange, temporary abode of purchasing power, or unit of account. Economists cannot agree, however, on the monetary function which should be given pride of place. We have different definitions of money according to the function thought most important. *The Federal Reserve publishes three money measures, conveniently called M-1, M-2, and M-3, which more or less correspond to measures of the media of exchange, temporary abode of purchasing power, and unit of account, respectively.*

The functional approach is conveniently summarized by the adage, "Money is what money does." According to the functional approach, alternative characteristics such as the physical properties of the commodity, the identity of the issuer, and so on are not important in determining whether or not some commodity is money. This is not to deny that the physical characteristics of money are important. Many people drink water from paper cups, but a few multimillionaires use gold goblets. Surely, there is a difference between paper and gold cups. Similarly, gold money may be preferable to paper money on some counts but certainly not all. Note carefully we said gold *money* and paper *money*. The money-is-what-money-does approach says the services performed by commodities are of primary significance; physical characteristics are secondary.

Money Measures Change over Time

The specific items which perform some monetary function change over time. For example, gold coins were, but no longer are, means of payment. Nevertheless, for many years money definitions remained fixed and straightforward, reflecting the static and simple financial structure. For all practical purposes, banks in 1960 offered only two types of deposits—demand and savings. Because of their relative simplicity and longevity,

---

[5]Some economists choose to list money's role as a standard of deferred payment as a separate function. This, however, seems to me to be merely an extension of its role as the medium of exchange.

the old definitions were widely known and, for awhile at least, took the aura of immutability. By the early 1970s, however, the shortcomings of the old definitions became apparent. The Fed responded in the traditional bureaucratic manner—it established the Advisory Committee on Monetary Statistics. The committee issued a scholarly report in June 1976. While the report was being dissected with great care, the innovations which were sweeping financial markets made the old definitions more obsolete and even rendered the report largely academic. The Federal Reserve finally met the need for new money definitions in February 1980. The Fed recognized that the new definitions possibly were not entirely accurate in 1980 and, in any case, would have to be revised as financial change continued unabated. Revisions have been minor, however. The current definitions basically were adopted in February 1980.

Before describing in detail the precise items in the various measures, consider why money had to be redefined in 1980. What precipitated the sweeping financial innovations of the 1970s? Why did banks and other depository institutions begin offering new and varied types of deposit accounts which made the simple definitions of the 1970s obsolete? Answering these questions first helps one appreciate the economic importance of seemingly minor and legalistic differences among deposit accounts and generally makes the new definitions much more understandable. Table 2–2 lists the six main reasons for the creation in the 1970s of new and varied bank accounts, which necessitated the 1980 redefined monetary aggregates. The importance of Table 2–2 extends far beyond money definitions, however. We will use it often. These six factors at least partially explain virtually every financial change in the 1970s and 1980s.

Circumvention of Regulation Q is perhaps the most important reason for recent financial innovations. All federally insured depository institutions are subject to *Regulation Q, which sets maximum interest rates they can pay on their deposits*. Virtually all deposits were subject to Regulation Q until 1970, when interest rate ceilings on one- to three-month CDs were abolished. (CDs are large, *negotiable* time deposits that cannot be redeemed by the issuing bank prior to maturity. However, there is a ready market where existing CDs are bought and sold.) Although the desirability

TABLE 2–2

Reasons for Creation of New and Varied Bank Accounts

1. Circumvention of Regulation Q.
2. High market interest rates.
3. Circumvention of reserve requirements.
4. The electronic revolution, especially advances in communications and computers.
5. More aggressive bank managers.
6. Depository institution losses and even bankruptcies.

of dismantling Regulation Q was apparent to many, the authorities relaxed Regulation Q only gradually and ever so slightly in the 1970s. However, regulations that greatly restrict firms are often evaded. Ingenious bankers, anxious to attract new deposits, created new types of accounts not anticipated by Regulation Q or subject to the highest interest rate ceilings. At long last the MCA of 1980 scheduled a dramatic phasing out of Regulation Q. Depository institutions now can pay any interest rate they want on most types of deposits. However, banks still are prohibited from paying any interest on demand deposits and truly competitive interest rates on passbook savings and other checkable deposits.[6]

Several factors listed in Table 2–2 often were *jointly* responsible for any single innovation. For example, Regulation Q became extremely restrictive in the 1970s because interest rates skyrocketed sharply and quickly. If loan rates had remained at their low 1950s level, banks would have had no incentive to raise deposit rates. In that case Regulation Q would have been of no practical significance. Profit-seeking banks in the high interest rate 1970s sought to offer higher deposit rates in order to attract new loanable funds and to stem the withdrawals of existing depositors, who began to purchase high yielding money market securities.

Some innovations were guided by attempts to avoid reserve requirements, that is, requirements that banks maintain a specified minimum cash ratio. Again, the strength of the reserve avoidance motive depends partially on market interest rates. The opportunity cost of holding zero-earning cash reserves rose with market interest rates. Banks reacted predictably by creating new accounts not covered by reserve requirements and by attempting to reclassify deposits from high to low reserve categories.

Computers and the electronic revolution generally have had a great impact on banking and other industries dependent on extensive record keeping. Deposits now can be transferred from New York to California inexpensively and virtually instantaneously. A bank's computer can be programmed to transfer funds from one type of account to another at the end of each day. For some transactions an 800 number telephone call makes a Massachusetts bank almost as convenient as my local Maryland bank.

The Great Depression of 1929–33 was harder on the banking industry than on practically any other industry. This may explain why the surviving banks turned into some of the most unimaginative and moribund firms. Bankers in the 1940s and 50s earned and cultivated the image of bespectacled, pin-striped exemplars of conservatism. But memories fade, and time has a way of homogenizing people and industries. In the 1960s,

---

[6]The distinction between demand and other checkable deposits will become clearer shortly. The main features of Regulation Q are reported monthly in the *Federal Reserve Bulletin*.

bankers began to copy their cousins in other industries. They became more aggressive lenders and better marketers. When banks noticed consumer finance companies lending to John Q. Public, loans to Argentina, Brazil, and the Philippines suddenly looked safe.

As we just mentioned, several factors listed in Table 2–2 are interdependent and jointly explain any single innovation. A combination of Regulation Q and high interest rates produced large losses at aggressive banks which took excessive risks. Regulators responded by letting banks imitate Procter & Gamble, the acknowledged marketing master. If a different soap for every perceived need is good for Procter & Gamble, why not let banks offer different types of deposits for different customers?

Current Definitions of Money

The three money measures, as amended through October 1984, are shown below.[7] More comprehensive definitions of money have higher numbers appended to M.

M-1 = C + TC + DD + OCD
= The public's *currency* plus *traveler's checks* plus net *demand deposits* at commercial banks plus *other checkable* deposits at banks and nonbank depository institutions

M-2 = M-1 + (ST+SD) + ORP + OED + MMMF + MMDA
= M-1 plus *small* denomination *time and savings deposits* plus *overnight repurchase* agreements plus *overnight "Eurodollars"* at foreign branches of U.S. banks plus *money market mutual funds* plus *money market deposit accounts*

M-3 = M-2 + (LT & SD) + TRP + TED
= M-2 plus *large time and savings deposits* plus *term repurchase* agreements plus *term Eurodollars*

Nonbank depository institutions are savings and loan associations, mutual savings banks, and credit unions.

M-1: Media of Exchange

According to the Fed, the narrowest definition of money, M-1, measures the media of exchange. Before justifying the other money definitions, a more complete description of the money components is appropriate.

[7] Since the definitions of money are not static and may have changed since October 1984, the reader should verify the text by looking at the *Federal Reserve Bulletin*. The Fed also publishes a liquidity measure called L. We shall ignore this measure because the Fed views it more as a proxy for short-term credit outstanding than money. In addition, the Fed currently tracks, but does not publish in the *Bulletin*, total nonfinancial debt.

M-1 includes currency, both coins and paper bills. Who issues currency in the United States? The Treasury issues all coins and a small amount of paper bills; the overwhelming proportion of paper money is issued by the Federal Reserve. Traveler's checks may be viewed as personalized currency. They are issued by corporations with credit ratings only slightly below the government. Thus, traveler's checks are accepted everywhere. They are personalized by your signature and payable only when signed a second time. Therefore, if you lose your traveler's checks before signing them a second time, the issuer will refund them.

Commercial banks still have a virtual monopoly on demand deposits, the old *original* checking account. Nonbank depository institutions, in addition to banks, offer other checkable deposits. Besides being the liabilities of commercial banks almost exclusively, *demand deposits, unlike other checkable deposits, do not pay interest and may be held by anyone.* Ownership of other checkable deposits is restricted.

Other checkable deposits are NOW (Negotiable Orders of Withdrawal), ATS (Automatic Transfers from Savings), CUSD (Credit Union Share Drafts), and Super NOW. All four basically stem from profit-oriented depositories attempts to avoid Regulation Q when interest rates were rising. NOW accounts, the oldest type of other checkable deposit, were first offered in 1972 by Massachusetts mutual savings banks. Mutual savings banks are almost exclusively located along the eastern seaboard from Massachusetts to Maryland. If you live in California and have never entered a mutual savings bank, you can think of it as an eastern savings and loan. Massachusetts mutual savings banks are strong, well-established institutions. Many are *not* insured by the FDIC (Federal Deposit Insurance Corporation); they are regulated and insured by state agencies exclusively. In 1972 the return that savings banks were earning on their mortgages and other assets rose substantially above their deposit rate. Profit-maximizing firms would have raised their deposit rate, thereby attracting more funds to be lent at the higher interest rate. However, the Massachusetts equivalent of federal Regulation Q was effective. Mutual savings banks already were paying the maximum permissible deposit rate. While mutual savings banks could have requested a relaxation of the Massachusetts equivalent of Regulation Q, they had a better idea. Instead of simply paying higher interest, why not offer a new type of deposit? Demand deposits then were the exclusive prerogative of commercial banks. Enterprising state savings banks began offering interest-paying savings accounts against which the depositor could write a negotiable order of withdrawal. Everyone except theologians, senators, and state banking officials trained to make the finest distinction agrees NOWs are equivalent to checks. The ability of Massachusetts officials to see the distinction was undoubtedly aided by *competition among regulators* and the desire to help "their" savings banks. For all practical purposes NOW accounts are interest-paying demand deposits. Because NOW accounts are technically savings deposits, which at the time could be held only by individuals and nonprofit organizations, ownership of NOW had to be restricted.

This new account was profitable and gave Massachusetts mutual savings banks a competitive edge for a short time. Authority to offer NOW accounts was quickly extended by federal authorities to commercial banks and all other federally insured depository institutions in Massachusetts and New Hampshire. This precipitated complaints of unfair competition from institutions in nearby states. Permission to offer NOWs was granted to institutions in the rest of New England and then in New York and then in New Jersey. Piecemeal extensions of NOW would only delay the inevitable. Banks and other depository institutions in all areas were able to offer NOW accounts beginning January 1, 1981.

Banks in areas where NOW accounts were prohibited before 1981 offered ATS accounts, where one maintains a zero checking balance and funds are automatically transferred from an interest-paying savings to the checking account in order to cover any checks written. Because the two ATS accounts require much more bookkeeping than a single NOW account, ATS has decreased significantly since 1981. To complicate matters for the novice, the NOW-like accounts offered by credit unions are called share drafts (CUSD). NOW, ATS, and CUSD are strictly nonbusiness accounts.

The newest type of other checkable deposit is the Super NOW, which was authorized to segment the consumer deposit market while at the same time giving banks a weapon to retaliate against money market mutual funds, an industry whose meteoric rise will be examined shortly. NOWs are subject to Regulation Q ceilings; the maximum interest rate federally insured depositories can pay on NOWs currently is 5¼ percent. However, Super NOWs, like money market funds, are not subject to Regulation Q. Banks can pay whatever deposit rate is necessary in order to attract Super NOWs. Due to the expressed intention to prevent a rapid increase in bank interest costs and decrease in bank profits, the federal government mandated a minimum denomination on Super NOWs. Only those with accounts greater than the minimum were likely to be aware of high market interest rates and withdraw their funds. By setting a minimum denomination for Super NOW, uninformed small depositors who would have maintained their low-earning deposits anyway were not allowed to benefit, for a while at least. Thus, Reg Q temporarily acquired a new dimension. To earn the substantially higher interest rate on Super NOWs, before 1985 one had to deposit at least $2,500. This sum was reduced to $1,000 in 1985, and is scheduled to be abolished on January 1, 1986.[8]

---

[8]Scheduled changes sometimes do not materialize. For any existing minimum denominations on various accounts, see the table (currently 1.16) on Reg Q ceilings in the *Federal Reserve Bulletin*.

Media of exchange or means of payment include those items which can be used in all, or nearly all, transactions and which *extinguish obligations between two parties*. Virtually any commodity can be purchased with currency, traveler's checks, and demand and other checkable deposits. To be sure the three means of payment are not equally desirable for all types of transactions. Distrusting the postal service or their own employees, some firms discourage the use of currency by customers who mail payments for bills. Payments with demand deposits are made by writing checks, which may not be acceptable without adequate identification. Considering such cases as anomalies, the media of exchange function of money seemingly leads to the M-1 definition.

Three qualifying comments are necessary. First, and most important, M-1 measures only the *public's* holdings. A typical commercial bank has plenty of cash in the till and also maintains deposits at several banks. The Treasury has accounts at thousands of banks. The money measures do *not* include the substantial quantity of currency and demand deposits held by the Fed, Treasury, and commercial banks. A money issuer's holdings of currency and demand deposits are excluded because its holdings serve an entirely different purpose than the holdings of the general public.[9] In this respect money is no different from bread: a baker's inventory of bread and the loaf in my pantry serve different purposes. Besides consolidating and excluding the currency and deposits of the government and commercial banks, the M-1 definition also excludes the domestic demand deposits of foreign commercial and central banks because these deposits are also viewed as being held for "peculiar" reasons. For example, M-1 excludes any deposits of London's Barclay Bank or the Bank of England at Chase Manhattan's New York office. The "public" whose currency and demand deposits are being measured is every economic unit *except* the Treasury, Fed, domestic commercial banks, and foreign commercial and central banks. To avoid double counting, checks deposited but not yet cleared are subtracted from total demand deposits to get net demand deposits.[10]

---

[9]The cash and demand deposits of nonbank depositories are included in the M-1 money supply because their other checkable deposits are a small portion of their total liabilities. Time and savings deposits still are the main liabilities of nonbank depositories. From the viewpoint of M-1, then, nonbank depositories are mainly nonmonetary financial institutions, like finance companies and mortgage banks, whose demand deposit holdings are also included in M-1.

[10]For example, when I deposit your $100 check, my demand deposit account is credited (increases), but it may take several days until your account is debited (decreases), particularly if our banks are a substantial distance apart. The amount of checks deposited but not cleared is equal to cash in the process of collection at commercial banks plus Federal Reserve Float. These terms will be discussed more fully in Chapter 17. For a more complete discussion of the items included in the money measures see Thomas Simpson, "The Redefined Monetary Aggregates." *Federal Reserve Bulletin,* February 1980, pp. 97–114 and current *Bulletins* for updates.

Second, many purchases are made with credit cards. The phrase "extinguish obligations between two parties" used above was not added accidentally. Unless you have a special credit card, which would be news to me, when you hand a merchant a credit card and walk out of the store with a package you have not extinguished all obligations. Approximately a month later you will get a notice (bill) that an obligation is due. And how do you pay this bill or debt? With a check, NOW, or currency. It may be convenient to think of credit card transactions as the simultaneous purchase of a good or service and a loan for an equal amount of money which is immediately used to pay for the good or service. A month or so later one repays the loan.

Third, nonbank (American Express Company, for example) traveler's checks are means of payment but, until July 1981, were not considered money for pragmatic reasons. (Bank traveler's checks were not isolated but were included for many years in the demand deposit component of the money supply.) Nonbank issuers of traveler's checks did not publicly publish the volume of their traveler's checks outstanding on a regular (daily or even monthly) basis. The Fed proposed that all companies confidentially report their traveler's checks outstanding so that an even better measure of the medium of exchange would be available. While the nonbank issuers knew the amount of their traveler's checks outstanding on a daily basis, they opposed the Fed's proposal on the grounds that it was costly and the first step towards unnecessary reporting requirements and regulation. The Fed won this battle. The fight between the Fed and the nonbanks is just one example where government regulators tend to understate and private firms tend to overstate information acquisition costs. The acquisition of information is costly and is justified only if the benefits exceed the cost. The need to be pragmatic and settle for the second best if the ideal measure is too costly to acquire extends beyond the narrow definition of money, as we shall see shortly.

M-2: Temporary Abode of Purchasing Power

What commodities are temporary abodes of purchasing power but not media of exchange? What items are held to bridge the gap between purchases and sales but are not actually used during the purchase? Such items must be extremely liquid; that is, readily salable at a highly predictable price. The sales price of liquid assets is hardly affected by the amount of time one spends finding a buyer: "forced and "leisurely" sales of liquid assets realize virtually the same price. A house and common stock are assets but not temporary abodes of purchasing power. Stock prices are quite volatile. Try to sell a house overnight and you will get much less than if you advertise and sit patiently. No one would buy a house or common stock to bridge the gap between income and desired (nonhousing) consumption.

Identifying items that are *not* temporary abodes of purchasing power is easier than identifying items that are. Difficult and somewhat arbitrary decisions must be made. "Small" time and savings deposits seemingly are stores of value but not means of payment and, therefore, are added to M-1 to get M-2. These deposits have been a reliable mainstay of depository institutions for many years and need no elaborate explanation. In financial circles, *small* means less than $100,000. That is, the small denomination time and savings deposits at banks and nonbank depository institutions include all such deposits under $100,000.

Overnight repurchase (RP) agreements and Eurodollars at foreign branches of U.S. banks essentially are one-day loans to banks. These accounts are testimony to firms' and banks' ingenuity in circumventing Reg Q and the prohibition on firms having other checkable deposits. Here is how RPs arise. A firm with temporarily excessive demand deposits could write a check and purchase government securities in the open market. If a firm did this, the gross earnings of the bank holding the firm's deposits would decline since deposits provide banks the wherewithal to make loans and earn interest. Firms found the direct purchase of government securities somewhat inconvenient and around 1975 conceived RPs. The bank debits (reduces) its customers' demand deposits and credits (increases) the RP account, so called because the bank pledges to repurchase at a predetermined price government securities that serve as collateral. If the bank were unable to repurchase the securities, they would become the property of the firm. So far, banks have always met their repurchase obligations. Firms earn "interest" because tomorrow's predetermined repurchase price and credit to the firm's demand account is greater than today's debit. Since deposits are loans to banks—the bank owes you the amount deposited—the shift from noninterest-paying demand deposits to interest-paying repurchase agreements simply is a change in the type of loan to banks. Bank interest costs do rise, but what is the alternative? Recall that banks created RPs to discourage firms from withdrawing their accounts altogether. Withdrawals reduce the amount of banks' earnings assets. Bankers have sharp pencils and attempt to maximize earnings. The higher interest cost is less than the interest income foregone without RPs.

Instead of a collateralized loan to a domestic bank, some U.S. residents and multinational corporations prefer to extend unsecured credit to the U.S. bank's foreign branch, which may be a different legal entity. Many foreign branches physically resemble domestic branches; people inside these branches are making deposits and getting loans. However, some foreign branches of U.S. banks are no more than post-office boxes. There may be no white marble edifice or red brick building or even a hut with friendly tellers to take your currency. Nevertheless, such "shell" branches have accounts because their parents in New York or elsewhere book for them. For example, a bank in New York will debit your local account and credit your *dollar* account in a leather-bound ledger marked "Shell Branch Accounts." The entries may be reversed the next day. *All dollar-denominated accounts outside the United States are called Eurodollars. However, only the overnight Eurodollars issued to U.S. residents by foreign branches of U.S. banks are included in M-2.*

The lack of physical branches and the large amount of such overnight Eurodollars relative to trade in the Caribbean and other areas suggest that smart lawyers and bankers seeking to avoid taxes and legal restrictions have joined forces in the Eurodollar market. However, there are many ordinary and perfectly legitimate reasons for Eurodollars. Cold-war politics, the needs of multinational corporations, and interest rate restrictions led European banks and branches of U.S. banks in Europe in the late 1950s to offer dollar-denominated deposits, hence Eurodollar.[11] The term *Eurodollar* has stuck, being used to describe dollar-denominated deposits in Europe and anywhere else outside the United States.

Creation of money market mutual funds (MMMF) in the mid-1970s opened a new world for the proverbial "little man."[12] Purchasers of any mutual fund receive pro-rata claims to the asset and income of the fund. In this case, the assets are exclusively very short-term, readily salable securities such as Treasury bills and commercial paper. These types of securities are called money market securities, hence the funds' name. The income of mutual fund holders, unlike depositors, is not predetermined but depends on the performance of the fund. Because MMMF assets are very short term, their income and value, while not perfectly certain, are highly predictable. Money market funds have minimum denominations—typically $5,000 when the industry started but often less today. While the funds' minimum denomination may seem large, it is quite small compared to the $100,000 minimum denomination of the money market instruments funds purchase. Indeed, the difference in minimum denominations is an essential element of MMMFs and explains this paragraph's first sentence. MMMFs let the little man participate in a market that previously had been the exclusive preserve of "fat cats." To increase their attractiveness, most funds allowed their holders to write checks against their account, though typically there was a $500 minimum check requirement.

Merrill Lynch's CMA (cash management account) triggered a period of explosive money fund growth. "Sweeps," made possible only because of inexpensive, powerful computers, are a distinguishing feature of CMAs. That is, each Monday the computer automatically transfers, or sweeps, any cash dividends received at Merrill Lynch during the past week into

[11]Chapter 8 elaborates on the factors that led to the creation of Eurodollars.

[12]We are aware, but have chosen to ignore, that "institution-only" money funds are excluded from M-2 and included in M-3.

your CMA money fund. You also can write an unlimited number of checks for any amount—without a $500 minimum. Some claim that Merrill Lynch and other brokerage firms, which have copied CMA in spite of patent infringement lawsuits by Merrill Lynch, have become banks. Money funds not managed by brokerage firms typically have retained the minimum check requirement.

Money market deposit accounts (MMDA) are the last item in M-2. The Federal Reserve in late 1982 granted banks and other depository institutions permission to offer these accounts in order to stop the encroachment by the funds. There is no interest rate ceiling on MMDAs so banks can match the funds' rate. Because it is a *deposit* account, the principal and yield on MMDA is prespecified, unlike MMMF. Individuals can write a maximum of three checks per month against their MMDA. This distinguishes MMDA from Super NOW.

There is little doubt that the items in M-1 are media of exchange. Are some of the items added to get M-2 also media of exchange? I would like to report that the answer is unequivocally no. Sharp, clear-cut divisions make life simple. Our life is not simple, however. Overnight RPs often are alleged to be disguised business demand deposits. The denomination of most overnight RPs is extremely large, much larger than you or I are ever likely to encounter. Let us admit forthrightly that the issues about RPs are complex and quickly proceed to accounts we are much more likely to know from personal experience.

Consider MMDAs and MMMFs. They certainly do have some means of payment features. Restrictions on the number or size of checks permitted by MMDAs and nonbrokerage firm MMMFs disqualifies them as universal media of exchange, but CMA and other brokerage firm MMMFs offer unlimited check writing privileges. However, for an item to be counted as a means of payment, you must be able to purchase virtually any commodity with the item, *and* you hold the item to purchase commodities. For example, the cash holdings and demand deposits of domestic and foreign banks are similar to ours in that they can be used to purchase virtually anything. Yet everyone agrees that banks' cash holdings should *not* be counted as money because banks hold cash primarily to pay off depositors rather than to buy goods. The lower turnover rate of CMAs and other MMMFs suggests that consumers do not hold them primarily for transaction purposes. In other words, withdrawals are considerably less frequent from MMMFs than from demand deposits. Demand deposits turn over frequently because consumers do use them to meet their daily transactions.

Why does M-2 include overnight Eurodollars only in foreign branches of U.S. banks? Why not include overnight Eurodollars in Swiss banks? We mentioned the need for pragmatism and a balance of costs and benefits. Data on Eurodollars of Swiss banks are not currently available, and the benefits of acquiring it may exceed the costs.

M-3: Unit of Account

The United States uses the dollar standard. Accountants' entries are recorded in dollars, and storekeepers quote values, commonly called prices, in terms of dollars. The prices of most commodities are not constant, as many of us have sadly learned. The price, or value expressed in terms of dollars, of shoes has risen substantially. Bond prices tumbled in the mid-1980s. However, the dollar value of some items is certain. Such commodities are necessary for the existence of a dollar or any other monetary standard, as we argued earlier. No one would use the dollar standard unless something is always worth a dollar.

The unit-of-account approach to defining money includes those items whose values are always fixed in terms of dollars. Currency and check deposits are fixed dollar assets, but M-1 is not sufficiently comprehensive. Time and savings deposits also are fixed dollar assets. The interest return on savings deposits can change but the principal is fixed, ignoring the possibility of default or assuming 100 percent insurance. The fixed dollar items added to M-2 to construct M-3 need little explanation. Large time deposits are time deposits over $100,000. Term RPs and Eurodollars have longer maturities than their overnight counterparts, typically 2 to 14 days for term RPs and less than 30 days for term Eurodollars. Two features distinguish these accounts. *First, all three are held almost exclusively by firms. Second, the overwhelming proportion of these three accounts cannot be redeemed prior to maturity.* Owners of large time deposits (typically negotiable certificates of deposit, CDs) in immediate need of cash must sell them in the open market. Banks redeem only small time deposits, subject to an early withdrawal penalty.

If you think money is all the stuff that is always worth a fixed number of dollars, select M-3 from the popular definitions of money.[13] We are *not* saying that money consists of fixed purchasing power assets: money has a fixed *dollar* value. The real value or purchasing power of a dollar is 1/P, where P is an index of (nonmoney) commodity prices. Inflations occur when the dollar value or price, P, of commodities increases. Precisely because money is worth a fixed number of dollars, the purchasing power of money declines during inflations.[14]

Table 2–3 summarizes the major features of the money components. One word of warning: virtually none of the components were perfectly

---

[13]M-2, like M-3, contains money market mutual funds, where you participate in any capital gain or loss and, therefore, are not guaranteed the value of your initial contribution. Nevertheless, the price variability of the very short-term assets held by money market funds is sufficiently small that as a good first approximation these funds may be considered fixed dollar assets.

[14]Knowledge of the three services performed by money will be used for the moment only to determine the appropriate definition of money. However, we shall see later that the

(Continued on p. 32.)

TABLE 2–3

Major Features of Money Components

Currency Issued by Federal Reserve or Treasury. Universally acceptable. Virtually impossible to prove ownership when lost.

Traveler's checks Issued by prime quality companies. Universally acceptable. Personalized currency; refund when lost.

Demand deposits Original type of check deposits. Issued by commercial banks almost exclusively. Noninterest paying. May be acquired by firms and consumers.

Other checkable deposits

NOW Negotiable orders of withdrawal. First issued by Massachusetts mutual savings banks in 1972. Available nationwide from banks and nonbanks in 1981. Pays interest subject to Reg Q maximum. Restricted to consumers and nonprofit organizations.

ATS Automatic transfers from savings. Funds are transferred from this interest-paying savings account to a companion demand deposit account when checks are written. Have been largely replaced by the simpler, single NOW.

CUSD Credit union share drafts. Credit union equivalents of NOWS.

Super NOW Similar to NOWs except are exempt from Reg Q and have a minimum denomination, $1,000 in 1985. Became available in 1982 as a competitive weapon against money market mutual funds.

Small savings deposits Consumer-oriented (less than $100,000) deposits often evidenced by a passbook. No fixed maturity. Subject to Reg Q.

Small time deposits Consumer-oriented (less than $100,000) deposits with a specified maturity date. Penalty if cashed prior to maturity. Not subject to Reg Q if maturity is greater than 31 days or amount exceeds $1,000 in 1985.

Overnight repurchase Overnight loan to a bank by a depositor, who gets a Treasury security as collateral. Bank repays the loan by repurchasing the Treasury security. "Interest," which is the difference between the sale and higher repurchase price on the Treasury security, is exempt from Reg Q. Typical denomination is at least $100,000. Not subject to reserve requirements.

Overnight Eurodollars at foreign branches of U.S. banks Overnight dollar-denominated deposits of U.S residents at foreign branches of U.S. banks. Typical minimum denomination is at least $1,000,000. Tax and legal factors strongly influence this account.

Money market mutual funds Mutual funds whose assets are exclusively short-term, prime quality, large denomination securities such as Treasury bills. Owner shares proportionally in the interest and asset value of the funds. Return not absolutely certain and not insured. At least some check writing permitted. Small minimum denomination. Established in early 1970s and grew explosively in late 70s and early 80s when computers made "sweeps" feasible.

Money market deposit accounts Similar to Super NOWs except owner may write a maximum of three checks per month, in contrast to unlimited check writing permitted by Super NOWs.

Large time and savings deposits Business-oriented (over $100,000) time and savings deposits, typically negotiable certificates of deposit, CDs. Initial maturity is at least seven days. Negotiable but not redeemable by bank. Denominations often exceed $1 million.

Term RPs RPs with maturities from 2 to 14 days.

Term Eurodollars Eurodollars with maturities typically from 7 to 30 days.

standard at any one time, and over time the meaning of some terms has changed. For example, some banks now offer so-called consumer (under $100,000) RPs and CDs, which originally were exclusively, and currently are normally, large denomination (over $100,000) accounts. Moreover, being a summary, Table 2–3 is incomplete but, I believe, convenient.

Justifications for Alternative Definitions of Money: The Empirical Approach

The second approach to the definition of money relies on empirical tests. *Collect data and estimate statistically the relationship between money defined in alternative ways and other economic variables. The appropriate definition of money is the money measure which yields the strongest statistical relationship.* We face a dilemma: the reader is not expected to be familiar with statistics, but he or she must be made aware of the empirical approach because most modern economists think it is far superior to the functional approach. With Caesar's remark on Gaul as our model, the empirical approach is divided into three parts. This chapter briefly summarizes the results of various tests of relationships between money, alternatively defined, and other variables. The two appendixes are for readers who want a deeper understanding of statistics in general and the empirical approach to money in particular. Appendix A presents an intuitive, graphical explanation of regression or least squares analysis, the statistical technique used most often by economists. That is, Appendix A discusses *how* relationships between variables, whatever they may be, are typically measured. Appendix B then uses the concepts developed in Appendix A toward the problem of defining money. Appendix B also extends the text by discussing empirical estimates of the elasticity of substitution among the monetary component. We do not, however, present tables full of regressions. Even there, results are summarized.

As stated, the empirical approach selects that particular money measure that is most closely associated with other variables. *Unfortunately, the empirical approach also does not lead to a unique definition of money because several empirical tests are reasonable.* In other words, several relationships involving money could reasonably be measured. Even for the same type of test, the best definition depends on the time period considered. What tests have been proposed? Two tests follow from the

---

great British economist, Lord Keynes, utilized these services of money in explaining how much money people want to hold. Keynes thought of total money demand as the sum of three components—transactions, precautionary, and speculative demands. Each component of money demand stressed one of the services performed by money. The transactions demand views money as a medium of exchange; the precautionary demand views money as a temporary abode of purchasing power; and the speculative demand strongly emphasizes the fixed dollar price of the unit of the account, which is held because of the risk of changes in the dollar price of bonds.

basic reason, boldly stated, for studying Money and Banking: the monetary authorities can control the quantity of money, and money affects the total value of currently produced goods and services—GNP. The last statement needs qualification. No monetary measure is perfectly controlled by the monetary authorities in the sense that money changes when, and only when, the monetary authorities take some deliberate action. Lack of perfect control does not imply the total absence of control. All three monetary measures vary in large part because of actions taken by the monetary authorities. Exactly how the authorities influence money is the subject of several chapters and can be ignored for the moment. (For those who remember the money and banking section of their principles course, an open-market purchase or sale is an example of a policy action.) *The first type of empirical test defines as money that measure whose variation is best explained by policy actions*. In other words, pick that definition of money which responds most closely to actions of the Fed and, consequently, is least affected by non-Fed actions. If money is not closely related to the Fed's actions, then the Fed will be unable to achieve its goals even if the goals always respond to money.

Several examples of this type of test are available, differing in details and the period covered by the data. *The overall empirical conclusion is that M-2 and M-3 are decidedly less well explained by policy variables than M-1*. More of the variation in M-2 and M-3 is uncontrolled by the Fed. The empirical results are not surprising. The Fed is phasing out its pre-1980 policy that treated demand and other checkable deposits differently for regulatory purposes. Both types of deposits now are subject to the same regulatory ratios, which we shall see later greatly facilitates their control. M-2 and M-3, on the other hand, include a hodgepodge of items that are regulated differently, if at all. RPs are not deposits and are largely uncontrolled. MMMFs escape Federal Reserve control because they are not banks. The control test then casts serious doubt on the M-2 and M-3 definitions. Money is a tool to achieve the desired level of income. However important money may be, one cannot attain the desired level of income unless one first can manipulate money.

The second type of empirical test measures the relationship between GNP, the main policy goal, and alternative definitions of money. You select the definition of money that has the strongest and most consistent relationship with GNP. By doing so, you maximize your chances of achieving any desired GNP. This type of test was the brainchild of Professors Milton Friedman and David Meiselman and was refined in 1968 by Leonall Andersen and Jerry Jordan of the Federal Reserve Bank of St. Louis.[15]

---

[15]Milton Friedman and David Meiselman, "The Relative Stability of Monetary Velocity and the Investment Multiplier in the United States," in Commission on Money and Credit, *Stabilization Policies* (Englewood Cliffs, N.J.: Prentice-Hall, 1963); and Leonall C. Ander-

Since that year it appears that everyone with ''free'' computer time, which includes most economists, has made one minor modification after another and estimated and reestimated the equations.[16] A thorough evaluation of all these studies would be a book by itself. The evidence is not conclusive. One can find a few periods several years long where M-1 has performed best. In most short periods M-2 performed best, sometimes decidedly so. *For long periods, such as 1900–84 or even 1960–79, the sweepstakes winner by a small but clear margin is M-2 followed in order by M-1 and M-3.*[17] The broader temporary abode of purchasing power concept of money explains a larger proportion of the variation of income.

In summary, the empirical approach to the definition of money tends to rule out M-3. The monetary authorities can control M-1 and M-2 better than M-3, and M-2 and M-1 better explain changes in GNP. The empirical approach eliminates one definition but has not presented us with a clear-cut winner, although M-1 seems to have the edge most of the time. *The substantially greater controllability of M-1 usually outweighs its somewhat weaker relationship with the goals.*

> [However] beginning in 1982, the behavior of M-1 in relation to economic activity had diverged sharply from historical trends, raising doubts about the usefulness of that aggregate as a policy target. . . . The Committee agreed that the uncertainties regarding M-1 continued to warrant the practice, begun in October 1982, of placing principal weight on the broader monetary aggregates—M-2 and M-3. . . . Less than customary weight would be assigned to M-1, at least until that aggregate had exhibited more regular and predictable behavior.[18]

These statements by the Fed demonstrate the importance of empirical relationships in the selection of the preferred money definition. By mid-1984 the Fed again seemed to prefer M-1 because its relationship with GNP became more normal.

Failure of the empirical approach to produce a clear-cut winner is particularly unfortunate because the services or money-is-what-money-does approach also fails to yield a unique definition of money. Therefore, if we are to proceed, we must make an arbitrary decision. Henceforth, money is defined as M-1. In our defense, which is not very strong, M-1 is the most popular definition of money because it ranks no worse than second in any empirical test and most people believe that the medium of

---

sen and Jerry Jordan, ''Monetary and Fiscal Policy: A Test of their Relative Importance in Economic Stabilization,'' Federal Reserve Bank of St. Louis, *Review,* November 1968. The St. Louis model, a major source of controversy between monetarists and Keynesians, is analyzed in detail in Chapter 30.

[16]Discretion suggests a lack of citations.

[17]David J. Bennett et al., ''Econometric Properties of the Redefined Monetary Aggregates,'' processed, Federal Reserve Board, February 1980.

[18]Federal Reserve, *1983 Annual Report,* pp. 12–13.

TABLE 2–4
Justifications for Alternative Definitions of Money

Criteria for Defining Money	*Appropriate Money Definition*
Functional approach:	
1. Medium of exchange	M-1
2. Temporary abode of purchasing power	M-2
3. Unit of account	M-3
Empirical approach:	
1. Controlled best by monetary authorities	M-1, M-2
2. Best explains income (GNP)	M-2, M-1
Preferred money definition	M-1

exchange function is paramount. Recognizing that our definition of money is arbitrary, the dependence of any fundamental analytical conclusions on a specific definition of money will be stated explicitly and highlighted. As you will see, this rarely happens. Usually the magnitude, but not the direction, of some monetary action will depend on the definition of money used. For example, a larger M-1 or M-2 increases the demand for goods and services, although not by the same amount. Small differentials due to a particular definition of money will be ignored.

Table 2–4 briefly summarizes this and the previous sections.

Money Growth: The Historical Record

Table 2–5 presents the December 1983 values and December 1976–December 1980 and December 1980–December 1983 *annualized* rates of growth of the money measures and their major components. (For more recent figures see a similarly titled table in the Federal Reserve *Bulletin.*) The full 1976–83 period was divided in half to show that monetary growth rates vary over time and by component. In recent years currency has been growing somewhat faster than demand deposits, reversing a long trend of lagging currency growth. Indeed, in the December 1980–83 period demand deposits actually declined as depository institutions nationwide were authorized to issue NOW accounts in January 1981. Other checkable deposits grew at more or less the same rate during the two periods. Because they were restricted to New England and New York in the earlier period, other checkable deposits had less of an impact on demand deposits during 1976–80. The explosive growth associated with the introduction of other checkable deposits cannot be sustained. Their rate of growth already began to decline significantly in 1983.

The explosive, if unsustainable, growth of a new instrument and its large impact on existing instruments is even more vividly illustrated by

TABLE 2–5
Money Stock Measures and Components

	December 1983 ($ billions)	*Annual Percentage Growth*	
		December 1976–December 1980	*December 1980–December 1983*
Currency	$ 146.0	9.6	8.0
Traveler's checks	4.8	10.5	6.2
Demand deposits	243.1	4.7	−3.2
Other checkable deposits	127.1	58.5	68.0
M-1	521.1	7.5	8.0
Savings deposits	312.3	−3.1	−8.7
Small time deposits	792.1	17.6	2.6
Overnight RPs and Eurodollars	56.1	24.3	25.6
Money market mutual funds	178.2	104.0*	−22.5†
Money market deposit accounts	372.4	n.a.	762.0†
M-2	2,184.6	9.4	11.1
Large time deposits	329.0	20.3	8.1
Term RPs and Eurodollars	89.1	22.3	26.5
M-3	$2,602.9	10.7	11.4

Note: M-2 is not the sum of its components because of a consolidation adjustment. Term RPs were estimated residually.
n.a. = not applicable.
*Annual percentage growth, December 1976–December 1982.
†Annual percentage growth, December 1982–December 1983.
Source: *Federal Reserve Bulletin*, various issues.

MMDAs and MMMFs. Between 1976 and 1982, MMMFs grew at an annual rate of 104 percent. Depository institutions started offering MMDAs on December 14, 1982. A little more than two weeks later, year-end MMDAs totaled $43 billion! In 1983, MMMFs declined 22.5 percent while MMDAs expanded 762 percent.

M-2 is always greater than M-1, by construction. The absolute and relative difference is also widening as M-2 has consistently grown faster than M-1. In the 1950s and early 60s savings deposits grew faster than the M-1 measures. Since then savings growth has decelerated and even turned negative by the late 70s as depository institutions offered new and more attractive small denomination time deposits, such as $10,000 certificates with deposit rates tied to six-month Treasury bills. Individuals were not just switching from savings accounts to small time deposits, however; the sum of savings and small time deposits grew faster than demand deposits. In the 1980s savings deposits continued to decline, and the growth of small time deposits was halted by MMDAs.

M-3 has grown faster than M-2 on balance, but not consistently so. The variability of M-3 growth was reduced in 1970 as Reg Q deposit rate ceilings on large time deposits, which are particularly sensitive to the deposit rate, were repealed.

Types of Money: Fiat versus Full-Bodied

Things acquire the status of money by their social acceptability. An individual accepts an item as money because other people so regard it. Table 2–6 illustrates that money is a social institution. Even an incomplete list of items that have served as money must be long because the number of societies is large and social institutions change over time. In the United States alone, tobacco, gold and silver coins, bank liabilities, and paper notes have served as money at various times. There must be consistency between the money a society uses and its institutions, ideas, and methods of production. Just as a currency of sheep and cattle would be inappropriate for a modern industrial state, so efforts suddenly to use bank deposits would be badly out of place in the interior of Haiti, which lacks the required framework of law and custom. Thus, while there are limits to the items that can be used as money, the limits are fairly broad. Surely gold and silver coins, if minted anew by the Treasury, would be generally acceptable today just as they were a few decades ago.

Are there any advantages in shifting from one form of money to another? Nearly everyone who writes about money has a list showing the desirable physical characteristics of money. It should be portable, divisible, durable, and easily recognizable, among other things. Portability is desirable in a medium of exchange; who wants to drag around hippopotamus carcasses? Since the prices of different goods vary considerably, divisibility without loss of value is clearly desirable. The advantages of the other characteristics are equally obvious. However, any list of items which have served as money shows many types of money not possessing all these desirable properties. Conventional wisdom says that diamonds were not used as money because they lose value on division. A two-carat diamond is worth more than two one-carat diamonds. Although the same is true about fish hooks, that is, an unbroken fish hook is worth more than the sum of all the pieces, Eskimos have used fish hooks as money. Physical characteristics are not of overwhelming importance in determining whether some specified commodity becomes money.

TABLE 2–6

Incomplete List of Items That Have Served as Money

boulders	cattle	bronze
cowry shells	goats	copper
fish hooks	pigs	gold
porpoise teeth	sheep	iron
salt	nonbank liabilities	nickel
tobacco	bank liabilities	silver
wool	paper notes	zinc

From the viewpoint of economic analysis and history, *the different kinds of money are most effectively classified by their cost of production and circulation. Full-bodied money* is money whose cost of production and circulation is as great as its value as money. The traditional example of full-bodied money in modern monetary systems is coins of the metal which a country uses as a standard. Prior to 1933 the United States was on the gold standard. The Treasury minted gold coins which contained bullion equal to the full value of the coins. The amount of gold in a $20 gold piece was purchased from metal dealers for $20. *Fiat money* is produced *and* maintained in circulation at zero cost. Paper money is approximately fiat money, the cost of production being exceedingly low. The nearest example of fiat money, however, is the Susan B. Anthony dollar coin. While coins cost more to produce than paper bills, the former last so much longer that coins cost less per year in circulation. The average life of a dollar bill is approximately 1 year, while a coin lasts 12 years. Indeed, the main justification for minting dollar coins was the saving to the Treasury, which obviously underestimated the public's unwillingness to accept new types of money.[19] With cash register drawers and vending machines designed for the old types of money, the new money is quickly returned to the Treasury for the old.

Pennies are the best current example of monies which clearly are neither full-bodied nor fiat. The cost of producing a copper penny obviously depends heavily on the price of copper. The price of copper originally was sufficiently low that pennies were almost fiat money. When the price of copper rose significantly in the early 1970s and the metallic value of a penny approached a penny, the Bureau of the Mint produced several

---

[19]Some economists express the difference between full-bodied and fiat money in terms of their nonmonetary value instead of cost of production. They say that the nonmonetary value of full-bodied money equals its monetary value, while fiat money has no nonmonetary value. In many cases both approaches are obviously identical. For example, the cost of producing a $20 gold coin was $20, and jewelers and dentists paid $20 for the gold in melted coins. Nevertheless, we prefer the cost approach because the nonmonetary value approach sometimes misleads people into believing that the intrinsic, nonmonetary value of gold establishes the value of coins when it is the reverse, the monetary value setting the nonmonetary value, assuming the coins circulate. That is, in the 1920s the Treasury was able to acquire gold for coins only because it set such a high price for gold that gold supply exceeded private nonmonetary demand. Since the Treasury was willing to buy any amount of gold at the high price, gold producers, who are not fools, did not sell to jewelers and others at a lower price. We also favor the cost approach because supporters of the nonmonetary approach invariably misclassify demand deposits as fiat money. Demand deposits barely have a physical existence, being entries in old-fashioned ledgers or a blip in a tape stored in a computer's memory. What is the nonmonetary value of something that barely exists? One's immediate reaction to classify such items as fiat money is wrong. While demand deposits may have no direct nonmonetary use at any moment in time, the maintenance of deposits over time requires resources which could produce nonmonetary goods. The present value of these foregone nonmonetary goods equals the value of the deposits. A more detailed justification for classifying demand deposits as full-bodied money is presented shortly, and U.S. gold policy is reviewed in a subsequent chapter.

proofs of aluminum pennies for a congressional committee investigating the feasibility of switching from copper to aluminum. Money that is more than full-bodied does not remain in circulation long. This is the fundamental fact underlying *Gresham's Law,* which is typically expressed as, "Bad money drives out good money." If the value of the copper in a penny were greater than one cent so that it costs more to produce a penny than its monetary value, private entrepreneurs would melt pennies for nonmonetary uses such as electric wires. The price of copper receded, the experiment with aluminum pennies was abandoned, and Americans had partially-bodied copper pennies throughout the 1970s.[20] However, in July 1981, when the cost of producing a copper penny rose to 0.8 cents, the Treasury announced that the copper penny was going the way of the dodo bird. Since 1982, pennies are 98 percent zinc slugs with a copper coating.

The difference between full-bodied and fiat money may alternatively be expressed in terms of *seigniorage,* the profits earned by money producers. Of course, the difference between the amount of money produced and the cost of production equals profits or seigniorage. *Producers of full-bodied money earn no seigniorage, while fiat money producers, typically the government, earn seigniorage equal to the amount of money produced.* What happens to the seigniorage? Regardless of type, fiat or full-bodied, money is placed in circulation by purchasing a physical commodity or financial asset, or as a gift from the money producer to other members of society. Much of advanced, pure monetary theory assumes fiat money enters the economic system as a handsome gift from the government; individuals gamboling through the woods pick up paper money dropped from helicopters. This assumption is convenient but unrealistic.[21] Governments usually use the *seigniorage* themselves to purchase some item. *Fiat money producers can acquire commodities equal to the value of money created. Full-bodied money creation does not enhance the producer; the cost of producing this type of money just equals the value of the commodities acquired when the money is spent.*

What are the advantages of fiat versus full-bodied money? Any commodity should be produced as cheaply as possible, thereby leaving a large quantity of resources available for the production of other commodities. Generally there is no such thing as a free lunch; more guns mean less butter. Money is the only commodity offering society the possibility of a free lunch. Why not take advantage of this possibility and use fiat money!

---

[20]A few of the aluminum penny proofs made in the early 1970s are lodged in coin collections. Although the congressional committee was supposed to return all the proofs to the Bureau of the Mint, a few proofs were "lost." The scarcity of the lost proofs makes them extremely valuable numismatically.

[21]This case is convenient because it holds constant the distribution of income, which usually has some effect on the equilibrium values of variables.

Worthless from the viewpoint of production costs, fiat money is good money because society as a whole can have money without any sacrifice. By switching from full-bodied money like gold coins to fiat paper money, the government can now hire miners and mining equipment and offer us an excellent subway system. Society would still have its medium of exchange, temporary abode of purchasing value, and unit of account and, in addition, a subway. A second advantage of fiat money is the ease with which the amount can be varied. Paper money can be quickly increased or decreased in order to smooth the business cycle or achieve other goals. Many, but not all, types of full-bodied money cannot be expanded rapidly. The value of gold mined each year is a small fraction of the current gold stock.

As just stated, *fiat money enables the government to acquire resources and provide society with services equal to the real value of money created.* Therein lies both the great advantage and disadvantage of fiat money. *Abuse of the resource acquisition power of fiat money has occurred all too often.* Many governments have preferred the impersonal printing press to the tax system because the latter makes the government's voracious appetite for resources more obvious.

Precisely because fiat money is costless to produce and the government acquires resources equal to the value of money created, some governments have viewed money as an easy way to get whatever they need. The real value or purchasing power of a unit of money is inversely related to the price level of commodities. If prices double, the real value of money is cut in half, by definition. The value of money created during some period and the resources acquired by a fiat money producer then equal the newly printed money divided by the price level. The last sentence is written algebraically as

$$R = \Delta M/P$$

For example, if the government prints an additional \$100 ($\Delta M = 100$) and each gizmo costs \$5 ($P = 5$), then it will acquire 20 gizmos ($R = 20$). The most dramatic examples of inflation are due to the seeming inability to understand that the acquisition of goods and services through monetary expansion is limited. In other words, some governments have acted as if the price level does not depend on the amount printed. *Given some price level,* the resources the government can purchase is directly related to the amount of fiat money printed. To get additional goods and services does the government simply print more money? Not necessarily. The price level probably will not remain fixed. Just as society will not use all its resources to produce full-bodied money, individuals will not sell unlimited quantities of goods and services to the government and simply hold the newly produced fiat money. The additional money balances will be spent, driving up prices. *The government cannot simultaneously control the nominal quantity of money and its real value.* By accepting fiat money society grants its government control of resources equal to the value of money created but retains the power to determine the value through the price mechanism. In terms of the equation, as the numerator increases so does the denominator, and at some point R reaches a maximum.[22]

The scenario of a typical hyperinflation goes something as follows. During a war or other time of crisis the government suddenly needs a large quantity of resources. Minting full-bodied money will not do the trick since the resources that can be purchased with additional full-bodied money only equal the resources used to produce the money. The tax system is inadequate to meet the enlarged government demand. The government cranks the printing press to pay soldiers, acquire guns, and so forth. To some extent the government is successful because prices will rise only *after* the money supply has increased. But the higher price level means that soldiers and munition makers must be paid more. To maintain its expenditures, the government prints even more money; prices rise at a faster rate; yet more money is printed; all prices, including paper, escalate upward faster; a one-unit bill approaches full-bodied money so the minimum denomination bill becomes 1 million units. How does the story end? The economy collapses, a large proportion of the population is at least temporarily impoverished, the rascals are thrown out, and the new government solemnly promises that new currency issues will be kept in check.

The ghost of the inflation after World War I still frightens many Germans today. Germany set the printing press at full speed and flooded the country with currency. The inflation rate hit a peak of 32,400 percent per month!

---

[22]See the first section of Chapter 16 for an analysis of fiat money creation and inflation as an alternative type of tax and necessary evil, at least during the Revolutionary War. Warning: the remainder of this difficult footnote is *only* for the potential monetary specialist. When will the government maximize the resources it acquires through the printing press? The equation in the text may alternatively be written as,

$$R = \frac{\Delta M}{M} \cdot \frac{M}{P} = \frac{\Delta P}{P} \cdot \frac{M}{P}$$

The first equality clearly holds since the M (money) terms in the numerator and denominator cancel. In a stationary state, which occurs when all real values remain constant, the rate of monetary expansion ($\Delta M/M$) will equal the rate of inflation ($\Delta P/P$). Thus, the second equality holds. If the demand for real money balances (M/P) were independent of the rate of inflation, then the government could always gain more resources by additional monetary expansion and inflation. That is not the case, however. As inflation rises, the demand for real money balances falls. A look at the equation suggests that resources acquisition is maximized when the percentage increase in the rate of inflation just equals the percentage decrease in the demand for real money balances. In the economist's technical terms, resource acquisition is maximized when the demand for real balances with respect to inflation is unit elastic. The familiar conclusion of microeconomics, that revenue maximization occurs at the point of unitary elasticity, is applicable to monetary economics.

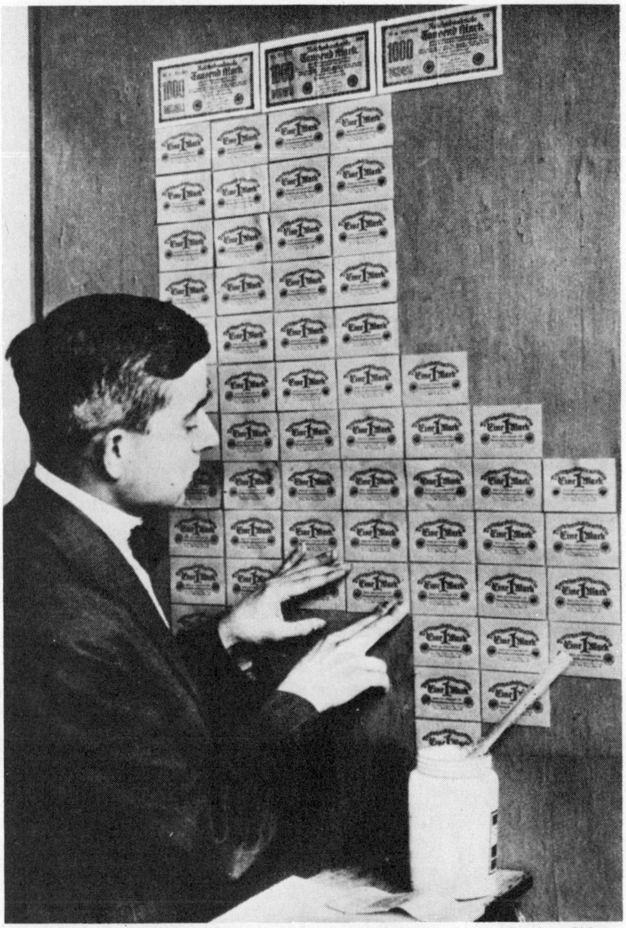

Historical Pictures Service, Chicago

Papering a wall with inflated one-mark German notes.

Prices in 1923 were 34 billion times what they had been in 1921![23] A bottle of German vintage wine cost less at night than the empty bottle the following morning.

But this was nothing compared with Hungary after World War II. From August 1945 to July 1946, the number of Hungarian pengos in circulation increased by a factor of 11.9 septillion (11,900,000,000,000,000,000,000,000). Over the same period, prices rose and the purchasing power of the pengo fell 3.81 octillion (3,810,000,000,000,000,000,000,000,000). Fairly boggles

[23]Philip Cagan, "The Monetary Dynamics of Hyperinflation," in *Studies in the Quantity Theory of Money,* ed. Milton Friedman (Chicago: University of Chicago Press, 1956).

the mind! Most of us unfortunately can only guess what a million dollars looks like and hope that we never will become billionaires, given the likely circumstance which would make such an outcome possible. A German billionaire in 1923 could not afford a cup of coffee. Some appreciation for these large numbers may be gained by noting that a million (1,000,000) seconds is equivalent to 12 days while a billion (1,000,000,000) seconds is equivalent to 32 years. Our earth did not exist 3.81 octillion seconds ago.[24]

Summary/Questions

All but the most primitive groups have assets that serve as a medium of exchange, temporary abode of purchasing power, and unit of account. Associating such assets with a bourgeois mentality which they hoped to eradicate, Lenin and other Communist leaders attempted to ban their existence and establish a "natural" economy. The resulting chaos convinced Lenin that all countries, capitalist as well as communist, need these assets, which are called money. Some assets perform one or two but not all three functions. For example, savings deposits at commercial banks are a temporary abode of purchasing power but not a medium of

---

[24]We said currency is fiat money, but are check deposits, the main form of money in the United States today, fiat or full-bodied money? Before answering this question, let us review the economic meaning of cost and profit.

An important cost often ignored by noneconomists is the opportunity cost of capital, that is, the return capital could earn in any competitive industry. Economic profit, the relevant profit concept determining whether money is fiat or full-bodied, is the difference between reported (accounting) profit and the opportunity cost of capital. Competitive firms do earn a normal return on their capital but do not earn any economic profit, by definition. The Federal Reserve earns substantial profits on its monetary operations, its currency virtually being fiat money. It is a monopoly. Indeed, fiat money *must* be produced by a monopolist. Congress has granted the Fed an exclusive license to manufacture costless money. If free entry existed in any industry with zero production cost, the capitalist spirit would induce firms to enter the industry until the commodity becomes worthless. Grant everyone the right to produce currency which is legal tender and the veritable outpouring of currency would make even the Hungarian inflation look mild. Of course, Congress realizes that everyone wants a money machine and spends a not inconsequential amount punishing those who cannot resist the temptation. Counterfeiting is a crime!

What type of money is a check deposit? While a check deposit may seem like fiat money, it is much closer to full-bodied money. The cost of producing any type of money includes both the cost of creating money and the cost of maintaining it in existence. The cost of creating check deposits typically is quite small. For example, if you come to a bank with currency and open a check deposit account, recording the deposit in a ledger sheet or computer is not costly. However, the implicit check deposit contract obliges the bank to send monthly statements, collect checks you deposit, pay checks you write, possibly pay you interest, and so on. Including as a cost the normal return on invested capital, the cost of serving check deposits approximately equals the earnings on assets made possible by check deposits. Banking is a relatively competitive industry; banks earn approximately zero economic profit.

exchange. Defining money by the asset's function or service leads to three measures of money corresponding to the service emphasized. If one places paramount importance on the medium of exchange, currency and check deposits definitely are money. Other measures of money correspond with the temporary abode of purchasing power and unit of account functions.

Lack of a unique money measure led many economists to abandon the functional approach and adopt an empirical approach. Collect data and estimate the relationship between money defined in alternative ways and other economic variables. The money measure selected yields the strongest statistical relationship. Unfortunately, the empirical approach also gives an ambiguous answer because economists cannot agree on the relationship to be estimated. Should we estimate the relationship between money and Federal Reserve policy actions or some other relationship? Contrary to nearly all principles courses and many advanced courses, lack of a definitive answer to the question does not cause us to ignore the empirical approach. *Quotations demonstrate that the Fed mainly relies on empirical tests for its preferred money definition.*

Disagreement on the definition of money is a source of constant amusement to nonmonetary economists. "If those monetary economists are uncertain what money is, they must be uncertain about everything else. Should we believe anything they say?" To monetary specialists the choice among money measures is similar to deciding among caviar, pâté, and shrimp cocktail—all are extremely good, and all are better than anything else. The general conclusions of economic analysis rarely depend on the specific money measure. For example, what is the effect, positive or negative, on interest rates of increasing the quantity of money? Though possibly not to the same extent, more money, however defined, causes lower interest rates, at least initially. The specific money measure chosen is less important than a knowledge of the alternative measures and their justification. *The Wall Street Journal* and other newspapers report weekly the behavior of the money supply. Suppose one reads that the annual growth rates of M-1 and M-2 were 4 and 8 percent, respectively. How does one understand economic policy unless one knows what M-1 and M-2 are and why these measures have been constructed?

1. What are the two basic reasons for exchanges?
2. List various exchange systems. What are their distinguishing characteristics?
3. Specific money measures change over time. For example, gold coins were, but no longer are, means of payment. State six reasons for the creation by financial institutions of new and diverse accounts, which necessitated the redefinition of money in 1980.
4. The three current measures of money are M-1, M-2, and M-3. State precisely what items are included in each money measure.

5. What are the three main functions or services performed by money, and what current money measures best perform these functions?
6. Are credit cards a means of payment?
7. What are the main *differences* between the following pairs: (*a*) demand and other checkable deposits, (*b*) NOW and Super NOW, (*c*) CUSD and NOW, (*d*) MMMF and MMDA, (*e*) overnight RP and Eurodollars, (*f*) small denomination and large denomination time deposits, (*g*) savings deposits and small time deposits, (*h*) Super NOW and MMDA, and (*i*) RPs and Super NOW.
8. The empirical approach to the definition of money has employed what empirical tests? What are the results of these tests?
9. Distinguish between full-bodied and fiat money. What are the main advantages and disadvantages of these two types of money?
10. Why are inflations common occurrences during wars and other times when the government's demand for resources increases significantly?

Appendix A: Regression Analysis

The purpose of this appendix is to convey a *commonsense* feel for the appropriateness of the empirical tests presented in the next section and in a few other chapters. This is not a statistics book: computational methods and the underlying mathematics are ignored here. The usefulness of knowing some basic statistical techniques and the meaning of a few statistical measures extends beyond money and banking to economics in general. Like it or not, economics is becoming more empirically oriented. This book would not give you an accurate flavor of modern money and banking if it totally ignored statistical techniques and tests. However, only limited space is given to empirical results because they are still inconclusive, partly because statistics is such an arcane science—there are lies, damn lies, and statistics, as Mark Twain said.

Suppose our theory says two variables, X and Y, are related. We purposely use general notation—the variables are called X and Y—because the principles to be discussed can be applied to virtually any problem. How does one test the theory? Are X and Y, in fact, related and, if so, precisely how?

The first step is data collection. The data for X and Y may be either time-series or cross-section. As their names suggest, time-series data are for the same economic unit at different time periods, while cross-section data are for different economic units at the same time period. For example, United States GNP from 1929 to 1984 is a time series, and 1984 GNP of United Nations member countries is a cross section. Hypothetical time-

TABLE 2A–1
Variables X and Y, 1980–1984

Year	*Variable Y*	*Variable X*
1980	2	1.5
1981	3	3.0
1982	4	3.0
1983	5	5.2
1984	6	3.8

series data for variables X and Y are presented in Table 2A–1. A preliminary notion of the relationship between the variables may be gained by a protracted examination of the table or by a quick glance at a graph. Each point in Figure 2A–1 graphs the annual values of X on the horizontal axis and Y on the vertical axis. Clearly, variables X and Y are positively related. Equally clearly, however, the relationship is not exact, that is, all the data points do not fall along a straight line such as LL′. The general equation for a straight line is

(2A–1)

$$Y = a + bX$$

where a and b are parameters (unspecified numbers). Tables and graphs are inconvenient and imprecise means of conveying information and showing inexact relationships. *Regression or least squares analysis is the statistical technique used most often by economists to describe an inexact relationship between two or more variables. The regression equation specifies the line* (that is, estimates the parameters a and b in Equation 2A–1) *which best describes the relationship between two variables. The regression line is closest to the data points and states the average value of the dependent variable Y for every value of the independent variable, X. In addition, regression analysis provides an R^2 (R squared or correlation coefficient squared), which measures how well the line describes the relationship between the two variables.*

Using the data shown in Table 2A–1, the regression or least squares estimate of Equation (2A–1), which is graphed in Figure 2A–1 as LL′, is

(2A–1′)

$$\underset{(0.46)}{Y = 0.92} + \underset{(0.30)}{0.934X} \qquad R^2 = 0.64$$

Temporarily ignore the numbers in parentheses and the term $R^2 = 0.64$. How this equation is computed is beyond the scope of this book.[1] One

[1]To learn how to calculate the regression equation, standard deviations, and R^2, see any economic statistics book. The regression line is also called the least squares line because it is closest to the data points in the sense that the line is constructed to minimize the sum of the squared differences between the points and the line.

FIGURE 2A–1
Graph of Data in Table 2A–1 and Regression Line, LL′

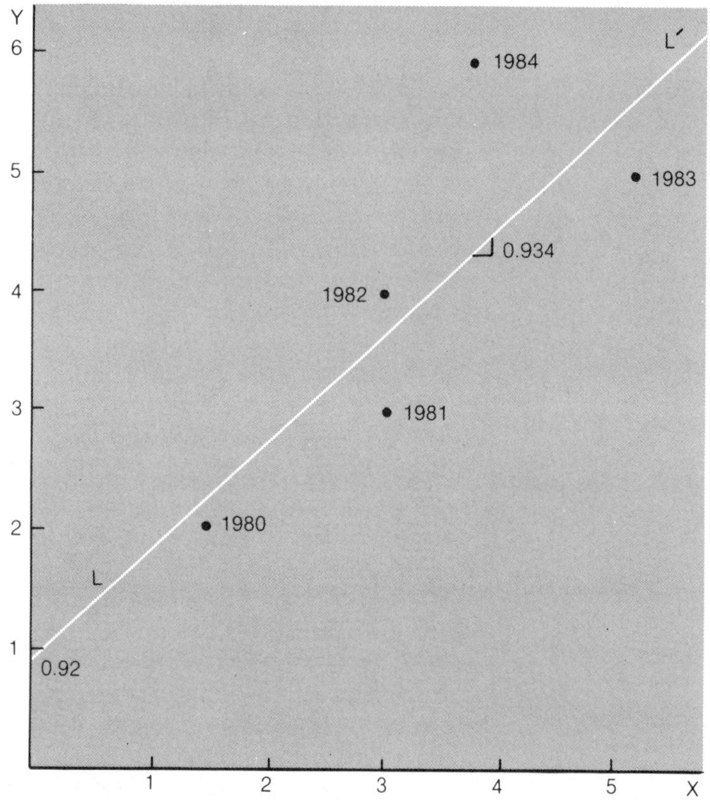

should know how to interpret the regression equation. It states the average value of the dependent variable for every value of the independent variable. In our example, when X equals 4, the average value of Y is 4.656 = 0.92 + 0.934(4). The intercept coefficient, 0.92, is the average value of Y when X is zero, and the slope coefficient, 0.934, measures the average change in Y per unit change in X. Being an average line, some of the points lie above and some below the line. Averages are informative but also hide a great deal. 0.934 is the average of 0 and 1.868 and also 0.924 and 0.944, yet the former pair is more widely dispersed than the latter. Each coefficient (average value) has a standard deviation, a measure of dispersion or variability usually written in parentheses under the coefficient. See Equation (2A–1′). Instead of reporting the standard deviation directly, many economists prefer to show in the parentheses the coefficient's t-value, which is the ratio of the coefficient to the standard deviation. The t-ratio of our slope coefficient is 3.11 = 0.934/0.30. A high t-ratio indicates predictability; the standard deviation (dispersion) is small relative to the regression coefficient (average value). The t-ratio reflects the likelihood that X has a systematic effect on Y. Generally, if the t-ratio is greater than 2, then the likelihood that an observed relationship between X and Y is systematic is greater than 95 percent or, equivalently, there is less than a 5 percent chance that X and Y are unrelated.

As just stated, each coefficient has its own standard deviation and t-ratio. It would be desirable to have a measure of overall "fit," the tightness of the total relationship between the variables. The correlation coefficient squared, R^2, is such a measure. It states how well the regression line describes the data or, equivalently, how close the line is to the data points. In statistical jargon, the R^2 measures how much of the variation in the dependent variable Y is explained by the independent variable X. The R^2 must take values between 0 and 1. When there is an exact relationship between X and Y so any variation in Y is due to X, all the data points lie along a line. In this case, the R^2 of the equation is 1. In virtually every case the relationship will be inexact and the R^2 will be less than 1. For example, the R^2 of the regression equation drawn in Figure 2A–1 is 0.64. We may think of the variation in Y as being explained by two forces: (1) X changes causing a movement along the line, and (2) other factors causing deviations from the line. The farther the data points are from the line and, therefore, the more important are the other factors, the smaller is the R^2. A low R^2 signifies a weak relationship as other factors besides the independent variable are influencing the dependent variable. If the scatter of data points is completely random so that there is no association between X and Y, then $R^2 = 0$. In this case none of the variation in Y is due to X. The R^2 is often used to judge the validity of theories. $R^2 = 0$ says there is no relationship between the variables, and the theory is incorrect. $R^2 = 1$ says the relationship is perfect or exact; the dependent variable always responds in the same manner to movements in the independent variable. Intermediate values imply some association between the variables, but the dependent variable is also related to other variables.

Many theories are more complicated than the one considered. We often believe that more than one factor causes variations in another factor. Hypotheses often include two or more independent, explanatory variables. For example, we may allege that the quantity of peanuts supplied, Y, depends on the peanut price, X_1, the price of fertilizer, X_2, the wage rate of farm labor, X_3, and so on. Regression analysis can be used to test these more complicated hypotheses, and the interpretation of the results is similar to the simpler case. The regression coefficient of the peanut price shows the average effect on the quantity supplied of a unit change in the peanut price *assuming all other factors* such as the price of fertilizer and so on *are constant*. The R^2 measures how well *all* the independent variables explain movements in the quantity supplied. If the theory specified every factor which causes changes in the quantity supplied, then the $R^2 = 1$. Why don't we include every factor which causes changes in the quantity supplied and, therefore, make the $R^2 = 1$? We simply do not know what factors to include. Indeed, a statistical analysis of the data would be unnecessary if we knew everything beforehand. Lack of knowledge forces us to estimate the parameters a and b and produces an R^2 less than unity.

Appendix B: The Empirical Approach to Defining Money

The text stated, "The first type of empirical test defines as money that measure whose variation is best explained by Fed policy actions. In other words, pick that definition of money which responds most closely to actions of the Fed and, consequently, is least affected by non-Fed actions." How does one measure the closeness of the relationship between money and Fed actions? Estimate by regression analysis the equation

$$\text{M-i} = a + b(B) \tag{2B–1}$$

where M-i is some measure of money and B is a Fed policy action variable. (We shall see shortly that the base, hence B, summarizes Fed policy.) Regression analysis yields estimates of a and b, standard deviations and, more important, the equation's R^2, which measures the closeness of the relationship between money and Fed policy actions. Select that money measure with the highest R^2 because a larger proportion of the change in that money measure is due to Fed policy and, therefore, a smaller proportion is due to non-Fed factors.

In terms of the graphical approach, different money measures, called M-i and M-j, are measured on the vertical axis, and some composite Fed policy action variable, Base, is measured on the horizontal axis. The small dots in Figure 2B–1 represent M-i, and M-j is represented by large dots. The first type of test toward defining money calculates the regression for both M-i and M-j. Looking at Figure 2B–1, which money measure would you select? The preferred money definition is M-i. Because M-i and M-j respond to non-Fed action, the points for neither M-i nor M-j lie along a straight line. Compared to the description of the relationship between M-j and Fed policy action given by the line for M-j, the straight line for M-i better describes the relationship between M-i and Fed policy. The M-i points are closer to its line, indicating the Fed policy actions account for a larger proportion of its variation, and other factors are less important. As stated in the text, the Fed controls M-1 best. M-2 and M-3 are less well explained by Fed policy.

FIGURE 2B–1
Relationships between M-i and the Base, a Measure of Federal Reserve Policy, and between M-j and the Base

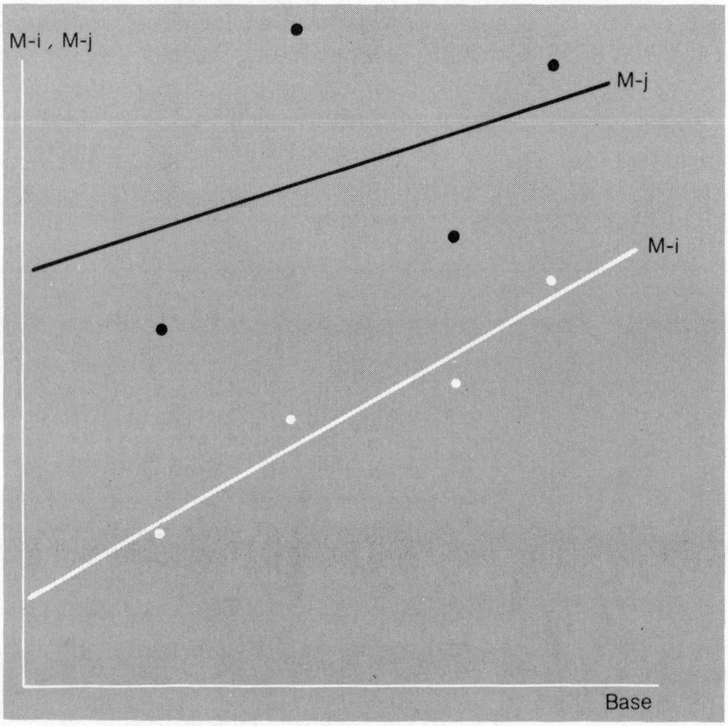

The second type of test estimates

$$\Delta GNP = a + b\Delta M \tag{2B–2}$$

where ΔGNP and ΔM are the changes in GNP and money, respectively, and b is the response of GNP to money. (Most equations also include lagged values of money and/or measures of fiscal policy.) For various technical reasons, the relationship is best estimated in terms of changes, Δs, instead of levels. Substituting different definitions of money in (2B–2) and reestimating the equation, one selects that definition of money which has the strongest and most consistent relationship with GNP, as measured by the R^2 of the regression equation.[1] In other words, money

[1]A backhand version of this test has become quite popular and may be appreciated by those with a *strong* statistical background. Those who have not mastered the forehand version can conveniently ignore what follows. Some economists estimate money demand functions by regressing alternative definition of money on GNP, interest rates, and possibly

cannot explain every movement of GNP; other things affect GNP. Choose that monetary measure which explains the largest proportion of the variation in GNP. The broader temporary abode of purchasing power concept of money, M-2, explains a larger proportion of the variation of income.

The third and final empirical test follows from the economic principle that the items to be classified as money, and the appropriate degree of aggregation in general, depend on the degree of substitutability between items. The narrowest definition of money, M–1, contains two items, currency and check deposits, which are not exactly alike. Nevertheless, why does everyone include at least currency and check deposits in their definitions of money? In other words, on what basis should we aggregate two assets, currency and check deposits, and consider them as one, money? Assets sufficiently similar that they can be substituted readily for each other should be aggregated. How does one measure similarity or substitutability? Other disciplines may consider explicitly the physical properties of the assets, when or how the assets are used, and so on. Economists oppose such approaches and rely on the price mechanism to reveal how society appraises commodities. *When society regards two assets as substitutes, a higher rate of return on one asset lowers the demand for the other. The cross rate of return elasticity, the percentage change in the quantity of asset J per percentage change in the rate of return of K, is the economic measure for the degree of substitutability between any financial asset J and K.* If the cross elasticity between two assets is highly negative, they are good substitutes, by definition, and can be effectively classified as one asset.[2] For example, bank time deposits and savings and loan deposits are good substitutes when a slightly higher bank time deposit rate of interest induces significant withdrawals from savings and loan associations, and vice versa. Currency and check deposits are included in every definition of money because it is generally believed that the cross elasticity between these two assets is high. Of course, this cannot be proved because currency bears no rate of return. Should one also include savings deposits? The amount of M–1 people want to hold depends on other factors besides the interest rate on savings deposits. The empirical approach says that you should estimate the parameters a, b, and c in the following equation:

---

other variables and then select that money definition which has the highest R^2. It is alleged that the monetary authorities' ability to hit an income target is directly related to the stability of the function as measured by the R^2. While the allegation may be true, the direct approach mentioned in the text avoids the difficulty of comparing R^2s when the dependent variables are different. The monetary measure best explained (highest R^2) may have a low partial correlation with income and a high partial correlation with interest rates.

[2]Traditional micro theory usually discusses cross *price* elasticities, which are positive for substitutes. Coffee and tea are substitutes because higher coffee prices *increase* the demand for tea. We are using rates of return, not prices. Bonds and money are substitutes when higher bond rates of return *reduce* the demand for money.

$$M-1=a-bi_s+cx \tag{2B–3}$$

where i_s is the rate of interest on savings deposits and x represents all other variables affecting M – 1.[3] If b were large so that M – 1 is highly responsive to the interest paid on savings deposits, and if the t-ratio of the b coefficient is large so that one can be confident that the effect of the savings deposit rate on M-1 is systematic, then add savings deposits to M – 1. You will not be disappointing your second grade math teacher: you are *not* adding apples and oranges. If b is large enough, you are adding golden delicious and red delicious apples to get just plain apples.[4] Proceeding in a similar manner one can estimate the degree of substitutability between M – 1 and RPs, and so on.

Estimates of (2B–3) and similar equations yield inconclusive results. Some studies find that b is zero and others find b is large. One reason for different results is that the world is not an ideal laboratory in which one can hold everything else constant and see how M – 1 varies with i_s. What we observe over time are different values of M – 1, i_s, and a whole host of other variables. Not knowing all the variables which affect M – 1 and, therefore, necessarily ignoring them, we may incorrectly attribute to i_s the effect of the unknown variables. In terms of Equation (2B–3), the inclusion of different x variables can affect the estimates of b. Tests of the degree of substitutability among assets are so mixed that they do little to pinpoint the appropriate money measures.

---

[3]Actually, the logarithms of the variables are used in (2B–3).

[4]The Divisia index approach, an old approach recently applied to money with very promising results, does reject this. Divisia aggregates weight the components by their estimated degree of moneyness. See William A. Barnett and Paul Spindt, *Divisia Monetary Aggregates: Compilation, Data, and Historical Behavior,* Federal Reserve Staff Studies, May 1982.

3

Elements of money supply analysis

> Let us control the money of a country and we care not who makes the laws.
>
> *Olde Maxim*

Measuring the quantity of money is relatively easy, even though tedious. For example, using the M-1 definition of money, the quantity of money can be measured by asking people to report their currency, demand deposits, and other checkable deposits. Because the number of money issuers is much smaller than the number of money holders, a more convenient approach becomes apparent: ask the issuers of money to report the amount of their monetary liabilities outstanding. Only the Federal Reserve and Treasury issue currency, and approximately 25,000 commercial banks and nonbank depositories issue demand and other checkable deposits. Even in these days of hand calculators and sophisticated computers, adding a column of 25,000 numbers is tedious but, in principle, a simple matter. Measurement requires patience, but little skill.

The money supply problem considered in this and in the following chapter is more interesting and does require some skill to solve. What are the determinants of the quantity of money? Why was the quantity of money in December 1983 \$525 billion and not, say, \$454 billion? Why did the quantity of money increase by approximately \$155 billion in the 1970s? What must be done to increase the money supply by another \$155 billion in the 1980s? *We shall see that the Federal Reserve, Treasury, banks, nonbank depositories, and the public—you and I—jointly determine the quantity of money.* This chapter basically reviews material. It admittedly perpetuates the rather stylized view of banks and the Fed presented in principles courses. The next chapter presents a more realistic analysis of bank behavior and stresses the important role of the public in determining the money supply. Subsequent chapters contain a much more detailed analysis of the Fed's actions. Since we are analyzing the money supply, we emphasize depositories' liabilities and largely ignore their loans and other noncash assets. Thus, a somewhat one-sided view of banks is presented in these two chapters.

The Balance Sheet

Familiarity with rudimentary bookkeeping is all but indispensable in the study of commercial banking.[1] The balance sheet identity discovered long ago says:

$$\text{Assets} = \text{Liabilities} + \text{Net worth}$$

The identity states compactly that all your valuable possessions (assets) are acquired by borrowing (liabilities) or with your own resources (net worth). A simplified balance sheet for Security Bank is shown below.

Security Bank

Assets		*Liabilities and Net Worth*	
Cash	75	Check deposits	200
Loans	275	Time deposits	250
Securities	150	Net worth	50

Traditionally, assets are listed on the left-hand side, and liabilities and net worth are on the right. From the viewpoint of a bank, check and time deposits are liabilities; it owes you the amount deposited. You can view check deposits as borrowings by banks at a zero or low interest rate but payable on demand. Does the "loans" account indicate Security lent \$275, or did Security borrow \$275? Being on the asset side of the balance sheet, loans represent Security's claim against people who were lent \$275. Throughout much of the book we will ignore net worth and present partial balance sheets called T-accounts to record the effect of a single transaction. Suppose a checking account customer deposits \$10 cash. The effect of this transaction is:

Security Bank

Cash	+10	Check deposits	+10

To provide the reader some practice before getting to more important problems, the following additional examples may be helpful. Betty deposits a \$10 check issued by Veronica, another depositor of Security.

---

[1]Bookkeeping is simply the recording of transactions; accounting is much more complex. Do not for one moment think that accountants spend their entire day working on problems similar to those illustrated in this book.

Security Bank

		Check deposits, Betty	+10
		Check deposits, Veronica	−10

Assets are unchanged in this case. A larger liability to Betty is matched by a smaller liability to Veronica.

A borrower pays back a $50 loan from the bank by writing a check on his account there.

Security Bank

Loans	−50	Check deposits	−50

A Commonsense View of the Money Supply

Before getting to some simple algebra, which should not scare anyone but often does, let us see what old-fashioned common sense tells us about the determinants of the quantity of money. We narrate with the aid of balance sheets a short history of banking designed to introduce the determinants of the money supply and show their general effect. The historical narrative keeps in the forefront the banks' ultimate objective, something often obscured by the algebra. Although we are interested in banks mainly because they are money producers and the amount of money affects GNP, banks are not directly interested in the amount of money they produce, as we defined money. Instead, they are mainly interested in making money as defined in the street. That is, expansion and contraction of check deposits, which we count as money, is not banks' ultimate objective but is only incidental in their quest for profits, which in street talk is referred to as making money.

This narrative should not be taken too literally. Some historical license was necessary. Because of the controversy about the definition of money, we want a *general* money supply framework which can be applied irrespective of the specific money definition selected. To accomplish this we introduce some terms whose precise measure and determinants depend on the money definition. In this and the next chapter we refer to money and nonmoney deposits. If the money measure were M-1, check, but not savings deposits, are money deposits. Savings deposits in this case are nonmoney deposits. If the money measure were M-2, however, both check and savings deposits are money deposits. Introduction of the generic items, money and nonmoney deposits, makes the analysis independent of the specific money measures. Similarly, the form of subsequent algebraic equations is independent of the specific money measure. Only the numerical value of the equations and the determinants of the variables depend on the money definition.[2] *Banks here are the generic name of all financial institutions which create money deposits*. Banks could include savings and loan associations.

Government-issued coins were the first type of money. Prior to the existence of banks, the money supply problem was extremely easy: the quantity of money depended simply on the government's decision to mint coins. Throughout this section we assume coins in circulation equal $200, a figure chosen for convenience. Assuming for simplicity the public has no nonmoney assets or liabilities, its balance sheet is shown below.

Public

Cash	200	Net worth	200

Mints do not produce individualized coins. Millions of quarters identical to the one in my pocket are in circulation. Consequently, it is virtually impossible to identify coins that are lost or stolen. Crime is not a recent phenomenon. Our forefathers spent substantial amounts on locks, window grills, and other devices to protect their coins from burglars. Some enterprising chaps saw this and said, "We can do a better job for less." These chaps were goldsmiths. Since goldsmiths already were weighing and assaying gold, had large secure vaults, and were trusted, they capitalized on their comparative advantage and became bankers. Just as banks currently rent safety deposit boxes, bankers levied a relatively large service charge on deposits. Individuals paid the service charge because their coins generally were safer in a bank than at home. Of course, some learned otherwise; a few bankers promptly absconded after accepting coins. Assuming honest bankers, depositors were given receipts and promised the coins were repayable on demand. Suppose individuals deposit $100. Figure 3–1 presents balance sheets for the consolidated banking system and public after the deposit.

FIGURE 3–1

Consolidated Banking System

Cash	100	Money deposits	100

Public

Cash	100	Net worth	200
Money deposits	100		

[2]We must at the outset explain our approach even though we recognize that it will become perfectly clear only when we actually use the formulas.

Depositing coins has no *immediate* impact on the money supply. One component, currency in the hands of the public, decreases while another component, money deposits, increases an equal amount. Remember that cash held by banks is not part of the money supply.

Check Collection and Reserves: A Digression

Initially, deposits were not transferable. People withdrew their deposits at banks and acquired coins prior to purchases. One could not write checks, which are orders to banks to pay a designated person. Since banks earned income on their deposits outstanding, they attempted to make deposits more attractive in order to encourage their use by the public. Transferable deposits expended by writing checks greatly enhanced deposit growth. Assume Adam writes a $10 check on his First National account to Zachariah, who has an account at the Last National. The effects of this transaction on the balance sheets of the two banks are shown below.

Last National

Assets		Liabilities	
Cash	+10	Money deposits of Z	+10

First National

Assets		Liabilities	
Cash	−10	Money deposits of A	−10

On behalf of its depositors, Last National collects $10 from First National and credits Zach's account. After paying Last National, First National debits Adam's account. Balance sheets cannot show the extra convenience to depositors from the ability to write checks. They do show that *issuing checks is identical to a cash withdrawal and subsequent cash deposit*. Check writing simply changes the order of withdrawals and deposits. Before checks were permitted, the transaction would initially affect the balance sheet of the First National and then the Last National.

The convenience to the public was not without additional cost and risk to banks, which now had to transfer cash among themselves. Wells Fargo was the leading "armored stagecoach" company in 19th century America. If you have seen any of John Wayne's old movies, you know just how costly the transfer of bank cash could be. Nevertheless, the additional income generated by making deposits more attractive presumably justified the cost. Still, if cash transfer costs could be reduced, profits would really skyrocket. Ingenious and profit-conscious bankers came upon a partial solution. Why not maintain deposits at Private Big Bank? When their depositors then wrote checks, the small banks just instructed Big Bank to transfer deposits between themselves.

Use of Private Big Banks for check clearing purposes was limited for two main reasons.[3] First, in a country like the United States where the geographic expansion of banks is severely restricted, small banks geographically distant are unlikely to agree on the Private Big Bank. Each bank wants a familiar nearby Big Bank to be the clearing agent. Second, even if the two banks agreed on The Big Bank, fear of the bank's failure in an era without deposit insurance made each reluctant to maintain sufficiently large deposits at Private Big Bank. While private banks still provide some check clearing services, the creation of a central bank like the Fed which prints cash and accepts banks' deposits nationwide overcame many problems. First National will retain some cash—appropriately called vault cash—since some depositors may want to switch back from deposits to cash, and any request for cash must be met on demand. However, First National will ship the overwhelming proportion of its cash holdings to the Fed and have its account credited.

First National

Cash	−10		
Deposits at Fed	+10		

Fed

		Cash	−10
		Deposits of First National	+10

The Fed issued the cash outstanding so its return to the Fed reduces its liability.[4] This is an important difference between the Fed and any private bank. The shipment of cash to Private Big Bank is recorded below.

Private Big Bank

Cash	+10	Deposits of First National	+10

Deposits at private banks increase an asset—vault cash—while deposits at the Fed only change the composition of its liabilities. Now, if Private Big Bank lends the cash unwisely and the borrower cannot repay, then it may become bankrupt, and First National will lose its deposits. Private banks do not print currency and may be unable to repay depositors.

As depositors write checks, a far more important way of expending deposits than depositor requests for cash, the Fed transfers banks' deposits. Assuming the transactions described earlier involving the First and

---

[3]Our historically accurate Chapter 16 unmasks early important Private Big Banks and exposes their precise modus operandi. The narrative at this point is designed simply to illustrate a few principles.

[4]Receipt by the Fed of Treasury-issued currency would require different account entries but does not change the essence of the argument.

Last National Banks, the latter sends the check deposited by Zach to the Fed, which credits Last National's account and debits First National's account.

Fed

	Deposits of First National	−10
	Deposits of Last National	+10

Of course, banks also record the transaction on their balance sheets, adjusting private check deposits and bank deposits at the Fed.

Bank Deposits at the Fed Are Equivalent to Vault Cash. Suppose Last National wants currency instead of a credit at the Fed. Can the Fed *always* provide Last National with currency? Yes, it is no more difficult for the Fed to crank the press than to write on a ledger sheet. From a legal as well as economic viewpoint, bank regulators treat vault cash and bank deposits at the Fed as equivalent.[5] It is convenient to give these two assets one name—*reserves*. Introduction of this term saves qualifying adjectives. Just plain currency henceforth means currency held by the public because currency held by banks is called reserves. The majority of bank reserves, in fact, are kept as deposits at the Fed. Assuming that all reserves are held as deposits at the Fed simplifies the exposition without affecting any of the conclusions. But do not be awed by such terms as reserves and deposits at the Fed. If you think of reserves as currency held by banks you cannot go wrong.

The Money Stock: A Multiplier Times the Base

Total currency, whether held by the public or banks as reserves, provides the foundation for the money supply. The public's currency is a component of the money supply, and banks must attract some currency, that is, acquire reserves, in order to issue deposits. No one would accept deposits if banks held no reserves and deposits were inconvertible into currency. Because they provide the foundation for the money supply, *currency and reserves are called the monetary base*.[6]

---

[5]This was not true prior to 1959, when the Fed began allowing banks to count their vault cash in meeting legally required minimum cash ratios. Thus one has the paradoxical situation where until 1959 bank deposits at the Fed were in some respects more like cash than cash itself. For *legal* purposes the deposits which some banks still maintain at other banks for check clearing and other purposes were counted as cash until quite recently. However, from the viewpoint of *economic* analysis, only vault cash and deposits at the Fed were, and are, identical.

[6]The term *monetary base* is not altogether standard. The St. Louis Federal Reserve Bank adjusts our definition for changes in legally required minimum cash ratios to get what it calls the monetary base. In your outside readings you may encounter the term *high-powered money,* which is the name some give to the monetary base.

$$\text{Monetary base} \equiv \text{Currency} + \text{Reserves}$$
$$B \equiv C + R$$

The identity symbol indicates that the above is true by definition. Since reserves are banks' currency holdings, whether in the green paper variety familiar to all or the equivalent deposits at the Fed, the monetary base identity in effect says that total currency is held by either the public or banks. The base in this example equals $200, the value of coins initially minted.

Provided bank reserves equal deposits, as has been implicitly assumed so far, the base also equals the money supply. Additional currency is either held by the public or deposited in banks, which do nothing but accept currency. In such cases, classifying the base as currency and reserves is of little practical importance. But banks no longer are currency warehouses holding 100 percent reserves, that is, reserves equal to deposits. Bankers quickly learned that not everyone simultaneously demands currency or writes checks. *Reserves equal to a fraction of check deposits are adequate.* In a fractional reserve system the money supply is greater than the base. This is readily apparent when the money supply and base definitions are written together. Letting D represent the deposits considered to be money,

$$M \equiv C + D$$
$$B \equiv C + R$$
$$M > B \text{ when } R < D$$

Economists loathe inequalities. They convert the $M > B$ inequality into an equality by saying that *money is the product of a multiplier, m, times the base.*

$$M = mB$$

The precise form of the multiplier depends on the behavioral assumptions made.

Open-Market Operations and Discounts

This and the next chapter emphasize the money supply multiplier. We assume the monetary base is determined by Fed policy. How does the Fed vary the base? Although we cannot simultaneously analyze the multiplier and base in detail, some knowledge about base changes is desirable before further discussion of the multiplier. We limit ourselves here to two Fed policy tools; a more complete analysis of other sources of the monetary base is postponed until Chapter 17.

You may have received the impression that the Fed increases the base by cranking a money machine. While the Fed does not act quite so crudely, the impression is basically correct. *Changes in the monetary base are accomplished largely through open-market operations, which is a fancy name for Fed purchases and sales of securities, typically Treasury bills or other short-term Treasury securities.* The side of the transaction from the Fed's viewpoint determines whether there is an open-market sale or purchase. That is, if the Fed buys a security, and a bank or individual sells the security, an open-market purchase has occurred. Conversely, sales of securities by the Fed are called open-market sales. Payment for open-market purchases is made by a check *issued by the Fed on itself.* The Fed need not own anything *before* buying securities or any other item. That is the beauty of being the money producer. The security seller may well accept larger deposits at the Fed, which are equivalent to currency. If this is unacceptable, the Fed will cash its check by printing money.

Open-market purchases increase the monetary base while sales decrease the base. Figure 3–2 illustrates the effect of an open-market purchase on the balance sheets of the Fed and banking system. Suppose the Fed buys $20 worth of Treasury securities from banks. This transaction is shown on line 1. Payment for open-market purchases is made by a check issued by the Fed on itself, which banks deposit. The open-market purchase increases the reserve component of the base. The fact that the Fed need not own anything before buying securities or any other item is somewhat obscured because banks usually collect from the Fed—the bankers' bank—by having their accounts credited. Were preferences to change, the Fed would cash its check by cranking a printing press, clearly revealing to all that it is a fiat money producer.

Suppose the Fed purchased the securities from individuals instead of banks. Individuals deposit the Fed's check at banks, which credit money deposits and collect the proceeds of the check by maintaining larger deposits at the Fed. See the transactions entered on line 2 of Figure 3–2.

FIGURE 3–2

Open-market purchase from (1) banks and (2) the public.

Banking System

(1)	Deposits at Fed	+20		
	Treasury securities	−20		
(2)	Deposits at Fed	+20	Money deposits	+20

Federal Reserve

(1)	Treasury securities	+20	Deposits of banks	+20
(2)	Treasury securities	+20	Deposits of banks	+20

If the Fed sells rather than buys securities, the entries are the same except that signs are reversed, that is, substitute − for + and vice versa.

The effect of an open-market purchase on the Fed's balance sheet is independent of the seller. The same is not true for the banking system, at least initially. In either case reserves increase, but purchases from banks reduce their securities while purchases from the public immediately increase deposits. The reader is warned not to make much of this initial difference. *Ultimately, after the banks and the public have had a chance to react to the increase in reserves, the money supply increase is independent of the identity of the seller.* This is not surprising. Since the Fed does not know who sells securities, its control over the money supply would be poor indeed if the particular seller mattered. The money supply depends on the monetary base; how or why the base was created has no ultimate effect.

The discount mechanism is a second source of the monetary base. Banks can borrow from the Federal Reserve. To make this sound more esoteric, the Fed says it has accommodated a bank with a discount.[7] The Fed is not altogether accommodating; it does not make interest-free loans. The Fed states that its loans to banks should be called discounts and, for consistency, refers to the interest rate on these loans as the discount rate. The Fed sets the discount rate and accommodates banks' demand, within limits to be discussed later. Figure 3–3 illustrates a $20 increase in discounts. The Fed credits a bank's deposit account by the amount of the discount. *Discounting, like open-market purchases from banks, has no immediate impact on the money supply.* Neither money deposits nor currency increases directly. Discounts clearly are negatively related to the discount rate. Banks borrow less when the discount rate is high. Any further discussion of the determinants of discounting and the relative advantages of

FIGURE 3–3
Discounts

Banking System

Deposits at Fed	+20	Discounts at Fed	+20

Federal Reserve

Discounts to banks	+20	Deposits of banks	+20

[7]In fairness to the Fed it must be stated that even before the Fed's existence the term *discount* was, and still is, widely used in banking circles to designate a type of loan where interest is prepaid. The public cannot borrow at the Fed except in extreme situations.

open-market operations versus the discount mechanism must be postponed. We simply needed to show how the monetary base can be changed.

General Money Supply Equations

Two basic equations for money supply analysis are the money definition, (3–1), and the equilibrium condition for the monetary base, (3–2).

$$M \equiv C + D \tag{3–1}$$

$$B^s = C^d + R^d \tag{3–2}$$

The identity symbol shows that, by definition, Equation (3–1) holds at all times. To emphasize that Equation (3–2) is an *equilibrium* condition, the equality notation and superscripts s and d are used. The base was just defined as reserves plus currency. We are not repeating ourselves; Equation (3–2) does not state a definition true at all times. Just as the peanut market is in equilibrium when the demand and supply for peanuts are equal, so the market for the monetary base is in equilibrium when the supply of the base, B^s, provided by the Fed and Treasury, equals the demand for the base by banks (reserves, R^d) and the public (currency, C^d). The importance of this equilibrium condition in the money supply process stems from the fact that if supply and demand for the base are not equal, then balance sheet adjustments by banks cause monetary changes. *The actual quantity of money equals the (equilibrium) money supply only when the monetary base market is in equilibrium.*[8] The validity of the last two sentences cannot be proven rigorously at this point but is supported by the subsequent analysis of adjustment processes and empirical observation.

At times we may wish to focus on the equilibrium *change* rather than the *level* of the money supply. Similar equations hold

$$\Delta M \equiv \Delta C + \Delta D \tag{3–1′}$$

$$\Delta B^s = \Delta C^d + \Delta R^d \tag{3–2′}$$

where Δ is the symbol for change or, technically speaking, the first difference. The equilibrium money supply change occurs only when the

[8]To emphasize that the actual *quantity* of money need not equal the money *supply*, and that the money supply is the outcome of an optimization process involving banks and the public instead of being mechanically determined, we often refer to the "equilibrium" money supply.

change in the base provided by the Fed and Treasury equals the change in the demand for reserves and currency.

Equations (3–1) and (3–2), or the corresponding equations for change, are the two central equations of money supply theory. One *always* begins with these two equations. *Throughout this chapter the supply of the base is exogenously determined by the authorities. The basic problem is determining the demand for the base, which is set equal to the given supply of the base.* To highlight the effect of each demand determinant, we begin with a simple model and introduce one determinant at a time. *When the demand for the base is determined and set equal to the given base supply, one readily gets the equilibrium money stock as the product of a multiplier times the base.* The form of the multiplier depends on the determinants of the demand for the base.

The Simple Money Supply Model

$$DER = 0, \ C = 0, \text{ and } NMD = 0$$

Let us assume, albeit unrealistically, that banks developed the perfect money deposit and are master marketers. As a result the public does not want to hold any currency ($C=0$), and banks do not have to offer non-money deposits ($NMD=0$) to attract additional funds. Money deposits are the only bank liability. Ignoring superscripts, with $C=0$ the two basic equations become

$$M \equiv D \tag{3–1.1}$$

$$B = R \tag{3–2.1}$$

The money supply and deposits coincide, given our assumptions. Deleting the superscripts makes the equation look less cluttered but the reader should not forget that *B stands for the exogenous supply of the base and R represents the demand for reserves. The two are equal only at equilibrium.* The Fed imposes required reserve ratios, or minimum ratios of reserves to money deposits. For simplicity, assume a *uniform* reserve ratio for all banks. In this model, banks hold reserves only to meet the legal requirements. Desired excess reserves are zero, $DER=0$. Thus the demand for reserves is a fraction of the deposits supplied by the banks; the fraction equals the required reserve ratio, r_m set by the Fed.

$$R = r_m D \tag{3–3}$$

Set the demand for reserves expressed by Equation (3–3) equal to a given base supply, B.

(3–4)

$$B = r_m D, \text{ or } D = B/r_m$$

Given the assumptions that individuals do not hold currency, nonmoney deposits do not exist, and banks demand reserves simply to satisfy legal requirements, Equation (3–4) is a specific example of the general Equation (3–2).

Substituting in Equation (3–1.1) gives the equilibrium money supply.[9]

(3–5)

$$M = D = \frac{1}{r_m} \cdot B$$

Since r_m is less than one, $1/r_m$ is greater than one and, consequently, called a multiplier. The money supply always is the product of a multiplier times the base. Given the assumptions of this model, the multiplier is $1/r_m$. Please take note, however, that *the money supply multiplier does not always equal* $1/r_m$ *but depends on the assumptions made.*

Equation (3–5) is the simple money supply relationship of your typical Principles course, where it is assumed the Fed and Treasury can peg the money supply at whatever amount they wish. Looking at the equation shows that the money supply is negatively related to the required reserve ratio. If the Fed cuts the reserve ratio in half, the money supply doubles.[10] The reserve ratio is easily changed; the Fed simply announces that henceforth the reserve ratio is, say, two percentage points higher. Nevertheless, the Fed rarely changes reserve ratios. Changes in the base largely explain money stock changes. The change or first difference form of the last equation is

(3–5′)

$$\Delta M = \frac{1}{r_m} \Delta B$$

If the reserve ratio is 20 percent (.20), according to Equation (3–5) the money stock is five times the base, and from Equation (3–5′) the same relationship holds for changes in the base.

---

[9]The reader may wonder why at this point we use the equality notation in the money supply equation. The reason is simple: we made use of the equilibrium condition $B = r_m D$. Assuming individuals do not hold currency, the money supply always equals deposits. Only at equilibrium does it equal B/r_m.

[10]Since we always will consider one change at a time, the qualifying phrase "other things being equal" is unnecessary. Throughout this chapter we assume that a change in one variable on the right-hand side of the equation will not cause another variable on the same side to change.

Money Supply Adjustments: An Aggregate View

The simple model is a convenient starting point, but only that. Before relaxing some assumptions, however, a specific example best illustrates the money supply adjustment process and the difference between individual and aggregate results. The initial balance sheets of all banks are consolidated and shown on Figure 3–4, line 1. The assumptions of the last section still hold. Assuming a 20 percent required reserve ratio, the demand for required reserves, \$100, equals the amount available, and the banking system is in equilibrium. Line 2 records a \$20 open-market purchase from commercial banks, which increases reserves to \$120. According to our formula the new equilibrium money supply is \$600, or, equivalently, the money supply increases by \$100. Let us see why this is so and how the equilibrium is reached.

Total reserves, TR, can be divided into required reserves, RR, and reserves not required by law, which are conventionally called excess reserves, ER.

$$TR \equiv RR + ER \tag{3–6}$$

This identity will be used often. We might even dignify it and call it the third basic relationship of the money supply process. Because of its importance, and because one usually solves the equation for excess reserves, rewrite it as follows:

$$ER \equiv TR - RR \tag{3–6'}$$

Immediately after the open-market purchase total reserves in this example are \$120, required reserves are \$100 (.2 × \$500), and excess reserves equal \$20. But by assumption, banks demand reserves only to meet the legal requirements. Therefore, the \$20 of excess reserves is undesired, and

FIGURE 3–4

(1) Initial equilibrium, (2) open-market purchase, (3) loan and deposit expansion, and (4) final equilibrium, sum of lines (1)–(3).

Consolidated Banking System

(1)	Deposits at Fed	100	Money deposits	500
	Loans and securities	400		
(2)	Deposits at Fed	+20		
	Loans and securities	−20		
(3)	Loans and securities	+100	Money deposits	+100
(4)	Deposits at Fed	120	Money deposits	600
	Loans and securities	480		

banks cannot be at equilibrium. Banks will adjust their balance sheets to eliminate the \$20 of unwanted excess reserves. It might appear the adjustment entails either a decrease in total reserves or an increase in required reserves totaling \$20. However, our assumption precludes a decrease in total reserves. Remember that bank reserves, whether held as vault cash or deposits at the Fed, are equivalent to currency. If the public does not want to hold any currency, banks cannot lose any reserves. The entire adjustment process involves an increase in required reserves. How does this come about? Banks make loans or purchase securities worth \$100 and credit the deposits of the public by an equivalent amount. These transactions are shown on line 3 of Figure 3–4. With money deposits now equal to \$600, banks want reserves of \$120. An equilibrium has been reached; unwanted excess reserves of the banking system have been eliminated. The equilibrium money supply change is \$100 (\$600 – \$500). This is precisely what our formulas (3–5) and (3–5′) say. In this example, $r_m = .2$, $B = 120$, and $\Delta B = 20$. Therefore, $M = 600$ and $\Delta M = 100$.

The following sketch without balance sheets shows that the same conclusion holds when the Fed purchases securities from the public. Recall that the immediate impact of a \$20 open-market purchase from the public is an equal increase in reserves and deposits. Required reserves on the deposits are \$4 in our example. Excess reserves are \$16. How are these unwanted excess reserves eliminated? Banks make loans and credit depositors' accounts by \$80. The total money supply changes by \$100 (\$20 + \$80).

Individual Bank Adjustments

Approximately 15,000 banks make up the banking system. What role does an individual bank play in the adjustment process? Assume all banks except one are in equilibrium. The \$20 of excess reserves is concentrated in bank A, from which the Fed bought a Treasury security.

(1) Initial equilibrium, (2) open-market purchase, (3) loan expansion, and (4) induced deposit withdrawals.

Bank A

	Assets		Liabilities	
(1)	Deposits at Fed	8	Money deposits	40
	Loans and securities	32		
(2)	Deposits at Fed	+20		
	Loans and securities	–20		
(3)	Loans and securities	+100	Money deposits	+100
(4)	Deposits at Fed	–100	Money deposits	–100

The initial position of bank A and the open-market purchase are shown by the top two lines of its balance sheet. Continue to assume the required reserve ratio is 20 percent. Total reserves are \$28 and required reserves are \$8, so excess reserves are \$20. Can bank A loan \$100 and credit the deposit accounts of its customer? (Remember we are assuming individuals do not hold currency, so the proceeds of bank loans must result in increased deposits.) Bank A could make such a loan, as shown on the third line of the balance sheet, and *temporarily* at least it would still meet the legal requirement. Money deposits now are \$140 and reserves are \$28, which is 20 percent of deposits and just what the Fed requires. However, an important word in the penultimate sentence is "temporarily." In the very near future bank A will be drastically short of reserves. Do individuals borrow and pay interest on their loans in order to keep deposits sitting in the bank? Of course not. An individual borrows in order to buy something. When the individual writes a check to purchase something, the seller of the item will deposit the check in a bank. But which bank? With 15,000 banks, the probability is virtually nil that the check will be deposited in bank A. The person who receives the check almost certainly has an account in another bank, called bank B. The final effect on the balance sheet of a \$100 check drawn on bank A and deposited at bank B is shown on the fourth line. *Bank reserve losses due to payment of depositors' checks are called clearing-house drains.*

Bank A would be deeply embarrassed if it made a \$100 loan. After borrowers spend the proceeds, the Fed would quickly note that payment of the check would overdraw bank A's account by \$72. (Bank A's deposits at the Fed are \$28, but it is supposed to pay bank B \$100 on behalf of its customer.) Failure to meet reserve requirements is bad enough but overdrawing an account is grounds for closure. The Fed does not extend overdrafts! Asking customers to repay recently made loans may be impossible and, in any case, will hardly enhance good will. While bank A may once have considered only the temporary effect of its loans and ignored the final effect, by now it has learned not to loan \$100 when its excess reserves are \$20. *An increase in bank loans or security holdings is almost immediately followed by an equal decrease in reserves. Therefore, deposit expansion by a single bank is limited by its excess reserves.*[11] Erase lines 3 and 4 in the previous balance sheet. Bank A will loan only \$20 in this example. The effect of this transaction on the balance sheets of banks A and B after the loan proceeds have been spent and checks have cleared is shown here.

Bank A

	Assets		Liabilities	
(3)	Loans and securities	+20	Money deposits	+20
(4)	Deposits at Fed	−20	Money deposits	−20

[11]This conclusion generally is independent of the type of asset acquired with the excess reserves. Suppose bank A placed an order to buy government securities instead of making loans. The people who sold securities most likely have accounts at other banks. When the sellers deposit bank A's check (called a cashier's check) at their bank and the check clears, we get the previous balance sheet.

Bank B

(4) Deposits at Fed	+20	Money deposits	+20

This is not the end of the story, however. While bank A is now in equilibrium, bank B is not. Bank B with \$20 in new deposits requires \$4 in additional reserves. Since it has acquired \$20 in reserves, \$16 represents unwanted excess reserves which can be lent to customers. The loan and subsequent payment by the borrower to a depositor at another bank, called bank C, is recorded next.

Bank B

Loans and securities	+16	Money deposits	+16
Deposits at Fed	−16	Money deposits	−16

Bank C

Deposits at Fed	+16	Money deposits	+16

Bank C now is in a disequilibrium position, and the adjustment process continues, affecting, in turn, banks D, E, F, and so on. The role played by each bank in the expansion process is shown in Table 3–1. In general, the expansion at the first step in this sequence is ΔB, and the expansion at each step equals the expansion in the previous step times the constant $(1 - r_m)$. The cumulative process may be represented by a geometric series.

$$\begin{aligned}\Delta M &= \Delta B + \Delta B(1 - r_m) + \Delta B(1 - r_m)^2 + \cdots + \Delta B(1 - r_m)^n \\ &= \Delta B[1 + (1 - r_m) + (1 - r_m)^2 + \cdots + (1 - r_m)^n] \\ &= 20[1 + .8 + .64 + \cdots + (.8)^n]\end{aligned}$$

TABLE 3–1

Summary of Deposit Expansion Process by Individual Banks, No Cash or Nonmoney Deposits*

Banks	*New Deposits Created by*	*New Loans Made by*	*New Deposits Retained by*	*Reserves Retained As Required Reserves by*
A	20.00	20.00	—	—
B	16.00	16.00	20.00	4.00
C	12.80	12.80	16.00	3.20
D	10.24	10.24	12.80	2.56
E	8.19	8.19	10.24	2.05
F	6.55	6.55	8.19	1.64
G	5.24	5.24	6.55	1.31
H	4.19	4.19	5.24	1.05
I	3.35	3.35	4.19	0.84
J	2.68	2.68	3.35	0.67
All other	10.76	10.76	13.44	2.68
Total by entire banking system	100.00	100.00	100.00	20.00

*Numbers have been rounded.

As n, the number of rounds in the expansion process, becomes sufficiently large, the value of such a series which decreases proportionally at each round approaches:[12]

$$\Delta M = \frac{\Delta B}{1-(1-r_m)} = \frac{\Delta B}{r_m} = \frac{\$20}{.2} = \$100$$

An optimist prefers an expansionary situation. A pessimist explaining a contraction would arrive at the same general result. Suppose bank Z's total reserves are \$20 less than required. This bank almost certainly would cover the reserve shortage by selling only \$20 of securities. The purchaser of the securities quite probably has an account at another bank, bank Y. Bank Z collects by having its account at the Fed credited by \$20. Of course, at the same time the Fed credits the account of bank Z it debits the account of bank Y. Now bank Y is short \$16 in required reserves or, equivalently, has excess reserves of \$ – 16. (Reserves at bank Y decreased by \$20, but the deposits of its customers also fell by the same amount, reducing required reserves by \$4.) The public reduces its money balances by another \$16 to buy the securities sold by bank Y. The story continues but you can anticipate the punch line. Many banks are involved before equilibrium is reached. Equilibrium often will be reached quite rapidly but at other times the lags are quite long.

Why can a single bank create deposits only equal to its excess reserves while the banking system expands by a multiple of the excess reserves? The public wants to hold money deposits—indeed in this example it holds nothing else—but it does not want all its deposits at a single bank. *From the viewpoint of a single bank, the clearing-house drain equals the increase in loans and newly created deposits, but the entire banking system faces no clearing-house drain, by assumption.* The reserves lost by one bank become the reserves of another bank. With banking system reserves fixed, multiple deposit expansion is necessary to transform the initial excess reserves into required reserves.

In subsequent chapters, the adjustment made by each bank in the expansion process generally is ignored because we are mainly interested in aggregate changes. The surveyor uses his chain to measure your property. To check the accuracy of his chain, the surveyor measures each link with a ruler and adds the measurements. Having done this once, he discards the ruler. We follow the same principle.

---

[12]Let $A = \Delta B[1 + (1-r_m) + (1-r_m)^2 + \cdots (1-r_m)^n]$.
Then, $(1-r_m)A = \Delta B[(1-r_m) + (1-r_m)^2 + \cdots + (1-r_m)^n + (1-r_m)^{n+1}]$.
Subtracting, $A - (1-r_m)A = \Delta B[1-(1-r_m)^{n+1}]$.
Dividing by r_m, $A = \Delta B[1-(1-r_m)^{n+1}]/r_m$.
As $n+1$ becomes very large, $(1-r_m)^{n+1}$ approaches zero since $(1-r_m) < 1$.

$$\lim_{n \to \infty} \Delta B[1-(1-r_m)^{n+1}]/r_m = \Delta B/r_m.$$

Summary/Questions

Stripped to essentials, open-market operations illustrate a fiat money producer's power to purchase whatever it may wish by cranking the press. The Fed purchases only securities, unlike some foreign fiat money producers whose tastes are more comprehensive. While payment for the security is made by check, Fed checks drawn against itself are equivalent to currency. Security sellers often prefer a credit (deposit) to Fed currency, obscuring the power of the Fed. Were preferences to change, the Fed would pay its creditors (depositors) by cranking the big green machine. Bank deposits at the Fed, called reserves, plus currency are the monetary base.

The marketing skill of bankers often is unrecognized. No one must hold money deposits, just as no one must hold savings bonds or Fly-by-Night stock. If individuals believed that bank deposits were completely inferior, the money supply would equal the currency base provided by the Fed. Bankers must sell their products like any other producer. At rock concerts you slip a $10 bill to someone in a cage and receive an admission ticket. You do something similar in a bank. You receive a deposit slip instead of an admission ticket. People purchase deposits because they are safe and convenient. We temporarily assumed that banks need offer only one type of deposit, called a money deposit, which the public "purchased" with *all* its currency. This had a strong effect on the money supply. Banks no longer are secured vaults with reserves equal to their deposits. Bankers learned long ago that fractional reserves are adequate. In other words, deposits are a multiple of reserves. Deposits and the money supply are positively related to the reserves that banks attract and negatively related to the required reserve fraction.

1. Assume the First National Bank (FNB) sells $25,000 of securities to:
a. A depositor of FNB who pays by check.
b. A depositor of FNB who pays in cash (currency).
c. A nonbank corporation.
d. Another bank.
e. The Federal Reserve.
What is the effect of each of the five transactions above on total reserves of (1) FNB and (2) the entire banking system? If not enough information is given for the answer to be certain, state what additional information is necessary.

2. Define the monetary base.

3. When did the money supply equal the monetary base? Is the money supply greater than, equal to, or less than the monetary base today?

4. What is the (1) immediate and (2) ultimate impact on the money supply of the deposit of currency?
5. Look at the balance sheet of any bank. Reserves always are a small fraction of money deposits. Therefore, any single bank can expand the money supply by a multiple of its excess reserves. True or False. Explain.
6. Go back to question 1. How do those transactions affect the *excess* reserves of (1) FNB and (2) the entire banking system?
7. Define open-market operations. Show the effect on the balance sheets of the Fed and commercial banks of a $100 open-market sale to an individual who pays for the security by writing a check.
8. What is the immediate impact of discounts at the Fed on (1) reserves and (2) the money supply?
9. Define clearing-house drain. Is the clearing-house drain the same for a single bank and the banking system? Explain your answer.
10. Assume that the public does not want any currency or nonmoney deposits and banks do not want any excess reserves. In this case what is the general formula for the money supply multiplier? If the reserve requirement is 10 percent, a $20 open-market *sale* will ultimately change the money supply by how much? A $20 open-market *purchase* will ultimately change the money supply by how much?

Determinants of the money supply: The multiplier

4

> Indeed, it will be found that so many and diverse are the forces causing variations in the reserve ratio . . . [and multiplier] that it is quite impossible to predict the magnitude of a change in the volume of money. . . .
>
> *Lauchlin Currie**

Our main quarrel with the simple money supply model is its false implication of precision. It suggests that the Fed controls money exactly since the money stock depends only on the required reserve ratio and the base, both of which are assumed to be controlled perfectly by the Fed. The opening quote illustrates, however, that for many years professional monetary economists have known that the Fed cannot hold money in a viselike grip. For just as many years they did not communicate this fact forcefully enough. Nonmonetary economics books typically presented only the simple model. A generation of nonmonetary economists and their students grew up thinking that only the Fed pulled the money strings.[1] This misconception will be cleared up as we examine various endogenous determinants of the money supply.

Money Multiplier I

$$r_m = \bar{r}_m; \quad DER = C = NMD = 0$$

Even if currency and nonmoney deposits do not exist (C = NMD = 0) and banks do not want any excess reserves (DER = 0), the Fed cannot

---

**The Supply and Control of Money in the United States* (Cambridge, Mass.: Harvard University Press, 1934), p. 71.

[1]This same generation claimed (incorrectly) that the Fed could not *push* the income string, that is, make money influence income.

control the money supply exactly because *the required reserve ratio is not uniform.* All money measures aggregate several components. In this case, "the" required reserve ratio for the aggregate is a weighted average of the components' ratios, where the weights measure the components' relative importance. As the public shifts from one component to another component with a different required reserve ratio, "the" aggregate reserve ratio changes. For example, assume there are two equally large deposit classes with required reserve ratios of 10 and 20 percent. The average reserve ratio is 15 percent. Suppose further that the public shifts all deposits from the high required reserve category to the low category. The average (and now uniform) reserve ratio falls to 10 percent.

Let the aggregate average required reserve ratio be $\bar{r}_m$. Total required reserves demanded can still be written as the product of the average reserve requirement times aggregate deposits.[2]

(4–1)

$$R = \bar{r}_m D$$

This looks extremely similar to Equation (3–3), the demand for reserves in the simple money supply model. Following the procedure used in Chapter 3, set the demand for reserves as given by Equation (4–1) equal to a given base and rearrange to solve for equilibrium deposits and money. When the public holds no currency, equilibrium deposits and money are the product of the inverse of "the" reserve ratio times the base.

(4–3)

$$M = D = \frac{1}{\bar{r}_m} \cdot B$$

Again, this looks extremely similar to Equation (3–5.1). There is an extremely important difference, however. *The Fed controls r_m perfectly in Equation (3–5.1) but not $\bar{r}_m$ in Equation (4–3).* The Fed does set the legal reserve ratio for a given type of money deposit. However, because reserve ratios vary by deposit type, and because the public ultimately determines what deposit type it holds, the public also influences the ag-

---

[2]Assuming n money components with different required reserve ratios, the total dollar demand for reserves is the sum of the demands by the n components.

(4–1′)

$$R = \sum_{i=1}^{n} r_{m_i} D_i = \sum_{i=1}^{n} r_{m_i} \frac{D_i}{D} D$$

The second equality clearly follows since D/D = 1. D_i/D is a component's relative importance. Inspection of Equations (4–1) and (4–1′) shows that

(4–2)

$$\bar{r}_m = \sum_{i=1}^{n} r_{m_i} \frac{D_i}{D}$$

gregate average requirement. See the example in the next-to-last paragraph. In that case the public's action reduced "the" reserve ratio, and money increased *without* any action by the Fed.

How much do reserve requirements vary across deposit classes? How large are variations in the aggregate average reserve ratio due to shifts from one money component to another? Prior to 1980 the Fed regulated the reserves of its members alone. Nonmember banks were regulated by state banking commissions, which set reserve ratios much lower than the Fed did. One of the main purposes of the Monetary Control Act (MCA) of 1980 was to eliminate the diversity of reserve ratios. MCA made all issuers of check deposits, including nonbanks such as savings and loans, subject to the Fed's reserve requirement policies. However, the new universal provision is being adopted gradually. Depositories brought under the Fed's regulations by MCA have until 1987 before their requirements will equal member bank requirements. Even then, reserve ratios will *not* be uniform in two respects. First, the reserve ratio on check deposits, which are included in every money definition, will continue to be higher for large banks than for small banks.[3] Second, reserve ratios vary by type of bank liability. Reserve ratios are high on check deposits, low on nonpersonal time deposits and a few other liabilities, and totally nonexistent on personal time deposits, nonbank traveler's checks, and many bank liabilities.

The value and, more importantly, the endogenous variability of the average required reserve ratio depends on the preferred money measure. The value of $\bar{r}_m$ decreases as the money definition widens. In M-1, only nonbank traveler's checks, which are a very small proportion of the total M-1, have no reserve requirements. On the other hand, many large items in M-2 have no or very low required reserve ratios. For similar reasons, the average reserve ratio also is much smaller for M-3 than M-1. Because both nonbank traveler's checks and the check deposits issued by small banks with low reserve requirements are a small proportion of M-1, the average required reserve ratio for M-1 varies very little, assuming the Fed does not intervene. In other words, *with two minor exceptions the reserve ratios on M-1 deposits are uniform, and, therefore, the average is largely independent of the public's asset choice.* M-2 is a hodgepodge. The reserve ratio varies considerably among deposit classes in M-2. No single type of deposit dominates M-2. Consequently, *the required reserve ratio for M-2 is significantly influenced by the public.* This is one important reason why the Fed can control M-1 much better than M-2, as we indicated in Chapter 2.

---

[3]The cut-off point between small and large banks and technical aspects of reserve requirement policy are discussed in Chapter 18.

Money Multiplier II

$$r_m = \bar{r}_m; \quad DER > 0; \quad C = NMD = 0$$

Bank depositors are fickle. They are continually writing checks and making deposits. As we saw in the last chapter, the change in check deposits *and* reserves at any one bank equals the difference between checks drawn on and payable to other banks. Assuming a bank's depositors are writing more checks than they are depositing so that there is a negative net clearing balance, required reserves fall by only a fraction of the decrease in deposits and reserves. Since total reserves decrease more than required reserves, a bank without excess reserves would no longer meet the legal requirements. It would have to sell liquid assets or gain reserves in some other way. A bank with sufficient excess reserve would avoid the bother and cost of selling assets. What is sufficient? Suppose the required reserve ratio is 20 percent and a bank suffers net check deposit withdrawals of $1. The deposit loss reduces reserves by an equal amount, and required reserves fall by 20¢. How much excess reserves does a bank need in order to avoid selling liquid assets? Continue if you said 80¢; otherwise, reread this paragraph. A bank cannot anticipate its deposit losses with certainty. Indeed, it may not even be sure that it will lose deposits as the bank's depositors could receive more checks than they issue. Nevertheless, there always exists some possibility of a deposit loss. The possible deposit losses are positively related to bank size. During the next week depositors might withdraw $100,000 from the First National Bank of Podunk. The Third National Bank of New York would not be altogether surprised if deposits fell $10 million tomorrow. As a first approximation then assume the amount of desired excess reserve, DER, is some fraction, $\bar{r}_{em}$, of money deposits.

(4–4)

$$DER = \bar{r}_{em} \cdot D$$

The fraction $\bar{r}_{em}$ is the average desired excess reserve ratio, as dividing both sides of Equation (4–4) by D confirms.

How does the introduction of a demand for excess reserves alter the money supply equations? Continuing to assume that the public does not want any currency, the two basic equations are:

(4–1.2)

$$M = D$$

(4–2.2)

$$B = R$$

This is similar to the preceding case so far. The difference lies in the demand for reserves, which is now made up of two components: (1) the demand for required reserves to meet the law, and (2) the demand for excess reserves to meet possible deposit outflows without having to sell securities or borrow.

(4–3.2)

$$R = \bar{r}_m D + \bar{r}_{em} D$$

Perform the substitutions shown in Case I. That is, set the demand for reserves expressed by Equation (4–3.2) equal to a given base supply B. One gets

(4–4.2)

$$B = \bar{r}_m D + \bar{r}_{em} D$$

(4–5.2)

$$M = D = \frac{1}{\bar{r}_m + \bar{r}_{em}} \cdot B$$

Case I could be viewed as a specific example of Case II where $\bar{r}_{em} = 0$. In this slightly more general case the money supply multiplier is $1/(\bar{r}_m + \bar{r}_{em})$, which clearly is smaller than $1/\bar{r}_m$. Suppose $\bar{r}_m = .20$ and $\bar{r}_{em} = .05$. If the monetary authorities increase the base by \$20, by how much does the money supply change?

$$\Delta M = \frac{1}{\bar{r}_m + \bar{r}_{em}} \cdot \Delta B = \frac{1}{.2 + .05} \cdot \$20 = \$80$$

The money supply would have increased \$100 if banks had not wanted any excess reserves. Since the required reserve ratio and the desired excess reserve ratio appear additively in the denominator, a reduction in either is expansionary, and vice versa. Note that *the reason why banks hold reserves has no effect whatever on the money supply; what matters is the total proportion of reserves to deposits that banks demand.* Let the Federal Reserve increase the required reserve ratio by 5 percentage points while, *by chance,* banks' desired excess reserve ratio falls by 5 percentage points.[4] What happens to the money supply? Nothing. Why? Required reserves plus desired excess reserves are unchanged.

Recognition of banks' demand for excess reserves is extremely important for monetary policy because it implies that the monetary authorities are unable to control the money supply at all times. Even if the Fed controlled the monetary base exactly and the required reserve ratio were uniform, the money supply would vary in response to the *bank-determined* desired excess reserve ratio. Banks file financial statements. From the statements the Fed can readily make *legal* distinctions between reserves. If the required reserve ratio is 20 percent in Figure 4–1, required reserves

---

[4]Do not for a moment think that an increase in required reserve *causes* desired excess reserves to fall by an equal amount. The Federal Reserve once made this mistake, and the nation suffered greatly, as we shall see shortly.

FIGURE 4–1

Commercial Banking System

Deposits at Fed		125	Deposits	500
Required reserves	100			
Excess reserves	25			
Desired excess	?			
Undesired excess	?			
Loans and securities		375		

are \$100 and excess reserves are \$25. *The seemingly mechanical separation of total reserves into required and excess reserves had economic significance when we assumed all excess reserves were undesired.* In such a situation the existence of excess reserves implies that the money supply would increase. Once we admit that banks demand excess reserves, can we state for sure what, if anything, will be happening to the money supply? We now must separate excess reserves, ER, into desired, DER, and undesired excess reserves, UER.

$$ER = DER + UER \tag{4–6}$$

With this separation of excess reserves, total reserves may be written as

$$TR = RR + DER + UER \tag{4–7}$$

It is difficult but essential for economic policy to make the *economic* distinction between required and desired excess reserves on the one hand and undesired excess reserves on the other. If banks demand excess reserves equal to 5 percent of deposits, will the money supply change, given the last balance sheet? No.[5] Reserves are just at the right level. Any adjustment by the system causes the reserve ratio to deviate from the desired value. Now suppose banks' demand changes and they do not want to hold excess reserves. The balance sheet no longer represents an equilibrium. Undesired excess reserves are zero at equilibrium by definition, so deposits and loans expand by \$125. At the new equilibrium money supply of \$625, banks want \$125 in reserves. Deposits increase when the actual reserve ratio is greater than the total desired ratio, which is the sum of the required and desired excess reserve ratios. Of course, *if* the Fed had realized that the desired excess ratio had fallen, a \$25 open-market sale reducing the base or an increase in required reserves to 25

[5]Substituting the values of this example in Equation (4–5.2), what does the equilibrium money supply equal? 500.

percent would have kept the money supply on course.[6] And *if* the Fed had done this, and *if*. . . . *The important point is: the Fed's inability to discriminate perfectly between desired and undesired excess reserves causes unintentional, and sometimes disastrous, money changes.*

Determinants of the Desired Excess Reserve Ratio

What determines the desired excess reserve ratio? Why did banks last year want excess reserves to equal, say, 1 percent of deposits while today they want 2 percent? Banks are uncertain about the behavior of their depositors and, therefore, whether they will be gaining or losing reserves. Many outcomes with different probabilities are possible. The desired excess reserve ratio depends on the distribution of deposit and reserve percentage changes.[7] Figure 4–2 graphs a simple distribution. The percentage change in deposits and reserves is plotted on the x-axis, and the y-axis shows the probability of the event. According to Figure 4–2, the three possible outcomes are a 1 percent loss, no change, and a 1 percent gain in reserves. Each outcome is equally likely; the probability attached to any one outcome is one third. An important characteristic of the distribution is its expected or average value. The expected value, which

FIGURE 4–2
Distribution of Deposit and Reserve Percentage Changes

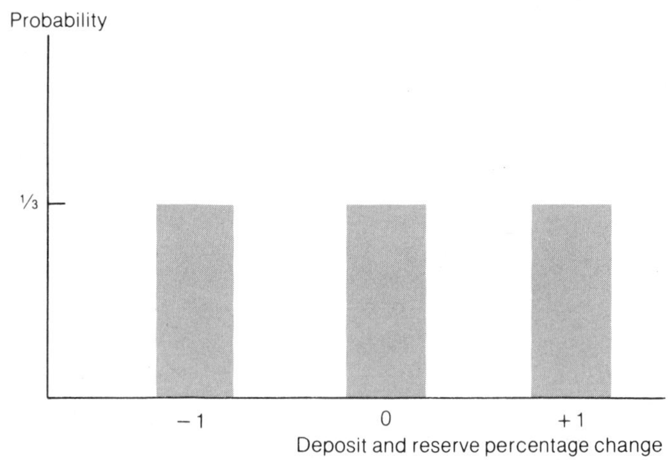

[6]Since $M = D = B/(\bar{r}_m + \bar{r}_{em})$, $M = 500$ when $\bar{r}_m = 0.2$, $\bar{r}_{em} = .05$, and $B = 125$. If $\bar{r}_{em} = 0$, $M = 625$, an increase of 125. To keep $M = 500$, make either $B = 100$ or $\bar{r}_m = 0.25$.

[7]The excess reserve *ratio* depends on the *percentage* change in reserves while the amount of excess reserves demanded depends on the dollar change in reserves.

is computed by summing the products of the probability times the outcome, is zero in this example. (Expected value = $1/3(-1) + 1/3(0) + 1/3(+1) = 0$.) Deposits sometimes rise and fall by 1 percent but remain unchanged on average. *The greater the expected percentage change in deposits, the smaller is the desired excess reserve ratio.* You demand *less* excess reserves today when you expect reserves and deposits to *increase* in the near future. Particularly at seashore resorts and other recreational areas, the expected deposit and reserve change varies considerably during the year. Suppose you are a banker in Ocean City, Maryland. Would you demand less or more excess reserves at the beginning of the summer, before the influx of tourists and temporary workers, than toward the end of the summer? If you said "less" you might just have a future in banking. At the beginning of the summer, the expected reserve and deposit percentage change is positive. Tourists bring their money to Ocean City and spend it on services provided by temporary workers who open bank accounts. Banks' demand for excess reserves is extremely low. There simply is no need for excess reserves now as they expect to gain reserves. By late August, however, the expected deposit change is negative, that is, banks expect withdrawals and want large excess reserves. The money leaves Ocean City when the temporary workers close their accounts and go home.

The variability of deposits and reserves, as measured by the range or standard deviation, is an important additional factor. Suppose the three equally likely outcomes are a 5 percent loss, no change, and a 5 percent gain in reserves and deposits. Compared to the situation illustrated by Figure 4–2, the expected or average change still is zero, but deposits are more variable. Wider deposit swings are possible. Again, see whether you would make a good banker. *How is the desired excess reserve ratio related to the variability or dispersion of deposits and reserves? A positive relationship exists*. Following a series of runs on banks and failures, vague rumors concerning the stability of one bank and then another are much more likely to induce individuals to shift their deposits among banks in hopes of finding a safe bank.[8] At such times banks in general will view their deposits as highly variable, and the aggregate desired excess ratio is high.

The careful reader probably noticed that the justification for desired excess reserves in terms of possible deposit losses was not sufficient. Even if a bank knows with certainty that it will lose reserves tomorrow, why should it hold excess reserves today? A bank could buy liquid assets with the excess reserves today and regain reserves by selling tommorow. Such a strategy would yield a bank interest income. There is a hitch,

---

[8]This was particularly true before deposit insurance. Even now, deposit insurance coverage is limited to \$100,000. While relatively few individuals or firms have accounts over \$100,000, large uninsured accounts are a substantial proportion of total deposits.

however. In buying and selling liquid assets the bank incurs brokerage costs. These costs include the commission paid to security dealers as well as the cost of bank executives' time spent arranging the transaction, which may be substantially more than commission charges. Clearly, brokerage costs must be balanced against the extra income earned by maintaining zero excess reserves and buying and selling liquid assets. *Excess reserves are positively related to brokerage cost.* It becomes profitable to hold more excess reserves and less liquid assets when brokerage costs are high. At the extreme situation where brokerage costs are zero, banks would demand no excess reserves. At another extreme, banks would hold only excess reserves if the rate of interest were zero. As interest rates rise, banks demand less excess reserves because the interest income from liquid assets surpasses brokerage costs. *Excess reserves and interest rates are negatively related.*

For those who like mathematical expressions, the discussion can be conveniently summarized.

$$\bar{r}_{em} = f(\underset{-}{\mu}, \underset{+}{\sigma}, \underset{-}{i}, \underset{+}{b})$$

where

μ = expected or average percentage change in money deposits
σ = variability of money deposits
i = interest rate on marketable securities
b = brokerage costs

The equation says the excess reserve ratio is a function of or depends on (that's what the letter "f" means) the variables in parentheses. The signs under the variables indicate the direction of the relationship between a variable and the excess reserve ratio. For example, larger expected deposits reduce desired excess reserves.

Desired Excess Reserves in the 1930s

Don't think that economists know everything about the desired excess reserve ratio. We know quite a bit, as the last few paragraphs demonstrated, but brokerage costs, interest rates, expected deposit changes, and the variability of deposits do not explain everything.[9] Other factors which

[9]Small banks hold proportionally more excess reserves than large banks. However, the distribution of deposits among banks does not change enough to have a significant effect on the average desired reserve ratio. Recent changes in required reserves have a *temporary* effect on desired excess reserves. The text, however, analyzes the *permanent* or long-run determinants of excess reserves. Even in the long run, desired excess reserves do depend on the required reserve ratio if variations in the latter are very large. For example, banks surely would hold some excess reserves (cash) even if required reserves were nonexistent, but, equally surely, they would hold no excess reserves when the required ratio is 100 percent. For practical purposes the effect of the required reserve ratio on the desired excess ratio may be ignored because variations in the former are quite small.

still have not been isolated cause the desired excess ratio to change over time. However, the Fed has come a long way since the 30s when it thought Case I existed—banks demand no excess reserves. Between 1933 and 1936 the unemployment rate fell from 24.9 to 16.9 percent, and the consumer price index (1929 = 100) rose from 75.4 to 80.9. The economy definitely was improving, but by any absolute standard it hardly was a period of prosperity. Nevertheless, the Fed feared that inflation would soon raise its ugly head. Banks were flush with excess reserves, which almost equaled required reserves. If all the excess reserves were undesired, as the Fed thought, the money supply would expand greatly and aggravate the "inflationary" potential of the economy. In a series of bold strokes the Fed doubled reserve requirements between August 16, 1936 and May 1, 1937. Naturally, excess reserves fell. The Fed sadly learned that banks did want large excess reserves. Bank loans and deposits fell because excess reserves, which were still substantial after the reserve requirement increase, were less than the desired amount.

The Fed relented nearly a year later, cutting required reserve ratios somewhat. Largely due to random factors which the Fed chose not to counteract, reserves increased steadily and dramatically. The reserve increase and moderation in requirements placed the money supply back on track by December 1938. Look at Table 4–1. Can you explain the behavior of the excess reserve ratio?

Could banks have demanded large amounts of excess reserves in June 1936? Individuals and bankers recalled the 1929–33 debacle. Demand deposits had fallen approximately one third. Expansionary policies by the Fed and Treasury during 1933–36 succeeded in restoring the 1929 level of demand deposits. Could the expansionary policies be temporary? Banks

TABLE 4–1

Check Deposits, Reserves, and Interest Rates, 1936–1938

Date	*6/30/36*	*12/31/36*	*6/30/37*	*12/31/37*	*6/30/38*	*12/31/38*
Check deposits*	23,780	25,483	25,198	23,959	24,313	25,986
Required reserve ratio†	.10	.15	.20	.20	.175	.175
Total reserves*	5,633	6,606	6,900	7,027	8,024	8,724
Required reserves‡	2,916	4,622	6,035	5,815	5,149	5,519
Excess reserves	2,717	1,984	865	1,212	2,875	3,205
Treasury bill rate (percent per year)	0.226	0.209	0.561	0.104	0.023	0.007
Excess reserve ratio	.114	.078	.034	.051	.118	.123

*Deposits and reserves, in $ millions, are for member banks only.
†The second row gives the check deposit required reserve ratio for reserve city banks.
‡Required reserves include those on both check and time deposits. Therefore, required reserves are greater than the product of check deposits and the check deposit required reserve ratio.
Source: Board of Governors of the Federal Reserve System, *Banking and Monetary Statistics* (Washington, D.C., 1943).

might have been expecting a policy reversal and reserve losses. In any case, confidence in the banking system was hardly at its high point, and banks viewed their deposits as highly variable. The second to last row in Table 4–1 contains no typographical mistake. If you had invested $1,000 in Treasury bills on June 30, 1936, your grand total three months later would have been $1,000.54.[10] Hardly worth the bother! All these factors suggest that desired excess reserves were large, and undesired excess might have been zero. The excess ratio was .114, seemingly just what banks demanded.

The reserve requirement increase between June and December 1936 naturally reduced excess reserves. Perhaps because banks had made prior loan commitments they were unable to reduce check deposits. Compare the first two columns, June 30, 1936, and December 31, 1936. By early 1937 banks started to reduce their check deposits and loans to restore the desired excess reserve ratio. Adjustments take time, however. Banks' attempts to increase excess reserves were counterbalanced by even higher required reserve ratios between January and June 1937. The excess reserve ratio continued to decline. Compare columns 2 and 3. Undesired excess reserves were negative or, equivalently, the desired excess ratio was greater than the actual ratio. In the fall of 1937 the Fed maintained high required reserve ratios but did not raise them further. Banks continued to contract and succeeded in raising the actual excess reserve ratio from .034 to .051, still far below earlier desired excess reserve ratios. Check deposits fell by nearly 6 percent between December 1936 and December 1937. Not altogether unrelated, the unemployment rate rose from 14.3 to 19.0 percent between 1937 and 1938. It appears the Fed recognized its folly. The increase in total reserves and the reserve requirement cuts in spring 1938 were so substantial that banks simultaneously were able to restore the desired excess reserve ratio and expand deposits. Compare columns 4 and 5. Total reserves continued to increase in fall 1938, and with the required reserve ratio constant, so did check deposits, in spite of a higher actual and presumably desired excess reserve ratio. It hardly seems possible that in December 1938 the annualized interest rate on 90-day Treasury bills was less than 1/100 of 1 percent! Millionaires had to dip into their capital; their interest income was a paltry $70 per year.

Excess Reserves in the 1970s and 1980s

Actual and presumably desired excess reserve ratios have been very low for many years. Knowledge of the determinants of the ratio suggests why this is so. Market interest rates and, therefore, the opportunity cost

---

[10]The interest rates in Table 4–1 are annualized. 0.226 percent per year is equivalent to 0.054 per quarter.

of excess reserves, have been high. Moreover, the development of new financial markets has reduced brokerage costs, making frequent purchases and sales profitable. For example, prior to 1930 the government typically balanced its budget and few government bonds were outstanding. Although the government issued bonds to finance moderate deficits during the 1930s, dealers failed to react immediately and did not create a wide market by standing ready to buy and sell large amounts of government bonds. Government bonds became highly marketable during World War II, when the deficit and bond issues soared. Readily salable assets like government bonds greatly reduced the need for excess reserves. Development of the federal funds market around 1960 further reduced the desired excess reserve ratio. Federal funds are bank deposits at the Federal Reserve.[11] In a typical federal funds transaction, a bank with excess reserves sells some of its deposits at the Fed to a bank with deficient reserves, on an overnight basis and at an agreed-upon interest rate. Thus, banks lend excess reserves directly to other banks instead of purchasing government securities or other assets.

Money Multiplier III

$$r_m = \bar{r}_m; \quad DER>0; \quad C>0, NMD>0$$

Look in your wallet. You probably are holding some currency. In addition, banks offer nonmoney liabilities which are subject to reserve requirements. It is time to drop the assumption that individuals do not hold currency or nonmoney deposits. We shall see that *currency held by the public reduces bank reserves, and nonmoney deposits reduce the reserves available to support money. Both tend to decrease the total money supply.*[12]

As a first approximation, *individuals always hold their desired proportions of money deposits, currency, and nonmoney deposits, which we call the preferred asset ratio.* The Fed and Treasury cannot force you to hold currency. Banks will gladly accept your currency and credit your account. While banks initially credit money deposit accounts when they purchase securities or make loans, individuals can readily convert the proceeds to currency or nonmoney deposits according to their preferences. It is true that banks have the legal prerogative of requiring 30-days' notice before savings accounts may be closed. However, banks rarely exercise this prerogative. Loss of interest (or even a negative interest) is

---

[11]Do not ask embarrassing questions: why introduce a new term, federal funds, when bank deposits at the Fed are also known as reserves? Inconvenient office hours and its own vocabulary are essential to sustaining the banking mystique.

[12]Banks are required to hold reserves against Treasury and interbank deposits, which are not considered to be money by any of the definitions. Thus, nonmoney deposits exist even for the broadest money measure.

the worst penalty for closing small time deposit accounts before maturity. CDs are one class of time deposits not payable before maturity. However, since CDs are negotiable, the rate of return adjusts rapidly to satisfy the preferred asset ratio. On balance, banks' liabilities are readily convertible into each other and into cash.[13] Using general notation to express currency and nonmoney deposits as a proportion of money deposits,

$$C = kD$$
$$NMD = nD$$

where k is the factor of proportionality between currency and money deposits or, equivalently, the ratio of currency to money deposits. The interpretation of n should be clear.

Note carefully what is and is not being said. Satisfaction of the public's preferred asset *ratio* at all times implies nothing about dollar amounts. Proportions can be correct even if the total is not. Consider an example which ignores nonmoney deposits for simplicity. Given income and other factors, suppose the desired money balances of a typical person are $1,350, composed of $350 in currency and the balance in money deposits. Might the individual be holding more or less money for a significant period of time? Definitely yes. An individual may not be holding the desired amount of money for some time because the costs of acquiring money are quite high. Whatever amount of money the individual may be holding, transferring funds from one account to another is sufficiently simple that the currency/money deposit ratio equals the preferred percentage except for fleeting moments. The currency/money deposit ratio, k, and the nonmoney/money deposit ratio, n, are not fixed numbers. Nevertheless, following the procedure of the last section, we first consider the effects of currency and nonmoney deposits on the money stock and then analyze the determinants of the ratios.

The fundamental money supply equations are:

(4–1.3)

$$M \equiv D + C \equiv D + kD \equiv (1 + k)D$$

(4–2.3)

$$\begin{aligned} B &= R + C = R + kD \\ &= \bar{r}_m D + \bar{r}_{em} D + \bar{r}_n nD + kD \\ &= (\bar{r}_m + \bar{r}_{em} + \bar{r}_n n + k)D \end{aligned}$$

---

[13]For short periods of time during the 19th century and the "bank holiday" of 1933, banks suspended payments, that is, banks refused to exchange currency for check deposits. Currency sold at a premium over check deposits. These periods where the actual currency/check deposit ratio was less than the desired ratio were quite short and can be ignored. We foresee no likelihood of such events recurring.

Equation (4–1.3) uses the preferred asset ratio, expressing currency as a fraction of money deposits. The monetary base equilibrium Equation (4–2.3) contains two new terms on the demand side. Besides the previously discussed average required and desired excess reserves against money deposits, $\bar{r}_m D + \bar{r}_{em} D$, the demand for reserves now includes required reserves against nonmoney deposits, which equal the average nonmoney deposit required reserve ratio, $\bar{r}_n$, multiplied by nonmoney deposits, NMD = nD. The average required reserve ratio usually is substantially smaller on nonmoney than money deposits. Currency, again expressed as a fraction of money deposits, is the nonbank demand for the base. The total demand for the base per dollar of money deposits is $\bar{r}_m + \bar{r}_{em} + \bar{r}_n n + k$, *given the public's preferences equal to n and k for nonmoney deposits and currency, respectively.*[14] The base equilibrium equation yields the quantity of money deposits. Rearranging (4–2.3) and solving for money deposits,

(4–4.3)

$$D = \frac{1}{\bar{r}_m + \bar{r}_{em} + \bar{r}_n n + k} \cdot B$$

The equilibrium values of the other variables follow readily. Substituting the last equation in (4–1.3) gives the equilibrium money stock.

(4–5.3)

$$M = \frac{1 + k}{\bar{r}_m + \bar{r}_{em} + \bar{r}_n n + k} \cdot B$$

From the proportionality assumptions, equilibrium currency and nonmoney deposits are[15]

(4–8.3)

$$C = \frac{k}{\bar{r}_m + \bar{r}_{em} + \bar{r}_n n + k} \cdot B = kD$$

(4–9.3)

$$NMD = \frac{n}{\bar{r}_m + \bar{r}_{em} + \bar{r}_n n + k} \cdot B = nD$$

Similar equations hold for the changes in the base and the items on the left-hand side. For example,

(4–9.3′)

$$\Delta NMD = \frac{n}{\bar{r}_m + \bar{r}_{em} + \bar{r}_n n + k} \Delta B = n\Delta D$$

---

[14]Banks may want excess reserves against nonmoney deposits as well as money deposits. We leave it to the reader to develop a money supply equation for such a case.

[15]Those who like algebra should solve for the equilibrium quantities of reserves and loans. Hint: balance sheets do balance. Ignoring net worth, money deposit + nonmoney deposits − loans = reserves.

Don't worry, these are our most complex equations. The money supply, Equation (4–5.3), still is expressed as the product of a multiplier times the base. However, recognition of nonmoney deposits and currency complicates the multiplier. Three new variables, $\bar{r}_n$, n, and k, have been introduced. How is the final money stock equation related to these three variables? From a purely mechanical viewpoint we see that $\bar{r}_n$ and n appear in the denominator of the money multiplier, so the money supply varies inversely with the average required reserve ratio against nonmoney deposits, $\bar{r}_n$, and the public's preferred nonmoney/money deposit ratio, n. Economically speaking, *as the nonmoney deposit reserve ratio or the quantity of nonmoney deposits rises, less reserves are available to support the money supply.* The currency/money deposit ratio appears in both the numerator and denominator of the money supply multiplier. Nevertheless, a larger ratio always reduces the money supply. With a fixed base, reserves decrease when people hold more currency. Since money deposits are a multiple of reserves, deposits ultimately fall by more than the increase in currency. Therefore, *the money supply falls when the currency/money deposit ratio rises.*[16]

Compared to the first model, this realistic model gives a substantially smaller money supply multiplier. Look at Equations (4–3), (4–5.2), and (4–5.3) and see how the multiplier becomes smaller as one introduces excess reserves, currency, and nonmoney deposits. The multiplier of Equation (4–5.3) shows how the Fed, banks, and the public *jointly* determine the money supply.

A Numerical Example

Let us give some economic flesh to these mathematical bones. A specific example illustrates the adjustment process.

The initial balance sheets of the banking system, the Fed, and the public are represented by the first line of Figure 4–3. Parameter values for this example are shown at the bottom of the figure. For example, the average required reserve ratios against money and nonmoney deposits are 0.18 and 0.05, respectively. Look at line 1 of Figure 4–3 carefully. Does it satisfy our equations and, thereby, represent an equilibrium? Given our assumptions, total (required and excess) desired reserves against money deposits are \$20 = (0.18 + 0.02)\$100. Required reserves against nonmoney deposits are \$10 = 0.05 × \$200. Therefore, bank reserves are at the desired level, \$30, and banks will not be adjusting their assets and liabilities, that is, banks are in equilibrium. According to the Fed's balance sheet, the monetary base is \$50. The Fed's balance sheet is convenient

[16]For those who are familiar with the calculus, $\delta M/\delta k = B(D - N)/D^2$, where D and N are the denominator and numerator, respectively, of the money supply multiplier. As $D < N$, then $\delta M/\delta k < 0$.

FIGURE 4–3 (1) Initial equilibrium, (2) open-market purchase from banks, (3) first-round bank expansion, and (4) the public's adjustment to the preferred asset ratio.

Banking System

	Assets		Liabilities	
(1)	Deposits at Fed	30	Money deposits	100
	Loans and securities	270	Nonmoney deposits	200
(2)	Deposits at Fed	+16		
	Loans and securities	−16		
(3)	Loans and securities	+80	Money deposits	+80
(4)	Deposits at Fed	−y	Money deposits	−x
			Nonmoney deposits	x−y

Fed

	Assets		Liabilities	
(1)	Treasury securities	50	Deposits of banks	30
			Currency in circulation	20
(2)	Treasury securities	+16	Deposits of banks	+16
(3)				
(4)			Deposits of banks	−y
			Currency in circulation	+y

Public

	Assets		Liabilities	
(1)	Money deposits	100	Loans from banks	100
	Nonmoney deposits	200	Net worth	500
	Currency	20		
	Treasury securities	80		
	Other assets	200		
(2)				
(3)	Money deposits	+80	Loans from banks	+80
(4)	Money deposits	−x		
	Nonmoney deposits	x−y		
	Currency	+y		

$\bar{r}_m = 0.18$ $\bar{r}_n = 0.05$ $n = 2.0$

$\bar{r}_{em} = 0.02$ $k = 0.2$

but unnecessary; the banking system's balance sheet is sufficient to determine the base. Since the currency/money deposit ratio is 20 percent, the $100 money deposit liability on the banking system's balance sheet implies currency is $20. Adding currency and reserves gives the $50 base. The first three assets are the important accounts in the public's balance sheet; the other accounts are listed for balance. The public's preferred asset ratio is satisfied, and the public is in equilibrium for purposes of money supply analysis. Money equals $120. Does our formula give this number? Rewriting the money supply Equation (4–5.3) and using the values in this example,

(4–5.3)

$$M = \frac{1+k}{\bar{r}_m + \bar{r}_{em} + \bar{r}_n n + k} \cdot B$$

$$M = \frac{1+.2}{.18+.02+(.05)2+.2} \cdot 50 = 120$$

Line 2 of Figure 4–3 shows a \$16 open-market purchase. How do banks and the public react? Concentrate first on the banking system's balance sheet. Reserves now are \$46 while the demand for reserves still is the same \$30. Banks attempt to eliminate the undesired excess reserves by expanding loans and money deposits. Required plus desired excess reserves equal 20 percent in this example. Therefore, the banking system expands loans and money deposits by \$80, thereby eliminating undesired excess reserves, \$80 = \$16/.2. The expansion shown on line 3, Figure 4–3, brings banks to a new equilibrium. (Sum lines 1–3. The demand for reserves, \$46, equals the amount available.)

If the public did not want currency or nonmoney deposits, as was assumed in the simple model and in this chapter's previous cases, the adjustment process would end here. The public would hold the additional money deposits, and the monetary increase is \$80.[17] Assuming a preferred asset ratio is more realistic, however, and causes further adjustments, this time by the public. *Do not for a moment think that banks automatically create assets in the proportions preferred by the public.* Banks create money deposits, but the ultimate recipients, presumably people other than the borrower, do not have to hold them. They immediately withdraw \$x from their money account, request \$y in cash, and place the balance \$x − \$y in nonmoney accounts, as shown on line 4, Figure 4–3.[18] *Step 4, which is necessary to satisfy the public's preferred asset ratio, distinguishes this case from prior cases, where the adjustment process ends at step 3.* Satisfaction of the public's preferred asset ratio changes both total and required reserves and throws banks *out* of equilibrium. The

---

[17]The Case II money supply Equation (4–5.2) is $\Delta M = (1/\bar{r}_m + \bar{r}_{em})\Delta B$. In this example, $\Delta M = (1/0.18 + 0.02)\$16 = \$80$.

[18]On the bank's balance sheet, −\$x = −\$55, −\$y = −\$5, and, of course, \$x − \$y = \$50. How did we get these numbers? Most readers will find the adjustment process quite difficult. Do *not* spend an inordinate amount of time on this footnote as subsequent material is much more important. Nevertheless, for those interested, the ratio of money deposits to money deposits equals one, of course. Therefore, the ratio of money deposits to total assets (money deposits, currency, and nonmoney deposits) is 1/3.2, where 3.2 is the sum of the three ratios: the money deposit ratio, 1; the currency ratio 0.2; and the nonmoney deposit ratio, 2. Whenever banks create \$1 in money deposits, the public retains only 1/3.2 and immediately uses 0.2/3.2 and 2/3.2 to acquire currency and nonmoney deposits, respectively. The three fractions sum to unity as the public must do something with the deposits banks create. Banks initially created \$80 in deposits, so the public retains \$25 = \$80(1/3.2). The public withdraws \$55 (the difference between the amount created, \$80, and retained, \$25) and gets currency, \$5 = \$80(0.2/3.2), and nonmoney deposits, \$50 = \$80(2/3.2).

public gains currency at the expense of total bank reserves, and the transfer from money to nonmoney deposits changes required reserves. We refrain from showing susbsequent steps.[19] There are many rounds of bank loan and money deposit expansion followed by the public's adjustment to restore the preferred asset ratio. The individual bank round-by-round adjustment shown earlier illustrates how the banking system reaches equilibrium. The sequential interaction presented here illustrates how the banking system *and* public reach equilibrium.

Many may wish to ignore the adjustment sequence, which is a pity but permissible. You cannot ignore the final effect of the open-market purchase. The first two lines of the previous set of balance sheets are reproduced in Figure 4–4. How did we get the line 3, which shows the changes induced by the $16 open-market purchase when the public demands additional currency and nonmoney deposits? Use the formulas. First, calculate the supply of the base after the $16 open-market purchase. The base is $66, $46 in reserves and $20 in currency. Rewriting the last five equations in level and first difference form and using the numbers given in this example we get:

(4–2.3)

$$\begin{aligned} B &= R + C \\ &= (\bar{r}_m + \bar{r}_{em} + \bar{r}_n n + k)D \\ 66 &= (.18 + .02 + (.05)(2) + .2)D = .5D \\ \Delta B &= \Delta R + \Delta C \\ &= (\bar{r}_m + \bar{r}_{em} + \bar{r}_n n + k)\Delta D \\ 16 &= (.18 + .02 + (.05)(2) + .2)\Delta D = .5\Delta D \end{aligned}$$

(4–4.3)

$$D = \frac{1}{\bar{r}_m + \bar{r}_{em} + \bar{r}_n n + k}B = \frac{1}{.5}B; 2.0(66) = 132$$

$$\Delta D = \frac{1}{.5}\Delta B = 32$$

(4–5.3)

$$M = D + C = (1 + k)D = \frac{(1 + k)}{\bar{r}_m + \bar{r}_{em} + \bar{r}_n n + k}B$$

$$= \frac{(1 + .2)}{.5}66 = 2.4(66) = 158.4$$

$$\Delta M = 2.4\Delta B = 38.4$$

---

[19]Combining lines 1 through 4 of Figure 4–3 with the numbers given in footnote 18 for x and y, reserves are $41. Legal (0.18) and desired excess (0.02) reserves against money deposits ($125) are $25. Legal reserves (0.05) against nonmoney deposits ($250) are $12.50. Therefore, total desired reserves are $25 + $12.50 = $37.50. Undesired excess reserves are $3.50 = $41.00 − $37.50. The banking system would continue to expand.

$$C = kD = (.2)132 = 26.4 \quad (4\text{–}8.3)$$
$$\Delta C = k\Delta D = (.2)32 = 6.4$$

$$NMD = nD = (2)132 = 264 \quad (4\text{–}9.3)$$
$$\Delta NMD = n\Delta D = (2)32 = 64$$

As stated, line 3, Figure 4–4, shows the *changes* due to the open-market purchase, and line 4, which sums lines 1–3, is the new equilibrium

FIGURE 4–4

(1) Initial equilibrium, (2) open-market purchase from banks, (3) equilibrium adjustments, and (4) new equilibrium values, sum of (1) – (3).

Banking System

(1)	Deposits at Fed	30	Money deposits	100
	Loans and securities	270	Nonmoney deposits	200
(2)	Deposits at Fed	+16		
	Loans and securities	−16		
(3)	Deposits at Fed	−6.4	Money deposits	+32
	Loans and securities	+102.4	Nonmoney deposits	+64
(4)	Deposits at Fed	39.6	Money deposits	132
	Loans and securities	356.4	Nonmoney deposits	264

Fed

(1)	Treasury securities	50	Deposits of banks	30
			Currency in circulation	20
(2)	Treasury securities	+16	Deposits of banks	+16
(3)			Deposits of banks	−6.4
			Currency in circulation	+6.4
(4)	Treasury securities	66	Deposits of banks	39.6
			Currency in circulation	26.4

Public

(1)	Money deposits	100	Loans from bank	100
	Nonmoney deposits	200	Net worth	500
	Currency	20		
	Treasury securities	80		
	Other assets	200		
(2)				
(3)	Money deposits	+32.0	Loans from banks	+102.4
	Nonmoney deposits	+64.0		
	Currency	+6.4		
(4)	Money deposits	132.0	Loans from banks	202.4
	Nonmoney deposits	264.0	Net worth	500.0
	Currency	26.4		
	Treasury securities	80.0		
	Other assets	200.0		

level. We checked the initial equilibrium and the reader should verify the new numbers in a similar manner. The difference between line 3 in Figures 4–3 and 4–4 arises from different assumptions about currency and nonmoney deposits. Comparing line 3 illustrates that when the public's preferred asset ratio is satisfied (1) the growth of the money supply is smaller, (2) the growth of bank credit is larger, and (3) the ultimate increase of reserves is less than the amount of the open-market purchase.

The Effect of the Money Definition on the Preferred Asset Ratio*

The left-hand side of the money supply Equation (4–5.3) is simply M without a number (1, 2, or 3) attached to it. The equation is valid irrespective of the preferred money definition, provided the terms in the equation are analyzed comformably. The term *currency* offers no special difficulty. It *always* is coins plus paper money. "Nonmoney" deposits, on the other hand, clearly depend on the money definition. Since money and nonmoney deposits depend on the money definition, the corresponding reserve ratios and the preferred asset ratios also depend on the money definition.

To clarify the previous paragraph and simultaneously fulfill our promise in Chapter 2 to highlight any factor that affects alternative definitions of money in different directions, consider the effect of a shift from demand to time deposits. Line 1 of Figure 4–5 illustrates the initial balance sheet. For simplicity, assume the public holds no currency and banks want no excess reserves. Let the legal reserve ratio on demand deposits be 16 percent, while the reserve ratio on (nonpersonal) time deposits is 6 percent. Given these assumptions, the initial equilibrium money supply Equations (4–5.3) for M-1 and M-2 become:

$$\text{M-1} = \frac{1}{\bar{r}_m + \bar{r}_n n} \cdot B = \frac{1}{.16 + (.06)(4/6)} \cdot 120 = 600 \tag{4–10}$$

$$\text{M-2} = \frac{1}{\bar{r}_m + \bar{r}_n n} \cdot B = \frac{1}{((.16)(6/10) + (.06)(4/10)) + 0} \cdot 120 = 1{,}000 \tag{4–11}$$

From the viewpoint of M-1, only demand deposits are money deposits, so $\bar{r}_m = .16$. Time deposits are nonmoney deposits. When money is defined as M-2, both demand and time deposits are money so that $\bar{r}_m$ is a weighted average of the two reserve ratios. In our example, $\bar{r}_m$ for M-2 is 0.12, the value of the term in parentheses in Equation (4–11). For M-2, there is no nonmoney in our example, $\bar{r}_n = n = 0$.

---

*This very technical section may be skipped without loss of continuity. Indeed, I recommend that most readers proceed directly to the next section.

FIGURE 4–5

(1) Initial equilibrium, (2) shift from demand to time deposits.

Banking System

(1)	Deposits at Fed	120	Demand deposits	600
	Loans and securities	880	Time deposits	400
(2)			Demand deposits	−100
			Time deposits	+100

Now suppose the preferred asset ratio changes. The public wants equal amounts of the two deposits and, consequently, shifts \$100 from demand to time deposits, as illustrated by line 2 of Figure 4–5. This *initial* shift by the public decreases M-1 by \$100 but has no effect on M-2. Advocates of the M-2 measure would claim that the shift only alters the *composition* of the money stock. Since reserve requirements are lower on time deposits than on demand deposits, the shift in the preferred asset ratio produces excess reserves and induces expansion by the banking system. The *ultimate* effect of the shift, *after* banks have expanded loans and deposits, is a *larger* M-2 but a *smaller* M-1. The bank expansion cannot compensate for the \$100 initial decrease in M-1. This is so because the larger time deposits require more reserves, making less available for demand deposits and M-1.[20]

Consistent with our preference for M-1, the implicit denominator in our discussion of the determinants of the excess reserve ratio was demand and other checkable deposits. M-2 and M-3 are sufficiently different from M-1 that the sections on the determinants of excess reserves are unreliable when the broader money measures are preferred.

Determinants of the Preferred Asset Ratio

When money is defined as M-1, the currency/money deposit ratio is essentially the currency/check deposit ratio. (Traveler's checks are a small component of M-1 and may be ignored.) The currency/check deposit ratio during an 80-year span is depicted in Figure 4–6. A quick glance reveals that the ratio has been far from constant. Looking at the broad outlines of Figure 4–6, the period up to approximately 1960 is characterized by almost uniformly declining currency ratios temporarily interrupted by two

[20] In terms of Equation (4–10) for M-1, the shift in this example increases n from (4/6) to 1 = (5/5). The new equilibrium M-1 then is \$545.45, which exceeds the value of M-1 immediately following the asset shift, \$500, because of the induced bank expansion. From the viewpoint of Equation (4–11) for M-2, this shift reduced the weighted average money reserve ratio, that is, $\bar{r}_m = 0.12$ becomes $\bar{r}_m = 0.11$. The new equilibrium M-2 is \$1,090.91.

FIGURE 4–6
Currency Ratio

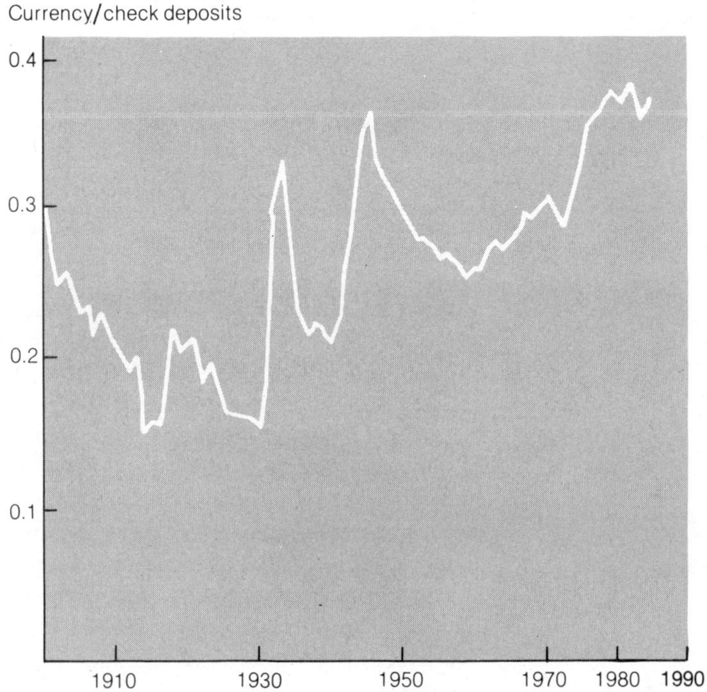

sharp rises. More specifically, the currency ratio fell more or less continually until 1930; rose sharply between 1930 and 1933; continued to decline between 1933 and 1941, albeit while at a higher level than 1930; rose dramatically between 1941 and 1946, surpassing all previous ratios; and reverted between 1946 and 1960 to a declining trend quite similar to the 1920s. Since approximately 1960, the currency ratio has risen slowly but steadily. Why has the currency ratio behaved in this manner?

The Currency Ratio

Income, expected deposit losses due to bank failures, market interest rates, tax rates, and the crime rate are the main determinants of the currency ratio. Market interest rates and expected bank failures influence the currency ratio because they determine the net rate of return on check deposits.

While we do not know in detail the causes of income growth, it is associated with lower information costs and an increase in the relative volume of transactions where checks are specially advantageous. Consequently, the currency ratio is *negatively* related to income. For example, higher incomes are associated with increased specialization. More people are engaged in the production of intermediate goods and fewer people produce and sell final goods and services. Check deposit transactions between firms who are familiar with each other increase relative to cash sales of final goods to strangers. Moreover, markets are narrow when incomes are low. Trades occur among neighbors. The technical progress which accompanies income growth reduces transportation costs and expands markets. California strawberries are shipped to Maryland supermarkets. Geographically distant payments are made by check to reduce the risk of loss. Technical progress also lowers information costs. Improved communication systems enable sellers to acquire information on your credit record quite inexpensively. Checks become more readily accepted, enhancing their use. We resist the temptation to give additional theoretical justification for the observed negative relationship between income and the currency ratio. Indeed, the growth of income by itself explains nearly all of the currency ratio's decline between 1900–29 and 1946–60. Even many of the wiggle-waggles of the currency ratio, particularly during 1900–29, are the result of the business cycle.

Why did the ratio rise sharply between 1930 and 1933? The United States and the rest of the world was in the Great Depression. Income fell dramatically, and the currency ratio rose as expected. There is a more important reason, however, for the 1930–33 rise in the currency ratio. Bank failures were an everyday occurrence. This made the net return on check deposits highly negative. In response to the falling net expected return on check deposits, individuals stood in long lines to withdraw their deposits.[21]

By 1934 income started to rebound, and the creation of the FDIC (Federal Deposit Insurance Corporation) restored *some* confidence in banks. Several years had to pass, however, before banks regained the public's full confidence. Deposit insurance was quite limited in the 1930s. (Deposit insurance is less than 100 percent even today.) The experience of 1930–33 was too fresh to be ignored altogether. The currency ratio in 1934 continued its decline from a high level because income was low but increasing, and expected deposit losses due to bank failures were high but decreasing.

The high currency ratio in the late 1930s is additionally explained by the very low market interest rates. (See Table 4–1 again.) The currency ratio clearly is inversely related to the return on check deposits; high yielding checking accounts induce the public to hold less currency. Abstracting from bank failures, the main determinant of the return on check

---

[21]Since depositors are wiped out by bank failures, the *actual* currency ratio mechanically rises with failures. However, failures increase the *desired* currency ratio even more.

deposits is market interest rates. Bankers will not pay much for funds that can be lent at, say, only 3 percent. In the 1930s banks routinely levied a service charge (a negative return) because market rates were so low. The high market interest rates and positive return on check deposits in the 1980s should lower the currency ratio, other things being equal. Look at Figure 4–6. Apparently, other things are not equal. What factors explain the high and rising currency ratio in recent years?

In 1940 the average personal tax rate was 3.3 percent. To finance World War II the federal tax rate rose to 12.1 percent in a five-year period and stayed more or less at this level until 1960. High tax rates encourage some people to hold check deposits rather than currency in order to have better records for the tax collectors. A canceled check is a good receipt for a deductible expense. On the other hand, some people may be willing to forego some deductions provided they are able to understate income even more. Many are unable to understate income because taxes are withheld on wages and salaries. Dividends and interest payments are reported to the IRS, making it somewhat risky to ignore such receipts. Public corporations that face independent auditors usually need accurate records. However, many independent professionals, skilled workers, and unincorporated businesses have good opportunities to cheat. It is a disheartening fact that tax chiselers predominate. Currency is ideal for no-questions-asked-and-no-records-please transactions. The higher tax rates are, the greater is the incentive to conceal income and make cash payments.[22] Because tax rates were high but approximately constant between 1945–60, the currency ratio was high but declined during this prosperous period.

Beginning around 1960 we embarked on what seems like a determined effort to make the United States the crime nation of the world. Some crimes are one-shot affairs; for example, a lover's quarrel becomes a homicide. However, some crime is a continuous business; for example, gambling, prostitution, and drugs. Although statistics on this "underground economy" are inevitably imprecise, I am told it is growing and is conducted on a strictly cash-and-carry basis. During the 1960s and 1970s personal tax rates increased steadily, and, allegedly, so did the underground economy. The higher tax rate and crime effect swamped the income growth and interest rate effect, producing a higher currency ratio.[23]

---

[22]Ideally we should be using the marginal rather than average personal tax rate. However, the former is difficult to compute and most likely both tax rates move together.

[23]The classic study of tax effects on the currency ratio is Phillip Cagan's, *Determinants and Effects of Changes in the Stock of Money, 1875–1960* (New York: Columbia University Press, 1965). Congress was sufficiently disturbed in 1947 by the possibility of tax evasion and black marketeering during World War II to introduce a bill creating a new currency. Individuals would receive new (blue) currency in exchange for the old demonetized green currency. Had the bill passed, the tax chiseler would have faced the dilemma of either abandoning his ill-gotten gain or swapping currency and attracting IRS attention. It may be best to accept the loss quietly in such situations. Several years ago the wife of a Dallas dentist, not knowing about her husband's financial affairs, threw out an old coffee can

Moreover, the tendency to cheat at any *given* tax rate may be greater since 1960. Crime statistics do not include tax evasion and bribes. Nevertheless, do certain basic forces cause parallel movements in blue- and white-collar crimes? Tendencies to steal at gun point and from governments at tax collection dates should run together.

A final point regarding the currency ratio. Do you think the currency ratio exhibits a seasonal pattern? Check your answer by looking at a *Federal Reserve Bulletin,* which is full of interesting statistics. What explains the seasonal pattern?

The Nonmoney/Money Deposit Ratio

The preceding section on the currency ratio would have to be modified considerably if the preferred money measure were M-2 or M-3. In those cases the currency ratio would *not* be a ratio of one means of payment to another means of payment. The currency ratio for M-2 would be the ratio of one means of payment to all stores of value. The precise determinants of such a ratio composed of conceptually distinct items are not well known. Even if the preferred money measure is M-1, *the determinants of the nonmoney/money deposit ratio are uncertain because of Federal Reserve policy changes*. Until 1980 all time and savings deposits were subject to reserve requirements. Since then reserves are required only on nonpersonal (corporate-owned, for example) time and savings deposits. The narrower focus on time deposits has been countered in recent years by an ever-widening collection of miscellaneous accounts that are subject to sporadic reserve requirements. For example, reserve requirements were imposed temporarily on consumer credit. Insufficient time has elapsed to learn the determinants of a ratio when changes in the types of accounts subject to reserve requirements are relatively recent and frequent. This does not vanish n from the money multiplier. What it does is make the Fed substitute back-of-the-envelope guesstimates for firm estimates.

Summary/Questions

Money, M, may be expressed as the product of a multiplier, m, and the base, B.

$$M = m \cdot B$$

stuffed with $20,000 in currency. On discovering that the can had been collected with the other trash, the dentist rented a bulldozer for $5,000 to sift the Dallas dump. The whole town was talking about it. The IRS was not far behind, much to the dentist's chagrin. He was sentenced to prison for tax evasion.

The Fed controls money mainly by changing the base. For this reason, we additionally write the change or first difference form of the money equation with a given multiplier.

$$\Delta M = m \cdot \Delta B$$

The money supply multiplier depends on the assumption of the model. Most principles courses begin and end with the simple model of Chapter 3, where the public holds only money deposits and banks hold reserves simply to meet uniform legal requirements. In this case, the base corresponds with bank reserves and the multiplier is the inverse of the uniform required reserve ratio. Money supply analysis becomes very mechanical. The Fed pulls some strings and a predictable outcome follows. Banks are the puppets of a monetary authority which always hits the target money supply by changing reserve requirements or the amount of reserves. However pedagogically useful the simple model may be as a starting point, realism requires going beyond it.

A multiplier that can reasonably accurately predict the impact of monetary base changes is much more complicated. Shifts among money deposits with different reserve requirements, banks' desired excess reserve ratio, and the public's preferred asset ratio for currency, nonmoney deposits, and money deposits enter the multiplier and can thwart monetary policy. In fact, *control of reserves and reserve requirements does not guarantee monetary control.* Banks and the public play an important role in the money supply process.

The money supply equation of our realistic Case III is

(4–5.3)

$$M = \frac{1 + k(\overset{-}{y}, \overset{+}{f}, \overset{-}{i}, \overset{+}{t}, \overset{+}{x})}{\bar{r}_m(\underset{-}{i}) + \bar{r}_{em}(\underset{+}{b}, \underset{-}{i}, \underset{-}{\mu}, \underset{+}{\sigma}) + \bar{r}_n n + k(\underset{-}{y}, \underset{+}{f}, \underset{-}{i}, \underset{+}{t}, \underset{+}{x})} \cdot B$$

This is the same equation we have used several times before. It may not look familiar because the determinants of the ratios are shown explicitly in order to emphasize that they are determined by banks and the public and are not fixed constants. The determinants are:

y = income
f = bank failure rate
i = market interest rate
t = tax rate
x = crime rate
b = brokerage cost of buying and selling securities.
μ = expected (percentage) change in money deposits
σ = variability of money deposits

The sign above or below a variable indicates the relationship between a variable and ratio. For example, the currency ratio, k, is negatively related to income and positively related to tax rates.

We saved something to make this somewhat more than a summary. Equation (4–5.3) indicates that the average money deposit required reserve ratio depends negatively on market interest rates. This is *not* so true today if money is M-1. We indicated that $\bar{r}_m$ now is approximately fixed for M-1 since reserve requirements on demand and other checkable deposits are identical. However, years ago the $\bar{r}_m$ for M-1 and to this day the $\bar{r}_m$ for M-2 depend negatively on market rates. Why is this so? As market interest rates rise, the opportunity cost of zero-earning reserves rises, and profit-oriented banks create new accounts with low or zero reserve requirements. This should sound familiar; it appeared in Chapter 2 in a more nontechnical manner. NOWs and RPs were created in part to evade reserve requirements when interest rates were high.

You answer two controversial questions to demonstrate mastery of the chapter. Does the money supply depend on market interest rates and, if so, for what reasons besides the effect of market rates on the average reserve ratio? Will the money supply vary over the business cycle even if the Fed sits on its hands? The answer is made easier by Equation (4–5.3), which shows explicitly the determinants of the money supply.

1. What conditions must exist in order for the Fed to control perfectly the money supply multiplier?
2. As the various assumptions are relaxed and we move from Case I (DER = C = NMD = 0) to Case II (DER > 0; C = NMD = 0) to Case III (DER > 0; C > 0; NMD > 0), does the size of the multiplier change? What does the multiplier equal in Cases I, II, and III? When is the multiplier largest?
3. Which is more variable, "the" required reserve ratio for M-1 or M-2? Why?
4. If banks have excess reserves, must the money supply be increasing?
5. Predicting is hazardous. Nevertheless, predict the behavior of the excess reserve ratio during the next five years. Carefully state the assumptions underlying your predictions.
6. If the required and desired excess reserve ratios on check and time deposits are identical, what is the effect of a shift from check to time deposits on (1) the M-1 money supply and (2) bank credit?
7. The *algebraic expressions* of the money supply multiplier for M-1 and M-2 are identical. Are the *numerical values* of the money supply multipliers for M-1 and M-2 also identical? Does the measurement and interpretation of the parameters in the algebraic expression depend on the money definition?

8. What are the determinants of the currency/check deposit ratio?

9. Does the money supply depend on market interest rates and, if so, why? Will the money supply vary over the business cycle even if the Fed sits on its hands?

10. The following information is necessary to answer parts *a–d* below.

Commercial Banking System

Vault cash	5,500	Money deposits	100,000
Deposits at Fed	24,500	Nonmoney deposits	180,000
Loans and securities	250,000		

Assume the public's preferred asset ratio, which is satisfied at all times, is $2 currency to $18 nonmoney deposits to $10 money deposits. The average reserve ratios are: $\bar{r}_m = 0.19$, $\bar{r}_{em} = 0.02$, and $\bar{r}_n = 0.05$.

a. Is the banking system in equilibrium? How much currency is in the hands of the public? What does the base equal? What does the quantity of money equal? Substitute the numbers in this example in the general formula (Case III). Does the quantity of money equal the equilibrium money supply given by the formula?

b. Assume an open-market purchase of $10,000 from banks. What is the (equilibrium) change of the following items: (1) money deposits, (2) currency, (3) money supply, (4) nonmoney deposits, (5) reserves, and (6) bank loans and securities?

c. Assume the Fed cuts the required reserve ratio on money deposits to 0.09. What are the new equilibrium values of the six items in part *b*? (In answering this part, assume the initial balance sheet, i.e., ignore the $10,000 open-market purchase.)

d. Suppose that, by coincidence, the desired excess reserve ratio rose to 0.12 when the Fed cut the required ratio to 0.09. What are the equilibrium values of the six items in part *b*?

PART TWO

Financial Institutions and Instruments

Financial markets and stock exchanges

5

It is usually agreed that casinos should, in the public interest, be inaccessible and expensive. And perhaps the same is true of Stock Exchanges.

*John Maynard Keynes**

The first part of this book focused on the liability side of banks' balance sheets; loan expansion was an incidental part of monetary expansion. The initial emphasis on bank liabilities was justified because the nature of their liabilities distinguishes banks from other financial institutions and private lenders. (Other checkable deposits still are a small proportion of nonbank deposits.) Virtually anyone can extend credit and lend money, but only banks can simultaneously lend and *create* money. Recognition of this distinguishing feature of banks is not a denial of the great importance of financial markets where banks *participate* with other institutions. Part Two examines the behavior of financial markets and, more generally, the process of transferring purchasing power among economic units. We look at the numerous institutions engaged in the transfer process and the numerous financial instruments which evidence the transfer. Even when the focus is on finance instead of money, more attention must be given to commercial banks because they are the largest member of the financial system.

This chapter first discusses the advantages stemming from credit markets and a financial system. The major types of financial instruments and markets are then described. We break with economic tradition in two important respects. In order to emphasize that our focus has shifted and

---

**The General Theory of Employment, Interest and Money* (New York: Harcourt Brace Jovanovich, 1936), p. 159.

broadened from money to finance, we analyze the direct finance market serviced by investment bankers and brokers and, for the moment, ignore banks and other intermediaries. Second, common stock, which banks do not hold, is the financial asset of interest instead of loans and debt instruments. To be sure, banks, other intermediaries, and debt instruments will follow.

The Benefits of Finance

Money and purchasing power are transferred from surplus to deficit units in financial markets. Surplus units are those economic units whose income from current production exceeds expenditures on currently produced goods and services, while deficit units spend more than their income. Although deficit household units are not uncommon, households on balance are surplus units. Their income exceeds consumption on currently produced goods and services. Households are net savers. Firms are deficit units; their net investment spending exceeds retained earnings. In recent years the consolidated government sector, that is, federal, state, and local, has invariably been a deficit unit. As fast as taxes have risen, they have failed to keep pace with government expenditures. While deficit sectors sometimes are denounced as profligates and surplus sectors are extolled as candidates for sainthood, the two types of economic units complement each other. *Without deficit units there would be no surplus units.* Total deficits must equal total surpluses because your expenditures are the receipts of another economic unit, and your earnings are someone else's expenditures. While surplus units are unlikely to want to keep accumulating money as their surpluses persist, they at least have the luxury of this option. Deficit units are not so fortunate. Lacking unlimited money balances, deficit units unable to issue financial claims against themselves eventually must continually balance their budgets. (Deficit units that sell common stocks or borrow issue financial claims against themselves.) Since total deficits equal total surpluses, lack of finance eventually forces every economic unit to continually balance its budget. *The essential aspect of finance is the transfer of money for claims on the future, which permits long-term unbalanced budgets. In other words, in financial markets claims against the future are issued or acquired so that current income and expenditures do not have to be equal.* Financial markets create bridges to carry us over time. We postpone until Chapter 34 discussion of the advantages and disadvantages of a balanced budget by government; the issues are too complex to be considered now. We will show how the two main private sectors, households and firms, benefit from finance and the ability to run relatively long-term deficits and surpluses.

First consider households strictly as consumers. Most people enter this world with nothing and leave behind little, so over their entire lifetimes most households are modest surplus units, approaching balanced-budget units. However, the typical household does not enjoy a modest surplus throughout its lifetime. During its early years following entrance into the labor market, the typical household incurs a large deficit as it acquires durable goods. A mortgage finances a home, and the household purchases its first automobile, TV, and washing machine on credit. With the stock of durable goods on hand and the repayment requirements so large that lenders refuse further extensions of credit, the typical household switches from a deficit to a small surplus unit. The surplus becomes larger as households anticipate the expenses of college for their children. Household incomes increase, but the surplus shrinks as children enter college and parents correctly decide they need one fling for the "good life." The long postponed Caribbean cruise, luxury car, and remodeled kitchen become reality. Having enjoyed the good life, the household runs its largest surpluses in anticipation of retirement and, if it anticipates correctly, ends its existence as a deficit unit with little to spare. This scenario clearly is preferable to living one's early adult years in parents' basements or a shack without TV, washing machine, and so on, which would be the likely result if one could not borrow. *Finance unties the knot linking consumption and current income. Consumer welfare increases when consumption and income patterns may differ.*

Now consider consumers strictly as savers. If financial claims were lacking, savers could accumulate cash or invest directly by starting their own firms. Neither alternative is appealing. Cash yields no return, and most households lack the management skills necessary to earn a high return on physical investments. Finance does not eliminate these options. It adds new ones. Because the average firm's return exceeds the return on direct investments by households, firms gladly offer, and households gladly accept, financial claims with interest and dividend payments above the household rate of return and below the firms' rate. *The separation of household/savers from firm/investors increases the rate of return on any given amount of saving.*

Besides increasing the return earned on any saving, the availability of financial claims usually produces greater saving. The household deciding whether to consume or save must consider what to do with the saving. Households that can purchase financial claims have an additional opportunity for their saving and tend to save more. Households deciding between consumption and saving may well save more, but what about those households who already have decided they want to spend the maximum? Finance increases the maximum. Nevertheless, the first effect dominates. Finance increases aggregate saving.

We can readily check the validity of the last statements. Household's saving must equal firm's investment, ignoring government. If our presumption about the effect of finance on saving is correct, we should come to the conclusion that finance increases the amount invested and its rate of return. In fact, we can come to this conclusion and, in the process, gain some extra insights. Finance clearly increases investment. History provides us many examples of inventors and entrepreneurs who initially did not have the resources to implement their ideas. While history recalls Henry Ford and other rare geniuses who started huge companies and even industries, thousands and thousands of small firms would not be in existence without finance. Indeed, finance often is the most crucial problem small firms face.

Even if finance only leads to a transfer of investment among firms, in our private capitalistic system finance increases the average rate of return on investment. Firms that earn high rates of return are able to pay high interest rates, and funds flow to firms that pay the highest interest. *Finance greatly raises the average rate of return on investments when economies of scale are prevalent so that the cost-minimizing/productivity-maximizing plant size is very large.* In this case the optimal size plant greatly exceeds the resources of any one person or socially cohesive group such as a family. Organized finance and the ability to draw resources from a widely diversified group are necessary for highly productive investments and economic growth. Even the Ford Motor Company eventually went public and sold stock in order to expand and remain competitive in an industry subject to economies of scale. *The ability of firms to issue financial claims even at onerous terms due to risk is one of the most important characteristics of a dynamic, progressive society.* A successful, growing firm repays its maturing debt by borrowing more and widening its deficit. The debt outstanding is not built on a house of cards. The additional output made possible by debt eventually generates the revenue to repay the debt and yield stockholders a return on their investment.

Main Types of Financial Instruments and Markets

Financial instruments evidence the transfer of funds and specify the rights and obligations of the parties. For example, they spell out the repayment terms. Perhaps the sharpest classification scheme based on the most important difference among financial claims lists them as debt or equity. *Debt instruments are contractual obligations to repay specified amounts in the future.* Debt instruments differ in the number of future specified payments, the certainty individuals attach to the fulfillment of the obligation, and in many other ways which will be discussed shortly. The essential aspect of debt, however, is the obligatory specified payments. Failure to make the payments forces the debtor to declare bankruptcy. Examples of debt are tuition loans, AT&T bonds, and Treasury bills. *Equity instruments are ownership claims.* Holders of equities participate in the management of the issuing firm, usually indirectly by voting for members of the board of directors. *Common stocks* are the most common type of equity, so common that the qualifying adjective is often ignored. Common stocks allow one to participate pro-rata in a firm's earnings and losses and in its assets if dissolution occurs. Some earnings typically are reinvested and some are distributed as dividends. Common stock is the residual claim; everyone from the firm's employees to its creditors is paid before stockholders. *Preferred stock,* the second major type of equity claim, stipulates the amount of future payments out of earnings, current or retained. Although debt instruments also stipulate the amount of future payments, preferred stock *dividends* are nonobligatory payments from earnings, while debt interest payments are an obligatory *expense*.[1] Preferred dividends must be made in full before paying common stock dividends. Preferred stock is purchased by those who want relatively certain and constant dividends while common stock, being the residual claim, appeals to those willing to bear risk in hopes of making a "killing."

The markets in which financial instruments are created and traded can be effectively divided into two types: (1) *the direct financial market* serviced by brokers, dealers, and investment bankers, and (2) *the intermediary market* where banks, savings and loans, and other intermediaries participate. Surplus units purchase in direct financial markets the claims issued by ultimate deficit units, often with the aid of brokers, dealers or investment bankers, who act as effective matchmakers. They reduce the search and information cost of finding surplus units who want the type of security being offered by deficit units. *In the intermediary market, as the name suggests, a financial institution such as a savings and loan stands between the surplus and ultimate deficit unit.* A surplus unit purchases claims issued by the intermediary, which then purchases claims issued by an ultimate deficit unit. For example, when a mother decides to no longer lend her son money and tells him to borrow at the bank where she just opened an account, finance switches from the direct to the intermediary market. The distinction between direct and intermediary finance is sufficiently important that a single name, *primary securities,* is given to all claims, whether equity or debt, issued by ultimate deficit units. *Intermediaries are financial tailors: they take in primary securities that do not fit and reshape them to suit the needs of surplus units.*

---

[1]Interest payments are treated like any other expense. They are deducted from revenue before paying taxes. Preferred stock dividends on the other hand are paid with after-tax dollars. For example, suppose a corporation's net *operating* income (income before interest, taxes, and dividends) is \$100, and the tax rate is 50 percent. If the interest payment on the debt is \$20, the corporation's net (after tax) income is \$40 = (\$100 − \$20) × 0.5. If the preferred stock dividend were the same \$20, net income would be \$30 = (\$100 × 0.5) − \$20. This tax aspect currently favors the issuance of debt instead of preferred stock. At the turn of the century, when there were no income taxes, the difference between expenses and dividends was irrelevant, and preferred stock was issued more frequently.

Direct Finance, Investment Bankers, and Brokers

Since money is produced mainly by banks, monetary economics books traditionally have emphasized intermediary finance. While we shall not break tradition, the direct finance market cannot be ignored altogether. Indeed, let's begin with direct finance. We will content ourselves with describing *how* purchases and sales are made and offer no advice on *what*.

Assume a firm is planning a new issue of primary securities, either debt or equity. The firm may be able to sell the new issue directly to one or more institutional buyers such as pension funds, in which case a *private* or *direct placement* has occurred. Normally, however, the firm will contact *an investment banker who finds buyers for the issue*. Some leading investment banking firms are Morgan Stanley, Merrill Lynch, Paine Webber-Blyth Eastman, and Salomon Brothers. Note that investment bankers are neither investors that hold securities for long periods nor bankers—at least not commercial bankers like Bank of America and Chase Manhattan. Indeed, commercial bankers are prohibited from being investment bankers, except for the general obligation issues of governmental units. *Investment bankers basically are marketers; they purchase newly issued financial instruments for immediate resale.*

The investment firm may be fortunate and contact one or more buyers who purchase the entire issue, in which case again a direct placement is said to occur. The new issue usually is too large for one buyer or even one investment banker. When this occurs, the contacted or lead investment banker forms a temporary partnership with other investment bankers to jointly market the new issue. Such a temporary association is called a *syndicate*. The syndicate usually *underwrites* the new issue, that is, it purchases all the new issue, either in a competitive (auction) sale or through direct negotiation, and then resells the securities in smaller units to the public. Of course, the underwriters' anticipated sale price is greater than the purchase price. Underwriters do assume the risk of general security price declines in the time interval following the purchase. Sometimes the risk is realized as the securities fail to fetch the anticipated sale price. Since the risk of loss depends directly on the length of the time interval between purchase and resale, and since the public's general lack of good information about small firms lengthens the time needed to resell their new issues, the new issues of small, less-well-known firms often are not underwritten but sold on a commission or "best-effort" basis.

The new issues or primary market functions so effectively in large part because of the existence of a secondary market where outstanding securities are traded. The prime example of a secondary market is the New York Stock Exchange where, in spite of its name, some bonds are also traded. Few individuals would buy new securities if they could not be resold. Participants in the secondary market are brokers and dealers. *A broker is a middleman* who finds buyers (sellers) for sellers (buyers) and is rewarded for his or her effort by a commission. Brokers do not own securities even for short time periods. So-called discount brokers, such as Charles Schwab, Inc., are strictly middlemen who simply execute buy and sell orders, while Merrill Lynch and other large, well-known financial brokers, like their cousins the marriage brokers, also offer advice, at a price. A dealer is a "used" investment banker. That is, *dealers purchase previously issued securities* hoping to sell them later at a higher price. Like the investment banker, the dealer bears the risk of a decline in the market value of his or her securities' inventory. Years ago, a firm concentrated on either the primary or secondary market; it was either an investment banker or a broker/dealer. Now nearly all large investment bankers are also brokers and dealers, and vice versa.

The precise form of middleman service, broker or dealer, that a firm offers in the secondary market depends on the type of market and security traded. The word "market" conjurs up a cavernous place filled with people. Financial markets of this type are called exchanges, for example, the New York and American Stock Exchanges. *Firms act as brokers when executing buy or sell orders for securities traded on exchanges.* Orders received at branch offices of brokerage firms such as Merrill Lynch are transmitted to the firm's floor representative, who physically meets another representative at the exchange floor and executes the order. The stock of most smaller companies and nearly all debt instruments are traded in the over-the-counter market. Unlike exchanges, *the over-the-counter market is not located in a specific place but is the network of individual broker and dealer offices located throughout the country and connected by telephone and computer. Firms behave as dealers and make the over-the-counter market by standing ready to buy and sell on their own behalf the securities in which they specialize.* The number of dealers specializing in a specific security varies with the value of the security outstanding. For example, a local brokerage house may be the only dealer for the securities of a small company while there are more than thirty dealers in government securities. No firm, however large, can be a dealer in every security. Nevertheless, you are able to purchase virtually any unlisted security because the nonspecialist brokerage firm knows who the dealers are. This suggests, however, that you can avoid one middleman and get a better price by trading directly with the specialist.

Common Stocks and the New York Stock Exchange (NYSE)

The primary market for stocks attracts great attention when a high-flying genetic engineering or personal computer firm offers a new issue. However, the primary stock market is rather small. The $40 billion raised in the new-issues equity market in 1983 broke all records, far surpassing the average $10 billion raised annually during the 1970s. Far more was raised in the corporate *bond* market. The stock market is predominantly a secondary market where outstanding securities are traded. In 1983 the volume of trading on the stock exchanges was approximately $4 billion daily. If trading on the OTC market were included, the total is nearly $6 billion *daily*. Contrast this with the $40 billion *annual* (1983) volume in the primary market. Large as the secondary equities market is, it is paled by the secondary market for government securities. The average *daily* transactions in Treasury bills alone by private, nonbank investors exceed $11 billion, and trades among dealers and banks approximate $12 billion daily.

All statistics on Treasury bill trades not withstanding, the stock market has captured the public's interest. We should take a closer look at the secondary market for stocks because many think economics *is* the stock market. Admit you are an economist to a layperson and the immediate response is a request for investment advice, particularly about stocks. Yet many economists have dismissed the stock market in a line or paragraph, as if it were simply a national casino where one's gambling instincts could be satisfied without traveling to Las Vegas or Atlantic City. Being ownership claims, stocks are risky; owners get the residual, if any, after everyone else is paid. But the stock market is much more than a national casino. While many firms do not issue bonds, every firm *must* have equity funds. Family and friends are the source of equity funds for most small firms. However, in order to take advantage of economies of scale, the equity funds of thousands nationwide must be gathered by investment bankers, and a secondary stock market must be maintained. A secondary market where "old" stocks can be bought and sold is especially important since these instruments are infinitely-lived securities without maturity date. We thoroughly disagree with this chapter's lead quotation.

There are 10 stock exchanges or organized, continuous auction markets for stock. The New York Stock Exchange (NYSE) is the largest with the American Stock Exchange a far distant second. The stocks of approximately 2,000 of the largest corporations are traded on the NYSE, and the stock of the giants in this select group are sometimes also listed in the small "regional" exchanges, particularly when the regional exchange and head office of the firm are located in the same city. An exchange will list a stock or admit it for trading if the company meets certain requirements, such as being larger than a specified size, publishing financial information, guaranteeing stockholders certain rights, and so on. Besides cross-listing stocks, the regional exchanges—for example, the Pacific Stock Exchange—also list the stock of small firms on an exclusive basis. The typical size of firms listed on the American Exchange falls between the size of firms on the New York and regional exchanges. Since the American Exchange is also located in New York, it does not duplicate the list of its bigger brother across the street. The approximate percentages of total dollar volume of stock transactions on exchanges is (1) New York Exchange, 75 percent, (2) American Exchange, 10 percent, and (3) regional exchanges, 15 percent.

The primary purposes of the exchanges are to provide various types of trading facilities and to regulate trading practices. The former include a building which houses the trading floor where brokers effect transactions for their customers, a ticker tape which reports trades and prices, and facilities for clearing and settling transactions. Concentrating on the dominant NYSE, the orders from thousands of customers of broker-dealers nationwide flow to the floor of the Exchange. The trading floor is as hectic as shown in the movies. In order to prevent total pandemonium, each stock is assigned a trading post where brokers with buy and sell orders congregate. There are two types of orders, *market and limit orders*. A market order instructs the broker to act in the customer's best interests immediately, buying at the lowest price or selling at the highest price, whatever it may be. Limit orders stress price instead of immediacy. They specify a maximum buying price below the current price or a minimum selling price above the current price so that the order cannot be executed immediately. Limit orders may be either good 'til canceled (GTC), or they may specify some time period.

Many transactions are effected smoothly by brokers representing their clients without any outside aid. Large market orders, however, are likely to cause unnecessarily large, short-run price fluctuations. Moreover, each of the hundreds of exchange member firms cannot conveniently have representatives at each trading post waiting for the price to rise or fall to limit prices. To minimize these problems, the exchange has assigned a specialist to each stock. The specialist "makes the market" by acting as a dealer, buying (selling) for his or her own account when there is a temporary imbalance of market sale (buy) orders. Thus, the specialist is supposed to stabilize the market. The specialist also "maintains the book" listing all limit orders. When the market price reaches the limit price, specialists buy or sell for the brokers who gave them limit orders.

Recent Stock Market Developments

Winds of change similar to those which are sweeping the commercial banking industry started earlier in the NYSE. *For many years the exchange was a cartel. Until the 1970s trading on the exchange was limited to members*. Nonmember broker-dealers had access to the trading facilities of the exchange only through members, which were required to charge the nonmember broker-dealer the same commission paid by the general public. Since nonmembers are not charitable institutions and must tack on their commission, the higher commission rates nonmembers charged their customers tended to restrict their participation in the exchange. *Moreover, the exchange rules tended to prohibit member firms from trading listed securities outside the exchange.* The impact of these rules produced two markets for listed stocks, the exchange for members and the so-called *Third Market, an informal, OTC market for listed securities among nonmembers. The rules which created two markets with different participants also prevented arbitrage,* which eliminates price differences on identical commodities.

The Third Market grew as the NYSE, like other cartels, fixed relatively high prices. The commission structure guaranteed that even the most inefficient brokers could make a profit. The commission rates were outrageously high on large transactions, which did not receive any discount. The commission on 10,000 shares (the minimum size "large block" as defined by the NYSE) was 100 times the commission on 100 shares (the typical "round lot") although resource costs increase only fractionally with transaction size. Unable to compete by price, the large brokerage houses in particular offered free research advice and financial publications, plush offices which pampered their customers, and other services designed to attract business. *Pressure from large institutional buyers and from exchange members themselves who were losing sales to the Third Market led between 1971 and 1975 to the abolition of fixed commission rates and the introduction of negotiable rates,* much as deposit rate ceilings are being eliminated in the banking market. Lower commission rates were accompanied with rule changes which reduced market segmentation and facilitated arbitrage between the Third Market and the NYSE.

The lower commission rates also were associated with an unbundling of services. Discount brokerage firms which simply execute your buy and sell orders were established. Full-service brokerage houses throw in some "free" market research with their higher commission structure. However, even the full-service houses now charge for newsletters and some services which formerly were free. This benefits consumers, who now can buy only those services they want. Moreover, even consumers who want the same bundle of services are better off because they can buy the various pieces from different firms. For example, consumers previously had to purchase transactions *and* research services from a full-service brokerage. Now they can purchase transactions services from a discount brokerage and research services from an investment advisory firm. Specialization of services should promote efficiency.

The extent to which a specialist should stabilize short-run price fluctuations and the restriction of information on limit orders to specialists are other controversial issues. Many claim that specialists lack sufficient capital to prevent unnecessary short-run price fluctuations, and the restriction of limit order information to specialists prevents others from speculating and stabilizing the market. These criticisms are partially valid, or at least Congress thought so. In 1975 Congress ordered the Securities and Exchange Commission (SEC) and the NYSE to develop as soon as possible a *national market system*, a computer-based information system which is supposed to (1) report the price and size of all transactions as they occur and (2) record all limit orders and construct a composite limit-order book which, after a person pressed a few buttons, would flash on a screen the limit-order information now available only to the New York specialist. The second objective of the national market system remains unfulfilled although a similar information system for OTC stocks has been developed.[2] In 1971, *NASDAQ, an acronym for National Association of Security Dealers Automated Quotations,* started displaying on TV screens in the offices of thousands of dealer-brokers the prices each dealer was bidding and asking for many nonlisted issues. This significantly improved the efficiency of the OTC market. Buyers can quickly call those selling at the lowest price, and sellers can put their shares on those buying at the highest price. Prices became more uniform, and the bid-asked spread narrowed. Moreover, the availability of a complete list of buyer and seller prices reduces the impact of large blocks on short-run prices as the owners of the blocks know whom to contact.

The SEC and Self-Regulation

The riskiness of stocks due to their residual nature cannot be reduced. However, the riskiness of stocks due to lack of information or even misinformation can be. Such a reduction was the basic objective of the Securities Act of 1933 and Securities Exchange Act of 1934. Potential buyers of goods can examine quality directly, but stock purchasers must rely almost completely on others for information about the future earnings and dividend stream to which stock ownership entitles one. The securities acts prohibited some of the unwise practices which in part enabled the stock market to climb to dizzying heights in the 1920s and to drop precipitously between 1929 and 1933. In particular, these acts outlawed the distribution of false reports, manipulative practices to move the stock price either up or down, exaggerated trading designed to suggest extraordinary interest, transactions based on insider information, and so on. To attain compliance, issuers of securities with few exceptions are required to register the issue with the SEC prior to sale to the general public. The registration process is designed to elicit fair and full information, rather than pass on the price and terms of the security. In other words, the SEC will not block the sale of extremely risky stock at very high prices provided potential buyers are made aware of the risk. Caveat emptor still reigns,

[2]The reason for the delay is explored later when we discuss self-regulation. The logical third step of the system is automated trading. The computer is programmed for continuous searches, and a trade is automatically executed when it finds an identical bid and offer.

and rightly so. In the early 1980s the necessity to register each issue was attacked as being too time consuming and expensive. Firms were granted on an experimental basis "advanced registration" authority, which would cover several issues up to two years.

For day-to-day compliance with security laws by firms, the SEC relies on "self-regulation" by the exchange or dealer association under the SEC's watchful eye. That is, the exchange and the National Association of Securities Dealers (NASD) are supposed to make and enforce rules consistent with SEC laws and regulations. Self-regulation of any industry is controversial. Self-regulators find it in their self-interest to penalize gross abuses; unpenalized gross abuses eventually lead to the termination of self-regulation. It is only natural, however, that at times self-regulators overemphasize the interests of their members and discount the harm to the general public. Many of the New York Exchange's cartel practices of the 1960s (for example, the restriction of trading to a limited number of members) were justified as necessary for self-regulation. Nine and a half years after Congress mandated the national market system, Wall Street continues foot-dragging. It still has not developed a computerized trading system which would allow investors to shop around for the best price nationwide.[3]

Summary/Questions

It is no accident that economists who downplay finance claim that consumption depends strongly and almost exclusively on *current* income. Without finance this would indeed be the case as budgets eventually would have to balance. Finance unties the knot tying consumption and current income. It lets you borrow (and spend) against future income. Recognition of finance suggests that spending depends on wealth or expected future income and the cost of finance, in addition to current income.

Because finance concerns claims against the future, which is more uncertain than the present, financial mistakes occur more often than consumption mistakes. This is especially true for common stocks, which are *residual* claims on the future. The future belongs to common stockholders,

---

[3]The SEC has hardly applied great pressure on Wall Street. In October 1979, four and a half years after the congressional mandate, the SEC chairman told the annual meeting of the National Security Traders Association to avoid "precipitous" development of a national market system. At the same meeting a year later the chairman did criticize the industry for foot-dragging. Interestingly, prior to the latter meeting, "The House Commerce Committee on Oversight and Investigations likened the SEC's go-slow approach to the pace of an 'arthritic gastropod on a drizzly day.' The SEC says there is no connection between the subcommittee's blast and its sudden tougher stance." (*Business Week,* October 27, 1980, p. 56).

after everyone else is paid their contractual claims. The SEC and stock exchanges attempt to aid consumers by insisting that firms provide accurate information. Since neither firms nor anyone else has a crystal ball, nothing can altogether eliminate financial mistakes. Why then is finance so pervasive? Because it is so beneficial. The cost of financial errors is inconsequential compared to the benefits of finance.

United States financial markets were much better developed than European financial markets around the mid-1950s. At the same time U.S. per capita GNP significantly exceeded European per capita GNP. Over the next 25 years European financial markets developed more rapidly than U.S. markets, and the GNP gap was closed. By 1980 deregulation and other factors produced new financial markets and instruments in the United States, and U.S. per capita GNP again rose above European per capita GNP. Was all this coincidental? Not entirely. Financial growth aids economic growth.

1. What is the effect of a financial system on the quantity of and rate of return on saving and investment? Does a financial system facilitate economic growth?
2. Explain, with the aid of examples, the benefits of finance to (*a*) consumer/households, (*b*) saver/households, and (*c*) investor/firms.
3. What are the main differences between (*a*) common stock, preferred stock, and debt; (*b*) direct and intermediary finance; (*c*) investment bankers, dealers, and brokers? Consider each part (*a*)–(*c*) separately.
4. What are the primary purposes of stock exchanges? What operating rules and practices has the NYSE adopted in order to meet its goals?
5. State the two main functions of the NYSE specialist.
6. What rules enabled the NYSE to act as a cartel for years? State the recent changes which have made the NYSE much more competitive.
7. Define: (*a*) over-the-counter market, (*b*) market order, (*c*) limit order, (*d*) the specialist's book, (*e*) the Third Market, and (*f*) NASDAQ.

Rates of return and other characteristics of bonds

6

Rates of return have more nooks and crannies than an English muffin. And the key to profitable investments is knowledge of the difference.

Since banks deal with debt instruments almost exclusively, let us take a closer look at these instruments. We take a broad view, however, because, as the last chapter stated, banks are only one participant in the credit market. Banks make loans, but so does Sears when I say, "Charge it." At this point let us look at the major characteristics or attributes of any debt instrument. Clearly, the most important feature of a loan/bond is the rate of interest or yield to maturity. We show how to compute the rate of interest and other measures of return. The existence of truth-in-lending laws confirms that computation of rates of return can be neither easy nor uniform. Other characteristics of securities and their relationship to a security's return are then explored. An analysis of the effect of inflation on interest rates concludes the chapter.

Rates of Return and Market Values of Bonds

The rate of return measures the annual percentage return on a debt instrument. There is universal agreement on this. When you try to apply the concept and calculate the rate of return on a specific debt instrument, disagreement becomes rampant. For example, suppose someone promises you $109 next year (365 days from today) in exchange for $100 today. What is the rate of return on such a loan? Nine percent is one correct answer. After all, $100 grows by 9 percent in order to equal $109 next year. Or does it? The instantaneous growth rate, or rate of return compounded continuously, is less than 9 percent, approximately 8.6 percent. The simple, annual rate of return is 9 percent; the $109 next year is 9 percent more than $100 today. Even assuming simple annual interest is appropriate, some would claim the rate of return on this loan is less than 9 percent because they assume (obviously incorrectly) that a year has 360 days. In our example the loan promises 9 percent in a "year" and 5 days, so the annual interest rate is less than 9 percent. While the assumption is bizarre in some respects, it is convenient to have a "standard" year instead of years with 365 or 366 days. We have just scratched the surface on the difficulties of measuring the rate of return on a particular security. Reams of paper were necessary to write truth-in-lending laws. There are more rate of return measures than nooks and crannies in an English muffin. We largely ignore technical issues in the remainder of this section and present a few popular return measures. Some measures admittedly are silly measures of return. Nevertheless, we must know them because they are used. If you don't know your M-1 from M-2 you may not do very well in a money and banking course. The consequences of not knowing your nominal return from your yield to maturity are worse.

Let us be sure we are familiar with bond market terminology before computing returns. Debt was defined as contractual obligations to repay specified amounts in the future. When the original term to maturity, that is, the time interval between the dates of issue and final payment, is more than one year, virtually all marketable debt instruments promise periodic payments, typically every six months, and a final larger payment. The periodic payments are called the coupon payments, and the final payment is the principal, par, or face value of the debt. Figure 6–1 pictures a bond, the name given to a debt instrument with a maturity greater than 10 years. Years ago nearly all bonds were bearer or coupon bonds like the one pictured in Figure 6–1. To receive payment the bondholder presents to the issuer the clipped coupon—the reason for scissors in most safety deposit booths. The issuer maintains no record of ownership, and the bearer of the bond is always presumed to be the rightful owner. Because of the risk of total loss due to theft or fire, many bondholders now prefer registered bonds, where the issuer maintains ownership records and automatically sends the periodic payments, which are still called coupon payments although no coupons are sent.[1] Coupon payments typically are not made on government and business debt when the original term to maturity is one year or less. In this case the only payment is the principal or face value.

---

[1]Coupon bonds are resurging largely because they are a convenient way to evade taxes. Issuers of coupon bonds cannot comply with the IRS requirement of reporting interest payments because they do not maintain ownership records and must pay anyone—the bond owner, his agent, or a thief—who presents the coupon. The IRS became so concerned in 1983 that the Treasury banned new issues of coupon bonds. Unreported coupon bonds were illegally yielding a tax-free income during life and were being bequeathed estate-tax-free at death.

FIGURE 6–1
Coupon Bond

Returns on Bonds with Coupons

We consider rate of return measures first for securities with coupons and face value and then for noncoupon securities. The simplest return measure is the (annual) *coupon yield or nominal return, which is the ratio of the (annual) coupon to the face value.*

$$\text{Coupon yield} = \text{Coupon/Face}$$

Since a bond's coupon and face value are specified at the date of issue, *the coupon yield remains fixed throughout the life of the bond.* The coupon yield is a peculiar measure of return. At the very least the return should be related to the price paid for the bond. The *current yield* accomplishes only the very least. It *expresses the coupon as a percentage of the current price.*

$$\text{Current yield} = \text{Coupon/Price}$$

Bond prices fluctuate, and, consequently, so do current or running yields. Inspection shows that the current yield exceeds the coupon whenever the bond is selling below par.

One problem with the current yield is that it ignores capital gains and losses. For example, assume that a $100 par value bond with $6 annual coupons and three years remaining to maturity is selling for $94.80. According to our formulas, its coupon yield is 6 percent (or 0.06), and its current yield is 6.33 percent. The current yield seems a low measure of return in this case. A good measure should take in account the $5.20 capital gain when the $100 principal is received three years hence. *The average total return to maturity (ATRM) is a good measure of return.* In general, let C = coupon, F = face, P_B = current price of bond, and n = maturity. ATRM is the sum of the coupon, C, plus the average annualized capital change to maturity, $(F - P_B)/n$, all relative to the "average" price during the maturity of the security, $(P_B + F)/2$.

(6–1)

$$\text{ATRM} = \frac{C + (F - P_B)/n}{(P_B + F)/2}$$

Using the numbers in our example where the current yield is 6.33 percent, the ATRM is 0.0793 or 7.93 percent.

(6–1′)

$$\text{ATRM} = \frac{6 + (100.00 - 94.80)/3}{(94.80 + 100.00)/2} = 0.0793$$

The problem with ATRM is the first letter/word, "A/average." It implicitly assumes that, say, a $20 capital gain over 10 years is the same as a $2 gain each year. Because $2 today is more valuable than $2

10 years from now, averaging has some elements of adding apples and oranges. *The best measure of return is the yield to maturity, which economists call "the" rate of interest. It is a growth rate. The rate of interest measures the percentage rate at which the current value must grow to equal the future receipts, or, equivalently, it is derived by computing the present value of the stream of future payments.*

The relationship between any present value (PV), annual interest rate written as a decimal (i), and future value one year hence (FV_1) is given below.

$$PV(1+i)=FV_1 \tag{6–2}$$

For example, what will \$100 today (PV = \$100) equal next year if the rate of interest is 10 percent (i = 0.1)? \$110, according to Equation (6–2). Continuing on, what will the \$100 equal two years from now assuming interest is compounded annually? \$121 (the interest earned in the second year is \$11, 10 percent of \$110). In general,

$$PV(1+i)^2=FV_2 \tag{6–3}$$

where FV_2 is a value two years hence. For any number n,

$$PV(1+i)^n=FV_n \tag{6–4}$$

where FV_n is the value n years hence.

Most people can readily compute the future value of a current sum. The reverse process for some reason is more troublesome, perhaps indicating that division is more difficult than multiplication. What does \$110 next year (FV_1 = \$110) equal today if the rate of interest is 10 percent (i = 0.1)? In other words, how much do I need today in order to have \$110 next year when the rate of interest is 10 percent? \$100. We can use Equation (6–2) although in this case it is more conveniently written as (6–2′) so the variable to be solved, PV, stands by itself.

$$\begin{aligned} PV &= FV_1/(1+i) \\ 100 &= 110/(1.1) \end{aligned} \tag{6–2′}$$

Similarly,

$$PV=FV_n/(1+i)^n \tag{6–4′}$$

The process of computing present value is also called discounting.

The price of a bond (P_B) is simply the discounted value of all coupons (C) and the face (F). Assuming an n period bond with a coupon each period, the price of the bond is given by

(6–5)

$$P_B = \frac{C_1}{(1+i)} + \frac{C_2}{(1+i)^2} + \cdots + \frac{C_n}{(1+i)^n} + \frac{F}{(1+i)^n}$$

Buyers and sellers of bonds, like any other commodity, quote the price. Since the bond contract specifies the coupon and face, the interest rate can be calculated when the price is given, although it is no easy task. Using the numbers in our previous example,

(6–5′)

$$P_B = 94.80 = \frac{6}{(1+i)} + \frac{6}{(1+i)^2} + \frac{6}{(1+i)^3} + \frac{100}{(1+i)^3}$$

What is the rate of interest on this bond? *The rate of interest* or yield to maturity is 8 percent. The difficulty of solving an equation like (6–5′) increases exponentially with n. Fortunately, bond tables which contain the answer to these equations are available. What do those without bond tables do? Use ATRM. Indeed, *ATRM was constructed precisely because it is an excellent approximation for the yield to maturity,* as our example illustrates.[2] For $n \geqslant 4$, Equation (6–5) is virtually insoluble, while the difficulty of solving (6–1) is virtually independent of the value of n.

Equations (6–2) and (6–5) show that bond prices and interest rates are negatively related. *When bond prices rise, the rate of interest falls, and vice versa.* Even if one did not see Equation (6–5), the negative relationship should have been clear provided one recalled that the rate of interest is the growth measure linking the current value and future payments. If the current price falls, then it must grow at a faster rate to equal the given future payments. Alternatively, if the growth rate falls, the current price must rise for it to equal the given future payments.

Perpetuities or consols are one case where the negative relationship between bond prices and the rate of interest is especially straightforward. Perpetuities have perpetual coupons (infinite maturity) but no repayment of the principal. Suppose the perpetuity offered $1 per year until the end of time. How much would you pay for such an obligation? You and your heirs will receive an infinite sum, assuming the payments in fact will be made, yet you should pay only a very modest sum. If the rate of interest were 10 percent, the price of this bond would be $10. For any perpetuity,

(6–6)

$$P_B = C/i$$

where the terms are as previously defined. The validity of Equation (6–6) may be appreciated by noting that $10 invested at 10 percent gives

---

[2]By averaging the capital gain and price, ATRM creates compensating errors and becomes an excellent approximation.

you \$1 each year without reduction in the principal. Although only a few perpetuities exist, economists often assume all bonds are perpetuities because Equation (6–6) is so simple and provides another useful short cut. When the maturity of a bond is 25 years or more and the interest rate is 10 percent or more, Equation (6–6) is a good approximation for (6–5). The present value of payments in the distant future is virtually nil when interest rates are very high.

Two aspects of the yield to maturity are most easily illustrated by the ATRM approximation. *The security price change necessary to induce any given change in the total return varies directly with the term to maturity.* This tends to make long-term bond prices more volatile.[3] For example, assume two securities, a 1-year and a 20-year bond; both have 8 percent coupon rates and sell at their \$100 face or par value. Assume further that the price of the one-year bond falls to \$97 so its total return to maturity rises to approximately 11 percent, the sum of the approximately 8 percent current yield and the 3 percent capital gain at maturity. If the price on the 20-year bond fell the same amount, its return would rise to only approximately 8.15 percent because the \$3 capital gain must be spread over 20 years. A 20-year, 8 percent coupon bond yields approximately 11 percent when its price falls to \$71.43, as substitution in Equation (6–1) shows.

$$\text{ATRM} = \frac{8 + (100 - 71.43)/20}{(71.43 + 100)/2} = .11 \text{ or } 11 \text{ percent} \qquad \mathbf{(6\text{–}1'')}$$

Second, the rate of interest is greater than, equals, or is less than the coupon rate according to whether the current bond price is less than, equals, or is greater than the face value. In our example, the 11 percent rate of interest exceeds the 8 percent coupon because a capital gain will be realized, that is, the current price (\$71.43) is less than the face value (\$100).

Failure to know the difference between the nooks and crannies of interest rates can be costly where it really hurts—in the pocketbook. For example, in the table "New York Stock Exchange Bonds," *The Wall Street Journal* has a column labeled "yield." Suppose it shows 6.33 percent for three-year Amorous Adventure bonds and 7 percent for otherwise identical Club Red bonds. Would you clearly be better off buying the Club Red bonds? Not necessarily. The highly respected *Wall Street Journal* unfortunately publishes the current yield, which is a poor measure of return. If the Club Red bonds have a 7 percent coupon, then the current yield and yield to maturity both are 7 percent. The 6.33 percent Amorous

---

[3]This is true even though the rates of return are more stable on long-term than on short-term securities.

Adventure bonds might correspond with our earlier example, that is, bonds with a 6 percent coupon but 8 percent yield to maturity. In that case Amorous Adventure are preferable to Club Red even though the yield column of *The Wall Street Journal* suggests otherwise.

Discount Yields and Returns on Noncoupon Bonds

The yield on Treasury bills and other securities with an original maturity of less than a year is conventionally computed in a peculiar manner. When the original maturity is less than a year, coupon payments are not made. These types of securities are called *discount securities* because they always sell below face, the difference between the current price and face being the interest. The return on these securities, which we shall call the *discount yield,* i_d, for reasons which will become clear immediately, conventionally is computed as follows,

(6–7)

$$i_d = \frac{F-P}{F} \times \frac{360}{\text{days to maturity}}$$

where F is the face value and P is the price of the Treasury bill. The term (F − P)/F is the percentage gain on the *face,* and (360/days to maturity) annualizes this gain, assuming 360 days is a year. For example, assume the price of a $10,000 Treasury bill maturing in three months (days to maturity = 90) is $9,760. What is the discount yield on this instrument? Using Equation (6–7), 0.096 or 9.6 percent.

(6–7′)

$$i_d = \frac{10{,}000-9{,}760}{10{,}000} \times \frac{360}{90} = 0.096 \text{ or } 9.6 \text{ percent}$$

Since the buyer of a discount security does not pay and the issuer does not receive the face value, the discount yield according to Equation (6–7), which measures the percentage gain on the face value, is misleading. Use Equation (6–8) to compute the effective rate of interest, defined as the rate of return on the current price. This is the rate at which the present value grows in order to equal the future value.

(6–8)

$$i = \frac{F-P}{P} \times \frac{360}{\text{days to maturity}}$$

In our example the discount yield is 9.6 percent but the true rate of interest is 9.84 percent.

(6–8′)

$$i = \frac{10{,}000-9{,}760}{9{,}760} \times \frac{360}{90} = 0.0984 \text{ or } 9.84 \text{ percent}$$

Equations (6–7) and (6–8) show that *a security's discount yield is always less than its effective rate of interest* since the face value always is greater than the current price. Given this, lenders prefer to quote the discount yield because it appears they are lending at lower interest rates. Years ago banks almost exclusively lent short term to firms, which made one payment at maturity. A $100 loan contract may have specified a 6 percent rate of interest, but, being a discount loan, interest was taken off the top; that is, the borrower received $94. The effective rate was more than 6 percent, specifically, 6.38 percent.

When quoting discount yields became standard practice, lenders dominated the market in the sense that the average lender could easily accommodate many average borrowers, and the average borrower borrowed relatively infrequently. These conditions no longer hold. In particular, Treasury debt is widely held; the assets of the largest financial institution do not begin to approach the value of Treasury debt outstanding. Moreover, the Treasury issues bills weekly. Nevertheless, the Treasury has been unable to change the way bankers and other major lenders quote the yield on its debt. The return on Treasury bills continues to be quoted on a discount basis although the Treasury and any other borrower prefer that the return on their debt be quoted on an effective interest rate basis. In our previous example the discount yield was 9.6 percent while the effective interest rate was 9.84 percent. Would you be more willing to buy a Treasury bill when you are told "the" interest rate is 9.6 or 9.84? Quoting the 9.84 percent effective interest rate instead of the 9.6 percent discount yield would facilitate the sale of Treasury bills.

While it is true that the financially sophisticated realize that a 9.6 discount yield equals a 9.84 effective interest rate, many are not financially sophisticated, and the side-by-side use of the two ways of measuring return may induce many to accept a lower return. The small money market certificates are a good illustration. For several years banks issued certificates with rates tied to the Treasury bill rate at the previous weekly auction. The formula tying the certificate and Treasury bill rates was complicated; depending on various factors the certificate rate equaled or marginally exceeded the Treasury bill rate. Assume for simplicity the certificate rate equaled the Treasury bill rate. The advertised returns may be equal, but should an individual be indifferent about the security purchased? Ignoring transactions costs, taxes, and other factors, an individual would be better off by purchasing a Treasury bill because the advertised return on the bill is its discount yield while the return on the certificate is an effective rate of interest. Consider another example. Suppose a six-month (days to maturity = 180), $10,000 Treasury bill sells for $9,500. Using Equation (6–7), the discount yield is 10 percent.

$$i_d = \frac{10{,}000 - 9{,}500}{10{,}000} \times \frac{360}{180} = 0.1 = 10 \text{ percent} \qquad \textbf{(6–7'')}$$

Banks then announce they will pay the same rate, 10 percent annually, and they do. The same $9,500 deposited in a bank would be worth only $9,975 six months later. (The interest income on $9,500 at 10 percent annually is $475 (= $950/2) for six months, which when added to $9,500 gives $9,975.) An individual is better off purchasing the Treasury bill because a 10 percent discount yield is a greater return than a 10 percent interest rate. In other words, the effective interest rate on the Treasury bill is more than 10 percent.

Relatively long-term noncoupon bonds with payment of principal alone, called *multiplier certificates,* are a very recent and popular wrinkle. For example, assume a six-year $1,000 par value certificate without coupons currently sells for $500. What rate of interest would you earn on such a certificate? One could solve an equation like (6–4) for i when PV = 500, FV = 1,000, and n = 6. This would give you an exact answer. With all the nooks and crannies you need a shortcut that gives a good approximation. Use the *Rule of 72, which states that the approximate annual return on an investment equals 72 divided by the number of years it takes for the investment to double in value.* Algebraically,

$$i = 72/n$$

or

$$n = 72/i$$

where n is the number of years it takes for the investment to double, and i is the rate of interest. In our example n = 6, so the rate of interest is 12 percent.[4] Alternatively, the second version of the Rule of 72 solves for n when you know i. The number of years it takes for an investment to double in value equals 72 divided by the rate of interest. The numerator is 72 instead of 100 because of compounding.

Attributes or Characteristics of Debt

The rate of interest is only one attribute or characteristic of any debt instrument. Other characteristics are sufficiently important that debt instruments differing in these characteristics often are given different names. For example, government securities with an original maturity of a year or less are Treasury *bills* while similar securities maturing within 1 to 10 years are Treasury *notes,* and those maturing beyond 10 years are Treasury *bonds*. At any moment in time interest rates vary from security to security to make each equally desirable to the average investor. For example, the demand for securities with a particularly desirable characteristic is high, and, consequently, their rate of interest is low. *When you look at a cross-section, the rate of interest summarizes the desirability*

---

[4]The Rule of 72 is a good approximation provided the rate of interest is less than 20 percent.

of all other characteristics. Let us consider the major attributes of securities and their impact on a security's rate of interest.

Default Risk

Risk is an important characteristic of debt. We should distinguish between two types of risk: (1) *default risk* and (2) *market risk*. Default risk is the probability that the contractual payments will not be made, or at best significantly delayed. Default risk is so important to investors, yet so difficult for them to estimate directly, that debtors pay public bond-rating firms, such as Moody's Investors Service and Standard & Poor's, to evaluate their debt. Although a firm may be quite confident its debt will receive a relatively low quality rating (high default risk rating), it gladly pays bond-rating firms because the sale of unrated bonds is virtually impossible. Investors first have to know the risk of default before deciding what compensation is necessary.

Standard & Poor's rates bonds currently paying interest from AAA (prime quality) to CC. Bonds in default are rated D. Bonds rated CC are not as risky as they may seem. The "outright speculations" which Standard and Poor's classifies as CC often have met their obligations on a timely basis. This is not surprising if you recall that only relatively strong firms can issue bonds in the first place. The Standard & Poor's ratings accurately reflect relative default risk. AAA bonds almost never default, at least while still rated AAA. Whoops, S&P does make mistakes but reacts quickly and lowers ratings prior to default.

Lenders demand an interest premium for default risk. The size of the default-risk premium clearly depends on the probability of default. As a result, the quoted yields to maturity are lower on AAA bonds than BBB (medium quality) bonds, which in turn offer a lower yield than CC bonds.[5] From the viewpoint of the lender, *collateral,* which increases recoveries during defaults, is equivalent to lower default probabilities. Consequently, borrowers offer collateral and thereby lower their borrowing cost. The specific property being financed almost always serves as collateral for real estate loans. In some cases the same property is collateral for several loans. In case of default and sale of the real estate, the first mortgage is paid in full before any payment on the second mortgage. Some debt has prior claim on all assets instead of being secured by specifically identified assets. Secured bonds of manufacturing firms generally are of this type. Bonds without collateral are called *debentures*.

---

[5]Throughout the remainder of this section "the" yield to maturity always refers to the *quoted* yield, which assumes that all payments are made and uses the formulas of the last section. The realized or ex-post yield may be less on a BBB bond than a AAA if the former in fact defaults. For simplicity, we shall let "bonds" represent any debt instrument regardless of term to maturity.

Bond ratings accurately measure relative default risk at all phases of the business cycle, but it appears the ratings overestimate default risk of low-rated bonds in the boom and underestimate default risk in the trough. Interest rates reflect this. The BBB interest rate is always greater than the AAA interest, but the spread narrows during a boom and widens during a trough. During a boom virtually any fool can make a profit. The default risk of marginal firms will appear quite low, and the BBB–AAA interest rate differential will narrow. Default risk rises across the board during a trough, especially for marginal firms. Earnings of blue-chip firms decline, often significantly, during recessions but the likelihood of default remains virtually nil. Marginally profitable firms on the other hand do not have the resources to weather a recession. A recession is an economic pneumonia: it temporarily debilitates the strong but kills the old and weak. Interest differentials widen during a recession.

Market Risk

Market risk is the current uncertainty of a security's value at the time one intends to convert it to cash. Bonds which one intends to hold to maturity are free of market risk. Bond price fluctuations are irrelevant if a sale is not anticipated. Long-term bonds do carry substantial market risk if the planned holding period is short, as is traditionally assumed. Long-term bond prices can fluctuate significantly over short periods of time. The possible market risk of short-term bonds often is not appreciated. If the planned holding period is 30 years, 1-year bonds bear market risk. Future interest rates are unknown. An individual with $1,000 to invest is uncertain about the value of this investment, including interest, 30 years hence if 1-year securities are purchased each year. In contrast, the value 30 years hence of a currently 30-year-to-maturity, $1,000 bond is a guaranteed $1,000 plus the coupons, abstracting from default risk.

The two kinds of risk typically are positively related but examples to the contrary exist. Treasury bonds are default-risk free—the government can always crank the big green money machine—but are *not* free of market risk. Conversely, check deposits over $100,000 (the current FDIC insurance maximum) are market-risk free—banks offer fixed dollar-denominated deposits—but are *not* free of default risk.

Market risk may be measured by the dispersion of the security's return over time. If the return was highly variable, predictions should be highly uncertain, and market risk is great. *A security's beta,* β, *is a relative measure of market risk* which has become increasingly popular. Many investment advisory firms report the beta for each stock, and betas have been calculated for some bonds. A stock's beta is the slope coefficient of the regression of a stock's return (dependent variable) on the return of a broad market index such as Standard & Poor's 500 stock index (independent variable). More simply, *beta shows the average change in the return of a stock per unit change in the return of the market index.* Over a short period of time the return on a stock may move contrary to the market, and its beta will be negative. Over longer periods of time the prices of most stocks move in the same direction, making nearly all betas positive. The common price pattern in the long run occurs because major economic events like booms, depressions, and inflations ultimately affect firms in a similar manner. Beta equals one when a security is as volatile as the market, and beta rises (falls) as its volatility rises (falls) relative to the market. Empirical studies have shown that high beta/market risk *stocks* earn a higher yield. The effect of market risk on *bond* returns is debatable, as the chapter on the term structure of interest rates will show. Most claim that bondholders demand compensation for bearing market risk.

Taxability

The taxability of returns effectively distinguishes many bonds. The interest payments of state and local governments currently are exempt from federal income taxes, and interest on Treasury securities is exempt from state and local income taxes. Largely because people are in different tax brackets, the quoted rate of interest always is computed on a pre-tax basis. However, individuals are interested in the after-tax return instead of the pre-tax return. To equalize the after-tax return on securities, the (quoted) rate of interest is low on securities which are lightly taxed. In particular, *the taxability effect lowers the rate of interest on (1) state and local securities (2) U.S. Treasury securities, and (3) low-coupon bonds.* As just indicated, state and local securities are exempt from federal income tax. Other things being equal, someone in the 40 percent tax bracket is indifferent between a 10 percent fully taxable bond and a 6 percent tax exempt bond.[6] State and local bonds typically yield 30 to 40 percent less than comparable fully-taxed securities. Thus, state and locals are not purchased by those in the lowest tax brackets but are tax "loopholes" for those in the highest tax brackets. States do not tax the interest on Treasury securities so the interest rate on these securities is low, *ceteris paribus*. Since the federal income tax rates are much higher than state and local tax rates, Treasury securities yield substantially more than state and locals on a pre-tax basis.

Taxability reduces the quoted rate of interest on low-coupon bonds. The total yield on any bond is generated by the coupon payments and capital gain, which is taxed at a lower rate than coupon (interest) income.

---

[6]Calling state and local securities "tax exempts" can be a misnomer because states tax each other's securities.

Consequently, individuals prefer capital gains to coupon payments. This reduces the yield on low-coupon, high-capital-gain securities, just as the lightly taxed state and local bonds offer a low return. An example may be helpful. Assume a recently issued 12 percent coupon security is selling at par so its total return is also 12 percent. Also assume a comparable 4 percent coupon security issued sometime ago when interest rates were lower. The latter security clearly cannot sell at par and yield only 4 percent when a comparable security is offering 12 percent. The price of the low-coupon security will fall in order to realize a capital gain at maturity. The price decline will *not* be enough to cause an annualized 8 percent capital gain and equalize the (quoted) rate of interest because the gain is taxed at a lower rate. Assuming interest and capital gains are taxed at 50 and 20 percent respectively, the high-coupon, 12 percent, bond yields 6 percent after taxes. To equalize after-tax returns, the low-coupon bond would have to yield only 9 percent, the 4 percent coupon plus a 5 percent capital gain. In summary, buyers are willing to pay a higher price for any lightly taxed security and, consequently, lower its pre-tax return.

Loan Size

After taxability, loan size is the most important determinant of cross-sectional interest rates for three reasons. First, because lenders are interested in their *net* after-tax returns, *the cost of making and administering loans,* like taxability, *influences the quoted or gross rate of interest.* Most loan-service costs do not increase proportionally with *loan size.* Some loan-service costs are fixed; it costs no more to record a $1 million loan than a $1,000 loan. Spreading these fixed costs over a large number of dollars reduces the loan-service cost per dollar lent. Some service costs even decline absolutely as well as relatively with loan size, at least up to a point. The information about small firms that a lender believes is necessary to evaluate a loan request often is costly to acquire, while similar information about large firms is readily available virtually free. Consistent with this, interest rates on consumer and other small loans are among the highest. Second, *small loans generally are riskier,* which further increases administration costs, such as the collection services of Badger and Browbeat (a firm that fell on hard times when aggravated assault was raised from a misdemeanor to a felony).

Loan and firm size clearly are positively related. A small firm that gets a large loan will no longer remain a small firm. In addition to high administration costs, *interest rates on small loans are high because lenders often exercise monopoly powers against small borrowers.* Unlike other industries where the degree of monopoly power depends almost exclusively on the type of firms in the industry, monopoly power in banking depends more on the customer than the bank. For example, the Bank of

America is the largest bank in the United States, yet it exercises virtually no monopoly power when dealing with IBM, AT&T, GM, GE, and other large companies. These large companies can borrow anywhere throughout the United States, indeed throughout the world. The thousands of potential lenders to large firms are disorganized and cannot form a cartel like the relatively few OPEC countries. Moreover, large firms maintain deposit accounts at many banks. If any one bank attempted to exercise monopoly power, the large firm would quickly find another bank only too willing to accept its deposits and make a loan.

Contrast the above with the opportunities available to small borrowers. Where can the owner of Joe's Diner borrow? Banks outside the immediate geographical area will not even consider the loan requests of small borrowers. Banks in New York lack information about small firms in San Francisco, and information costs increase with the distance between small borrowers and lenders. If a small California firm were audacious enough to inquire about a loan at a New York bank, it would be told politely but firmly that it should maintain its banking ties in California. Given the existence of only a handful of banks in most local markets, banks do organize against small borrowers. Both large and small banks exercise monopoly power against small firms. The Bank of America with numerous competitors in San Francisco probably is less of a monopolist than the First National Bank of Podunk, a one-bank town. While small firms are discriminated against, discrimination is less important than administrative costs in explaining the differential between interest rates to large and small borrowers. Empirical estimates are presented in Chapter 14.

Marketability

Marketability measures the ease and cost of being "in and out," that is, buying an item and selling it shortly thereafter. An item must satisfy two conditions to be readily marketable: (1) the brokerage and other transactions cost associated with it must be low, and (2) the purchase and sales price should be relatively independent of the time spent searching for sellers and buyers. One should think before purchasing nonmarketable instruments because mistaken purchases are costly. Nonmarketable instruments are suitable only for those with long holding-period horizons. Houses and other real estate are not readily marketable assets. Houses that must be sold within a week typically fetch a price much lower than one would get by standing pat and keeping the house on the market for six months. Moreover, the usual realty commission is 6 percent of the sales price, making a buy and sell strategy costly. Treasury bills, in contrast, are readily marketable. Treasury bills worth billions of dollars are sold daily, and the commission rate is quite small, especially on large denomination bills. Standardized items that are widely held often are marketable. Investors coined words to express compactly a debt instrument's degree of marketability. What is the main difference between a loan and a security? Loans are nonmarketable, while securities are readily marketable debt instruments. Marketability reduces the rate of interest.

Liquidity

Everyone recognizes the importance of liquidity while simultaneously disagreeing on its precise qualities. Generally, *liquid securities are said to encompass two characteristics already mentioned: (1) ready marketability and (2) little short-term market risk*. That is, a liquid security can be sold on short notice easily and at little cost, and the near future sales or redemption price is known with a high degree of certainty. Treasury bills, commercial paper, and certificates of deposit are examples of liquid securities. Most liquid assets are short term which, by definition, mature in the near future and are free of short-term market risk. U.S. savings bonds are a conspicuous exception. The Treasury stands ready to redeem savings bonds at predetermined prices, which effectively makes them riskless and marketable even if they cannot be sold to other individuals. Many securities possess one but not both qualities of liquid securities. For example, the common stock of large companies listed on the New York Stock Exchange and long-term government bonds are readily marketable but possess significant short-term market risk. Stock and bond prices sometimes change more than 10 percent in a quarter. Short-term consumer-oriented money market certificates, like the six-month certificates tied to the Treasury bill rate, are free from short-term market risk but lack marketability. A substantial interest penalty is incurred in cashing these certificates before maturity.

Term to Maturity

Term to maturity is the characteristic of bonds that economists have analyzed most extensively. Do 1-year bonds yield more or less than otherwise identical 10-year bonds? The effect of all the economic analysis has not been a consensus but several theories, each with some empirical support. The next chapter looks exclusively at the term to maturity.

The Historical Record

Figure 6–2, which graphs several long-term bond yields, confirms the major assertions of this section. State and local government bonds have offered the lowest yields since 1940 because federal income tax rates have been high. Prior to 1940, however, a combination of very low tax rates and high default risk drove the yield on state and local government bonds

FIGURE 6–2
Long-Term Bond Yields

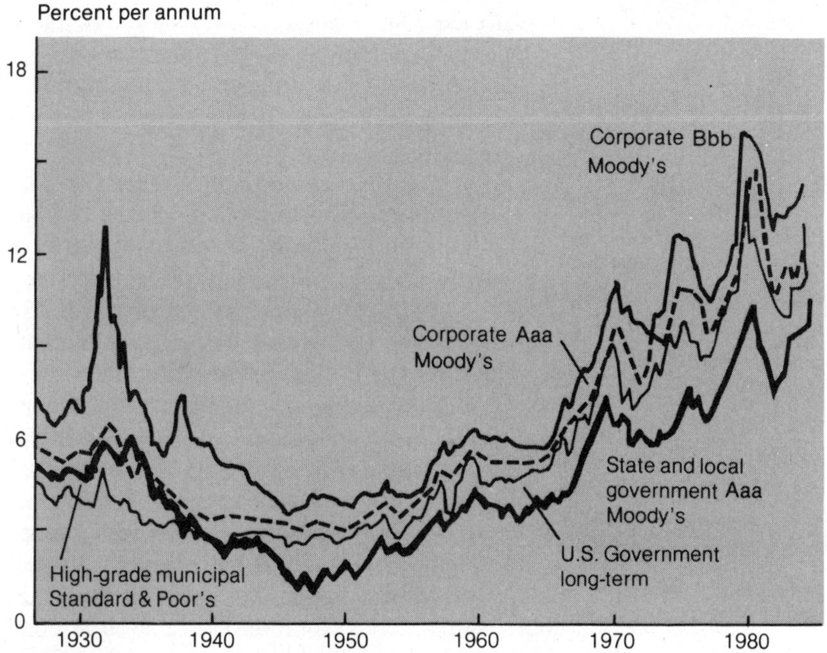

Source: Federal Reserve, *Historical Chart Book, 1984*, p. 97.

above the yield on riskless U.S. Treasury bonds. Note the width of the BBB–AAA interest rate differential throughout the entire 1930s and particularly during the depth of the Great Depression of 1929–33. The differential again widened during the 1974–75 and 1982–83 recessions.

Nominal Rates, Real Rates, and Inflation

The analysis so far has been limited to the variability of interest rates across securities at any one moment in time. We must postpone a detailed analysis of each factor that causes interest rate variations over time. Inflation, a time-series phenomenon of prices rising over time, is one such factor. It is convenient and important, however, to consider at this point the effects of inflation on the rate of interest on a "standard" loan.

"The" rate of interest, or yield to maturity, as defined earlier and as published in *The Wall Street Journal* and other financial publications, is the *nominal* rate of interest. That is, we defined the rate of interest as the growth rate linking a current *dollar* sum and a future *dollar* sum. When prices are constant, the nominal rate also equals the *real rate of interest,* that is, *the additional goods a lender can purchase in the future by sacrificing consumption today.* Inflation creates a wedge between nominal and real rates of interest. As a first approximation for inflation rates that are not too high, the realized nominal rate of interest equals the real rate of interest plus the rate of inflation. Algebraically,

(6–9)

$$i_{nominal} = i_{real} + \pi$$
$$i_{real} = i_{nominal} - \pi$$

where π is the rate of inflation.[7] For example, someone who lends \$100 and receives \$110 at the end of the year earns a 10 percent nominal return. If goods cost 6 percent more at the end of the year (π = 6 percent), then the lender can purchase only 4 percent more goods a year hence (i_{real} = 4 percent).

Does inflation reduce the real rate of interest, raise the nominal rate, or produce some combination of the two? When the rate of inflation changes, which term adjusts to satisfy Equation (6–9)? The answer depends on whether inflation is unanticipated or anticipated. Bonds and loan contracts specify the nominal rate of interest. Unanticipated inflation, by definition, catches people by surprise; behavior is not adjusted for any unanticipated event. *When inflation is unanticipated, loans continue to be made at the old nominal rate of interest, and the real rate of interest falls.* Unanticipated inflation benefits borrowers at the expense of lenders. Inflation is likely to be unanticipated when it starts or, more accurately, whenever the rate of inflation changes sharply.

Matters are quite different when inflation is anticipated. Although loan contracts continue to specify nominal interest rates, the nominal rate is adjusted upward for inflation because *borrowers and lenders ultimately are concerned about goods and services rather than dollars. As a first approximation, the nominal rate of interest shifts upward by the rate of anticipated inflation, and the real rate of interest remains constant.* Look at Figure 6–3, which plots real (adjusted for the price level) loanable funds on the horizontal axis and the nominal rate of interest on the vertical axis. Let the solid curves represent behavior prior to inflation. Now assume a 6 percent rate of inflation is anticipated. *As a first approximation,* the loan-

[7]The precise formula is:

$$1 + i_{real} = (1 + i_{nominal})/(1 + \pi)$$

where the interest and inflation rates are expressed in *decimal* form. The equation says that the goods one can buy in the future per dollar lent (left-hand side) equal the number of dollars one has in the future per dollar lent today (numerator of right-hand side) divided by the future price of goods currently worth one dollar (denominator of right-hand side). Expanding the equation,

$$i_{nominal} = i_{real} + \pi i_{real} + \pi$$

Equation (6–9) ignores the interaction term, which is small when the rate of inflation or real rate is small. For example, if the real interest rate and rate of inflation are both 10 percent (written as 0.1 in the equation), then the interaction term is 0.01. The correct nominal rate is 0.21 while Equation (6–9)'s approximation is 0.20.

FIGURE 6–3
The Demand and Supply of Loanable Funds Shift Upward by the Rate of Anticipated Inflation

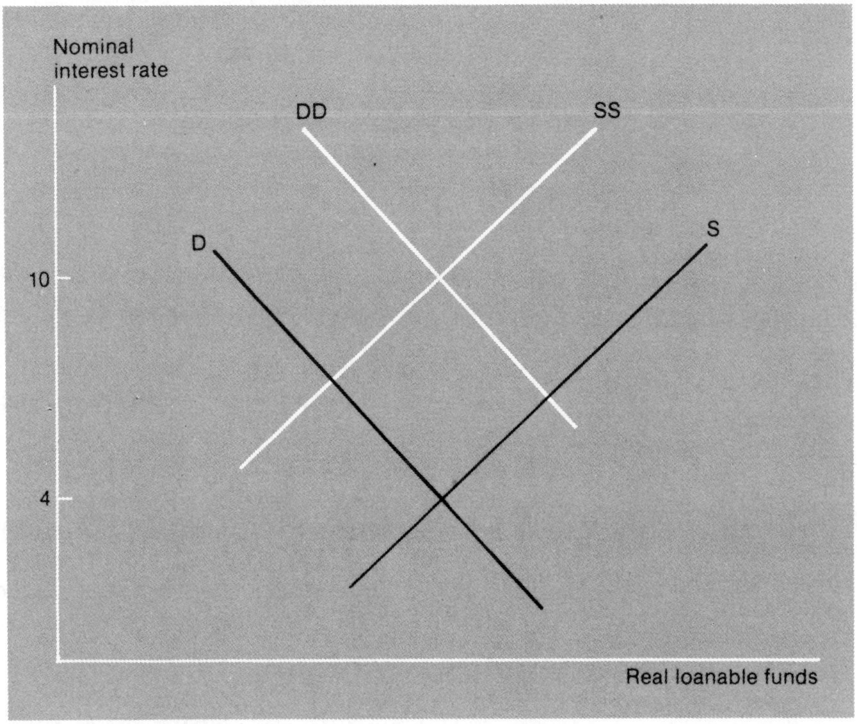

supply curve shifts upward by 6 percent as lenders are interested in their ability to purchase goods and services. Will the loan-demand curve also shift upward by 6 percent as a first approximation? Yes. Borrowers can afford to pay 6 percent more dollars because each dollar purchases 6 percent less. When inflation persists and becomes anticipated, the nominal rate of interest rises and neither borrowers nor lenders gain in real terms.

This section is admittedly incomplete. Subsequent parts of the book analyzes how other factors besides inflation affect the real rate of interest. Moreover, we have stressed that the one-for-one relationship between anticipated inflation and nominal interest rates is only a first approximation, as Figure 6–4 confirms. The gap between the corporate AAA bond rate of interest and the expected rate of inflation lines is not constant. (Expected inflation is estimated by averaging the past three years' rates of inflation.) Chapter 28 takes a closer look at inflationary expectations and introduces such "real world" complications as taxes, which make the relationship inexact. Nevertheless, Figure 6–4 shows there is a very strong, if inexact, positive relationship between nominal interest rates and expected inflation.

FIGURE 6–4

Long-Term Bond Yields and the Rate of Inflation

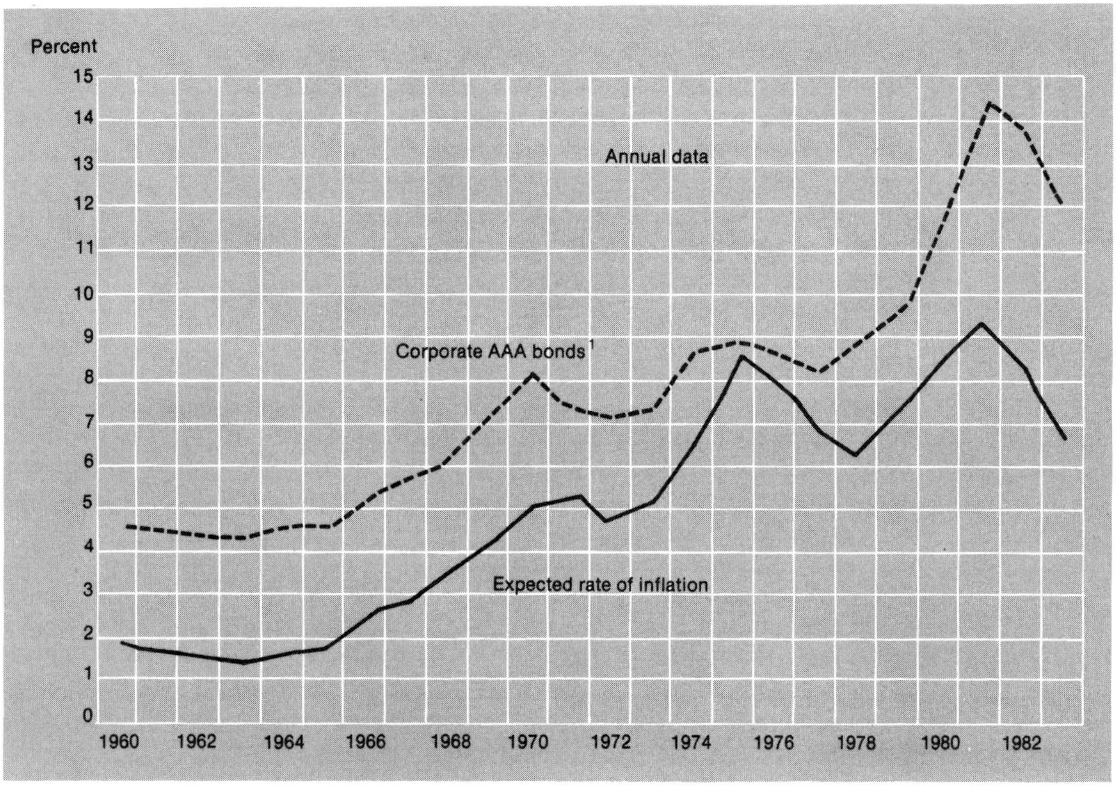

Source: Federal Reserve Bank of St. Louis *Review*, August/September 1980, p. 19; and recent *Federal Reserve Bulletins*.

Summary/Questions

In financial markets money is exchanged for promises to be fulfilled in the future. The rate of interest is the link between the two. Because finance is extremely beneficial, virtually everyone participates in financial markets. Some purchase cars on credit, while others help finance the deficit by buying Treasury bonds. The breadth of financial markets is reflected by the cross-sectional diversity of interest rates, as any issue of *The Wall Street Journal* confirms. Prime quality corporations promise less because their promises are more believable. In other words, the rate of interest is less on AAA bonds than CC bonds.

Intangibles are prone to different interpretations. Rates of interest, which link intangible future promises to the present, are no exception. Truth-in-lending laws confirm that many people encounter measurement and conceptual difficulties with interest rates. We discussed several peculiar ways of measuring interest. Perhaps the best known interest rate, the prime rate, is easily measured, but its relevance is becoming increasingly unclear. Until about 1975, the prime rate was the rate of interest on short-term bank loans to the highest quality borrowers. Some consumer organizations and small firms claim that by the late 1970s banks' best customers were paying less than the prime rate, which simply became a base for scaling other interest rates upward. Perhaps the bank critics are correct. One large New York bank adopted a new definition: the prime rate is the rate that the main office says is the prime rate!

1. Assume that a 10-year to maturity, $100 par value bond with a $7 annual coupon currently sells for $80. What is this bond's (*a*) nominal or coupon yield, (*b*) current yield, and (*c*) average total return to maturity, ATRM, which is a good approximation of its yield to maturity or rate of interest? If bond tables are available, compute the exact rate of interest.

2. What is the relationship between a bond's price and its rate of interest? How is the magnitude of the change in bond prices necessary to produce any *given* interest rate change related to the term to maturity of the bond?

3. Assume the price of a six-month (180 days), $10,000 par value Treasury bill is $9,400. What is the bill's (*a*) discount yield, and (*b*) effective rate of interest?

4. Define the Rule of 72. List two other "quick-and-easy" approximations used in finance to compute interest rates.

5. List the major characteristics of debt instruments and their effect on the rate of interest.

6. Distinguish between default risk and market risk. Give examples of securities that have one type of risk but not the other.

7. What is the relationship between market risk, marketabililty, and liquidity? Give examples of securities which possess (*a*) one of these characteristics but not the others and (*b*) all three characteristics.

8. What three types of securities offer low yields because of tax features? Explain your answer.

9. Give three reasons for the inverse relationship between loan size and the rate of interest.

10. What is the relationship between the nominal rate of interest, real rate of interest, and rate of inflation? How, if at all, does (*a*) unanticipated and (*b*) anticipated inflation influence the real and nominal interest rate?

Term structure of interest rates

7

> Rather more can be said on our present methods about the differences between rates of interest which arise from differences in the duration of loans.
>
> *John Hicks**

The term to maturity is the attribute of government debt that can be changed most easily at the date of issue. For this reason and others, economists interested in government policy have analyzed most extensively the effect of term to maturity on the rate of interest. *The term structure of interest rates curve or yield curve shows the relationship at any one instant between the yield to maturity and term to maturity on otherwise comparable securities.* Several yield curves are plotted in Figure 7–1. The interest rate or yield to maturity is on the vertical axis and term to maturity is on the horizontal axis. Traditionally, the yield curve of marketable Treasury securities is computed because the Treasury has issued securities spanning a wide maturity range. Comparability except for maturity is most likely satisfied by securities of the same issuer. To repeat, *the yield curve utilizes cross-section data; it shows interest rates at any one instant.* The four yield curve patterns most often encountered are illustrated in Figure 7–1. The yield curve typically is (1) upward sloping, (2) flat, (3) downward sloping, or (4) humped, rising at first and then declining.

Playing the Yield Curve

More practical financial analysts also are interested in the yield curve, though for different reasons than economists. They see the yield curve

---

**Value and Capital*, 2d ed. (Oxford: Oxford University Press, 1946), p. 144.

FIGURE 7–1
Term Structure of Interest Rates or Yield Curves

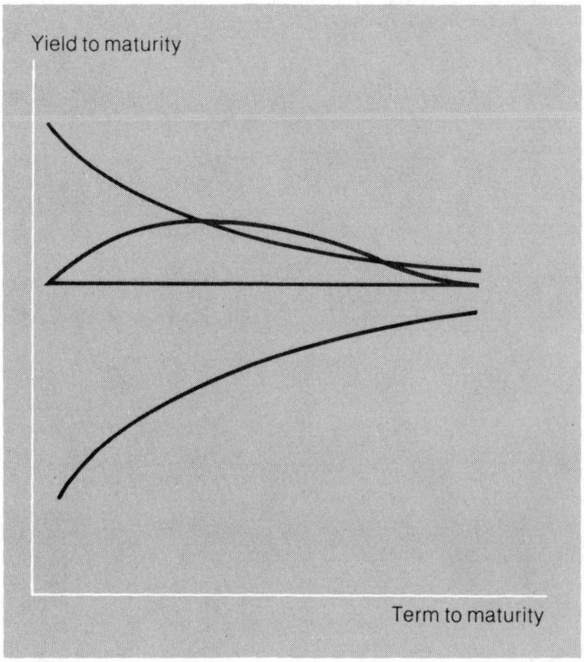

as something to be played for profit, particularly when it is steeply rising or steeply falling. *One plays the yield curve by borrowing in one end of the market and lending or buying securities in the other end.* Brokerage houses in particular allow their customers to play the yield curve for high stakes. You can borrow short term at rates just above the prime rate from Merrill Lynch and other brokers in order to buy long-term bonds. The down payment or, in the technical language of Wall Street, margin requirement for government bonds typically is only 5 to 10 percent. (The margin requirement for stocks is much higher.) For example, $10,000 will buy you $100,000 government bonds; your broker will gladly lend you the $90,000 difference. Especially if the yield curve is sharply upward sloping, should you borrow the $90,000 at, say, 8 percent for a year, buy a 20-year government bond yielding, say, 12 percent *to maturity,* and sell the bond a year later? Will the 20-year bond yielding 12 percent to maturity also yield 12 percent *this year*? The profit potential on your $10,000 is enormous. Will the potential be realized? What profits can you realistically expect from playing the yield curve?

The opportunities for playing the yield curve in the reverse direction were more limited until quite recently, when new interest rate futures and options contracts widened the playing field. The limited opportunities of old did have the strong advantage of being understandable to many. For example, my friendly bank has advertised for many years that it makes (long-term) second mortgages so that its customers may use the equity in their homes to finance exotic trips and their children's education. I am sure my friendly bank would not object to my buying T-bills with the proceeds of a second mortgage.

What determines the term structure of interest rates? Why does the yield curve have a particular shape this year and a different shape next year? We immediately present the three main theories of the term structure that answer these questions and simultaneously draw the implications of the theories for players of the yield curve. We then have a section on Operation Twist for those more interested in the yield curve for economic policy and history purposes. The final section presents some empirical evidence for and against the various theories of the term structure.

Theories of the Term Structure of Interest Rates

There are three main theories of the term structure of interest rates: (1) the market segmentation or hedging or supply and demand hypothesis, (2) the expectations hypothesis, and (3) the risk premium hypothesis.[1]

Market Segmentation Hypothesis

Extreme risk aversion and institutional restrictions are the fundamental assumptions underlying the market segmentation hypothesis of the term structure of interest rates. As indicated earlier, market risk depends on the relation between the bond's term to maturity and the holder's planned holding period. *Investors reduce market risk by more closely matching the security's term to maturity with their planned holding period.* Extremely risk-averse bondholders will buy bonds that they intend to hold to maturity. Five-year and 30-year bonds are risky to an individual who plans to hold securities for 20 years. The proceeds of the 5-year bond will have to be reinvested for 15 years at an uncertain rate of interest, while the current 30-year bond will still have a 10-year term to maturity when it is sold 20 years hence, and the sales price of every item 20 years hence is uncertain. Similarly, borrowers incur risk when the maturity of the bond issued differs from the life of the asset being financed. For example, assume the life of a steel mill is 40 years; over that period the steel company expects to recover the cost of the mill and earn a normal return.

---

[1]The risk premium hypothesis is more often called the liquidity preference hypothesis. We believe the former name is less confusing. "Liquidity preference" often is equated with Keynes's speculative demand for money, which assumes that risk-neutral individuals maximize expected return. This is the assumption of the expectations hypothesis, as we shall see shortly. The risk premium or liquidity preference hypothesis *of the term structure* assumes partial risk aversion.

The steel mill will not generate sufficient revenues in one year to cover its construction cost. The steel company that issues one-year bonds to finance the mill runs the risk of not being able to "roll over" the bonds next year. On the other hand, a firm that issues 30-year bonds in order to purchase inventories which are liquidated in three months incurs the risk of finding a suitable investment for the funds thrown off by the inventory liquidation. Such a firm could buy its outstanding bonds, but the purchase price would be uncertain. *Extreme risk averters match their planned holding period and a security's term to maturity, irrespective of interest rates.*

Advocates of the market segmentation hypothesis recognize that not everyone is extremely risk averse. Indeed, some are not risk averse at all. Las Vegas was built for risk lovers. Some investors purposely mismatch the maturity of their assets and liabilities and play the yield curve. Nevertheless, market segmentation supporters claim that yield curve players and other risk lovers account for an inconsequential proportion of total borrowing and lending. *They claim the loan market is dominated by naturally extremely risk-averse individuals and individuals who act extremely risk averse due to institutional and legal factors.* For example, suppose someone is willing to bear the risk of financing a house with successive one-year loans. Such an individual almost certainly will not be accommodated. Savings and loans traditionally make long-term mortgages, and restrictions on savings and loans and other financial institutions close whatever avenues tradition left open.

Assuming for simplicity two types of loans, short- and long-term, extreme risk aversion implies that the short-term (long-term) interest rate is totally irrelevant to bondholders with long (short) holding periods. The short- and long-term interest rates can be analyzed with ordinary supply and demand curves. Figures 7–2a and 7–2b graph on the horizontal axis the quantity of short- and long-term loanable funds, respectively, and the corresponding interest rate is graphed on the vertical axis. (Loans and loanable funds are identical; borrowers demand loans or loanable funds. While brevity would suggest a preference for loans, economists are contrary minded in this respect.) The demand for short-term loanable funds is downward sloping because at lower short-term interest rates borrowers are encouraged to undertake more *short-term* projects. The demand for short-term loanable funds is *not* downward sloping because borrowers *temporarily* finance long-term projects with short-term credit. A change in the *short-term* interest rate has no effect on the *long-term* supply and demand for loanable funds. The markets are segmented, at least the *private* part of the market. *The term structure of interest rates simply reflects the strength of the demand and supply for loanable funds by term to maturity.*

The market segmentation hypothesis suggests that the Treasury can significantly influence the term structure of interest rates by changing the

FIGURE 7–2

Segmented Markets Approach to the Term Structure of Interest Rates

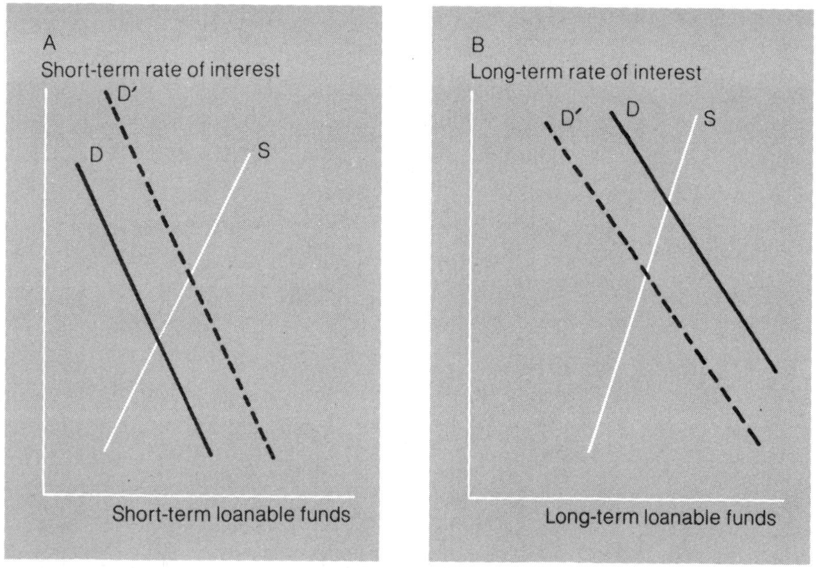

composition of its debt. When the Treasury borrows short-term, it supplies short-term bills, or equivalently, *demands* short-term loanable funds. If the Treasury borrows short term instead of long term, the short-term demand for loanable funds and its rate of interest increase, and the long-term demand and its rate of interest fall, as illustrated by the dashed curves in Figures 7–2a and 7–2b, respectively. The reasons for and the results of the Treasury's experiment in the early 1960s to twist the yield curve by changing the composition of its debt are presented after analyzing all the term structure theories.

The market segmentation hypothesis implies that the *few* individuals who are not extremely risk averse and do play the yield curve earn profits by borrowing cheap and lending dear. *Arbitrage profits exist in segmented markets*. For example, suppose the short-term rate is 10 percent and the long-term rate is 14 percent. Clearly, if interest rates at the end of the period are unchanged, you will profit by borrowing at the cheap 10 percent short-term rate and lending/buying securities at the dear 14 percent long-term rate. By not suggesting how the interest rate level and short-term/long-term differential will change over time, *the hypothesis implicitly assumes interest rates will remain constant*. Thus profits will be earned by borrowing cheap and lending dear *whether the cheap interest rate is the short-term or long-term rate*. If you can lend short term at 14 percent and borrow long term at 10 percent, do so. Exploitable profits exist when the vast proportion of the population is extremely risk averse. Exactly where the profitable opportunities lie depends on the relative numbers of borrowers and lenders arranged by their preferred holding period. For example, if the short-term rate is above the long-term rate because a relatively large demand for short-term funds is not being met by extremely risk-averse suppliers who have a long-term horizon, then those who meet the demand and lend short term will profit.

Expectations Hypothesis

The expectations hypothesis is the second major theory of the term structure of interest rates. *The expectations hypothesis assumes individuals (1) form expectations about future interest rates and (2) are risk neutral, deciding solely on the basis of the highest expected rate of return.* For example, this theory assumes that individuals are indifferent between earning a certain 10 percent and a 50-50 chance of nothing or 20 percent. Given the two assumptions, it follows that *(1) long-term interest rates are an average of current and expected future short-term interest rates, and (2) the expected holding period yield is independent of the security held.* An example best demonstrates that the two conclusions do follow from the assumptions. Temporarily assume everyone forms identical expectations about the future. For simplicity there are only two time periods, t and t + 1, called "years." Let the rate of interest on one-year loans at time t be 8 percent, and the expected, at time t, interest rate on one-year loans in period t + 1 is 12 percent. Algebraically,

$$i_{1,t} = 8 \text{ and } i^e_{1,t+1} = 12 \tag{7–1}$$

where i is the rate of interest, the first subscript following i is the length of the loan, the second subscript is the time period, and e is expected. Given (7–1), what is the interest rate on a two-year loan in period t?

$$i_{2,t} = ? \tag{7–2}$$

A two-year loan may be viewed as a one-year loan today and a one-year loan a year hence. Viewed in this manner, a two-year loan will be competitive only if its return over two years equals the expected return on two successive one-year loans. In other words, the interest rate on two-year loans must be an average of the current one-year interest rate and the expected interest rate a year hence, assuming risk-neutral individuals. Ignoring compounding, in our example[2]

[2]The long-term interest rate is not a simple *arithmetic* average of the current and expected future short-term interest rates when compounding is taken into account. Nevertheless, the long-term rate is *an* average of the short-term rates, the precise type of average depending on the pattern of payments. Assuming discount loans or zero coupon bonds with the only payment at maturity, the long-term rate is a geometric average of the short-term rates. In

$$i_{2,t} = (i_{1,t} + i^e_{1,t+1})/2 = (8 + 12)/2 = 10 \tag{7–2'}$$

Arbitrage drives the two-year rate of interest to 10 percent. Suppose the interest rate were above 10 percent, say 11 percent. A two-year loan would bring the lender a total of 22 percent over the two years while a succession of two one-year loans would bring only a 20 percent expected return, again ignoring compound. Such a situation cannot persist. Lenders intent on maximizing their expected return will shift to the two-year loan market and drive the interest rate down to 10 percent. Similar reasoning indicates that arbitrage prevents the rate of interest from being below 10 percent. Generalizing Equation (7–2′)

$$i_{n,t} = (i_{1,t} + \sum_{j=1}^{n-1} i^e_{1,t+j})/n \tag{7–3}$$

The n–period interest rate is an average of the expected one-year interest rates during the period. *This implies that the yield curve is upward sloping when interest rates are expected to rise in the future, flat when interest rates are expected to remain constant, and downward sloping when interest rates are expected to fall.*

The explanation for the two-year rate being 10 percent in our case indicated that the expected return earned by those who lend for two years is independent of the type of loan, that is, a two-year loan or two one-year loans. Is the same true for one-year lenders? Will the bondholder earn the same expected return in period t whether he or she owns a one-year or two-year bond? Yes. In our example, the holder of a one-year bond earns 8 percent in period t, and the holder of a two-year bond who sells the bond at the end of the first year expects to earn the same 8 percent in period t, *not* the 10 percent Equation (7–2′) might suggest. The annual interest rate for the two years t *and* t + 1 is 10 percent, but the expected rate of return on two-year bonds in period t *alone* is only 8 percent. Let us see why this is so. The two-year bond at period t becomes a one-year bond at period t + 1. If expectations are correct so one-year bonds are offering 12 percent in period t + 1, the "old" two-year (10 percent coupon) bond will be purchased in period t + 1 only if it offers a 2 percent capital gain. What then must happen to the capital value of the two-year bond during period t? Its capital value must fall from 100 to approximately 98. In this manner the bondholder earns 12 percent in period t + 1; a 10 percent coupon plus a 2 percent capital gain when the principal is repaid at the end of period t + 1.[3] But if this occurs, the

---

the normal case with coupon and principal payments and interest compounding, the precise averaging formula is very complex—not a geometric average as is often incorrectly assumed.

[3]We are ignoring taxes and other complications.

investor in two-year bonds earns only 8 percent in year t; a 10 percent coupon minus a 2 percent capital loss as the bond price falls from 100 to 98. Figure 7–3 illustrates the expected price of the two-year bond between t and t + 2. *The expected return is a function of the holding period; it does not depend on the maturity of the bond purchased.* In our example the bondholder earns 8 percent in period t and 12 percent in period t + 1 irrespective of the bond purchased.

Reread the last paragraph; most find it quite difficult. It makes no mention of the amount of short-term and long-term bonds because the expectations hypothesis denies that changes in the composition of the debt *directly* affect the yield curve.[4] If long-term Treasury borrowing tended to drive the long-term rate up, arbitrage by profit maximizers would occur until the long-term rate equaled an average of current and expected future short-term rates. Changes in the composition of Treasury debt may *indirectly* affect the yield curve by changing expectations. For example, if long-term Treasury borrowing is interpreted as indicating that a more restrictive policy of higher future rates will be adopted, the yield curve should become steeper.

Of course, everyone's expectations are not identical as we have been assuming so far. Differences of opinion make horse races and financial

FIGURE 7–3
Bond Prices over Time

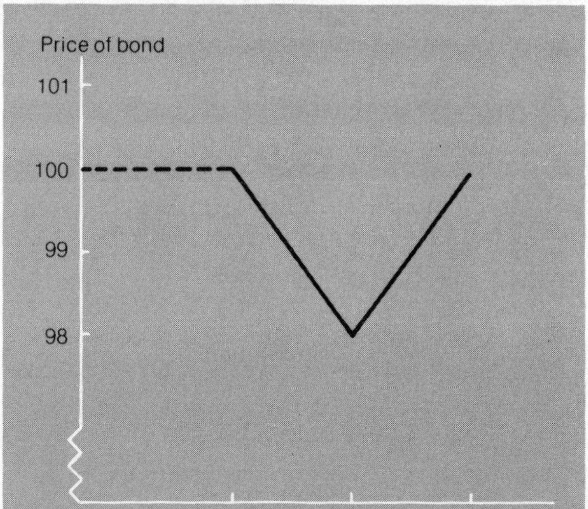

[4]We are assuming expectations are approximately homogeneous.

markets, causing one person to sell and another to buy. Recognizing differences of opinion simply means that the two major implications of the expectations hypothesis should be expressed only for the representative or marginal individual. That is, (1) long-term interest rates are an average of the current and expected future short-term interest rates of the representative person, and (2) the expected holding period yield for the representative person is independent of the security held.

Suppose you are the representative or marginal person, where your expectation of future interest rates just equals the average expectation of all other financial market participants. More important, *as the representative person you do not have any better or worse basis for forming accurate forecasts of future interest rates than the other financial market participants*. What profits will you earn playing the yield curve? First, being a representative participant in *financial* markets is no put down. There are many very savvy investors looking from San Francisco to New York to London for an extra 1/8 percent. *According to the expectations hypothesis the representative person cannot expect to earn anything from playing the yield curve*. Indeed, the representative person is indifferent to short- and long-term bonds since, according to (2) in the last paragraph, the expected holding period yield for the representative person is independent of the security held. In terms of our example, the representative person gains nothing by borrowing short-term at 8 percent in order to buy long-term bonds yielding 10 percent to *maturity*. If the long-term bond is held to maturity, the average cost of *repeated* short-term borrowings is the same 10 percent as the bond yield. On the other hand, a long-term bond held only for a short time will yield the same 8 percent as the borrowing cost. Of course, the representative person will make a better than average forecast on occasion and profit from playing the yield curve. At other times, however, he will incur losses. The representative person may ponder at length over the choice of maturities, but a decision based on the flip of a coin will be as profitable on average.[5]

Suppose you are not the representative person. Your expectations of future interest rates are much *higher* than the expectations of others. In this case you will *not* be indifferent between short- and long-term bonds. In your mind long-term interest rates are too low; they incorporate the low expected future rates of the representative person. You believe short-term securities will offer a higher yield than long-term securities. Therefore, you borrow long term to purchase short-term securities. Conversely, suppose your expectations of future interest rates are much *lower* than the expectations of others. In this case you will prefer long-term over

[5]The reader familiar with the investment literature will note the similarity between the expectations hypothesis of the term structure and the random walk hypothesis of common stock prices.

short-term securities. *You can expect profits so long as your expectations are more accurate than the expectations of the representative person.* Indeed, profits are the reward for accuracy.

Risk Premium Hypothesis

The risk premium hypothesis of the term structure is an intermediate hypothesis incorporating elements of the other two hypotheses. The risk premium hypothesis assumes *(1) individuals are moderately risk averse, and (2) long-term bonds are risky to bondholders because, on balance, their planned holding period is short.* According to this hypothesis, the rate of interest on two-year bonds is *greater than* an average of the current and future interest rates on one-year bonds in order to compensate bondholders for the riskiness of two-year bonds. The hypothesis says that Equation (7–2′) should be

$$i_{2,t} = (i_{1,t} + i^e_{1,t+1} + \alpha)/2 = (8 + 12 + \alpha)/2 > 10 \tag{7–2″}$$

where α is the positive risk premium. Equation (7–2″) replaces the final equality in Equation (7–2′) with an inequality. *In this case, the expected yield for any holding period is less for liquid, short-term bonds than long-term bonds which earn a risk premium.*[6] Equations (7–1) and (7–2″) clearly show the implications of the risk premium hypothesis for a two-year holding period: the two-year bond yields more than a succession of two one-year bonds. The somewhat more difficult one-year holding period case is made easier by letting the risk premium α take a specific value, say, two. The yield to maturity on two-year bonds is then 11 percent. In our example, a one-year bond yields 8 percent while a two-year bond held for the first year yields 10 percent, assuming correct interest rate expectations. The capital value of a two-year, 11 percent coupon bond must fall 1 percent this year—making the total return 10 percent—in order to raise its total yield to 12 percent next year. The 8 percent return on a one-year bond is two percent ($\alpha = 2$) less than the 10 percent *expected* return on two-year bonds held for a year because the expected rate of interest next year is uncertain and may not materialize. If interest rates rise markedly next year, causing bond values to fall dramatically this year, the *realized* yield on a two-year bond held for a year could be less than 8 percent. Bondholders must be compensated for this risk.

Why do borrowers (bond issuers) willingly pay long-term rates which are higher than the average expected yield on one-year bonds? *The risk*

---

[6]Note that the sentence mentions holding period yields, not yields to maturity. The risk premium hypothesis does *not* state that the yield to maturity is always less on short-term bonds, that is, it does *not* state that the yield curve is always upward sloping.

premium theory implicitly assumes borrowers in general are financing long-term projects. Given this, short-term credit is risky from the viewpoint of the borrower. Long-term bonds avoid the risk of not being able to borrow at some point in the future. Risk-averse borrowers willingly pay a premium to *avoid* this risk. The risk premium of the lender is a safety premium to the borrower.

What are the implications of the risk premium hypothesis for players of the yield curve who are solely concerned about profit *and* have the same information as everyone else? Because according to this hypothesis the expected holding period yield is greater on long-term securities, *someone who is not risk averse can always expect (on average) profits by borrowing short-term and buying otherwise identical long-term securities*. This is so even if long-term rates are less than short-term rates. In this case interest rates are expected to fall. That is why the long-term rate, which is an average of the current and expected future rates *plus* a risk premium, is less than the short-term rate. Assuming expectations are realized and interest rates fall, holders of long-term bonds have a capital gain and claim the risk premium as their profit. A numerical example is helpful. Reverse the values of the current and expected one-year interest rates in the last example so that $i_{1,t} = 12$ and $i^e_{1,t+1} = 8$. Assuming the risk premium, α, still is 2 percent, $i_{2,t} = 11$. In words, the interest rate on two-year bonds is 11 percent. In this case one still *expects* a 2 percent profit, the risk premium, by borrowing short term at 12 percent in order to buy a two-year 11 percent bond! One expects a 3 percent (11 − 8) capital gain during the year because the one-year interest rate is expected to fall to 8 percent next year. The total *expected* return on a two-year bond held the first year is 14 percent, the sum of the 11 percent certain coupon plus the 3 percent *expected* (uncertain) capital gain. Of course, the expectation will not be realized at all times; the investor will not *always* profit by borrowing short term and investing long term. On average, however, the investor profits from borrowing short term and investing long term, and this is so whether the long-term rate is above or below the short-term rate.

Operation Twist, Recession, and the Balance of Payments

The term structure of interest rates has been analyzed most extensively by economists because major economic goals are alleged to be influenced by the rate of interest on specific term to maturity bonds. In particular, GNP and employment are supposed to be influenced mainly by the long-term rate of interest while the balance of payments is supposed to be influenced mainly by the short-term rate of interest. In subsequent theoretical chapters, where we abstract from the myriad of interest rates, we shall learn that "the" rate of interest effect on investment spending is a major link between money on the one hand and GNP and employment on the other. Investment spending here means the (1) acquisition of new plant and equipment by firms; (2) construction of homes, apartment buildings, and other structures; and (3) additions to firms' inventories. The value of new plant and equipment and structures overwhelms additions to inventories. The former types of investments are long lived, while inventories typically are held for a short period of time and then sold. This suggested to many economists, particularly those who adhered to the market-segmentation theory of the term structure of interest rates, that the long-term interest rate was "the" interest rate influencing investment spending. In order to increase GNP and employment, monetary policy had to induce more investment spending by lowering long-term interest rates.

Throughout much of the 1950s the United States incurred a balance-of-payments deficit. At first, the deficit was viewed as a temporary phenomenon without cause for alarm. By 1960, however, the Fed and other officials became concerned and decided the deficit had to end before the United States lost its entire gold stock or the dollar depreciated. In order to prevent a balance-of-payments deficit from becoming even larger and simultaneously maintain the exchange rate, the Treasury had to induce foreigners to hold and not sell their dollar-denominated assets. What would induce foreigners to hold more dollar assets and reduce the balance-of-payments deficit? Higher interest rates in the United States than abroad. In particular, it was thought that foreign holdings of short-term dollar assets were sensitive to short-term rates in the United States.

The United States seemingly faced a dilemma. 1960 also was a recession year. To stimulate the economy, long-term interest rates should fall, but short-term interest rates should rise for balance-of-payments purposes. In order to simultaneously achieve both balance-of-payments equilibrium and full employment the yield curve had to be twisted clockwise, raising short-term interest rates and lowering long-term rates. The Federal Reserve and Treasury thought the task was relatively simple. They, like many bond dealers and financial analysts at the time, adhered to the market segmentation hypothesis of the term structure, which suggested that the yield curve can be twisted by changing the composition of Treasury debt in private hands. The Fed and Treasury engaged in Operation Twist or, as some prefer to call it, Operation Nudge. Up until 1960, Federal Reserve open-market operations were executed almost exclusively by buying and selling short-term Treasury bills. On February 20, 1961, the Fed abandoned this policy, announcing, "The System Open-Market Account is purchasing in the open market U.S. Government bonds and notes of varying maturities, some of which will exceed five years." For its part, the Treasury could accelerate the natural shortening over time of the average term to maturity by concentrating new issues in the short-term area. In addition, both the Treasury and Federal Reserve could engage in outright swaps of Treasury bills for outstanding long-term bonds.

Operation Twist was only modestly successful, if not a total failure. Some blame the lack of success on insufficient effort. Federal Reserve swaps of shorts for longs as well as its net purchases of longer maturities were limited in scale. Moreover, the Treasury offset these operations to some extent by redeeming some of its maturing securities, which are necessarily short term, with long-term securities. Nevertheless, statistical studies indicate that anything short of a massive change in the composition of Treasury debt outstanding would have an insignificant impact on the term structure.[7]

Term Structure Evidence

While the statistical studies generally do not support the market segmentation hypothesis, the behavior of certain financial institutions suggests that the hypothesis has an element of truth. Consider life insurance companies. The premiums of a growing life insurance company will outstrip its current payments, and both its assets and contingent liabilities will increase. Since the time of death of its policyholders is staggered but primarily in the distant future, the market segmentation hypothesis suggests that insurance companies will be holding mainly long-term assets. The prediction is verified repeatedly: all insurance companies throughout history have held mainly long-term bonds. This fact is consistent with the expectations hypothesis only if all insurance companies' expectations of future interest rates always were less than the expectations of others, which is unlikely.

If the behavior of insurance companies contradicts the expectations hypothesis, changes in the shape of the yield curve over the business cycle strongly support the expectations hypothesis. Figure 7–4 shows that short-term rates are much more variable than long-term rates because the yield curve typically is upward sloping during a recession and downward sloping during a boom. This is precisely what the expectations hypothesis predicts. Interest rates in general are low during a recession because firms are not borrowing due to poor sales. Interest rates are lowest on short-term securities. Recessions are temporary phenomena, by definition; recessions occur when output falls and then rebounds. During a recession people should be expecting higher future interest rates as the economy and borrowing rebound. Therefore, according to the expectations hypothesis, the yield curve should be upward sloping. Conversely,

---

[7]Franco Modigliani and Richard Sutch, "Debt Management and the Term Structure of Interest Rates: An Empirical Analysis of Recent Experience," *Journal of Political Economy*, August 1967, supplement, pp. 569–89.

FIGURE 7–4
Yield Curves during Booms and Recessions

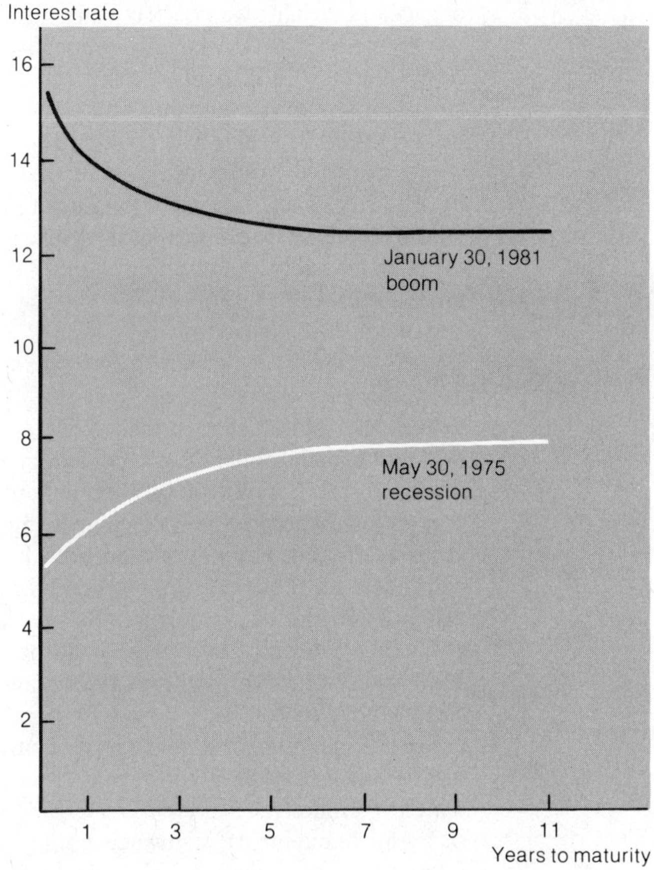

Source: *Treasury Bulletin*. (Fitted by eye to produce a smooth curve.)

during a boom people should be expecting a return to normal times and lower future interest rates, making the yield curve downward sloping. Stated somewhat differently, people realize that current (short-term) interest rates, like income, fluctuate up and down. Given this, (average) expected future rates (plural) of interest should be (1) relatively stable, and (2) above (below) the current short-term rate when the latter is low (high). If long-term interest rates are an average of current and future expected rates (plural) of interest, then long-term rates should be more stable than short-term rates. The yield curve should shift from upward sloping to downward sloping as the economy moves from recession to boom.[8]

The general pattern of yield curves over the business cycle is also consistent with the risk premium theory, which is basically a modification of the expectations theory. One may distinguish between the two theories by constructing a yield curve averaged over many years, say 50 to 75 years. *The expectations hypothesis predicts the long-run average yield curve will be flat.* Sometimes the current short-term rate will exceed expected future rates and vice versa. Averaged over many years, the current and expected future rates should be approximately equal, giving a flat yield curve. Advocates of the risk premium theory agree that current and expected future rates averaged over many years should be approximately equal. Given this, however, *the risk premium theory concludes that the yield curve should be upward sloping because long-term rates include a risk premium. The recent evidence supports the risk premium hypothesis. The average yield curve for 1930–84 is upward sloping,* even ignoring the period when the Fed pegged interest rates. However, during other relatively long periods, for example, 1900–30 in this country and throughout much of the 19th century in England, yield curves were flat.

In summary, each theory has some empirical support. Risk premiums do seem to exist, at least recently, but they are not very large. Short-term liquid securities do offer a somewhat lower rate of return on average. However, the simpler expectations hypothesis is a fairly good approximation for the more complex risk premium hypothesis. Unless you have much better information than other market participants, expect only a modest profit by borrowing short term and investing long term. Although the behavior of insurance companies is consistent with the market segmentation approach, the failure of Operation Twist casts serious doubt on this approach.

Summary/Questions

Rates of interest on alternative securities move together over time. During a business cycle peak, for example, interest rates in general are high. However, all interest rates do not change equally, which causes the spread between them to vary and sometimes produces what appears to be "really good deals." Were three-month Treasury bills yielding 15 percent in 1981

[8]Undoubtedly, the upward shift in the 1975 and 1981 yield curves illustrated in Figure 7–4 is partially explained by inflationary expectations, which was discussed in the last chapter.

really good deals when the rate of interest on long-term government bonds was only 14 percent? Was either one a good deal when one considers the rate of inflation? The very practical orientation of this chapter helps answer such questions. When short-term interest rates in the following years fell much more than the average investor expected, then the person who temporarily passed up 15 percent in order to lock in a 14 percent return for the long run is a savvy investor.

1. Define and draw the term structure of interest rates or yield curve. Explain the three main theories of the term structure, paying particular attention to the fundamental assumptions of each theory.
2. Suppose the current one-year interest rate is 12 percent and the expected one-year rate next year is 14 percent. Ignoring compounding, what does the expectations hypothesis say the current two-year interest rate equals? According to the expectations hypothesis, what rate of return is earned by the average investor in the first year assuming he or she held a two-year bond? For the next two questions answer: greater, less, equal, or uncertain. Compared to the expectations hypothesis, the risk premium hypothesis says the two-year rate is ______ . Compared to the expectations hypothesis, the hedging or market segmentation hypothesis says the two-year rate is ______ .
3. Define playing the yield curve. What do the three theories of the term structure say about the profits earned from playing the yield curve and the number of players? In particular, which theory generally advises: *(a)* borrow cheap and lend dear, *(b)* borrow short term and lend long term, and *(c)* do not simultaneously borrow and lend?
4. According to the risk premium theory of the term structure, only what type of person should borrow long term and invest short term? How often should this strategy be adopted?
5. Define Operation Twist. What factors led the Treasury and the Fed to attempt Operation Twist?
6. Present some evidence in favor of each of the three theories of the term structure of interest rate.

A closer look at financial instruments

8

Chapter 6 listed the major characteristics or attributes of financial claims and the interrelationships between these characteristics and yield to maturity. We did not, however, strongly link the major characteristics with specific financial instruments. That is, we offered only few examples of securities containing any given characteristic. This chapter focuses on the major types of securities and their issuers. We state the main characteristics of each major security and explain how its creation filled a void in the financial system. U.S. Treasury securities are classified first because the value outstanding and the value traded in any period dwarf other securities. Moreover, U.S. Treasury securities play a crucial role in the conduct of monetary policy. *Private money market instruments* (readily marketable securities maturing within a year) and *capital market instruments* (marketable long-term debt) are then described.

U.S. Treasury Securities

Table 8–1 lists the gross public debt of the United States Treasury by type and holder. Both dollar amounts and percentages of the total are shown for December 1983. A comparison of the percentage figures for December 1954 and December 1983 shows the trend in the relative importance of each component over nearly 30 years. As mentioned earlier, *Treasury bills,* nicknamed T-bills, are Treasury securities with an initial maturity under a year which are sold at a discount. The minimum denomination is $10,000. The Treasury *auctions* 91-day and 182-day bills

TABLE 8–1
Gross Public Debt of the U.S. Treasury: Type and Ownership

Type and holder	*Billions of Dollars, December 1983*	*Percent of Total, December 1983*	*Percent of Total, December 1954*
Marketable:	1,050.9	75.0	56.6
Bills*	343.8	24.5	17.2
Notes	573.4	40.9	10.0
Bonds	133.7	9.5	29.3
Nonmarketable:	350.0	25.0	43.4
Savings bonds	70.7	5.0	20.7
Government accounts series	231.9	16.6	15.3
Miscellaneous	46.7	3.3	7.4
Total†	1,400.9	100.0	100.0
By holder:			
U.S. agencies and trust funds	245.3	17.5	17.8
Federal Reserve Banks	163.2	11.6	8.9
Private investors:	994.2	71.0	73.3
Commercial banks	168.5	11.8	24.8
Insurance companies	47.5	3.3	5.4
Mutual savings banks	n.a.	n.a.	3.2
Other corporations	n.a.	n.a.	6.9
State and local governments	138.5	9.6	5.2
Individuals:	129.2	9.2	22.8
Savings bonds	70.5	5.1	17.9
Other securities	58.7	4.1	4.9
Foreign and international units	177.1	12.6	n.a.
Other miscellaneous investors	273.3	19.6	5.0
Total	1,400.9	100.0	100.0

n.a. = not available.
*Certificates of indebtedness, which had an original maturity of less than a year, are included in bills in 1954.
†May not add due to rounding and data discrepancies.
Source: *Federal Reserve Bulletin.*

every week, and nine-month and one-year bills are auctioned monthly. The submitted bid prices determine the discount yield earned. The Treasury does *not* set a price and adopt a take-it-or-leave-it approach. Since many feel uncertain about the price they should bid, the number of competitive bidders is small relative to the amount auctioned, about $12 billion weekly, composed almost equally of 91- and 182-day bills. The 30 or so government security dealers are the active bidders. Many middle-size banks and nonfinancial corporations prefer to buy from the dealers who are successful in the primary auction market. Most "little" people enter *noncompetitive* bids and pay that week's average bid price. In addition to the "regular" Treasury bills, the Treasury sporadically offers so-called tax anticipation bills (TABs). These are similar to Treasury bills except that they always mature one week after corporate income taxes are due.

Although TABs are discount securities and sell below par prior to maturity, the Treasury accepts them at full face value on the tax date.[1]

Even the huge amount outstanding, more than $340 billion, underestimates the importance of Treasury bills. These securities are the major money market trading instrument. The average *daily* value of Treasury bills bought and sold by *private nonbank* investors was over $11 billion in December 1983, or approximately the value of the weekly new issues.[2] Although T-bills are short term, they often are sold before maturity. To reduce the transaction and safekeeping costs of transferring beautifully engraved negotiable certificates, bills are sold in book-entry form on computer at the Treasury's Bureau of Public Debt or at Federal Reserve Banks. Purchasers receive nonnegotiable receipts, and ownership changes are recorded on the computer. The New York Stock Exchange has been pondering the adoption of such a system, but continues with its cumbersome system because the volume on the stock exchange does not begin to approach the volume of the government securities market.

Treasury Notes and Bonds

Treasury notes, the most common type of government debt, currently have initial maturities of between 1 and 10 years, and bonds mature beyond 10 years. Notes and bonds are virtually identical except for original maturity. The change in the relative importance of notes and bonds between 1954 and 1983, as shown in Table 8–1, is in part illusory. The Treasury has been raising the arbitrary maturity demarcation line between notes and bonds. In 1954 the maximum maturity of a note was five years. It subsequently was raised to seven years and now is 10 years. Although these securities are default free and quite marketable, they differ in many respects from T-bills. For example, notes and bonds are coupon instruments, the denominations of which are in multiples of $1,000. Notes and bonds are issued less frequently and regularly than the weekly T-bills. Two-year notes are issued monthly, for example. The ratio of transactions to value outstanding is much smaller for these instruments than for T-bills. The value of notes and bonds outstanding is about twice T-bills outstanding, but average daily transactions are only about one half.

Years ago the Treasury almost exclusively offered bonds on a fixed price, take-it-or-leave-it basis. Sometimes the price was set too high given

---

[1]This special feature of TABs is not altogether without precedent. The Treasury accepts in payment of estate taxes a limited number of long-term bonds at full face even though they are selling below face. These are called flower bonds: the taxes saved can be spent on nicer flowers at the funeral.

[2]Most new issues are refinancing or "rolling over" maturing issues instead of raising new money. The trading value was estimated from the *Federal Reserve Bulletin* by eliminating dealer and bank transactions, which amount to approximately $12 billion.

the coupon, and the yield to maturity was too low. In this case the Treasury issue "failed," that is, only a small proportion of the issue was sold. Because new issues are marketed just a few days before the Treasury needs the funds, a market failure is a great embarrassment and inconvenience as the Treasury must scurry for other sources of funds. As a result, the price often was set sufficiently low to minimize failures. Once in the early 1970s the Treasury mistakenly set a truly bargain basement price, and it was flooded with buy orders. Hundreds of thousands of people with small orders inundated a market normally patronized by a few hundred people ordering bonds worth millions. The Treasury offered for sale $3 billion and received buy orders for $29 billion! The excess demand was met by limiting each buyer to $200,000. Those who did notice the Treasury's mistake were handsomely rewarded. Within a day after issue the price of the bonds rose 1.5 percent. If one could find such bonds every day, the annual return would be over 500 percent! Since that fiasco, Treasury bond offerings generally are made at auction, which guarantees the issue will not fail without the Treasury having to estimate the market clearing price.[3]

The secondary market for Treasury securities is so broad that *The Wall Street Journal* and leading nonfinancial newspapers such as the *Washington Post* publish daily quotations for all Treasury issues. Table 8–2 is a

TABLE 8–2
Treasury Issues: Bonds, Notes, and Bills

Rate	*Mat.*	*Date*	*Bid*	*Asked*	*Bid Chg.*	*Yield*
9⅞s	1984	Nov. n.	99.25	99.29		10.01
9¼s	1985	Jan. n	99.5	99.9	−.1	10.09
8s	1985	Feb. n	98.8	98.16		9.67
9⅝s	1985	Mar.	99.8	99.16	−.1	10.12
10s	1986	Dec. n	97.8	97.12	−.3	11.10
3½s	1990	Feb.	91	91.16	+.8	5.18
11½s	1995	Nov.	96.18	96.26	−.13	12.01

Mat.	*Discount Bid*	*Discount Asked*	*Yield*	*Mat.*	*Discount Bid*	*Discount Asked*	*Yield*
1984:				1984:			
3– 1	8.69	8.61	9.00	6–28	9.21	9.15	9.57
3– 8	8.74	8.66	8.80	7– 5	9.28	9.24	9.68
3–15	8.67	8.57	8.72	7–12	9.30	9.26	9.72
3–22	8.86	8.67	8.83	7–19	9.32	9.28	9.76
3–29	8.71	8.65	8.83	7–26	9.33	9.29	9.79

Source: *The Wall Street Journal*, February 29, 1984.

[3]Although bills had been sold at auction for many years, the Treasury resisted the auction approach for longer-term issues because it feared auctions discourage small participants, who purchase most other goods on a fixed-price basis. The Treasury wants a broad market where bonds are widely held.

sample of quotations from the February 29, 1984 copy of *The Wall Street Journal*. For bonds and notes, the rate column shows the issue's coupon or nominal yield. The next two columns are the maturity year and month. The letter *n* following the month designates a note; otherwise the issue is a bond. The fourth and fifth columns give the dealers' bid and asked price expressed in that quaint financial unit, the 32d. The figures to the right of the decimal point are in 32ds instead of 100ths. Thus the 99.29 asked price in the first row indicates that dealers are selling the note at \$99.91 or \$99 29/32 per \$100 par value.[4] The asked or selling price is always greater than the bid or buying price, the difference between the two being the dealers' profit. The next-to-last column shows how bid prices changed from the previous day. The final column is the interest rate or yield to maturity based on the asked price. For Treasury bills, rates alone are quoted explicitly, and the prices are implicit. Following the maturity date is the bid and asked *discount yield* as defined in Chapter 6. Since the bid price always is less than the asked price, the bid yield is greater than the asked yield. The last column shows the effective, coupon equivalent yield to maturity based on the asked price. Note that the asked discount yield is always less than the effective yield to maturity. (Recall that the discount asked yield computes the return on the par value while the effective yield computes the return on the current asking price.)

Nonmarketable Debt

About 25 percent of the current federal debt is nonmarketable according to the traditional classification scheme whereby marketability depends on the existence of a broad secondary market. This way of measuring marketability can be misleading, however. *U.S. savings bonds* are the best known "nonmarketable" debt. While these cannot be traded to others in a financial market, they are extremely marketable and liquid because the Treasury redeems them prior to maturity at stipulated prices through commercial banks and other financial institutions. There are two types of savings bonds, Series EE and HH, which were introduced in the days of double-digit inflation (January 1980) to replace the single-letter series. The EE bonds are purchased at a discount like Treasury bills and upon maturity pay face value, which may be a small sum. These are favorite wedding and graduation gifts, perhaps because they prominently display the face value instead of the lower purchase price. The HH bonds are now issued only in exchange for E or EE bonds. They are bought at face value, pay interest semiannually, and typically are a larger denomination than EE bonds.

---

[4] 1/32d equals 3.125 basis points, another quaint financial measurement unit. 1 percent equals 100 basis points, or 1 basis point equals 0.01 percent.

In general, savings bonds have proven to be quite popular. The value of savings bonds outstanding jumped from $6.1 billion in December 1941 to $48.2 billion in December 1945 as the flag was wrapped around them during World War II. While their patriotic appeal has diminished, they continue to be popular with small savers. Nearly $70 billion worth of savings bonds are currently outstanding. Provided one had the ability to save money one received and did not need payroll deductions, savings bonds were not particularly attractive investments for many years. The administratively-determined interest rates often were far below market-determined interest rates. Many claimed the Treasury was "ripping off" the small saver, particularly when inflation hit double digits. The relative importance of savings bonds dropped sharply between 1954 and 1983, as Table 8–1 shows. Congress realized that there was some validity to the criticism and tried to stem the decline in the importance of savings bonds by giving the Treasury authority to pay higher interest rates. A complicated and variable formula currently is used to set the savings bond rate. Without going into the details, the rate earned increases the longer savings bonds are held and equals 85 percent of the average rate on five-year Treasury notes if held to maturity.

The government account series, the largest nonmarketable component of the federal debt, is held almost entirely by U.S. government agencies and trust funds such as the FDIC and the Federal Old Age and Survivors Insurance Trust Fund (Social Security). These trust funds are the captive pawns of the Treasury; they are legally required to hold only U.S. government securities. In some respects the very issuance of the series and interest payments are a purely internal, bookkeeping matter of robbing Peter to pay Paul. Nevertheless, the Treasury plays the game honestly, paying interest at a rate equivalent to the rate on marketable securities.

Ownership of Treasury Securities

The *gross* debt in December 1983 was approximately $1,401 billion. The *net* debt held by the public was "only" about $1,000 billion because the Federal Reserve Banks and U.S. government agencies and trust funds held $408 billion, or 29 percent of the debt. The increased share of the Fed reflects the excessive money supply created through open-market purchases, which consequently generated inflation. Private ownership of U.S. Treasury securities declined but remains widespread. Let us abstract from the hodgepodge which makes up the "other miscellaneous investor" class. *Foreign and international organizations are the most important private holders of marketable Treasury securities*. Although U.S. citizens' holdings of Treasury securities are not far behind those of foreigners, the majority of individuals own nonmarketable savings bonds. Matters were quite different in 1954. Foreign holdings were so small that the Fed did not list them separately. Foreigners' share has been increasing steadily for the last 30 years as a result of the persistent U.S. balance of payments deficit. The turmoil in the international monetary system and the quadrupling of OPEC prices in 1973–74 accelerated the upward trend.

Commercial banks are the next most important private holders of Treasury securities. A comparison of the second and third columns of Table 8–1 indicates, however, that their importance is declining. During World War II the private loan market was at a virtual standstill as the war effort totally dominated the economy. Without a demand for private loans and severely limited in their choice of earning assets, commercial banks, insurance companies, and mutual savings banks turned to Treasury securities. The war's end saw the banking system and other financial institutions swollen with Treasury securities. As the private sector expanded, commercial banks accommodated the private demand by dumping large quantities of Treasury securities or not subscribing to refunding issues. One still observes this pattern of holding long-term Treasury securities only when nothing better is available. The insurance companies' and mutual savings banks' downward pattern of Treasury security holdings has paralleled the commercial bank pattern, even if their absolute holdings have always been much smaller. Mutual savings banks have declined in importance so much that they no longer are listed separately.

State and local government units have been expanding their holdings of Treasury securities, holding approximately $139 billion in December 1983. Some portion of these holdings are long-term bonds held for retirement programs for local government employees. The remainder are temporary investments held between tax receipts and expenditures. For many years state and local governments were notoriously poor money managers. A combination of high interest rates and pressure from various organizations when state and local taxes fell behind expenditures led local officials to manage their funds more efficiently, switching from cash to U.S. Treasury bills and other short-term securities.

Money Market Instruments

Money market instruments are short-term (less than a year), *large denomination, readily marketable debt instruments.* The participants in the money market can be virtually any individual, firm, or government unit with temporarily excessive or deficient money balances.

Certificates of Deposit (CDs)

Ranked by the amount outstanding *and* trading volume, certificates of deposit (CDs) perhaps are the second most important money market instrument, following T-bills. *CDs are large*—the minimum denomination is at least $100,000 and generally $1 million—*negotiable time deposits issued mainly by banks*. They are evidenced by a certificate issued to the depositor, hence their name. The amount outstanding on December 31, 1983, at large (weekly reporting) commercial banks equaled approximately $90 billion, and other banks and nonbank depositories probably issued an additional $50 billion. These numbers are particularly impressive when one considers that CDs were developed only in 1961. Besides the CDs, there are more than $180 billion worth of time deposits over $100,000 that are nonnegotiable.

The negotiability factor explains the development of CDs. In 1961 banks lacked an instrument to compete effectively for the temporarily excess money balances of large companies. Interest was not paid on demand deposits, and corporations were reluctant to hold nonnegotiable time deposits, which would tie up their funds unconditionally until maturity or be subject to a significant penalty if withdrawn. Ever sharp bankers developed a secondary market for CDs, which enables investors to sell their CDs and acquire cash from someone other than bankers.

The growth path of CDs has been strongly upward but quite variable because Regulation Q ceilings fixed maximum interest rates banks could pay. When the rate of interest on similar negotiable instruments rose above the Reg Q ceiling rate, banks were unable to roll over their maturing CDs, which shrank precipitously. Between 1970 and 1973 the Fed phased out the rate restrictions on CDs, and their growth path has become much more stable.

Nearly all CDs are coupon instruments and trade on a 360-day basis. The minimum initial maturity is 30 days. Because the denomination of most CDs exceeds the FDIC insurance maximum, the financial condition and reputation of the issuing bank influence the rate of interest. CDs of larger, prime quality banks generally carry a lower interest rate than those of smaller, regional banks.

Table 8–3 shows the dollar amounts of the main money market instruments at the beginning of the 1970s and mid-1980s and the percentage change during the interim.

TABLE 8–3

Money Market Instruments, January 1970 and December 1983 ($ billions)

	January 1970	*December 1983*	*Percent Change*
Treasury bills	80.6	343.8	326
Certificates of deposit*	10.9	91.9	743
Commercial paper	32.6	180.2	453
Bankers acceptances	5.5	72.9	1,225
Eurodollars†	24.7	369.9	1,397

*At large (weekly reporting) banks only.
†At foreign branches of U.S. banks only.
Source: Federal Reserve *Bulletin* and *Flow of Funds Accounts: Assets and Liabilities Outstanding, 1959–82.*

Commercial Paper

Commercial paper is the unsecured promissory note of a nationally known, prime quality corporation with an initial maturity of less than 270 days, generally between one and two months.[5] Minimum denominations are $100,000. Commercial paper is a substitute for short-term bank loans. It is an old money market instrument in England and on the Continent that has staged a strong resurgence in the United States since the 1960s. Firms had to find new sources of funds as banks abandoned the tradition of concentrating on short-term business loans and entered the consumer loan and mortgage markets. Similar to their long-term cousin the corporate bond, large issues of commercial paper are evaluated by credit rating firms.

The name *commercial paper* stems from the fact that the original issuers of this instrument were predominantly commercial firms financing inventories or accounts receivable from customers. The paper or IOUs might more correctly be called finance paper today. Approximately 75 percent of commercial paper is issued by financial companies, for example, finance companies, mortgage bankers, and commercial bank holding companies. Sales finance companies, which extend credit for the installment purchase of such major consumer items as cars and which may be a subsidiary of a manufacturing corporation, are the largest issuers of commercial paper. General Motors Acceptance Corporation (GMAC) is such a company. The method of primary sale largely depends on the degree of the issuer's activity in the market. By participating in the market on a virtually continuous basis, sales finance companies know the large, ready buyers of commercial paper and place their issues directly. The occasional issuer places its commercial paper with one of six regular commercial paper dealers, who sells it to others.

Commercial paper is a substitute for bank loans from the viewpoint of the issuer and, perhaps surprisingly, from the viewpoint of banks. That is, banks were the major purchasers of commercial paper until the 1950s and still continue to purchase significant amounts. The market has broadened considerably, however. Nonfinancial firms now are the major purchasers of commercial paper, but many other types of institutions participate in the commercial paper market.

Bankers Acceptances

Bankers acceptances are short-term time drafts on a bank issued by less well-known corporations and guaranteed by the bank. The guarantee of the bank raises the credit quality of the draft and makes it negotiable.

---

[5]The term to maturity is less than 270 days in order to avoid the expense and delay of registering the issue with the Securities and Exchange Commission.

Let us look at the function of these instruments and the mechanics of their creation. Assume a relatively small American firm cannot pay cash and needs credit in order to import goods. To sell its wares, the foreign producer generally is willing to extend credit but is reluctant in this case due to its inability to assess the credit worthiness of the importer. If the importer can guarantee repayment, the foreign producer would extend credit for, say, 90 days. The importer gets such a guarantee from its banker. It issues a draft on the bank ordering it to pay the foreign producer the amount due in 90 days. At this point the draft is simply a postdated check; on the future date the bank will not honor it unless the importer has the funds on deposit. However, the importer then takes the draft to its bank, which stamps "accepted" across its face. By accepting the note, the bank has obligated itself to pay the draft when it comes due, whether or not the importer has sufficient funds on deposit. The bank charges the importer for guaranteeing payment. Moreover, the bank may require collateral. Acceptance by the bank has made the draft a negotiable, marketable instrument. The foreign producer may hold the acceptance until the due date or sell it at a discount. On the due date, whoever is holding the acceptance presents it for payment. If all went well, the importer deposited funds by the due date, and the bank simply transfers the funds from the account of the importer to the holder of the acceptance.

For many years bankers acceptances were primarily associated with foreign trade (hence our example of the importer) because information and contract enforcement costs are high when firms are located in different countries. In recent days, however, less than half of the bankers acceptances arise from foreign trade. Domestic firms in growing numbers are unwilling to rely on another firm's word and require banker acceptances. The acceptance market is small—about 40 percent—compared to the commercial paper market, but both are growing rapidly.

Federal Funds

Federal funds, or fed funds for short, *are commercial bank deposits at the Federal Reserve system.* As mentioned in Chapters 3 and 4, cash and these deposits (fed funds) are the bank reserves which the Fed requires. Fed funds are a means of adjusting reserves to satisfy the Fed requirement. Banks which would have failed to meet the reserve requirement borrow or, as the participants prefer to say, "purchase" fed funds from banks which would have had excess reserves. For example, Main Street Bank may agree to lend or "sell" Morgan Guaranty $1 million in fed funds for a day at a 10 percent annual rate. Since the two banks typically are aware that each is in excellent financial condition, the loan (sale) usually is unsecured. There are degrees of excellence, however. The fed funds rate at any moment depends somewhat on the reputation of the purchaser, with prime quality banks such as Morgan Guaranty paying slightly lower rates. After reaching agreement, Main Street simply instructs the Fed by telephone to transfer $1 million from its reserve balances to Morgan. The Fed does so immediately through its electronic transfer system. The next day Morgan repays Main Street the $1 million plus interest. Yes, $1 million is the typical minimum denomination in the fed funds market, and one day is the typical maturity of the loans (sales), though the loan may be extended from day to day if the seller and buyer agree.[6]

Although an incipient fed funds market existed in the 1920s, it became significant only in the 1950s as the excess reserves of the banking system were reduced. In the 1950s fed funds were used most exclusively by the largest banks as a means of adjusting reserves to satisfy Fed requirements. While the fed funds market still serves this function, it now is also a permanent source of funds for the largest banks, and small banks participate indirectly. That is, the largest banks are net purchasers of Fed funds almost continuously. Demand deposit fluctuations and consequent reserves fluctuations determine the extent to which the largest banks are net purchasers. By increasing the liability "fed funds purchased," the largest banks can make even more loans or acquire other assets. While the size of the minimum denomination precludes smaller banks from participating directly in the market, the large banks readily buy outside the organized fed funds market any amount, however small, from their respondents, that is, small banks which maintain deposits at large banks as a means of implicit payment for check collection and other services. The largest banks retain what they need for their own purposes and sell the remainder, if any, to each other.

[6]A careful reading of footnotes is becoming more important in understanding the fed funds account on banks' balance sheets as published in various Federal Reserve tables. Often the fed funds account will include the type of transaction described in the text as well as repurchase agreements to nonbank bond dealers and banks. For example, suppose a nonbank dealer has excess deposits for a few days which it would rather *not* use at the moment to increase its bond inventory. A search for short-term investments begins. The dealer approaches its banker, who is mindful that the dealer has excess deposits which will be withdrawn if the dealer is not accommodated. The dealer and banker come to a repurchase agreement. That is, the dealer relinquishes the excess demand deposits to purchase some of the bank's government securities, which the bank guarantees to repurchase at a higher price on some specified date. The transaction *should* be recorded by decreasing demand deposits and increasing the liability "securities sold under repurchase agreements." However, in many Federal Reserve tables this transaction would reduce demand deposits and increase "fed funds purchased," which footnotes state also include securities sold under repurchase agreement. Fed funds are not shown in Table 8–3 precisely because the data are unreliable.

Strictly speaking, fed funds are not money market instruments because they are not negotiable. However, their maturity is so short, typically one day, that they are always classified as money market instruments.

Eurodollars

The Eurodollar market is the largest international money market. *Eurodollars are dollar-denominated deposits of banks outside the United States, including foreign branches of U.S. banks*. The deposits sometimes are demand deposits but usually are time deposits, with maturities from 7 to 90 days being most common. Most foreign countries do not prohibit interest payments on demand deposits, and both Eurodollar demand and time deposits earn interest. As stated in Chapter 2, Eurodollars are somewhat of a misnomer. European banks, particularly London banks, were the first to offer dollar-denominated accounts, hence Eurodollars. Banks in the Caribbean, Hong Kong, Singapore, Tokyo, and Canada now offer dollar-denominated accounts, which are also considered Eurodollars. This market is strictly for big spenders. The minimum denomination is at least $1 million and sometimes $10 million. (U.S.-based banks do not offer mark or pound-denominated accounts. Thus, there are no Americomarks or Americopounds. The U.S. has only Americodollars.)

Statistics about the size of worldwide Eurodollar market are relatively unreliable, but it probably equaled about $550 billion in 1983. Table 8–3 shows that the Eurodollar deposits of foreign branches of U.S. banks were $370 billion. Approximately 70 percent of this amount, however, was owed to banks, including the parent bank and sister branches. Private firms and citizens of every country do participate actively in this market, but less so than in the Treasury bills market.

The Russians initiated the Eurodollar market in the early 1950s. They needed dollar accounts since the dollar was the universally accepted currency in international trade and finance. However, they feared at the height of the cold war that their bank deposits in the United States might be expropriated. The fear was not entirely irrational; German assets had been expropriated just a decade earlier. The Russians convinced London banks to accept dollar-denominated deposits and transferred their deposits from New York to London. The London banks now owned the deposits of the Russians in New York. The fear by Russians and others that their deposits will be expropriated by the United States continues to play a minor role in explaining the existence of Eurodollars. The Ayatollah undoubtedly was sorry that Iran had any U.S. deposits, which were blocked though not expropriated.

There currently are three major reasons why firms and individuals who want dollar accounts prefer Eurodollars to Americodollars. (1) Interest rates are unregulated and typically higher on Eurodollars than U.S. based money market instruments; (2) Eurodollars are more convenient than Americodollars for anyone located abroad; and (3) Eurodollars offer tax and legal advantages compared to Americodollars. The small Russian-created Eurodollar market received a big boost until 1973 from United States Reg Q interest rate ceilings on CDs, which are comparable to

Eurodollars in terms of denomination and maturity. When the interest rate ceiling became particularly binding and banks suffered severe runoffs in their CDs, large New York banks encouraged their depositors to acquire Eurodollars in their branches abroad instead of commercial paper or some other money-market instrument.

Figure 8–1 shows the balance sheet effects of maturing CDs and the creation of Eurodollars. Line 1 records the *initial* effect of a maturing CD which is not renewed. Assuming Mammoth Bank was at equilibrium and reserves equaled the desired value, the bank subsequently would have to sell earning assets. To prevent this, Mammoth Bank induces firm XYZ, a depositor, to transfer its maturing CD to its foreign branch, as recorded in lines 2 and 3. The parent and subsidiary are supposed to be operated as independent, profit-maximizing firms. A noncaptive foreign bank would not pay interest on its Eurodollar while simultaneously holding an *equal* amount of sterile demand deposits in the United States. The branch may want to retain a small amount of U.S. deposits as (unrequired) reserves, just as a U.S. bank not subject to any reserve requirement would hold some cash. Ignoring any demand for reserves, the branch can lend the $100 to anyone—U.S. or foreign consumers, firms, or banks. Suppose the subsidiary lends the funds to its parent, as recorded on line 4. Everyone benefits, as they must in any arms length transaction. Firm XYZ accepts Eurodollars because the return on Eurodollars, including an allowance for risk, convenience, and other loan terms, is greater than the return on alternative money market instruments. Consolidating the bank and its foreign branch, interest is paid to firm XYZ, but presumably the

FIGURE 8–1

(1) Maturing CDs which are not renewed, (2) and (3) maturing CDs are used to acquire Eurodollars, (4) branch makes loan to its parent.

Mammoth Bank

(1) Reserves	−100	CDs	−100
(2)		CDs	−100
		Demand deposits, firm XYZ	+100
(3)		Demand deposits, firm XYZ	−100
		Demand deposits, foreign branch	+100
(4)		Demand deposits, foreign branch	−100
		Eurodollar borrowing	+100

Mammoth Bank, Foreign Branch

(1)			
(2)			
(3) Dollar deposits, home office	+100	Dollar deposits, firm XYZ	+100
(4) Dollar deposits, home office	−100		
Loans to home office	+100		

interest paid is less than the interest earned on the bank's assets.[7] While the transaction illustrated in Figure 8–1 is not unusual, note well that most Eurodollars are borrowed by someone other than the parent of a foreign branch.

Although the dollar depreciated considerably in the 1970s, it remains the currency of international trade. Because of this, a foreign exporter who receives dollars and expects to need dollars in the near future may prefer to hold dollars in the interim rather than convert the dollars to local currency and then reverse the process when dollars are needed. Foreign exporters and especially foreign subsidiaries of U.S. multinational companies find Eurodollars extremely convenient. A firm based in Brussels, for example, prefers having its dollar account in a Brussels bank where the firm does all its other business. You and I find nearby banks more convenient, *ceteris paribus,* and foreign companies feel likewise. *While an interest rate differential in favor of Eurodollars may have been necessary at first, the mundane convenience factor is perhaps the most important explanation of its continued growth in an era when Eurodollar interest rates have occasionally fallen below U.S. money market rates.*

The complicated accounting and legal system is another important explanation for the Eurodollar market, particularly in "offshore" or "shell" branches located on some remote island. As was mentioned in Chapter 2, billion-dollar post office box branches cannot be explained by local economic needs.

Capital Markets

Capital markets are the markets for long-term, relatively marketable financial instruments. Bonds are one type of capital instrument. Bonds have many different characteristics or attributes, as discussed in Chapter 6, and are issued by many groups, mainly commercial firms, the Treasury, federal agencies, and state and local governments. Nevertheless, to paraphrase the inimitable Gertrude Stein, "A bond is a bond is a bond." *All bonds are long-term marketable debt instruments issued by economic units other than households.* The paraphrase of Gertrude Stein suggests that we can be brief at this point, in view of our earlier discussion on bond attributes, the direct finance market, and government securities. The suggestion indeed is correct. We should mention, however, that the type of bond underwriter and secondary market varies by issuer.

Treasury and federal agency new issues nearly always are sold directly, with the Fed accepting bids for auction sales. The new issues of com-

---

[7]Another advantage of these transactions in the early 1970s was the reduction in required reserves because Eurodollar borrowings were not subject to ordinary reserve requirements. The MCA of 1980 set the same reserve ratio on Eurodollar borrowings and nonpersonal time deposits so that the transactions in Figure 8–1 do not reduce required reserves today.

mercial firms and *some* state and local governments are marketed by investment bankers. Commercial banks are prohibited from underwriting private bonds, but they are the main underwriters of general obligation state and local government bonds. General obligation bonds, also called full faith and credit bonds, technically have up to a 100 percent tax lien on all property within the issuer's jurisdiction. The term also means that the issuer will exert every effort to collect taxes in order to repay the debt. Commercial banks routinely underwrote all types of new issues until the 1930s, when the restrictions were set in order to reduce abuses to be discussed later. The prohibition on investment banking activities by commercial banks was not complete because municipal bonds were not that prevalent in the 1930s—state and local governments still believed in a balanced budget—and because many local issuers were believed to require special aid. While virtually every locality has a bank, most do not have investment bankers/dealers. The commercial bank is considered to perform a public service when it underwrites issues for small local government units, which borrow infrequently and are unfamiliar with the intricacies of investment banking.

Banks have agitated in recent years for the restoration of full investment banking powers. They claim it is only just since investment bankers have invaded their turf by sponsoring money market funds. We examine this complex issue in a subsequent chapter.

The secondary market for private bonds is quite thin. Many private bonds are held to maturity, so the ratio of sales of bonds outstanding to new bond issues is quite low. A small fraction of private bonds outstanding is listed on the New York Exchange. However, the secondary market for even listed private bonds typically is the communications network among dealers called the over-the-counter (OTC) market. All nonlisted and most listed private bonds, as well as all federal, state, and local government bonds, are sold in the OTC market. *The Wall Street Journal* publishes transaction data daily for Treasury securities, federal agency securities, and bonds listed on the exchanges. Price and other information about other bonds is not readily available to small investors.

The Mortgage Market and Housing Agencies

Mortgages are long-term, somewhat marketable debt instruments issued to purchase real estate, which serves as collateral for the loan. Mortgages are the least marketable capital market instrument but the largest in terms of the value outstanding. Financial intermediaries, particularly savings and loans, are the main holders of mortgages. Nearly everyone issues a mortgage in order to buy a home; few have that much cash. The term to maturity of mortgages is between 15 and 40 years, usually 30 years, but the average life of a mortgage is substantially less, about 10 years. Average life is less than maturity because most mortgagors may prepay with little or no penalty, and mortgagees may require full payment when a house is sold and not allow the new homeowner to assume the mortgage.

Residential mortgages, more than mortgages for apartment buildings and other large structures, were quite illiquid, at least until the 1970s. Lack of knowledge of the credit worthiness of the typical household greatly reduces the marketability of individual outstanding mortgages. Moreover, mortgages do not have standard denominations, which help develop a broad market. The relative illiquidity of mortgages also stems from their substantial servicing requirement, which many lenders are incapable or unwilling to perform. For example, the higher delinquency rates on mortgages may require the wise counsel of the legal firm of Dewey, Cheatem, and Howe and the collection services of Badger and Browbeat. More accountants are needed to record the more frequent payments, maintain escrow accounts for property tax payments, and so on.

As part of the package to encourage home ownership after World War II, the Veterans Administration (VA) and Federal Housing Administration (FHA) guaranteed mortgage payments, the former at no fee for qualified veterans and the latter for a premium. With the guarantee, mortgagees lent to potential homeowners who otherwise would not qualify for a mortgage. While the programs were designed to increase the origination of mortgages, they had the side benefit of making outstanding mortgages more marketable. A California mortgage banker could more easily sell a VA or FHA insured mortgage to, say, a Chicago insurance company because the guarantee reduced the insurance company's uneasiness about its inability to appraise the credit worthiness of the California mortgage.[8] Most mortgages, however, continued to be "conventional" or uninsured mortgages that never became readily marketable nationwide.

In the face of several housing crunches in the late 1960s and 1970s and large losses by savings and loans during the early 1980s, the "old-line" Federal National Mortgage Associate (FNMA or Fannie Mae) greatly expanded its scope of operations, and several new housing agencies were formed. We postpone discussion of these developments until Chapter 11, where recent innovations to aid savings and loans are analyzed.

Summary/Questions

At any moment the overwhelming majority of economic units are simultaneously debtors and creditors, often with the same economic unit. For example, most homeowners have issued a mortgage (debt) and own de-

[8]Since payments from an insurer inevitably must be delayed, any lender prefers timely payments from the borrower.

mand and time deposits (credit to commercial banks), and often the bank holds the mortgage. The simultaneous debtor-creditor relationship occurs because within broad limits economic units can tailor debt to their needs. The tailoring of debt to particular needs has accelerated, thereby widening the menu of assets available to economic units in their role as creditors. For example, prior to World War II banks passively waited for demand and time deposits to come their way. When the demand for bank loans increased following the war and demand and time deposits failed to keep pace, banks introduced CDs. This increased the availability of money market instruments. Money and capital market instruments often offer the consumer a higher return than time and savings deposits but are dismissed as too complicated. That simply is not the case. We hope this chapter will aid the reader in the very practical quest for the best asset.

1. What are the main differences between Treasury bills, notes, and bonds? Do *not* limit your answer to their term to maturity.
2. Are U.S. savings bonds marketable? What are the main differences between Series EE and HH savings bonds?
3. State the major trends in the relative importance of different classes of holders of U.S. Treasury securities.
4. Compare the main money market instruments. In particular, state how they differ from each other by (1) issuer, (2) minimum denomination, and (3) overall market size.
5. What explains the birth of Eurodollars? What factors explain their continued growth?
6. How are the various types of bonds marketed, and what organizations market them?
7. State the impact of VA and FHA guarantees on the marketability of mortgages.
8. What money or capital market instrument is most closely associated with; (*a*) short-term debt of prime quality corporations, (*b*) long-term corporate debt, (*c*) debt of medium-size firms guaranteed by banks, (*d*) interbank loans, (*e*) accounts at foreign subsidiaries of U.S. banks, and (*f*) long-term debt secured by real estate.

Banks and other financial intermediaries

9

Necessity is the mother of invention.

Financial intermediaries are firms with mainly financial assets—for example, stocks, bonds, and mortgages. Intermediaries stand between surplus units (lenders) and deficit units (borrowers). They purchase primary securities issued by deficit units (borrowers) with funds acquired from surplus units (lenders), who prefer the claims issued by intermediaries to primary securities. This chapter describes the factors which led to the creation of various intermediaries and their primary characteristics and functions.

We begin with commercial banks, the largest intermediary. This being a descriptive chapter, we simply present in graphical form past and current balance sheets and income statements for the banking system in order to learn what banks *actually* do. The next chapter on bank management analyzes various problems banks face and states what banks *should* do. We then examine nonbank depositories such as savings and loans and, finally, nondepositories such as finance companies. Compared to commercial banks, the other intermediaries are specialized institutions. We emphasize their main differences and the void in the financial system which they were designed to fill.

The Banking System's Balance Sheet and Income Statement

Commercial banks are the oldest form of depository. The first bank in this country of a modern type was the Bank of North America, which was established in 1781 in Philadelphia. Perhaps because they had a head start on other intermediaries, banks are by far the largest intermediary. This section reviews in graphic form some important features of banks' balance sheets and income statements. Look at the asset side first. The left-hand panel of Figure 9–1 shows the dramatic *decrease in the relative importance of cash and securities and the increase in total loans during the postwar period.* Using 1950 as a starting point can be misleading since it followed a most abnormal period, World War II. Shifting the starting point to the late 1950s, by which time the effects of World War II and the less important Korean War should have vanished, the trend in the total loans and securities ratios is still visible. However, the later starting point eliminates most of the upward trend in the commercial and industrial loan ratio. *Relatively speaking, over the past 25 years banks have been substituting other loans for securities while keeping commercial loans ap-*

FIGURE 9–1

Commercial Banks' Balance Sheet Ratios

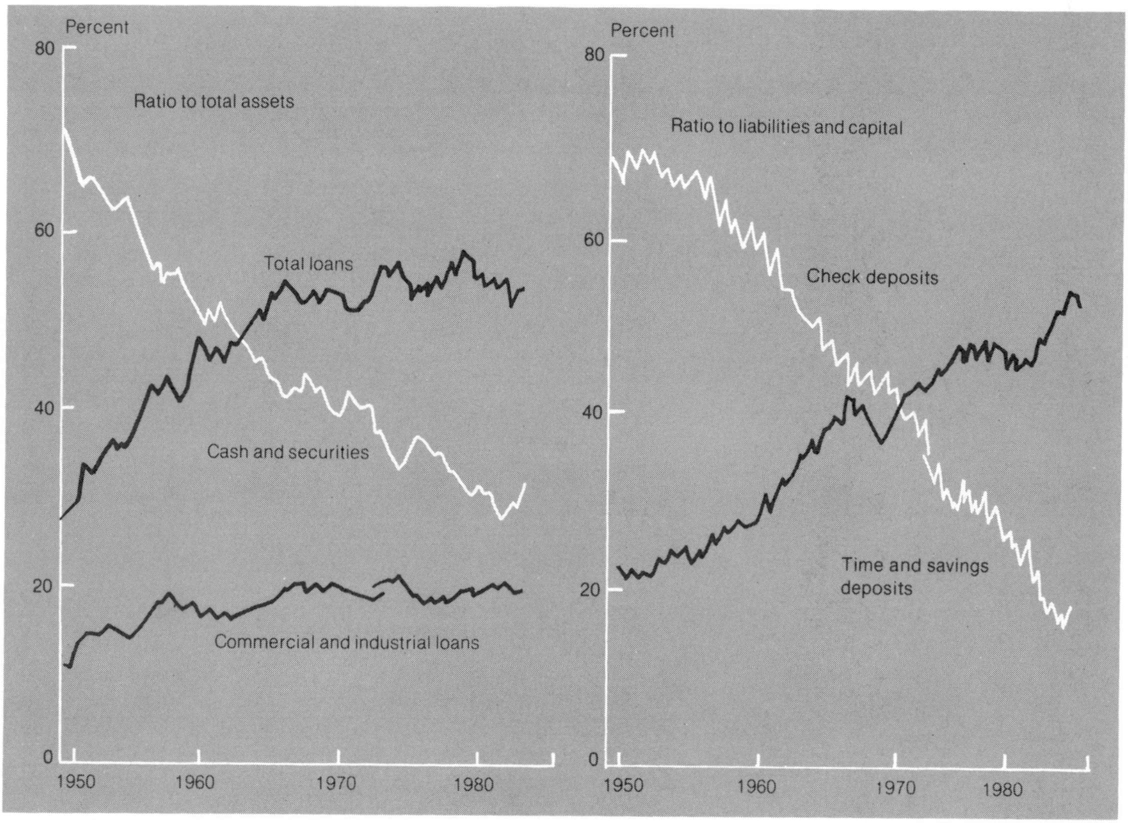

Source: Federal Reserve, *Historical Chart Book, 1984,* p. 83.

proximately constant. Consequently, the ratio of commercial to total loans has fallen.

Figure 9–2 shows the principal classes of loans and securities. *Banks are department stores of finance; their asset portfolio is well diversified.* The vertical axis in Figure 9–2 is a logarithmic scale, so the slopes of the lines measure growth rates. Real estate and other loans to individuals have been growing faster than commercial and industrial loans, causing the just mentioned decline in the ratio of commercial to total loans. The annual growth rates of loans to nonbank financial institutions and for real estate have been the most variable and stable, respectively. The latter

FIGURE 9–2

Principal Classes of Commercial Bank Loans and Securities

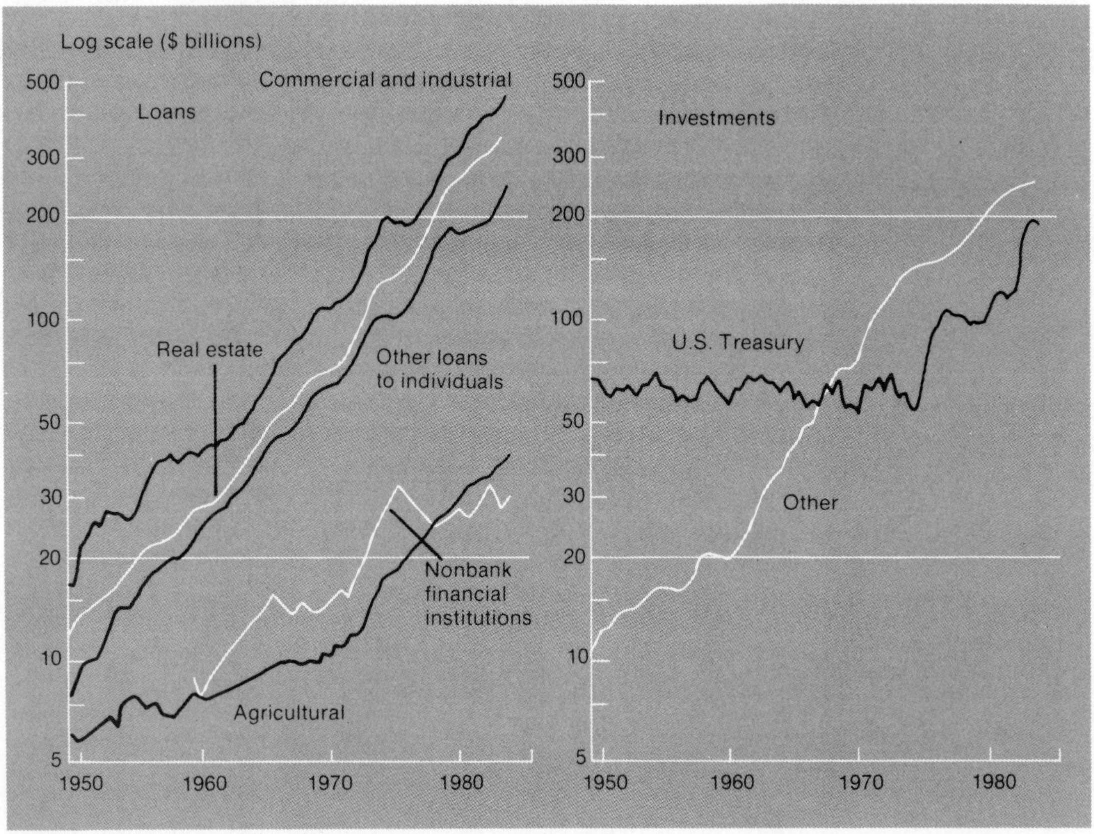

Source: Federal Reserve, *Historical Chart Book, 1984*, pp. 80–81.

fact may be surprising, in view of the well-publicized sensitivity of the real estate industry to monetary policy. *The instability in the supply of real estate loans is due mainly to nonbanks, particularly savings and loans, while banks are a reliable source of real estate loans,* at least relative to other loan classes. The decline in the total securities ratio hides significant differences among principal security classes. Up to the mid-1970s the ratio fell because the amount of U.S. Treasury securities remained relatively constant while total assets grew. Other securities, principally state and local government securities, grew almost as fast as loans until the mid-1970s, when the relative growth pattern of securities was reversed. From the mid-1970s, the growth of other securities has lagged, which explains the continued decline of the total securities ratio. Treasury securities, on the other hand, have kept pace with total assets. This may be due to the absolutely and proportionally larger federal deficits.

Turning to the sources side of the balance sheet, pronounced changes in the relative importance of check and time (and savings) deposits began in the late 1950s and have continued more or less unabated to the present. (See Figure 9–1.) The spectacular growth of consumer certificates, MMDAs, and CDs explains why *time deposits have surpassed check deposits*. NOW accounts have not been able to arrest the decline in the relative importance of check deposits.

The left-hand panel of Figure 9–3 shows that the capital/asset ratio was greater than 12 percent in the 1920s, fell sharply during the Great Depression, and continued to slide until the end of World War II, when it began to increase slightly. Around 1960 the trend in the capital ratio again turned downward, but this time quite gently. *The capital ratio currently is approximately 6 percent of total assets*. Other sources of funds such as RPs and discounts at the Fed explain why check deposits, time and savings deposits, and capital do not sum to 100 percent.

Banking is not a particularly profitable industry. Banks did earn nearly $200 billion in 1983, but expenses (mainly interest payments) ate up the overwhelming proportion of this sum. The right-hand panel of Figure 9–3 shows operating income (operating revenue less expenses) and net income (operating income minus taxes, loan losses, and charge-offs) expressed as a percent of capital. Operating income has been positive even during the Great Depression, when large loan losses did produce a negative net income. Between 1945 and 1965, net income as a percent of bank capital averaged about 9 percent, a rate of return exceeded by many other industries. *The (nominal) rate of return in banking, as in other industries, has risen in this inflationary age but is still less than 12 percent. Some market instruments yield a higher return.* Net income as a percent of total assets is much less, about 0.70 percent.[1]

---

[1]This can be deduced from the fact that the income/capital and capital/asset ratios are about 12 and 6 percent, respectively.

FIGURE 9–3
Banks' Capital/Asset and Income/Capital Ratios, 1920–1983

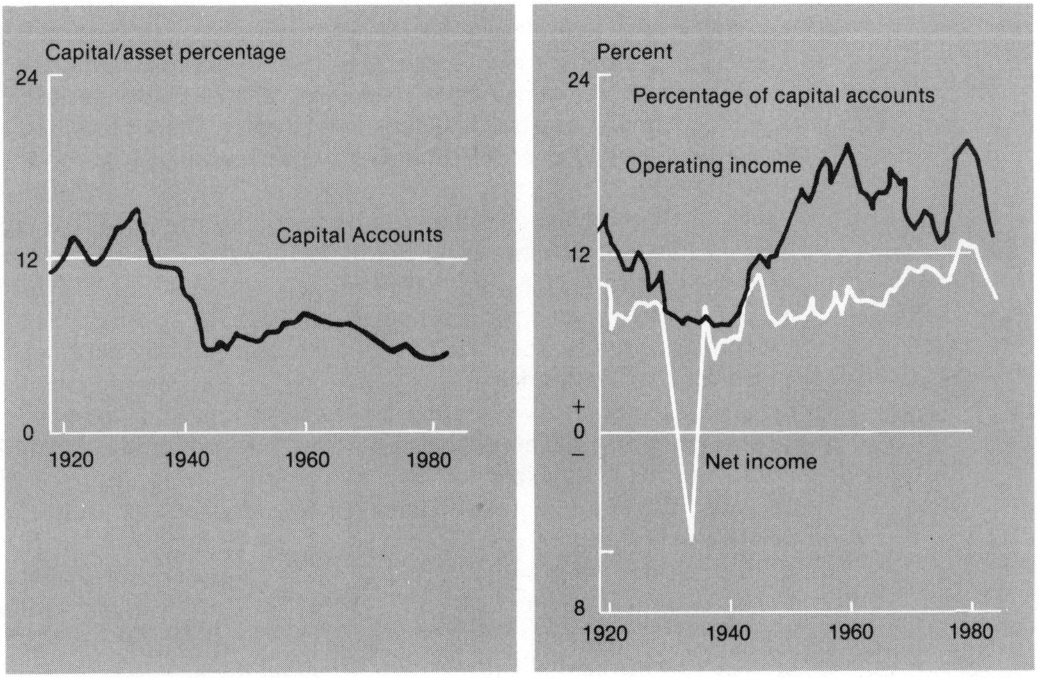

Source: Federal Reserve, *Historical Chart Book, 1984*, p. 85.

Depository Intermediaries

Table 9–1 shows the asset size and growth during the post-World War II period of the four depository intermediaries and summarizes their current balance sheet. Although banks continue to outrank other financial intermediaries by a wide margin, their postwar growth rate has lagged, particularly in comparison to savings and loans and credit unions. Consequently, *the share of commercial banks in the depository market has fallen significantly.* The proportion of bank assets to total depository assets was 86 percent in 1945 but only 68 percent in 1983. Banks' slide was particularly pronounced during the early postwar period but has been arrested. Their annualized growth rate rose from only 3.2 percent between 1945 and 1960 to 9.2 percent between 1960 and 1983. The different subperiod growth rates are largely explained by the introduction around 1960 of new types of time deposits and money market instruments, such as CDs and Eurodollars. The growth rate in the latter period would have

TABLE 9–1
Size, Growth, and Summary Balance Sheet of Depositories

Intermediary	*Total Assets, December 1945 ($ billions)*	*Total Assets, October 1983 ($ billions)*	*Percent Change*	*Average Size, 1983 ($ millions)*
Commercial banks	160.3	2,039	1,175	136
Savings and loans	8.7	755	8,578	212
Mutual savings banks	17.0	188	1,055	460
Credit unions	0.37	81	21,791	4

Commercial banks (percent of total)

Cash items	8.7	Check deposits	16.8
U.S. government securities	8.9	Small time and savings	36.5
Other securities	12.2	Large time and savings	18.3
Commercial loans	19.9	Funds purchase and other debt	14.2
Real estate loans	16.2	Other liabilities	6.9
Consumer loans	10.5	Net worth	7.3
Other assets	23.6		

Savings and loans (percent of total)

Mortgages	64.1	NOW	2.1
Cash and securities	13.3	Small time and savings	71.7
Other assets	22.6	Large time and savings	8.5
		FHLB advances and other borrowings	11.6
		Other liabilities	2.2
		Net worth	3.9

Mutual savings banks (percent of total)

Mortgages	54.0	NOW	2.8
Bonds	25.9	Small time and savings	83.6
Consumer and commercial loans	6.7	Large time and savings	3.7
Cash items	7.1	Other liabilities	3.3
Other assets	6.3	Reserves (net worth)	6.6

Credit unions (percent of total)

Consumer credit	54.5	Check deposits (CUSD)	5.5
Cash assets	16.6	Small time and savings	86.3
Other assets	28.9	Reserves (net worth)	7.8

Sources: U.S. League of Savings Associations, *Fact Book;* Credit Union National Association, *Yearbook;* FDIC, *Annual Report; Federal Reserve Bulletin* and *Flow of Funds,* various issues.

been even higher except the interest rate prohibition and other restrictions on demand deposits prevented banks from making them competitive in an era when market interest rates rose to historical heights. The ability of banks nationwide to offer NOW accounts beginning in January 1981 and MMDA in December 1982 increased their growth rate and market share during the early 1980s. In a brief three years, from 1980 to 1983, banks' share of total depository assets grew from 62 to 68 percent.

The second section of Table 9–1 shows that compared to banks other depositories are specialty boutiques. Commercial banks are department stores of finance. Banks long ago stopped emphasizing short-term business loans, although they still are the dominant force in this market. The percentages of total assets by major classes do correctly indicate the importance of the asset classes to an intermediary's operations, but the percentages are a misleading measure of the importance of an intermediary in the various asset markets unless one considers the intermediary's size. For example, consumer loans amounted to only 10.5 percent of bank assets in October 1983 but were 54.5 percent of credit union assets. However, because banks are much larger than credit unions, they made more than four times the consumer loans of credit unions. *Banks are the dominant force in the municipal bond market, holding approximately 45 percent of the outstanding issues.* Differences in the tax brackets of other depositories and banks explain why the former do not and the latter do purchase tax-exempt municipal securities. Most other depository intermediaries are mutuals or cooperatives that do not issue common stock. They can accumulate an equity cushion only by retaining earnings. Tax laws allow nonbank intermediaries to classify a larger proportion of their earnings as nontaxable "reserves for losses" so that they can accumulate an adequate equity cushion while paying competitive deposit rates. Banks, however, are stock companies subject to federal corporate income tax regulations.

Mutual Savings Banks

Mutual savings banks (MSBs) are the next oldest intermediary. In 1804 the Farmers Bank of Annapolis, Maryland, became the first commercial bank to pay interest on its deposits. The practice of paying interest on deposits, at least on small local deposits, did not become widespread immediately. *MSBs were organized by wealthy individuals or social groups in order to encourage saving among the poorer classes by providing convenient facilities and paying interest on their deposits.* The first MSB and currently the largest, Philadelphia Savings Fund Society, was established in 1816. The names of many MSBs still reflect their origin as depositories for small amounts by working classes. New York City still has the Emigrant, Bowery, Dime, and Dollar Savings Bank, and Boston has the Five Cent Savings. The Dollar is larger than the Five Cent but smaller than the Dime.

MSBs have not expanded much geographically. *They are concentrated in New England and the Middle Atlantic states,* with approximately 75 percent of the 409 MSBs in the three states of Massachusetts, New York, and Connecticut. Thirty-four states do not have a MSB. There are several reasons for their failure to expand geographically. First, until very recently all MSBs were state chartered, mutual or cooperative institutions with a semi-public-service outlook. Lacking stockholders and a strong profit motive, charters were denied MSBs but given to stock-issuing commercial banks, which had more to gain from a charter and could *offer* state officials more. In an example of Gresham's Law, MSBs also lost out to savings and loan associations, which were granted broader branching powers and had smaller net worth requirements.

Regulatory relief may change matters. In 1978 Congress granted MSBs the option of converting to federally chartered organizations, and the less restrictive federal regulations have encouraged some to do so. In the early 1980s, several states allowed MSBs to incorporate and issue stock. By 1984 nearly 150 savings and loans actually converted to MSBs.

A second reason MSBs lagged is because commercial banks did meet the competition. *Interest-bearing time and savings deposits at commercial banks became standard and eliminated the need for MSBs.* Even in those areas where MSBs became established, the industry shrank numerically. The average age of MSBs exceeds the average age of other intermediaries, including banks, as few new MSBs were founded. Less than 10 percent of MSBs were organized after 1900, not counting the recent savings and loan converts. For these reasons and because MSBs are located along the eastern seaboard, which has grown less rapidly than other areas in the postwar period, they have been eclipsed by their kissing kin, savings and loan associations. MSBs should not be dismissed lightly, however. Their geographic concentration and age make them much more important collectively and individually than the aggregates may suggest. In Boston, New York, and several other eastern metropolitan areas and states, the MSB industry in general and many individual MSBs are powerhouses. As is often the case, old firms are large firms. *The average size of MSBs is approximately $460 million, which is over three times the average size of commercial banks.*

Mortgages and government and corporate bonds comprise approximately 55 and 25 percent, respectively, of MSBs total assets. Thus, *compared to banks, the assets of MSBs are much longer lived.* The maturity structure of liabilities is also somewhat longer for MSBs than banks. Although Massachusetts MSBs have been offering NOW accounts for more than 10 years, these accounts equal only about 3 percent of total liabilities. Regular time and savings deposits equal about 87 percent of total liabilities and capital in 1983. The savings deposits of both intermediaries are effectively payable on demand, but MSBs have a larger proportion of time deposits, which are more stable due to the interest penalty on withdrawals prior to maturity. There still remains a substantial imbalance in the maturity structure of the long-term assets and relatively short-term liabilities.

The conservative, public service, little-person attitude of MSBs *compared to savings and loans* is clearly seen by the liability structure. *MSBs make much less use of large time and savings deposits and borrowings, and their net worth ratio is almost twice that of savings and loans.*

Savings and Loan Associations (S&Ls)

The first S&L, Oxford Provident Building Association, was organized—guess where?—in Philadelphia in 1831 to *finance residential housing,* something shunned by commercial banks at the time.[2] Mortgages were only incidental to MSBs, which had to own some earning asset in order to pay interest on their deposits, but mortgages were the *raison d'être* for S&Ls. The first S&Ls were mutuals patterned after British building societies. Each member of some affinity group contributed the same specified amount per period. When the savings pool reached a certain amount, it was lent to the member willing to pay the highest interest rate, with the proviso that it be used to finance a house. The first house financed by Oxford Provident still stands at 4276 Orchard Street, Philadelphia. This small—500 square feet—2½-story frame house was a steal at $375. With the proceeds from members' additional contributions and the repayment of mortgages, the association continued making mortgages until each member became a homeowner, at which time the association was dissolved with each member receiving an equal share.

S&Ls did not spread rapidly. Six years passed before the second S&L was established. Another six years passed before there was a third. Following the Civil War, however, S&Ls changed their method of operations and took off. Membership and the equal "deposit" requirements were eliminated; now anyone could walk in and "deposit" any amount. (In view of their earlier method of operations, S&Ls technically issue shares, although these shares have the same characteristics as time and savings deposits at banks.) The new, open-to-all S&Ls often were sponsored directly or indirectly by builders, who naturally continued to emphasize mortgages to the virtual exclusion of other assets. However, the strong link between the two sides of the balance sheet was broken. Depositors were no longer guaranteed mortgages. Operations became more profit oriented. This greater profit orientation became most obvious when some new S&Ls chose to be stock firms instead of mutuals. About 22 percent of S&Ls are private stock companies. They hold about 30 percent of the industry's assets, being somewhat larger than the average S&L. The percentage of stock associations rose in the early 1980s as S&Ls needed to raise large amounts of capital funds to forestall bankruptcies. The desperate measures undertaken to save S&Ls is the subject of Chapter 11.

The attempt by S&Ls to appeal to a deeper market was not altogether successful prior to 1950. Although concentrated in a few states, in 1930 MSBs were about as large as S&Ls, which were located throughout the country. Thus, S&Ls had a very small share in virtually every geographic

---

[2]Actually, Oxford Provident originally was located in Frankford, Pennsylvania, a suburb which officially became a part of Philadelphia 23 years later in 1854.

market, while MSBs either had a large share or did not participate. The reasons for the nationwide weakness of S&Ls are not well known. The assets and liabilities of MSBs and S&Ls are quite similar. Why were S&Ls weak competitors in the markets where MSBs did not participate? While there is no definitive answer, their inability to shake the popular view—misconception?—that they were not altogether safe and reputable certainly did not help them attract deposits. A few S&Ls did sacrifice deposit safety by making risky mortgages in order to help builders sell houses. Guilt by association was prevalent prior to deposit insurance. The Great Depression hit S&Ls particularly hard in spite of governmental efforts to shore them up. Their relatively poor reputation induced larger withdrawals than usual. The small net worth of many households caused them to default on their mortgages shortly after becoming unemployed. By 1935 real estate acquired through foreclosures equaled 20 percent of S&Ls assets. S&Ls became landlords as well as lenders. Various federal housing and credit agencies were established to help S&Ls. The newly created Federal Savings and Loan Insurance Corporation (FSLIC) surprisingly was unable to instill confidence in S&Ls in the 1930s. On the other hand, MSBs were regarded as pillars of strength. From parity with MSBs in 1930, S&Ls fell to half the size in 1945.

Increased insurance coverage of S&L accounts, the strengthening of the FSLIC itself in 1950, and the postwar boom were the catalysts that launched S&Ls into orbit. Besides the direct benefit of the higher coverage, the expanded insurance was interpreted by many as a sign of government approval. Would the government consent to lend the FSLIC more and increase the insurance on S&L accounts if the likelihood of bankruptcies were high? Is it not true that only the healthy can buy life insurance and the rich borrow? The greater concentration of S&Ls in California and other Sun Belt states is a second fortuitous reason for their postwar takeoff. Finally, S&Ls grew more rapidly than other intermediaries because they were relatively unregulated. S&Ls, free until 1966 from the maximum interest rate ceilings which shackled commercial banks, consistently offered higher deposit rates. They attracted funds away from local and distant intermediaries. New Englanders became an important source of funds for California S&Ls.

The severe restrictions on both sides of S&Ls balance sheet are being relaxed. On the asset side, mortgages no longer must equal at least 85 percent of total assets in order for S&Ls to qualify for important tax benefits. *They have been allowed to issue credit cards, extend more consumer credit, and even make some commercial loans.* In time S&Ls may become an important source of consumer and commercial loans. However, they still are largely mortgage lenders that hold a little cash and marketable securities for liquidity purposes. Table 9–1 underestimates the importance of mortgages to S&Ls; a substantial proportion of "Other assets'' are mortgage-backed securities. *The most important development for the liability side was the imposition of Reg Q in 1966 and its dismantlement in the early 1980s.* NOW accounts are a small proportion of total deposits but are an important competitive tool to retain the deposits of those who want ''one-stop banking.'' FHLB advances also are a small but important source of funds during periods of credit tightness. Advances let S&Ls maintain their portfolio when they experience deposit outflows. Off the balance sheet altogether, the Monetary Control Act (MCA) gave S&Ls trust powers and, thereby, another source of income totally free of interest rates. Chapter 11 looks at all these developments much more closely. Their overall effect is easily summarized: *S&Ls are becoming more like banks.*

Credit Unions

Credit unions are consumer/employee-oriented saving and lending institutions. The general lack of consumer credit prompted Monsignor Pierre Hevey and Mr. Alphonse Desjardins to organize Saint Mary's Cooperative Credit Association in Manchester, New Hampshire, in 1908. *All credit unions are mutuals which accept deposits from and primarily make loans to their members.* Common employment is the membership characteristic of approximately 85 percent of credit unions. In other words, the vast majority of credit unions are sponsored by firms and government agencies on behalf of their employees. The remaining 15 percent are operated by social and fraternal organizations. Credit union ''deposits,'' technically shares since credit unions are mutuals, may be insured by the National Credit Union Share Insurance Fund for the same $100,000 coverage as other depositories' accounts.

Credit unions are the newest and smallest yet fastest growing depository. Several factors explain their extraordinary growth. First, *the deposit rate ceilings were higher for credit unions than other depositories.* Of course, the ceiling rate need not be paid. In practice, the ceiling becomes a floor. This is particularly true for credit unions because employers often regard them as a fringe benefit. Employers usually provide the facilities and release employees from their other duties to work ''free'' for the credit union. With their lower expenses, credit unions are able to pay higher deposit rates, *ceteris paribus.* Second, besides low expenses, a high interest income lets credit unions pay high deposit rates. Although credit unions typically charge lower rates than consumer finance companies, their earnings are high because of their relatively low default rate. Credit unions pride themselves on being able to assess correctly the credit worthiness of borrowers. It is doubtful, however, if credit unions are any better than other intermediaries at assessing risk. *Their default rate is low probably because the personal and employment ties between credit unions and borrowers induce the latter to pay the former first, before other creditors*. Delays and defaults are embarrassing. When one can meet some but not all his or her obligations, one selects to default on those loans which minimize the damage to one's reputation. Defaults are *not* selected at random. One deliberately chooses to pay the furniture store instead of the doctor, knowing full well that the former can repossess the sofa while the latter cannot repossess your gall bladder. Third, credit unions can pay high deposit rates because *they are the only financial intermediaries which are not subject to any income taxes.*[3] *Finally, the rapid growth rate of credit unions is explained by the convenience factor.* They typically are located where the depositor works.

Credit unions are much smaller than other intermediaries. Their median size is about $4 million. Membership restrictions severely limit the growth of any one institution. Regulatory changes reducing specialization and homogenizing depositories have touched credit unions. In April 1977 credit unions were empowered to make 30-year mortgages. Until then they only had made relatively short-term home improvement loans. On the liability side, in August 1974 the National Credit Union Administration permitted credit unions to offer interest paying checkable deposits called share drafts.

Nondepository Intermediaries

The liabilities of depository and nondepository intermediaries are quite different. I often "cash" bank liabilities but fortunately have not cashed, and never want to cash, life insurance company liabilities. Nevertheless, insurance companies and other firms fall within our definition of intermediaries, that is, firms with mainly financial assets. Let us look at these institutions.

Life Insurance Companies

Philadelphia is the mother of the financial system, having given birth to the first bank, MSB, and S&L. She also gave birth to the first life insurance company in 1757, more than 20 years before she bore the first bank. The first insurance company was The Corporation for Relief of Poor and Distressed Presbyterian Ministers and of the Poor and Distressed Widows and Children of Presbyterian Ministers. Its name has mercifully been shortened. The company now is simply The Presbyterian Minister's Fund.

Life insurance companies are the oldest and second largest nondepository intermediary. They provide two major, diametrically different prod-

[3]Another peculiar feature of credit unions is the voting scheme at general meetings. Each depositor (shareholder) has one vote irrespective of the amount deposited.

ucts: (1) life insurance, or financial protection against dying too soon, and (2) annuities, or financial protection against living too long. Their name clearly implies that the first product distinguishes these companies; many non-life-insurance firms offer annuities. The insured and annuitants contribute over a period of time. The beneficiary collects when the insured dies, while annuitants receive monthly payments as long as they live. Issuance of both types of policies insures the insurance company. If its policyholders die sooner than expected, the company "loses" on life insurance but "wins" on annuities.

Two basic types of life insurance are offered, (1) term and (2) ordinary or whole life. A term policy grants protection for a limited period and contains no savings fund accumulation. The company pays, say, $1,000 in the event of death during the term, nothing being paid in case of survival. The premiums each term equal the expected mortality costs (death benefits) plus operational expenses and a normal return. Since expected mortality costs increase with age, the insured's term premiums increase over time. The whole life premiums on the contrary are fixed. Such a policy requires the company to charge premiums higher than on term insurance during the early years of the policy. The difference between the whole life and term premiums is the insured's savings fund, called the insurance "reserve" or the policy's cash and surrender value. This reserve will be drawn down in later years when, due to the increased death rate, the uniform annual premiums become insufficient to meet current cost. If the policy is surrendered, the insured receives the reserve. Whole life contracts let the insured borrow the reserve at a specified interest rate, usually quite low. Consequently, insurance policy loans rise during periods of tight money.

Insurance companies grew quite rapidly until 1945, at which time they were the second largest intermediary, more than three times larger than S&Ls. In spite of the Great Depression, the assets of life insurance companies increased from $18 to $30 billion between 1930 and 1940. Since 1945, however, the life insurance industry has grown quite slowly compared to other intermediaries. Table 9–2 presents data similar to Table 9–1 for nondepository intermediaries. Why have life insurance companies grown more slowly than other intermediaries? With the breakdown of the extended family there is a greater need for annuities or insurance against living too long. Can you trust your children to provide for you in your old age? Although the need for annuities has grown, it increasingly has been provided by noninsurance sources such as Social Security (technically, Old Age and Survivors Insurance Fund) and noninsurance pension funds. Individuals previously purchased annuities singly. Similar coverage now is compulsory (Social Security) or provided for a group, most often by noninsurance companies. Insurance companies now manage one quarter of pension fund assets, down significantly from 1945. Second, term in-

TABLE 9–2

Size, Growth, and Summary Balance Sheet of Nondepositories

Intermediary	*Total Assets, December 1945 ($ billions)*	*Total Assets, December 1983 ($ billions)*	*Percent Change*
Life insurance companies	43.9	567.5	1,293
Other insurance companies	6.3	204.5	3,146
Pension funds	5.4	605.8	11,119
Mutual funds	1.3	89.5	6,784
Finance companies	4.3	229.6	5,240

Life insurance companies (percent of total)

Assets		Liabilities	
Bonds	43.4	Life insurance reserves	41.8
Mortgages	25.0	Pension and annuity reserves	40.3
Stocks	9.8	Capital and other liabilities	17.9
Policy loans	9.3		
Other assets	12.5		

Other insurance companies (percent of total)

Assets		Liabilities	
State and local bonds	42.5	Policy payables	70.4
Corporate and Treasury bonds	24.6	Capital	29.6
Stocks	18.8		
Other assets	14.1		

Pension funds (percent of total)

Assets		Liabilities	
Stocks	43.0	Pension reserves	100.0
Bonds	50.7		
Other assets	6.3		

Mutual funds (percent of total)

Assets		Liabilities	
Stocks	54.6	Shares outstanding	100.0
Bonds	40.7		
Other assets	4.7		

Finance companies (percent of total)

Assets		Liabilities	
Consumer credit	48.8	Commercial paper	32.3
Business loans	41.8	Bonds	25.3
Other assets	9.4	Bank loans	12.5
		Capital and other liabilities	29.9

Sources: Federal Reserve, *Flow of Funds and Assets and Liabilities Outstanding, 1945–1972,* and *1959–1983.*

surance has become increasingly more popular than ordinary insurance. Term insurance generates substantial revenues, but almost equal expenses, so that it is not a significant source of life insurance company *assets,* which Table 9–2 measures.

Since purchasers of life insurance and annuities tend to be young households who collect when they are old, insurance companies match their long-term liabilities with long-term assets, as the segmented markets theory of the term structure suggests. Table 9–2 indicates that bonds and mortgages equal approximately 45 and 25 percent, respectively, of life insurance assets. Insurance companies are the major holders of corporate bonds with one third of corporate bonds outstanding. Stocks, equal to nearly 10 percent of assets, are held mainly because some prefer variable rate annuities dependent on the stock market. High interest rates induced policyholders to borrow from their insurers and explain the final major asset.

Other Insurance Companies

The companies called "other insurance" in Federal Reserve publications are mainly property/casualty and health insurance companies. These companies provide insurance against damage to property by fire, floods, and other natural catastrophies; auto accidents; burglary and embezzlement; personal liability for injury to others; and illness. There still is substantial specialization in the provision of life and other insurance, though less so than several decades ago.

Table 9–2 indicates that the other insurance industry is smaller than the life insurance industry but has grown faster in the postwar period, perhaps because individuals feel that they need greater protection against the higher crime rate and an increasingly litigious society. Burglary and personal liability insurance are almost essential. Sharply higher medical costs have prompted the overwhelming majority to buy health insurance.

The proportions of mortgages and state and local bonds in the portfolios of life and other insurance companies are quite different. Other insurance companies have acquired virtually no mortgages but hold state and local bonds equal to nearly half of their assets. Two factors explain the portfolio differences. First, most other insurance companies are stock corporations, the earnings of which are subject to federal corporate income tax. This makes tax-exempt state and locals very attractive. Many life insurance companies, on the other hand, are mutuals whose earnings are regarded by the federal tax code as nontaxable reserves to be paid to policyholders instead of taxable income. State and locals are poor investments for life insurance companies or anyone else in low tax brackets. Second, floods, earthquakes, and other risks that other insurance companies insure are less predictable than deaths. Given this, other insurance companies avoid mortgages, which are the least liquid capital market instrument.

Pension Funds and Mutual Funds

As just stated, noninsurance company pension funds are similar to the annuities and pension funds managed by insurance companies except for the fund manager, which is not an insurance company, by definition. Pension funds are established by private companies, unions, or state and local governments. They may manage the funds directly or, more frequently, hire an outside trustee such as an investment company or bank. Table 9–2 shows that pension funds grew so fast during the post-World War II period that by 1983 they were the largest nondepository.[4] Even if the percentage contribution per capita had remained constant, an increasing labor force and pay scale enlarge the aggregate pension fund. But employer and employee contributions also increased, both absolutely and relatively. We already mentioned that the breakdown of the traditional family has contributed to the growth of pensions. *The deferred taxability of employer contributions and the earnings of the fund greatly increase the desirability of fringe benefits, such as pensions, relative to salary.* The data in Table 9–2 do not include IRAs (individual retirement accounts) and Keogh retirement accounts of the self-employed. Tax factors explain the very rapid growth of these personal retirement accounts as well.

The amount of the pension/retirement payment may either be stipulated in the contract (defined benefit) or depend on the contributions and earnings of the fund (defined contribution). Most state and local government retirement funds and a significant portion of private pension funds are defined benefit funds, where the benefit is generally related to the participant's final years' income and the number of years employed.

Defined contribution pension funds are quite similar to mutual funds (open-end investment companies) insofar as the payoff depends on the funds' performance. The main difference between pension and mutual funds is that the former place restrictions on the assets being cashed, while the latter redeem their shares on demand at the current pro rata net asset value of their portfolio. The assets of most mutual funds are relatively homogeneous; they tend to specialize in a particular segment of the financial market. Most still are equity funds, but stocks now comprise about 55 percent of mutual fund assets, down from 90 percent a quarter century ago. (The data in Table 9–2 *exclude* money market funds, which in a few years became twice as large as all other types of mutual funds.) Corporate bond and balanced (stocks and bonds) funds existed for many years and are becoming more important. Nontaxable municipal bond funds are the newest and fastest growing mutual funds.

The overall postwar growth rate of mutual funds has been relatively high because mutual funds grew extremely rapidly in the first 25 years. The portfolio of equity funds naturally increased during the long bull market of 1945–70. Moreover, during that period an increasing number

---

[4]The pension fund data in Table 9–2 sums the private pension and state and local retirement fund data shown separately in flow-of-funds statistics. Contributions to pension funds increased even more rapidly than asset values, which were held back by the dismal performance of the stock and bond markets from about 1970 to 1982.

of people regarded stocks as *the* investment and inflation hedge. This was reflected by the higher direct participation rates in the stock market and higher indirect participation rates through mutual fund purchases. During the 1970s, however, the stock market went nowhere, and many became disillusioned with common stocks. The image of mutual fund managers as sages of Wall Street was tarnished by their inability to outperform the market. Nonmoney market mutual funds actually declined slightly. The annualized growth rate was 11.4 percent between 1950 and 1970 but −0.1 percent during the 1970s. Similar problems beset the portfolio of pension funds, which managed to grow only because contributions greatly exceeded benefits paid.

Two factors explain the mutual fund turnaround during the early 1980s. First, funds capitalized on the higher interest rates by creating new bond funds, particularly municipals. Second, the bull stock market that began on August 13, 1982, made stocks glamorous again.

Finance Companies

These intermediaries directly or indirectly finance consumer purchases. We should distinguish between consumer and sales finance companies. Consumer finance companies, often called small loan companies, lend directly to consumers for the purchase of specific items or for "debt consolidation." Small loan companies often are the last resort; they accept risks that banks, credit unions, and other intermediaries turn down. Given this and the small size of the typical loan, consumer loan rates are quite high. Household Finance and Beneficial Finance are the two largest small loan companies with offices throughout the United States. Sales finance companies sometimes directly finance the purchase of durable goods at lower rates than small loan companies. All the largest sales finance companies are "captive" firms owned by manufacturers of consumer goods or by retailers; for example, General Motor's GMAC, Ford Motor Credit, General Electric Credit, and Sears Roebuck Acceptance. You may not realize that your friendly Cadillac dealer is simply acting on behalf of GMAC when those E–Z payments are extended. Sales finance companies also lend indirectly to consumers by financing the inventories of and leasing equipment to consumer-oriented firms such as auto dealers and apparel manufacturers.

As indicated in the last chapter and shown in Table 9–2, commercial paper is an important source of funds for finance companies. These intermediaries also sell bonds and borrow at banks. Finance companies more than other intermediaries "denominate downward," that is, the amount of the average liability greatly exceeds the average asset. Mutual funds on the other hand denominate upward; the average size of the assets in their portfolio exceeds the average fundholder's position.

TABLE 9–3

Relative Importance of Intermediaries over Time (Percent of assets to total intermediary assets)

Intermediary	*Year*			
	1950	*1960*	*1970*	*1983*
Commercial banks	51.9	38.9	38.5	35.5
Savings and loans	5.9	12.0	13.4	17.1
Mutual savings banks	7.6	6.9	6.1	4.2
Credit unions	0.3	0.8	1.4	2.1
Life insurance companies	21.8	19.6	15.3	13.7
Other insurance companies	4.2	4.4	3.8	5.0
Pension funds	4.1	9.8	13.0	12.7
Mutual funds	1.0	2.9	3.7	2.2
Finance companies	3.1	4.6	4.9	5.6

Note: Columns may not add to 100 due to rounding.
Source: Federal Reserve. *Flow of Funds Accounts*, various issues.

Summary/Questions

Table 9–3 summarizes some of the discussion in the last two sections by showing the relative importance of all intermediaries over time.

The majority of people do not have any contact with the direct financial market, but virtually everyone deals with intermediaries, particularly depositories, on a regular basis. For example, I'll bet that nearly every reader has some type of deposit account, but only a small percentage own stocks and bonds directly. However, many own them indirectly through mutual funds, the savings provision of an ordinary life insurance policy, or a pension fund. This is not to say that direct finance is unimportant. The value of stocks owned directly still exceeds the value of stocks owned by intermediaries, in spite of the growth of pension funds. Some markets, however, are thoroughly dominated by intermediaries. You and I as consumers and possible homeowners would find little credit and mortgage funds if intermediaries did not exist. Few people lend directly so others can buy cars and homes. Because credit is so beneficial as we argued in Chapter 5, intermediaries, which increase the availability of credit, also are extremely beneficial.

1. What are the major items on bank's balance sheets, and how have they changed over time? In particular, how, if at all, have the following changed relative to total assets: (*a*) cash and securities, (*b*) total loans, (*c*) check deposits, (*d*) time deposits, (*e*) commercial loans, (*f*) real estate loans, and (*g*) capital?
2. List three nonbank depositories and five nondepository intermediaries.

3. For each of the three nonbank depositories, state (1) the circumstances which led to their creation, (2) their main assets and liabilities, and (3) any distinguishing characteristics.
4. Explain how the sale of annuities reduces risk for life insurance companies.
5. State the main assets and liabilities and any distinguishing characteristics of nondepository intermediaries.
6. Which intermediary is most closely associated with the following terms: (*a*) department store of finance, (*b*) mortgages, (*c*) consumer credit, (*d*) interest on deposits, (*e*) denominate downward, (*f*) denominate upward, (*g*) protection against dying too soon, and (*h*) protection against living too long.
7. What factors explain the very different pre- and post-World War II growth rates of mutual savings banks and savings and loans?
8. What factors explain the different post-World War II growth rates of (*a*) life insurance companies, (*b*) other insurance companies, and (*c*) pension funds?
9. What factors explain the different growth rates of the (nonmoney) mutual fund industry between (*a*) 1945–70, (*b*) 1970–82, and (*c*) 1982 to the present?

Banking theories

10

Those who can do, those who cannot become bankers.
Very old-fashioned teacher[*]

In spite of its title, this chapter is more descriptive than theoretical. We begin by describing banks' objectives in an uncertain world where current events are largely shaped by past actions. How should an *individual* bank operate in such an environment in order to best achieve its objectives? Answers to the last question, which have changed significantly over time, are elevated in financial circles to the status of "banking theories." Statements of the currently most widely practiced management policies become the accepted "theory" of the day. This suggests that to some extent banking theories are rationalizations. Yet it is unclear that during any period something other than actual banking practice would have made the average bank more successful. Banking theories changed largely because the entire financial system and range of alternatives available to banks have changed and only in small part because of a fundamental change in the bank's objectives.

Banking in an Uncertain World with a Memory

Although economists and financial analysts are interested in banks because they create money and extend credit, these actions are only incidental to banks themselves. In an uncertain world where accounts are related at any one time and over time, *banks attempt to maximize short-run profits subject to solvency and liquidity constraints*. Note that banks, or other firms for that matter, are *not short-run profit maximizers exclu-*

---

[*]With due apologies to G. B. Shaw.

sively. To be sure, a bank may well attempt to maximize profits in the *long run*. Let AZ in Figure 10–1 represent the long run. Shouldn't a bank intent on maximizing profits over interval AZ attempt to maximize profits over every shorter interval such as EF? Not necessarily because uncertainty exists, and accounts are linked functionally.

Before explaining the last sentence, consider the environment in which banks operate. Banks clearly are uncertain about the rate of return on their assets and the size of deposit flows. Banks will realize low returns or even losses on their long-term assets when interest rates rise unexpectedly. Defaults may be higher than expected, reducing banks' rate of return. A bank's inability to predict perfectly the actions of its depositors produces unexpected deposit inflows and outflows. To complicate matters more for bankers, the consequences and distribution of an uncertain event depend on previous and current decisions in other areas. Let deposit flows be the example of an uncertain event. The *consequences* of the random *deposit* flows that are realized depend in part on the *asset* decisions the banker made. Banks without excess reserves or very liquid assets may incur losses in selling securities to raise cash to meet deposit outflows. Moreover, the realized *value* of deposit flows, or the likelihood attached to the various possible deposit inflows and outflows, depends on *past* loan decisions. An inability or unwillingness to meet depositors' loan requests yesterday greatly increases the likelihood of deposit outflows today.

Clearly, uncertainty implies that banks do not always maximize *actual* profits. Mistakes will be made at times. Less obvious but equally true, banks may not even attempt to maximize *expected* short-run profits. Strict maximization of expected profits requires actions based on the expected or average outcome of uncertain events such as future interest rates and loan default rates. However, bankers realize that an unfavorable outcome, instead of the expected or average outcome, may well occur. Because there will be no long run unless they survive unfavorable outcomes in the short run, banks may not want to act simply on the basis of expected or average values.

A bank's accounts are linked *functionally* at any one moment and over time, and not simply linked mechanically by the balance sheet constraint. For example, suppose short-run profit maximization requires denying de-

FIGURE 10–1

positors' loans and placing funds in the money market at higher rates of interest. What will happen in the future? The denial of loans to depositors is almost guaranteed to cause subsequent deposit outflows to more accommodating banks and lower long-run profits. *Because uncertainty exists and accounts are interrelated, continuous attempts to maximize profits can be counterproductive.*[1] On the other hand, a bank cannot altogether ignore short-run profits since long-run profits are the sum of short-run profits. Banks maximize short-run profits subject to solvency and liquidity constraints.

Defining terms, banks remain solvent so long as their assets exceed their liabilities or, equivalently, their net worth or capital is positive. For solvency purposes, assets are valued at the prices they would fetch given a reasonable selling time (say, six months or a year) rather than at immediate, distress sale prices. Remember that net worth represents the bank owners' investment in the bank. Banks with a small net worth tend to earn high profit rates when uncertain events are favorable. However, insolvent banks with a negative net worth are closed by bank regulators. *The solvency constraint says that in order to remain in business in the long run, when some strongly unfavorable events are bound to occur, banks sacrifice short-run profits by increasing net worth and reducing risk taking.*

According to the liquidity constraint, banks must be able to meet depositors' withdrawals and legitimate loan requests immediately and continuously without incurring sizable costs. "Legitimate loan requests" admittedly is a somewhat nebulous concept. Nonmafia types can make illegitimate loan requests. Legitimate loan requests are those which, if denied, generate a high probability of future withdrawals. While commercial and industrial firms also face liquidity constraints, the constraint is more severe for banks because of the nature of their products. When General Motors overestimates its sales and produces too many cars, its inventories rise and cash balances fall. General Motors' inventories and cash balances would fluctuate much more if it also gave current owners the option of returning existing cars for cash on demand. The owners of most bank products do enjoy an instant return privilege. Demand deposits are by law, and savings deposits are in fact, immediately convertible into cash.[2]

---

[1]The fundamental but complex idea that long-run profit maximization does *not* imply short-run profit maximization because of uncertainty and the interrelationship of accounts over time is not unique to banking. Indeed, the success of Japanese automakers and other Japanese industrialists is often credited to their acute awareness of this fundamental idea.

[2]There often is safety in numbers. When many banks are simultaneously illiquid but solvent, they stop or limit convertibility of deposits to cash, creating a so-called bank holiday. Convertibility resumes when the demand for cash returns to normal levels or after the passage of sufficient time for an orderly liquidation of assets. The last nationwide bank

Assets are such that a trade-off usually exists in their contribution to the three banking goals. When is a bank most liquid? A bank is most liquid and can clearly meet any cash or loan request when it is holding only cash. However, cash yields no income, and a bank without revenues but with expenses eventually will fail. Liquidity may also be attained by owning readily marketable short-term securities such as Treasury bills. The risk premium hypothesis of the term structure of interest rates states that the holding period yield is less on short-term Treasury bills than on long-term bonds, and marketable Treasury bills generally yield less than nonmarketable short-term assets such as consumer loans, even after adjustment for default risk. A trade-off also exists between income and solvency. Since forecasts are much more accurate for the near than for the distant future, and since banks expect loans to be repaid while recognizing the risk to the contrary, risky loans tend to increase current income as banks charge higher interest on risky loans yet few defaults occur immediately. Defaults are prediction errors which are less likely in the near future. As time passes, the bank's mistakes will manifest themselves, and some borrowers will default. Particularly if the default risk is underestimated, the initial additional income will be less than the subsequent losses, which could cause bankruptcy.

Banking Theories over Time

This section presents the precise policies banks are supposed to follow in order to maximize profits subject to a liquidity and solvency constraint.

Real Bill or Commercial Loan Theory

From the time of its initial exposition by Adam Smith in *The Wealth of Nations* until approximately 1910, the *real bills or commercial loan theory* reigned supreme. The real bills doctrine encompasses elements of bank management and monetary policy. Discussion of the latter aspect is postponed until the section on the discount rate. Regarding individual bank management, *the real bills theory states that banks should make short-term, self-liquidating loans to finance the current production, transportation, or storage of physical goods, either manufactured or agricultural.* Short-term inventory loans to a toy retailer in early fall and

---

holiday occurred in 1933. All banks were temporarily closed but most subsequently reopened. Localized holidays occur nowadays after a natural disaster which disrupts the flow of cash from the Fed to banks. For example, banks in Mississippi's Gulf Coast region suspended convertibility following Hurricane Frederick in 1979. The governors of Ohio and Maryland imposed holidays on state insured S&Ls in mid-1985.

agricultural loans for the purchase of seed and other variable factors of productions are examples of ideal loans according to the theory. These loans are self-liquidating in the sense that they finance goods which the borrower does not intend to consume personally and which, therefore, will be sold directly (toys in our example) or indirectly after further processing (seed). What types of loans were forbidden by the real bills theory, a name we prefer to the commercial loan theory because agricultural loans were not precluded? *Any* long-term loans, consumer loans, and loans to purchase stocks or other financial assets were taboo.

Yesterday's bankers, like today's merchandisers, were guilty of exaggeration in claiming that real bills *guarantee* bank liquidity. Real bills need not be *monetarily* self-liquidating in the sense that such loans definitely will be repaid and, thereby, yield a large, predictable cash flow. True, physical goods always can be *quantitatively* self-liquidating—anything can be sold at some sufficiently low price—but no loan is *monetarily* self-liquidating because the monetary value of the (nonmoney) goods being financed may fall. Nevertheless, if bankers had more frequently practiced what they preached, they would have been illiquid less frequently. Prior to the early 1900s, there was no well-organized securities market where banks could readily sell large quantities of securities when they needed cash. Banks had to look to their loan portfolio for liquidity. During any given short-time period, a portfolio consisting of long-term loans generates little cash flow, by definition. But all short-term loans are not equally desirable. Particularly in an era when financial markets were relatively undeveloped and workers could be readily fired, short-term financial loans and consumer loans were more risky and generated less certain cash flows than real bills.

Bankers sometimes violated the spirit while maintaining the letter of the real bills doctrine. Officially short-term loans often were effectively long-term loans. Firms counting on their short-term loans continually being renewed purchased long-lived assets, which even in the best of circumstances did not generate sufficient cash to repay the loan in the short run. Even when firms were less daring and, in fact, used loans to finance short-term assets, banks could be forced to continually renew loans.[3] Our toy retailer must maintain some inventory at all times. This perpetual need for short-term assets may create a perpetual need for short-term loans which banks must satisfy. Nevertheless, real bills were less risky and generated a larger cash flow than other types of loans. They also strengthened depositors' ties to a bank since firms held the vast proportion of deposits. Consumers in those days preferred currency.

---

[3]Ascertaining the specific asset financed by a loan is an extremely difficult task, as we shall show later.

Shiftability

By the beginning of this century a national market for various types of assets had developed to the point that "shiftability" became possible. *The shiftability hypothesis states that a bank's portfolio of marketable assets is its main source of liquidity.* This hypothesis received big boosts from the U.S. entry into World War I and the long bull market of the roaring 20s. In order to finance the war effort the Treasury issued large—by previous standards—quantities of bonds. The Fed encouraged banks to purchase government bonds along with real bills by allowing them as collateral for Fed discounts. Throughout the 19th and early 20th centuries banks made some stock market loans, contrary to the real bills doctrine. The public's enhanced participation in the market made stocks more liquid. A broad and deep stock market makes exercise of the demand or call provision typical on such loans less likely to trigger a financial panic. While the Fed opposed stock market loans, it did not have the tools to prohibit or even discourage banks from making such loans. The Fed could hardly base its objections on the real bills doctrine when it had encouraged similar violations so banks would buy government bonds.

The hypothesis is aptly named because satisfaction of one bank's liquidity needs by selling liquid assets shifts the problem to another bank. For example, a bank with a large quantity of Treasury bills can readily meet its depositors' requests for cash by liquidating part of its portfolio. Provided payment for the bills is made by check, as is most likely, the reserves of another bank will fall, requiring it to adjust. Liquid assets do not prevent *multiple* contractions and expansions. The money creator is the only economic agent to which the entire banking *system* can shift depositors' requests for cash. More simply, the Fed currently is the main source of liquidity for the banking system. Chapter 4's analysis of excess reserves in 1936–38 is one of several illustrations of the Fed's failure to meet its duties.

In view of legal constraints and the depositor-borrower relationship, the shiftability theory states that the profitability, liquidity, and solvency objectives will be met by allocating assets in the following order.

1. Maintain the required or primary reserves. Cash and deposits at the Fed yield no income, but bankers must make some sacrifice if they want to remain in business.
2. Acquire open-market, short-term securities often called secondary reserves. The interest earned usually compensates for the reduction in liquidity brought about by smaller cash holdings.
3. Make customer, both consumer and business, loans. These assets tend to be more profitable. While they decrease liquidity, they also reduce the need for liquidity by tying depositors more closely to

the bank. Generally, customer loans are more risky than open-market securities and increase the likelihood of insolvency.

4. Invest the remainder, if any, in open-market, long-term securities, such as government bonds.

The asset management sequence is made more concrete by considering the adjustment pattern in response to an exogenous deposit increase. The immediate impact of the deposit increase is an equal cash increase. After setting aside any required amount, the banker will invest the remainder in the shortest money market instrument. For example, the bank may sell overnight Federal funds, that is, lend the cash to another bank for a day. The deposit inflow today may be an outflow tomorrow, so the bank cannot afford to make illiquid, if profitable, customer loans immediately. As time passes and the deposit inflow seems more permanent, the banker shifts the funds to the longer end of the money market and then makes customer loans or, lacking customer demand, enters the capital market.

Anticipated Income

As the composition of bank assets paralleled the shift of resources from the government to the private sectors following cessation of World War II, the anticipated income hypothesis gained popularity. This hypothesis formulated in the late 1940s repudiates the real bill doctrine while simultaneously and implicitly accepting the shiftability hypothesis that liquid assets are a single bank's best source of liquidity. *The anticipated income hypothesis states that the likelihood of loan repayments, which generate a cash flow that supplements bank liquidity, depends on the anticipated income of the borrower instead of the type of borrower or the use made of the funds.* To some extent this was well known; some real bills always default—ask those who lent to Penn Central and Braniff—while Horatio Alger repays his consumer loan. While everyone recognizes the possibility of exceptions to any rule like the real bills theory, the anticipated income hypothesis is a statement about the average or typical borrower and loan in the late 1940s. It states that no particular *large* class of borrowers or loans is much more likely to produce a stable and predictable cash flow. Thus, the hypothesis suggests that banks should evaluate loan requests on an *individual* basis because rough-and-ready rules of thumb are not very accurate.

Real estate loans in particular, and term loans in general, are good examples of the validity of the anticipated income hypothesis.[4] Structural

---

[4]The anticipated income hypothesis is associated with Herbert Prochnow, *Term Loans and Theories of Bank Liquidity* (Englewood Cliffs, N.J.: Prentice-Hall, 1949).

changes since 1900 have increased the liquidity of mortgages. The typical mortgage in 1900 was not amortized, that is, the borrower paid the loan principal in full at maturity instead of making periodic payments. Moreover, the typical interest payment was made less frequently than monthly. Amortization and monthly interest payment have increased the short-term cash flow from mortgages and reduced their *duration, which is the weighted average of the maturity of every payment associated with a loan, coupon interest as well as the principal.*[5] Besides changes in the contract terms, the creation of housing insurance and intermediaries such as FHA, which we mentioned in Chapter 8, have increased the liquidity of mortgages to the point that they are not categorically unsuitable investments.

Liability Management

Prior to 1960 the liability side of banks' balance sheets provided little liquidity and did not respond to short-run profit opportunities. Demand and passbook savings deposits made up the overwhelming proportion of bank liabilities. In reponse to withdrawals by one group of depositors, a bank could not change the terms of its deposits and attract another group. Many deposit terms (for example, the number of tellers and the length of the banking day) cannot be readily adjusted in the short run although they strongly influence the amount of bank deposits. Regulation Q often precluded use of the deposit rate, the term most easily adjusted in the short run. Even if Reg Q were not binding or banks could quickly lower service charges, net deposit rate changes would have been very costly because demand and savings deposits are not very responsive to the deposit rate. Moreover, the higher deposit rates would be earned by *all* demand and savings deposits, new as well as existing ones. Beginning around 1960, with the development of the CD and Fed funds markets, and continuing with the Eurodollar and RP markets, large banks created money market liabilities which *normally* could be adjusted readily without increasing the cost of already existing deposits. This led to the liability management theory of banking. *In its infancy the extreme form of the liability management theory stated that banks could satisfy any liquidity need and short-run profit opportunity by issuing money market liabilities such as CDs.* In other words, liability management stated that banks in

[5]Some important concepts are discovered only to be lost and repeatedly rediscovered. Such is the case with duration. The concept was publicized at the beginning of the century, rediscovered by the anticipated income hypothesis, and quite recently rediscovered by GAP analysts. While the *maturity* of a loan considers the date of only the final (face or principal) payment, the *duration* of a loan considers the dates of all payments, interest and principal. The duration of all bonds with coupons is less than their maturity; duration equals maturity only for discount bonds with a single payment. GAP analysts, who are concerned about mismatches in the asset and liability structure of intermediaries for reasons we shall explore in depth in the following chapter, now focus on duration instead of maturity because the former recognizes the entire cash flow associated with a loan.

need of cash should borrow instead of selling assets (shiftability hypothesis) or planning an orderly cash flow (anticipated income hypothesis). Although Reg Q generally was less binding on bank money market instruments than savings deposits, it became binding during the so-called credit crunches of the 1960s and at other times when banks needed to borrow most. With the dismantlement of Reg Q, institutional impediments to liability management will diminish but not vanish altogether. The *moderate* version of the liability management theory recognizes these impediments and states that money market bank liabilities should be used along with bank assets to meet liquidity needs.

Computer Models

The four banking theories presented so far are rules of thumb relative to what has recently been classified as the latest banking theory: the computer or statistical model of banking. A banking model here means a set of mathematical equations describing the interrelationship among bank assets, liabilities, and income over time. The equations are estimated with a computer programmed to perform regressions or some other type of statistical analysis. The models are large scale, complex, quantitative versions of back-of-the-envelope models that bankers and economists guesstimated before the computer. For example, we mentioned that assets and liabilities are not independent as depositors expect their loan requests to be honored. A computer model's estimate of the income effects of selling a short-term, open-market instrument in order to make a relatively long-term consumer loan will incorporate measurement of the deposit flows associated with different assets, forecasts of future interest rates, and other factors besides the obviously important current interest rate differential between the two assets. Computer models also calculate duration gaps or differences between the *entire* cash flow associated with a bank's assets and liabilities. Computation of duration gaps is difficult since it must incorporate the uncertainty of mortgage and other loan prepayments and early time deposit withdrawals. The computer model differs from the four earlier banking models in two important respects: (1) the computer model forecasts liquidity needs in addition to indicating how the needs should be met, and (2) computer models are flexible and do not indicate that some course of action is always best, irrespective of the characteristics of the individual bank, local economy, and the financial system.

Summary/Questions

A recurring theme of this book is that banking can be an exciting, imaginative profession. The banker/robot of Chapter 3, who responds mechanically to every Federal Reserve action, is a gross caricature of the modern banker. Narrow rules of thumb such as the real bills doctrine gave way years ago to the broader, more eclectic anticipated income theory. The latter in turn has been replaced by management techniques using the most sophisticated computers. Large, money market banks in particular are dynamic firms.

1. Are banks pure profit maximizers in the short run? What are their objectives?
2. While balance sheets balance, the individual accounts are unrelated. True, false, or uncertain. Explain your answer.
3. List the five main banking theories in chronological order.
4. Describe the major banking theories and explain their relationship to the structure of the economy.
5. According to the shiftability theory, in what order should assets be allocated?
6. Associate the following items with a banking theory: (*a*) self-liquidating loans, (*b*) liquid assets, (*c*) CDs and RPs, and (*d*) quality borrowers of all types.
7. What is the difference between a loan's maturity and duration?

11 Disintermediation and deregulation: Depositories at the brink of bankruptcy

To rescue savings and loans from the fate of the dodo bird, a distinction without a difference was created.

Most financial intermediaries are profit-*oriented* firms (even if not profit *maximizers*). The return on their assets exceeds the interest they pay on their liabilities. Since individuals can purchase securities directly and earn higher returns than intermediaries pay, intermediaries must transform unwanted primary securities into desirable claims in order to exist. How can they do this? The first part of this chapter is relatively theoretical. It discusses the fundamental reasons for the existence of financial intermediaries. The discussion will show that the desperate plight of depositories, particularly savings and loans (S&Ls), in the early 1980s was to some extent inevitable. The transformation of undesirable primary securities to desirable deposits, which is the very reason for the existence of S&Ls and other depositories, is extremely unprofitable during periods such as the early 1980s.

The difficulties of depositories that are inherent to their very existence were compounded by unchanging regulations in a changing financial system. Deregulation proposals of the 1961 Commission on Money and Credit, the 1971 Hunt Report, and the 1976 FINE Report went largely unheeded because the "need" was not urgent enough. And yet, very shortly thereafter, Congress and the Carter and Reagan administrations feared that sharply higher market interest rates would lead to the collapse of depositories as a whole. Although subsequent chapters criticize regulatory authorities for their overconcern about the failure of *individual* institutions, the failure of an entire *industry*, such as the S&L industry, would be good cause for concern. The mortgage market is thoroughly dominated by S&Ls and other intermediaries. This market is also distinguished by its close ties to the commodities market. If consumer credit suddenly were unavailable for whatever reason, the demand for automobiles, other durables, and even services would fall significantly. However, the percentage decline in the demand for consumer goods would be small compared to the percentage decline suffered by the construction industry if mortgages were no longer available. The final section presents the main features of the Depository Institutions Deregulation and Monetary Control Act (MCA) of 1980, the Garn-St. Germain Depository Institutions Act (GSt.G) of 1982, and other less comprehensive legislation and regulatory reforms designed to help depositories.

Deregulation has been so sweeping that the listing of main reforms is admittedly incomplete, and you are not expected to remember every detail. Order to the seemingly crazy and farflung patchwork of financial deregulation in the early 1980s is gained by always keeping firmly in mind one of its objectives: *rescue S&Ls and other depositories, many of which were at the brink of bankruptcy.*

The Rationale for Financial Intermediaries

Why can intermediaries exist? Why do individuals acquire intermediaries' securities instead of purchasing primary issues directly? *Financial intermediaries exist because by pooling funds they are able to take advantage of (1) the law of large numbers, and (2) economies of scale.* The law of large numbers states that as the number of independent random (uncertain) events increases, risk is reduced relative to the expected outcome. As the number of uncertain events becomes infinitely large, the average or expected outcome becomes highly predictable. In other words, *the law of large numbers states that although the outcome of any one event may be highly uncertain, the average outcome of many events is predictable.* While the law is important to every intermediary, it is absolutely essential to the life insurance industry, so much so that the law of large numbers is sometimes called the *insurance principle*. How can insurees be extremely confident that insurance companies will meet their obligations when premiums equal, say, 2 percent of the insurance in force and the likelihood of death is only somewhat less than 2 percent? If the company insures only one person, it either earns the 2 percent premium—the person lives—or it loses the amount insured—the person dies—which may bankrupt the company. When the company insures many people, it can be quite confident that somewhat less than 2 percent of its policyholders will die. Increases in the number of policyholders aid the company in predicting the percentage of deaths but not the specific people who will die.

The law of large numbers affects both sides of the balance sheet and the income statement of depositories. The last paragraph considered large numbers and the liability/expense side of insurance companies. The analog for commercial banks and other depository intermediaries is *relative* certainty of the percentage outflows and inflows of total deposits, compared to the uncertainty about the behavior of any one depositor. Of course, the expected percentage flows and their predictability vary over time, as the analysis of desired excess reserves in Chapter 4 indicated. During any particular time period, however, *the reduction in the uncertainty of expected deposit flows due to the law of large numbers enables depository institutions to issue highly liquid liabilities although the overwhelming proportion of their assets are illiquid.* For example, suppose a bank or savings and loan estimates that 10 percent of its many depositors will withdraw their funds. Knowing full well that deviations from the 10 percent expected value will be small and the likelihood of a 20 percent outflow is virtually nil, the institution can effectively, if not legally, make its deposits payable on demand even though 80 percent of its assets are illiquid mortgages. *On the asset side, the law of large numbers reduces the risk of default on the portfolio although each asset is risky.* That is, the law of large numbers turns the *risk of default on one asset* into a more *certain portfolio default rate.* Ignoring capital gains and losses, a depository intermediary can guarantee the rate on its liabilities even though the return on any one asset may be quite unpredictable due to default risk. In summary, large numbers (diversification) of depositors and assets let the intermediary purchase illiquid, uncertain return assets while simultaneously issuing liquid, guaranteed return liabilities.

The existence of economies of scale is the second reason why surplus units prefer intermediary claims to those issued by ultimate deficit units. While economies of scale are important to all intermediaries, they provide the almost complete rationale for mutual funds or open-end investment companies, where one acquires pro rata shares of the assets and earnings of a fund of financial instruments. Unlike depository intermediaries, the assets and liabilities of which have different characteristics, the asset portfolio and claims issued by mutual funds are, of necessity, virtually identical since the latter are pro rata shares on the former. For example, higher interest rates and lower bond values have no effect on savings deposit rates, at least in the short run. However, bond market behavior is directly and immediately passed through to bond mutual fund owners. Since the products that mutual funds offer are identical to the products they own, individuals willingly pay the mutual fund a management fee because the fund either (1) acquires information on financial instruments relatively inexpensively, or (2) administers the portfolio more inexpensively than individuals can. By pooling funds, intermediaries realize economies of scale of information and administration. For example, the cost of *The Wall Street Journal,* the literally thousands of stock market newsletters, and other sources of information is independent of the size of one's portfolio. However, their value is proportional to the portfolio. The prince and the pauper pay the same amount for *The Wall Street Journal,* but the former gains more by reading it. Those with small sums to invest should not spend the time and money trying to ferret out the best investment, considering the size of the possible benefits. Their time would be better spend on other pursuits. Managers of large sums, however, find the acquisition of information profitable. Administration costs, the second category of costs, are broadly interpreted here to include the transaction costs of buying and selling, bookkeeping costs, safekeeping costs, and so on. Specialization and the frequent repetition of the same operation produce economies of administration. Moreover, now that brokerage costs on the New York Exchange are negotiated, administration costs relative to assets should decline further.

While all intermediaries, and not just mutual funds, take advantage of economies of scale, we shall discover in subsequent chapters that economies of scale in banking are exhausted quite rapidly. Beyond a certain point, a bank's average cost is approximately constant. Given this, let us abstract from economies of scale and assume that anyone can earn the same rate of return as the intermediary does on its assets. Under these circumstances an intermediary can exist and earn a profit *only* by acquiring assets which are less liquid and longer term than its liabilities. The characteristics of its assets and liabilities *must* differ. This is made possible by the law of large numbers.

Disintermediation

Depository intermediaries normally function quite smoothly. However, because of the mismatch in liquidity and term to maturity (duration) between their assets and liabilities, depositories incur severe problems whenever interest rates rise sharply and rapidly. What is the effect of higher interest rates on the interest income of *current* holders of outstanding bonds and fixed rate mortgages? Nothing. Only new lenders gain higher interest income. Are holders of existing long-term assets affected by higher interest rates? Yes, the value of their assets tumbles. Particularly when intermediaries' deposits are *de jure* or *de facto* highly liquid and pay a fixed rate, the higher market interest rates are likely to cause disintermediation. *Disintermediation is the withdrawal of funds from depositories in order to purchase primary securities when primary yields rise substantially above deposit rates.* Disintermediation forces depositories to recognize their capital losses. To meet their depositors' withdrawals, depositories have to sell assets just when they have fallen in price. If disintermediation and the resultant capital losses are large enough, bankruptcy occurs. Assuming no prohibitive regulations, deposit rates could be raised in order to stem disintermediation. However, what will be the effect of such a policy on operating profits? They fall because deposit costs rise while interest income is approximately constant due to the long life of the assets.

The last paragraph is so important that a detailed example is justified to guarantee that it was perfectly understood. To sharpen the illustration, assume the depository's single earning asset is a perpetuity paying $1 per period so its price, P_B, is 1/i, where i is the yield to maturity. Assume the interest rate had been constant at 5 percent so the cost and market price of each bond was $20. According to line 1 of Figure 11–1, the deposit rate was 4.5 percent ($46.125/$1025) so depositors sacrifice a modest return, 0.5 percent, in order to hold more desirable deposits instead of perpetuities. So long as the interest rate remains constant, the depository

FIGURE 11–1

Effect of Rising Interest Rates and Disintermediation on Balance Sheet and Income Statement of Depository Institutions

Initial *accounting and economic* statements, (2) *economic* statements after interest rate rises, (3) *accounting* statements after interest rate rises with $50 withdrawals and bond sales at end of period, (4) *accounting* statements after deposit rate is increased, (5) *accounting* statements after interest rate rises with $50 withdrawals and borrowing.

Depository Balance Sheet

	Assets		*Liabilities and Net Worth*		*Income Statement*	
(1)	Cash	$ 75	Deposits	$1,025	Interest income	$50.000
	Perpetuities	1,000	Net worth	50	Deposit expense	46.125
	(50 bonds)				Dividends	3.875
	Total	$1,075	Total	$1,075	Retained earnings	0
(2)	Cash	$ 75	Deposits	$1,025	Interest income	$ 50.000
	Perpetuities	500	Net worth	−450	Deposit expense	46.125
	(50 bonds)				Dividends	3.875
	Total	$575	Total	$ 575	Capital loss	500.000
					Retained earnings	−500.000
(3)	Cash	$ 75	Deposits	$975	Interest income	$50.000
	Perpetuities	900	Net worth	0	Deposit expense	46.125
	(45 bonds)				Dividends	3.875
	Total	$975	Total	$975	Capital loss	−50.000
					Retained earnings	−50.000
(4)	Cash	$ 32.75	Deposits	$1,025.00	Interest income	$50.00
	Perpetiuties	1,000.00	Net worth	7.75	Deposit expense	92.25
	(50 bonds)				Retained earnings	−42.25
	Total	$1,032.75	Total	$1,032.75		
(5)	Cash	$ 75	Deposits	$ 975	Interest income	$50.000
	Perpetuities	1,000	Borrowings	50	Interest (deposit and	
	(50 bonds)		Net worth	50	borrowing) expense	46.125
	Total	$1,075	Total	$1,075	Dividends	3.875
					Retained earnings	0

earns a 7.75 percent return on its net worth—quite tidy considering the return on perpetuities is only 5 percent.

Now assume the interest rate doubles to 10 percent with the value of each bond cut in half to $10. An *economic* balance sheet which values assets at market prices would record a capital loss of $500 at the end of the period. From an economic viewpoint, the depository is bankrupt; its assets equal $575 while its liabilities are $1,025. The depository has a negative net worth of $450, which equals the initial $50 net worth and the negative retained earning of $500. (See line 2 of Figure 11–1.) Except for a very few bonds held in so-called trading accounts, however, the regulatory authorities allow depositories to mark at cost. From a legal and accounting viewpoint, capital losses are recorded only when they are realized. Provided depositors continue to hold 4.5 percent deposits in spite of the current availability of 10 percent perpetuities, the depository could operate exactly as before. (See line 1 again.) The higher yield does *not* increase the depository's interest income because the coupon is fixed. The higher yield simply means one has to pay less (the bond price fell) for the given stream of coupons. The depository surely will incur withdrawals if it does not raise deposit rates. Line 2, the economic balance sheet, would be realized if deposit withdrawals were complete. That is, the withdrawal of the $1,025 in deposits bankrupts the depository, and the depositors receive $575. This too is unrealistic. Something between no withdrawals and complete withdrawals will occur. Line 3 of Figure 11–1 assumes withdrawals equal $50, which equals 5 percent of liabilities but 100 percent of net worth. Even from a legal and accounting viewpoint, the depository is brought to the verge of bankruptcy as its net worth plummets to zero. Assuming the depository wishes to maintain $75 cash, no amount of creative accounting can hide the fact that five bonds valued at $100 must be sold in order to raise $50, causing a $50 capital loss.[1] We shall ignore for now the possibility that the perpetuities may not be readily marketable.

If maintaining deposit rates and realizing *capital losses* is not appealing, the alternative of raising deposit rates and incurring *operating losses* is not much better. Line 4 assumes the depository doubles its rate so that

---

[1]While the depository may well draw on its cash balances to meet some withdrawals, the fundamental principle being illustrated here remains valid: relatively small deposit withdrawals can bankrupt a depository when its assets are overvalued. Even if a depository could operate without any cash, 12.5 percent withdrawals would bring the depository to the edge of bankruptcy in our example. The super-creative accounting permitted by federal regulatory authorities in order to hide realized losses is hard to believe. Instead of reducing net worth by the amount of the loss, regulators suggested that S&Ls capitalize the loss, which would be amortized over the life of the asset sold and no longer held! This was too much for the accounting profession, which told S&Ls that their financial statements would no longer be certified if they adopted the federal proposals. S&Ls have two sets of books, one for regulators and another for accountants.

relative rates of return remain constant. This should stem any deposit outflow, but it causes an operating loss of $42.25 and reduces net worth to $7.75. Another $42.25 loss next period and the depository is bankrupt. It could be saved from capital losses and operating losses by tapping a new source of funds to counterbalance the deposit outflow, as line 5 assumes. If the depository can borrow at the deposit rate instead of having to sell bonds, or if it creates new deposits which people find more desirable and are willing to hold at the existing low deposit rate, then it can continue its operations. Lines 1 and 5 are effectively identical.

Which depositories face the greatest difficulty when market interest rates rise? S&Ls and MSBs, for three reasons. First, S&L and MSB assets, mainly mortgages and bonds, are longer lived. The average maturity (duration) of commercial bank and credit union assets is shorter, so their income responds sooner to interest rates, and the capital loss is smaller. Second, S&L and MSB assets are less marketable. Quite apart from the interest rate/maturity effect, any large "forced" sale of unmarketable assets will produce large losses. At least until relatively recently, S&Ls and MSBs were almost forced to adopt the strategy of paying higher deposit rates while incurring operating losses because their mortgage assets were so unmarketable. They simply did not have enough assets that could be sold readily. Third, demand deposits, an important liability of commercial banks, are less responsive than time and savings deposits to market interest rates. Therefore, when market interest rates rise, commercial banks experience less disintermediation than other depositories.

To make matters worse for all depositories, the newly created money market funds encouraged disintermediation. They made the public aware of the extremely high rates of return on money market instruments and other primary securities. In the eyes of depositories, money funds were the vultures ready to pick them clean just as they were down, and nearly out. Between S&Ls and MSBs, higher market rates probably impose a greater hardship on S&Ls because they hold a larger proportion of less marketable mortgages and more interest-sensitive deposits.

Table 11–1 presents data confirming some of these assertions. The first three rows show the very large interest rate increase between 1977 and 1981 and the subsequently smaller decrease. As our previous discussion of the term structure of interest rates indicated, short-term rates are more volatile than long-term rates. This is particularly troublesome for depositories because their deposit flows are more responsive to short- than long-term interest rates.

The next two rows present profits as a percent of total assets. S&Ls were slightly more profitable than *commercial* banks in 1977 and 1978 but then entered a protracted earnings slump. The 1981 and 1982 S&L losses would have been even worse if regulatory authorities had failed to adopt some policies spelled out shortly. The losses brought the already low S&L

TABLE 11–1

Market Interest Rates, Profits, and Selected S&L Data, 1977–1983

	1977	*1978*	*1979*	*1980*	*1981*	*1982*	*1983*
Market interest rates (percent):							
Three-month T-bill	5.27	7.19	10.07	11.43	14.03	10.61	8.61
AAA bond rate	8.02	8.73	9.63	11.94	14.17	13.79	12.04
Mortgage rate	9.02	9.56	10.78	12.66	14.70	15.14	12.66
Profits, percent of assets:							
Banks	0.71	0.76	0.80	0.79	0.76	0.72	0.72
S&Ls	0.77	0.82	0.67	0.14	−0.73	−0.62	0.24
Net worth, percent of S&L assets	5.45	5.51	5.58	5.25	4.23	3.70	4.04
Number of S&Ls	4,761	4,725	4,684	4,613	4,292	3,833	3,645
FSLIC payments ($ millions)		1	36	167	988	1,131	1,048
S&L mortgages repaid (percent)	14	13	11	8	7	8	13

Sources: *Federal Reserve Bulletin;* Federal Home Loan Bank Board, *Annual Report;* United States League of Savings Institutions, *Savings and Loan Sourcebook;* National Council of Savings Institutions, *Economic Update,* various issues.

net worth/assets ratio down to dangerously low levels. Note that the higher interest rates had no impact on commercial bank profits. Their short-term assets and other features served them well.

The next two rows show the impact of the losses on the industry structure and their insurer. The number of S&Ls held approximately steady between 1977 and 1980 but then decreased sharply as some S&Ls failed and, more importantly, others merged with their profitable brothers and sisters. Insurance payments by the Federal Savings and Loan Insurance Corporation (FSLIC) due to individual S&L failures are small relative to the S&L industry's total assets. Even in 1981 the insurance payments/S&L assets ratio was only about 0.15 percent. However, insurance payments grew significantly and were a large absolute amount, nearly $1 billion annually in the early 1980s. FSLIC payments remained high even though S&L profits rebounded somewhat by 1983.

Mortgagors, largely households, soften S&Ls for the money market vultures. They do not repay their mortgages when interest rates rise because either they cannot sell their homes or they choose to remodel their old house and hold on to their low rate mortgage instead of moving to a new, better house at a high mortgage rate. Look at the last row. Although the term to maturity of the typical mortgage is 30 years, the average mortgage in 1977 was repaid in about 7 years, or, equivalently, 14 percent of S&L mortgages were repaid as people moved and sold their homes. By 1981 the average life of S&L mortgages doubled, and repayments were cut in half. The long-lived assets of S&Ls became even longer lived. With fewer mortgagors repaying, S&Ls were unable to benefit from the higher market rates.

Regulation Q

The problems that S&Ls and other intermediaries face when interest rates rise were made more difficult by (1) asset restrictions to improve housing and (2) regulations displaying a depression-era mentality, particularly Reg Q.

Good housing is a long-established policy goal. This goal is reflected in many ways: (1) public housing and other forms of housing subsidies to the poor, (2) mortgage interest and property tax deductions for home-owners and landlords, and (3) accelerated depreciation and other tax benefits for landlords. In terms of financial intermediaries, this good housing goal was reflected in restrictions on the nonmortgage assets that S&Ls and MSBs could acquire. Restricting nonmortgage assets increased the availability of mortgages and lowered mortgage rates. However, it also had the effect of lengthening the average maturity of intermediary assets and intensifying disintermediation.

Reg Q, which prohibits interest payments on demand deposits and sets positive ceilings on time and savings deposit rates, also aggravates matters. The regulation initially applied only to commercial banks. The reasons for both the initial enactment and subsequent extension of Reg Q illustrate that poor policy occurs when government officials and politicians act before analyzing events and examining the data. We elaborate on the last sentence before linking Reg Q and disintermediation. Reg Q, initially enacted in 1933, was part of an impressive array of regulations designed to subvert the free market system, which was alleged to have fostered the Great Depression. So-called fair trade laws set floors on product prices, and Reg Q set ceilings on bank costs. The advocates of Reg Q claimed that banks were too competitive. Left to their own devices in the 1920s, banks *supposedly* paid excessively high deposit rates, and profit margins tumbled in spite of high-yielding risky loans made in an attempt to compensate for the high deposit costs. Hemorrhaged by a protracted period of below normal earnings, a larger than normal number of banks succumbed to the Great Depression. This theory could be correct. However, it has one basic flaw: it is wrong. The data do *not* show a significant decline in profit margins during the 1920s. Without the benefit of foresight, no one in 1929 would have claimed banks were weaker than in 1925.[2] The sound loans of 1929 were the defaults of 1933 through no fault of the banks. Lack of empirical support for the theory should have been antic-

---

[2]George Benston, "Interest Payment on Demand Deposits and Bank Investment Behavior," *Journal of Political Economy,* October 1964, pp. 431–49.

ipated since it attributes schizophrenia to bankers. When managing their liabilities, bankers supposedly allow their competitive instincts to rival the self-destructive tendencies of lemmings leaping to their deaths. Yet the collusive, fraternal attitude of bankers supposedly is so strong when they extend credit that society must be protected by usury laws.

Deposit rate ceilings were extended to S&Ls in 1966 in an effort to support the housing industry. Although low by the standards of the late 1970s, interest rates rose rapidly and sharply during 1965 and 1966. The higher interest rates had a strong impact on the housing industry, which is especially sensitive to the rate of interest. In view of the good housing policy, the government attempted to insulate the housing industry by (1) lowering the Reg Q ceiling on bank deposits, and (2) installing somewhat higher (0.75 percent originally) ceilings on S&L deposits. These two acts were supposed to increase the flow of credit to the housing industry by giving S&Ls, which are specialists in the mortgage market, a competitive edge over the generalist commercial banks. Moreover, the two acts supposedly would reduce the overall (bank and S&L) mortgage rate because intermediary deposit costs were lower, assuming the ceilings were effective. Granting S&Ls a competitive edge over banks did soften the perverse impact of the Reg Q extension on the housing industry. In other words, *given* that ceilings were placed on S&L deposit rates, the good housing policy was served by a positive differential in favor of S&Ls. However, the good housing policy would have been better served by not imposing any ceiling on S&L deposits.

Consider why the financial authorities incorrectly thought that a deposit rate ceiling and lower intermediary costs would reduce mortgage rates and stimulate housing. Everyone knows that when the wage rate or fertilizer costs fall, the cost curves for peanuts shift downward, and the peanut price falls. Shouldn't intermediary prices, that is, the mortgage rate, also follow costs, or are banks and S&Ls that different from peanut farmers? No, S&Ls and peanut farmers indeed are similarly motivated, but S&Ls will not reduce the mortgage rate in this case. There is an important difference between the *ability to buy* inputs at low prices and the *necessity of paying* lower prices for inputs. In the former case the farmer can buy more inputs and produce more, which lowers price. In the latter case, however, the ceiling reduces the amount of input (deposits) that can be purchased, reduces output (mortgages), and *raises* the product price (mortgage rate). Lines 3 and 4 of Figure 11–1 confirm the last sentence, particularly when the assumption of an exogenous loan rate is dropped. Line 3 illustrates that when intermediaries do not raise deposit rates or cannot because of Reg Q, their costs are lower but so are their holdings of perpetuities. Mortgages are the S&Ls earning asset equivalent of the perpetuities in Figure 11–1. Therefore, Reg Q *reduces* the mortgages S&Ls can make. Moreover, the bond sales (lower mortgages) due to Reg Q will *raise* interest rates further. Some intermediaries in an unregulated economy would respond to higher market rates by raising their deposit rates, as illustrated by line 4 of Figure 11–1. When intermediaries act in this manner, they can make more loans. Reg Q prevents any banks from responding and intensifies disintermediation.

New Mortgage Instruments and Housing Agencies

Proposals by various monetary commissions in the 1960s and 1970s to reduce disintermediation were largely ignored. However, the creation of new housing agencies and the strengthening of existing ones did help S&Ls and other depositories. Depositories did not wait for the regulators; they created new financial instruments to reduce disintermediation and increase their earnings when interest rates rise. Foremost among these were new mortgage instruments.

Until the 1970s the interest rate and monthly payment were fixed throughout the life of mortgages. Variable rate mortgages (VRMs), also called adjustable rate mortgages (ARMs), and graduated payment mortgages (GPMs) are now becoming popular although the fixed-rate, fixed-payment mortgages still are most prevalent. VRMs adjust the mortgage rate up and down periodically to reflect the current level of interest rates. Some home buyers want VRMs in order to avoid being saddled with a 16 percent mortgage for 30 years—interest rates some day may fall back to 6 percent. But buyers with VRMs also run the risk that rising rates will push their loan payments still higher.[3] GPMs allow lower monthly payments in the early years of the mortgage and higher monthly payments later. For example, the monthly payment on a $100,000, 13 percent GPM mortgage at its inception might be $792, or $236 lower than the fixed payment mortgage, but by the sixth year the monthly payment rises above the fixed payment to $1,136. GPMs were developed in order to facilitate home ownership, or better housing, in an inflationary environment. Recalling our earlier discussion about inflation and interest rates, anticipated inflation raises the mortgage rate and monthly payment. A 5 percent higher interest rate on a $100,000 loan increases the monthly payment by approximately $400. *Inflation raises monthly mortgage payments relative to current income and makes home ownership more difficult.* However, in an inflationary environment with rising incomes, any fixed payment

---

[3]Shared appreciation mortgages are a still newer and not yet common type of mortgage. In this case the mortgagor receives a mortgage rate that is one-third lower than the prevailing rate but gives the mortgagee one third of the profits from the eventual sale of the house. If the real mortgage rate were zero, that is, the nominal interest rate equals the inflation rate, the mortgagee would be indifferent between standard and shared appreciation mortgages, ignoring taxes. Tax considerations may lead the mortgagee to prefer shared appreciation mortgages even when the real rate of interest is positive.

declines relative to income. *Thus GPMs are a means of keeping housing expenditures as a percent of income approximately constant instead of declining sharply from a high initial level.*

VRMs and GPMs benefit the mortgagee as much as the mortgagor. From the viewpoint of S&Ls and other mortgagees, VRMs make the current yield on mortgages depend on current market conditions and effectively transform long-term mortgages into short-term loans, at least with regard to their yield.[4] By facilitating home ownership when interest rates are high, GPMs increase housing sales, the repayment of mortgages, and the flow of funds which can be invested at high rates.

Government agencies directly and indirectly lent more to depositories and made mortgages more marketable. The "old-line" Federal National Mortgage Association (FNMA or Fannie Mae) greatly expanded its scope of operations.[5] Fannie Mae issued larger quantities of bonds and used the proceeds to acquire mortgages from banks and savings and loans, which now had the funds to originate mortgages or meet deposit outflows. Fannie Mae was joined by the Federal Home Loan Bank System (FHLB), the regulatory agency for federally chartered savings and loan associations. It lent more to its member associations. Contrary to the Fed, which also lends to depositories, the FHLB cannot create money; it first must sell its bonds in the capital market and then lend to savings and loans. Fannie Mae and the FHLB could not do the job alone, so in 1968 and 1970 Congress created the Federal Home Loan Mortgage Corporation and the Government National Mortgage Association, dubbed Freddie Mac and Ginnie Mae, respectively, by the wags on the Street. While Freddie Mac and Ginnie Mae differ in many respects, our interest centers on their common feature: both guarantee and sell pass-through mortgage certificates which the originators of the mortgage continue to service. That is, mortgage makers form a mortgage pool, and Freddie Mac and Ginnie Mae guarantee the payment of interest and principal on pass-through mortgage certificates based on the pool. As payments are made on the mortgages in the pool, the proceeds (interest plus principal), less a service charge, are passed through to the certificate holders. Certificates with standardized terms are traded on the secondary market.

S&Ls could sell few mortgages directly to ultimate surplus units such as households. Yet, they have sold huge quantities to the federal agencies as collateral for pass-through certificates. The latter have proven very popular. First, pass-throughs are guaranteed by the government and come

---

[4]While there are some regulatory limits to the variability of mortgage rates, any stickiness on VRMs is mainly self-imposed in order not to alienate mortgagors.

[5]Fannie Mae was established by Congress in 1938. It was an agency within the Department of Urban and Housing Development when it was spun off and became a quasi-independent firm. Its shares are listed on the New York Stock Exchange.

in standardized terms. Second, those who live off their interest receipts prefer the monthly payments of pass-throughs to semiannual bond coupons. Moreover, the amortization of mortgages makes their annual payments larger than bond coupons. Surprisingly perhaps, S&Ls themselves have purchased large quantities of pass-through certificates after selling the mortgages which stand behind the certificates. Mortgage-backed securities now equal about 11 percent of S&L assets, up from virtually nothing a decade ago.

The MCA of 1980 further extended the governmental sources of funds available to depositories. The Federal Reserve's discount window was thrown open to *all* depositories that issue check deposits. Discounting previously had been limited to Fed member banks.

Major Innovations and Regulatory Reforms

The MCA of 1980, the GSt.G of 1982, various regulatory reforms, and financial innovation have reduced the severity of the periodic crises which engulf depository institutions. Consolidate material presented in this and previous chapters by preparing *a comprehensive list of financial innovations and regulatory reforms designed to reduce disintermediation and the sensitivity of depository profits to higher interest rates*. Complete your list before continuing to read.

1. Abolish Reg Q. This has occurred gradually, beginning in 1973 with market rate large CDs. In the MCA, Congress instructed the financial authorities to eliminate Reg Q ceilings no later than 1986 on all deposits except demand, NOW, and passbook savings.
2. Create new types of mortgages which transform legally long-term assets into economically short-term assets (VRM) or increase the likelihood of housing sales and mortgage payment (GPM).
3. Strengthen government housing agencies which lend to intermediaries, for example, the Fed and FHLB, and make a secondary mortgage market by purchasing and pooling mortgages, for example, Freddie Mac, Ginnie Mae, and old Fannie Mae.
4. Allow intermediaries to acquire a broader range of assets, particularly short-term assets. MCA let S&Ls place up to 20 percent of their assets in credit card loans, other consumer credit, commercial paper, and other corporate debt. Prior to 1980 S&Ls held less than 2 percent in such assets. GSt.G increased in 1982 the allowable S&L ratio of nonmortgage loans to 30 percent.
5. Let each depository offer demand deposits or other checkable deposits since these are a new source of less interest-sensitive funds. MCA let nonbanks offer NOW accounts, and GSt.G let them offer demand deposits to their *business* borrowers.

6. Let each intermediary offer a wide variety of time accounts so that it can tap new sources of funds. In the 1970s depositories began to issue six-month and two-and-a-half-year consumer-oriented certificates at interest rates tied to the comparable government security rate. These time deposits proved extremely popular to consumers; they quickly supplanted passbook savings deposits as the major source of depository funds. These time deposits proved extremely popular to depositories as well. When market interest rates rose, depositories now could raise the deposit rate on *new,* interest-sensitive time accounts while keeping the rate constant on less sensitive and existing passbook accounts. MMDAs made possible by GSt.G were a powerful weapon against money market funds. Depositories lower their interest costs by segmenting the market and offering an account matching each person's preferences.
7. Stiffen the penalty for the early withdrawal of time accounts in order to lengthen their maturity and better match asset lives. The maximum penalty for early withdrawals in the 1970s was foregone interest; in the 1980s one could receive less than the amount deposited when funds were withdrawn prematurely. (The precise magnitude of the penalty depends on the initial term of the account.)
8. Increase the ability of depositories to take advantage of higher market rates by overriding state usury ceilings (MCA of 1980) and preempt or severely limit state laws which allow a new homeowner the right to assume an old mortgage at below market rates (GSt.G of 1982).
9. Increase noninterest rate earnings. The Federal Reserve has expanded its list of "closely related" markets which bank holding companies may enter. (Specifics are in Chapter 13.) MCA granted S&Ls authority to issue credit cards, engage in trust operations, and invest in mutual funds and service corporations.
10. When all else fails, encourage creative accounting to make matters look better and avoid other regulations. Most examples, and indeed there are many, are very complex, but here are two you will appreciate.[6] According to FHLB regulations S&Ls must maintain a net worth equal to at least 3 percent of their liabilities. When many associations' net worth fell below this minimum, the FHLB suddenly realized that several liabilities were not liabilities after all but instead were negative (contra) assets. By reclassifying these accounts S&Ls met the net worth/liabilities ratio. Second, GSt.G provided a capital assistance program for savings institutions and

[6]Cf. footnote 1.

commercial banks. Institutions with a net worth deficiency were allowed to issue special certificates which, after being exchanged for FDIC or FSLIC promissory notes of *equal* value, are counted toward net worth. Instead of simply relaxing the net worth requirement, regulators swap paper between themselves and depositories until the requirement is met.

Summary/Questions

The first section on the reasons for the existence of intermediaries implies that nothing can totally prevent disintermediation since depositories must differentiate their deposits from their assets. However, regulations enacted in the 1930s or later by depression-era-mentality regulators greatly aggravated matters. When Congress and regulators finally recognized this, they acted aggressively on many fronts. For example, to forestall any impending panic the FSLIC in 1982 began publishing FSLIC = Safety in Spanish, Portuguese, and Polish translations. Much more substantive are MCA and GSt.G, two generally excellent legislative acts that reflect a post-Depression mentality appropriate for the 1980s.

Table 11–1 shows that by 1983 the financial position of S&Ls had improved greatly, in part because of deregulation and because interest rates stabilized. Note carefully that *higher* (upward change), *and not high,* interest rates produce problems for depositories. When the return on their assets has been high for some time, they can afford to pay high deposit rates. In spite of their improved condition, new proposals to aid depositories surface virtually daily. Some of the proposals seem worthwhile, but others are pure boondoggles. Which, if any, of these proposals will be adopted is uncertain at this time without a crystal ball. Let's hope that regulators who fought deregulation for so long do not overreact now. One thing is certain: *the sweeping financial deregulation of the late 1970s and early 1980s occurred because S&Ls and other depositories were at the brink of bankruptcy. In the process of rescuing depositories, they were made more homogeneous.* S&Ls currently offer checkable deposits and make some commercial loans. Table 11–2 shows two important ways in which deregulation and financial innovation have radically changed S&L operations in a brief seven-year period. S&L deposits subject to Reg Q interest rate ceilings fell from nearly 90 to 25 percent. VRMs, which make earnings responsive to current interest rates, are a growing, but still small, proportion of *total* assets because existing assets are long lived and repaid slowly. However, more than half of *new* mortgages were VRMs in 1983. The sharp drop in fixed rate mortgages between 1982 and 1983 is somewhat illusory as pass-through certificates based on fixed rate mortgages have

TABLE 11–2
Selected Savings and Loan Data, 1977–1983, (As percent of total assets)

	1977	*1978*	*1979*	*1980*	*1981*	*1982*	*1983*
Fixed ceiling (Q) liabilities (including NOW)	87	75	56	38	26	22	24
Small, market-rate liabilities	0	9	25	41	49	53	47
Managed liabilities	9	12	15	18	22	20	24
Fixed rate mortgages	86	86	86	80	78	75	60
Variable rate mortgages	n.a.	n.a.	n.a.	4	6	6	8

n.a. = not available.
Sources: *Federal Reserve Bulletin;* Federal Home Loan Bank Board, *Annual Report;* United States League of Savings Institutions, *Savings and Loan Sourcebook;* National Council of Savings Institutions, *Economic Update,* various issues.

replaced about 10 percent of S&Ls direct holdings of these fixed mortgages, as explained earlier.

1. What are the two main reasons financial intermediaries can exist even though the interest rate they pay is less than the rate on primary securities?
2. Define the "insurance principle." What is its more technical name?
3. Define "disintermediation." (How many other words have 17 letters?)
4. Illustrate with the aid of balance sheets and income statements that a depository with long-term assets and short-term liabilities must incur capital and/or income losses when market interest rates rise. What action avoids capital losses? What action avoids income losses?
5. Reg Q deposit rate ceilings reduce depository costs and, therefore, reduce loan and mortgage rates. True or false. Explain your answer.
6. VRM and GPM are acronyms for what? Compare VRMs and GPMs with the traditional fixed-rate, fixed-payment mortgages.
7. Describe various government programs and agencies which have increased the marketability of mortgages.
8. Prepare a comprehensive list of innovations and regulatory changes designed to reduce disintermediation and aid depository institutions.

PART THREE

Regulation, Structure, and Performance of the Banking Industry

General reasons for regulation, with specific applications to banking

12

We begin a series of four chapters on the regulation, structure, and performance of the banking industry. This chapter reviews the basic reasons for the regulation of banking or any other industry. Then each of four currently "hot" banking topics receives a full-chapter or mini-chapter treatment. Some of the specific banking issues important today were not the specific issues important 20 years ago, and some issues important today may be forgotten within 20 years. However, the basic reasons for government regulation in 20 years will be the same as they are today. Knowledge of the basic reasons for regulation is the best preparation for the currently unknown specific topics that will be "relevant" 20 years hence.

The material is divided into four chapters to accommodate the selective reader. I hope you will read the entire section; I think you will find it surprisingly interesting and challenging. Nevertheless, readers with little time and greater interest in other topics covered in the book should read this chapter if they have a somewhat theoretical bent, and then sample one or two of the following chapters. In order for those who sample only one chapter to get an adequate diet, two mini-chapters, 13–A and 13–B, are consolidated into a chapter of regular length. The more practically-oriented reader should proceed directly to a "specific issue" chapter. Here is your selection.

Chapter 13

A Who should regulate banks? In particular, should there be a single all-powerful bank regulator or several regulators with limited authority?

B	What are the appropriate product market limitations for banks? Should banks be allowed directly or indirectly through holding companies to offer a wide range of products such as insurance, investment banking, and mutual funds?
Chapter 14	What are the appropriate geographic limitations for banks? Should interstate or, at least, statewide branch banking be permitted?
Chapter 15	Is reform of deposit insurance necessary? In particular, should the amount of insurance coverage be changed, and should deposit insurance premiums depend on the riskiness of the bank?

Lack of Information and External Effects

Under most circumstances an unregulated industry achieves maximum *productive* efficiency in the long run. In other words, costs normally are minimized in the *absence* of any regulation. Cost minimization simply is in the producer's self-interest. In this case Adam Smith's dictum is valid: the pursuit of one's self-interest benefits society. Cost minimization benefits society because it increases the availability of resources for other uses. *Considering an industry's productive efficiency alone, there exists a strong presumption against regulation.* In order to reduce costs, firms call consultants and not their well-meaning regulator, who typically is not a better manager and technician than the average business person. Although regulations typically increase average costs, they can be justified on four grounds:

1. Lack of information about the product.
2. External effects.
3. Economies of scale, also called natural monopolies.
4. Monopolies not explained by economies of scale.

We consider the first two reasons for regulation and the type of regulation adopted before discussing economies of scale and monopoly.

Lack of product information misallocates resources. Products whose value and quality are underestimated are produced and consumed suboptimally. When economies were largely agrarian, there was a pronounced disparity in information about financial and nonfinancial products. Consumers could more easily evaluate the relative merits of tangible commodities such as varieties of wheat than intangible deposits at the First or Second National Bank. This partially explains why banking has long been one of the most highly regulated industries. Increasing productivity has produced additional as well as more sophisticated products and, as a result, spawned a broader based consumer protection movement.

Private firms realize the importance of information; many are in the business of providing it. Nevertheless, if an information void still exists, and if the problems caused by the lack of information are sufficiently great, then government intervention is justified. Two general types of regulation are prevalent. First, some regulations are designed to provide information directly. For example, cigarette packs warn us of the health hazard, and stickers on windows of new cars provide mileage information. The second type of regulation reduces the consequences of lack of information by making the industry more homogeneous. For example, newcomers to town need be less fearful when doctors are licensed. They can thumb through the Yellow Pages and with some confidence select a doctor on the basis of a surname similar to theirs or some other nonprofessional criterion.

Regulations address the information problems faced by three important banking participants: bank investors, borrowers, and depositors. At least with respect to large banks, the bank regulatory agencies have largely—not entirely—abdicated to the SEC their authority to provide investment information. The SEC defines and enforces "full disclosure" by large firms, including banks, to current and potential stockholders. (The extent of the additional information forthcoming because of the SEC's full disclosure laws is debatable.) Bank borrowers and other debtors have fared somewhat better in gaining information due to the bank agencies. The Federal Reserve administers the truth-in-lending laws, which have provided more and better interest rate information.[1] While SEC full disclosure and Fed truth-in-lending laws are designed to provide bank stockholders and borrowers with more information, regulations quite properly have *not* been designed to provide depositors with an important piece of information—the likelihood of bank failures.[2] Instead, regulations making banks more homogeneous and deposit insurance greatly reduce depositors' need for information. Restrictive chartering and asset and liability limitations, which are checked during bank examinations, are a few of the many ways of producing more homogeneous banks.

External effects occur when the *private* cost and benefit do not equal *social* cost and benefit because someone other than the producer or consumer of the product incurs a cost or benefit. The classic example of external effects in principles of economics is the air pollution generated by the production of steel. In this case the social cost of steel exceeds the private cost by the cost of dirty air, and an external *dis*economy occurs. There is a much better example of external effects: the creation of bank

---

[1]The greater information gain from Fed truth-in-lending than SEC full disclosure may simply reflect the greater demand for information by unsophisticated borrowers rather than better administration by the Fed.

[2]The FDIC, however, has sporadically and misguidedly in my mind proposed that its *estimate* of a bank's condition be made public.

credit and money. Banks' actions affect not only them and their customers but the entire economy. The next section on central banking analyzes the regulations to control money and credit.

Bank failures are a second important example of external effects. Any bankruptcy may generate some external effects as the full costs of the bankruptcy are not borne by the owners. The bankrupt firm's employees and suppliers may be temporarily unemployed, and its customers may lack alternative sources of the product. The external effects of failures are positively related to the size of the bankrupt firm. For example, the Detroit job market cannot quickly place thousands of laid-off auto workers, while the disruptions in the labor and products markets are short lived when a small pencil producer fails. Thus the Chryslers and Lockheeds in the economy are aided while ma and pa operations are left to fend for themselves.

For any size firm, the rippling effect of *bank* failures is wider and produces greater external diseconomies, at least prior to the FDIC. Depositors rarely lost everything when a bank failed; they simply did not recover the full value of their deposits. Typically, however, the partial recovery was significantly delayed. During the interim depositors were greatly inconvenienced and forced to reduce their spending, which in turn had negative effects on the suppliers to the depositors. Lack of information aggravated the external effects of bank failures. The sight of one failure generated widespread suspicion in everyone's mind. When one bank fails, is it not likely that some other banks are suffering from the same ailments? True, some negative factors are industrywide, but some are particular to a bank, for example, theft or poor management. Lacking information about the quality of the loan portfolio and other aspects of banks, depositors unable to distinguish between industrywide and particular factors ran and tested all banks. The outcome often was a banking panic which induced a recession.

Just as in the case of lack of information, there are two general types of regulations dealing with external effects. One attempts to stimulate occurrence of events which generate external *economies* or prevent occurrence of events which generate external *diseconomies*. Reserve requirements are a banking example of this type of regulation. They reduce the likelihood of "undesired" monetary changes that generate external *diseconomies*. With respect to bank failures, minimum capital requirements and asset restrictions are examples of this type of regulation. The second type of regulation reduces the consequences of the external effects. Deposit insurance clearly is an excellent way of reducing the external effects of bank failures.[3] With deposit insurance many bank failures pass virtually unnoticed.

---

[3]The distinction between policies which prevent failures and mitigate their effects is not perfectly sharp. Deposit insurance also clearly reduces failures by preventing runs on banks.

Economies of Scale and Monopoly

We mentioned earlier that cost minimization is in a banker's self-interest. This entrepreneurial quest to minimize cost naturally leads to a monopoly when there are *economies of scale*, so that total costs increase less than proportionally with output or, equivalently, average unit costs decline. When economies of scale are pervasive, cost minimizing firms merge and eventually become a monopoly, which maintains itself by blocking entry through its ability to produce at lower unit costs than new, small firms.

A monopoly is no more profit oriented than any other firm; it simply is in a better position to achieve its goal. Lacking rivals and restricted only by the demand for the product, the monopolistic firm raises price, reduces output, and earns excessive profits. *Monopoly creates external or allocative inefficiency*. Compared to other products, too little of the monopoly product is produced, precisely because the monopolist charges and earns too much. *In a free market system with economies of scale, attainment of internal or productive efficiency causes external or allocative inefficiency*. Regulation must strike a balance between the low cost-low price objectives.

Economies of scale are not a necessary condition for monopoly. Since a monopoly, however achieved, can earn supernormal profits, self-interest creates a tendency toward collusion and monopolistic industries whenever possible. Monopolies not explained by economies of scale generate all the evils of monopolies without yielding any benefits. Regulations which prevent or terminate monopolies are justified, although in some cases they may be unnecessary because monopolization may not be feasible. For example, an unregulated wheat industry is unlikely to act monopolistically because entry is easy and collusion among large numbers is difficult.

Charter, merger, branching, and holding company policies are the main tools used by banking regulators to achieve the twin objectives of letting banks take advantage of any economies of scale while preventing monopolies. These policies work indirectly; they create the industry structure most consistent with efficiency and competition.[4] Bank regulators have

---

[4]While charter, merger, branching, and holding company policies can strongly influence the structure of the banking industry, other general policies beyond the control of bank regulators can have equally powerful effects but often go unrecognized. For example, the "double taxation of dividends"—that is, profits are taxed first at the corporate level and then taxed again at the personal level (aside from a small exclusion) when distributed as dividends—coupled with the lower tax rate on capital gains than on dividend income, has probably increased the size of banks and other firms more than antitrust policy could reduce it. An example is helpful. Assume a corporation's pretax earnings are $100, the corporate and personal tax rates are 50 percent, and the capital gains tax rate is 20 percent, where the tax rates are representative for the well-to-do. As matters now stand, the corporation's posttax earnings in our example are $50 whether it pays dividends or retains earnings. If the corporation distributes the $50 earnings as dividends, the stockholder will have $25 after personal taxes. On the other hand, suppose the corporation retains the $50 and expands. Assuming for simplicity that this strategy raises the value of its stock by the same $50 it

exercised charter and branching powers for many years, although often *not* to promote a competitive environment because external effects interfered, as we shall see later. Merger restrictions are relatively new for banking even though they are a traditional tool of antitrust policy. Holding company policies also were developed only recently.

Questions

1. List four factors that justify the regulation of banking or any other industry.
2. Define "economies of scale" and "external effects."
3. Precisely what regulations can be explained by lack of information and external effects in banking?
4. In a free enterprise society economies of scale are a necessary and sufficient condition for monopolies. True or false. Explain your answer.

---

invested, the stockholder will be $40 richer when the stock is sold and the capital gains tax is paid. Thus the stockholder wants the corporation to retain earnings and grow instead of paying dividends. If dividends are taxed only once and the corporation does not pay taxes on earnings distributed as dividends, then a dividend policy would net the stockholder $50, which is more than the retained earnings-growth policy yields. In the 19th century prior to income taxes one bought "a cow for her milk, a hen for her eggs, and a stock by heck, for her dividends." Now stocks are for retained earnings and growth. While the double taxation of dividends may be justified on the basis of its progressivity or some other grounds, its effects on the structure of the banking or any other industry should not be ignored.

Bank regulators and product markets

13

Real estate magnates must be very superstitious; their tall buildings rarely evidence a 13th floor. Authors are less superstitious. Indeed, we effectively have two Chapter 13s. The subjects covered in the two mini-chapters, 13–A and 13–B, are quite different. The two are officially consolidated into a single Chapter 13 because each is quite short. The longer chapter is the minimum adequate dose of regulatory and structural issues.

13–A: THE CASE FOR AND AGAINST MULTIPLE BANK REGULATORS

> The dual banking system: The banking practice of paying high wages to loan officers, usually males, and low wages to tellers, usually females.
>
> *Anonymous student who failed Money and Banking*

We are not sure that the student who gave the above definition of the dual banking system deserved to fail a money and banking course. There certainly is much truth to that observation of bank hiring practices. Nevertheless, the dual banking system does refer to something altogether different. It is time to learn more about the regulators of the banking industry.

Bank Regulators: Who Are They?

The dual banking system is a banking system chartered, regulated, and supervised by federal and state agencies. The historical circumstances that led to the dual banking system in 1863 are presented in Chapter 16. For our purposes it is sufficient at this point to note that by 1863 all banks were chartered and regulated by their state bank commissions, which varied greatly in their approach to regulation.[1] Some state bank commissions were exceedingly strict, while others were lax. In 1863 a new federal agency, the Comptroller of the Currency, began chartering "national" banks.

Initially, the dual banking might better have been called the dichotomous banking system because from a bank's viewpoint the regulatory powers of the federal and state banking authorities did not overlap for all practical purposes. A bank was either a state bank regulated by a state bank commissioner exclusively or a national bank regulated solely by the Comptroller of the Currency.[2] Although the specific regulatory functions performed by state bank commissioners have changed over time, each state has managed with a single bank regulator. Not so for the federal government. When a major, new banking regulation was necessary, the federal government created a new banking agency. *The three federal banking agencies, with the date of their establishment shown in parentheses, are: the Comptroller of the Currency (1863), Federal Reserve System (1913), and the Federal Deposit Insurance Corporation, FDIC (1933).* Congress gave each new agency an immediate constituency by requiring all banks already subject to federal regulations to join the new agency. Moreover, it gave *state* banks an opportunity to join too. The availability of discounts and deposit insurance encouraged many state banks to become members of the Federal Reserve System and FDIC, respectively.[3] While state banks joined these agencies for special reasons, as members they became subject to the full regulatory and supervisory power of the *federal* agency, in addition to their state commissioner. For example, state banks joining the FDIC in order to purchase deposit insurance were subject to Regulation Q limiting deposit rates and other regulations. Not wanting to "rock the boat" as the federal regulatory base expanded, the

---

[1]The federal government had chartered two banks prior to 1863, but they no longer were in existence by that date. See Chapter 16.

[2]When the Office of the Comptroller of the Currency, an agency within the Treasury Department, was established by the National Bank Act of 1863, its name was appropriate. The comptroller did control, or at least significantly affect, the amount of currency. As we shall see in Chapter 16 on commercial and central banking history, the Office of the Comptroller was created to charter a class of banks which would issue a safe, uniform type of currency called national bank notes. With the creation of the Federal Reserve System, national bank notes were supplanted by Federal Reserve notes. Thus, the charter and supervision of national banks no longer is a means of controlling currency.

[3]Discounting no longer is the main reason for Fed membership.

FIGURE 13–1
Bank Regulatory Authorities and Bank Classes, December 1982*

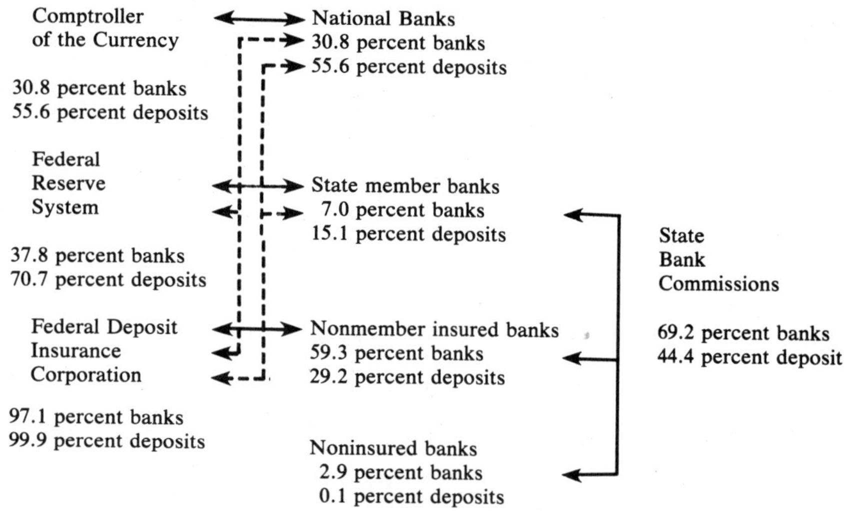

*Solid arrows connect bank class and effective supervisor. Broken arrows connect existing bank class and new nominal supervisor as bank class was automatically brought under control of federal agency.
Source: FDIC, *Statistics on Banking*, 1982.

new agencies assumed *primary* responsibility for the banks brought under federal control for the first time and let existing federal agencies continue to regulate their banks.

Figure 13–1 shows this layering of regulators and the relative importance of bank classes as measured by the percent of all banks and deposits. For example, Figure 13–1 shows that all national banks must be members of the Federal Reserve System and the FDIC, and the old-line Office of the Comptroller has been allowed to continue supervising national banks largely without the interference from the "new" federal agencies. Federal and state authorities have failed to achieve effective cooperation. Insured state banks, which are virtually all state banks, are supervised by a state authority *and* either the Fed or FDIC. Thus, the dual banking system has moved from a state or federal supervisory system to a state and/or federal system.

Besides the information presented directly, Figure 13–1 indirectly shows the relative size of banks in each class by comparing the percent of banks and percent of deposits. For example, national banks tend to be large since they make up approximately 30 percent of all banks yet hold over half of total deposits. Summarizing the more important features of Figure 13–1:

1. The Comptroller of the Currency is the most important banking agency as measured by the percent of deposits subject to its *primary* supervision.

2. The Federal Reserve regulates a largely captive group of banks; only a few large state banks have voluntarily joined the system. In 1982 approximately 70 percent of total deposits were held by Fed member banks.
3. Membership in the FDIC is largely voluntary but virtually complete.
4. Nonmember insured state banks tend to be small.
5. Noninsured banks are the only class of banks nominally and effectively regulated by a single agency. These banks tend to be very small.

Monopolistic and Competitive Regulations

Some banking tasks are performed by one regulator exclusively. The bank regulators along with the regulations which they determine exclusively or which significantly distinguish the regulators in terms of their effect on bank profitability, the structure of the bank industry, and bank performance are:

— *Comptroller of the Currency:* Charters national banks.
— *Federal Reserve System:* Sets reserve requirements and regulates all bank holding companies.
— *FDIC:* Insures deposits, and, thereby, has effective veto power over state banking commissions' charter decisions.
— *State Bank Commissions:* Charter banks and determine the extent of branching within the state.

Note that the Fed and the FDIC do *not* charter banks. When the Comptroller grants a charter, the FDIC more or less automatically insures its deposits. However, the FDIC is not so accommodating to the state bank commissions, the other issuers of bank charters. The FDIC seriously evaluates state bank applications for insurance. Since most new banks believe that deposit insurance is essential for their operation, the FDIC has effective veto power over state bank commissions' chartering decisions. The Federal Reserve exercises several important powers not shown above because they have little effect on banking structure and relative bank profitability, for example, open-market operations and discounting.

In contrast to the distinguishing regulatory tasks just outlined, there is a common set of tasks performed by all banking agencies. For example, each regulator is responsible for annually examining its banks, setting limitations on their activities, and evaluating merger proposals, among other things. *Monopolistic (applicable to all banks) regulations are much less frequent than competitive regulations applicable to only a subset of banks*. Competitive regulations dealing with the *same* banking issue often differ significantly. Reserve requirements were far-and-away the best example of such a situation prior to 1980. Up to that date only *member* banks had to meet the reserve requirements set by the Fed. The reserve requirements for nonmembers were set by their respective state bank commissions. *Nonmember bank reserve requirements generally were lower and could be satisfied by liquid assets such as T-bills.* The MCA, which set uniform reserve requirements for *all* banks *and* nonbank depositories, abolished an example of competitive regulation.

Important but less well-known examples of competitive regulation still exist. All state and federal regulators restrict the assets that their banks may acquire. For many years national banks have been more severely restricted than state banks. National banks were prohibited from making mortgages until the 1920s, long after states lifted such a restriction. In mid-1984 California let its banks directly purchase any type of real estate. National banks, on the other hand, can directly purchase only their own office buildings. (All banks can acquire real estate through foreclosures.) In another example of competitive regulation, South Dakota embarked on the wild plan of becoming the financial capital of the United States. In 1982 it broke ranks with all other states and allowed its banks to underwrite insurance. Bank of America (California) and Citicorp (New York) bought South Dakota banks with the intention of using them as a base to sell insurance nationwide. The ploy was unsuccessful because the South Dakota banks became subsidiaries of the banking giants' holding companies, and the Fed as sole regulator of holding companies scotched the idea of mixing banking and insurance. The Fed was able to intervene only because holding companies were involved. South Dakota banks not owned by a holding company technically can still underwrite insurance, though none are large enough to do so economically. Examples of competitive regulations can be quite technical. You may ignore the details but not the basic point: competitive regulations over important matters still vary greatly among banking authorities.

Competition: Destructive or Beneficial?

Some believe that competitive regulation produces a type of Gresham's Law—weak regulators drive out strong regulators. That is, banks search out permissive regulators and make whatever legal changes are necessary to come under the permissive regulator's authority. Even originally strict regulators become lax to remain in business and have some firms to regulate. The experience with reserve requirements does support the destructive competition viewpoint. The higher and strictly cash (nonearning) reserves of Fed member banks reduced their profits relative to nonmember banks prior to 1980. For example, in 1978 Walter Wriston, Chairman of

Citicorp, New York's largest bank, estimated that his bank's annual pretax income would increase by $80 to $90 million if it withdrew from the Fed and used its reserves for loans and investments.[4] Ninety-nine banks using similar calculations actually did relinquish Fed membership during that year. The ratio of member bank deposits to total deposits fell from 90 to 70 percent between 1945 and 1980 as some Fed member banks withdrew from the System and new banks opted for a state charter and nonmembership. The Fed responded by lowering its reserve requirements and loosening its regulatory grip over its dwindling members until MCA subjected all banks to its reserve requirements. At that point the Fed began tightening subsidiary features of reserve requirements and other regulations.[5]

Others argue that multiple authorities and competitive regulation facilitate innovations and a dynamic system. According to this viewpoint, a single, all-embracing authority may enact foolish regulations without impunity and, in any case, would be unresponsive to change. Advocates of diversity point to interest earning NOWs and the avoidance of *federal* Regulation Q by *state* MSBs. Chapter 11 explained why Reg Q never should have been enacted and why its extension to S&Ls was counterproductive. Nevertheless, that silly regulation was imposed by all federal banking agencies. Since most banks need deposit insurance, and the FDIC adopted Reg Q, noninterest paying checking deposits became the rule for many years. *NOW accounts were introduced in the 1970s in spite of opposition by the FDIC, Fed, and Comptroller.* Consumers earn interest on their checking accounts only because Massachusetts and New Hampshire commissioners were responsive to change, and mutual savings banks in those states were sufficiently well established that they did not need federal insurance.

We presented examples for and against multiple regulators. Where does this leave us? It is difficult to state unequivocably whether competitive regulation is desirable. The answer largely depends on one's views about regulation in general and the role of government. Those who view existing regulations as beneficial and seek a larger role for government generally favor a single regulator in order to prevent end runs by banks. Those contrary minded, who prefer the abolition of all regulat*ion*, claim that if regulat*ors* must exist, one all-powerful goose is worse than a gaggle of geese, each with limited authority. Consistency requires those who oppose regulation in general to support competition everywhere, regulators being no exception. Competition, to them, is always beneficial.

---

[4]"Banking in Transition," *The Bankers Magazine*, September–October 1978, p. 35.

[5]The shift from lagged to contemporaneous reserves, which is discussed in Chapter 18, is one example supporting the sentence in the text.

13–B: BANK HOLDING COMPANIES AND PRODUCT MARKETS

The bank is dead; long live the financial services institution!
*Martin Mayer**

The bank holding company movement inevitably triggered debate about the appropriate product market for banks. The movement began in the early 1960s and spread rapidly. Virtually every nationally known bank currently is a subsidiary of a *bank holding company (BHC), a corporation which controls one or more banks and possibly a nonbank business*. More simply, a BHC is a specialized conglomerate which has at least one subsidiary bank. To explain the growth and importance of BHCs, one should distinguish between two types of holding companies, one-bank and multibank. While the names should be sufficient to explain the difference between the two types, lack of definitions occasionally causes misunderstanding. A one-bank holding company (OBHC) owns only one bank subsidiary, which may have several branches, however. A multibank holding company (MBHC) owns more than one bank subsidiary. Both OBHCs and MBHCs may own one or more nonbank firms.

Table 13–1 presents absolute and relative measures of BHCs. The extent of the BHC movement often is underestimated by the public because the subsidiaries of multibank companies are legal entities with separate names, and the nonbank subsidiaries generally keep a low profile. More than one half of the banks with about 85 percent of total deposits are controlled by BHCs. Large banks in particular have found the holding

TABLE 13–1
Bank Holding Companies and Subsidiary Banks, December 31, 1983

	Bank holding company		
	One-bank	*Multibank*	*Total*
Number or dollars:			
Holding companies	4,444	615	5,059
Subsidiary banks	4,444	3,277	7,721
Deposits ($ billions)	474	805	1,209
Percent of insured banks:			
Holding companies	30.0	4.2	34.2
Subsidiary banks	30.0	22.1	52.1
Deposits	32.0	54.3	86.3

Source: Federal Reserve, *Annual Statistical Digest, 1983*, Table 83.

**The Money Bazaars: Understanding the Banking Revolution Around Us* (New York: Truman Talley Books, 1984), Chapters 1 and 2.

company structure advantageous. Should this cause concern? The BHC movement is widespread. Is it also economically important?

The Rationale for Bank Holding Companies

First consider OBHCs. While a few OBHCs existed for many years, prior to 1960 the bank typically was the junior subsidiary. For example, a large manufacturing firm in a relatively small town may have owned a bank largely for the convenience of its employees. The company bank has not been glorified in song but it did exist. The relative importance of the bank and nonbank subsidiaries changed as the BHC movement got underway around 1965. Large banks formed holding companies in order to acquire nonbank firms, some quite large and in industries totally unrelated to banking. Many feared that this was the beginning of *zaibatsus*, Japan's vast bank-industrial combines. Would these vast combines engage in cutthroat practices until they had driven out the competition and then exercise monopoly power? While attempts to monopolize the economy do explain a few OBHCs, much more mundane factors explain the creation of most of them. First, Reg Q restrictions in the late 1960s often made CDs an unreliable source of funds. Banks formed holding companies to acquire reliable sources of funds and circumvent Reg Q. In particular, the holding company could float its commercial paper not subject to these ceilings, using the proceeds to acquire loans from the bank subsidiary. Second, *de novo* entry in "closely related" industries let OBHC improve banking services and simultaneously take advantage of complementarity in production. For example, a bank may not have sufficient business to justify purchase of a computer. However, the establishment of a bookkeeping and data processing subsidiary may justify the computer and lead to better service for the bank's customers.

The apparition of potential *zaibatsus* was temporarily put to rest by the 1970 amendments to the Bank Holding Company Act of 1956, which stated that BHCs could engage only in those businesses "so closely related to banking as to be proper incident thereto." All BHCs came under the Fed's control, although the subsidiary banks still are supervised by their primary regulator as shown in Figure 13–1. For example, the Comptroller examines national banks owned by a BHC. Fed regulation of BHCs means that the Fed (1) specifies the "closely related" nonbank businesses which a BHC may enter, and (2) determines whether a BHC may purchase a specific nonbank or bank, which then would become a subsidiary. The Fed's list of permissible activities includes finance companies, mortgage banking, credit life insurance, financial advising, leasing, and data processing. Of course, a bank/closely-related-nonbank combine may decrease competition, though perhaps not to the extent of *zaibatsus*. Any decrease in competition is supposed to be outweighed by increased convenience and efficiency.

MBHCs were established mainly to surmount state branching restrictions and the prohibition on interstate banking. Many thought the bank subsidiaries of MBHCs effectively were branches although legally distinct, independent banks. Thus it seemed incongruous that some unit and limited-branching states would permit statewide MBHCs, and the federal government would ban interstate banking while permitting holding companies to operate across state lines. In recent years, however, it has become clear that circumvention of branching laws is not the sole purpose of MBHCs, some of which now operate entirely within a single statewide branching state. In some cases complicated tax laws favor the MBHC route to branch banking. Second, banks in relatively small towns in particular are alleged to lose substantial goodwill when they merge with a large city bank, so these banks retain their "independent" status. To be sure, banks under the holding company umbrella are not totally independent; management does set some guidelines for subsidiary banks. MBHCs exist in statewide-branching states because management believes the limited autonomy of subsidiaries enhances performance. The optimal degree of decentralization varies from firm to firm and, consequently, so does the position of subsidiary banks in the spectrum of decision making from independent bank to branch. Perhaps because of this diversity, the effect of affiliation within a MBHC is inconclusive.[6]

Controversy about the appropriate product for banks flared up anew during the early 1980s primarily because of the phenomenal growth of MMMFs and the acquisition of nonbank financial companies by large nonfinancial firms such as Sears and National Steel. As banks see it, MMMFs that offer limited check writing options are invading their territory, which simultaneously is being circumscribed tightly by Sears and other powerful nonfinancial giants with national chains. Banks argue that they must enter new product markets merely to survive. The Fed in response has widened its list of permissible, "closely related" activities open to BHCs, though not wide and fast enough to suit banks. *They are clamoring loudest for full investment banking and insurance privileges and the ability to sponsor mutual funds.*

Miscellaneous Bank Products in the 1930s

A review of bank product markets years ago helps us understand the pros and cons of bank entry into the three areas just mentioned. *Banks have traditionally been defined as firms which make commercial loans and offer checking deposits.* While this definition was supposed to distinguish banks from nonbanks, banks have routinely engaged in activities that have nothing to do with making loans on their own account or offering deposits.

---

[6]See Robert J. Lawrence and Samuel H. Talley, "An Assessment of Bank Holding Companies," *Federal Reserve Bulletin*, January 1976, pp. 15–21.

One such activity is *trust services*. Basically, the trust department of a bank manages other people's funds for a fee. At the turn of the century banks had an almost complete monopoly on the provision of trust services and derived a significant proportion of their income from such services. Banks remain the largest providers of trust services, but with the passage of time the relative importance both of banks in the funds management industry and of trust income to total bank income has declined greatly. The banks with the largest trust departments are Morgan Guaranty, Bankers Trust, and Chase Manhattan. None, however, gets as much as 10 percent of its income from trust services. First insurance companies and then mutual funds established departments that manage huge sums for individuals, corporations, and unions.

Investment banking was a second important activity of commercial banks prior to 1933. Even if the level of financial markets as measured, say, by the Dow Jones average remains constant, investment banking is a risky business. Profits are earned by being able to estimate (guess) the price at which new issues can be sold to the public. If investment bankers overestimate the selling price, they will bid too high and incur a loss. The riskiness of investment banking obviously increases during any unexpected and protracted decline such as 1929–33. Investment banking losses contributed to a number of commercial bank failures during the Great Depression.

The riskiness of the investment banking department stands in sharp contrast to the safety of the trust department's income, which typically is determined solely by the sum managed. That is, most trust departments charge a small percentage, say, 1 percent, of the amount managed irrespective of the return earned by the funds in trust. There is one easy way to reduce the riskiness of investment banking: stick it to the trust customers. In other words, have the trust department buy for its clients those issues which the investment banker priced too high and was unable to sell on the open market. The loss is shifted from the investment banking department to trust customers. Of course, such behavior is strictly illegal. The proverbial Chinese Wall is supposed to isolate the trust department from all other departments in the bank. The suspicion, right or wrong, that trust departments were willing accomplices coupled with the indisputable fact that investment banking is essentially risky led in 1933 to the *Glass-Steagall Banking Act, which generally provided for a separation of commercial and investment banking*. An exception for general obligation municipal issues was granted for reasons stated in Chapter 8.

New Product Markets for Banks

Banks quietly accepted the Glass-Steagall Act until recently, when they were joined by the Comptroller of the Currency, and to a lesser degree the Fed and congressional committees, in seeking repeal of Glass-Steagall.

The repeal process is slow and contested at every step. For example, in 1980 the Fed gave banks authority to underwrite commercial paper, which the Fed ruled was not a security under Glass-Steagall. The securities industry filed suit, which filtered its way through the legal system for years. The Supreme Court at long last overruled the Fed. Immediately thereafter congressional banking committees in their legislative packages specifically said that commercial paper is not a security and authorized banks to underwrite it. The full Congress is likely to agree when it considers the bill.

On what bases have banks sought repeal of Glass-Steagall?

1. Trust departments will be totally isolated from investment banking. Without admitting any wrongdoing in the past, banks claim that better monitoring procedures currently available do make possible a Chinese Wall.
2. The Securities Exchange Act, which requires full disclosure, has reduced the riskiness of investment banking. According to banks, investment banking is no more risky than commercial banking, where the repayment ability of firms up to 20 years from now must be estimated.
3. Even if denied full investment banking powers, banks have sought to underwrite revenue bonds issued by municipalities. They claim that the Glass-Steagall Act ignored revenue bonds simply because they were inconsequential at a time when local government believed in a balanced budget and tax rates were very low. The same reasoning that allows banks to underwrite general obligation bonds should apply to revenue bonds. The Senate Banking Committee recently agreed. Its 1984 legislative package, which Congress probably will pass, lets banks underwrite revenue bonds, in addition to commercial paper.
4. Justice, or tit for tat, is the fourth basis for repeal. Banks point out that investment bankers are some of the largest sponsors of MMMFs with check writing privileges. Equity demands that banks be able to offer a full range of services. Banks did not wait for repeal of Glass-Steagall before entering some aspects of the securities business. Many now have a stock brokerage department, which does not underwrite securities but does execute orders for its customers.[7] Charles Schwab, the largest discount broker, is a subsidiary of Bank of America, the largest bank.

Years ago trust accounts were separate; banks set up a distinct account for each customer. Now, however, banks often commingle small trust accounts. The distinction between a commingled trust fund and mutual fund is a fine one indeed. Banks claim that their experience in commingled

---

[7]For the difference between brokers and dealer/investment bankers, see Chapter 5.

trust accounts justifies their management of mutual funds. They buttress their claim with the same tit for tat argument—mutual funds as sponsors of large MMMFs have already indirectly entered the banking business.

Banks also make the tit for tat argument when they request authority to sell life and property and casualty insurance. Ordinary life insurance has a savings element, which banks claim would be most ably managed by their trust department. Large banks further point out that their size lets them take maximum advantage of the insurance principle.[8] The insurance department would be one of a bank's safest operations. Insurance companies do not deny this. They resurrect the old arguments behind the 1970 amendments to the Bank Holding Company Act. Insurance companies fear that the convenience of one-stop shopping will induce bank customers, who are nearly the entire population, to purchase insurance from banks. Moreover, banks may make the purchase of insurance an implicit precondition for a loan. It is difficult to say whether these fears are real or imagined. One thing is certain—banks do want to enter the insurance industry and are doing so indirectly. Banks have recently started renting office space in their lobbies to insurance companies. Banks charge square foot rental rates high enough to capture for themselves whatever advantages they may have had in selling insurance.

Questions

A1. List the four bank regulators and state the relative number and size of the banks for which each regulator is primarily responsible.

A2. What are the main responsibilities which distinguish the bank regulators?

A3. Explain the pros and cons of competitive regulation by multiple authorities. Give examples.

A4. Define the dual banking system. How has it changed in the past century?

B1. What are bank holding companies? Do they control a large part of the industry?

B2. What are OBHCs and MBHCs? Why were they formed?

B3. Why did the Glass-Steagall Act separate commercial and investment banking?

B4. What arguments do commercial banks give for reentry into investment banking?

B5. What other industries besides investment banking are banks especially eager to enter? How do they justify entry into these markets?

[8] See Chapter 11.

14 Nationwide branch banking?

As Maine goes, so goes the nation. Or will it be, as Maine goes, so goes Vermont.*

New York's Chemical Bank ad (see Exhibit 14–1) and similar ads in *The Wall Street Journal,* a nationwide newspaper, have prompted many to sound the alarm: nationwide branch banking is coming. Or, should they say, salvation is at hand: nationwide branch banking is coming. Before evaluating branch banking, the next section presents some current measures of the structure of the banking industry. It is followed by a review of the current branching status and the recent trends which led to outcries that nationwide branching is coming. There is a clear trend toward greater statewide and regional banking, but I, like Mark Twain on hearing reports of his death, believe reports of nationwide banking are exaggerated at this time. Whether nationwide or just regional, greater branching will significantly increase the average size of banks and reduce their number. Because of this, we review the data on economies of scale in banking and the relationship between industry structure and bank loan rates. From these empirical results we draw implications concerning not only branching but also charter and merger policies which can best create a structure consistent with low cost, efficient production on the one hand and low interest rates and competitive credit allocation on the other. In the final part of the chapter we discuss miscellaneous issues about branching.

---

*Adapted from James Farley's November 4, 1936, press statement.

EXHIBIT 14–1

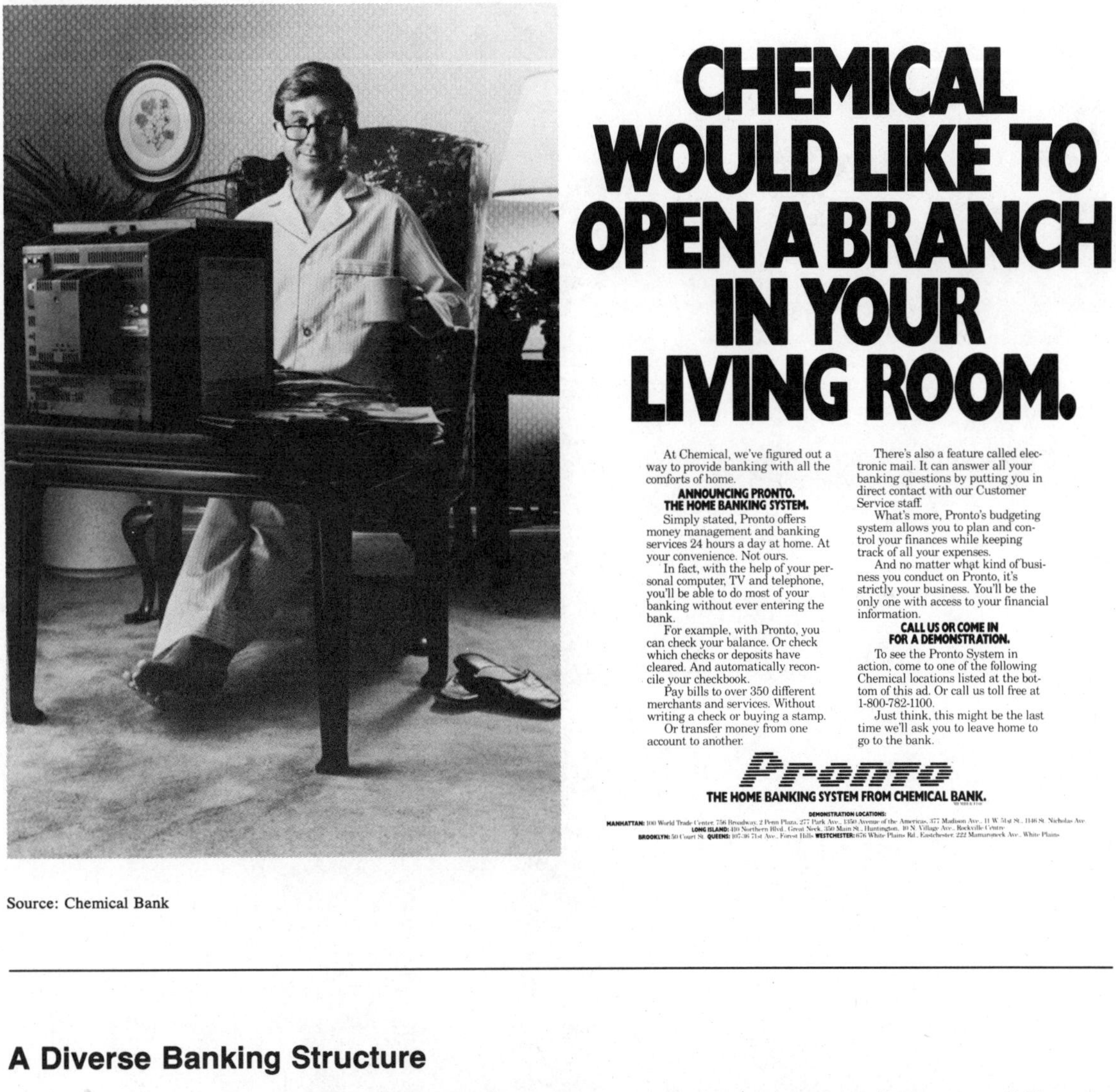

Source: Chemical Bank

A Diverse Banking Structure

Banks are hardly homogeneous. Perhaps the most important difference among banks is size, as measured by total assets. Table 14–1 presents absolute and relative measures of the importance of different size banks. The table shows that the United States is a country of thousands of pigmy banks and hundreds of giant banks. Each of the 10,000 small banks, or approximately 65 percent of all banks, has assets under $50 million. The

TABLE 14–1

Number, Assets, and Percent of Commercial Banks Grouped by Asset Size, December 31, 1982

Banks Assets	*Number*	*Number as Percent of Total*	*Total Assets ($ billions)*	*Total Assets as Percent of Total*
Less than $5 million . . .	510	3.4	1.7	0.1
$5.0–$9.9 million	1,517	10.1	11.6	0.6
$10.0–$24.9 million. . . .	4,332	29.0	73.3	3.6
$25.0–$49.9 million. . . .	3,773	25.2	135.2	6.6
$50.0–$99.9 million. . . .	2,505	16.8	172.4	8.5
$100.0–$299.9 million . .	1,576	10.5	252.1	12.4
$300.0–$499.9 million . .	258	1.7	99.1	4.9
$500.0–$999.9 million . .	216	1.4	151.0	7.4
$1.0–$4.9 billion	219	1.5	452.6	22.3
$5.0 billion or more . . .	45	0.3	685.0	33.7
Total.	14,951	100.0	2,034.0	100.0

Source: FDIC, *Statistic on Banking*, 1982, p. 19.

combined assets of these 10,000 small banks are approximately 10 percent of total industry assets or not even twice the assets of the single largest bank, the Bank of America! This structure is in sharp contrast to that found in most developed countries, where the industry comprises one or two dozen banks, and most are fairly large. If the United States has many small banks, it also has many large banks. Given the size of the U.S. economy, it is hardly surprising that U.S. banks rank among the largest in the world. What is surprising is the result of the more valid comparison of U.S. banks versus firms in other industries. No other industry comes close to having 45 firms with assets over $5.0 billion. Banking is a big business! Table 14–2 lists the true giants. Some are household names, but others maintain a low profile. Unmask the industry and learn the name of a bank a day. The bank ranked seventh in Table 14–2 will surely drop from the select top 10 list next year.

Tables 14–1 and 14–2 present static, single-period measures of the structure of the national banking industry. Has the structure changed over time? Are banks becoming more homogeneous? Tables similar to 14–1 and 14–2 for different dates would shed little light on these questions. Such tables would show that banks are becoming larger, but so are other firms, particularly in this inflationary environment. (Of course, the assets and income of other firms may be increasing *because* bank assets and deposits—money—expand.) Instead of dollar benchmarks we need relative measures. Such measures show that first, the banking industry is not growing faster than the economy as a whole. The ratio of total bank *assets*

TABLE 14–2
Assets of Ten Largest U.S. Banks ($ billions)

Bank	Assets	Bank	Assets
1. Bank of America (California)	$117.7	6. Chemical (New York)	$46.9
2. Citibank (New York)	109.6	7. Continental Illinois	41.0
3. Chase Manhattan (New York)	79.5	8. Bankers Trust (New York)	40.6
4. Manufacturers Hanover (New York)	57.6	9. First National, Chicago	35.1
5. Morgan Guaranty (New York)	57.2	10. Security Pacific (California)	34.0

Source: *Polk World Bank Directory,* Midyear 1983.

to GNP has remained roughly constant during the past 25 years.[1] Second, the structure of the entire banking industry has remained relatively stable. If anything, banking is becoming more competitive. One of the empirical regularities since the 1950s was the approximate 50/50 split of the industry between the top 100 and the remainder. That is, the 100 largest banks had consistently controlled approximately 50 percent of the industry's assets.[2] In recent years, however, the split has become 55/45 in favor of the smaller banks. Banks as a whole are marching in step with the rest of the country, but, perhaps surprisingly, smaller banks are running faster.

Branching

Each state determines the extent of branching within its borders, whether by state or national banks. Branching laws traditionally divide states in three classes: (1) unit banking, (2) limited branch banking, and (3) statewide branch banking. Unit-banking states prohibit branching altogether; a unit bank is located in one spot.[3] Statewide branch-banking states, as the name implies, allow banks to operate a branch anywhere within the state. Between these two extremes are limited branch-banking states. The limitation usually concerns geographical dispersion rather than number of branches or some other factor. Limited-branching states typically let banks operate branches within the county of the main office and contiguous counties. Figure 14–1 shows the type of branching permitted in 1984

[1]The ratio of demand deposits to GNP has fallen, but time deposits and the newer bank liabilities have made up the difference.

[2]Benjamin F. Kleboner, "Recent Changes in the Structure of Banking," in Federal Reserve Bank of Chicago, *Bank Structure and Competition, 1970*; and Bernard Shull, "Multiple Office Banking and Competition: A Review of the Literature," in United States Senate Committee on Banking, Housing, and Urban Affairs, *Compendium of Issues Relating to Branching by Financial Institutions*. Notice that our Table 14–1 also supports this empirical regularity.

[3]The "one spot" rule is often interpreted broadly. Illinois permits two *drive-in* facilities within two miles of the main bank office, yet Illinois is traditionally classified a unit-banking state.

FIGURE 14–1
State Branching Laws, 1984

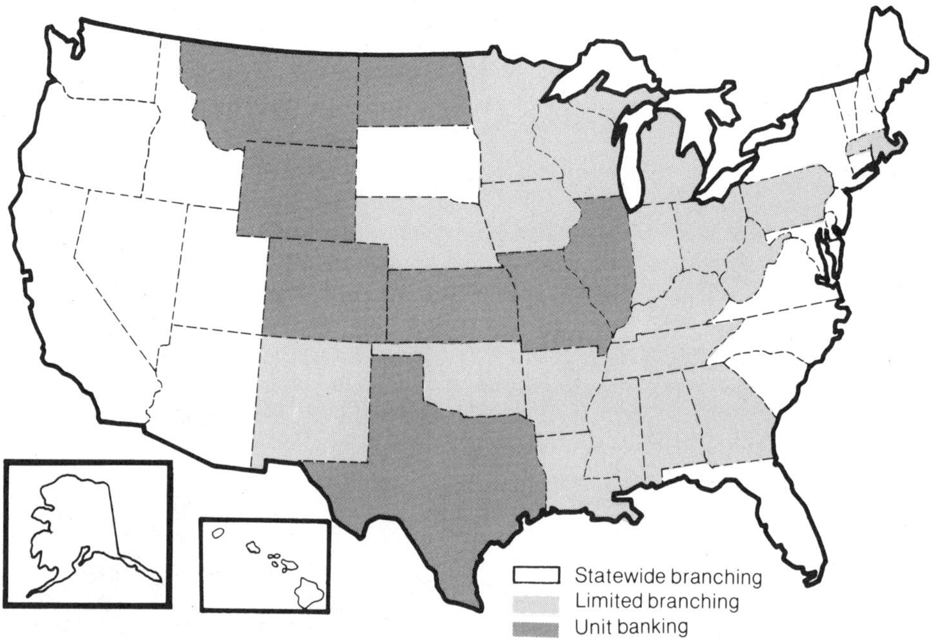

by the 50 states. A pattern to this crazy quilt of state branching statutes emerges: (1) the Atlantic coast states generally permit statewide branching, (2) the remainder of the states in the eastern half permit limited branching, (3) the Great Plains states are mainly unit-banking states, and (4) statewide branching prevails in the Far West.

Years ago the pattern of state branching statutes was quite simple: *unit banking virtually blanketed the country.* The liberalization of branching laws and the banking system's response is one of the more dramatic banking developments of this century. Figure 14–2 shows that in 1920 the United States was a nation of unit banks, which even more than today were *nonmembers* of the Federal Reserve System. Throughout the 1920s the number of small nonmember banks decreased significantly, largely due to bank failures, while branches increased moderately. The shakeout of the banking industry during the Great Depression had a more or less permanent effect on the number of banks; the number of banks has remained approximately constant since 1934. In contrast, the Depression

FIGURE 14–2
Banks and Branches, 1917–1983

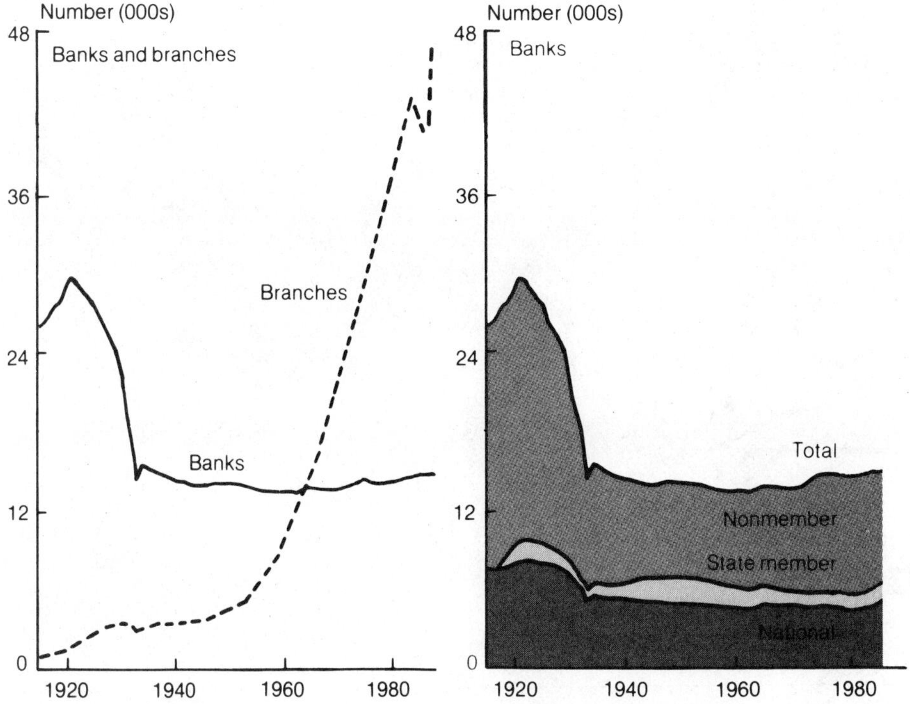

Source: Federal Reserve, *Historical Chart Book, 1984*, p. 82.

slowed the growth of branching temporarily, but by the mid-1950s a strong upward trend emerged. The typical bank now operates four branches. According to an old saw, as soon as a company was formed—and three is company—California's Bank of America opened a branch. An exaggeration, of course, but it does have about 1,000 offices.

Deregulation temporarily halted the strong trend toward branching in the early 1980s. Previously, when banks could not pay competitive interest rates, they offered their depositors extra convenience in the form of branches. With the relaxation of Regulation Q, however, banks began using interest payments instead of convenience to attract customers. Changes in state branching laws, population growth, and other forces quickly overpowered the reaction to deregulation, making the upward trend visible again. In the early 1980s alone, Figure 14–1 had to be modified to show that West Virginia, Oklahoma, and Nebraska switched from unit banking to limited branching. Is Figure 14–1 still accurate for your state?

The Beginnings of Nationwide Branch Banking

For many years most academic economists and others thought that federal law absolutely prohibited interstate branching, except for a few "grandfathered" cases. Numerous bank actions prior to 1980 were viewed as containing elements of interstate banking which, however, clearly stopped short of full interstate banking due to the prohibition. For example, wholesale banks such as Citicorp and Morgan Guaranty opened nationwide loan office systems. Their loan officers in Houston and other large cities throughout the United States made million-dollar loans. While they did not accept deposits, their possible suggestion that Houston borrowers open deposit accounts in New York could be very persuasive. More distant cousins of nationwide branches are the offices of "closely related" holding company affiliates. For example, consumer finance, factoring, and leasing affiliates of Manufacturers Hanover Bank, affectionately called Manny Hanny on the Street, have over 700 offices in 33 states. Affiliates of Citicorp, the largest of them all, have 1,000 offices in 40 states.

Bank failures and the electronic revolution accelerated the semblance of interstate banking in the early 1980s. When several banks on the verge of failing were too large for local banks to swallow, the FDIC engineered their purchase by out-of-state money market banks. Although "failing firm" exceptions to antitrust laws have a long history, their application to banking made it clear that any federal prohibition was not absolute. Moreover, the out-of-state purchasers were well known as aggressive banks that would do anything, including buying a failing firm, to get a foothold in another state. Systems linking automatic teller machines (ATM) in various states are another example of indirect interstate banking. Some allow, say, a depositor of the Bank of New York to withdraw funds while at a New Jersey supermarket. Finally, if a branch is defined as a facility where one conducts banking business, then personal computers and an 800 telephone number can readily turn your home into a bank branch, as the Chemical Bank ad indicates.

The nonbank-bank movement greatly heightened the semblance of interstate banking. The last chapter stated that a bank was traditionally defined as a depository which makes *commercial* loans and offers *check* deposits. Loan offices are not banks and have operated nationwide for many years because they do not accept deposits. The "nonbank-bank" of the early 1980s is the opposite of a loan office; it offers check and all other deposits but does not make commercial loans. Consumer loans and mortgages are its specialties. A nonbank-*bank,* as such a monstrous name suggests, is closer to a bank than a loan *office*. Hundreds of nonbank-banks crossing state lines were provisionally approved by the Comptroller of the Currency virtually before anyone knew what was going on. These nonbank-banks became subsidiaries of *large* bank holding companies with "true" banks and of mutual funds.

The Fed opposed the nonbank-bank movement. As sole regulator of bank holding companies, the Fed attempted to overrule the Comptroller. However, laws and regulations were such that the Fed could not single-handedly stop the nonbank-banks. Ingenious lawyers and *large* bankers found a loophole which the Fed and *small* bankers are desperately trying to plug. First, they turned to Congress. Pending legislation is attempting to halt the nonbank-bank movement by redefining a bank as a firm with deposit insurance or by making the definition of "commercial loans" so comprehensive that virtually no current nonbank-bank could survive without them. For example, commercial paper and federal funds sold would be commercial loans under the pending legislation. Second, small bankers, encouraged by the Fed, turned to the courts. In early 1985 a District Court ordered the Comptroller to withhold *final* approval of nonbank-banks while simultaneously allowing the Comptroller to issue additional *provisional* approvals.

The outcome of the nonbank-bank movement is clouded. Nevertheless, it appears in early 1985 that at least some nonbank-banks will permanently survive. Nearly all pending legislation has a grandfather clause. If large banks have their way, the growth of nonbank-banks will rival the earlier growth of branching so long as restrictions on true nationwide branching exist.

The semblance of interstate banking took substance with Maine's reciprocal banking law in 1980. Maine granted New England banks the right to buy Maine banks and open branches provided the other state granted Maine banks the same privilege. Maine's reciprocal banking law made it clear that federal law *per se* did *not* ban interstate banking; it only upheld state laws banning interstate banking. All states had laws banning interstate banking until Maine broke ranks. Many states then imitated Maine by passing, or at least considering, similar regional banking laws. Regional banking is often viewed as a temporary step necessary to strengthen regional banks before true nationwide branching and the onslaught by money market banks (particularly the New York banks) takes place. Sentiment for regional banking is especially strong in New England and the southeastern states from Maryland to Florida.

Maine, always the leader, has since graduated beyond regionalism. *Any* bank now may purchase a Maine bank, and several New England and New York banks have done so. Massachusetts banks have been especially expansionary in Maine and the rest of New England. At the same time, Massachusetts banks vehemently oppose entry by the large New York banks.

Semblance becomes substance which feeds back on semblance. Changes in the ownership and name of several institutions grandfathered years ago increase the semblance of interstate banking. In the 1970s the legendary Rothschilds purchased the BanCal Tri-State Corporation, which is the oldest commercial bank in the West and is licensed to operate in California, Oregon, and Washington. They sold the bank in the 1980s. Why would the Rothschilds, the first family of high finance, purchase the bank and sell it a decade later? Some thought that nationwide banking must surely be at hand. The Rothschilds were bailing out before nationwide banking greatly diminishes the value of the bank's unusual prerogative to operate in three important states.

The grandfathered First Interstate Bancorporation is the largest *multi-state* bank holding company—it has over 20 banks with 900 branches in 11 western states. Its banks previously had distinctly different names, for example, United California Bank and First National Bank of Oregon. In the early 1980s the holding company changed its name from Western Bancorporation to First Interstate, and affiliated banks became the First Interstate Bank of ______ (fill in any western state). Moreover, like McDonald's, it started selling franchises. For a fee *your* bank (*you* still own it) can be called First Interstate of ______. (It has been much less successful than McDonald's in selling franchises. Only five have been sold so far.)

In summary, greater statewide banking and some regional banking are already here. Will other states follow Maine and allow nationwide banking? I think so, but it will take many years.

Banking Structure and Economies of Scale

Are there economies of scale? Would an industry structure resembling that found in most other developed countries reduce operating costs and promote efficiency? Are there too many small banks? Recall that economies of scale exist when total cost increases less than proportionally with output, so average unit cost declines with output. A problem immediately arises: what is bank output? We have repeatedly referred to banks as department stores of finance because their diversified asset portfolio makes them similar to multiproduct firms. Small consumer loans, which are costly to service per dollar lent, may be viewed as a different product than large industrial loans to prime companies. The diversity on the liability side is almost as great. If the banking products were produced in fixed proportions, then total output would still be well defined, and product diversity would not be troublesome. But such is clearly not the case. A typical large bank is *not* simply a magnified small bank. Borrowers at large banks include the Fortune 500 giants, stock brokers, and wealthy individuals financing tax shelters, while farmers and consumers purchasing used cars are the customers of small banks. Care must be exercised

FIGURE 14–3
Relationship between Average Cost and Bank Size

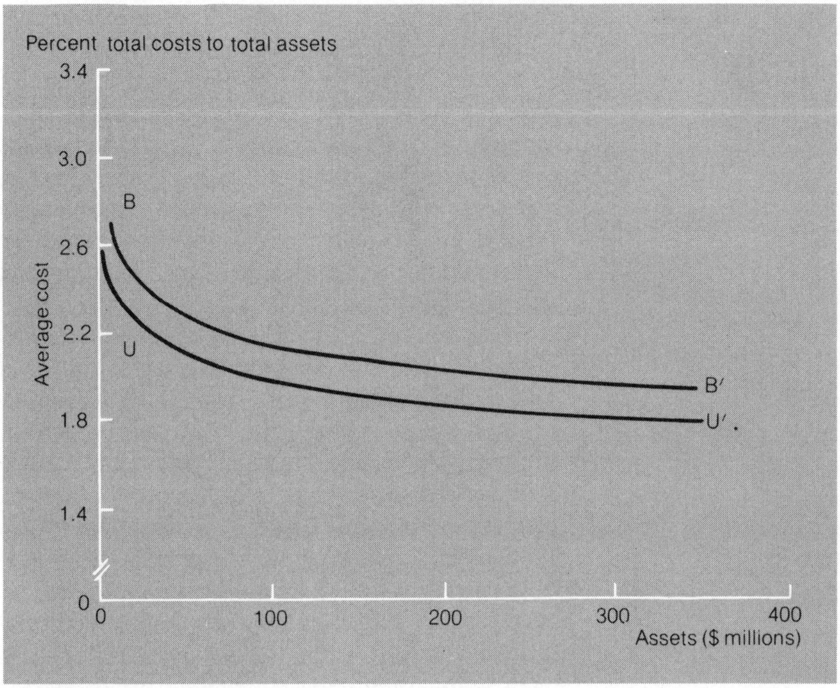

to distinguish true economies of scale from cost differences due to product mix.

One of the earliest studies was by Lyle Gramley, who collected data for *unit* banks.[4] After standardizing for product mix by including such variables as the ratio of consumer to total loans, regression or least squares analysis was used to analyze the relationship between average cost and size, as measured by total assets.[5] The curve UU′ in Figure 14–3 graphs

---

[4]Lyle Gramley, *A Study of Scale Economies in Banking,* Federal Reserve Bank of Kansas City, 1962. The appendix at the end of the book presents the regression equation which the text illustrates graphically.

[5]Two approaches to the measurement of output have been followed. First, the approach mentioned in the text, where a *dollar* measure of total output, typically total assets or sometimes deposits, is standardized for product mix. The second approach rejects the concept of "total output" altogether. Numerous *physical* measures of output are constructed, such as the *number* of demand deposit accounts, and cost accounting data allocate costs to each output measure. While the second approach is methodologically preferable, the diversity of results makes it difficult to summarize. Fortunately, the conclusion of the more rigorous second approach confirms the simpler total assets/product mix approach. The

the estimated relationship for unit banks. The graph indicates the existence of economies of scale: average costs decrease with bank size. The magnitude of economies of scale is not uniform, however. Economies of scale are significant when banks are small but rapidly diminish as bank size increases. Economies of scale are virtually exhausted when the bank attains assets of $100 million. Diseconomies do not set in, that is, the curve does not turn upward.

Another study by Schweiger and McGee arrived at essentially the same conclusion about economies for *branch* banks.[6] However, for any given size bank the average cost is greater for a branch bank. This is as expected. For example, the costs of operating a $100 million asset branch bank with, say, 10 branches should be greater than the cost of operating the same size unit bank. The curve BB′ graphs the economies of scale relationship for branch banks.

Given the efficiency objective, the implications of Figure 14–3 for merger policy are clear, assuming mergers are not associated with changes in the type of bank organization. *Mergers between small banks should be encouraged.* There are many to encourage. According to Table 14–1 the assets of approximately 85 percent of all banks are less than $100 million, the point at which economies become less pronounced. The cost savings through mergers of large banks are minimal, but diseconomies of scale do not set in. The implications for charter policy are somewhat less clear. A liberal charter policy increases the number of banks and reduces average size since the new small banks take some business away from the established large banks. Therefore, a presumption against chartering banks is appropriate, assuming operating efficiency is the sole objective. The presumption must be tempered, however, by the realization that the regression equations which the graph illustrates give average or mean relationships for all banks. The costs for some banks will be less than the graph suggests, and it may be that the banks attempting to enter are precisely the efficient ones.

Contrary to the first impression one may get from Figure 14–3, *branching does not increase average cost and reduce operating efficiency.* If bank size were independent of the type of banking organization, or, equivalently, if branch banking did not facilitate the existence of larger banks than would otherwise exist under unit banking, then the operating efficiency criterion would indicate that branching should not be permitted.

---

pioneering studies using physical measures of output and cost accounting data are George Benston, "Economies of Scale and Marginal Costs in Banking Operations," *National Banking Review,* June 1965, pp. 507–49; and Frederick Bell and Neil Murphy, *Costs in Commercial Banking: A Quantitative Analysis of Bank Behavior and Its Relation to Bank Regulation,* Research Report No. 41, Federal Reserve of Boston, April 1968.

[6]Irving Schweiger and John McGee, "Chicago Banking," *Journal of Business,* July 1961, pp. 320ff.

However, branching increases average bank size. Branch banks could not attain their large size without also incurring the extra costs of branches. In terms of Figure 14–3 the alternative is many banks up the low UU′ curve or one bank down the high BB′ curve. Are the average costs of a branch bank less than the costs which the branches would incur as unit banks? A priori, the answer is yes. In some ways branch banks are an assemblage of unit banks. The recording of checks by individual branches and the duplication of other functions inhibit the specialization possible in a similar size unit bank. However, like in a unit bank, the management of the investment portfolio of a branch bank is centralized, and specialists on various industries approve large loans. Empirically, the answer is a *qualified* yes. For example, using Schweiger and McGee's regression, average costs per $100,000 assets of a $240-million branch bank are $154 lower than the average costs of an assemblage of two $60-million and six $20-million unit banks. While it is possible to find a combination of unit banks with lower costs than an equal size branch bank, branching reduces costs *somewhat* for many bank size combinations. The efficiency gains from branching typically are *not* that large, however.

Banking Structure, Monopoly, and Loan Rates

Bank loans to *large* firms are made in a national market. A large firm is well-known throughout the United States. Its financial position can be ascertained by *all* potential lenders at minimum costs. The cost of acquiring information which a bank feels is necessary in order to evaluate risk is small and independent of the distance between potential lender and large borrower. Similarly, convenience does not dictate that the large borrower select a nearby bank. The large firm usually maintains deposits in several banks within a city, banks in different cities, and banks in different regions. Moreover, the large firm's officers are aware of the "going" rate on bank credit substitutes.

Although the number of effective banks to large firms is substantially smaller than the approximately 15,000 banks—small banks cannot service the needs of large firms—there are a sufficient number of large banks to assure competitive credit allocation to large firms. Look at Table 14–1 again. The assets of about 250 banks exceed $1 billion! The 100 largest banks control only 45 percent of the industry's assets. Such a statement could be made about few other industries. The national market for large loans is extremely competitive. Anything less than nationwide branching *coupled with the approval of all mergers* is unlikely to change the competitive structure of the large-loan market. Mergers between medium size banks will make *them* more competitive in the market but will not increase competition. It is immaterial if the assets of 250 or 251 banks exceed $1 billion.

The geographic boundary of the bank-loan market for consumers and small firms is not national. Indeed, many bank-loan markets exist. Small firms generally are known only by the banks in the immediate location. Banks lending to small firms outside their immediate area encounter additional information costs, and their risk evaluation will probably be greater. As the extra costs and higher risk evaluation of lending interregionally would have to be passed forward in terms of higher loan rates, interregional loans become poor substitutes for local loans. Thus, the market for loans to consumers and small firms is fragmented. These fragmented markets explain why small banks can exist in spite of economies of scale. Some small banks have the entire market and are more profitable than money-market banks.

The banking market in most small towns and SMAs (standard metropolitan areas) is not a monopoly in the strictest sense of the term. There typically are several banks. However, observation of the structure of local banking markets indicates that monopolistic elements could be present. Three structural measures of local markets influence loan rates paid by *consumers* and *small firms*.[7]

1. Number of banks in the area.
2. Concentration ratio, defined here as the percentage of the area's banking deposits held by the three largest banks.
3. Average deposit size of banks in the area.

Consider first the effect of banking structure in towns and small cities. In such areas, the concentration ratio typically is 100 percent: few towns have more than three banks. *The number of banks is the best means of distinguishing structure in towns*. Schweiger and McGee used data gathered by comparison shoppers for standard automobile loans in towns surrounding Chicago.[8] Illinois is a unit banking state, so each banking office sets its loan rate. The "shopped" banks' rates were averaged on the basis of the number of banks in the town. They found that *the average rate on identical loans was negatively correlated with the number of banks in a town*. For example, the average rates on automobile loans in one-, two-, and three-and-more-bank towns were 11.7, 11.0, and 10.7 percent, respectively. Note that the most dramatic reduction in consumer loan rates occurs when the number of banks increases from one to two. Further bank expansion does not bring as significant rate reductions. A second bank reduces loan rates by 0.70 percentage points or approximately 7

---

[7]Because the banking market for large firms is the national or even international market, the structure of the local market has no effect on loan rates paid by large firms. The use of assets instead of deposits in the concentration and size variables does not affect any of the conclusions.

[8]Ibid., p. 261.

percent. This is substantial considering that this area near Chicago is quite densely populated. In more sparsely populated areas where cities are farther apart, the interest rate differential should be larger.

What are the implications of this study for policy, *assuming competitive credit allocation is the sole objective*? In rural areas charters should be freely granted and mergers *between banks already in the market* should be prohibited, particularly when there are only two banks. Mergers between unit banks in small towns and branch banks that did *not* previously operate in the market will *not* reduce competition as the number of banks is unchanged. Indeed, it may even increase competition and lower loan rates. Although the small loan market typically is more monopolistic in small towns than large cities, the branch bank can exercise only the smaller degree of monopoly power because administrative reasons dictate a common rate schedule at all branches. A second reason for branching is the increase in the number of banks in *small* areas. Branches can operate profitably in areas where a unit bank cannot. Branching encourages charter applications.

The results for small towns, showing that loan rates fall more sharply in going from one to two banks than from two to three banks, suggest there is some critical number of banks beyond which additional banks do not reduce loan rates. The analysis for SMAs confirms this suspicion. Unlike rural areas, the number of banks in metropolitan areas is not significant because it exceeds the critical number. *In SMAs, the (three-bank) concentration ratio and average size of banks are the structure variables which influence loan rates to small firms.*[9] Bankers are aware that their decisions and rivals' response determine loan rates. The large market share of a few banks in highly concentrated markets facilitates collusion and the exercise of market power. Loan rates indeed are higher in the more concentrated local markets. Concentration in local markets does not influence the loan rate to large firms, which borrow in the national market. Consequently, concentration increases the difference between small and large borrower loan rates. On average for all local markets, concentration explains about 25 percent of the difference in the loan rate to small and large borrowers.

Average bank size is the second market structure determinant of loan rates in SMAs. The relationship between average bank size and loan rates is parabolic, as illustrated in Figure 14–4. Increasing average bank size first lowers and then raises loan rates. Loan rates are minimized with respect to bank size when the latter equals approximately $110 million. *Economies of scale and gains from market power explain the parabolic*

---

[9]Paul A. Meyer, "Price Discrimination, Regional Loan Rates, and the Structure of the Banking Industry," *Journal of Finance,* March 1967, pp. 37–48. The appendix shows the regression equation of loan rates on the concentration ratio and average bank size.

FIGURE 14–4
Small Borrower Loan Rates and Average Bank Size in SMAs

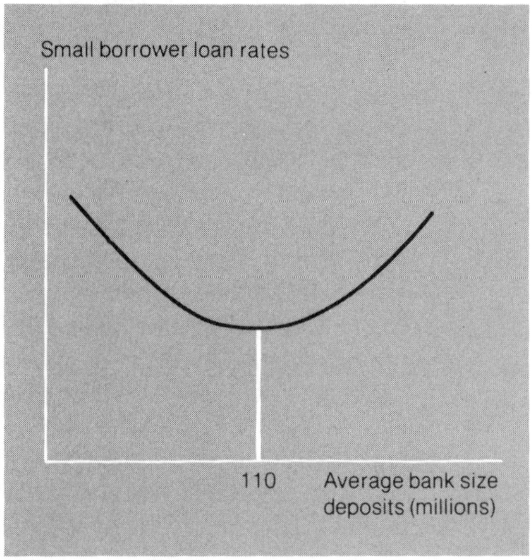

relation between bank size and loan rates. When the average bank is small, expansion places a large downward pressure on rates as economies of scale are substantial, and there is little incentive to curtail competition. As bank size increases, economies of scale become less pronounced, but the profits to each bank from restricting competition increase. The prospect of large profits encourages tacit agreement to limit competition. Banks are more likely to use their market power and restrict competition when average bank size is large. Past a certain size the net effect on interest rates of larger banks is positive because the small downward pressure on rates due to economies is more than offset by the upward pressure of a decrease in competition that enhances bank profits.

What are the implications of these results for charter, merger, and branching policy in metropolitan areas, assuming competitive credit allocation is the sole objective? Unqualified answers are impossible because of the parabolic relationship between loan rates and average bank size. For example, entry reduces, or at least does not increase, concentration so charters should be granted freely, *ceteris paribus*. However, entry also reduces average bank size, the effect of which depends on whether the market is on the downward- or upward-sloping portion of the curve. If the average bank is larger than the size minimizing loan rates so that the upward-sloping portion of the curve is applicable, then entry should be encouraged. However, a too liberal charter policy could create an overbanked city with too many small banks. Mergers have the opposite effect on size; they increase it. Just as in the case of entry, the desirability of the size effect of mergers is ambiguous, depending on the size of existing banks. Mergers in areas with a preponderance of small banks are desirable, *ceteris paribus*. Mergers involving one of the three largest banks or mergers between relatively large banks which leapfrog into the top three are undesirable because concentration is increased.

In small areas such as towns, branching increases the number of banks, decreases average bank size, and *reduces* concentration as distant banks establish branches which would be unprofitable independent banks. In large areas such as an entire country, the converse is true. While branching produces more banks in a small area, the same branch banks are in the many small areas which compose the total. Nationwide branching is the major force explaining the previously stated difference between the banking structure in the United States on the one hand and Western Europe, Canada, and Japan on the other. From the viewpoint of the effect of branching on structure, are SMAs small or large areas? Branching produces "large area" effects in SMAs. The lowest deposit concentration is found in SMAs in unit banking states. The magnitude of branching is largely irrelevant, however. For example, the median concentration ratio is approximately 74 percent in SMAs in statewide branching states, 71 percent in SMAs in limited branching states, and 60 percent in SMAs in unit banking states. Other measures show even less difference between SMAs in statewide and limited branching states.[10] *Branching is associated with higher banking concentration in SMAs and leads to high loan rates for small borrowers. The extent of branching, limited area, statewide, or nationwide, has little influence on concentration in SMAs.*

Consistent with its "large area" effect on concentration, *branching is associated with larger banks in SMAs,* counting only deposits within the SMA.[11] The desirability of such an effect again is ambiguous, depending on the size of the average unit bank in the SMA relative to the size minimizing loan rates. *Greater convenience is a definite plus for branching.* The factors which produce more *banks* in small towns located in branching states produce more *banking offices* in SMAs located in branching states, where either a branch or unit bank is one banking office. For example, in New York City and Chicago there are 9,000 and 34,000 people,

---

[10]Alan E. Grunewald, "Economic Necessity for Interstate Banking," in Federal Reserve Bank of Chicago, *Proceedings of a Conference on Bank Structure and Competition, 1979,* p. 241.

[11]Average bank size and the three-bank concentration ratio are not necessarily related. For example, suppose an area has three $100-million deposit banks and five $20-million deposit banks. Average bank size is $50 million ($400 million/8), and the three-bank concentration ratio is 75 ($300/$400). If all five small banks merged, average bank size would increase to $100 million, but concentration remains constant.

respectively, per banking office.[12] New York permits branching while Illinois does not.

If SMAs are the markets for small firms and the nation is the market for large firms, are states the market for medium-size firms? Since certainly statewide and very possibly interstate branching increase statewide concentration, should they be prohibited? The answer to both questions is no. There are firms that can borrow outside the city in which they are located but not throughout the entire country. However, states with boundaries often determined by the whim of a monarch 200 years ago are the banking markets for few such firms. Because states are not banking markets, statewide concentration ratios are meaningless. Moreover, the theory of linked oligopoly—which alleges that performance is enhanced by different oligopolists in each market, as occurs in unit and limited branch-banking states, instead of a common set of oligopolists in all markets, as would occur under interstate branching—is untested. In *United States* v. *Marine Bancorporation* the Supreme Court rejected statewide banking markets and the linked oligopoly theory.

> There has been no persuasive showing that the effect of the merger on a statewide basis may be substantially to lessen competition within the meaning of Section 7 [of the Clayton Act]. The Government's underlying concern for a linkage or network of statewide oligopolistic banking markets is, on the record at least, considerably closer to "ephemeral possibilities" than to "probabilities." To assume, on the basis of essentially no evidence, that the challenged merger will tend to produce a statewide linkage of oligopolies is to espouse a per se rule against geographic market extension mergers like the one at issue here. No Section 7 case from this Court has gone that far, and we do not do so today.[13]

Branching and Bank Failures

The 1920s generally were prosperous years for most Americans except small-town bankers, particularly those in farming areas. The growing use of automobiles and greater mobility generally reduced the monopoly power of small-town banks as individuals now had access to banks a few miles down the road. Moreover, the continuing relative decline of agriculture and farm income led to out-migration, reduced the average size of deposits, and lowered the quality of assets of banks in farm areas. Inability to adapt to these changes in demand and population is the main explanation for the failures of the 1920s. It often is not appreciated that *unit banking laws are artificial constraints severely hampering adaptability to demand shifts.*

---

[12] *Ibid.*, p. 234.

[13] 418 U.S. 602 (1974) as quoted in *ibid.*, pp. 236–37.

The high concentration of the 1920s bank failures in the Plains States from Texas to North Dakota supports this demand shift explanation for the failures. Moreover, Figure 14–2, which shows that branching was rare in the 1920s, is consistent with the hypothesis that unit banking magnifies the consequences of any given shock, hampers adaptability, and increases failures. Branching is a means of diversification; branch banks draw on a wider geographical area, which reduces the consequence of many shocks. The decline of one branch due to, say, a new highway bypass is not catastrophic when it is one of 10 branches. In fact, the decline of one branch may aid another branch, leaving the total system relatively unaffected. Mergers in branching states are a possible response to demand shift. Large banks could purchase small banks encountering temporary difficulties and convert them to branches. A branch office may be profitable although it will fail as an independent bank because branching facilitates the transfer of funds and loans. In order for a unit bank to succeed, it must find both a source of funds and a demand for loans. Branch banks on the other hand may have some branches which effectively act as collectors of deposits to be lent by other branches where loan demand is high. In unit-banking states, however, mergers typically are not a viable response because the banking office must be closed.[14]

Questions

1. Describe the current structure of the overall U.S. banking industry with respect to (1) the number and size distribution of banks and (2) the extent of branching. How has the structure changed over time?
2. Give some illustrations supporting the hypothesis that nationwide branching is coming.
3. Appropriate measures of the structure of the banking industry depend on the size of the borrower. Explain.
4. Do economies of scale exist? What charter, merger, and branching policies promote economies of scale and operating efficiency?
5. What measures of local banking structure influence loan rates paid by consumers and small firms in (*a*) small towns, and (*b*) SMAs? What charter, merger, and branching policies promote competitive credit allocation in local markets?
6. Discuss the relationship between branching and bank failures.

[14]The recent, well-publicized difficulties of Continental Illinois, located in a unit banking state, support the text. With only one office, Continental Illinois had virtually no "retail" banking and was highly dependent on large uninsured deposits, which are highly responsive to any rumors of bankruptcies.

15 Deposit insurance and policies to prevent bank failures

Bankers are not supposed to be smart. Bankers are supposed to be safe.

Chapter 11 indicated that concern about the solvency of financial institutions, particularly S&Ls, helped prompt the financial deregulation of the late 1970s and 1980s. The same concern plus heightened awareness by regulators that bank deposit insurance, like any other insurance, creates a moral hazard has led to a reevaluation of FDIC policies, which is the chapter's first topic.

A moral hazard occurs when insurance entices the insured to act in a manner that increases the likelihood of the event being insured against. For example, insurance creates a moral hazard when smokers become more careless after buying fire insurance or when bankers take greater risks after acquiring deposit insurance. What policies will reduce the moral hazard of deposit insurance, and what are the consequences of such policies? These are some questions about deposit insurance answered in the first part of this chapter. Although we explicitly discuss the FDIC and *bank* deposit insurance, many policy issues apply virtually intact for the Federal Savings and Loan Insurance Corporation (FSLIC) and *nonbank* deposit insurance. The FDIC, however, is in much better financial condition.

Regulators did *not* acquire a totally new concern in the late 1970s, and the possibility of a moral hazard had *not* escaped them altogether. *The prevention of bankruptcy has been the most important objective of bank regulation since at least the 1930s.* Deregulation and a reevaluation of deposit insurance occurred because by the late 1970s current policies were no longer meeting that objective, not because the objective changed. The last part of the chapter discusses some policies initiated years ago to reduce bank failures that are still in effect today.

Can We Count on the FDIC?

Federal deposit insurance came into existence in 1933 with the creation of the FDIC. Note: Congress created a *new corporation* specifically to provide insurance. The Treasury does not *explicitly* insure deposits. It did contribute capital to get the FDIC started and agreed to lend it $3 billion should the need arise. Like all insurance companies the FDIC collects premiums. *Deposit insurance is not a free good.* The uniform (applicable to all banks) legal premium is 1/12 percent of *total domestic deposits*. Again, like many insurance companies, the FDIC rebates part of the premium when it has a "good experience." For many years the effective premium was one half of the legal premium. Due to recent losses and a provision of Garn-St. Germain, the rebate has been substantially reduced.

Premiums have consistently exceeded losses. As a result the FDIC's reserve or capital accumulation fund has grown. Still, the reserve is somewhat less than 1 percent of total deposits. Is this reserve adequate? Some feel the question is silly. After all, we are talking about *federal* insurance, and the government always could print money to pay depositors. What the government can and will do may differ, however. The Treasury does *not* have a legal obligation to rescue the FDIC. Indeed, a corporation was created to leave space between the Treasury and insurance. While I am confident that Congress will authorize the Treasury to cover whatever losses the FDIC cannot sustain, the FDIC is less certain. The chapter, "Adequacy of the Insurance Fund and Revisions to Assessment Procedures," in the FDIC's report, *Deposit Insurance in a Changing Environment,* attempts to prove that the FDIC can do the job alone.

The FDIC is correct; chances are small that the Treasury will need to rescue the FDIC. Its reserve equal to 1 percent of total deposits should be adequate to cover the failure of banks with 10 percent of total industry deposits. This is so because a failed bank's assets are not totally worthless; they typically are worth 90 percent of deposits. The FDIC has to make up only the remainder. Since it is unlikely that banks with 10 percent of total industry deposits will fail, we can count on the FDIC.

What Is the Appropriate Amount of Insurance?

Reducing the external effects of bank failures is the major justification for deposit insurance. Insurance immediately frees deposits at failed banks. Insured depositors of failed banks can continue spending without interruption, and the insured depositors of existing banks do not have to test their banks' solvency. Although the external effects argument calls for complete, 100 percent deposit insurance, it is incomplete, at least from a legal viewpoint. Depositors' accounts at *each* insured bank currently (1984) are insured for $100,000. Although the deposits of insured banks nearly equal total deposits according to Figure 13–1, only 70 percent of total deposits are insured.[1] This is explained by the existence of large accounts exceeding the insurance limit.

What is the rationale for the $100,000 limit? Why isn't deposit insurance complete in order to reduce more fully the external effects of bank failures? A subsidiary reason for insurance and moral hazard suggest that deposit insurance be limited. First, there is the "only little people lack information" argument. According to this argument, society has, in effect, compelled nearly everyone to have a bank account. Small depositors cannot be expected to have good information and should be protected. Large depositors, on the other hand, should be able to evaluate the solvency of banks and need no more protection than little people need. Perhaps $100,000 insurance already is too much for "little people."

The second argument says that 100 percent deposit insurance creates the moral hazard of encouraging excessive risk taking by banks, given the current insurance premium structure. Risk-loving banks can pay higher deposit rates and offer other inducements because they expect to earn a higher average return. Risk-loving banks, whether insured or not, are unlikely to attract funds from a large number of *small* depositors. The higher deposit *rates* or other inducements offered by these banks have little impact on the *dollar* income of small depositors and, consequently, do not compensate them for the inconvenience of dealing with distant or unknown banks. On the other hand, fully insured *large* depositors with nothing to lose would be highly responsive to risk-loving banks' inducements. Risk-loving banks clearly fail more frequently. Insurance is limited in order to prevent risk-loving banks from expanding by taking large depositors away from their conservative colleagues. Uninsured large depositors sharply limit the ability of risky banks to dominate the industry. With little to gain and much to lose from risk-taking bankers, the uninsured large depositor selects the conservative banker with a gray pin-stripe suit. In order to maintain their uninsured large depositors and grow, bankers limit their risk taking, and, *ceteris paribus,* bank failures are less likely.

The *ceteris paribus* condition in the last sentence is extremely important. Because the condition often will not be satisfied, limited deposit insurance does *not* necessarily reduce bank failures. Anything less than 100 percent deposit insurance does not altogether stop withdrawals when

---

[1]Stanley Silverberg, "Implications of Changes in the Effective Level of Deposit Insurance Coverage," in Federal Reserve Bank of Chicago, *Proceedings of a Conference on Bank Structure and Competition, 1980.*

a bank's condition is thought to be precarious. Particularly when banks are illiquid, massive withdrawals and the forced sale of assets enhance the likelihood of failure. Continental Illinois, the giant (see Table 14–2) which ran into grave difficulties in 1984, vividly illustrates this. *Compared to 100 percent insurance, limited deposit insurance increases the likelihood of bank failures due to bank runs and illiquidity while reducing bank failures due to risk taking by bankers.* Which of these factors dominate? While adoption of the current limited deposit insurance system clearly has reduced bank failures, it is unclear that extension to 100 percent insurance will further decrease failures.[2] One can get too much of a good thing. Continental Illinois, however, could not get enough. The FDIC broke *legal* tradition by publicly announcing that all Continental depositors, however large, would be 100 percent insured. Even this did not stop massive deposit withdrawals. Anything less would certainly have caused instant failure and possibly a nationwide liquidity crisis.

Methods of Handling Bank Failures and the Ex-Ante/Ex-Post Dilemma

Is the Continental Illinois case truly unique from the viewpoint of deposit insurance? Had deposit insurance *in fact* been limited up to that time? No, but large depositors thought that insurance was effectively limited, at least until the early 1970s. In 1974 the Franklin National Bank failed, the first truly large bank to do so since the 1930s. In the five months between publication of the Franklin's precarious financial condition and its official closure, the Fed lent the Franklin $1.7 billion in an effort to keep the bank afloat as large depositors were closing their accounts. However, no depositor or general creditor, however large, incurred any loss because of the way the FDIC handled the failure. *The FDIC has handled the majority of bank failures and all large bank (over $100 million deposits) failures prior to 1982 through purchase and assumption (P&A).* In the P&A method another bank bids to purchase some or all of the assets and assumes *all* the deposit liabilities of the failed bank. Since a bank fails because its liabilities exceed assets, the FDIC makes a cash payment to the highest bidder equal to the liabilities assumed minus the amount bid for the assets. The payment often is quite small because expansion-minded banks seeking new customers and facilities bid a premium for the assets. *In P&A cases every depositor in a bank that fails today holds equal deposits in a solvent bank tomorrow.*

The alternative method of handlng failures is the payout, where the FDIC immediately pays off the *insured* deposits, acquires but eventually liquidates the assets, and shares the loss with uninsured depositors to the extent the liquidated assets are short of deposits. The method of disposal,

---

[2]Technically speaking, the relationship between bank failures and the insurance limit may not be monotonic.

P&A or payout, supposedly is selected to minimize FDIC cost, but the exclusive use of the P&A method for large banks prior to 1982 indicates that external effects weigh heavily in the FDIC's mind. It does not want a bank failure to disrupt the economy. Because large depositors do suffer losses when the payout method is adopted, the payout method had been applied only to small banks, which have few large depositors—if there were many, the bank would not be small.[3]

By 1980 nearly everyone believed that *all* deposits at *large* banks were effectively 100 percent insured. Failing or risky banks hired money brokers to funnel large deposits their way and keep them afloat. Money brokers could easily deliver millions of dollars because large depositors did not evaluate the condition of large banks using brokers. In 1982 the FDIC decided the practice had to stop. It used the payout method to close the Penn Square, a large Oklahoma bank that made too many risky loans to oil companies. Large depositors suffered greatly.

The FDIC reverted to the P&A method in the next large failure, the United American Bank of Knoxville. Nevertheless, large depositors remained wary of money broker operations following their loss in Penn Square. Always enterprising and adaptable, money brokers changed their operating method. They became retail brokers, dividing huge sums into many $100,000 pieces and placing each piece in a different bank. In this manner the large sum was legally insured. The FDIC lashed out at money brokers once more. In 1984 it proposed that deposits be insured for $100,000 only if the depositor opened the account directly. If a money broker opened $100,000 accounts at First National for, say, 50 customers, then according to the FDIC proposal all 50 accounts would be insured for $100,000 or, equivalently, each account would be insured for $2,000. The courts ruled against the FDIC proposal even before it was implemented. The FDIC is appealing, and it may still prevail. It continues to view money brokers as the scourges of the deposit insurance system. Who are these money brokers? Hardly any are pariahs in anyone's mind except the FDIC. Indeed, many are highly respected. The leading money broker is Merrill Lynch.

A conflict between the basic objective of deposit insurance and the moral hazard that insurance creates causes the cat and mouse games by the FDIC and money brokers. Insurance should be *limited ex-ante* in

---

[3]In mid-1984 the FDIC adopted a variation of the payout method with elements of a P&A. When a bank failed, another immediately assumed all insured deposits and the *fraction* of uninsured deposits that the FDIC estimated would eventually be recovered. Compared to the old payout method, this benefits both the FDIC and the local economy in two ways. First, the FDIC's net losses are reduced. Expansion-minded banks which assume the *insured* deposits bid a premium for the assets of the failed bank. This reduces the FDIC's net losses since insured depositors must be paid in any case. Second, the local economy is disrupted less because uninsured depositors receive immediate funds, which may be augmented later if the FDIC underestimated asset liquidation values. This is a variation of the payout method because uninsured depositors do *not* come out whole.

order to reduce the moral hazard of excessive risk taking by banks. Depositors should *anticipate* losses from failures. However, elimination of the external effects of bank failures, which is the main objective of deposit insurance, suggests that insurance be *unlimited ex-post, that is, depositors actually suffer no losses*. For many years depositors seemingly were fooled by the law. Ex-ante decisions were guided by the legally limited insurance although insurance was ex-post unlimited, at least at large banks. In recent years depositors realized that some laws make distinctions without differences. *Ex-post experience instead of the law has more strongly and quickly influenced ex-ante anticipations,* making cat and mouse games necessary. The FDIC tries to maintain a difference between ex-ante and ex-post insurance in spite of private behavior which produces a convergence of the two.

What Is the Appropriate Premium Structure?

Premium receipts are the product of the premium base times the premium rate, just as tax receipts are the product of the tax base, such as income or sales, times the tax rate. Given this, there are two issues regarding the premium structure:

1. What is the appropriate base? The base chosen has a differential impact on banks.
2. What is the appropriate rate structure? In particular, should insurance premiums be uniform or graduated according to the risk taken by the bank? Risk-based insurance rates clearly discourage excessive risk taking by banks.

Total (domestic) deposits now are the base against which the insurance rates are levied. Because large banks have bigger accounts and not simply more accounts, the proportion of insured to total deposits is less at large banks than small banks. Therefore, large banks want the base changed to insured deposits. They claim that they are effectively subsidizing small banks because the insurance base is all deposits although all deposits are not insured. The proposal by large banks seems reasonable. Shouldn't you only pay for what you get? With a total deposit base, large banks pay a higher rate premium on insured deposits.

How do small banks and the FDIC justify the current system? First, small banks point to the P&A method of handling large bank failures. Large banks in fact are not subsidizing small banks because virtually all large bank deposits are *de facto,* even if not *de jure,* insured. Second, if a subsidy does exist, it is justified in order to encourage entry. Entrants, which inevitably are small, have a special need for insurance since lack of information about them is most pronounced. Without a subsidy from large banks, entry would be reduced and the industry eventually would be monopolistic.

Most private insurance premiums vary according to risk. For example, the elderly pay more for life insurance. Why should conservative and well managed banks pay the same insurance rate as their risk-loving cousins? Why not offer unlimited insurance with premium rates based on risk? In this manner banks do have something to lose from accepting too much risk. *One hundred percent deposit insurance and the complete elimination of the external effects of bank failures create no moral hazard when insurance rates are risk based.* In this case, risk-loving banks with high insurance payments could not afford to pay high deposit rates.

The FDIC's argument against risk-based insurance premiums relies almost exclusively on the difficulty of measuring risk. The counterargument recognizes this by calling for the establishment of only a few risk classes. A finely graduated premium structure is inconsistent with the difficulties in measuring risk. The counterargument says that risk already is being assessed, however imperfectly, in bank examinations and other ways. Moreover, risk premiums already are being collected implicitly through capital adequacy requirements, asset and liability restrictions, etc. According to the counterargument, an admittedly imperfect risk-based premium (price mechanism) is preferable to some government regulations as a means of allocating risk among banks. Regulation, the *alternative* to a risk-based graduated insurance structure, implicitly sets prices at zero if some action is permitted, or infinitely high if some action is prohibited. Risk-based insurance premiums can substitute for *some* regulations, though certainly not all regulations.

Select Policies to Reduce Bank Failures

The concern about bank failures by the FDIC, the insurer of banks, certainly is understandable. However, concern about bank failures extends beyond the FDIC to all other bank regulators. *While bank regulators have multiple goals, bank solvency is their premier goal.* The multitude of government regulations and examinations can be understood only against the backdrop of regulators' overwhelming desire to prevent bank failures. Is a vigorous policy aimed directly at reducing bank failures desirable now that insurance has largely eliminated its external effects? Bankruptcies often are the termination of a long string of losses. During relatively prosperous times losses are signs that resources are being misallocated, since the value of goods produced is less than the cost of resources used. Viewed in this manner, bankruptcies are worthwhile, signaling that "no more good money is being thrown after bad." To be sure, it would have been best not to have created the firm in the first place, thereby avoiding the losses and ultimate death. Can bank regulations prevent the formation of banks which ultimately become insolvent? Generally, what is the best safeguard against insolvency? Recall that solvency is one of the bank's objectives. *Honest bankers' desire to succeed, rather than any regulation, is the most effective safeguard against failure*. If bankers wanted to fail, it is doubtful that regulations could be devised to prevent them from doing so. Honest bankers and their managers suffer significant hardships when a firm is bankrupt. Besides the immediate loss of jobs, the future prospects of the insolvent bankers are dim. Visualize the following résumé: Previous employment: President, U.S. Prestige Bank (now bankrupt). Hardly a résumé likely to gain one job offers. Besides the loss of jobs, the insolvent bank's stockholders lose their investment.

We mentioned at several points that *honest* bankers have no incentive to fail, but the *dishonest* banker is successful if the bank does fail. Bankruptcy may occur precisely because the dishonest banker stole too much and made too many loans to the wrong people. *Blatant dishonesty is a major reason for bank failures nowadays, and less obvious dishonesty enters in many failures officially diagnosed as mismanagement*. For example, are delinquent loans to one's friends and relatives examples of dishonesty or mismanagement? Banking history shows that the industry has attracted some crooks. The portability of the product and the difficulty in ascertaining quality made banking a nightmare in the 1850s, as we shall show later. Merely passing laws barring crooks from the banking industry would be as successful in achieving its objective as legislation against foreign aggression prevents wars. *The bank charter and annual examination gather information that depositors often cannot acquire. The charter and examination process should and does check the honesty and reputation of management. This has made banks more homogeneous and reduced failures*.

To be sure, honest bankers like other people do make mistakes, and some fail. Regulators should be quite blasé about honest failures which do not produce external effect. What should be and what is do not always coincide. Regulations severely restricting risk taking and protecting the banking industry have indeed reduced bank failures, but at the cost of more commercial firm failures and a more monopolistic, uninnovative banking sector. Banks are intermediaries and a major source of funds for small firms. *For every conservative bank there are dozens of small firms which failed for lack of financing*.

Bank Charter Policy

A liberal charter policy would foster a dynamic environment. In fact, charter policy is geared more to the creation and maintenance of monopolies than to their elimination. A 1980 report prepared by the Democratic staff of the Senate Banking Committee is one of many studies claiming that recent Comptrollers of the Currency were "more interested in protecting existing banks during this period (1970–77) than in promoting and meeting the banking needs of the public.''[4] In order for a new bank to acquire a charter, regulators must be convinced that it will be profitable and not significantly harm existing banks. Many charter applications are denied on the grounds of alleged unprofitability. Who is the best judge of future success, the detached regulator or the (honest) entrant willing to commit funds? Charters are rarely, if ever, granted when some banks in an area are unprofitable, on the grounds that losses are prima facie evidence of overbanking. While this may be the case, this policy ignores the real possibility that the existing banks are unprofitable because they are poorly managed. The (honest) entrant who has every hope of succeeding should not be denied the opportunity. Sheltering the market from the rigors of competition is undesirable when external effects are absent.

Bank Examinations

The periodic bank examination in general and the ''capital adequacy'' aspect of the exam are integral elements of this policy of preventing failures. Bank examiners spring unannounced at a bank. The examination has some elements of a financial audit. Cash, securities, and other assets which may become attached to sticky fingers are audited to verify that they are on hand. They typically are.[5] While attempting to ferret out dishonest bankers by its financial audit aspects, *the bank examination primarily is designed to verify compliance with banking regulation and, more important, be an early warning system.* For example, the examiner will check compliance with size of loan and interest rate limitations. Above all, the examination is supposed to identify potential problems while still minor and correctable.[6] An appraisal of the quality and collectibility of the loan portfolio has traditionally been one of the key elements of the exam as an early warning system. Loans are classified as good, substandard, doubtful, and loss. The usual rule of thumb used in interpreting these categories is that virtually all loans categorized ''good'' will be collected; losses will be incurred on 20 percent of the substandard loans,

---

[4]The classic study to arrive at this conclusion is Sam Peltzman, ''Bank Entry Regulation: Its Impact and Purpose,'' *National Bank Review,* December 1965, pp. 163–77. The Banking Committee report is summarized in the *Washington Post,* October 27, 1980, p. D3.

[5]The movies may have the bank vice president packing a suitcase full of cash and securities and flying to Rio, but this is rarely how defalcations actually occur. The suitcase approach can be tried only once. An essentially similar scheme can be used repeatedly and will likely net one more than a suitcase full. Even in crime, bankers adhere to double-entry bookkeeping. The dishonest banker takes the cash and books a loan to the ABC company. When the examiners arrive there is no cash, which is just what the records indicate because ABC got a loan. The problem is: ABC is a fictitious company or a company headed by the banker's relative, who has no intention of paying off the loan. By the time this is discovered the banker has gone through the alphabet and lent to XYZ.

[6]Because examinations occur only periodically, the quarterly financial statements banks submit to regulators are incorporated in the early warning system.

50 percent of the doubtful loans, and virtually 100 percent of the loss loans.

While there always was some diversity among regulators in the loan evaluation process, congressional hearings following the Franklin National Bank debacle in 1974 uncovered significant diversity in the other factors analyzed and in the bank rating system. This made evaluation of the condition of the overall banking system difficult. Uniformity was achieved in 1978 with the new Uniform Interagency Bank Rating System which assigns ratings from 1 to 5, with 1 indicating "strength" and 5 "unsatisfactory and in need of immediate remedial attention," to five aspects of a bank's operation and condition: (1) *C*apital adequacy, (2) *A*sset quality, (3) *M*anagement and administration, (4) *E*arnings quantity and quality, and (5) *L*iquidity level.[7] While the five performance dimensions are somewhat interdependent, each is rated separately. An acronym: examiners want a Number 1 CAMEL. In addition, examiners offer a composite judgment incorporating these five aspects and other factors, such as local economic conditions and affiliation with a bank holding company. The composite rating also is scaled from 1 to 5. A composite 1-rated bank receives little attention between examinations while a composite 5 bank is subject to constant monitoring. Examiners usually "suggest" a corrective action program for 5 banks. Banks are not legally required to adopt the corrective program, but they usually find it advantageous to do so. One does not fool with bank examiners. They can get a cease and desist order or ultimately cancel a bank's deposit insurance, often the kiss of death.

At this point the reader should have a general impression of the factors examiners consider in evaluating the five performance dimensions except possibly the quality of earnings and capital adequacy. The main factor in the quality of earnings is the amount of the bank's additions to valuation or loss reserves so that at each moment in time the balance sheet shows reasonably accurate valuations, and realized losses do not cause a "surprise."

Bank Failures and Capital Adequacy

Capital adequacy was the performance dimension mentioned first because it is the heart of the bank examination process. Capital is the owners' contribution and measures the magnitude of mistakes honest bank managers can make before bankruptcy occurs. The capital adequacy problem entails estimating the capital/asset ratio consistent with a "small" likelihood of insolvency. Capital adequacy is especially controversial within banking circles because the capital/asset ratio has important but opposite

---

[7]Geoge G. Juncker, "A New Supervisory System for Rating Banks," Federal Reserve Bank of New York *Quarterly Review,* Summer 1978, pp. 47–50.

FIGURE 15–1
Banks' Capital/Asset Percentage, 1920–1983

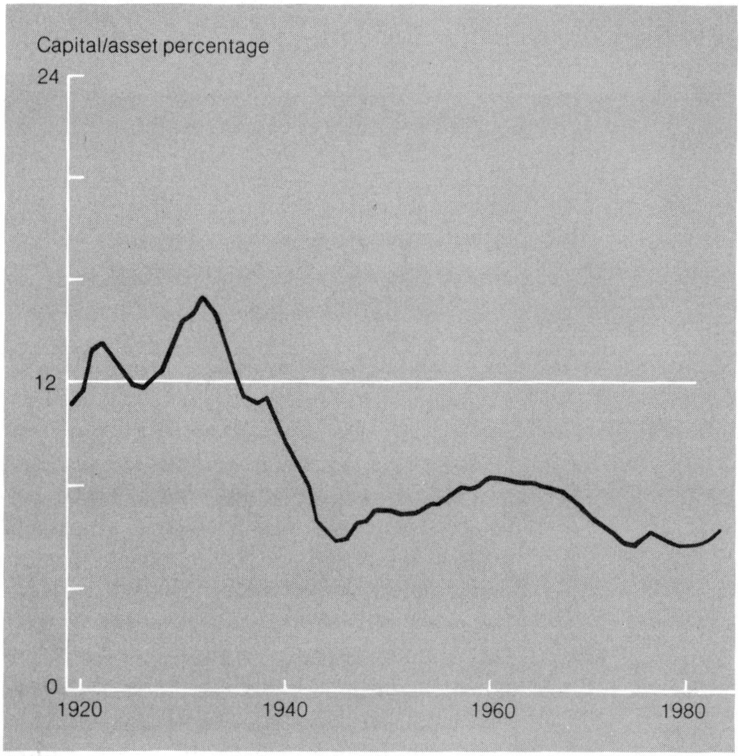

Source: Federal Reserve, *Historical Chart Book 1983*, p. 85.

effects on bankers' profitability and solvency. This is seen most clearly when we write the rate of return on stockholders' capital as

$$\text{Rate of return} = \frac{\text{Profits}}{\text{Assets}} \cdot \frac{\text{Assets}}{\text{Capital}}$$

Although a low capital/asset ratio (high asset/capital ratio) may increase the likelihood of failures, the equation shows that, *ceteris paribus,* it also increases the owners' rate of return. As Chapter 10 on bank objectives and banking theories stated, bankers do estimate the trade-off. Regulators, however, do not participate in the bank's profits and ignore the opportunity cost of a high capital/asset ratio. They are praised when bank failures are low, not when bank profits are high.

The capital adequacy tug-of-war between bankers and bank regulators has continued for so long because, besides disagreeing on what constitutes a "low" probability of failure, the relationship between failure and capital is imprecise. Figure 9–3, which graphs banks' capital/asset ratio from

TABLE 15–1
Average Annual Number and Percentage of Bank Failures

Time Period	*Failures, Number*	*Failures, Percent*
1920–22	346.0	1.17
1923–29	692.0	2.57
1930	1350.0	5.81
1931	2293.0	10.76
1932	1453.0	7.88
1933	4000.0	28.68
1934–40	47.0	0.31
1941–74	4.6	0.03
1975–79	10.8	0.07
1980–84	47.8	0.32

Source: Federal Reserve, *Banking and Monetary Statistics* (Washington: National Capital Press, 1943) for data up to 1939, and FDIC, *Annual Report, 1984* for data since 1940.

1920 forward, is reproduced for convenience as Figure 15–1. Table 15–1 shows the average annual number and percentage of bank failures for selected years since 1920. Clearly, a high capital/asset ratio is no guarantee against failure. In the prosperous 1920s about 700, or 2.5 percent, of the banks failed annually, and the capital/asset ratio averaged 13 percent. In the 1960s and 1970s about six banks, or 0.05 percent, failed annually, and the capital/asset ratio was only 7 percent. The bank failure rate quadrupled between the late 1970s and early 1980s although the capital/asset ratio remained virtually constant.[8] However, one should not conclude from the figure and table that the capital/asset ratio does not influence the failure rate. During the Great Depression years of 1930–33, failures were a common occurrence. Yet the capital/asset ratio was *increasing* because the banks with a low capital/asset ratio were failing.

Why are banks able to operate with less capital nowadays? What factors influence how much capital is ''adequate,'' that is, the capital consistent with a given small probability of failure? Answers to these questions are presented in tabular form in Table 15–2. According to Table 15–2, the decline of the *actual* capital/asset ratio should not be a source of great concern. *With the possible exception of asset quality,* which may have decreased as banks made more high-risk foreign loans, *all factors which reduce the adequate amount of capital have increased.* Consequently, the adequate capital/asset ratio very probably has also fallen. Further reductions in the *actual* ratio are undesirable, however, particularly if the government stops aiding borrowers on the verge of default, e.g., Chrysler Corp.

---

[8]The higher failure rate reflects special factors rather than a general deterioration of the banking industry. Fraud, loans to insiders, mismanagement, and a collapse in farming and petroleum explain nearly all recent failures. Table 11–1 showed that the banking industry's profit rate remained virtually constant between the late 1970s and early 80s.

TABLE 15–2

Factors Reducing the Adequate Capital/Asset Ratio and Their Change over Time

Factors	*Change over Time*
(1) Adaptability to demand and population changes.	Increase as (1) banking markets expanded due to greater branching, (2) management techniques improved, and (3) banks became less specialized lenders.
(2) Economic stability.	Increase, perhaps because government is committed to full employment.
(3) Bank liquidity	Increase due to (1) the development of organized, national financial markets, and (2) greater commitment by the Federal Reserve to aid banks at the discount window, e.g., Franklin National Bank.
(4) Asset quality	Probably decrease as banks made more high-risk foreign loans. Impact of loan quality has been reduced, however, as government aids defaulters, e.g., Argentina and Chrysler Corp.
(5) Deposit stability	Increase due to (1) deposit insurance and (2) a higher time deposit ratio.

Questions

1. Discuss the adequacy of the FDIC reserve fund. Is the federal government (Treasury) required to rescue the FDIC if its reserve fund is depleted?
2. Carefully evaluate the pros and cons of 100 percent deposit insurance.
3. Explain the difference between the purchase and assumption (P&A) and payout methods of handling bank failures.
4. Deposit insurance is legally limited but effectively unlimited at large banks. Explain.
5. What are the advantages of risk-based deposit insurance? Why are premiums uniform?
6. Assuming external effects do not exist, what types of policies which reduce bank failures are justified? What are the disadvantages of policies which attempt to reduce bank failures by limiting risk taking by banks?
7. What are the main purposes of bank examinations? What factors are considered when banks are evaluated?
8. Why is there a capital adequacy controversy, and what factors influence the "adequate" amount of capital?

PART FOUR

Central Banking

Central banking history and the Federal Reserve System

16

Money does not manage itself. About President Woodrow Wilson's signing into law with three gold pens the Federal Reserve Act at 6:02 P.M. on Tuesday, December 23, 1913, Wilson's biographer Arthur Link said, "Thus ended the long struggle for the greatest single piece of constructive legislation of the Wilson era and one of the most important domestic acts in the nation's history."[1] While Link may be guilty of some literary license, the banking situation often was chaotic in the 19th and early 20th century. This chapter should give us an appreciation of our central banking accomplishments since the birth of this country. But study of banking history fulfills more than our collective need to stroke our egos. Knowledge of the past gives order to the present. For example, the seemingly bizarre system of 12 Federal Reserve Banks, each of which may be charging a different discount rate, can be better understood if one is aware of the rural idealism versus urban reality and states' rights versus federal power conflicts, two conflicts ever present in American history but fortunately less intense nowadays. Past social and political controversies shape present economic institutions. Dispensing with further justifications, we proceed directly to a history of banking and the structure of the Federal Reserve System.

---

[1]Arthur Link, *Wilson: The New Freedom* (Princeton, N.J.: Princeton University Press, 1956), p. 238.

Colonial America and the First Banks

The financial sector sometimes leads and sometimes lags behind the real sector, but most often the two sectors mirror each other. The real sector in colonial America is easily characterized: it was agrarian. Benjamin Franklin conjectured that for one artisan or merchant there were at least a hundred farmers. The enormous expanse of empty and fertile land and a poor transportation system made the colonial farmers much more self-reliant than their English cousins. Consistent with an economy largely composed of self-sufficient farms, the financial sector in colonial America was quite primitive. The English pound was the unit of account but not the medium of exchange. That is, prices were quoted and records were kept in terms of pounds, shillings, and pence, but this money did not circulate. Spanish, French, and Portugese coins and paper money issued by some of the colonies were the means of payment. The notes of most colonies were issued to finance specific projects. They remained in circulation for a short period of time and then were withdrawn. English currency did not circulate because there was a perennial trade deficit with England. As soon as a merchant acquired an English pound, it was used to finance imports from England. Moreover, European coins were quite scarce. To supplement the supply of specie (gold or silver coins), wealthy and respectable individuals or temporary partnerships operating in a side office issued notes which did circulate as money. However, *colonial America had no banks in the modern sense. There were no incorporated firms with a permanent and specialized staff and separate office which issued notes, accepted deposits, and made loans.*

The American Revolution radically changed this monetary scene. With few exceptions, Rhode Island being the most notable, the notes (paper currency) of the prerevolutionary colonies did *not* depreciate relative to specie. A Pennsylvania one-pound note could be exchanged for one pound sterling, when available, or the equivalent in European coins. The notes issued by the Continental Congress during the Revolution did depreciate. Continental notes are an excellent example of Chapter 2's analysis of fiat money. "Regular" tax systems typically are inadequate whenever there is a dramatic increase in the government's need for resources, such as during wars. The alternatives the patriots faced were quite simple: issue fiat money to finance the Revolution or give up the struggle. The war effort did demand significant resources, and the country was flooded with continental notes. The outcome was inevitable: prices in terms of continentals skyrocketed to the point that anything valueless was said not to be worth a continental. Inflation was the price the country had to pay to win the war.

The patriots well recognized the power of fiat money. David Ramsay, a member of the Continental Congress and author of *History of the United States,* first published in 1789, said,

> America, having never been much taxed in any direct way, and being without established government, and especially as she was contending against what was lately lawful authority, could not immediately proceed to taxation. Besides, as the contest was on the subject of taxation, the laying of taxes adequate to the exigencies of war, even though it had been practicable, would have been impolitic. The only plausible expedient, in their power to adopt, was the emission of bills of credit [paper money].
>
> * * * * *
>
> [These paper notes] circulated for several months, without any depreciation, and commanded the resources of the country for public service, equally with the same sum of gold or silver. The United States derived for a considerable time as much benefit from this paper creation of their own, though without any established funds for its support or redemption, as would have resulted from a free gift of as many Mexican dollars. While the ministry of England were puzzling themselves for new taxes, and funds, on which to raise their supplies, Congress raised theirs by resolutions directing paper of no intrinsic value to be struck off, in form of promissory notes. But there was a point, both in time and quantity, beyond which this congressional alchymy ceased to operate. The time was about eighteen months from the date of their first emission, and that quantity about twenty million of dollars.[2]

Benjamin Franklin recognized that Congress acquired resources because it indeed was taxing its citizens by printing money and inflating. *Inflation is a tax. An inflation which reduces the purchasing power of money by, say, 50 percent is identical to a 50 percent tax on money balances*. This point is sufficiently important to risk the charge of being wordy. Suppose the price of widgets goes from 50 cents to $1 so that the purchasing power of money falls 50 percent. A dollar formerly purchased two widgets but now purchases one. Instead of that scenario, suppose a dollar is taxed 50 percent but prices remain constant, so after taxes the moneyholder can purchase one widget. The moneyholder is indifferent between inflation and taxation. Both policies reduce one's command over goods and services equally. Franklin said,[3]

> The general effect of the depreciation [inflation] has operated as a *gradual tax*. . . . Every man has paid his share of the tax according to the time he retained any of the money in his hands, and to the depreciation within that time. Thus it has proved a tax on money.

Were we fighting for or against taxation without representation?

Although the English continued to occupy selected areas and a peace treaty was two years away, fighting in the Revolutionary War ceased with

---

[2]David Ramsay, *History of the United States* (Philadelphia: M. Carey, 1817), vol. 3, appendix 4, pp. xvii, xviii.

[3]Benjamin Franklin, *The Writings of Benjamin Franklin,* ed. Albert H. Smyth (New York: Macmillan, 1907), vol. 9, p. 234. Franklin goes on to say that he favors the inflation tax. Italics in original.

the Battle of Yorktown on October 18, 1781. The government's need for resources was much reduced but not totally eliminated. Considering that continentals had become worthless and the tax system remained inadequate, another revenue source was necessary. On December 31, 1781, the Continental Congress meeting in Philadelphia chartered the Bank of North America, the first modern bank in America. The powers of Congress being uncertain, for safety's sake the Pennsylvania legislature also chartered the bank a month later. Private citizens and the Congress subscribed to the bank's capital. Consistent with the ownership distribution, the bank was supposed to lend to the private and government sectors, generally by creating its own notes (paper currency). *There is no essential difference between note and deposit expansion.* In one case the borrower's account is credited, and in the other case the borrower is given fresh notes (paper currency). In neither case did the bank have these items beforehand. Banks usually created notes because borrowers and the public in general preferred them to deposits. Recall that the currency/deposit ratio is negatively related to income. When incomes are low and transportation and communication systems are poor, currency is preferable to deposits. The reserves of the Bank of North America were specie. Just as its modern counterparts, the bank operated with fractional reserves because not everyone demanded specie for notes and deposits. At the same time, some people always want specie for their notes. This meant that the bank could not expand without limit; it held some specie although it was not required to do so. The bank was cautious. It did not expand its loans and notes beyond the amount its reserves could support. The bank's notes circulated at par with specie. The conservatism which allowed its notes to circulate at par meant that the bank largely failed in its objectives of being an important source of loanable funds for the government, which sold its bank stock shortly after the bank began operations. The Bank of North America's success inspired the formation of other banks in major cities. The respective state legislatures chartered the Bank of New York in 1784, the Bank of Massachusetts (Boston) also in 1784, and the Bank of Maryland (Baltimore) in 1790. Thus in 1790 the United States had four banks—not many but the same number as in England.[4]

The First Bank of the United States, 1791–1811

The Revolutionary War ended in 1783, but the Republic as we know it was not created until 1789. The six-year interval was marked by a struggle between states' rightists (Jeffersonian Republicans) and Federalists over the appropriate form of government. The political struggle reflected a

---

[4]Banks here mean incorporated firms. Numerous partnerships extended credit in England.

more fundamental and enduring social conflict which we shall call rural idealism versus urban reality. The expression of these two social forces has varied over time. Rural idealism initially elevated the farmer to mystical superiority. Benjamin Franklin, a successful businessman, espoused the rural position as if he were a farmer. He said, "There seem to be but three ways for a nation to acquire wealth. The first is *war*. . . . This is *robbery*. The second by *commerce* which is generally *cheating*. The third by *agriculture*, the only *honest way*, wherein man receives a real increase . . . as a reward for his innocent life and his virtuous industry."[5] With the shift away from agriculture, rural idealism embraced any occupation, provided it entailed hard work and self-reliance, and any small business.

> His brow is wet with honest sweat,
> He earns whate'er he can,
> And looks the whole world in the face
> For he owes not any man.
>
> "The Village Blacksmith,"
> Henry Wadsworth Longfellow

Rural idealism extolls the free, simple, and unregulated life, the little person, and the competitor who slays the monopolist. Urban reality stresses industrialization and large-scale production as a means of material progress. While urban reality does not advocate monopolies and oppression, it tolerates such conditions if they aid growth. Urban reality never captured the imagination of the masses; large corporations, advanced technology, and profit maximization are not inspirational. The pastoral poetry of rural idealism contrasts sharply with the matter-of-fact aphorisms of urban reality: the business of America is business.[6] Although not logically related, urban reality in its early years strongly supported federal power. Presumably, a strong central government and national economic market are more profitable than the small protected markets under states' rights. Conflicts between conservationists and international oil companies and between service-oriented local stores and chain discounters are modern examples of the rural idealism versus urban reality conflict. In the monetary area, the conflict years ago between hard specie and soft currency has shifted to one between visible checks and invisible automatic transfers.

The interests of the small urban class coincided with those of patriots like George Washington, Alexander Hamilton, and James Madison, who argued that the confederated government was too weak. After much de-

---

[5]Benjamin Franklin, *The Papers of Benjamin Franklin,* ed. William B. Wilcox (New Haven: Yale University Press, 1972), vol. 16, p. 109. Italics in original.

[6]Calvin Coolidge, in a speech before the Society of American Newspaper Editors, January 17, 1925.

bate, which we do not even begin to summarize, the Constitution finally was adopted, and urban realists and Federalists came to power. The monetary clauses of the Constitution give Congress the power "to coin Money, regulate the Value thereof." A mint which produced gold and silver coins was established in 1791. The unit of account was a dollar patterned after the Spanish dollar, that is, the silver content of the U.S. and Spanish dollars both equaled 371.25 grains. Gold was to be coined at a ratio of 1 gold to 15 silver, the prevailing market ratio at the time. When the relative price of gold increased shortly thereafter, the United States adopted a de facto silver standard until 1834, illustrating Gresham's Law: bad (overvalued silver) coins drove good (undervalued gold) coins out of circulation. Most believed the Constitution barred the federal government from issuing paper money. Hamilton and a few others disagreed, but the sorry record of the continentals was too fresh in people's minds to permit the issue of *government* paper money.

The rural idealism versus urban reality conflict resurfaced in the debate about the [First] Bank of the United States, the major political controversy following ratification of the Constitution.[7] The main protagonists were Secretary of the Treasury Alexander Hamilton and Secretary of State Thomas Jefferson. Hamilton urged Congress to charter a national bank. Jefferson argued against the bank. Hamilton won the debate.

In 1791 Congress chartered the First Bank of the United States for 20 years. The bank garnered a congressional majority for various reasons. *First, and most important, it became a symbol of federal power.* Confederation had just been defeated, but the principle of a strong central government was still not firmly established. Hamilton needed a major issue. He finally selected banking, which was totally abhorrent to the agrarians. Hamilton argued that Congress could charter a national bank under the constitutional clause giving it all the powers "necessary and proper" to perform its responsibilities. Congress lacked only those powers *specifically denied* in the Constitution. Jefferson responded that the federal government had only those powers *specifically granted* it by the Constitution, with the states retaining all power not specifically relinquished. Since the Constitution was silent about congressional incorporation of banks or other types of firms, Jefferson said the First Bank was unconstitutional. While the states' rightists may have opposed the establishment of other national institutions, the opposition to an incorporated national bank verged on the irrational. Any corporation was an "unnatural" organization, and an incorporated bank was additionally immoral. President John Adams said that "banks have done more injury to the religion, morality, tranquility, prosperity, and even wealth of the nation

[7]The bank became the First only after it ceased to exist and the Second was chartered.

than they can have done or ever will do good."[8] The bank violated the agrarian principles of a natural and moral life.

Second, political and philosophical principles aside, Hamilton argued for the bank on the grounds of convenience. The new federal government levied taxes and spent. *It needed a fiscal agent*, that is, an organization which would collect the taxes, hold the government's funds, transfer funds among regions and offices, and make authorized payments. While the existing state banks could have performed these services, a single nationwide bank could do them more efficiently.

Third, any bank tended to foster commerce and industry. While the real bills doctrine never precluded agricultural loans, particularly in the early days, commercial loans were banks' first priority.

Fourth, debtors and others favoring higher prices supported the bank on the grounds that any fractional reserve bank expands the money supply and is inflationary. Each dollar that a bank acquires supports multiple notes and deposits.

Finally, Secretary Hamilton was anxious to have some unit more or less committed to extending credit to the Treasury whenever necessary. He hoped the First Bank of the United States would fulfill for the federal government the same role the Bank of North America was supposed to play for the confederation.

The capital stock of the First Bank was $10 million, five times more than the next largest banks, the Bank of North America and Manhattan Company, the forerunner of the Chase Manhattan Bank. The bank was an early example of joint private and public enterprise. The federal government subscribed for stock worth $2 million, and the remainder was oversubscribed by private individuals. Government and private directors were allocated on the same one-fifth/four-fifth basis. The stock was a good buy. Within three months of its issue the bank's stock rose from $25 to $300 per share! Fully one third of Congress owned bank stock, creating the suspicion that Congress chartered the bank to enrich itself. The bank was headquartered in Philadelphia and eventually had eight branches from Boston to New Orleans. It was extremely large relative to other banks and commercial firms.

In most respects the First Bank acted like a private bank. It made loans, accepted deposits, and issued notes. It considered itself the exemplar of a well-managed conservative bank, and justly so. It had a high capital ratio, made sound loans, and always maintained adequate reserves (specie). Its notes circulated at par throughout the country. Besides its private functions, the First Bank performed two functions normally associated with a central bank. First, as already mentioned, it was the fiscal

---

[8]John Adams, *The Works of John Adams,* ed. Charles Francis Adams (Boston: Little, Brown, 1856), vol. 10, p. 375.

agent for the Treasury. Second, it adopted policies to create a sound, default-free banking system. The tools on hand in order to accomplish its second objective were quite primitive. It could not set required reserve ratios, examine banks, or specify a capital ratio.[9] Much like any large firm or wealthy person, the First Bank maintained large credit balances with the state banks. *The First Bank created a sound banking system mainly by frequent unannounced large calls on its credit balances.* Aware that the First Bank might be testing their liquidity and solvency by withdrawing its deposits, the state banks maintained large (excess) reserves, held a more liquid loan portfolio, and reduced their note and deposit expansion. As Chapter 4 indicated, the demand for excess reserves is negatively related to the expected change in deposits (and in those days, bank notes) and positively related to deposit (and note) variability. The First Bank with its branches throughout the country was sufficiently large that its customers were continually bringing in notes and depositing checks drawn on every state bank. With the liabilities of state banks always on hand, it could continually test them by demanding payment in specie. If a bank repeatedly passed the test, the First Bank would maintain the bank's notes in circulation instead of redeeming them. Thus, the state bank had a strong incentive to be especially prudent.

The 20-year charter of the First Bank of the United States expired in 1811 and was not renewed. The debate on recharter largely echoed the debate 20 years earlier, with the same constitutional issues paramount. Two new issues did surface. First, a significant portion of the bank's stock had been purchased by foreigners. Some feared that foreigners would gain control of the First Bank, the largest corporation of its day, and thereby dominate the economy. Second, state bankers who resented the First Bank's control formed a coalition with debtors and others favoring higher prices, who came to realize that the First Bank over its short lifetime had shifted from being an inflationary to a deflationary force because the banking system had grown rapidly. Only four state banks existed when the First Bank was chartered in 1791. By 1811 there were 90 banks. When few banks exist, the creation of new banks, often in bankless areas, reduces the demand for specie as individuals find bank notes and deposits more convenient. Given a fractional reserve banking system, the new bank expands the money supply. When there are many banks, however, an entrant has little effect on the money supply, *ceteris paribus,* because it acquires deposits at the expense of existing banks instead of specie. In other words, the effect of a new bank on the currency/deposit ratio de-

---

[9]The banks did report their condition to the states; Massachusetts set reserve requirements in 1792, and other states followed; and bank charters typically specified a capital ratio. However, these requirements imposed by the *states,* and not the First Bank, were often ignored.

pends on the number of existing banks. When few banks exist, a new bank significantly increases convenience, reduces the currency ratio, and increases money and prices. By 1811 the slight positive effect of the First Bank on the money supply due to the convenience factor was outweighed by its control tactics which forced state banks to hold larger reserves. *Unreconstructed states' rightists, rural idealists, anti-foreigners, expansionary-minded bankers, and debtors defeated recharter by one vote in each house of Congress.*[10] The First Bank was dissolved in 1811.

The Second Bank of the United States, 1816–1836

The demise of the First Bank made banking more profitable as banks could operate with less specie and more earning assets. As expected, the number of state banks increased dramatically, from 90 in 1811 to approximately 250 five years later. From the viewpoint of the Treasury, dissolution of the First Bank could hardly have come at a more inopportune time. A year later the United States was embroiled in the War of 1812. As in other wars, government expenditures increased, and greater regional transfers of funds were necessary. The loss of a fiscal agent with branches throughout the country hampered smooth money management. The government maintained accounts in many state banks. Transfer of the funds among banks and regions was difficult. The War of 1812 was financed mainly through the sale of bonds. Here again the First Bank, partially owned by the government, would have been preferable to private banks. To be sure, the state banks did issue some notes to buy government bonds.

The quest for victory overrides constitutional principles during wartime. The government discovered that it did have the authority to issue paper money. Between 1812 and 1815 the Treasury issued $36 million, which had limited circulation because its denomination was quite large. The Treasury notes were promptly redeemed after the war. The monetary expansion by the Treasury and banks reduced the currency ratio to dangerously low levels in the best of times, and times were not the best. The English attack on Washington and Baltimore induced runs on banks for specie. Except in New England, a general suspension occurred; banks stopped converting their notes and deposits into specie. Bank notes sold at varying discounts.

The peace treaty with England in December 1814 did not restore convertibility or a smoothly functioning banking system. By early 1816 President Madison, Speaker of the House Henry Clay, and Congressman John

---

[10]James Madison, president in 1811, and other Jefffersonian Republicans, but not Mr. Jefferson himself, put principle aside and favored recharter in 1811 on the grounds of economic convenience. Conservative banks like the Bank of New York also supported recharter.

C. Calhoun led the fight for a Second Bank of the United States. The arguments pro and con remained essentially unchanged since 1791, but the emphasis shifted. The fiscal agent, reliable credit source, and bank regulatory functions were highlighted instead of constitutional principles. The bill chartering the Second Bank of the United States passed in 1816. The Second Bank was quite similar to its predecessor—it was headquartered in Philadelphia, had a 20-year charter, and one fifth of its capital was subscribed by the government. It was much larger, however. The Second Bank's capital was $35 million, and it eventually had 25 branches.

The Second Bank embarked on stormy seas. Baltimore tried but failed in its bid to be headquarters of the Second Bank. Determined to surpass Philadelphia, James Buchanan, president of the Baltimore branch, lent large amounts to local firms in an early effort at "regional development." Buchanan's honest mistakes were compounded by James McCulloch, cashier of the same Baltimore branch, who embezzled a significant sum. After McCulloch and Buchanan were replaced in 1819, the Second Bank began competently performing the functions of a private and central bank. It lent and issued notes prudently. It was the government's fiscal agent and tested the state banks' solvency and liquidity by frequently presenting notes for redemption.

By 1828 members of the rural movement grew tired of being governed politically by squires from Virginia, Pennsylvania, and Massachusetts, and of being economically subservient to the urban elite. They elected Andrew Jackson, who interpreted his election as a mandate to humble the economic power structure and eradicate monopolies. Labeled as a menace to American democracy, the large and powerful Second Bank became Jackson's prime target. Personality clashes intensified economic and political differences. The president of the Second Bank was Nicholas Biddle, the patrician scion of a Philadelphia family. General Jackson, a self-made man of humble origin, belonged to the aristocracy of the frontier. The birth and breeding of the Philadelphia gentry clashed with the cockfighting, horse-racing, whisky-drinking frontier aristocracy. Clearly aware of Jackson's opposition, the Second Bank's supporters thought its only salvation lay at the polls. Since its charter expired in April 1836, the November 1836 election was too late. The bank began its defense early. Henry Clay, President Jackson's opponent in the 1832 election, pushed through Congress a bill extending the Second Bank's life. Jackson promptly vetoed the bill. Inconsistency, disingenuousness, and outright sham riddled his veto message. The battle lines were drawn. *The Second Bank became the major issue in the 1832 presidential campaign.* Jackson put together a coalition which, incongruities and strange bedfellows notwithstanding, proved most effective. He won resoundingly. We met many elements of the Jacksonian coalition at the execution of the First Bank. The coalition deserves enumeration again because the influence of many elements extended beyond banking to 19th century political and economic history in general. The Second Bank was killed by:

1. States' rightists, who said the federally chartered bank violated the Constitution.[11]
2. State bankers, who were restrained by the central banking functions of the federal bank. They were joined by speculators and other advocates of inflation.
3. Moderate rural idealists, who claimed that all banks aided urban enterprise at the expense of farmers and artisans.
4. Extreme rural idealists, for whom all corporations were unnatural and all banks were immoral. The Second Bank was a monopoly monster which oppressed the little person. The Equal Rights Party, or Loco Focos as they came to be called, held this position.
5. Anti-foreigners, who saw foreign control everywhere. The American Party, or Know Nothings, exemplified this viewpoint.

The previously mentioned personality clash between Jackson and Biddle rates first place in the category of special factors associated with the Second Bank. Second place goes to regionalism based on pride and especially economic interests. Philadelphia was both the political and financial capital when the republic was born. Washington soon replaced Philadelphia as the political capital. Baltimore suffered a flight of fancy in 1819 when it sought financial leadership. New York was a more likely contender. It surpassed Philadelphia in population by 1820. The opening of the Erie Canal in 1825 further accelerated New York's growth. The unchallenged financial supremacy, with its accompanying rewards, of New York's upstart Wall Street would be long delayed, however, so long as the mammoth Federal Bank remained in Philadelphia's staid Chestnut Street. Wall Street enlisted the services of its native son, Martin Van Buren, who resigned the governorship of New York to become, in turn, Jackson's first Secretary of State, second Vice President, and successor as President of the United States. Van Buren ranks near the bottom on every poll of presidents. He would rank near the top of a business lobbyist's poll. He helped New York deliver the coup de grace to Philadelphia.

The 1832 election sealed the bank's fate. Jackson did not wait for its official death in 1836 before dismembering it. In 1833 President Jackson withdrew the U.S. government deposits from the Second Bank and distributed them among several private banks. Roger Taney, a Maryland

---

[11]The Baltimore branch of the Second Bank refused to pay a tax levied by the state of Maryland and was sued in the name of James McCulloch, the dishonest cashier. The Supreme Court clearly affirmed in the famous *McCulloch v. Maryland* case of 1819 that Congress had the power to incorporate a bank and that states could not interfere with its operation. Thus the constitutional issue was raised over a decade later merely to stir passions.

gentleman who subsequently was appointed Chief Justice of the Supreme Court, was the Secretary of the Treasury at the time. Mr. Taney was a stockholder of Baltimore's Union Bank, which just happened to receive government deposits. The other banks were equally well-connected politically and came to be called "pet banks."

Free Banking, 1837–1863

The rural idealism, antielitism, and antimonopoly spirit which contributed to the demise of the Second Bank next challenged the state banks, and with good reason. *Every state bank had been chartered by a special act of the legislature*. Most incorporation acts stipulated that stockholders pay the state a significant "license" fee, the bank lend the state certain amounts on demand, meritorious organizations (often colleges) be allowed to purchase bank stock at favorable prices, and so on. The incorporation act did not stipulate, but it was clear to all, that bribes, or at least good political connections, were often essential. While not universally true, banks were means to reward political friends and punish political enemies. The charter of most banks purposely was quite short. Political meddling on the wrong side was grounds for denial of charter extensions. To correct these abuses, Michigan in 1837 and New York in 1838 passed so-called *free banking laws, which automatically granted bank charters upon satisfaction of specified requirements*. A key word is *automatically*. A special act of the legislature was no longer required to establish a bank. Anyone who qualified could become a banker. Virtually all the states soon followed the example of Michigan and New York.

If Michigan and New York were co-leaders of the democratic spirit in banking, they were at opposite ends of the spectrum in terms of the quality of their banks. The banking laws of the two states were quite similar. In terms of regulations and the CAMEL of modern bank examination, free banking laws typically did specify capital ratios, asset quality, and liquidity ratios.[12] However, enforcement in Michigan and many other states was almost nonexistent. Taking the free banking and equal rights spirit to its ridiculous extreme, Michigan did not check the honesty and capability of management and the bank's earnings potential—the M and E of CAMEL. New York banks generally were pillars of integrity, while *bank* in Michigan was a four letter word. Any crook could become a Michigan banker in 1840. We shall return to the diversity of bank operations shortly.

During this period there was neither a nationwide bank nor a federal banking authority. Relatively small private banks or state agencies attempted to perform four tasks associated with a central bank. In particular, a central bank:

---

[12]See the previous chapter's section on bank examinations.

1. Acts as a fiscal agent for the Treasury,
2. Fosters an efficient payments system,
3. Supervises and regulates the banking system, and
4. Controls money, interest rates, and/or other financial variables in order to achieve ultimate goals such as high employment.

Some of these tasks occasionally were performed successfully but most often unsuccessfully.

The Independent Treasury System

The free banking period officially began in 1837, but in some respects it began in 1833 with the dismemberment of the Second Bank and the creation of pet banks. The effective death of the Second Bank ushered in a period of profitable bank expansion. Between 1834 and 1837, 194 new banks were organized, increasing the banking system by approximately one third. The normal increase in the demand for specie associated with the banking expansion—recall our friend of Chapter 4, the currency ratio—was fictitiously augmented by the July 1836 specie circular forbidding anything but specie in payment of public lands. The inevitable occurred. Banks could not meet the demand for specie and in concert suspended convertibility. Inconvertibility remained widespread for three years.

The blatant favoritism of the pet banks scheme and the general suspension of convertibility convinced many that state banks were inappropriate fiscal agents. The government needed unbiased and safe depositories. Lacking a federal bank, the Independent Treasury system was adopted in 1840, only to be repealed the following year. But in 1846 the system was adopted again and, with some modification in 1867, remained in effect until the creation of the Federal Reserve System in 1913. *In order to divorce government finances from the banking system, the Independent Treasury system stipulated that (1) all payments to the government were to be made in specie or government notes, and (2) all, later revised to most, government funds would be held in "safety deposit boxes" constructed throughout the country.* The goldsmiths of old would have been proud!

What was the effect of the Independent Treasury? It hampered monetary stability. Specie and government notes were the reserves of the banking system. An excess of government receipts over expenditures filled the strongboxes but drained reserves from the banking system. This produced a multiple money contraction in a fractional reserve system. Government deficits had the opposite effect. *Lack of synchronization of government receipts and expenditures, particularly during relatively short time periods such as quarters, made the money supply quite volatile.* If banks had continued to function as fiscal agents, tax payment simply would have reduced private deposits and increased Treasury deposits at the banks. As time passed and the effect of deficits and surpluses on the money supply became clearer, several Secretaries of the Treasury diligently attempted to synchronize receipts and expenditures. A few even became primitive central bankers practicing open-market operations. That is, any surplus was expended on the few government bonds outstanding. Moreover, the spirit of the law sometimes was ignored with impunity. The Independent Treasury system eventually did let the Treasury maintain small deposit balances for special reasons. Some Secretaries interpreted "small" and "special" quite liberally.

Cooperative Schemes

Banks developed several cooperative practices which made the payments and banking systems more efficient and profitable and simultaneously lowered bank failures. Many of these practices began during the era of the Second Bank but flourished after it ceased to exist. The Suffolk Bank of Boston pioneered a regional deposit and note redemption and collection system. Country banks around Boston opened accounts at the Suffolk Bank. Instead of sending checks and notes directly to each other, it was much cheaper and faster for each bank to send them to a central location. The Suffolk Bank debited and credited the appropriate bank's account. The country banks did hold some specie for over-the-counter redemptions. However, the deposits at the Suffolk Bank and similar banks in other areas became the principal reserves of the country banks. Thus began the *pyramiding of reserves, where deposits at a city bank are the reserves of a country bank.* The Suffolk Bank treated bank and other deposits similarly. It maintained the same specie (reserve) ratio against all deposits. Consequently, pyramiding reduced the ratio of banking system cash holdings to deposits and notes outstanding and increased the vulnerability of the banking system to shifts in the public's currency ratio. In time, the Suffolk Bank extended the variety of services it offered the country banks. We still have a *correspondent banking system whereby small banks maintain deposits at large banks in exchange for collection and other services.* Since most checks and notes that a bank receives are drawn on nearby banks, it would be silly for, say, a Georgia bank to have a Massachusetts collection agent. Lacking a nationwide bank, banks in each region produced their versions of the Suffolk system. *Nationwide check collection remained difficult.*[13]

Bank insurance schemes are the second major example of industry cooperation. In response to bank depositors' and note holders' pleas for a liquid and solvent banking system, the New York legislature passed the

---

[13]Cf. the role of "Big Bank" in the check collection process outlined in Chapter 3.

Safety-Fund Act of 1829. The act established the first precursor to the FDIC. The banks contributed to a fund administered by the New York bank commissioner, who made payments to failed banks' noteholders and depositors. Bank diversity toward risk taking made the safety fund controversial, just as the FDIC is today. The insurance premiums reduced profitability. However, insurance enhanced bank solvency and liquidity from the viewpoint of depositors and reduced deposit instability. Banks were able to hold more relatively illiquid, high-return assets. The conservative New York City banks already enjoyed the public's confidence. In their minds, the premiums exceeded the value of the insurance, in terms of their ability to operate with less zero-earning cash due to greater public confidence. The risk-taking smaller upstate banks, which deservedly were somewhat less well-regarded, did favor insurance from its inception. With the passage of several crises, even the city banks came to favor the safety fund, which was dissolved with the establishment of the national banking system in 1863. The New York safety fund remained solvent, although barely so at times, because other New York bank regulations emphasized safety. In the chaotic national market the New York banks chose to project a conservative image. Most other state bank insurance schemes failed within a few years.

The Chaos of State Bank Notes

To appreciate the diversity and problems under the free banking system, let us examine the process of organizing a bank in Michigan and New York. *Some Michigan bank promoters would proceed to a distant and inaccessible county and request a certificate of incorporation from the secretary of state*. The free banking laws specified that at least 30 percent of the capital stock had to be paid in specie, while the remaining 70 percent could be subscribed by a personal bond (IOU). In other words, loans to stockholders could finance up to 70 percent of a bank's capital or net worth. Line 1 of the balance sheet illustrates the establishment of New Bank. Bank commissioners then verified that New Bank had specie, took possession of the bonds of stockholders, and countersigned $700 in notes beautifully engraved by the New Bank. *Each bank issued personalized notes (paper currency)*. The signature of the bank commissioner verified the possession of collateral (stockholders' bonds) equal to the notes outstanding. Line 2 illustrates that notes are placed in circulation by the acquisition of bonds, mortgages, or something else.

(1) Establishment of the bank, and (2) notes are placed in circulation.

New Bank of Michigan

Assets		Liabilities	
(1) Specie (cash reserves)	300	Net Worth	1,000
Bonds of (loans to) stockholders	700		
(2) Assets acquired with notes	700	Notes in circulation	700

Were the New Bank's notes safe? Could they be converted dollar-for-dollar into specie or other assets? At first glance the answer seems yes. The capital (net worth) ratio was extremely high. Assets were $1,700 while notes equaled only $700. The bank commissioner held $700 in bonds of stockholders which could be sold to pay off note holders. The similar regulations in Michigan and New York were strict enough if administered and enforced. True, the law requiring only a 30 percent cash payment was somewhat lax, but "payment" of a bank's capital stock by a loan from the bank itself is not necessarily any more reprehensible than bank credit for purchases of other companies' stock. The difference between Michigan and New York was that New York bank operators were persons of means who were required to offer sufficient collateral *other than the bank stock,* while some Michigan bank operators were deadbeats without collateral except the stock being financed. The IOUs backing some Michigan bank notes were worthless. The Michigan authorities should have known something was amiss: why would any *honest* person establish a bank in an inaccessible place? There is only one conclusion: the banker was dishonest. When the ordeal of examination had been safely passed, specie was promptly withdrawn. "The specie found by them [examiners] in one bank was sent by hurried journey ahead of them to be counted at the next. Gold and silver flew about the country with the celerity of magic."[14] Conservative New York banks purchased high-quality canal or railroad bonds with their notes. The *wildcat banks,* so called because of their location in areas more heavily populated by wildcats than humans, placed their notes in circulation by satisfying their whims for high living. Very simply, wildcat bankers were given a license to steal. "Perjury and direct robbery of associates seem to have been frequent in the history of these associations, and no legal penalties appear to have been inflicted."[15] When holders of wildcat notes attempted to redeem them, they found the bank's cupboard bare or at least less than full.

Similar swindles would be discovered sooner today because bank liabilities are deposits, which do not circulate. That is, checks are cashed or deposited but rarely endorsed payable to someone else. Currency circulates, passing through various hands before finally reaching a bank. Given the poor communications system of the 19th century and the location of wildcat banks, partially valuable or even worthless notes stayed in circulation for a long time.[16] Speculators purchased wildcat notes from

---

[14]John J. Knox, *A History of Banking in the United States* (New York: Bradford Rhodes & Company, 1903), pp. 733–34.

[15]Ibid., p. 734.

[16]Most crook/bankers found that they could embezzle a larger amount by making some legitimate loans, which gave their notes some value. Use of all notes for strictly nonbanking purposes attracts attention and reduces the time period of circulation.

TABLE 16–1
Percent Change of State Bank Notes and Deposits, 1834–1861

Period	*Bank Notes*	*Deposits*	*Total Notes and Deposits*
1834–37	+56	+68	+61
1837–43	−60	−56	−58
1843–48	+120	+84	+102
1848–49	−11	−12	−11
1849–54	+110	+107	+109
1854–55	−29	+2	−12
1855–57	+13	+21	+18
1857–58	−28	−20	−23
1858–61	+30	+38	+35

Source: John J. Knox, *A History of Banking in the United States* (New York: Bradford Rhodes & Company, 1903), p. 312.

the knowledgeable at deep discounts and, like holders of the Old Maid card, passed them off on the unsuspecting. Personalized notes compounded the chaotic currency situation. Counterfeit notes of safe banks easily duped a citizenry unfamiliar with the notes of all 1,600 banks existing in 1860. In any economic environment, however gloomy, enterprising people see a need and make a buck. Thompson saw a need. His *Bank Notes Reporter and Counterfeit Detector* became required reading. Still, the marvel is how long some wildcat notes circulated, particularly at the beginning of the free banking era. Thompson's *Reporter* and public outcries for a safe currency eliminated the worst abuses by 1860, but outcries for further reform justifiably continued.

Table 16–1 shows the variability of state bank notes and deposits between the effective demise of the Second Bank in late 1833 and 1860. A rapid expansion following termination of the Second Bank's restraining influence started the period on its roller-coaster path.

The National Banking System, 1863–1913

Many of the controversies which engulfed the First and Second Bank of the United States came to a head in 1861. The Civil War erupted. It was financed through taxes and bond sales at first. The Continental Congress's experiment with paper money was such a disaster that it deterred the federal government until there was no alternative. In 1862 the federal government issued *greenbacks,* the popular name given to the *first government-issued paper money of any real consequence (large amount).* Greenbacks were more successful than continentals; they always had some value. Nevertheless, the detrimental side effects of large greenback issues were predictable. Within a few months prices rose, and the United States went off the gold standard. No government can maintain a fixed-price for gold, as required by the gold standard, during inflation. When the prices for commodities in general rise, gold at a fixed-dollar price appears cheap, and the public attempts to convert its dollars into gold. The government eventually runs out of gold. Just as overexpansion by banks ultimately made their deposits inconvertible into currency, so overissued paper money became inconvertible into gold at a fixed-exchange rate. Between 1862 and 1879 the United States was on an inconvertible paper standard, much as it is today. Gold was like any other commodity. Its dollar price rose and fell instead of remaining constant, as the gold standard requires.

Important as greenbacks were, the so-called National Banking Act of 1863, amended in 1864 and 1865—Congress was determined to get it right—influenced currency and banking more strongly.[17] This act was designed to (1) reduce bank abuses and create a safe banking system, (2) correct the chaotic state bank note situation, and (3) aid the federal government's financing of the Civil War. In order to fulfill these objectives, the act provided for the creation of a national banking system while simultaneously attempting to abolish the state banking system.

The National Banking Act accepted the principle of free banking. It established the Office of the Comptroller of the Currency, which would charter any bank meeting certain minimum standards. *The act created a sounder banking system by setting minimum standards higher than those of most states and by enforcing the standards vigorously.* The act also encouraged the free flow of information. The more prominent regulations were:

1. Organizers of all national banks had to pay cash for the bank's stock. This prevented assetless deadbeats from gaining control of banks by having the bank itself finance its capital stock. Moreover, the capital requirement was high.
2. Reserve requirements against deposits were high, and bank notes were fully backed by government bonds at all times, which made them convertible into specie. We shall return to these requirements later.
3. Assets were restricted in order to improve quality and encourage diversification. In particular, real estate loans, which often were quite speculative, and loans exceeding 10 percent of the bank's net worth were prohibited.
4. National banks were required to file reports of condition with the Comptroller and publish the reports in newspapers accessible to their stockholders and depositors.
5. Banks were examined to verify compliance with the law. Penalties for regulatory violations ranged from harassment to closure, and

[17]The act is officially the National Currency Act but is now called the National Banking Act because it had a more lasting effect on banking than currency.

the legal authorities were promptly advised of embezzlements and other crimes.

Establishment of higher standards accomplishes nothing per se unless a mechanism is devised whereby banks join the system and become subject to the standards. What inducement did the National Banking Act provide for the state banks to become national banks? A national bank could issue notes, appropriately called national bank notes, equal to 90 percent of the par or market value of special government bonds, whichever was lower. The bank's bonds were deposited with the Comptroller, who would sell the bonds and pay noteholders if the bank could not redeem its notes. Possession by the Comptroller of pledged bonds always exceeding by at least 10 percent the amount of bank notes outstanding guaranteed the notes' convertibility. Aside from affixing the name of the issuing bank, the notes were uniform and well designed. This made detection of counterfeits easier. Since banks earned the interest on the bonds, which the Comptroller held merely for safekeeping, the government thought banks would find the note-issue privilege extremely profitable. The interest-earning bonds provided the basis for notes, which could be lent out again to earn more interest. The notes issued could equal a bank's net worth (capital). *The carrot to join the banking system would have produced a safe currency and helped finance the war by increasing banks' demand for government bonds.* A minor problem arose: the carrot was insufficiently sweet. Banks also kept the interest on the assets pledged for their state bank notes. While most states limited bank notes to a fraction of a bank's capital, the ability of national banks to issue notes equal to their capital was insufficient compensation for the onerous federal regulations.

In 1865 the stick was applied. State bank notes were taxed 10 percent annually. The Comptroller thought this surely would kill all state banks. Since the assets the notes were financing earned less than 10 percent, state bank notes became unprofitable and were quickly retired. Many banks immediately changed status from state to national in order to issue the untaxed national notes. *Tax avoidance created a uniform, safe currency and increased the demand for government bonds.* Within two years, however, the rush to join the national banking system ended. Many banks decided that the lower reserve requirements and generally less exacting regulations of the states outweighed their need to issue notes. Deposit banking was on the rise. Look at Table 16–1. In most subperiods deposits rose more or decreased less than notes. By 1867 a dual banking system was firmly rooted.

The National Banking Act did correct the main monetary problem of its time, an unsafe currency system. *It had a major fault: the quantity of currency was inelastic.*[18] *This fault was compounded by a flaw of the free*

[18]The fault often is inaccurately labeled an inelastic money supply.

TABLE 16–2
Reserves under the National Banking System, 1863–1913

Type of Bank	*Required Reserve Ratio*	*Composition of Reserves*
Central reserve city (New York, Chicago, and St. Louis)	25	All cash in vault
Reserve city (47 other large cities)	25	Up to one half of reserves (12.5 percent of deposits) as deposits at central reserve city banks and remainder as vault cash
Country	15	Up to three fifths of reserves as deposits at central reserve or reserve city banks and remainder as vault cash

banking period which was uncorrected by the act, namely, the pyramiding of reserves due to an inefficient check-collection process. Consider the pyramiding of reserves first. For purposes of reserve requirements, the National Banking System established three bank classes determined by location. The information is presented in Table 16–2. Although the *quoted* reserve ratios were quite high, the bank currency/deposit or *effective* reserve ratios were relatively low because banks did pyramid reserves as allowed by the law. Banks held reserves in the form of deposits at larger banks instead of currency because (1) larger banks paid interest on deposits, and (2) deposits at larger banks facilitated check clearance and collection.

Three types of currency circulated: (1) gold and silver coins, (2) government paper money (greenbacks), and (3) national bank notes. *All three types of currency were inelastically supplied, that is, currency was virtually fixed in the short run and did not respond to seasonal and cyclical needs.* Little gold and silver can be mined or imported in the short run. An 1878 statute placed a ceiling of $347 million on greenbacks outstanding. Greenbacks are reissued periodically to satisfy the demand for a crisp currency, but the amount outstanding remains fixed at this amount. National bank notes were secured by special (circulation privilege) government bonds. These bonds were relatively fixed, and any change was dictated by the government's surplus or deficit instead of seasonal or cyclical needs for currency. The inelastic currency supply was particularly troublesome because the agrarian economy and lack of deposit insurance produced large seasonal and erratic variations in the desired currency/deposit ratio. Because currency was inelastic, the public's greater demand for currency could be met only through decreases in bank currency reserves and a multiple deposit contraction. The pyramiding of reserves meant that banks held little currency. Any pressure within the system was quickly transmitted and magnified at the apex, particularly the New York City banks. These banks typically called their stock market loans when country banks withdrew their deposits. Of course, borrowers for stock market purposes did not have sufficient idle money and were forced to sell their stock. If enough calls were made, stock prices fell precipitously, producing a so-called panic or crisis. Even this could be insufficient. The seller of stock typically was paid by check, which was deposited to pay off the loan. Banks needed currency, however. Banks sometimes halted the multiple contraction process by universally agreeing on suspension and inconvertibility. So long as the public demanded large amounts of currency, banks in unison agreed not to provide it. They simply could not. Convertibility resumed when the public no longer wanted to convert deposits into cash. Major panics and suspensions of currency payments occurred in 1873, 1884, 1893, and 1907. The panic of 1907 was the last straw. *The country needed an elastic currency.*

Structure of the Federal Reserve System

The National Monetary Commission established in 1908 undertook a broad and exhaustive study of America's financial needs. While a consensus on the need for a central bank existed, disagreement on the structure of the Federal Reserve System was so intense as to almost block its creation. Five years elapsed between creation of the National Monetary Commission and passage of the Federal Reserve Act. Congress and bankers recognized that the structure of any organization, which sometimes is dismissed as a mere mechanical detail, has great practical importance. For example, who should select Federal Reserve officials, bankers or the President? The answer to this question clearly would influence the objectives and operational methods of the system. Rural idealists favored a decentralized organization managed by officials who were appointed by the President and confirmed by the Senate and whose primary allegiance was to the public. They were convinced that control of America's banking and financial system rested in the hands of a small Wall Street cadre, the so-called Money Trust. A decentralized, geographically dispersed Federal Reserve System would be less likely to come under the Money Trust's control. The agrarians wanted a public-oriented Federal Reserve to regulate the Money Trust out of existence. Urban realists on the other hand denied the existence of a Money Trust. They favored a centralized, banker-dominated organization free from government interference and guided by the nation's laissez-faire economic policy. The structure of the Federal Reserve System reflects the carefully crafted compromise between rural idealists and urban realists.

FIGURE 16–1

The Federal Reserve System: Boundaries of Federal Reserve Districts and Their Branch Territories

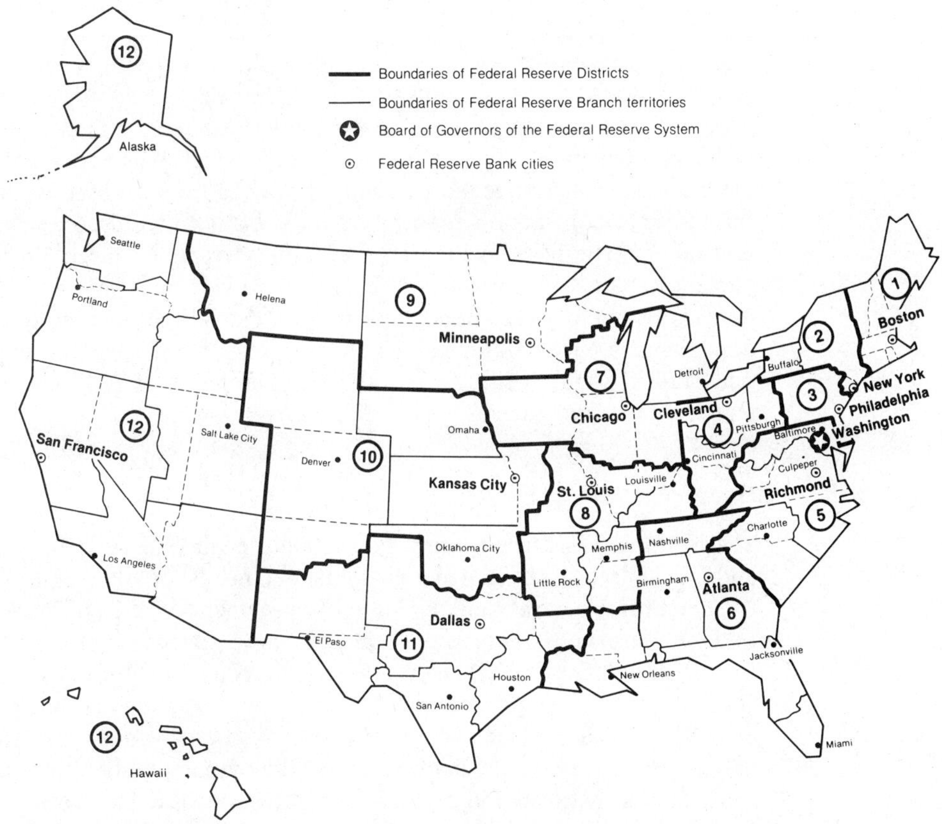

Federal Reserve Banks

The full title of the Federal Reserve Act is, "An Act to provide for the establishment of Federal reserve banks, to furnish an elastic currency, to afford means of rediscounting commercial paper, to establish a more effective supervision of banking in the United States, and for other purposes." Although the Fed's precise goals, instruments, and operating procedures have varied significantly over time, the act's full title alludes to its two constant and general goals: (1) management of currency, money, credit, and/or interest rates; and (2) creation of an efficient and smoothly functioning banking and financial system. The Fed has performed the second goal so efficiently that it now is unappreciated and taken for granted. The early banking history was presented in part to dispel the all too common view that the unglamorous second goal matters little. The Fed's main "housekeeping" chores which maintain a smoothly functioning financial system and, thereby, economy are (*a*) the supervision and regulation of the banking system, (*b*) the clearance and collection of checks, and (*c*) the fiscal agent function for the Treasury. Part 3 discussed the first housekeeping chore, which the Fed shares with other banking authorities, and the next chapter describes how the other two chores are performed.

Banks had to be established. A Washington-based board could supervise commercial banks, but only (Federal Reserve) Banks can create currency, accept deposits, extend discounts to commercial banks, collect checks, and be an efficient fiscal agent. The Federal Reserve Act (and amendments in 1914) divided the country into 12 districts, with each district having a Federal Reserve Bank and typically some branches. Figure 16–1 shows district boundaries, bank cities, and branch cities. (In what district do you live? Districts are identified by number or by the bank city.) The boundaries of the Federal Reserve districts were drawn "with due regard to the convenience and customary course of business and shall not necessarily be coterminous with any State or States."

Each of the Federal Reserve Banks is a corporation. Member banks subscribed to the capital stock of their district Federal Reserve Bank an amount equal to 6 (subsequently 3) percent of their own net worth. With this net worth the Fed Banks were able to operate from their inception without congressional appropriations. The rural/urban compromise granted sole ownership to the member banks but effectively made the Fed Banks' stock preferred stock paying a 6 percent dividend. The member banks do not have the proprietory rights, powers, and privileges that belong to stockholders of private corporations. After payment of the required dividend, virtually all profits are distributed to the Treasury.

The management selection process also reflects the private and public nature of the Fed Banks. Each Fed Bank has nine directors divided into three classes, A, B, and C. The three class A directors are bankers, and the three class B directors are merchants, industrialists, or farmers who are not directors or controlling stockholders of banks. The class A and B directors are elected by member banks, one director of each class being elected by small banks, one of each class by medium-size banks, and one of each class by large banks. The three class C directors, who must be nonbankers, are designated by the Washington-based Board of Governors, whose members are selected by the President and confirmed by the Senate. One of the class C directors is designated as chairman of the Reserve Bank's board. The directors are responsible for the conduct of the affairs of the Reserve Bank. They appoint the Reserve Banks' operating officers, but the law requires that the president and first vice-president be approved by the Washington-based board.

Besides performing the important housekeeping functions, the Reserve Banks participate in monetary and interest rate policy decisions. Indeed, *the Federal Reserve Act specified that the Banks should be the main, or at least an equal, partner in the monetary policy decision-making process.* The full title of the act indicates that an elastic currency and, therefore, monetary base was to be provided by the rediscounting of commercial paper or real bills. Banks could borrow (discount) at the Reserve Banks and acquire currency or a deposit credit by offering real bills as collateral.[19] (The balance sheet effects of discounting were illustrated in Chapter 3.) *The discount rate for each district is jointly determined by the district Bank and the Washington-based board. The district Bank proposes discount changes, which must be approved by the board.* Thus, in (agrarian) principle, one could simultaneously have 12 different discount rates. Principle has never corresponded with reality. Discount rates have not always been uniform, but differences typically have been short-lived.

In the early years of the Federal Reserve System, the board routinely acquiesced to the Banks, which were led by the New York Bank. Although the organization chart has remained constant, officials change, and by force of personalities *the board gradually seized power over discounting. By the late 1920s, the board did not immediately approve Banks' proposed discount rate changes.* The board now dominates discount policy. The board tells the Banks what it believes the appropriate discount rate is, and most Banks are sufficiently compliant to "request" the board's desired rate. The remainder then quickly fall in line for the sake of unity within the system. The Banks' diminished role in the discount process understates their decline in monetary policy decison making. *The framers of the Federal Reserve Act envisaged that discount policy would be the main monetary policy tool. However, discounting has long been eclipsed by reserve requirement policy and open-market operations, particularly the latter.*

Board of Governors of the Federal Reserve System

The board is composed of seven members appointed by the President and confirmed by the Senate. The term of office is 14 years. Members who have served a full term may not be reappointed. The members must come from different Federal Reserve districts, and in making appointments the President is to "have due regard to a fair representation of the financial, agricultural, industrial, and commercial interest and geograph-

---

[19]Because the real bills which served as collateral typically were discounted, that is, interest was prepaid so the borrower received less than the face value of the loan from the commercial bank, the Fed was said to "rediscount" the bills.

ical divisions of the country.'' It is incongruous that an economic policy board existed for nearly 50 years before a practicing economist was appointed a member in the early 1960s! Economists have been represented ever since, often by several members. The President designates one of the members as chairperson. Arthur Burns was the first economist to assume the chair.

The Board of Governors, and particularly its chairperson, is the central controlling authority within the Federal Reserve System. While the board's power grab over the discounting mechanism began in the 1920s and was based solely on the force of personalities, the general activism of Franklin D. Roosevelt's presidency in 1933 and ''the need to do something'' to lift the economy from the depression doldrums officially centralized control within the board. The Banking Act of 1935 gave the board (1) *sole* authority to set reserve requirements, within broad ranges specified by Congress, and (2) a majority on the Federal Open Market Committee.[20] Until 1935 reserve requirements were set by Congress and could *not* be changed by any unit within the Fed. Reserve requirements were phased in, becoming fully effective in 1917, and remained constant until 1936, when the board raised reserve requirements to reduce excess reserves and eliminate the ''inflationary potential'' of an economy suffering more than 15 percent unemployment. (See Chapter 4.) Fortunately, subsequent reserve requirement policy has been more judicious. Requirement changes still occur relatively infrequently. Open-market operations are the main monetary policy tool.

Federal Open Market Committee (FOMC)

The Federal Reserve Act gave the system the power to buy and sell government securities and a few other types of marketable financial instruments. This power was granted almost as an afterthought of little

---

[20]Broadly defined privileges of office and other auxiliary information, which often are better indicators of power than job descriptions, confirm the shift of power from the Banks to the board. For example, in banking circles governor is a more prestigious title than president. Prior to the 1930s, the head of each Fed Bank was a governor, while only the head of the five-member, Washington-based Federal Reserve Board was a governor. The Banking Act expanded the Federal Reserve Board to seven members (the two ex-officio members were dropped) and rechristened it the Board of Governors of the Federal Reserve System. Each member of the board was elevated to governor status, and the head officer of the Banks was demoted to president. In addition, the governors received a significant salary increase, and their term of office was lengthened from 10 to 14 years. However, even after the increase, Board of Governor salaries were only about one third the salaries of Bank presidents because the Banks officially are private firms which are not bound by civil service regulations. By 1980 Bank salaries were only somewhat higher than board salaries. Significant salary differentials between government employees and employees of government-sponsored agencies still exist today. For example, the heads of Fannie Mae and the Synthetic Fuel Corporation earn much more than cabinet secretaries.

consequence. The act was passed during calm times when belief in the automaticity of the gold standard ruled supreme. Banks themselves thought that active intervention in financial markets generally was inappropriate and would occur only on special occasions. However, within a year the world became embroiled in a war, and many countries were forced off the gold standard, making intervention much more feasible. By the time the United States entered the war in 1917, the Reserve Banks were conducting modest open-market operations in order to support the government bond market and for the very practical reason that they needed some income.[21] Bank discounts, the other Fed earning asset, were insufficiently large to cover the Fed's operating costs. Surprisingly enough, the Fed in its early years did not realize that open-market purchases have the same effect on currency and reserves as discounts. The effect of discounts is clear because the Fed immediately credits the commercial bank's deposit account. However, the effect of open-market purchases on currency or reserves appears only after the seller deposits the Fed's check. Although the time interval between open-market purchases and check collection is very short, several years passed before the Fed clearly recognized that purchases increase reserves.

The Banks in 1923 formed a committee of five eastern Fed Bank presidents, expanded in 1930 to all 12 Bank presidents, which coordinated open-market operations. Prior to that date individual Banks engaged in independent open-market operations, some Banks selling while others were simultaneously buying. The Banking Act of 1935 sealed the transfer of monetary powers from the Banks to the board by creating a Federal Open Market Committee (FOMC). Like its predecessor committee, the FOMC has 12 voting members, but the 7 Bank presidents added in 1930 were replaced by the entire Board of Governors. The president of the New York Bank retained a permanent seat on the FOMC. The remaining four slots on the FOMC are rotated annually among the other 11 Bank presidents. The seven nonvoting Bank presidents attend the FOMC meetings and participate in the debate. Consistent with the FOMC's makeup, the committee's staff, who also attend the meetings and advise the members, is drawn from the entire system. Although the FOMC officially determines only open-market operations, discount and reserve requirement policy are discussed at the meetings in order to coordinate all three monetary policy tools.

---

[21]Support of the government bond market came mainly through relaxation of the real bills requirement and allowance of discounts secured by government bonds. The Fed preferred the lesser visibility of this indirect means of supporting the bond market to direct purchases.

Advisory Committees

The Federal Reserve System has two formal, legislated advisory groups, the Federal Advisory Council and the Consumer Advisory Council. The creation of a Federal Advisory Council was inserted into the Federal Reserve Act to appease the American Bankers Association, which had denounced a "public" board as communistic, confiscatory, un-American, and, generally, a snake in the grass. The Federal Advisory Council consists of 12 *bankers*, one from each Federal Reserve district, who meet quarterly in Washington and serve as a liaison between the Reserve Banks and the board. The Consumer Advisory Council, which is composed of approximately 30 creditors, consumers, and others, was established in 1976 pursuant to the Equal Credit Opportunity Act to advise the board on consumer matters. Besides these legislated advisory groups, the Fed has created several informal committees. While not a committee, no mention of advice received by the Fed would be complete without mention of its staff. As far as government staffs go, the Fed staff clearly is one of the best.

Monetary Power beyond Organization Charts

Who shapes monetary policy? Open-market operations have totally eclipsed discounting as a source of currency and reserves, and reserve requirements are changed quite infrequently. Thus, the shapers of open-market policy largely set monetary policy. The seven to five majority on the FOMC enjoyed by the board suggests that it sets monetary policy. Voting strength does facilitate the exercise of power. However, numbers of potential voters do *not* always equal power, as political analysts or anyone who has served on a committee knows. Limitations on campaign contributions are attempts to transform "one person, one vote" into "each person equal." Power does not necessarily require a vote, as the phrase "power behind the throne" implies. Given this, who actually sets monetary policy? The best answer was given by someone intimately involved. Sherman J. Maisel, professor of economics at the University of California at Berkeley and a governor of the Federal Reserve from 1965 to 1972, estimated that during his tenure monetary power within the Federal Reserve System was shared in the following proportions: (1) the chairman, 45 percent; (2) the staff of the board and FOMC, 25 percent; (3) the other governors, 20 percent; and (4) Federal Reserve Banks, 10 percent.[22] According to Maisel, the paid staff of advisers advise, while the two legislated advisory committees scurry the corridors of power unable to find an attentive ear.

---

[22]Sherman J. Maisel, *Managing the Dollar* (New York: W. W. Norton, 1973), p. 110.

We caution the reader that these percentages are not immutable. Power depends partially on personalities. William McChesney Martin and Arthur Burns were the chairmen between 1965 and 1972 while Paul Volcker is the current chairman. Nevertheless, the percentage estimates remain reasonably accurate today. Why is the chair so powerful? First, to the outside world "the" Federal Reserve is the chair and a group of faceless people. As titular head and spokesperson of the Fed, the chair testifies before Congress and participates in many decisions which never come before the board. For example, overall economic policy sometimes is coordinated by the Quadriad, who are the Secretary of the Treasury, chair of the Council of Economic Advisers, director of the Office of Management and Budget, and the Federal Reserve Board chair. The chair's power outside the system attracts votes and reinforces its power within the system. Second, the chair in any committee system is strengthened by its ability to select the agenda and shape the debate.

Summary/Questions

The Federal Reserve Act established a central bank the goals and structure of which have changed considerably over time. The framers of the act primarily wanted an elastic currency so that an increase in the demand for currency did not lead to a decrease in reserves and a multiple money contraction. In terms of the analysis of Chapters 3 and 4, a higher currency ratio reduces the money multiplier and money supply, *ceteris paribus*. The framers of the act wanted to break the *ceteris paribus* condition. They wanted a higher currency ratio to be countered by a monetary base augmented by discounting, thereby keeping the money supply constant. Over longer periods they wanted the money supply to follow the dictates of the gold standard and *passively* adjust to economic activity. The Fed continues to neutralize the effect of shifts in the currency ratio. However, such offsetting policy is now considered a technicality, albeit important. Monetary policy now *actively* manages the money supply with a view to full employment and price stability.

The change in goals affected and was affected by the structure of the Fed. A passive monetary policy was consistent with decentralized decision-making and discounting, which is at the discretion of commercial banks. Although the board and the 12 Fed Banks legally continue to share power over the discounting mechanism, the Fed Banks now effectively are very junior partners. The Banking Act of 1935 legitimatized the centralization of power and the activist orientation of the Fed. Creation of a board-dominated FOMC officially recognized the importance of open-market operations. Moreover, the board alone was granted the power to change reserve requirements. The Fed has lost its rural idealist roots.

1. Describe the colonial monetary system. What was the unit of account? What was the medium of exchange? Did the Revolutionary War significantly change the financial structure?
2. Explain how inflation is a tax.
3. What are the essential elements of the rural idealism versus urban reality controversy? How has its precise expression changed over time?
4. State the arguments for and against the First Bank of the United States which resurfaced when the Second Bank's charter was considered. The charter of each bank was not renewed largely because the political strength of their advocates declined during the interim. However, in each case some new issues arose which contributed to its demise. For both the First and Second Bank, state some issues discussed during the charter *renewal* period but not during the original charter *issuance* period.
5. What two functions normally associated with central banks did both the First and Second Bank of the United States perform?
6. Define the Independent Treasury system. How did it affect the stability of the monetary system?
7. Define free banking. When did it exist? What are the pros and cons of free banking?
8. What were the two main cooperative practices developed by banks during the free banking period?
9. What were the main reasons for the establishment of the National Banking System? Did it meet its goals?
10. What were the major faults of the National Banking System which the creation of the Federal Reserve System was supposed to rectify?
11. How does the organizational structure of the Federal Reserve reflect the rural idealism versus urban reality controversy?
12. Precisely what group within the Federal Reserve System determines (1) open-market operations, (2) the discount rate, and (3) reserve requirement ratios? Describe the decision-making groups in terms of appointment procedures, term of office, and so on.
13. State the changes in the decision making responsibilities within the Fed that occurred during 1933–35.

17 Determinants of the money supply: The monetary base

This chapter explains the final link in the money supply, the monetary base. Thus, in some respects it should have immediately followed Chapter 4, where we analyzed the money supply multiplier. In other respects, however, this chapter is an extension of the preceding one. We describe with the aid of balance sheets two major Federal Reserve housekeeping chores, check collection and the fiscal agent function. Important as these housekeeping chores are, the Fed was created primarily to provide an elastic currency, as the last chapter stated. Creators of the Fed stressed the need for elasticity because changes in the demand for currency and the composition of a *fixed* base produce monetary instability in a fractional reserve system. The Fed was supposed to neutralize currency demand shifts by varying the supply of currency and the base. This chapter shows how the Fed neutralizes the effect of currency shifts, but it goes further. The overwhelming proportion of *the chapter analyzes the variables uncontrolled by the Fed which influence the monetary base*. Contrary to the assumption of Chapter 4, the base is not perfectly controlled by the Fed. Indeed, we learned in Chapter 3 that discounts increase reserves and the base, and discounts are initiated by commercial banks themselves. In some ways the base now is too elastic; discounting is only one of several uncontrolled sources producing variations in the base. The final section explains how the Fed manipulates the base in order to (1) offset the effect of uncontrolled influences such as discounting, and (2) neutralize the effect of currency shifts.

This chapter is for specialists. Those little interested in identifying the specific uncontrolled factors which cause variations in the base should proceed directly to the summary.

Balance Sheets and the Monetary Base Equation

Currency is issued by and is a liability of the Federal Reserve or the Treasury, and reserves are vault cash and bank deposits at the Fed. *Therefore, the monetary base is the liability of either the Fed or the Treasury and is included within Tables 17–1 and 17–2, which present the Fed and Treasury monetary account balance sheets, respectively. In particular, lines K and L in Table 17–1 show the Fed's contribution toward the base, and line Q in Table 17–2 shows the Treasury's contribution.*

The balance sheet identity says that

$$\text{Assets} = \text{Liabilities} + \text{Net worth}$$

In the case at hand, some of the liabilities are the monetary base. Calling the remaining liabilities *and* net worth "other liabilities," the balance sheet identity for the monetary authorities may be expressed as

$$\text{Assets} = \text{Other liabilities} + \text{Base}$$
$$\text{Assets} - \text{Other liabilities} = \text{Base}$$

Our explanation of the monetary base relies heavily on the fundamental principle of double-entry bookkeeping that every transaction must affect

TABLE 17–1

Federal Reserve System Balance Sheet, August 31, 1984 ($ millions)

Assets		
(A) U.S. government securities		$162,046
(B) Discounts to banks		8,276
(C) Float		326
Cash in process of collection	6,808	
Deferred availability item	6,482	
(D) Miscellaneous assets		8,290
(E) Gold certificates		11,098
(F) Special drawing rights certificates		4,618
(G) Treasury currency		454
Total assets		$195,108
Liabilities and Net Worth		
(H) Treasury deposits		$ 4,029
(I) Foreign and other deposits		1,802
(J) Miscellaneous liabilities and net worth		6,140
(K) Federal Reserve notes in circulation		161,551
(L) Bank reserve deposits		21,586
Total liabilities and net worth		$195,108

TABLE 17–2
Treasury Monetary Account Balance Sheet, August 31, 1984 ($ millions)

Assets	
(M) Gold	$11,098
(N) Treasury currency outstanding	16,220
(O) Federal Reserve notes	225
Total assets	27,543
Liabilities and Net Worth	
(P) Gold certificates	$11,098
(Q) Treasury currency in circulation	15,980
(R) Treasury cash	465
Total liabilities and net worth	$27,543

at least two accounts. Any change in the base must be accompanied by a change in some other item on the monetary authorities' balance sheets. Stated somewhat differently, a change in any other item on the balance sheets *might* change the base. If Fed or Treasury assets increase *and* other liabilities are constant, then the base increases. An increase in other liabilities with assets constant implies that the base falls. The last two sentences suggest calling Fed and Treasury assets factors supplying the base, and other liabilities factors absorbing.[1] The new nomenclature expresses the balance sheet identity as

$$\text{Factors supplying} - \text{Factors absorbing} = \text{Base}$$

Of course, an increase in a factor supplying does not necessarily increase the base; the compensating double-entry bookkeeping account could be a decrease in another factor supplying or an increase in a factor absorbing. For example, suppose a transaction increases gold and Treasury cash, which are items (M) and (R), respectively, in Table 17–2. In this case the base remains constant as factors supplying and absorbing increase. However, the compensating balance sheet entry associated with changes in many factors supplying and absorbing is a change in the base. Do not let the new nomenclature for the balance sheet obscure the identity of the individual items. What items, and only what items, are factors supplying or absorbing the base? Federal Reserve and Treasury assets and liabilities.

The opening sentence stated that the monetary base would be explained. However, this chapter does not "explain" the base in any profound sense. Explaining the base simply means showing *how* the base changes. *We illustrate the series of balance sheet entries associated with a change in a factor supplying or absorbing, paying particular attention whether the compensating change on the balance sheet is the base or*

[1]Some call factors supplying "sources" of the base, and factors absorbing are called "uses" or "negative sources."

some other account. Giving the word *explain* this meaning involves a simplification. To a substantial extent we are deliberately avoiding a difficult question (why?) and substituting an easy question (how?). Don't be disappointed; the easy question is not that easy and it is enough for one chapter. In addition, illustrating how all the accounts in Tables 17–1 and 17–2 change is time consuming. At this point our only concession to the difficult (why?) question is answering the following: is the specific factor supplying or absorbing under the direct and immediate control of the monetary authorities, or does it change due to random events or forces only indirectly affected by the authorities? We also consider whether any change is somewhat long lasting or is likely to be reversed immediately. If a factor is not directly controlled by the monetary authorities, we attempt no elaborate explanation of the variables causing the factor to vary. Our concession to the difficult question is necessary for the extremely important discussion of monetary control in subsequent chapters. Can the Fed counteract the effect of all factors and control the base and the money supply? The message of this and previous chapters is: monetary control is not easy and requires some agility.

In some respects this is the book's most technical chapter up to this point. To breathe some life into what can be a series of sterile bookkeeping entries, we present substantial historical and institutional material. This blend of technical and institutional matter may blur the primary objective of this chapter. Therefore, the objectives deserve special emphasis. *The reader should learn (1) what items are included in the Fed and Treasury balance sheets, and for each item learn (2) the typical compensating entry required by double-entry bookkeeping, (3) whether the item is controlled directly by the Fed or changes for various reasons, and (4) the relative size and importance of each item as a contributor to short-run variations of the base.*

The sizes of the two balance sheets, Tables 17–1 and 17–2, suggest that the Treasury is decidedly the junior monetary authority. This is indeed the case. Therefore, let us begin with the Fed's balance sheet. Since all transactions are symmetric, we discuss only increases in the factors. Substituting words like *sell* for *buy* changes the sign of the entries.

The Fed's U.S. Government Securities Account and Discounts

The first account in Table 17–1, U.S. government securities held by the Fed, is easy to analyze and can well illustrate our approach to the monetary base. What is the typical compensating balance sheet entry when the Fed's holdings of U.S. government securities change? Do changes in the U.S. government securities account reflect policy decisions, or does the account change because of random forces and actions by others? The U.S. government securities account on the Fed's balance sheet equals the cumulative net open-market purchases. Although the mechanics of open-market purchases were presented earlier, they are repeated here. U.S. securities may be purchased from banks, line 1 in Figure 17–1, or from the public, which deposits the Fed's check, as illustrated in line 2. In either case, the deposit-of-banks-at-the-Fed component of the base increases. The U.S. government securities account is directly controlled by the Fed; it does not change unless the Fed makes a deliberate decision to buy or sell.[2]

As stated earlier, the Fed has purchased on the open market a minor amount of securities issued by such U.S. agencies as the Federal Home Loan Bank and Federal National Mortgage Association (Fanny Mae). Strictly speaking then, the U.S. government securities account is somewhat of a misnomer. From the view point of the money supply, however, the specific item purchased is irrelevant. The Fed could just as well purchase IBM shares or mosquito nets. *When the private sector (banks or the public) receive checks issued by the Fed, the base increases irrespective of the Fed's motive for issuing the check.*

Like open-market operations, discounting needs no long explanation at this stage. Figure 17–2 shows that discounts increase the base. The Fed does *not* directly control discounts. The Fed sets the discount rate but banks decide how much to borrow at the Fed, and their response to the discount rate is not always the same.

The discount figure in Table 17–1 is atypical. About $7 billion of the $8 billion in discounts was an ''extended credit'' to the failing Continental Illinois Bank. The function of discounts will be discussed in the next chapter. For our current purposes it is sufficient to note that discounts normally are a minor factor supplying the base. During the past several years discounts have averaged less than 1 percent of the base. During

FIGURE 17–1

Open-Market Purchases from (1) Banks and (2) the Public

Banking System

(1) U.S. securities	−100		
Deposits at Fed	+100		
(2) Deposits at Fed	+100	Check deposits	+100

Fed

(1) U.S. securities	+100	Deposits of banks	+100
(2) U.S. securities	+100	Deposits of banks	+100

[2]The existence of repurchase clauses for some securities does not contradict the text since the Fed must agree to the repurchase clause.

FIGURE 17–2
Discounting

Banking System				Fed			
Deposits at Fed	+100	Discounts at Fed	+100	Discounts to banks	+100	Deposits of banks	+100

relatively short periods of time, however, changes in the volume of discounts are substantial, both absolutely and relative to the base. For example, in early August 1977 market interest rates started rising quite sharply. In the week ending August 24, 1977 discounts averaged $1.7 billion. Four weeks earlier, when market interest rates were substantially lower, bank discounts averaged only $295 million. The volume of discounts is small relative to the base, but sometimes discounts are a major source of short-run monetary instability.[3]

Float: Cash in the Process of Collection Minus Deferred Availability Items

Float, which is the difference between cash in the process of collection and deferred availability items, stems from time lags in clearing checks. As stated in the last chapter, check collection was no simple matter before the existence of the Federal Reserve because all banks did not directly or indirectly maintain accounts at one bank, which would clear checks by debiting one bank's account and crediting another bank. It could involve the Wells Fargo Company shipping coins and currency around the country.[4] Indeed, check collection was sufficiently expensive and time consuming that many checks were not paid at par. That is, the bank against which a check was drawn paid a small (say, 50 cents) amount less than the stated amount of the check although it debited the check issuer's account by the full face value of the check, the difference between the amount debited and paid being a service charge. These *nonpar banks* were not uncommon in various regions up to the 1950s. Today only a few (about 10) small banks in Louisiana have refused to give up their check collection service charges.

---

[3]The sentence in the text may sound incorrect because the important distinction between current values and changes is often confused. Suppose that discounts increase from 1 to 2 during some time period, and the base changes from 100 to 101. Discounts are always small compared to the base—1 percent at the beginning and about 2 percent at the end of the period—but the change in discounts is a substantial proportion (100 percent in this case) of the change in the base.

[4]More often, however, check collection involved an elaborate system of correspondent banks.

The Federal Reserve Act provided for an efficient and rapid system of check collection through Federal Reserve Banks and branches scattered throughout the country. The Fed's check collection system, which is available to all par banks, is one of the least glamorous housekeeping operations performed by the Fed. Nonetheless, it is vital to the proper functioning of the financial sector. Ignoring nonpar banks, suppose you deposit at the Union Trust Company of Maryland a $100 check drawn on the Bank of Winnemucca (an exciting little town in northern Nevada). Union Trust forwards the check to the Baltimore branch of the Federal Reserve for collection.[5] Note that the Fed does not immediately increase the reserves of Union Trust and decrease the reserves of the Bank of Winnemucca. Because of this some banks do not allow you to write checks against very recent deposits. The Fed debits cash in the process of collection, funds it is attempting to collect from the bank of Winnemucca, and credits deferred availability items, a temporary account showing the amount to be credited to Union Trust in the near future.

FIGURE 17–3
Check Collection

Union Trust				**Fed**			
Cash in the process of collection	+100	Check deposits	+100	Cash in the process of collection	+100	Deferred availability items	+100

Why doesn't the Fed immediately credit the account of one bank and debit the account of the other? The answer is simple but not obvious. It has nothing to do with rubber checks. The Fed does not immediately decrease the deposits of the Bank of Winnemucca because *reserve management is complicated by debits unbeknown to a bank.* Banks are required to hold reserves at least equal to a specified fraction of deposits. A bank unaware of debits to its reserve account would have substantial difficulty meeting the reserve requirement. You surely would have a difficult time balancing your checkbook if you were unaware of debits to your account. Therefore, the Fed does not debit the Bank of Winnemucca's account until the bank receives its depositor's check. But when will this check be presented to the Bank of Winnemucca? It has to be pro-

[5]Some banks clear directly with the Fed but many others clear indirectly by means of a correspondent. From our viewpoint of the effect on check collection on the base, direct or indirect collection is equivalent. The actions of the Union Trust in our example are independent of the type of depositor. We ignore the interdistrict settlement accounts among Federal Reserve Banks as these are bookkeeping accounts of no consequence whatsoever to the money supply or any other economic variable.

cessed, flown across the country, and then delivered to the Bank of Winnemucca. If all goes well, the Bank of Winnemucca receives the check within two days. *However, a check processing staff inadequate to handle the peak volume of checks, bad weather delaying the transportation process, mechanical failures, and other unexpected events could delay the check for several days.*

Just as reserve management is complicated by debits unbeknown to a bank, lack of knowledge when one's account will be credited complicates reserve management. To eliminate this uncertainty and the cost of tracking each check, the Fed has established a deferred availability schedule indicating when payment will be made. The schedule is based on the location of the bank against which the check is drawn and the location of the bank receiving the check. Union Trust will have its account credited the same day, one, or at most, two days following delivery of the check to the Fed. The deferred availability schedule is relatively optimistic. It often takes longer than the scheduled time for checks to reach banks. This is immaterial to the Union Trust as on the second day, in this case where the banks are very distant, the following entries are recorded.

FIGURE 17–4
Check Collection (*continued*)

Union Trust			Fed		
Cash in process of collection	−100			Deferred availability items	−100
Deposits at Fed	+100			Deposits of Union Trust	+100

At this point float has increased $100. Combining Figures 17–3 and 17–4, the Fed shows that cash in process of collection still is $100 but there is no deferred availability item. On the Fed's balance sheet, Table 17–1, deferred availability items, shown as a negative item on the asset side, is subtracted from cash in the process of collection to give float. The base varies directly with float. In this example, Union Trust has larger reserves while reserves of the Bank of Winnemucca are unchanged. Float is no inconsequential amount, averaging around $3 billion in recent years. More important, *random factors such as bad weather cause float to vary by literally hundreds of millions of dollars from day to day.*

Float is a short-run phenomenon. Continuing this illustration, the entries shown in Figure 17–5 (p. 306) are recorded when the Bank of Winnemucca finally receives the check.

Consolidation of the last three balance sheets confirms that *in the final analysis checks simply shuffle reserves between banks. During the process*

FIGURE 17–5
Check Collection
(concluded)

Bank of Winnemucca				Fed			
Deposits at Fed	−100	Check deposits	−100	Cash in process of collection	−100	Deposits of Bank of Winnemucca	−100

of collection, checks may (not must) give rise to float and increase the base. Not every check generates Fed float. However, the number of checks written is sufficiently large that float always is positive if variable due to bad weather, and so on.

Large payments formerly made by check are now made through Fed wire transfers, which may be viewed as an instantaneous check collection system through computers linked nationwide. For example, suppose a Houston oillionaire in search of a tax shelter purchases a Vermont ski lodge. The Houston bank, following the oillionaire's instructions, tells the Fed's Houston branch to reduce its account and credit the account of Green Mountain National, the bank of the former owner of the ski lodge. Through a computer system linking all the Fed units, the appropriate transactions and notifications are effected virtually instantaneously, eliminating the possibility of float.

In principle, float could be negative if the deferred availability schedule were lengthened. The check would reach the Bank of Winnemucca before the account of Union Trust is credited. The Fed has retained an optimistic deferred availability schedule but attempts to minimize the impact of its optimism on its earnings. Soon after commercial airlines started bumping bags of checks in favor of other cargo, the Fed contracted a cargo airliner to transport checks more expeditiously. There was reason for this apparent madness. Float, like discounts, is a short-term extension of credit by the Fed to a commercial bank. Until 1981 there was an important difference, however. Float was an interest-free credit to the banking system. In our example Union Trust Bank did not pay interest on the reserves it acquired due to the Fed's optimistic deferred availability schedule. The Fed is primarily a macroeconomic policy and bank regulatory authority; its actions generally are not motivated by a desire to maximize profits. However, the Fed objected to extensions of interest-free credits and contracted for the airplanes in order to reduce float. To provide the same amount of the base with a lower level of float, the Fed could own a larger quantity of interest-bearing securities and earn greater profits. The Fed now is more blatantly opposed to letting float reduce its profits. It recently started charging banks for float, much as it charges banks that discount.

Is the Fed's more profit-oriented attitude desirable? In recent years the Fed's interest receipts have been about $16 billion annually. Since the Fed's expenses are less than 10 percent of its receipts, the Fed like all fiat money producers makes a substantial profit. What happens to these profits? They are transferred back to the Treasury, about $15 billion recently, and reduce the taxes necessary to finance any given expenditure. The new Fed policy benefits the general taxpayer and reduces somewhat the budget deficit.

The Fed's check clearing and collection facilities are rarely used, and consequently float rarely occurs, when the two parties to a check are local banks. In this case it is much simpler for each bank to send a messenger to a designated place with all the checks it received that were drawn on all other local banks. The designated place is called a clearinghouse, which may have a permanent location or be as transient as a floating crap game. The clearinghouse may be the back room of Security National this week, Fidelity Trust next week, and so on. Wherever the bank representatives meet, each picks up the checks drawn on it that the other local banks have brought. The clearinghouse officer then instructs the Fed to transfer the net clearing balance for each bank. For example, suppose First National takes to the clearinghouse $100 in checks drawn on local banks, and the local banks bring $120 in checks issued by First National depositors. The clearinghouse officer instructs the Fed to reduce First National's account by $20 in this example. When banks are nearby, sending checks to the Fed would be a waste of time and resources, especially now that the Fed charges for its check collection services.[6] Full cost pricing and profits are no longer dirty words at the Fed.

Miscellaneous Asset and Liabilities

The Federal Reserve balance sheet contains a hodgepodge of small asset and liability accounts ranging from spartan steel desks and the latest computers to accrued wages and salaries. In addition, the Fed's net worth or capital account is quite small. These accounts are consolidated in the accounts "miscellaneous assets" and "miscellaneous liabilities and net worth." It is not worth analyzing these items in detail. *Changes in these accounts often are accompanied by corresponding changes in the base.* Occasionally, however, a transaction is recorded by offsetting entries in these small accounts, leaving the base unaffected.

We postpone discussion of the Fed's last three assets, namely, gold certificates, special drawing rights certificates, and Treasury currency, until we analyze the Treasury balance sheet. The Fed's "Treasury cur-

---

[6]Banks do not bear higher check processing costs by clearing directly. You don't just drop checks into a bag and take them to the Fed; the Fed insists that checks be sorted.

rency'' measures the stockpile of coins and a few greenbacks which the Fed holds for the convenience of banks and the public. It is segregated from miscellaneous assets because it will be subtracted from the Treasury's account ''Treasury currency in circulation'' when the Fed and Treasury balance sheets are consolidated. Gold certificates also cancel when the two balance sheets are consolidated, being a Fed asset and Treasury liability.

Treasury and Nonbank Deposits at the Fed

We begin by outlining the rationale for the Treasury's current cash management policies, which avoid the instability of the Independent Treasury system while utilizing the Fed as a fiscal agent.

The United States government may be viewed as a huge business employing millions of people and spending and receiving billions of dollars annually. Large firms have hundreds of demand deposit accounts, and the largest business of them all has thousands, called tax and loan (T&L) accounts. These accounts derive their name from the fact that taxes and bond sales are the principal sources of Treasury receipts. The accounting entries associated with either taxes or bond sales are identical for all practical purposes. *T&L accounts at thousands of commercial banks and the elaborate system of transferring funds from commercial banks to the Fed is explained by the lack of synchronization between Treasury receipts and expenditures and by a seemingly impartial system of selecting the commercial banks which will get the Treasury's business.* Treasury receipts from taxes and bond sales initially are redeposited in the same bank against which a check is drawn. For example, the check which you mail to the Treasury on April 15 because insufficient taxes were withheld is forwarded by the Treasury to your bank. An advantage of this system is the minimum impact of taxes and bond sales on *individual banks*. Government receipts do not redistribute deposits and reserves among banks.[7] To prevent possible loss to the Treasury from bank failures, banks are required to own U.S. securities as collateral against T&L accounts.

From the viewpoint of the entire banking system, this system mitigates the effects of unsynchronized receipts and payments on the money supply. Treasury receipts must *temporarily* reduce the money supply, which is defined to exclude Treasury deposits. Conversely, Treasury expenditures must *temporarily* increase the money supply. Therefore, whenever Treasury receipts are greater (less) than payments, the money supply falls (rises).[8] According to the last balance sheet (Figure 17–6), the money

---

[7]The statement in the text is not completely accurate. Most, but not all, banks are *special depositories* that have T&L accounts.

[8]According to the money supply formula of Chapter 4, increases in any nonmoney deposit, such as T&L deposits, decrease the money supply.

FIGURE 17–6

Treasury Deposits Tax or Bond Receipts in Bank

Your Bank		
	Treasury tax and loan account	+100
	Private check deposits	−100

supply falls by $100 if the Treasury is not spending during the tax payment period. Reserves, however, are unchanged when the Treasury keeps its funds in T&L accounts. Were the Treasury to deposit the tax receipts at the Fed, or place the receipts in a cash warehouse reminiscent of the Independent Treasury, the money supply *and* reserves would decline. See Figure 17–7.

Larger (smaller) Treasury deposits at the Fed decrease (increase) the base. Figure 17–7 does not show the disruptive multiple contraction of private deposits that would follow the reserve loss. To prevent violent money supply fluctuations, the Treasury allows its T&L accounts to rise during tax payment periods.

In principle, the Treasury could make payments by writing checks against its T&L accounts. If it did this, Treasury receipts and expenditures would affect the money supply but not the monetary base. Treasury cash management is facilitated, however, by a single disbursing agent, the Fed. Treasury T&L accounts at the thousands of banks are feeder accounts for the Treasury's account at the Fed, against which all payments are made. Figure 17–8 illustrates the Treasury's cash management policies.

The relative size of the numbers in lines 1 and 2 reflects unsynchronized receipts and expenditures. Taxes are collected during somewhat widely spaced discrete time intervals, while expenditures occur at a more or less continuous rate. During a tax collection period, receipts to T&L accounts are $100 (line 1) while anticipated expenditures are much less, only $20 in our example. *The Treasury transfers to its Fed account (line 2) an amount equal to anticipated expenditures.* The T&L account increase of $80 (lines 1 and 2) equals the amount receipts exceed anticipated expenditures. Assuming the Treasury correctly anticipates its payments, debits to Treasury deposits at the Fed exactly match credits, leaving the Treasury

FIGURE 17–7

Treasury Deposits Tax Receipts at the Fed

Commercial Banks				Fed			
Deposits at Fed	−100	Check deposits	−100			Deposits of banks	−100
						Treasury deposits	+100

FIGURE 17–8

(1) Treasury deposits receipts at banks, (2) transfers anticipated amount spent to Fed, and (3) spends by drawing its deposits at the Fed

Commercial Banks				Fed			
(1)		Tax and loan accounts	+100	(1)			
		Private check deposits	−100				
(2) Deposits at Fed	−20	Tax and loan accounts	−20	(2)		Treasury deposits	+20
						Deposits of banks	−20
(3) Deposits at Fed	+18	Private check deposits	+18	(3)		Treasury deposits	−18
						Deposits of banks	+18

account and the base unchanged. In other words, Treasury expenditures of $20 are recorded by reversing the entries in line 2. Figure 17–8 assumes that the Treasury overestimates expenditures by $2; according to line 3 expenditures equal only $18. *When the Treasury overestimates (underestimates) its expenditures, additions to Treasury deposits at the Fed are greater (less) than subtractions, Treasury deposits rise (fall), and bank reserves and the monetary base decrease (increase).*

The Treasury's payment projections are often incorrect. If nothing else, the time interval between receipt and deposit of Treasury checks by individuals is not constant. More important, daily Treasury expenditures do vary substantially. It would be impractical to phone banks across the country every day to tell them the amount to be transferred from T&L accounts to the Treasury's account at the Fed. The Treasury has established a schedule indicating when transfers are to be made. Since the schedule covers some future time interval and is drawn up before the exact dates of payments are known, Treasury deposits at the Fed vary in spite of attempts to maintain a constant level. Nonetheless, the system of maintaining deposits in the banking system lessens the variation of the base associated with unsynchronous Treasury receipts and expenditures. *Treasury deposits are similar to discounts in that (1) their variability is largely unintentional, (2) they are small relative to the base, and (3) during short periods of time they change significantly, both absolutely and relative to changes in the base necessary to achieve moderate (2 to 8 percent) annual rates of monetary growth.*[9]

---

[9]The Teasury practiced the cash management policy outlined in the text until 1967 and then adopted it again in 1978. In the interim the Treasury did not vary its T&L accounts in

In view of our subsequent discussion of fiscal policy, it is worth emphasizing that government spending and taxes only temporarily affect the money supply and need not have any permanent effect. Suppose the government shifts from a balanced budget to a deficit because either taxes are cut or expenditures rise. Assuming the Treasury sells bonds to the public in order to finance the deficit, the money supply decline during the bond sales program is quickly reversed when the proceeds are expended. Similarly, a Treasury surplus used to retire the national debt has no permanent effect on the money supply.

Selected nonbanks, e.g., foreign governments and international organizations, also maintain accounts at the Fed. From the viewpoint of monetary control, nonbank deposits at the Fed are similar to Treasury deposits. Transfers of deposits from commercial banks to the Fed, whether by the Treasury or selected nonbanks, invariably affect the reserve components of the base. *Nonbank deposits are an uncontrolled factor absorbing the base.* The Fed selects the organizations whose deposits it will accept.

---

order to cushion the effect of unsynchronized receipts and expenditures on the monetary base. Instead, all receipts were almost immediately deposited at the Fed, causing the base to fall precipitously, *ceteris paribus*. The base rebounded slowly as the receipts were spent. Why did the Treasury manage its funds between 1967 and 1978 by imitating the Independent Treasury system? Critics finally convinced the Treasury in 1967 that commercial banks were robbing it, in a perfectly legal manner of course. By transferring to the Fed only the funds it anticipates spending, the Treasury's T&L accounts at banks were variable and, most important to bankers, quite large on average. *Banks earn income on the assets made possible by T&L accounts.* (Remember the balance sheet identity.) Synchronization problems aside, if the Treasury were to maintain deposits only at the Fed *while the Fed provides the same base,* the Fed's U.S. government securities account would increase by the average amount of T&L accounts at commercial banks. In other words, to prevent the reserve loss that would occur from Treasury withdrawals of T&L accounts from commercial banks to the Fed, the Fed can buy government securities from banks, thereby enlarging its portfolio at the expense of banks. This is precisely what the critics wanted. The Fed instead of commercial banks would earn the interest on the securities. The Independent Treasury system produced monetary instability when there was no central bank to offset withdrawals of cash and reserves from the banking system.

After 10 years of maintaining virtually all its deposits at the Fed, commercial banks finally recognized that the Treasury indeed was determined to tap every source of income. If the banks were again to have large T&L accounts, they had to devise a way of sharing with the Treasury the income made possible by these accounts. The Treasury favored a cooperative arrangement with the banks as it realized that the policy of immediately depositing receipts at the Fed had a disruptive effect on the base. A thorny legal issue arose: precisely how should the Treasury/banks income-sharing agreement be expressed so as not to suggest a kickback, collusion, or some other action illegal if one of the parties were not the Treasury? Although interest payment on demand deposits was prohibited in 1978, the wise Solomons decided that banks could pay the Treasury interest on its T&L accounts because T&L accounts were a "special" non-demand account. One advantage of being the regulator is having the ability to classify items to one's benefit. Unable for political reasons to exempt itself from the law prohibiting interest payment on demand deposits, the Treasury simply changed the name of its deposits, which now bear interest. The authorities extended this ploy to *consumers* by legalizing NOW accounts. Firms still cannot earn interest on their check deposits.

After doing this, the organization manages its deposit balances without Fed interference. Just as your deposits are not controlled by your bank, foreign deposits at the Fed are not controlled by the Fed.

Having completed discussion of the Fed's nonbase accounts, we now turn to the Treasury's balance sheet.

Gold, Gold Certificates, and Other International Assets

Gold has long been an important asset in settling international accounts and is the major Treasury monetary asset. The Treasury's posture on gold during this century has covered the whole map. Due to repayments and other technical reasons the Treasury is occasionally alloted some gold nowadays. On balance, however, it is a small seller of gold. The Treasury currently is unable to buy gold because its official price is much lower than the world market price.[10] Since there is no telling what the Treasury's position on gold will be as you read this book, and since official prices change by edict, a brief review of gold policy is in order before analyzing the effect of gold transactions.

Prior to 1933 the United States was on a strict gold standard. Gold circulated freely as money and was the basic form into which all other types of money could generally be converted. Gold certificates and other forms of currency circulated because they were more convenient than gold coins. Paper bills are less likely than gold coins to make holes in your pockets. Anyone could buy or sell one ounce of gold at the Treasury for $20.67 paper money. 1933 and 1934 were years of infamy for gold bugs. A series of Executive Orders devalued the dollar by 40.94 percent in terms of gold (to $35 per ounce of gold), demonetized gold coins, and transferred title of the Fed's gold to the Treasury in exchange for gold certificates. Private gold ownership was forbidden except in limited amounts for licensed purposes—for the manufacture of jewelry, teeth, and for a few other uses. Even the Fed was prohibited from owning gold. The Treasury bought gold from domestic and foreign suppliers but sold unlimited amounts of gold at $35 per ounce only to official foreign organizations such as central banks. In terms of Figure 17–9, D_{P+F} and S_{P+F} are the private domestic and foreign demand and supply curves, respectively. Prior to 1933 the gold standard committed the Treasury to make up any excess supply or demand for gold at $20.67 per ounce. The Treasury purchased AB in our graph. The 1933 and 1934 Executive Orders raised the gold support price and reduced demand, illustrated by the dashed

---

[10]In January 1976, the "official" gold price was formally abolished at the International Monetary Fund meetings in Kingston, Jamaica. However, the history of gold makes it convenient to entertain the fiction of an official price. International payments systems are discussed in more detail in Chapters 32 and 33.

FIGURE 17–9
Gold Standard Demand and Supply of Gold

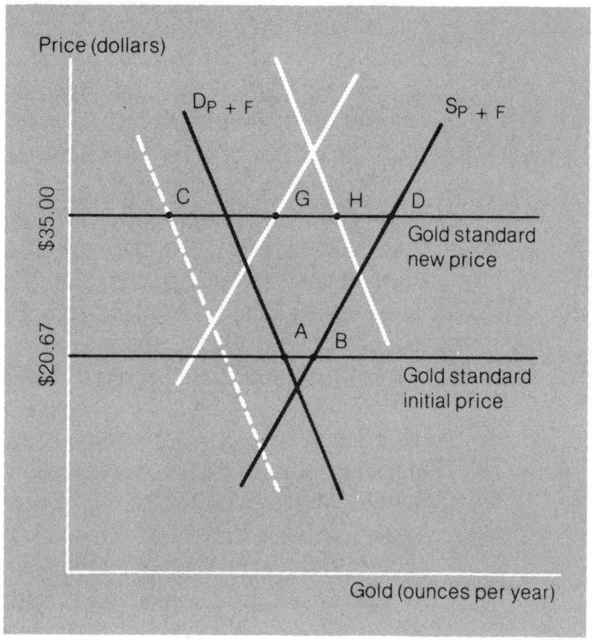

curve, by placing restrictions on gold usage. Treasury gold purchases jumped to CD. Until 1967 incremental demand for gold at $35 per ounce was less than annual gold production or could easily be met from the coffers of the world's central bankers. Consequently, except for a few isolated instances, the free market price of gold stayed at the official price throughout this period, and central bankers on balance augmented their gold pool.

The modified gold standard of the 1930s remained essentially unchanged until 1967–68, when increases in the worldwide private demand for gold at $35 per ounce began to significantly outstrip the production of gold. In terms of Figure 17–9, higher wages and other costs made gold production more expensive, shifting the supply curve inward, and higher prices for other commodities at home and abroad made gold an attractive substitute, shifting the demand curve outward. The demand and supply curves intersected above $35. Although the Treasury did not sell gold to the private sector, other central banks did. As foreign central banks lost gold to meet their citizen's request, they made more frequent calls on the Treasury in order to replenish their dwindling gold supplies. The Treasury and the central banks of a majority of the world's leading countries were jointly drawn into a losing proposition. Frustrated by their losses of gold to the private sector (GH in Figure 17–9) as they attempted to maintain the official price, the world's central bankers finally decided in March 1968, amid much fanfare, to throw in the towel. In brief, like many losers at Atlantic City casinos, they picked up what chips were still theirs and refused to play any longer. They agreed in blood not to sell to or buy any more gold from the nasty private speculators and producers. All transactions within the charmed circle of central bankers took place at the pegged official price. As for the private speculators, they could do as they jolly well wished. With the sore losers out of the game, the free market price of gold fluctuates with the tides of private supply and demand, at times hitting unthought-of-heights. So long as the two circles do not come in contact with each other or with intermediaries, the official and free market prices go their separate ways, like a divorced couple.[11]

Policy changes occurred frequently in the 1970s. On August 15, 1971, what many thought impossible became reality. In a televised speech President Richard M. Nixon announced that the Treasury would stop playing the gold game even within the charmed circle. The dollar became totally inconvertible as all U.S. Treasury gold purchases and sales were suspended. To realign foreign exchange rates, in December 1971 the Treasury devalued the U.S. dollar and raised the official price of gold to $38 per ounce. Since the Treasury maintained its hands-off-gold policy, the devaluation was largely symbolic. The dollar was further devalued in 1973 (to $42.22 per ounce of gold); ownership of gold no longer was a crime on January 1, 1975; and the Treasury resumed modest gold sales to the public. Treasury gold sales have been insufficient to drive the price of gold to anywhere near the official price, $42.22 per ounce. The official price of gold is the Treasury's *buying* price, at which no purchases are made. The Treasury has not let the official price interfere with its sales, which are made at market prices. *In summary, the Treasury's gold position has shifted from (a) unlimited purchases and sales to all comers; to (b) unlimited purchases and limited sales to special groups; to (c) no transactions; and to (d) Treasury initiated sales but no purchases.* While we are not forecasting a purchases and no sales policy, the only policy so far not followed by the Treasury, let us show the effect of gold purchases on balance sheets. Gold sales simply reverse the entries in Figure 17–10.

The accurate accounting of gold transactions is quite complex and peculiar. For this reason, I suspect, most books adopt a simple, straight-

---

[11]Is gold that different from other commodities? Consider what would happen if your local supermarket advertised steak at $1.09 a pound. Earnest citizens would quickly clean the shelves of steak. Suppose the supermarket refused to restock the shelves. Who would be criticized, the supermarket for false advertising or the earnest citizens? The answer is clear, yet the gold mystique is so strong that in similar circumstances the private participants typically are derogatorily characterized as speculators, while the central bankers are defenders of the currency.

FIGURE 17–10

(1a) Gold purchase, (1b) Treasury monetizes gold by issuing gold certificates, which is equivalent to printing money in order to pay for the gold, and (2b) Treasury finances the gold purchase by selling bonds.

Treasury

	Assets		Liabilities	
(1b)	Gold	+100	Gold certificates	+100
(2b)	Gold	+100	Treasury cash	+100

Federal Reserve

	Assets		Liabilities	
(1a)			Treasury deposits	−100
			Deposits of banks	+100
(1b)	Gold certificates	+100	Treasury deposits	+100
(2b)			Treasury deposits	+100
			Deposits of banks	−100

Commercial Banking System

	Assets		Liabilities	
(1a)	Deposits at Fed	+100	Check deposits	+100
(1b)				
(2b)	Deposits at Fed	−100	Check deposits	−100

forward but inaccurate approach. I reject that approach. Accuracy is paramount. Moreover, the accounting is not so complex provided one keeps firmly in mind that what matters for purposes of explaining the base is the Treasury's *monetary account* balance sheet. This balance sheet includes only those items associated with gold and coins. Thus, the Treasury's monetary account is an incomplete Treasury balance sheet. Look at Table 17–2. Excluded are the "ordinary," nonmoney items that the Treasury acquired as the fiscal authority and the associated financial instruments. For example, 1600 Pennsylvania Avenue, Yellowstone National Park, and F-111 airplanes do not appear in the asset column, and billions of Treasury bonds are glaringly absent from the liability side. Treasury deposits at the Fed is a liability of the Fed but does not appear as a Treasury asset because it is assumed that all Treasury deposits at the Fed arise from the Treasury's taxing authority and bond sales. The assumption may not be altogether accurate; any division of receipts by functions is bound to be somewhat arbitrary. Nevertheless, from the viewpoint of the money supply, the Treasury monetary account as shown is precisely what we want.

Gold purchases clearly increased the currency component of the base when the Treasury financed the purchase by minting gold coins of equal value. Although the Treasury stopped minting gold coins in 1933, gold purchases typically increase the base because they are financed essentially by printing money. Suppose miners, gold speculators, or foreign governments bring gold nuggets worth $100 to the Fed. Line 1a in Figure 17–10 illustrates the impact of gold purchases. Unlike you and me, the Fed follows the 1930s laws and does not own gold, which is purchased on behalf of the Treasury. Thus, the Fed debits Treasury deposits and credits deposits of banks when the sellers of gold deposit the Fed's check in their commercial banks.[12]

The Fed now notifies the Treasury that it is the proud owner of $100 additional gold. The Treasury has two alternative ways of financing the purchase. First, the Treasury usually monetizes the gold by issuing gold certificates or claims against the gold. The Fed purchases the certificates and credits Treasury deposits. See line 1b of Figure 17–10. The consolidated effect of lines 1a and 1b is an increase in gold and bank deposits at the Fed, which are equivalent to cash according to Chapter 3. Second, the Treasury could treat the gold purchase as an "ordinary" expenditure, which we argued in the last section has no permanent effect on the base or money supply. In this case, the Treasury would finance the gold purchase by taxes or, more likely, bond sales. See line 2b of the Fed's balance sheet, which assumes the public uses a check to buy bonds. The Treasury in turn debits gold and credits its monetary net worth, called Treasury cash. It may appear that the Treasury should credit bonds outstanding instead of Treasury cash. However, the latter account does not even appear on the Treasury's *monetary account*, the incomplete Treasury balance sheet appropriate for analyzing the monetary base. When the Treasury purchases gold by selling bonds, the Treasury's fiscal net worth, which is not illustrated in Figure 17–10, decreases but its monetary net worth, Treasury cash, increases.

Table 17–2 shows that the Treasury now cannot afford the luxury of treating gold as an ordinary commodity. It has issued gold certificates equal to the gold stock. In the past, however, the Treasury sometimes issued bonds to finance gold purchases. It created a wedge between the gold stock and certificates. The difference between gold and gold certificates is called sterilized gold, an appropriate term because gold purchases increase the base and the failure to issue gold certificates *while maintaining constant Treasury balances at the Fed* decreases the base. *Ster-*

---

[12]Private sellers of gold must deposit the Fed's check in commercial banks, but foreign governments may have their deposit accounts at the Fed credited. However, foreign governments hold the proceeds of gold sales in their Fed accounts for only a short period, if at all. Gold is rarely sold to permanently increase foreign balances at the Fed. Foreign governments typically will purchase interest-bearing dollar-denominated assets such as Treasury securities with the proceeds of gold sales. When foreign governments do this, the first line of Figure 17–10 shows the impact of gold purchases.

ilized gold is also called free gold as certificates equal to this amount can be issued.

The mechanics of gold transactions would be simplified if the Fed bought gold directly. In such an event, the Fed would debit a Gold account and credit Deposits of banks. This is equivalent to consolidating the two balance sheets and summing lines 1a and 1b, Figure 17–10. Can the Fed, like the Treasury, sterilize gold if its policies call for an unchanged quantity of reserves? Surely. The Fed instead of the Treasury sells bonds. In either case the private sector acquires additional bonds in exchange for gold. The possible desirability of sterilizing gold is no handicap to Fed ownership of this international asset.

The Fed follows the more direct approach when buying or selling other assets used to settle international balance of payments, for example, special drawing rights (SDRs) and foreign currency assets such as German mark or Swiss franc securities.[13] SDRs are created by the International Monetary Fund and are sometimes referred to as paper gold. These assets appear on line F of the Fed's balance sheet, Table 17–1. When the sellers of these assets deposit the Fed's check at commercial banks, the Fed debits special drawing rights certificates and credits bank reserve deposits.

Under current policy the Treasury cannot buy gold because its official and buying price is substantially below the world market price. The Treasury certainly would find eager buyers for the entire gold stock if it agreed to sell at the official price. The Treasury prefers small sales at world market prices. Most important, all the sales have been strictly at the Treasury's initiative. *As matters now stand, the monetary authorities exert direct control over this source of the base.* This may not be true in the future, and it certainly was not true prior to 1971. The association of gold with international transactions is enough to suggest that events in this country *and* abroad influence gold flows. However much one thinks the Fed and Treasury determine events in this country, attributing to them a major impact on some foreign events is a flight of fancy. People and gold responded to Nazism by fleeing to the United States. While the Fed has often been criticized, and justly so, blaming it for Nazism would be going too far. Throughout much of our history the Fed had little direct and immediate impact on gold flows. Unlike float, gold is a relatively long-lasting uncontrolled source of the base. The direction of gold flows is not reversed quickly. The United States gained gold throughout the 1930s and lost it during the 1960s.

---

[13]In fact, SDRs are handled somewhat analogously to gold. However, because we want to abstract from the allocation of SDRs by the IMF to the Treasury, which has no effect on the money supply, it is convenient to assume the Treasury does not participate in SDR sales by other countries.

Treasury Currency Outstanding and Treasury Currency in Circulation

The relatively recently created Federal Reserve was not granted exclusive rights over all the functions a central bank normally performs. The Treasury retained its earlier authority to issue coins and currency. *Treasury currency outstanding measures the net amount of Treasury coin and currency issued, whether in circulation or still in the Treasury's vault.* The rationale for this account has puzzled many. Treasury currency is an example of Treasury debt. Therefore, the liability account "Treasury currency in circulation" in Table 17–2 is not surprising. But why is Treasury currency outstanding an asset? The answer is made more concrete by showing immediately the accounting associated with Treasury currency creation. For simplicity, we assume money creation is costless. None of the principles illustrated are altered by recognizing the small cost of minting coins. The immediate impact of minting coins is shown on the first line of Figure 17–11. That is, line 1 shows the effect of money creation while it is still in the Treasury's possession. Keeping recently minted coins in the vault has no effect on any economic variable. The Treasury created an asset and credits its net worth since the currency (coinage) is not yet in circulation. Factors supplying and absorbing the base increase by the same amount. Of course, the Treasury does not mint coins to keep them in the vault; coins are minted to be spent *directly or indirectly*. Line 2 assumes the coins are spent *directly* on some item, increasing the currency component of the base. The net impact of lines 1 and 2 is an equal increase in Treasury currency outstanding and Treasury currency in circulation.

Why does the Treasury follow this accounting system? Why bother making any entry when newly created currency is still on hand? Why not leave line 1 blank, and debit on line 2 the *actual* asset acquired and credit Treasury currency in circulation when the newly minted money is spent. The proposed accounting would be simpler—only one line—and seemingly more accurate: it would show the actual asset acquired instead of the peculiar account, Treasury currency outstanding. The proposed accounting would indeed be simpler, but it would not be more accurate. It would be more arbitrary. This is so because the Treasury also is the fiscal authority, while we here are interested only in its monetary power. Indeed, the vast majority of the federal government's assets arise from its fiscal powers. Any attempt to segregate assets according to the source of finance, tax collection or money creation, is bound to be arbitrary. The Treasury is not different from you or me in this respect. Suppose you work part-time at the library and dining hall, and purchase a ticket to a rock concert and a record album. Who acquired the ticket, you the librarian or you the cook? And who owns the record? Clearly, any attempt to match the source of receipts and expenditures invites criticism. Instead

FIGURE 17–11 (1) Treasury mints coins, (2) Treasury spends currency directly, (3) Treasury transfers currency to the Fed, and (4) Treasury spends deposits received in exchange for currency.

	Treasury			Fed	
(1)	Treasury currency outstanding +100	Treasury cash +100	(1)		
(2)		Treasury cash −100 Treasury currency in circulation +100	(2)		
(3)		Treasury cash −100 Treasury currency in circulation +100	(3)	Treasury currency +100	Treasury deposits +100
(4)			(4)		Treasury deposits −100 Deposits of banks +100

of listing an arbitrary set of assets acquired by the Treasury as a monetary authority, the value of all assets so acquired are recorded in a common account, Treasury currency outstanding. That is, Treasury currency outstanding includes whatever assets were acquired with Treasury currency.

Contrary to the assumption of line 2, the newly minted Treasury money probably is spent *indirectly*, giving rise to lines 3 and 4. The Fed maintains a stockpile of coins to meet the demands of banks and the public. Suppose a larger demand for coins depleted the Fed stockpile so it requests additional coins from the Treasury. Such a request is the most common impetus for currency creation. As expected, transporting cash from the Treasury to the Fed, as recorded on line 3, has no effect on the base. The Treasury's net worth fell because from its viewpoint more currency is in circulation. However, the currency is held by the Fed, which credits the Treasury deposits. Line 4 assumes the Treasury spends the deposits which were received in exchange for coins. As individuals deposit the Treasury checks, bank reserves increase.

As the name implies, Treasury currency is minted/printed exclusively by the Treasury. Therefore, Treasury currency outstanding, which changes when additional currency is created, is a controlled factor supplying that has a somewhat delayed effect on the base. During the short period between printing and disbursal, Treasury currency outstanding is neutralized by a factor absorbing, Treasury cash. When the currency is spent directly or indirectly, the base increases.[14] The manner of spending only influences which component of the base, currency in circulation or deposits at the Fed, increases.

Although the Fed's stockpiling of Treasury coins and its own notes does not affect the base, this important housekeeping chore deserves more than the brief mention in the next-to-last paragraph. The Fed's stockpile lets you transform any denomination of old limp currency into new crisp currency. Banks ship excess vault cash to the Fed, which credits their deposit account. Dirty bills are shredded, burned, and reissued. When banks are short of vault cash, the entries are reversed except that banks receive clean money. (This is *not* an example of laundering money, however.) Millions of dollars flow to and from the Fed daily as banks shift the composition of their reserves from vault cash to deposits and adjust the denominations of their vault cash.

Treasury Holdings of Fed Notes and Treasury Cash

The Treasury holds Federal Reserve notes for the same reasons individuals and firms do; Fed notes are a convenient means of payment for some transactions. We may ignore illustrating how this Treasury account changes since it does not appear separately when the Fed and Treasury balance sheets are consolidated.

Analysis of all other accounts in a double-entry bookkeeping system makes unnecessary independent analysis of the final account, Treasury cash. We already indicated all the events which cause Treasury cash to adjust. It is desirable, nevertheless, to show that Treasury cash does correspond to monetary net worth as alleged. A rearrangement of the Treasury's balance sheet, labeled Table 17–3, and our previous discussion imply that *Treasury cash generally equals the Treasury's holdings of currency, including its own, and free gold, which was positive for many years but currently is zero*. But its currency holdings and free gold equals the amount the Treasury as the monetary authority can spend without borrowing, which is what net worth or wealth measures.

---

[14]Since the Treasury always could issue coins, Figure 17–11 may *incorrectly* suggest that currency was elastic prior to the creation of the Fed. Currency was not elastic because the Treasury could readily and cheaply mint only a few types of coins, for example, pennies, while it specified that all types and denominations of currency could be convertible one for the other. If the Treasury attempted to place only additional pennies in circulation when the demand for currency in general increased, some pennies would quickly return to the Treasury in exchange for greenbacks and gold coins. The public wanted more currency, not just more pennies. Since greenbacks were restricted and gold coins could not be readily produced, the Treasury was unable to put the pennies in circulation and provide an elastic currency. The ability of the Fed to create complementary notes that can be exchanged for Treasury currency makes total currency completely elastic today. This line of reasoning indicates that currency was less elastic prior to 1933 when the United States was on a strict gold standard. Paper money could not be expanded too fast then because individuals would exchange paper money for gold, drawing down the Treasury's limited supply.

TABLE 17–3
A Rearrangement of the Treasury Monetary Account Balance Sheet

(N)	Treasury currency outstanding	
− (Q)	Treasury currency in circulation	= Treasury currency at Treasury
+ (O)	Fed notes at Treasury	= Fed notes at Treasury
+ (M)	Gold − (P) gold certificates	= Free gold
	Total	= (R) Treasury cash

Summary/Questions

The two balance sheets, Tables 17–1 and 17–2, are consolidated and rearranged as Table 17–4 in order to show more compactly all the accounts that could possibly affect the base. Table 17–4 expresses the base as the difference between Fed and Treasury factors supplying (assets) and factors absorbing (other liabilities). An additional column shows changes in factors supplying and absorbing between July and August 1984. The consolidated balance sheet does not show gold certificates since this account

TABLE 17–4
Consolidated Federal Reserve and Treasury Balance Sheet; Monetary Base Equation; Base, Federal Reserve Credit, and Related Items, August 31, 1984, and Change from July to August 1984 ($ millions, monthly average of daily figures)

	August 31, 1984	*Change, August 1984–July 1984*
Factors supplying (assets):		
U.S. government securities held by Fed (A)	$162,046	−2,511
Discounts to banks (B)	8,276	+2,072
Float (C)	326	−405
Miscellaneous Fed assets (D)	8,290	−462
Gold (M)	11,098	0
Special drawing rights certificates (F)	4,618	0
Treasury currency outstanding (N)	16,220	+39
Total	$210,874	−1,267
Factors absorbing (other liabilities):		
Treasury deposits (H)	$ 4,029	−438
Foreign and other deposits (I)	1,802	−67
Miscellaneous Fed liabilities and net worth (J)	6,140	−142
Treasury cash (R)	465	−39
Total	$ 12,436	−686
Monetary base = Factors supplying − Factors absorbing	$198,438	−581
Monetary base composition from Fed and Treasury balance sheets:		
Bank reserve deposits (L)	$ 21,586	−405
Currency held by public and banks (K+Q−G−O)	176,852	−176
Monetary base composition from Fed, Treasury, and banks balance sheets:		
Bank reserves: Deposits at Fed and vault cash	$ 42,368	−781
Currency in the hands of the public	156,070	+200

*Letter in parentheses following account indicates similar account in Tables 17–1 and 17–2.

cancels, being an asset of the Fed and a liability of the Treasury. According to the balance sheets of the Fed and Treasury, currency in circulation is $161,551 and $15,980 million, respectively. However, the Fed and Treasury hold $679 million of each others currency. (Lines G and O in Tables 17–1 and 17–2, respectively.) From the viewpiont of the Fed *and* Treasury, currency in circulation is $176,852 ($161,551 million plus $15,980 million, minus $679 million).

Economists cannot agree on terminology. Table 17–4 is called the (1) consolidated Federal Reserve and Treasury balance sheet, (2) monetary base equation, and (3) base, Federal Reserve credit, and related items.[15] If the table does not look much like an equation, on a long horizontal line write the factoring supplying (positive sign) and factors absorbing (negative sign) and place an equality before the base. Table 17–4 includes a memorandum not derived directly from the Treasury and Fed balance sheets. Banks report their vault cash positions to the Fed and Federal Deposit Insurance Corporation. From these reports and the Treasury and Fed balance sheets, currency held by the public is calculated as a residual.

The reader should be able to construct the monetary base equation. The exact numbers in Table 17–4 are unimportant; they vary from day to day. What is important to gain from the table is knowledge about what transactions augment or reduce the base, the relative size of the accounts, and above all, why each account varies. Does float change because of conscious Fed policy or because of some random factors? Is the gold stock immediately and directly affected by Fed and Treasury policy? Familiarity with Table 17–4 is essential in order to answer a controversial question in monetary economics: can the Fed control the quantity of money?

The monetary base equation indicates that the monetary authorities do not have perfect control over the base, where perfect control means that a change occurs if, and only if, the Fed initiates some positive action. Treasury currency outstanding, being the amount of currency minted by the Treasury, and the Fed's holdings of U.S. government securities, which is the cumulative net amount of open-market operations, are directly controlled by the monetary authorities. Gold currently is under Treasury

---

[15]The Fed publishes a table entitled "depositories' reserves, Federal Reserve credit and related items," or something similar. (The precise title of the table has varied recently.) The Fed table differs from our table by shifting currency held by the public *and* banks up "above the line" to join other uses. In terms of the balance sheet identity, Bank reserve deposits = Assets − Other liabilities − Currrency held by the public and banks. Continued publication of this table over the past 25 years is a sign of a sclerotic Fed. The table was somewhat useful prior to 1960, when only deposits at the Fed counted as member bank reserves. Now that currency also counts as reserves, the Fed should not highlight one component of reserves.

control, but future gold policy is uncertain. The other accounts in Table 17–4 are factors supplying or absorbing the base which are not directly controlled by the Fed. These uncontrolled accounts typically are quite small; U.S. government securities is the overwhelming source of the base. However, monthly and even longer period *changes* in these accounts are significant compared to *changes* in the base. Even after ignoring the discounts associated with Continental Illinois as being truly atypical, Table 17–4 shows that the reduction in float accounted for nearly 75 percent of the decrease in the base between July and August 1984. Treasury deposits changed slightly more than float during that month. In other months Treasury deposits and float are virtually constant and "normal" discounts cause large changes in the base. The Fed cannot set some dial, take a Rip Van Winkle nap, and expect the base or the money supply multiplier to remain constant until it awakens. The Fed has to continuously manipulate some dials to control the money supply.

Defensive Open-Market Operations

Open-market policy is the dial the Fed manipulates to counteract the effect on the money supply of (1) uncontrolled factors supplying or absorbing the base, and (2) currency ratio shifts. Such open-market operations are called defensive. *Defensive open-market operations keep the base and money supply on target.* When the currency ratio increases and bank reserves fall, defensive open-market purchases replenish reserves and prevent a multiple contraction. When an uncontrolled factor increases the base, the Fed sells securities to decrease the base. The Fed buys securities when uncontrolled factors reduce the base. Is the Fed successful? Can it counteract the uncontrolled factors and keep the base on target? Yes, provided the target period is not unreasonably short. The Fed cannot react instantly. Defensive open-market operations do not keep the base at its desired value minute by minute or hour by hour. Given an appropriate period, however, Table 17–4 correctly suggests that the base will equal its desired value. *The U.S. government securities account overwhelms all other items in the monetary base equation.* Additional evidence on control is presented in Chapter 20, where we carefully analyze the meaning of control and reintroduce the multiplier for a complete analysis of the money supply. Control of the base is only the first step in controlling money.

1. Define factor supplying and factor absorbing the base and give some examples of each.
2. What is the largest factor supplying the base? How does it arise?
3. Are discounts at the Fed a factor supplying or absorbing the base? Are discounts important in explaining either the level or change in the base?

4. What is float? Why does it arise? What is its effect on the base? What events cause float to vary?
5. Describe the Treasury's current money management policy. What is the impact of Treasury receipts on individual banks and the banking system? Compare the Treasury's current money management policies with those of the mid 1970s.
6. Briefly summarize U.S. gold policy since 1930.
7. Explain why Treasury purchases of gold generally tend to increase the base while purchases of "ordinary" commodities do not affect the base. When do gold purchases not affect the base? What is sterilized or free gold? How does one get free gold?
8. How can Treasury currency outstanding be an asset of the Treasury when the Treasury issued the currency?
9. Define Treasury cash. When will it be unaffected by gold purchases and currency creation?
10. For each of the following items state whether it is a factor supplying or absorbing of the base. If it is a factor supplying or absorbing, state whether an *increase* in the item causes the base to increase or decrease, and state whether the item is controlled or uncontrolled by the Fed. The items are: (*a*) check deposits at banks, (*b*) Eurodollars, (*c*) Treasury deposits at the Fed, (*d*) Treasury deposits at commercial banks (T&L accounts), (*e*) foreign deposits at the Fed, (*f*) U.S. government securities held by the Fed, (*g*) U.S. government securities held by commercial banks, and (*h*) gold held by dealers.
11. Define defensive open-market operations.

18 The instruments of monetary policy

Monetary policy follows a tortuous path because the goal variables or ultimate targets, such as GNP and the consumer price index, are buffeted by exogenous forces in addition to *the three major instruments or tools of monetary policy: (1) open-market operations, (2) reserve requirements, and (3) discount policy.* Some exogenous, nonmonetary forces have a strong and immediate impact on the goals, while others affect the ultimate targets with a long lag. In order to judge monetary policymakers fairly in this complex environment, we must know more than the broad outlines of the policy instruments. Do the authorities have sufficiently sharp tools? This chapter takes a detailed look at the three major instruments.

Open-Market Operations: An Introduction

We begin, if only briefly, with the most important tool: open-market operations. The last chapter stated that open-market policy is the premier *defensive* tool, whereby the Fed offsets the effect of uncontrolled factors on the base and money supply. But open-market operations are much more than a defensive tool. The Fed actively conducts some open-market operations in order to achieve proximate and ultimate goals. What name should one give to these activist, goal-oriented open-market operations, given that the passive, constancy-oriented operations are called defensive? Although the logic for "offensive" open-market operations is compelling, such terminology thoroughly vexes the Fed. The Fed prefers the term "dynamic open-market operations." *Dynamic open-market pur-*

chases and sales are conducted in order to achieve the goals. Note that dynamic operations may be contractionary—sales—as well as expansionary—purchases. It is convenient to entertain the fiction that all uncontrolled factors are first offset by defensive operations before the Fed engages in dynamic operations. Viewed in this manner over 95 percent of all open-market operations are defensive. In point of fact, the uncontrolled factors influencing the base are not offset if they work in the direction of the desired change. For example, suppose float increases by $400 million and, in view of the desired money supply and rates of interest, the Fed wants the base to increase by $500 million. In this case, there is no need for a $400 million defensive sale to counteract float *and* a $500 million dynamic purchase. A single $100 million purchase is adequate since *the balance sheet effects of defensive and dynamic open-market operations are identical.* The two types of open-market operations differ solely with respect to their immediate objectives.

The balance sheet effects of open-market operations were illustrated almost from the beginning of the book and need not be repeated.[1] Chapter 16 described the composition of the Federal Open Market Committee (FOMC). Significant mention of open-market operations had to be made along the way because it clearly is the most important monetary tool, so much so that monetary policy often is equated with open-market policy. We postpone until the next chapter an analysis of the *strategy* of open-market policy, that is, the criteria and objectives guiding the FOMC's dynamic operations. At this point we simply want to portray realistically the *mechanics* of open-market operations. Exhibit 18–1 puts you in the trader's desk and shows you how to do it.[2] Would you like to work at the New York Fed? Many find the purchase and sale of Treasury bills worth billions exhilirating, and jobs at the Fed are scarce.

EXHIBIT 18–1

The Trading Desk: They Do It Daily

Each day presents a new challenge to the account manager and his colleagues. Yet each day has much in common with every other day. It is Tuesday before Thanksgiving. On this day, as on all days, the manager must bear in mind the instructions given him at the last FOMC meeting. Suppose the short-run directives call for growth of total reserves con-

---

[1]See Chapter 3.

[2]Exhibit 18–1 is taken unabashedly from Paul Meek, *Open-Market Operations* (Federal Reserve Bank of New York, 1978). Meek, monetary adviser in the New York Fed Bank's Open-Market Operations and Treasury Issues Division, tells the inside story better than anyone. The Meek pamphlet and numerous other publications are available free from the Federal Reserve Bank of New York, 33 Liberty St., New York, N.Y. 10045.

sistent with a 3–5½ percent growth of M-1 provided the federal funds rate is between 9 and 13 percent.

The trading room's business day begins at 9:00 A.M. News tickers are pounding out the overnight financial news. Securities traders are reorienting themselves by scanning yesterday's closing quotations on the board facing the open end of the trading desk. Two officers hurry to a 10th floor conference room for separate meetings with representatives of three dealer firms. Fed officers directly responsible for open-market operations meet with the dealers on a rotating basis every business day. The dealers comment on market developments as well as matters of particular interest to their firms. The Fed officers listen and ask questions. The meetings, brief and to the point, are conducted in market jargon. The dealers leave at 9:15. Two senior partners of a second dealer firm enter the conference room. They comment on the market's inactivity during the last few days and other matters. On leaving at 9:30, the two senior partners bump into the vice president of a New York wholesale bank, who covers much the same material. At 9:45 the Fed officers take the elevator down to their eighth floor offices to prepare for the daily Treasury call.

Shortly after 10:15 each day, the fiscal assistant secretary of the Treasury and the account manager use a direct telephone line to compare notes on the immediate outlook for the Treasury's balances at Reserve Banks. Their objective is to coordinate changes in Treasury balances with the system's management of bank reserves. Scheduled transfers from tax and loan accounts to the Treasury's Fed account are $350 million but an expenditure drain of $600 million is projected. The net effect is a $250 million decrease in Treasury deposits and increase in unborrowed reserves.

At 10:45 the account manager joins the desk officer in reviewing a research report, received only moments before, which projects factors affecting bank reserves and the base over the next six weeks. The projections are based upon the behavior of factors over the same calendar period during the past several years. The projections indicate that during the next week float will decline $1.5 billion in accordance with end-of-month patterns. A seasonal rise in currency in circulation increases the need to expand reserves.

The projections are just that, projections, and not certainties. The officers get a feel of the market by looking at the federal funds and Treasury bill rates for signals of the timing and magnitude of the reserve pressures actually at work on this particular day. Two clerks update the quotation board with the latest "runs" of prices and yields obtained by telephone from dealers. The Fed's traders anticipate from their conversations with dealers what the board shows: interest rates are a shade higher. The officers begin to formulate the day's plan of action. The manager writes out the day's program. Meanwhile, a staff call is made to the Board in Washington and to the office of one of the Reserve Bank presidents currently on the FOMC. Today is San Francisco's turn. The officers hurry to an adjoining office to participate in the key telephone conversation—the 11:15 conference call—that formalizes the day's strategy.

"Washington and San Francisco are standing by," announces the telephone operator, completing the three-way telephone hookup that enables the account manager to review developments with the staff of the Board and the Reserve Bank president on call. Participating in the conversation at the New York end today are the president of the bank, the manager of the system account, and the officers of the securities department. Seated directly behind a telephone microphone, the manager speaks:

> Yesterday, we had a shortfall of reserves that more than offset what we put in. We look for a sharp decline in reserves today and tomorrow as currency in circulation increases and float drops. This will be offset somewhat by a decline in Treasury deposits. The uncontrolled tightening is confirmed by the Federal funds rate, which opened at 12⅛ percent bid, ⅝ percentage point above yesterday's close. In view of the expected stringency in reserves, the account plans to purchase as much as $500 million of Treasury bills.

The Board participant and San Francisco Reserve Bank president may express their views and report about possible money supply revisions. The call is usually completed by 11:30. A Board staff member promptly summarizes the call in a memorandum sent to each Board member, and a telegram is sent to each Reserve Bank president.

With the decision made and explained to Fed officials outside New York, the manager turns to the officers and securities traders who sit before telephone consoles linking them to the more than 30 dealers in U.S. securities. "We're going to ask for offerings of all types of bills for cash," the manager says. Each person is quickly assigned two to four dealers to call.

Joan, a Fed trader, presses a button on her telephone console, sounding a buzzer at the corresponding console of a government securities dealer.

"Jack," Joan says, "we are looking for offerings of all bills for cash delivery."

Jack replies, "I'll be back in a minute." The salespersons of his firm quickly contact customers to see if they wish to make offerings. Jack consults the partner in charge about how aggressive he should be in offering the firm's own holdings.

Ten minutes later Jack calls back. "Joan, I can offer you for cash $5 million of January 5 bills to yield 8.85 percent—$20 million of January 26 bills at 8.90—$10 million of March 23 bills at 9.05—and $30 million of May 30 bills at 9.14."

Joan says, "Can I have those offerings firm for a few minutes?"

"Sure. It's firm for 20 minutes."

Within minutes the "go-around" is completed. The traders have recorded the offerings obtained from their calls on special preprinted slips. The officer-in-charge arrays the individual dealer offerings on an inclined board atop a stand-up counter. A tally shows that dealers have offered $1.8 billion of bills for cash sale, that is, with delivery and payment today. The officer then begins circling with a red pencil the offerings that provide the highest rate of return—lowest price. An associate keeps a running total of the amounts being bought. When the desired amount—$500 million—has been circled, the individual slips are returned to the traders, who quickly telephone the dealers.

"Jack, we'll take the $5 million of January 5 bills at 8.85 and the $30 million of May 30 bills at 9.14, both for cash; no, thanks, on the others," Joan says.

Only the paper work remains. The traders write tickets, which provide the basic authority for the Bank's government bond department to receive and pay for the specific Treasury bills bought. The Federal Reserve credits to the dealers' banks immediately add $500 million to reserves and the base. A large part of the increase in reserves is transferred the same day over the Fed's wire network from the dealers' checking accounts to the reserve accounts of banks in other cities: $10 million is wired to Hartford by a dealer to pay off an insurance company loan, $25 million to a San Francisco bank to redeem securities held by it, and so on. Thus, reserves spread quickly across the country. And banks gaining reserves may redistribute part of them temporarily by lending them in the federal funds market.

Exhibit 18–1 says it all, except for other means of supplying and absorbing reserves besides cash delivery transactions, which involve delivery and payment the same day. A "regular" delivery transaction involves delivery and payment the next business day. Years ago, outright transactions—either cash or regular—predominated, but they currently account for less than 5 percent of open-market operations. The Fed now supplies reserves mainly by making *repurchase agreements* with dealers, where the Fed purchases securities and the dealer agrees to repurchase the same securities at the original price plus interest within an agreed period of up to 15 days. Repurchase agreements are made only at the Fed's initiative. Conversely, the Fed can absorb reserves temporarily through matched sale-purchase, also called reverse repurchase. These transactions involve the Fed first selling Treasury bills and subsequently purchasing the same issue at a predetermined price.

Reserve Requirement Policy*

The establishment of uniform reserve requirements was one of the more important features of the Depository Institutions Deregulation and Monetary Control Act (MCA) of March 1980. Prior to the act, the Fed set required reserves on demand, time and savings, and, occasionally, on other deposits of only its *member* banks. The reserve ratio was significantly less on time than on demand deposits. Member bank reserves had to be held in the form of deposits with Fed Banks or vault cash. Reserve requirements for *nonmember* banks were set by the 50 state bank commissioners, whose vigilance over their loss of power, or even its appearance, prevented cooperation and uniformity. *In general, nonmember banks had lower reserve requirements, and at least part of the reserves could be held in the form of deposits at other banks or interest-earning liquid assets.* Since large correspondent banks offered their depositors more and better services than the Fed did, and since the Fed let nonmember banks use its facilities indirectly through correspondents, the effective reserve

*Those who read the optional Chapter 13–A will have to excuse the repetition in the first two paragraphs of this section.

requirement was much lower for nonmembers. Nonmember banks earned explicit interest on part of their reserves or received more services. Reserve requirements for *nonbank* depository institutions were set by the corresponding federal or state regulatory authority. Like nonmember banks, the required reserves for nonbanks were low and could be held in the form of deposits at other banks or liquid assets. For reserve requirement purposes, NOW and other similar checkable deposits were considered as time deposits by all regulatory authorities until 1980. Since other checkable deposits were highly restricted through 1980, their classification for reserve purposes was largely irrelevant then. The nationwide expansion of other checkable deposits in 1981 made their reserve classification an important issue.

The higher and stricter reserve requirements imposed by the Fed reduced bank profitability and discouraged membership. The ratio of member bank to total bank deposits fell from approximately 90 percent after World War II to 75 percent by 1979. The membership decline together with the expansion of NOW and similar accounts by nonbanks convinced the Fed that it was losing control over the quantity of money. Over the opposition of many nonmember banks and nonbank depositories, the MCA set reserve requirements, subject to some Fed discretion, for *all* depository institutions. Reserves are held in the form of vault cash or deposits at the Fed.[3]

The Structure of Reserve Requirements

Table 18–1 shows the current (1984) reserve requirements. Net transaction accounts, which have the highest ratio, approximately equal net

TABLE 18–1

Depository Institution Reserve Requirements, Effective June 1, 1984

Type of deposit	*Percent*
Net transaction accounts:	
Under $29 million	3
Over $29 million	12
Nonpersonal time deposits, by original maturity:	
Under 1½ years	3
Over 1½ years	0
Eurocurrency liabilities:	
All types	3

[3]To cushion nonmember banks and thrift institutions from the shock of reserve requirements, their requirements are being phased-in over a seven year period, so only after September 3, 1987, will all depository institutions have truly identical requirements. Moreover, nonmember banks and nonbank depositories (respondents) unfamiliar with the Fed may hold reserves in the form of complete pass-through deposits at member banks (correspondents). In this case, the correspondent's required reserves increase by the full amount of the respondent's deposits. Such pass-through deposits are economically equal to deposits at the Fed.

check deposits, as defined in M-1 (see Chapter 2). In other words, as an excellent first *approximation* net transaction accounts are M-1 minus currency and traveler's checks.[4] Because this is only an approximation, we shall use the official Federal Reserve term, net transaction accounts.

Transaction account reserve requirements are graduated, 3 percent on deposits up to $29 million and 12 percent on the remainder. The reserve cutoff point ($29 million in 1984) is raised annually by 80 percent of the percentage increase in aggregate net transaction accounts. For example, if aggregate transaction accounts increase 10 percent in 1984, the reserve cutoff point in 1985 is raised 8 percent, to $31.32 million. This procedure guarantees that *relatively* small banks always will have lower reserve requirements in spite of *absolute* growth.

Political necessity partially explains the structure of transaction account reserve requirements. As Chapter 13–A showed, nonmember banks on average are significantly smaller than member banks. The 3 percent required reserve ratio for small depositories is sufficiently low as not to reduce the profitability of the typical nonmember bank, which for the first time was brought under the Fed's required reserve policy by MCA. Indeed, the MCA reduced required reserves and increased profits for *small* nonmember banks in *some* states. The numerically few but economically important *large* nonmember banks, which had much to lose by the 12 percent reserve requirement set by MCA, were isolated. Without opposition to the MCA's reserve requirement provisions by their small brothers and sisters, the large nonmember banks were brought kicking and screaming into the Fed's clutches. Moreover, the large nonmember banks could not enlist the support of member banks because the MCA generally lowered member bank reserve requirements. Reserve requirements for the largest member banks were reduced from 16 to 12 percent.[5]

Nonpersonal time deposits and Eurocurrency liabilities are also subject to required reserves. Nonpersonal time deposits are, with a few exceptions, time or savings deposits that are not transaction accounts and in

---

[4]Transaction accounts, but not M-1, including savings deposits on which the account holder is permitted to make withdrawals by telephone and preauthorized transfers (in excess of three per month). Telephone withdrawal and preauthorized transfer accounts, which were authorized nationwide *before* NOW accounts, are relatively small. Most probably, banks will be replacing them in the near future with checkable deposits. These telephone transfer accounts are not ATS accounts, which are transaction account and are included in M-1. Moreover, these telephone transfer accounts are not MMDAs, which are time deposits for reserve purposes and are included in M-2 but not M-1. Nonbank traveler's checks are included in M-1 but are not transaction accounts for reserve requirement purposes.

[5]The Fed's long-standing policy of setting lower reserve requirements for small banks does not contradict the text. Small banks have had a powerful lobby for many years. MCA reduced reserve requirements for small banks to the point that the requirement is virtually meaningless. MCA reduced reserve requirements less for large banks. The benefits from lower reserve requirements were offset to some extent by the imposition of charges for Fed services previously provided free.

which beneficial interest is held by a depositor that is not a natural person. For example, CDs held by corporations are nonpersonal time deposits. Eurocurrency liabilities basically are (*a*) net dollar borrowings by domestic banks from their foreign offices, (*b*) dollar assets sold by domestic banks to their foreign offices, and (*c*) dollar or foreign currency loans to United States residents by foreign offices of domestic banks. Some nonpersonal time deposits are small and, consequently, are included in M-2. However, most nonpersonal time deposits are included only in M-3 because they are large. Most Eurocurrency liabilities are not included in any of the monetary aggregates.

In addition to these "basic" reserve requirements the Board may, after consulting with the appropriate congressional committees, impose additional "emergency" reserve requirements on depository institutions at *any* ratio on *any* liability. Consultation does not necessarily imply approval, but it is unlikely that the Fed would implement emergency measures denounced by Congress. The Board may also set a "supplemental" reserve requirement of not more than 4 percent on transaction accounts. Supplemental reserve requirements may be imposed if they are deemed "essential" for monetary policy by five members of the Board. The fine difference between "emergency" and "essential" conditions is unspecified but important to bankers because emergency reserves, like basic reserves, do not earn interest while the supplemental reserves that are essential for policy participate in the Fed's earnings. The exact rate of interest earned by supplemental reserves is unspecified, but it will be positive. The Fed *after* the fact must justify to Congress any imposition of supplemental reserves. Emergency and supplemental reserves have not yet (mid–1984) been levied, and we expect they rarely will. Late 1976 was the last time the Fed Board changed required reserve ratios prior to changes dictated by the MCA effective from November 13, 1980. Since the Board rarely chose to exercise its exclusive prerogative over reserve requirements prior to the act, the current necessity for congressional consultation should reduce the frequency of changes even more.

We have followed tradition by painting the reserve requirement as one that *must* be met. What penalties are incurred by failing to meet reserve requirements? Does the Fed chop bankers' hands—or worse? Officially at least, the penalty for reserve deficiencies is quite minor. Fed Banks are authorized to assess penalties on required reserve deficiencies at a rate of 2 percent *above* the current discount rate. If banks could borrow unlimited amounts at the discount window, the penalty would be meaningless; banks would borrow at the discount rate. However, discounting is restricted, as we shall see shortly. Since federal funds and other reserve adjustment assets sometimes cost more than 2 percent above the discount rate, and since banks rarely are short on required reserves, the 2 percent official penalty must understate the effective penalty. The higher effective penalty arises because the Fed has other regulatory powers, and failure to meet reserve requirements affects the administration of other regulations. For example, holding company applications would be denied any bank often deficient on reserves. Even if there were no other regulatory considerations, the Fed, like most other regulators, is sufficiently adept at harrassment to make compliance the course of least resistance. The Board ultimately may initiate cease and desist proceedings against reserve violators.

Contemporaneous or Lagged Reserve Accounting

Required reserves do not have to be met continuously and instantaneously. Depositories always have been allowed to average required reserves over some period. Prior to 1968 *contemporaneous reserve accounting, CRA,* with a one-week period existed. That is, *average* deposits during a week (beginning on Thursday) determined *average* required reserves during the *same* week. Member banks petitioned for *lagged reserve accounting, LRA*. The Fed, fearful that banks would leave the System and avoid its regulations, as was possible in 1968 before MCA, granted its member banks' request. Under LRA, in effect between November 1968 and January 1984, average deposits during a week determined required reserves two weeks hence. For example, daily required reserves, computed by multiplying the appropriate reserve ratio times end-of-day deposits, are averaged for, say, the week of June 1–7 (the "computation period"). The requirements are satisfied when the computation period's required reserves equal daily average reserves for the week of June 15–21.[6] *The required reserve target under LRA is known during the entire week, having been determined by deposits two weeks earlier.* Under CRA, random deposit flows during the week affect *both* reserves and the required reserve target. Since any target is hit more readily when the target is known, banks can satisfy their reserve requirements with *less* excess reserves and low-yielding liquid assets to guard against the random deposit flows. That is why banks agitated for LRA.

LRA dominated the discussion of reserve requirements from the mid-1970s to early 1980s. *Monetarists in particular claimed that LRA made money and interest rates much more volatile*. The Fed, on the other hand, said that volatility was independent of the type of reserve accounting and retained LRA to please banks. Loud and persistent monetarist attacks on LRA coupled with MCA's closure of the reserve requirement escape hatch—*all* depositories became subject to the Fed's requirements—finally induced a reluctant Fed to return to essentially CRA in January 1984. The lag was shortened from two weeks to two days. However, in order to

---

[6]We are ignoring the fact that vault cash was not lagged and that the lag was longer for banks with deposits under $15 million, which make up less than 4 percent of total deposits.

weaken CRA, the Fed lengthened the averaging period from one to *two* weeks. In particular, *since January 1984 average deposits during a two-week period, running from Tuesday to the second Monday (say, July 1 to July 14), determine required reserves from Thursday to the second Wednesday (July 3 to July 16).*[7]

For purposes of short-run control where timing is crucial, the type of reserve accounting, contemporaneous or lagged, does matter, as monetarists claim.[8] Assume the Fed does not engage in open-market operations or in any other way counteract bank actions, irrespective of the reserve rule. The unit of analysis is the *aggregate* banking system. Suppose the demand for business loans increases this week. Under either reserve system, banks accommodate their customers and create additional deposits. Deposit expansion under a contemporaneous reserve rule increases required reserves, which banks first attempt to acquire by borrowing in the federal funds market. This raises the federal funds rate and interest rates generally. However, the federal funds market simply shuffles reserves among banks without affecting the total. The higher interest rates do induce banks to discount at the Fed and demand less excess reserves. In this manner they meet their higher reserve requirements. Contrast this situation with the lagged reserve rule, where banks can create deposits this week without any restraining influence from *predetermined* required reserves. Although current reserves place no constraint on current loan and deposit expansion, the expansion is finite because banks realize that required reserves rise in the future, at which time the cost of reserves may be high. Nevertheless, *without the discipline of contemporaneous requirements, deposit expansion under the lagged rule is likely to be greater.* Because deposits and required reserves increase more in the lagged case, two weeks hence the federal funds rate, and interest rates generally, must rise more than they did in the coincident case in order to increase discounts and reduce excess reserves more. The lagged reserve rule increases the interest rate volatility associated with any degree of monetary control or, more likely, reduces the degree of

---

[7]This is true only for transaction accounts, which due to their high reserve ratio explain the major proportion of required reserves. Reserve requirements on other accounts continue to be set on a lagged basis.

[8]This is true when the monetary base, unborrowed reserves, total reserves, the Fed's portfolio of Treasury securities, or some other dollar-valued measure of Federal Reserve credit is the Fed's anterior intermediate or operating variable, as defined in the next chapter. In these cases, the Fed cannot control either money or interest rates perfectly; both are endogenous variables. The rest of this section assumes for simplicity that the Fed's portfolio of Treasury securities is the operating variable. The type of reserve accounting, LRA or CRA, does not prevent the Fed from using interest rates as the operating variable. The rate of interest becomes exogenous in this case, and the issue of (endogenous) interest rate instability is moot. The choice between LRA and CRA has virtually no effect on money supply instability when interest rates are the operating variable.

monetary control exercised, given the Fed's aversion to interest rate volatility. In other words, the Fed validates the large money supply increase under LRA by providing banks two weeks hence with the additional reserves necessary to prevent much higher interest rates. *The monetary and/or interest rate stability associated with CRA is reduced as the reserve averaging period is lengthened.* Current reserves are less of a constraint when there is more time to meet reserve requirements.

The last paragraph admittedly is very difficult, so consider another example. Assume float or some other uncontrolled source increases the base and reserves. Whatever the reserve system, the entire unexpected reserve increase *initially* is excess, which causes banks to expand. Abstracting from discounts, loans and the money stock must expand enough, and the rate of interest must fall enough under LRA, to transform the *entire* amount from undesired to desired excess reserves. No adjustment by the banking system decreases excess reserves (increases required reserves) in this case. Under CRA, however, the monetary expansion and interest rate decline are less because the expansion reduces excess reserves. *The equilibrium increase in desired excess reserves is less than the initial unexpected increase in excess reserves when CRA exists.*

Required Reserves, Liquidity, and Solvency

What is the main purpose of reserve requirements? Originally, reserve requirements were viewed as important means of increasing the liquidity and solvency of banks. Although most people now are *mechanically* conditioned to deny that the main objectives of reserve requirements are more liquid and solvent banks, even bank regulators, when they let their guard down in informal discussions, revert to the old view about reserve requirements. *Relatively low, say, about 10 percent, required reserves do not significantly increase a bank's liquidity and solvency.* The two banking measures are improved only to a minor degree by reserve requirements.

Consider first the relationship between required reserves and liquidity. For our purposes here, liquidity means sufficient cash to be able to meet deposit outflows without selling earning assets. Suppose a depositor withdraws $10, causing total reserves to fall $10. With CRA and a 10 percent requirement, required reserves fall $1. Relatively low required reserves do provide some liquidity because, assuming no excess reserves, the amount of earning assets that must be liquidated is the complement of the reserve ratio. For example, if the reserve ratio were twice as high (20 percent rather than 10 percent in our example), the $10 deposit outflow would require the sale of earning assets worth $8 instead of $9. Because reserve ratios are low, significant (100 percent in our example) reserve changes cause only minor (11 percent) changes in the amount of earning assets associated with deposit flows. *Excess reserves, and not required reserves, are the ultimate liquid asset. Can regulations require excess reserves? Of course not. Required excess reserves are a contradiction in terms.* Second, required reserves provide some liquidity because requirements are averaged over two weeks rather than satisfied continuously. In our example, the bank could operate with a $9 reserve shortage for a few days, provided it had a positive excess some other days. In such a situation, we may view the $9 required reserves against $90 of other deposits as providing short-run liquidity which eliminates the need for immediate sale of earning assets.

Let us now examine the relationship between required reserves and bank solvency. Look at the balance sheets for the two banks. On the

First National Bank

Reserves	5	Check deposits	100
Loans	115		

Second National Bank

Reserves	15	Check deposits	100
Loans	95		

basis of the two balance sheets, can you state with a high degree of confidence that the Second National Bank, with its high reserve ratio, is less likely to fail than the First National, *assuming similar loan quality at both banks?* No. Recalling the discussion of Chapter 15, what regulation has the greatest impact on reducing bank failures? If you could require a minimum ratio of items on the balance sheet, what ratio would you specify in order to minimize bankruptcy? Balance sheets should balance. The previous balance sheets purposely do not balance because we did not want to give away the answers to the questions. *Capital adequacy requirements are the simplest and most effective means of reducing failures.* Since capital (net worth) equals assets minus liabilities, and since insolvency occurs when assets are less than liabilities, the capital/asset ratio measures the maximum percentage loss the bank could incur prior to bankruptcy. *Reserves do reduce the short-run likelihood of failure somewhat because they are perfectly safe and lower the amount of risk assets.* In our example, the First National's unillustrated capital account equals $20. Its loans (risk assets) could decrease in value approximately 17.4 percent ($20/$115) before it is bankrupt. Although the Second National's reserve ratio is 15 percent, 10 percent more than the First National's, it is more likely to fail, *ceteris paribus*. Its loans could decrease in value only approximately 10.5 percent ($10/$95). As just stated, reserves have a minor effect on failures in the *short run* by reducing risk assets. For example, if the Second National's capital account also were $20 and its loans were $105 (so the balance sheet would balance), then it would remain solvent provided losses did not exceed 19 percent ($20/$105), somewhat higher than the 17.4 percent maximum loss for the First National. In the *long run,* however, reserve requirement may actually increase failures because requirements reduce profits.

Monetary Control and the Existence of Reserve Requirements

The main purpose of reserve requirements is to aid monetary control. We first shall examine how the mere *existence* of reserve requirements aids monetary control and then shall examine how reserve requirement *changes* influence monetary and credit conditions. Recall that the Fed could not change reserve requirements prior to 1935. It rarely changed them between 1935 and 1980, when any variation did not have to be justified. Reserve requirement variations are more unlikely now because the 1980 regulation specifies Congressional consultation. In view of this, *reserve requirements would be a virtually worthless monetary instrument unless their mere existence facilitated monetary control.* Yet, surprisingly, the primary benefits of constant, positive reserve requirements are often ignored while the secondary benefits of reserve variations are stressed. The existence of reserve requirements aids monetary control in three ways.

First, reserve requirements lessen the effect on the money supply of all the uncontrolled factors supplying and absorbing the base. The required reserve ratio appears in the denominator of the money supply multiplier, making the multiplier smaller. Since the money supply is the product of the multiplier and the base, required reserves reduce the volatility of the money supply due to variations in the base. Algebraically, $M = mB$, where the terms are as defined in Chapters 3 and 4. Required reserves lower m and, therefore, $\Delta M/\Delta B$. The higher the required reserve ratio, the smaller is the disruptive effect of uncontrolled sources of the base.

Second, required reserves reduce the effect on the money supply of fluctuations in the currency/check deposit ratio. For example, when the public decides to hold less cash, the banking system gains an equal amount of reserves which can support a multiple expansion. The size of the multiple expansion depends negatively on the required reserve ratio. *The money supply is less responsive to currency/deposit fluctuations when the required reserve ratio is high.* The extreme proposal of 100 percent required reserves, which seeks to transform modern bankers into the goldsmiths of old with cash warehouses, is an attempt to eliminate altogether the effect of currency shifts on the money supply.

Finally, *required reserves reduce the effect of fluctuations of the excess reserve ratio on the money supply.* An example best illustrates this feature of required reserves. For simplicity, assume the second money supply case in Chapter 4, where individuals do not hold currency or nonmoney deposits. Money deposits are banks' only liability. In this case, the money supply equation is

$$M = \frac{1}{\bar{r}_m + \bar{r}_{em}} B,$$

where $\bar{r}_m$ and $\bar{r}_{em}$ are the average required and excess reserve ratios, respectively. Suppose the bank determined excess reserve ratio fluctuates randomly between 0.05 and 0.1, and that the optimal money supply is \$450. If there were no reserve requirements so that $\bar{r}_m = 0$, then the optimal constant policy would set the base at \$30. Excess reserve fluctuations, however, prevent continual attainment of the monetary target. With $\bar{r}_m = 0$ and $B = \$30$, the money equation shows that the money supply equals \$600 when $\bar{r}_{em} = 0.05$ and \$300 when $\bar{r}_{em} = 0.1$. On average, the monetary authority hits its target. The multiplier varies between 10 and 20. Now suppose a 15 percent reserve requirement is instituted. Given the same monetary target and excess reserve fluctuations, the Fed would increase the base to \$100 in order to hit the monetary target on average. The important point, however, is the reduction in monetary fluctuations about the average due to the reserve requirements. When $\bar{r}_m = 0.15$ and $B = \$100$, the money supply equals \$500 when $\bar{r}_{em} = 0.05$ and \$400 when $\bar{r}_{em} = 0.1$. The imposition of reserve requirements reduces the range of monetary fluctuations from \$300–\$600 to \$400–\$500. In terms of the multiplier, *the same fluctuations in the excess reserve ratio produce smaller variations in the multiplier when required reserves exist*. In our example, the multiplier varied 100 percent (between 10 and 20) prior to the imposition of reserve requirements but only 25 percent (between 4 and 5) afterward. The required reserve ratio acts as an anchor stabilizing the multiplier and money supply.

Monetary Control and Reserve Requirement Changes

We shall not illustrate again the effect of reserve requirement variations. One point merits emphasis, however. *Reserve requirement changes have no immediate impact on any item on banks' balance sheets or the money supply.* Shortly thereafter, reserve variations do have an impact because banks are profit maximizers, subject to some constraints. Lower reserve requirements produce sterile undesired excess reserves. In order to earn more interest income, banks lower the loan rate and expand loans and deposits.

Are reserve requirement variations an effective way of changing money and interest rates? First, compared to other money policy instruments, *the impact of reserve requirement variations is more widespread geographically and across institutions*. Reserve requirements affect all depository institutions throughout the country. Open-market operations initially affect only those banks that have security dealers' accounts. While the final effects of open-market operations are filtered through the federal funds and government securities markets to all large banks quite rapidly and broadly, the final monetary impact on small banks and nonbank depositories is somewhat delayed for open-market operations compared to reserve requirement variations. Second, the current policy of specifying basic requirements which may be modified by emergency and supplemental measures suggests that neither frequent nor small reserve requirement variations are possible. Thus, reserve requirements are *not* sharp tools for short-run control. But if these characteristics often are desirable, *reserve requirements are ideal when one needs a blunt instrument for long-run monetary variations*. Precisely because reserve requirement changes are infrequent, have a large effect on the money supply, and must be justified, depository institutions and economic actors generally will interpret them correctly. In the parlance of economists, reserve requirements have desirable *announcement effects. Inferences about the future derived from a policy action are its announcement effects*. Since economic actors recognize that monetary policy at least indirectly affects their lives, they search for clues on the future posture of monetary policy. Policy tools which are used continually typically do not generate announcement effects. Some policy tools which are used infrequently engender false announcement effects; they suggest a fundamental change in policy when there is none. The Fed purposely has saved reserve requirements for the cleanup spot—other tools are the leadoff batters—so that its objective when changing requirements is clearly understood. Finally, the assumed permanency of reserve requirement variations may induce depository institutions to expand more rapidly into illiquid and long-term assets, which may have a greater economic impact than an equal expansion of liquid assets.

Reserve Requirement Reforms

For many years the Federal Reserve gave three reasons for its advocacy of reserve requirement uniformity across institutions. (Temporarily ignore the variability of requirements across deposit types.) First, uniform requirements eliminate the impact on the money supply of shifts in the public's preference for different types of institutions. As stated in Chapter 4, when reserve requirements are not uniform, "the" required reserve ratio in the multiplier can only be the average ratio. The shift of deposits from banks with low to high requirements would raise the average required ratio, reduce excess reserves, and generate a monetary contraction. Although reserve requirements still are not perfectly uniform, the MCA of 1980 significantly reduced the variability across institutions by bringing nonmember banks and all nonbank depositories within the fold. Moreover, graduation by size was substantially reduced. Second, uniformity across institutions was viewed as a prerequisite to the imposition of the high reserve requirements that facilitate monetary control. While this argument for uniformity is correct—the unprofitability of high reserve requirements induces banks with the option to escape them—the necessity for political compromise produced the precise opposite. *Uniformity was accompanied by a general lowering of reserve requirements.* Third, uniformity across institutions is desirable on equity grounds. Equals should be treated equally.

We introduce the next topic in the form of a problem. Suppose you are a Fed official with sole and complete authority over the required reserve ratio on nonpersonal time deposits maturing within one and one-half years. The current reserve ratio is 3 percent, but you can set it at any level between 0 and 100 percent. What ratio would you select and why? Do answer the question before reading on. Start with the "why" question. We must specify the reason for reserve requirements before determining their optimal value.

Reserve requirements should be imposed in order to facilitate monetary control. Assuming M-1 is the appropriate monetary aggregate, then the reserve requirement on nonpersonal time deposits should be abolished. In that case, changes in nonpersonal time deposits would not affect the reserves available to support check deposits and would not produce monetary instability. In terms of the advanced money supply equation in Chapter 4, variations in n are irrelevant when $\bar{r}_n = 0$. (Recall that n in Chapter 4 represents all nonmoney liabilities subject to reserve requirements.) If M-3 were the appropriate monetary aggregate, then nonpersonal time deposits, all of which are included in M-3, and transaction accounts, which approximately equal check deposits, should have *identical* reserve requirements. Uniformity of reserve requirements among the monetary components eliminates the effect of shifts in composition. Of course, this line of reasoning implies that reserve requirements should be extended to all the items in M-3. *Current reserve requirements cannot be justified as the optimal values in order to control any monetary aggregate, unless the Fed has some secret and complex money supply measure such as M-1.7KJ.*

Discount Policy

Discount policy has two dimensions: (1) price, and (2) quantity. The price dimension is simply the discount rate depository institutions pay on their borrowings at the Fed. The quantity dimension places limits on the amount depositories can borrow at any given discount rate. Banks cannot borrow at the discount window whatever amount they want. The Fed calls itself the lender of *last* resort. It says discounting is a *privilege* and not a right.

The quantity dimension has taken various forms over time, but basically *it attempts to specify "legitimate" purposes for discounts*. More specifically, the quantity dimension originally took the form of the *real bills or commercial loan doctrine,* which among other things required specific collateral in order to discount. The quantity dimension now monitors bank's recent balance sheet adjustments in order to ascertain that banks are borrowing *out of need and not for profit*. While formerly limited to member banks, the discount window was opened in 1980 to all depositories.

Why are there two dimensions to discounting? The Fed feels two dimensions are necessary because (1) banks have different objectives than the Fed, (2) discounting is at the initiative of banks, and (3) the Fed favors discount rate stability. The Fed sets the discount rate with a view toward full employment and price stability. Are these the objectives of depository institutions? Of course not. They seek to make profits. At any discount rate banks may decide to borrow too much, given the Fed's objectives, so reserves and the money supply expand excessively. One solution is obvious: change the discount rate. The Fed, however, favors stable interest rates in general and a stable discount rate in particular. Given this objective, the other solution is to ration quantity through some nonprice dimension of discounting.

As stated earlier, discounting was the most important tool when the Fed was created in 1913. The Federal Reserve Act established reserve requirements but did not give the Fed the authority to change them. Open-market operations were largely dismissed because financial markets were underdeveloped. Although the issuance of government bonds in order to finance World War I significantly broadened the bond market, open-market operations remained a minor tool throughout the 1920s because it was contrary to the prevalent laissez-faire, antidiscretion philosophy of the time. Discounts are at the initiative of banks, although banks' behavior clearly depends on Fed policy. This made discounting compatible with the laissez-faire philosophy. Even those who favored a somewhat activist, discretionary policy still evaluated discounting positively because the banks' initiative provided the Fed with information on the appropriate policy. At a time when few statistics were collected and when the statistics collected often were unreliable and dated, monitoring banks and their demand for loans was a good way of knowing the current and future state of the economy.

The Quantity Dimension: Real Bills*

The creators of the Fed wanted it to copy the Bank of England, which in the early 20th century administered its discount window according to

*Warning: This difficult section is for economic historians. Those interested in current policy should proceed directly to the next section.

the precepts of the real bills or commercial loan theory. The Fed did abandon strict adherence to the real-bills doctrine shortly after it came into existence in order to aid Treasury financings. However, it practiced a flexible version of real bills at least until the early 1930s, and modern adaptations appear sporadically. Real bills as a theory of commercial bank management was discussed in Chapter 10. Basically, it says that banks will be liquid when they make short-term productive loans (acquire real bills). It also is a theory of central bank management. *The real-bills doctrine states that a central bank will create the appropriate noninflationary amount of money when it discounts the real bills presented by commercial banks*. The three fundamental assumptions of the real-bills doctrine are:

1. The money supply is a constant multiple of the base.
2. Banks' requests for discounts at the Fed are a constant proportion of their inventory loans and other real bills.
3. Inventories and other goods financed by real bills are a constant proportion of total output.

If the base is provided solely by discounts so that the base is a constant proportion of inventory loans, it does follow, given the three assumptions, that the money supply changes will parallel income changes. Contrary to the assertion of the real-bills doctrine, proportionality between money and income does *not* guarantee price stability. On the other hand, many modern detractors of the real-bills doctrine are wrong in alleging that the real-bills doctrine always is destabilizing. *Whether or not the real-bills doctrine is stabilizing depends on the source of the income change. Monetary policy which follows the precepts of the real-bills doctrine destabilizes an economy buffeted by demand shocks but stabilizes an economy buffeted by supply shocks*. If income increases because aggregate demand increases, then the inflationary potential of a larger demand is augmented by monetary expansion. However, if income increases because aggregate supply increases, then the deflationary potential of a larger supply is averted by a real-bills policy.[9]

Figure 18–1 illustrates these ideas. Suppose the initial demand and supply of commodities in general are represented by the solid curves in Figure 18–1. If for any reason demand now increases to D′, income will increase. Banks will accommodate firms' need for higher inventories by discounting real bills and increasing the money supply. Monetary expansion further increases the demand for commodities, shifting the demand curve to D″. The real-bills doctrine is destabilizing in this case. It induces demand shifts in the same direction as the original disturbance. Now

---

[9]In terms of the quantity theory equation to be presented later, if higher incomes are associated with a proportionally higher velocity, then monetary expansion is destabilizing. However, if higher incomes are associated with a constant or lower velocity, then monetary expansion is stabilizing. Policy is destabilizing whenever any random or exogenous change induces a policy change in the same direction.

FIGURE 18–1
Real Bills Is Destabilizing when Demand Shocks Predominate but Stabilizing when Supply Shocks Predominate

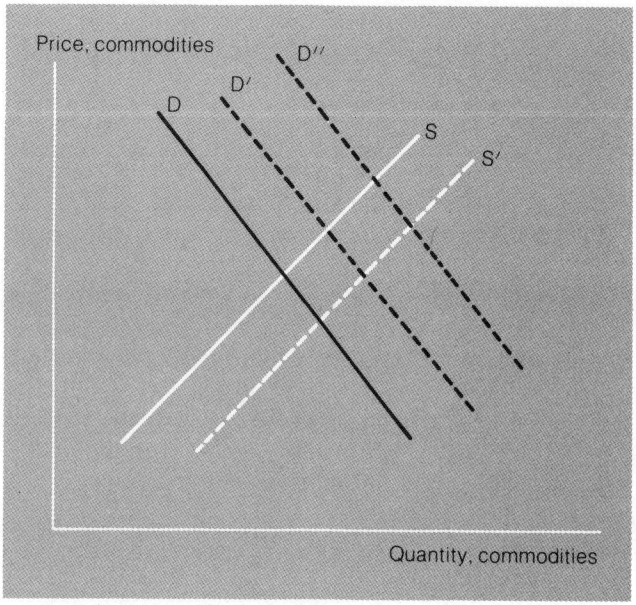

suppose the disturbance originates on the supply side. Supply shifts from S to S′. The higher income also leads to more loans and monetary expansion. Again, monetary expansion shifts demand, this time from D to D′. In this case the real-bills doctrine is stabilizing. The demand increase is necessary in order to keep prices stable.

What types of shocks, demand or supply shocks, tend to predominate? Is monetary policy conducted according to the real-bills doctrine stabilizing or destabilizing? Over time, both demand and supply shift out. The shocks illustrated by the shifting curves in Figure 18–1 are the deviations from the long-run supply and demand trends. Most economists during the period from World War II to the 1970s thought that demand always was considerably more unstable than supply and, consequently, denounced the real-bills doctrine. While demand shocks did predominate immediately following World War II, more recent experience has shown that supply shifts cannot be totally ignored. Crop failures and oil embargoes and cartels are examples of (inward) supply shifts. Higher oil prices increase the quantity of commodities we must export to pay for our oil imports and reduce real income. If the monetary authorities had been determined to stabilize the general price level and followed the real-bills doctrine, the money supply would have *fallen* with income. The higher oil prices would have been accompanied by lower prices in other sectors, keeping the general level of prices more or less constant. Instead, the monetary authorities were unwilling to accept a reduction in our standard of living due to higher real prices for oil. Reacting almost as if higher OPEC prices and a lower standard of living were immoral, the inward supply was countered by monetary *expansion* and an outward shift in demand. If this had been the end of the story, the monetary expansion and inflation may have been worthwhile. At least output would not have fallen much. However, the strengthened OPEC cartel which initiated the disturbance was not going to be outdone. OPEC raised oil prices in order to purchase more commodities. If the United States and other countries inflated, thereby temporarily reducing the real price of oil and the imports OPEC could acquire, then OPEC would raise prices again. An inflationary spiral got underway. Inward supply shifts were followed by outward demand shifts, which were followed by inward supply shifts, and so on.

OPEC did not exist when the real-bills doctrine was widely accepted. However, in those days the economy was largely agricultural. The weather and other random factors have a much more important effect on supply in agricultural economies. Therefore, the real-bills doctrine was *not* so destabilizing in the early years. Indeed, it actually may have been stabilizing, contrary to the assertions of many current economists. Adam Smith (the father of the real-bills doctrine and economics in general), the creators of the Federal Reserve, and most early 20th century economists were not your run-of-the-mill dummies. They advocated the real-bills doctrine because it sometimes was stabilizing.

The Quantity Dimension: Need, Not Profit

The quantity dimension has a new twist. The Fed no longer requires real bills as collateral.[10] The quantity dimension is reflected today by the Fed's attempting to determine the reason for bank borrowing. According to the Fed, banks borrow either for "need" or "profit." *Banks are allowed to borrow out of need but not for profit.* In some sense all discounting is for profit. Arms-length transactions must make an economic unit better off or the transaction would not be made. No one forces banks to borrow at the Fed. They do so instead of selling liquid assets or issuing CDs because they are better off borrowing. Nevertheless, *the Fed does not view banks as borrowing for profit when either (1) deposits are falling, or (2) "customer" loans are increasing.* When either condition holds,

---

[10]Strictly speaking, only bank borrowings at the Fed which are secured by real bills are discounts or, as called years ago, rediscounts. Banks' borrowings at the Fed on the basis of their own promissory note secured nearly always by government securities are technically called advances, instead of discounts. Advances predominate by a wide margin. From an economic viewpoint, the two types of borrowings are identical.

banks are said to borrow out of need. Customer loans basically are loans to depositors, particularly small depositors. The Fed views banks as having an obligation to lend to their customers. According to Chapter 10, customer loans are obligations in the sense that failure to lend to depositors leads them to place their deposits elsewhere. Banks borrow for profit according to the Fed when discounts are financing security purchases or national loans. *Surveillance against borrowing for profit explains why market interest rates often remain considerably above the discount rate.*[11]

The Fed formalized somewhat its need concept and surveillance procedures in 1973 by establishing a seasonal credit privilege. To be eligible for this new borrowing privilege, deposit institutions must exhibit a seasonal pattern in loans and deposits that persists for at least eight weeks. The seasonal privilege is available to institutions with deposits under $100 million. The small depositories must arrange for the credit prior to the seasonal need. The primary beneficiaries are depositories in rural and resort areas.

The Relationship between the Discount Rate and Money Market Interest Rates

The price dimension of discounting attracts the most attention, particularly in the popular press. Requests, indeed groveling appeals, to the Fed for a lower discount rate are quite frequent, presumably because lower market interest rates will follow. The Fed discount rate and money market interest rates, such as the three-month Treasury bill and CD rates, are highly positively correlated. See Figure 18–2. Why do the rates move together? What cause and effect relationship is responsible for the statistically positive correlation? *The high positive correlation is due in part to a causal relationship from the discount rate to money market rates. First, higher discount rates discourage discounting, which reduces the monetary base. The initial effect of a lower base and money supply is higher market interest rates. Second, a higher discount rate sometimes provides the necessary political justification banks were seeking in order*

---

[11]Some observers of the banking scene claim that such surveillance is unnecessary because banks are "naturally reluctant to borrow." Prior to the existence of the Fed, borrowing by banks was universally interpreted as a sign of weakness. Particularly in an age without deposit insurance, banks needed to project an image of strength and, consequently, rarely borrowed. The Federal Reserve, which looked at itself as a lender of last resort and not a permanent source of funds for banks, naturally strengthened banks reluctance to borrow through nonprice dimensions and surveillance. The strongest version of the reluctance hypothesis, which says that banks are naturally reluctant to borrow, is contradicted today by the liability management techniques of virtually all large banks. Strong reluctance now may be a characteristic of many small banks of little consequence. The weak version of the hypothesis has much truth: banks have become so accustomed to borrow less than the profit-maximizing amount from the Fed that suspension of surveillance procedures would induce little additional borrowing in the short run.

FIGURE 18–2
The Discount Rate and Short-Term Interest Rates

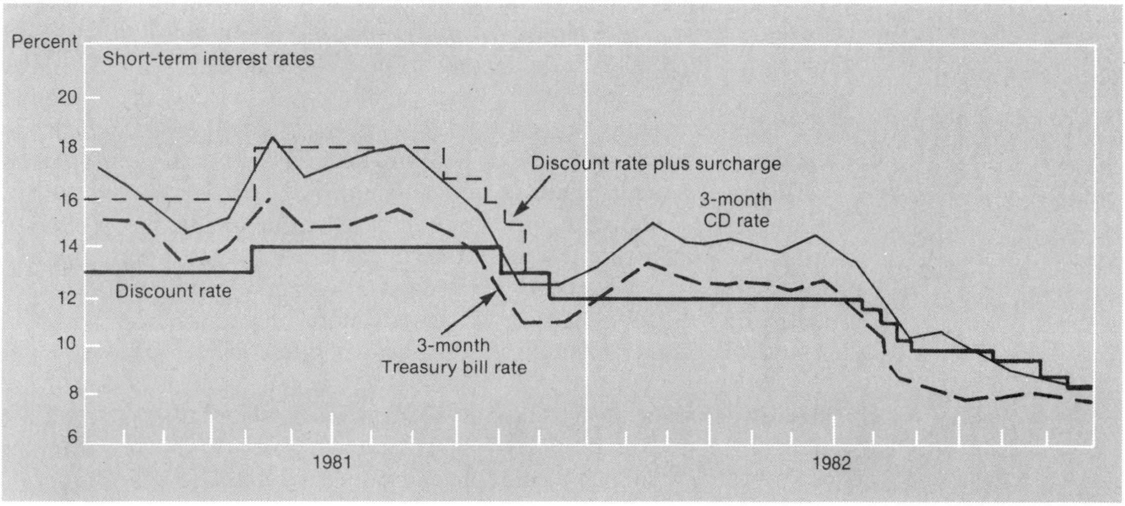

Source: Federal Reserve Bank of New York, *Annual Report,* 1982, p.14.

to raise interest rates. High interest rates are politically unpopular. For this and other reasons, banks sometimes ration credit. That is, the rate of interest is below its equilibrium value, and banks allocate credit on the basis of other variables. When the Fed raises its discount rate, banks can stop rationing credit and revert to employing the interest rate as an allocation tool. Banks can effectively respond to any criticism, "Look, we are simply following the example of the Fed." Since prices and interest rates are better allocation tools than years in business, asset size, skin color, sex, or yet other allocation devices, any reduction of credit rationing is a real plus for discount rate changes.

The positive association between the discount and market rates is also due to causation going the reverse direction, from market interest rates to the discount rate. *When business is booming and market interest rates are rising, countercyclical economic policy dictates that the Fed raise the discount rate in order to prevent the monetary expansion that would result from the positive relationship between discounting and the differential between the market and discount rates.* In symbols,

$$D = (i_m - i_d, \ . \ . \ .) \qquad \textbf{(18–1)}$$

where D is discounts, i_m and i_d are the market and discount rate, respectively, and the ellipses indicate that discounts depend on other factors besides the rate differential. While the Fed may rail against borrowing for profit and has set up some mechanical rules to detect such reprehensible conduct, the naked empirical truth is that discounts do depend on the rate differential. Aggregate deposit balance is associated with inflows and outflows at the micro level. When market rates exceed the discount, institutions incurring deposit outflows will borrow at the Fed, which will adjudge the banks needy. The Fed raises the discount rates in order to halt the reserve and monetary expansion during business peaks.

Figure 18–2 shows that the discount rate lags behind market rates. For example, the CD rate fell more than 5 percentage points (from approximately 18 to 12½ percent) between August and December 1981. The decline in the discount rate was much more moderate, from 14 to 12 percent. The first reduction in the discount rate occurred on November 2, 1981, more than two months *after* the CD rate started its downward slide. Moreover, another reduction occurred on December 4, 1981, by which time market rates were starting an upward climb. While timing patterns are not infallible guides to causation, *this lagged pattern suggests that causation generally runs from market rates to the discount rate*. Two important implications follow from this finding. First, *discount rate changes generally do not have expectational or announcement effects*. Your TV anchorperson may announce in solemn tones that the Fed changed the discount rate. Most people will ignore the statement, not even knowing what it means. But how will the financially sophisticated who play the market interpret the Fed's action? They rarely will be surprised by discount rate changes. The discount rate lags market interest rates enough that sophisticated market participants have acquired earlier signals of the overall posture of monetary policy. Discount rate changes generally are viewed as technical adjustments to keep policy on course, rather than as a change in policy.

We sprinkled the last paragraph with several "generally's" because the discount rate can have announcement effects. The most dramatic example of a discount rate change with an announcement effect occurred in late 1931. In 1930 and early 1931 the Fed repeatedly cut the discount rate, and justly so. The United States was in the midst of the worst depression in its history, so that any expansionary policy was welcome. In 1931 Britain went off the gold standard. The Fed was determined that the United States would remain on the gold standard, if necessary at the expense of employment and economic recovery. It feared, however, that foreigners might suspect that the United States would copy Britain. Talk is cheap. The Fed had to convince the public that it meant business about gold glittering. In one fell swoop the Fed more than doubled the discount rate. The market got the message that the Fed had new goals. The dollar strengthened, and the economy weakened further.

The second major implication of the lagged response of the discount rate to market interest rates is that discounting and, ceteris paribus, *the money supply tend to be procyclical.* That is, discounts and the money supply increase during booms because the greater borrowing by firms during business expansions raises market interest rates. Needless to say, but said nevertheless, the appropriate policy is countercyclical. Money should contract, or expand less rapidly, during business expansions. To be sure, the procyclical pattern is not that long and strong because the Fed does not delay closing the interest rate differential inordinately.

Discounting: Escape Hatch or Safety Valve?

Open-market operations and discounting are negatively related in the short run. Whenever the Fed sells securities, thereby reducing the base and money supply and raising market interest rates, banks respond to the reserve loss by borrowing more, thereby offsetting some of the monetary and interest rate contraction. Open-market purchases also are partially offset in the short run by less discounting. Is the negative relationship between open-market operations and discounts a bane or a boon? This question has been debated for some time. As occasionally happens, the debaters get sidetracked on irrelevant issues and ignore the fundamentals. Most economists claim that the negative relationship makes discounting an escape hatch which reduces the effectiveness of open-market operations and overall monetary policy. The Fed must compensate for the negative relationship by engaging in larger open-market purchases and sales initially. A minority view the identical phenomenon as a safety valve. They view the larger open-market operations as positively beneficial.[12] The debate degenerated into a semantic controversy because the debaters concentrated on irrelevant *averages*. The government securities market is so large that the Fed can readily compensate for *average* discounts. While this may keep the base on target on average, the negative relationship is not known *exactly* at all times. *Discounting is at the initiative of banks, and their behavior is not always forecast correctly.* Discounting, like other uncontrolled sources of the monetary base which cannot be predicted exactly, causes short-run fluctuations about the target. Unintentional fluctuations are *not* necessarily undesirable. The monetary authority may set such poor targets that deviations about the targets may be welcome. However, any random deviations from optimally set targets are undesirable, by definition. While the Fed's targets may well be nonoptimal, they probably are not so poor that uncontrolled deviations are

---

[12]The minority also claim that the offsetting effect of discounting on open-market operations induces the Fed to act sooner. The rationale for this allegation is not spelled out and far from obvious. Moreover, even if the allegation were true, a trigger-happy Fed may be very undesirable, as advocates of monetary policy rules argue.

an improvement. *Discounting thus is an escape hatch instead of a safety valve.*

Since analogies have always been popular in this debate, let me offer a new analogy while recognizing that no analogy is perfect. Suppose static interference hinders reception of a radio station. Is this desirable or not? Should you attempt to eliminate the interference? The answer largely depends on how much you enjoy the radio program. If the program is really worthwhile, you will attempt to eliminate the static immediately. On the other hand, the program may be so bad that the static dulls a cacophony of sound and actually improves matters.

Reform Proposals

Most of the reform proposals assume that the Fed is a sufficiently good fiddler, although certainly no concert violinist, that we want to listen to its music. The static from discounting is annoying. One proposal goes all the way: *abolish discounts.*[13] Let's hear the tune just as the Fed is playing it. The main criticism of this proposal focuses on its microeconomic consequences, particularly for small banks. Critics allege that small banks have few ways of adjusting their balance sheets and must rely on discounts at the Fed when they are buffeted by large shocks. The Fed accepts this position and has formalized and extended it to large banks. Besides the usual adjustment credit granted to banks with moderate short-run needs, in the 1970s the Fed established a new discounting category called special circumstances, which basically is for banks with immoderate long-run needs. The main beneficiaries of special circumstances discounting have been Franklin National Bank and Continental Illinois. Professor Friedman, and others who want to abolish discounting, claim that discounting is a vestige of the past. They concede that a few banks will be hurt by the proposal, but they claim that, contrary to years ago, virtually all banks, including small banks, have alternative credit sources. The Franklin National Bank case exemplifies the possibility that discounting may extend too much credit for too long and simply postpone the inevitable.

The second major reform proposal would tie the discount rate to market interest rates in the very short run. This proposal would change discount rates frequently, say, weekly, in order to maintain a constant differential between the discount and market interest rates. *Tying the discount and market rates would largely eliminate the procyclical effect of discounting.* If this proposal were adopted, lack of knowledge of the precise relationship between discounts and the interest rate differential would be irrelevant. Since the differential would remain constant, its effect, whatever

---

[13] Milton Friedman, *A Program for Monetary Stability* (New York: Fordham University Press, 1959), p. 44.

it may be, would also be constant. Of course, discounting depends on other factors besides the interest differential. (Recall the ellipses in Equation 18–1.) The current proposal does not totally eliminate the unpredictable aspects of discounting.

The tying proposal has wide support. Its opponents are mainly domiciled at the Fed, which is somewhat surprising considering that the proposal would increase the likelihood of the Fed's hitting its target. The Fed has raised numerous "technical" issues such as how often should the discount rate be adjusted, to what specific market interest rate should the discount rate be tied, and what should the interest rate differential equal? While people not intimately involved in an operation often dismiss various real complications as mere technicalities, the issues raised by the Fed are important yet not readily answered. However, implementation of the proposal should not await determination of the *optimal* adjustment period, the *optimal* market rate, and the *optimal* differential. Improvements in any area should be adopted, and some (nonoptimal) tying scheme which improves the current administration of the discount mechanism can be readily found. One suspects that the Fed objects to the tying scheme because it reduces its discretionary power. No one who has savored power wants to be reduced to a robot.

The third proposal, which is a logical extension of the second, would have *the Fed pay interest on commercial banks' excess reserves at the tied discount rate*. In our discussion of the money multiplier and excess reserve ratio in Chapter 4, we said that excess reserves depend on market interest rates, among other variables. At that point we were implicitly assuming that excess reserves earned no interest so the market interest rate was the opportunity cost of excess reserves. If excess reserves earned interest at the discount rate, then the opportunity cost and excess reserve determinant would be the rate differential. *Extension of the tying proposal to excess reserves would eliminate another important source of short-run monetary variations.*

Recent Changes

All three proposals were made more than 20 years ago but remain just that, proposals, because of Fed opposition. The Fed is not against all change, however. With little prior notice it instituted the seasonal and special circumstances borrowing programs just mentioned. Compared to the traditional short-term adjustment discounts, the new programs offer longer term credit and, in the seasonal case, must be arranged beforehand. Perhaps in order to emphasize the special nature of these programs and to forestall more frequent discounting, the Fed in 1980 began applying a surcharge to short-term adjustment discounts by large institutions (deposits of $500 million or more) which borrow in successive weeks or in more than four weeks in a calendar quarter. The surcharge of up to four percentage points was eliminated in late 1981.

Figure 18–3 presents some recent though limited empirical evidence on the magnitude of the effect of interest rate differentials on discounting. The horizontal axis measures the difference between the federal funds and the discount rates. The vertical axis measures the amount of discounts at the Fed. The regression equation, which best describes the relationship between the two variables, is illustrated along with the raw data for July through December 1980. The strong positive relationship would be eliminated by the tying proposal which keeps the interest rates differential

FIGURE 18–3
Relationship between the Amount of Discounts at the Fed and the Difference between the Federal Funds and Discount Rates

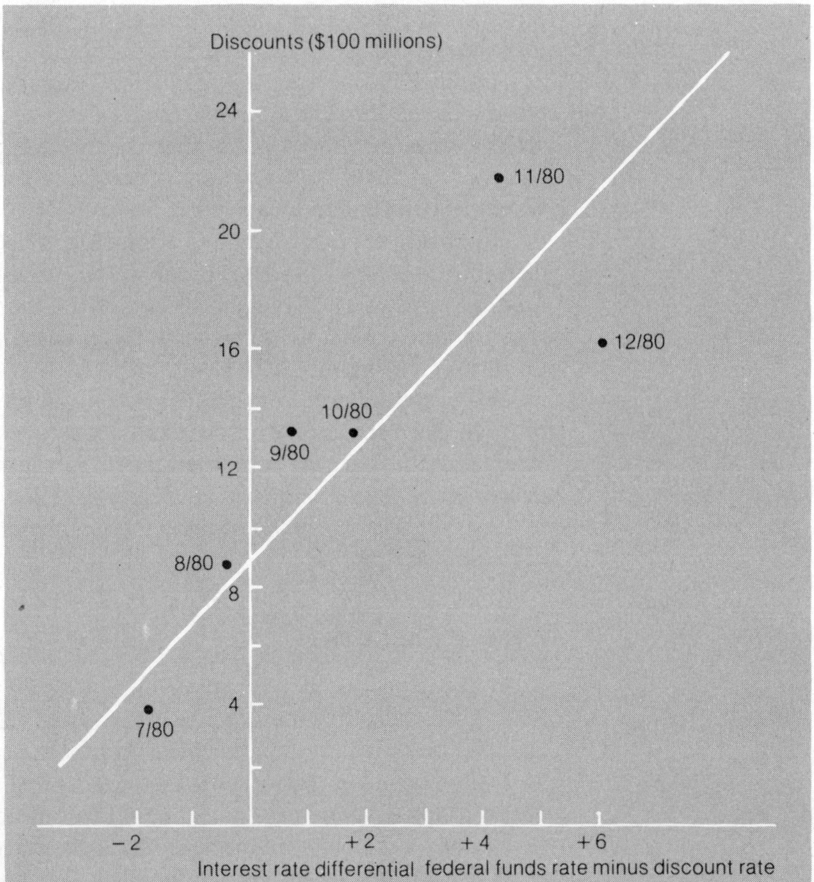

constant.[14] More precisely, the tying proposal would eliminate about 75 percent of the variation in discounts. The unknown ellipses in Equation 18–1 explain 25 percent of the variation in discounts.

Summary/Questions

The three main monetary policy instruments are open-market operations, reserve requirements, and the discount mechanism. To the novice the three instruments are simply alternative means of accomplishing the same end. If the Fed wants less money and higher interest rates, it simply sells securities in the open-market, raises reserve requirements, or raises the discount rate. While the three tools can be used interchangeably to achieve the same *general* targets, the sophisticated student of the financial system knows that the *specific* effects of the tools vary considerably. For example, the novice says that the Fed simply raises reserve requirements in order to reduce monetary growth. But can the Fed raise requirements? How will the general public and depository institutions react to the announcement of higher reserves? Will the reserve requirements be broadly based or fall on selected institutions? Will the reduced profitability from higher reserves cause a reduction in the number of financial institutions and higher service charges? The answers to similar questions about open-market operations are quite different.

1. Define defensive and dynamic open-market operations.
2. With the passage of the Monetary Control Act, what financial institutions are subject to the Fed's reserve requirement ratios? What liabilities have reserve requirement ratios, and what do the ratios equal? What assets count as reserves?
3. Do reserve requirements have to be met instantaneously and continuously? State the current and previous (pre-1984) time patterns between deposits and required reserves and the length of the reserve averaging period.
4. Define CRA and LRA. Carefully explain why the money stock and interest rates are more volatile under LRA than CRA.

---

[14]The regression equation is

$$D = 9.03 + 1.92(i_{FF} - i_d), \qquad R^2 = 0.767 \tag{18–1'}$$

where D is discounts in $100 millions and $i_{FF} - i_d$ is the interest rate differential. The t statistic of the slope coefficent (1.92) equals 3.67, indicating that there is a high likelihood (over 95 percent) of a systematic relationship. The value of R^2 indicates that approximately 75 percent of the variation in discounts is explained by interest rate differences. The results are only illustrative; the sample size could well be expanded.

5. What are the main means of enhancing bank *(a)* solvency, and *(b)* liquidity? How, if at all, do required reserve ratios affect bank solvency and liquidity?
6. State three ways by which the mere existence of reserve requirements aids monetary control and reduces the volatility of money.
7. What are the advantages of uniform reserve requirements applicable to all depositories?
8. Discuss the real-bills doctrine of central banking. What are its basic assumptions? Does it tend to stabilize or destabilize the economy?
9. How does the Fed distinguish between borrowing for need or profit? What empirical evidence suggests that, in fact, some discounts are motivated by profits?
10. Explain the causal relationships which produce a positive association between the discount rate and short-term money market rates.
11. State and evaluate critically various proposals to reform the discount mechanism.
12. Under what two conditions may banks discount at the Fed for longer than the very short run?

Monetary policy: Strategy, targets, and independence

19

Both this and the next chapters analyze the strategy of monetary policy formulated during FOMC meetings. The chapters emphasize the appropriate intermediate or operating targets, such as money and interest rates, in order to achieve ultimate goals such as GNP. In other words, the chapters emphasize the *short-term, dynamic* objectives of the FOMC account manager in his daily decisions to buy or sell securities. Although the topics in the two chapters are similar, the chapter divisions are justified on the grounds that they provide convenient stopping places. The student more interested in the ultimate goals of monetary policy may skip both chapters and proceed directly to Chapter 21. Most students interested in Federal Reserve decision making should read this chapter now, but some will prefer to postpone the chapter until immediately after Chapter 28. In any case, the next chapter admittedly is for the specialist.

This chapter is difficult and imprecise, filled with qualifying statements and much hemming and hawing. Yet the difficulty and imprecision are inevitable, given the topic. Brace yourself: economists and other policymakers are *not* all knowing and all powerful. *The fundamental theme of this chapter is that the economic structure is uncertain and lags exist.* Given these disheartening but undeniable facts, optimal policy is not easily ascertained, if indeed it exists at all. Different opinions about lags and the structure of the economy yield different policy prescriptions. This is not to say that all opinions are equally valid. Uncertainty does not mean total ignorance about the economic structure. This chapter first describes some of the difficulties *any* policymaker faces and rationalizes the two-stage strategy whereby an intermediate (sometimes called operating) target is selected. The second section looks at FOMC meetings as an illustration of a two-stage monetary strategy. We then describe and attempt to grade several of the previously and currently most popular monetary policy targets. In view of the topic's difficulty and indefiniteness, we shall hit only the highlights. The last section shifts from "what" and "why" questions to "who." In particular, it discusses the pros and cons of an independent Federal Reserve.

Some simplification is absolutely necessary. We shall assume universal agreement on a well-defined ultimate goal, which may be one dimensional or a unique, feasible combination of various variables.[1] In fact, most serious disagreements stem from very different goals. Nevertheless, the assumption is made because such disagreements are more properly viewed as political instead of economic, as Chapter 1 argued.

Economic Policy in a World of Uncertainty and Lags

Monetary policy and economic policy in general involve the manipulation of certain policy tools or instruments (the cause variables) which influence some ultimate targets or goals (the effect variables). Why don't policymakers quickly go about their business of achieving the well-defined goal at all times? Temporarily place policymakers in their paradise: assume they always can achieve their goals. When will they be in this paradise? *When lags exist, policymakers must have perfect knowledge about the economic structure in order to achieve their goal.* The value and effect on the goal of both the policy instruments *and* every exogenous variable must always be perfectly predictable. Figure 19–1 presents a simple schematic representation of these ideas. Time is being measured along the horizontal axis. The causal policy tools precede the goals by some distance because their impact is neither immediate nor direct. *Policy works with a lag*. The precise, if lagged, relationship between the tools and goals is illustrated by a solid line connecting the two. The figure shows the monetary policy tools and goal variables, but the analysis is applicable to other policies as well. Exogenous, from the viewpoint of the policymaker, factors also influence the goals. The lags of the various exogenous factors, represented by E in Figure 19–1, may be either shorter or longer than the policy lag. Provided the policymaker can predict the *value and impact* of the exogenous variables exactly, then the goals still can be achieved exactly. However, the relationship between tools and goals will no longer be simple. When the exogenous factors are expansionary, the instruments

[1]Chapter 29 analyzes some of the problems associated with multiple goals. Except when confusion may arise, we follow traditional practice of not distinguishing between "goal" as a variable (say, GNP) and "goal" as a specific value of the variable (full employment GNP).

FIGURE 19–1
Policymaking in a Certain Environment

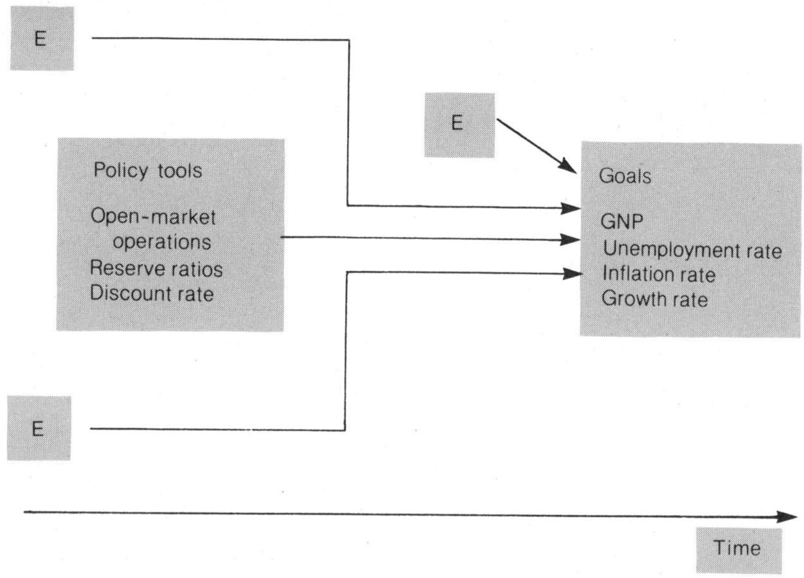

must be set lower than normal. Numerous instrument settings are compatible with given goals, depending on the value of the exogenous variables.

The policymaker's world, however, is characterized by uncertainty or imperfect knowledge about the economic structure, in particular, uncertainty about the relationship between instrument and goal and uncertainty about the value and impact of exogenous variables. Indeed, policymakers may not even know precisely what some of the exogenous variables are. At times they will admit this and call these exogenous variables "random variables." At other times unknown exogenous variables are given mysterious names such as "animal spirits." The question marks about the exogenous variables and the multiple broken lines between variables in Figure 19–2 attempt to portray the uncertain world of the policymaker.

Uncertainty would pose no problem if, contrary to fact and the assumption of the last two paragraphs, lags did not exist. *Lack of any lags whatsoever is a second sufficient condition which places policymakers in paradise.* If policymakers were continuously aware of the value of the goal variable, and if policy instruments had an instantaneous impact on the goal variable, then policymakers could adjust and readjust the policy instruments continuously. This would keep the goal variable on target in spite of the exogenous variables and the occasionally unpredictable effects of the instruments.

FIGURE 19–2
Policymaking in an Uncertain Environment

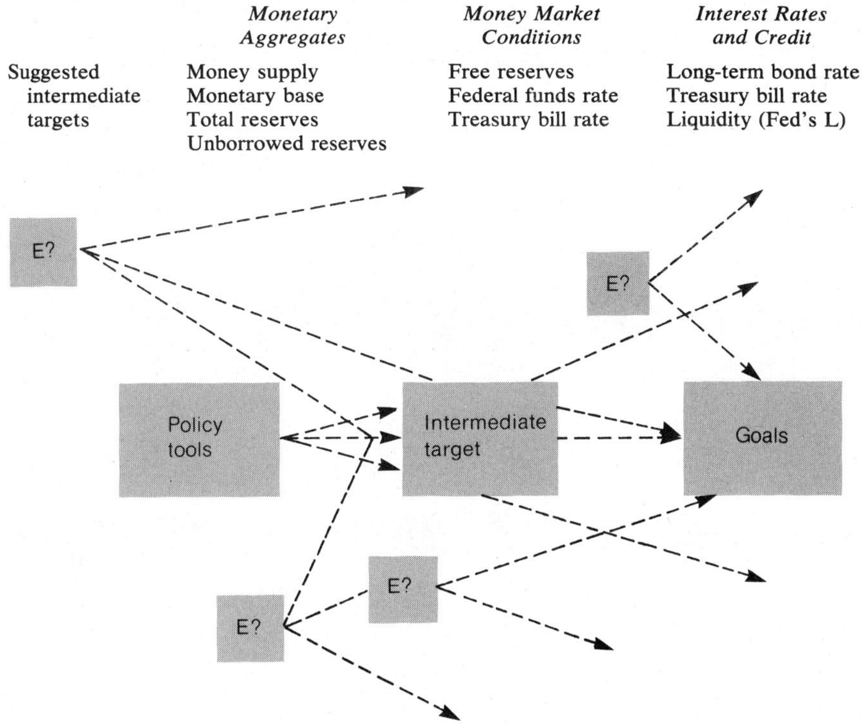

Of course, neither sufficient condition exists. Lags *and* uncertainty exist, and the problems caused by each are reinforced by the other. In a world of lags and uncertainty, what operating strategy should the policymaker follow? What method of operation maximizes the likelihood of hitting the goals, given one's estimate of the relationships among the variables? One operating strategy focuses *directly* on the goals. *Policymakers who follow a direct, single-stage strategy closely monitor the goal variable and manipulate the instrument if, and only if, the current and desired values of the goal variable differ.* For various reasons many people recommend a *two- (or more) stage strategy, where the policymaker focuses on at least one intermediate target which the policymaker treats, for purposes of a short-run operating guide, as if it were the true goal or ultimate target.*[2] The (at least) two-stage monetary policy strategy is de-

[2]Much of the literature on monetary policy strategy and targets and indicators is confused and confusing. A notable exception, both in terms of its high quality and conclusion against uncritical acceptance of intermediate targets and indicators, is Benjamin Friedman, "Targets, Instruments, and Indicators of Monetary Policy," *Journal of Monetary Economics,* October 1975, pp. 443–73.

picted in Figure 19–2 by a box between the instruments and goals. The intermediate target should be a *readily observable* variable which responds to the policy instruments *before* the goal responds. The intermediate variable(s) may respond to exogenous variables in addition to the policy instruments. However, there should be a *strong* link between the intermediate and goal variables. The top portion of Figure 19–2 identifies some candidates for the monetary policy intermediate variable. Given the goals and the policymaker's best estimate of lags, exogenous variables, and the economic structure, the optimal value of the intermediate target is selected. The policymaker then focuses on this variable and adjusts the instruments to hit the optimal value. *Periodically,* the value of the intermediate target is adjusted to reflect different goals or different estimates of the exogenous variables. In contrast to the single-stage strategy, however, a decline in the ultimate goal variable need *not immediately* induce expansionary instrument settings. Indeed, followers of a two-stage strategy on occasion will *correctly* adopt a *contractionary* policy even though the goal variable is currently *below* target.

Let's look at the minutes of FOMC meetings to verify that the Fed does follow a two-stage strategy and make this section more concrete.

FOMC Meetings: They Do It Monthly

By the time the FOMC assembles at 9:30 A.M. around the 30-foot mahogany table in the Federal Reserve boardroom, each member is well prepared to deliberate. Since the last meeting a little over a month ago the members and nonvoting Fed Bank presidents have received daily, weekly, and occasional special reports which (1) describe past and prospective economic and financial developments, both domestic and international, and (2) present the staff's view of the direction of the economy and the probable effects of alternative policies. A few days before the FOMC meeting, the staff organizes the information in three differently colored books, namely, green, red, and blue books.

Perhaps because some members fail to do their homework, or because the reports are so voluminous—up to 250 pages—that the members need a refresher, the meeting begins with the famous 5S, staff statistical "summary" and slide show. For example, at the January 30–31, 1984 meeting, the staff reviewed the behavior and rated the accuracy of existing forecasts of real GNP, the price index for gross domestic business product, the dollar value of total retail sales, unit sales of new automobiles, the index of industrial production, and so on. As we shall see later, the FOMC has a strong propensity to consider everything, and the large staff has to justify its existence. A special 5S is presented once each quarter. The senior staff unveils *detailed new* forecasts of the economy over the next year or so, given a continuation of existing policy. Both the regular and special

FOMC boardroom

5S end with a review of last month's monetary policy decisions, comparisons of the target and actual values of the monetary variables during the past months, and predictions of the effects of alternative policy proposals.

Armed with data about the present and forecasts of the future, decision making now begins. What shall we do? Which, if any, of the staff-prepared policy proposals should be adopted, and how should open-market operations be executed in order to implement the selected proposal? Your dedicated FOMC members again ask themselves, "What shall we do?" The specific items debated have varied over time with changes in FOMC membership, economic trends, and special events, such as the isolated failure of an important bank.[3] Nevertheless, some issues are debated repeatedly yet never resolved because (1) goals are not precise and uniform, (2) forecasts of the value and effect of policy and nonpolicy variables are uncertain, and (3) lags exist.

---

[3]Excellent sources of FOMC inside information are Paul Meek, *United States Monetary Policy and Financial Markets* (Federal Reserve Bank of New York, 1982) and Sherman Maisel, *Managing the Dollar* (New York: W. W. Norton, 1973).

A decision, however difficult, must be reached. Following the debate, which the chair shapes and ends at its pleasure, each of the principals states what policy should be adopted. The chair then puts before the FOMC for final consideration and vote the *policy directive* that in the chair's mind best embodies the committee's views. (Chapter 16's mention of the power derived from chairing committees may be better appreciated now.) The chair's directive invariably is adopted although, for reasons to be stated shortly, in recent years dissenting votes are more common.

The FOMC Directive: Summary and Call for Action

The directive, which has been lengthened over the years but still is less than a page, has three parts. The first briefly and incompletely reviews the data presented by the staff. The second part *briefly* states the *general* policy goals or ultimate targets. For example, at the January 30–31, 1984 meeting, the expressed goals were:

> The Federal Open Market Committee seeks to foster monetary and financial conditions that will help to reduce inflation further, promote growth in output on a sustainable basis, and contribute to an improved pattern of international transactions.

These goals are hardly precise. As we shall argue later, committees are unsuited to more precise decision making. Perhaps because the goals are so general, the wording of this section changes somewhat but the substance remains constant throughout the years. For example, about 13 years before, on August 18, 1970,

> It is the policy of the Federal Open Market Committee to foster financial conditions conducive to orderly reduction in the rate of inflation, while encouraging the resumption of sustainable economic growth and the attainment of reasonable equilibrium in the country's balance of payments.

Immediately following the goal statement is the set of authorizations and instructions to the manager of the system open-market account thought to be most compatible with the general goals. This section of the directive is the most important to economists and speculators. At the same January 1984 meeting the FOMC told the Account Manager for Domestic (Open Market) Operation:

> In the short run, the Committee seeks to maintain the existing degree of pressure on bank reserve positions, anticipating that approach will be consistent with growth of M-2 and M-3 each at annual rates of about 7 percent during the period from December to March. Lesser restraint would be acceptable in the context of a shortfall in monetary and credit growth from current expectations, while somewhat greater restraint might be acceptable with more rapid expansion of the aggregates . . . .

> The Chairman may call for Committee consultation if it appears to the Manager for Domestic Operations that pursuit of the monetary objectives and related reserve paths during the period before the next meeting is likely to be associated with a federal funds rate persistently outside a range of 6 to 10 percent.

The quotations verify a two-stage policy, as we claimed. The Account Manager was instructed in the short run to adjust "pressure on bank reserve positions" to achieve primarily monetary (M-2 and M-3) and secondarily interest rate objectives. The FOMC would reconsider its decision if, in pursuit of the monetary objectives, interest rates, which were *not* an ultimate goal, moved outside the prescribed range. New data on inflation, output, and international transactions—the ultimate goals—would not, however, call for Committee consultation in the short run.

Rationale for a Two-Stage Strategy

The two-stage strategy is proposed mainly because it provides information about the unknown exogenous variables in an economy characterized by (1) data or recognition lags, and (2) impact lags. Accurate estimates of some variables are available virtually immediately. For example, interest rate data are virtually contemporaneous, and relatively accurate estimates of today's money supply are known within a week. Data lags for other variables are considerably longer. A calendar quarter is the shortest period for GNP estimates, and reasonably accurate estimates are first available approximately two months *after* the quarter ends. Policymakers must first know the *current* value of the goal and exogenous variables. Then they can determine the setting of the policy instrument consistent with the *desired* value of the goal variable. Even if the policy instruments had an immediate impact on the goals, *data lags imply that policymakers will be unable to achieve the goals because they cannot compensate for the unknown effect of the exogenous variables*. A readily available intermediate target may signal the behavior of the goal variable and indicate how policy should be adjusted. For example, suppose some exogenous variable reduces both the intermediate and goal variables. The intermediate variable selected is readily observable, but the exogenous and goal variables are observed with a long lag, if at all. By concentrating on the intermediate variable, the authorities are forewarned in this case that a more expansionary policy is necessary.[4] The admonition to ball players to keep one's eye on the ball is a good one, provided the ball can be seen before it

---

[4]Particularly when the distinction between intermediate targets and indicators is blurred, control by the authorities is supposed to be a characteristic of a good target. If this were the case, the targets would *not* provide information about the exogenous variables and thereby would defeat one of their main functions. We shall discuss indicators later.

crosses the plate. If one cannot see the ball, then one should search for clues about when to swing.

Of course, the instruments do not have an immediate impact on the goal; impact lags exist. Even if there were no data lag with respect to the goal variable, the authorities would be unable to compensate for the unpredicted effect of exogenous variables. Policy instrument adjustments affect the goal variable only *after* the passage of some time—the impact lag. *Focusing on an intermediate target may be desirable because the exogenous variables are correlated over time,* instead of being totally unrelated over time. In technical terms, impact lags, together with serially correlated exogenous variables, may justify a two-stage monetary policy. This difficult proposition is best justified by an example. Policy instruments as well as the exogenous variables influence the intermediate variable before they influence the goal. Suppose today's policy instruments and exogenous variables affect the intermediate target next month and the goal next year. Serial correlation means that today's exogenous variables are related to prior exogenous variables. The strength and consistency of the relationship between the current and prior values of the exogenous variables depends *directly* on the length of the lag between the two values. For example, knowledge of economic history up to 1898 is valuable, but the more recent past is a better guide to the future. Consequently, monitoring the intermediate target yields better information on the proper setting of the instruments necessary to compensate for today's exogenous variables. In our example, the current value of the intermediate (goal) variable depends upon last month's (year's) exogenous variables. The current value of the exogenous variables, which the policy instruments must counteract in order to achieve the goal next year, is more closely related to last month's value than last year's value. Therefore, focusing on the intermediate variable instead of the goal may provide better information on the unknown current value of the exogenous variables and increase the likelihood of setting the policy instrument at the value proper for the goal.

Let's continue with our example and show the difference between a one-stage and two-stage strategy. If the goal variable currently were *below* target while the intermediate variable were *above* target, the two-stage strategy would *reduce* the instrument settings because the intermediate variable is above its target value. This may well be the appropriate policy even though the goal variable currently is *below* target! With our one-year impact lag the issue is: what are today's appropriate instrument settings, which will affect the goal one year hence, and not today. Because the goal one year hence will also be influenced by today's unobserved exogenous variables, we must estimate today's exogenous variables. Today's above-target intermediate variable indicates the exogenous variables were expansionary last month, while today's below-target goal variable indicates the exogenous variables were contractionary last year. Neither last month's nor last year's variable is an infallible predictor of today's variable. Nevertheless, with serial correlation, today's exogenous variables are more likely to be expansionary, in which case a two-stage policy is countercyclical but a single-stage policy is procyclical. A procyclical policy adds fuel to the fire when it should be dampening the flames; it expands the instrument settings when the exogenous variables already are expansionary.[5]

Another justification for the two-stage strategy is different degrees of uncertainty about the economic linkages between instruments and goal. If the policymaker is reasonably certain about the relationship between the intermediate target and goal, then in the short-run the policymaker may treat the intermediate target as if it were the goal and concentrate his or her energies on the difficult task of hitting the optimal value of the intermediate target.[6]

The major issues in this two-stage strategy are:

1. Assuming a single intermediate target, which one is the best? The candidates are money market conditions, particularly free reserves, interest rates, and the money supply.
2. Are multiple intermediate targets, either at the same or different points in the chain linking instruments and goals, feasible and desirable? In terms of Figure 19–2, may one have numerous items in one intermediate target box and several boxes at different horizontal positions?

Complete answers to these questions depend on one's estimate of the structure of the *entire* economic system. In some respects, therefore, we should answer these questions only *after* examining in detail the linkages between intermediate variables and goals. For practical purposes, how-

---

[5]The information gathering property of the intermediate variable does not depend on positive serial correlation, as we implicitly assumed. If serial correlation is negative, the two-stage (one-stage) strategy in our example would increase (decrease) the instrument settings but still be countercyclical (procyclical). If the private sector's behavior incorporates the structural serial correlation so that reduced form equations are serially uncorrelated, as the rational expectations hypothesis assumes, then the choice of strategies is a matter of indifference. Neither strategy can systematically influence the goal according to rational expectations, as we explain in some detail in Chapter 29. Serial correlation of exogenous variables is *not* a sufficient condition for a two-stage strategy when, contrary to the implicit assumption in the text, the sets of exogenous variables influencing the intermediate and goal variables differ. In this case one could view the intermediate variable as being a proxy of the true, from the viewpoint of the goal, exogenous variable. A good estimate of the proxy may be worse than a poor estimate of the true variable.

[6]The two justifications for a two-stage strategy—the information content of the operating target and a reasonably certain relationship between operating target and goal—may be mutually contradictory.

ever, the detailed relationships are unimportant for our two *qualitative* questions. Their answers often require only widely accepted general relationships, for example, both monetary expansion and lower interest rates tend to increase GNP.[7] In view of this, a separation of monetary policy issues into the linkages between instruments and intermediate variables and between intermediate variables and goals has become standard. In those few cases where even qualitative answers depend on controversial relationships, we shall present pros and cons.

In contrast to the goal variables, the intermediate variables have changed considerably over time. We analyze in chronological order the post-World War II intermediate variables of the Fed.

Free Reserves Strategy

One could argue that *monetary* policy did not exist throughout the 1940s. The Treasury instructed the Fed to *peg interest rates,* which became both the intermediate and ultimate variable. The Fed ignored money. It dutifully bought whatever government bonds the private sector refused at the pegged interest rate structure. This policy was adopted for the pure convenience of the Treasury. Interest rates were set at a low level in order to minimize the Treasury's interest expense and deficit. For example, the annual interest rate on 90-day Treasury bills was 3/8 percent. The effect of the rate of interest on other sectors and goals was irrelevant, at least until the late 1940s.

The Fed did not seriously object to pegging interest rates during World War II and shortly thereafter. The extremely low rates helped finance the war, and everyone was 100 percent behind the war effort. Raising interest rates after the war was considered unpatriotic. Those who had purchased bonds and helped the war effort would incur capital losses from higher interest rates. The Fed also favored a continuation of the low interest rate policy because it would avert the major postwar depression many were forecasting. Montgomery Ward has earned a permanent place in the history of business blunders for not expanding and falling far behind Sears because it forecast a depression. *The postwar depression did not materialize by 1950, however. Forecasts were revised* in 1950 as the United States became embroiled in the Korean War. Sharply higher defense expenditures and other increases in aggregate demand, combined with the low pegged interest rates, now produced an inflationary situation. At this point the Federal Reserve and Treasury sharply disagreed. The Fed acquired new ultimate goals, price stability and full employment. The Treasury was willing to sacrifice price stability for low interest rates. The Fed

---

[7]To be sure, the *magnitude* of the superiority of one intermediate variable over another depends on the detailed relationships.

was not so disposed. It claimed that patriotism now called for a high interest rate policy. While bondholders would suffer *nominal* capital losses from such a policy, high interest rates would arrest inflation and *real* capital losses. By once again wrapping its objectives in flag and country, the Fed regained its independence in the famous Federal Reserve-Treasury Accord of 1951. The Fed was no longer committed to pegging interest rates.

The Fed did not altogether abandon interest rates after 1951. *It adopted a money market strategy. Money market conditions officially are some combination of (a) the three-month Treasury bill rate, (b) the federal funds rate, (c) free reserves, and (d) something normally eloquent central bankers can only describe as the "tone and feel of the market." Free reserves, which may be positive or negative, are excess reserves minus discounts at the Fed.* Negative free reserves are often called net borrowed reserves. Immediately after the Accord the T-bill rate was a significant aspect of money market conditions. This was not surprising since continuity is a frequent characteristic of policy. Soon thereafter, however, free reserves became the most important determinant of money market conditions by far. Whatever weight the other variables may have had in some official definition of money market conditions, *in reality money market conditions were equivalent to free reserves.*

The official intermediate target included variables with different dimensions. The T-bill rate is a percent, while free reserves are a dollar magnitude. Not being able to add apples and oranges, *monetary policy operating instructions were extremely vague. Easier, constant, or firmer (sometimes called tighter) money market conditions were the order of the day.* Given the actual intermediate variable, easy (firm) money market conditions existed when free reserves were large (small or even negative).

The Fed never stated explicitly why free reserves became the intermediate target. Nevertheless, the argument for free reserves is seemingly based on its being a good predictor of future money supply and interest rate movements and, ultimately, income and prices. Open-market purchases or increases in uncontrolled sources of the base have a positive immediate impact on excess reserves and, therefore, on free reserves. Banks' initial reaction may be partial repayment of their discounts. This has no effect on free reserves. Drawing down excess reserves to repay discounts keeps the difference between the two constant. The high free reserves generated by the open-market purchase are only temporary. Banks will shortly make loans and create deposits, causing lower interest rates and a larger money supply.

The Fed's free reserves strategy was severely criticized, particularly by Professors Karl Brunner and Allan Meltzer in a 1964 study.[8] What is

---

[8]See *The Federal Reserve's Attachment to the Free Reserves Concept* (Washington, D.C.: House Banking and Currency Committee, 1964).

wrong with a free reserve target? The Fed totally ignored, or at least significantly underestimated, the effect of the exogenous factors on free reserves, which is somewhat surprising since one reason for an operating target is the information it yields about the unknown exogenous variables. The significant underestimate made the money supply procyclical and reduced the normally moderating behavior of interest rates. For example, suppose firms suddenly become more pessimistic about the future and start spending less. A recession gets under way. The spending decline is accompanied by a reduction in the demand for credit and lower market interest rates. Recalling the determinants of excess reserves and discounts, what will happen to free reserves? Lower market interest rates increase banks' demand for excess reserves and reduce discounts, particularly since the discount rate lags market rates. Both large excess reserves and small discounts increase free reserves.

The Fed did not realize that banks' demand for free reserves depends significantly on market rates. Consequently, the larger free reserves alarmed the Fed. It feared that the monetary base was expanding too rapidly, and that the money supply would be rising and interest rates falling too rapidly in the near future. The Fed responded by *selling* securities, which reduced the money supply and prevented a rapid interest rate decline. Of course, in time the Fed realized that a recession was under way and that the larger free reserves were not expansionary because the demand for free reserves had risen. However, *the general underestimate of market interest rate effects on free reserves and the lagged awareness of economic conditions made the money supply procyclical about turning points and reduced the interest rate fluctuations which help stabilize the economy.*

A free reserve target was equally objectionable during the expansionary phase of a business cycle. As the boom got under way and market interest rates rose because firms were borrowing more, the demand for free reserves fell, often to negative levels. Unaware of the business boom due to data lags and uncertain about the demand for free reserves, the Fed responded by open-market purchases in order to maintain free reserves at the constant target value. The open-market purchase increased the money supply and partially offset the higher market rates which help stabilize the economy during booms. This clearly was undesirable. Remember, however, that neither the Fed nor anyone else sees aggregate demand curves; only actual GNP is observed, with a lag to boot. The existence of lags and economic uncertainty, which provides a justification for an intermediate target, also implies that policymakers will not achieve their ultimate goals at all times. We cannot expect perfection from policymakers. Yet, we must demand that they adopt procedures which minimize large deviations from the goal. The Fed's commitment to free reserves should not be questioned just because it is as silly as the deaf man who heard the mute person say that the blind woman saw the crippled person run–on water.

Experimenting with Multiple Targets: 1966–1975

Largely in response to the critics, the operating instructions were modified in June 1966 to include what has been called a *proviso clause*. The account manager was directed to keep "money market conditions at about their recent ranges; *provided,* however, that if required reserves expand considerably more than seasonally expected, operations shall be conducted with a view to attaining some . . . firming of money market conditions."[9] *For the first time the account manager was instructed to consider explicitly, if only conditionally, an item, required reserves, well known to be closely related to money.*

The proviso was supposed to distinguish between supply and demand effects on free reserves. For example, lower free reserves coupled with higher required reserves signal aggregate expansion and an increase in the private sector's demand for credit and money. Free reserves decrease as banks reduce their excess reserves and borrow more at the discount window in order to accommodate their customers' demands. The same lower free reserves coupled, however, with lower required reserves signal monetary contraction and a decrease in the supply of the base and reserves. The supply contraction reduces excess and free reserves immediately and, shortly thereafter, required reserves as banks respond by contracting money and credit.

The specific provisional item changed frequently because none is capable of distinguishing between every type of supply and demand shock. Required reserves were quickly replaced by reserves available to support private deposits and then by bank credit, which is virtually identical to total deposits. At the January 1970 meeting, which followed Professor Arthur Burns's nomination to the Fed chair but preceded his installation, the proviso at long last mentioned money explicitly. Less than two months after assuming office, at the March 1970 FOMC meeting, Professor Burns succeeded in bringing money out of the shadows to center stage. The FOMC sought "to promote some easing of conditions in *credit* markets *and* somewhat greater growth in money over the months ahead" (our emphasis). *Money* officially *was on par with credit market conditions in 1970.* Compared to *money* market conditions, *credit* market conditions place much greater weight on interest rates and downgrade free reserves. The 1970 change in operating strategies illustrates well that the Chairman often *is* the System.

---

[9]Federal Reserve, *Annual Report, 1966,* p. 151. Our italics. The directive of the February 1966 meeting of the FOMC instructed the account manager to operate "with a view toward a gradual reduction in reserve availability." Subsequent meetings determined that the account manager and many committee members interpreted "reserve availability" as free reserve availability, although the proponents of the reserve clause had in mind total or required reserves, which are approximately equal.

Money and Interest Rates

Was the early 1970s *official* operating policy feasible? Can the Federal Reserve simultaneously hit both a money and interest rate target? Figure 19–3 draws the demand and supply of money as functions of interest rates. We do not wish to get sidetracked explaining the shape of these curves. Good old-fashioned common sense supports the proposition that the amount of loans and money supplied by banks increases and the amount demanded by the public decreases when interest rates rise.[10] Although the Fed expresses the monetary target as a growth rate, there is a one-to-one relationship between growth rates and current values, with the previous period's value as the given base. From a diagrammatic viewpoint, money levels are more convenient than growth rates. Suppose r_0 and M_0 are the Fed's multiple interest rate and money targets, respectively. Are multiple precise intermediate targets feasible? Generally, no. The Fed's instruments influence the supply curve. Lower reserve require-

FIGURE 19–3
The Federal Reserve Generally Cannot Control Both Interest Rates and Money

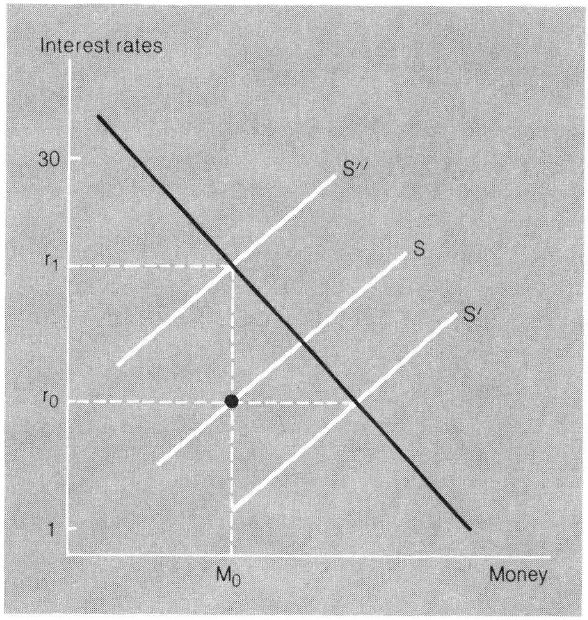

[10]We do not want to suggest that money is a loan (credit). However, we are aware that the reader may recognize the similarity between Figures 7–2 and 19–3. Figure 19–3 purposely has interest rates (plural) on the vertical axis because the argument against multiple targets is independent of the specific interest rate selected.

ments, for example, shift the supply curve outwards from S to S′; banks are able to supply more money at any interest rate. The Fed can set the instruments so that the supply curve goes through the point (M_0,r_0). However, the Fed's instruments do not *directly* influence the demand curve. Except in the fortuitous situation where the demand curve passes through the point (M_0,r_0), these two targets are incompatible. The supply curve S leads to small errors in both targets. Figure 19–3 shows that one could hit *either* target exactly at the expense of larger errors in the other target. For example, money supply S″ gives the desired M_0, but the interest rate is r_1, which is substantially greater than r_0. *Because the equilibrium money-interest rate combination must lie on the uncontrolled demand curve, a money-interest rate target generally is not feasible.*

The Fed's targets are not precise, as we have been assuming so far, but are ranges. (We explore shortly the rationale for ranges.) General Custer's men were sharpshooters when they used sufficiently big targets. Similarly, wide ranges increase the likelihood of the Fed's hitting multiple targets. For example, the money supply M_0 is feasible according to Figure 19–3 provided the interest rate can range between 1 and 30 percent. In this case, interest rates are not an effective target, in the sense that it does not constrain use of the policy instruments.

A Reluctant Fed Is Introduced to Monetarism: 1975–1978

Policymakers respond reluctantly to criticism, which is loudest during bad times. Events in early 1975 confirm this observation. Early 1975 was approximately the trough of the deepest post-World War II recession up to that time. Economists were virtually unanimous in claiming that monetary policy was too restrictive in 1974 and contributed to the deepening recession. For example, Paul Samuelson, the dean of American economists, charged, "If we go into a depression, the Fed will justly bear much of the blame."[11] Widespread agreement that the Fed's policy rated an F was accompanied, perhaps surprisingly, by widespread *dis*agreement about both the actual and optimal policies. Everyone gave the Fed an F, but for different reasons. Franco Modigliani, professor of economics at MIT and an acknowledged leader of the Keynesian camp, proclaimed before Congress:

> I think the mistakes of last year came from the fact that the Fed was looking at the money supply instead of looking at what really bites the economy. *No one, no one except a few fools perhaps on Wall Street are directly affected by the money supply,* but the people do pay higher interest rates, people do have

---

[11]Paul A. Samuelson, "A Burns Depression?", *Newsweek,* March 3, 1975, p. 63.

> to pay higher mortgage rates, and that is where monetary policy bites, not through the change of the money supply.[12]

Monetarist Milton Friedman strongly disagreed: money matters, but the Fed was looking at interest rates.

> From June 1974 to January 1975, M-1 has grown at the average rate of 1.1 percent per year. This has surely contributed to the recent deepending of the recession. I believe that we need stability in monetary growth, [but] wide fluctuations from one side to the other . . . [occur because the Fed] insists on operating as it now does by controlling an interest rate such as the Federal Funds rate.[13]

How did the Fed respond to these criticisms? The Fed, which has a long history of being overly sensitive, was deeply hurt by the accusations of its Keynesian allies that it was paying too much attention to the money supply. It confessed its basically Keynesian orientation. "In particular, we pay close attention to interest rates because of their profound effects on the workings of the economy."[14] It went further in the February 25, 1975, Statement to Congress. It claimed that it could not control the money supply, even if it wanted to.

> The Federal Reserve can supply the banking system with reserves through open-market operations or through reserve requirement changes (sic); but if banks choose to repay debt or rebuild their liquidity, these actions will have little impact on the public's money supply. The Federal Reserve can have a marked influence on short-term interest rates and may have some indirect influence on other terms of credit. But it cannot force businesses or consumers to borrow from their banks and thus to expand the volume of bank loans. The Federal Reserve cannot force people to hold money in the form of demand deposits when they prefer to hold . . . income-earning assets. These limitations are inescapable and they need to be understood.[15]

Certainly, the fact that the Fed was *officially* attempting the impossible—to control money and interest rates—contributed to the widespread disagreement about actual Fed policy. But don't the unofficial Fed statements confirm beyond doubt that interest rates were the effective intermediate variable? How could someone as distinguished as Professor

---

[12]U.S. Congress, Joint Economic Committee, *The 1975 Economic Report of the President,* 94th Cong., 1st sess., February 5, 6, 7, and 14, 1975, p. 542. Italics added.

[13]U.S. Congress, Senate Committee on Banking, Housing and Urban Affairs, *Monetary Policy Oversight,* 94th Cong., 1st sess., February 25 and 26, 1975, p. 59–60.

[14]"Statement to Congress," *Federal Reserve Bulletin,* February 1975, p. 64. This and the past several quotes were in Nancy Jianakoplos, "The FOMC in 1975; Announcing Monetary Targets," Federal Reserve Bank of St. Louis *Review,* March 1976.

[15]Arthur Burns, "Statement to Congress," *Federal Reserve Bulletin,* March 1975, p. 152.

Modigliani possibly claim that the money supply was the intermediate target in view of Chairman Burns's statement? Analysts quickly discover that the Fed speaks with forked tongue. Contradictions to you and me are perfectly logical statements to the Fed. One can find several Fed quotations which contradict the latter two Fed quotes and support Modigliani's viewpoint. For example, in the *very same* February 25, 1975, Statement to Congress, only one page after saying that it cannot possibly control money, Chairman Burns proclaims:

> As this committee knows, the Federal Reserve System has given very close attention in recent years to the behavior of monetary aggregates. We are well aware that an expanding economy needs an expanding supply of money and credit and that any protracted shrinkage of the money stock could lead to or exacerbate a shrinkage of economic activity.[16]

Moreover, the Fed went so far as to question its ability to control interest rates, despite having pegged interest rates throughout the 1940s. Although the Fed said that it " . . . can have a marked influence on short-term interest rates," it also claimed that its " . . . ability to influence interest rates is far more limited than is commonly believed."[17]

Let's pause briefly to speculate on the reasons for the Fed's contradictory statements. Contradictory statements may be explained by (1) frustration from attempting to do too much, namely, control both money and interest rates, (2) uncertainty about the variable, money or interest rates, it should control when it recognizes it cannot control both, and (3) the difficulty in controlling money when it attempts to do so, or (4) the desire always to be at least half right, ex post.

Long-Term and More Precise Targets

We shall postpone analysis of the appropriate intermediate target, money or interest rates, and the degree of monetary control. Pressing on with our history of monetary strategy and intermediate targets, Congress accepted the monetarists' criticism that the Fed was paying too much attention to interest rates. Congress introduced a reluctant Fed to monetarism by passing Concurrent Resolution 133 on March 24, 1975. Among other things, *the resolution required the FOMC to adopt long-term (one-year) target growth rates for the monetary aggregates, with the targets for the year ahead disclosed publicly each calendar quarter before congressional committees*. This minor resolution produced major changes. First, one year is hardly very long term, but up to this the Fed had never explicitly

---

[16]Ibid., p. 153.

[17]"Statement to Congress," *Federal Reserve Bulletin,* March 1975, p. 152, and February 1975, p. 64.

considered intermediate variable values beyond the next monthly meeting.[18] *Year-ahead targets were long-run targets for the Fed.* Second, the long-term money targets had to be expressed as growth rate ranges, for example, 4 to 7 percent. The Fed no longer could seek an "easier" or "tighter" monetary policy. *The more precise objectives extended to the short-run intermediate variables, money and interest rates.*[19] Third, *the Fed had to publicly announce its intentions beforehand.* Up to this time the Fed's intentions were made known in minutes of FOMC meetings released years later.

The Fed objected to this and similar resolutions, as expected.

> If we focused solely on the money supply or guided our operations entirely by the money aggregates, the Federal Reserve would fail to fulfill its responsibilities for helping to achieve the economic goals of our Nation.
>
> Finally, the Board objects to the last paragraph . . . , which calls for . . . reports to the Congress by the Federal Reserve of its plans for future monetary policy. Such a requirement could . . . undermine the capacity of the Federal Reserve to exercise its best judgment in adapting policies to changing circumstances.[20]

The Fed, aware that it is a creature of Congress, did comply punctiliously with the letter of Resolution 133, but it avoided the spirit whenever possible. The Fed's long-run money targets between 1975 and 1978 were characterized by the *forgiveness principle and short-run base drift,* which caused the Fed to miss its money target. The meaning of these terms is best understood in the context of a day with Arthur Burns, Fed Chairman when Resolution 133 was passed. One day each calendar quarter Chairman Burns would dutifully traipse up to Capitol Hill and reveal to Congress the FOMC's one-year monetary targets. For example, in May 1975 Chairman Burns solemnly announced that between March 1975 and March 1976 M-1 should grow between 5 and 7.5 percent. Three months later the same Chairman Burns announced that the M–1 target range was still 5 to 7.5 percent, this time from the end of the second quarter 1975 to the second quarter 1976. During the second quarter of 1975, however, M-1 had grown at an 11.2 percent annual rate. *The forgiveness principle and base drift apply when the one-year forward target range remains constant although money growth in the recent past has been wide of the target.* The Fed simply forgives the error and accepts the new, in this case higher, level of the money supply as the base to compute future growth rates.

---

[18]The constancy of the intermediate variables over many meetings during the 1960s and early 1970s suggests that the FOMC implicitly had a longer-run outlook.

[19]Concurrent Resolution 133 mandated a *long-run* money target but did not prohibit a *short-run* interest rate target.

[20]"Statement to Congress," *Federal Reserve Bulletin,* March 1975, p. 154.

(Base drift has nothing to do with the monetary base.) The forgiveness principle and base drift strongly suggest that long-run money growth was not an important operating variable. True target or desired values should be adjusted in response to recent errors.

The Fed's Forced Conversion To Monetarism: October 6, 1979

Senator Hubert H. Humphrey, a true old-fashioned Keynesian if ever there was one, sponsored the Balanced Growth Act of 1978, better known as the *Humphrey-Hawkins Act,* which ironically forced the Fed to convert to monetarism. The Act, which still is in effect, *requires the Fed to formulate a money growth target each February for the calendar year.*[21] *Furthermore, the following February the actual money growth during the year just ended is compared with the annual monetary growth target formulated the previous February.*

Compare these new requirements with the old ones. As just outlined, under Resolution 133 each *quarter* the Fed formulated money growth targets for the *year* ahead. When the Fed appeared before Congress the next quarter, it was *not* required to compare the actual growth during the past quarter with last quarter's projected growth for the year. Of course, many things that are not required occur routinely. While one certainly would expect Congress to ask the Fed for the just mentioned comparison, it generally did not do so. Congress generally did not inquire about a discrepancy between the actual and targeted growth.[22] If a discrepancy was noted, the Fed begged forgiveness, as we just stated. *The likelihood of forgiveness by Congress was abetted by the fact that each quarter the Fed was targeting money growth for the year ahead.* An example illustrates why different *policy formulation* (a quarter in our case) and *target evaluation* (one-year) periods facilitate forgiveness. Suppose the Fed appears before Congress on February 15 and states that the money supply during the calendar year should grow between 5 and 7 percent. Next May 15 the Fed again testifies and again states that money should grow between 5 and 7 percent from last April to next April. Suppose further that under clever congressional questioning the Fed acknowledges that money grew at a 10 percent annual rate during the first quarter. If the Fed were scolded by a Congressperson or anyone else, it could rightly claim that the year is not yet up, and that there is no *necessary* contradiction between high

---

[21]The Fed is also required to appear in July to (1) reaffirm the prior February's target or explain why a change is necessary, and (2) give a *preliminary* estimate of next year's target.

[22]Congress's inattention to the discrepancy may be partially explained by the provision of Resolution 133 that the Fed alternate the presentation of its congressional testimony each quarter from House to Senate committee. Thus, no committee ever benefited from successive Fed testimony.

actual growth and the constant target growth. For example, if money grew at a 5 percent annual rate from April onward, the growth rate for the entire calendar year would be 6.25 percent, which is within the 5 to 7 percent range. Because Congress had a short time horizon and never looked back more than one policy formulation period, which was a quarter, even though target values were for a year, the Fed could continuously miss the target while simultaneously claiming that it intended to hit the target. Stated somewhat differently, any given calendar quarter, such as January–March 1976, was included in four target evaluation periods, which increases the likelihood that money growth during the quarter is consistent with one target growth rate.

There was no day of reckoning prior to Humphrey-Hawkins. Monetary growth rates were always set for "next year," which kept shifting and never arrived. One always looked forward and did not look back because "next year" changed each quarter. Under Humphrey-Hawkins a day of reckoning does arrive. At the end of the year the money supply will be compared with the calendar year target. The greater accountability requirements of Humphrey-Hawkins forced the Fed to amend its errant ways in the historic October 6, 1979, FOMC meeting. February 1979 was the first time the Fed was required to specify money growth ranges under the 1978 Humphrey-Hawkins Act. Using the 1978 fourth quarter as a base, the FOMC stated that in 1979 the money supply was going to grow between 1.5 and 4.5 percent. Look at Figure 19–4, where we show the actual money supply and desired money supplies assuming 1.5 and 4.5 percent growth. The actual money supply in the beginning of 1979 was considerably below the minimum desired level, as illustrated by the 1.5 percent growth line. The Fed took the shortfall in stride; it had several months to correct the situation. From March through September monetary growth accelerated dramatically. By late September the money supply was above the upper 4.5 percent target. It became clear that with three months remaining the Fed would not hit its stated annual objective if it continued its course of action. What an embarrassment! At the very inception of the mandate to specify monetary growth ranges for a given calendar period, the Fed was not meeting its own stated objectives because it was overly concerned about interest rates.

Something had to be done quickly. The Fed would lose face before Congress in the near future unless it changed its policies. To make matters worse, foreign exchange speculators had already lost much confidence in the Fed. Speculators correctly recognized that an inflation would follow the Fed's extremely rapid monetary expansion and dumped their dollars in order to purchase relatively stable foreign currencies. In September 1979 the once almighty dollar sank daily to new bottoms. Monetary policy had to change. *Paul Volcker,* who was appointed Chairman just a couple of months earlier, saw that the change was made. A man of Volcker's

FIGURE 19–4
Actual Money Supply and Desired Money Supplies, Given 1.5 to 4.5 Percent Target Growth Rate, 1979

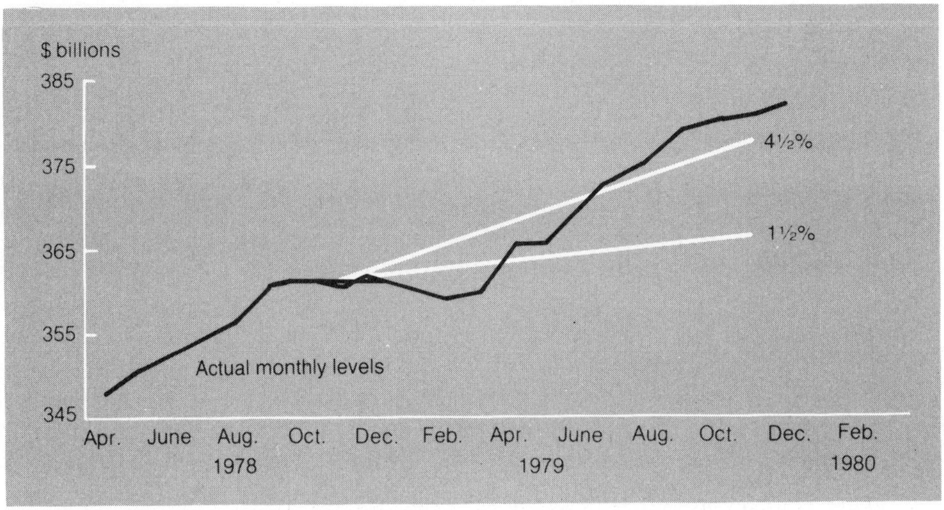

Source: Federal Reserve Banks of St. Louis *Review*, March 1980, p. 9.

stature did not want to admit defeat in what would have been his first February appearance before Congress, as mandated by Humphrey-Hawkins. *At the October 6, 1979, FOMC meeting the Fed revised its strategy.*[23] *The meeting was "historic" for two reasons. First, the Fed stated in blood that it would pay much more attention to the money supply and less attention to the federal funds rate. Second, to underscore its commitment to the money supply, the Fed said it would begin controlling the supply of bank reserves more directly.*

The October 6, 1979, statement was widely interpreted as the Fed's official announcement of conversion to strict monetarism. Careful readers recognized, however, that the statement promised reform and not adherence to orthodox monetarism. Interest rates would be decidedly downgraded but not ignored altogether. According to the first part of the 1979 statement, when the issue is either money or interest rates, money now will be selected more *frequently*. In terms of Figure 19–2, money and interest rates seemingly are in the same box/position in the time path linking the tools and goals, with money above interest rates in importance.

[23]The Fed also revised its targeted money stock upwards, on the grounds that it overestimated the growth of other checkable deposits. Simple revision of the targeted values was insufficient, since it is widely known that targets constantly revised are always hit.

Second, the federal funds rate will not be even a *major* target preceding money. In other words, in any *three-stage* strategy the Fed would focus *mainly* on reserves instead of the federal funds rate in order to hit the target money supply, which in turn would hit the ultimate goal.[24] Reserves would be one of the multiple intermediate variables along the time path linking tools and goals.

Recent directives follow the formula adopted at the October 1979 meeting. For example, take another look at part of the official operating directive of the January 30–31, 1984, FOMC meeting.

> The Committee established growth ranges for the broader aggregates of 6 to 9 percent for both M-2 and M-3 for the period from the fourth quarter of 1983 to the fourth quarter of 1984. The Committee also considered that a range of 4 to 8 percent for M-1 would be appropriate for the same period. . . .
>
> In the short run, the Committee seeks to maintain the existing degree of pressure on bank reserve positions, anticipating that approach will be consistent with the growth of M-2 and M-3 each at annual rates of 8 percent and M-1 at an annual rate of about 7 percent during the period from December to March.
>
> The Chairman may call for Committee consultation if . . . the federal funds rate persistently [is] outside a range of 6 to 10 percent.

Summarizing the important differences between this and earlier directives:

1. Monetary aggregates (M-1 through M-3) are "long-run" (one-year) intermediate targets. The Fed did not set long-run intermediate targets before the mid-1970s, when Congress mandated them. Up to that time the Fed account manager had only a one month time horizon. The long-run intermediate target initially placed little effective constraint on policy because the target applied to the forever movable "next year." The *calendar-year* monetary growth ranges required by Humphrey-Hawkins made the constraint more effective.
2. The short-run intermediate targets are monetary aggregates and the federal funds rates. Money market conditions have been reduced to the federal funds rate, and the monetary aggregates are considered. In order to achieve the targeted monetary aggregates, the account manager now is supposed to focus on reserves. The targeted short-run and long-run rates of monetary aggregates may differ.
3. Tolerance ranges of "about X percent" are specified. Thus, the directive, while not absolutely precise, is more definite than years ago when easier or firmer conditions were prescribed.

---

[24]When multiple intermediate targets exist, the anterior intermediate variable often is called the operating variable, and the posterior/third-stage intermediate variable is simply the intermediate variable.

The Fed's Monetarism Wanes in the 1980s

The Fed *seemed* to be living up to its word immediately after October 1979. It did pay *more* attention to the money supply and *less* attention to the federal funds rate. Note, however, that the money supply never was and is not now the Fed's only intermediate target. Look at Figure 19–4. Monetary growth came to a halt in October and November 1979 but, because the Fed had other targets, monetary growth resumed in December although the money supply already exceeded its desired level. The M-1 growth ranges were raised to 4–6.5 percent in 1980. The 1980 pattern of actual monetary growth relative to the target growth ranges is a near clone of the 1979 pattern although the Fed was operating throughout 1980 under the new operating procedure which focuses on reserves more directly! Look at Figure 19–5. In 1980, however, the Fed did hit, although just barely, the upward range by reducing the money supply in December.

When multiple targets are specified, the width of the targets and the frequency and size of errors provide clues concerning the effective target.

FIGURE 19–5

Actual Money Supply and Desired Money Supplies, Given 4 to 6.5 Percent Target Growth Rate, 1980

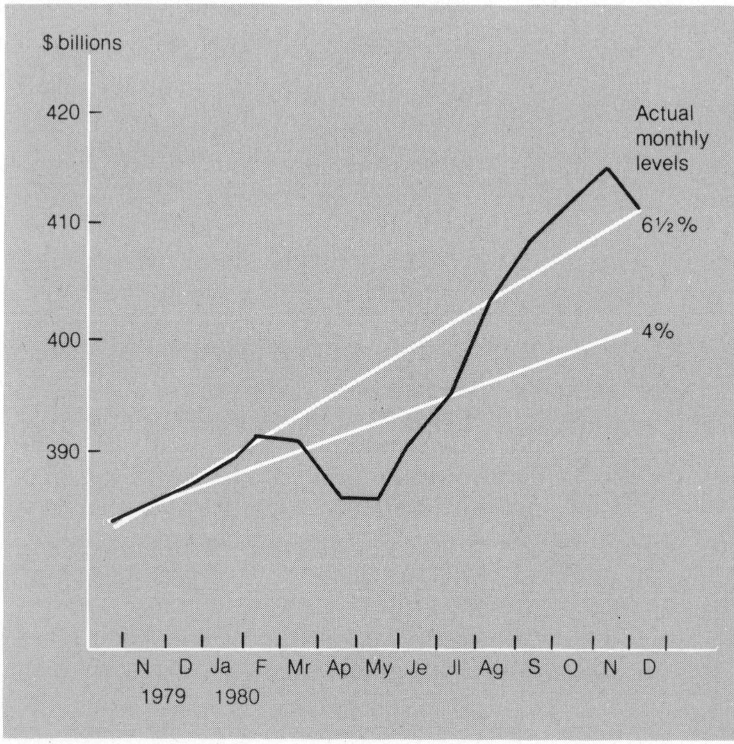

Source: Federal Reserve *Bulletin*, April 1981, p. 278.

FIGURE 19–6
1979 Federal Funds Rate, Actual and FOMC Target Range

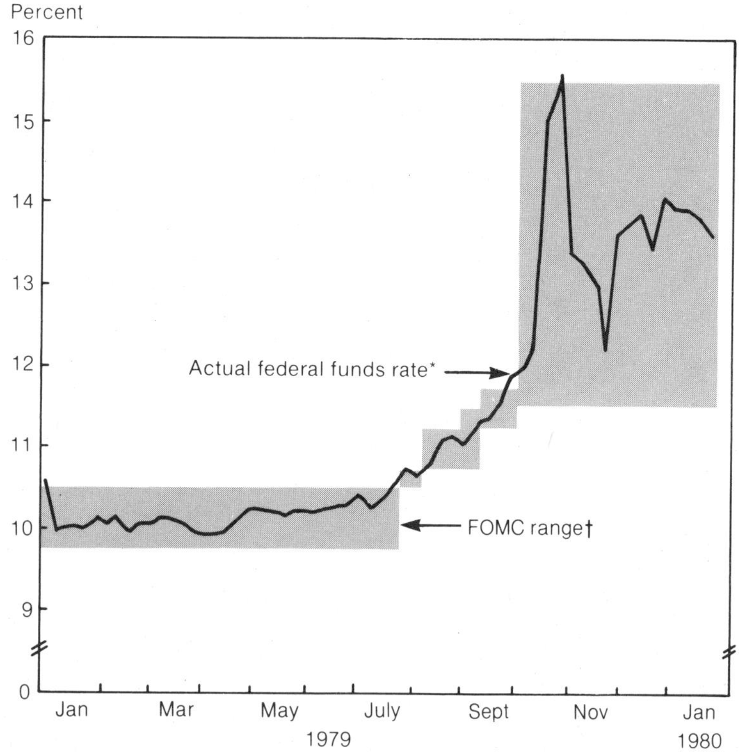

*Weekly averages of effective daily rates
†At each meeting during 1979 the FOMC established a range for the federal funds rate. These ranges are indicated for the first full week during which they were in effect.
Source: Richard Lang, "The FOMC in 1979: Introducing Reserve Targeting," Federal Reserve Bank of St. Louis *Review*, March 1980, p.12

They are not infallible clues for various reasons. For example, presumably no one knowingly selects unattainable targets. One target may be hit more frequently simply because it is easier to predict.[25] Nevertheless, when the size of the *relative* ranges and errors differ significantly over time, we may reasonably assume shifts in the main operating target.

Figures 19–6 and 19–7 corroborate a shift in operating targets as alleged at the October 6, 1979, FOMC meeting. Prior to the meeting, the FOMC range for the federal funds rate was no more than three quarters of one percent, and the target always was hit. Moreover, the range was relatively

[25]Even the measurement of targets is controversial. Why should money be seasonally adjusted? Is the seasonal pattern *created* by the Fed and then expunged by seasonally adjusting? Is the commitment to interest rates disguised by seasonally adjusting money but not interest rates?

constant across the monthly FOMC meetings. In contrast, the FOMC tolerance ranges for monetary growth rates before October 1979 were quite wide—at least 4 percent—and the Fed hit the range in only one month, and then barely so. The Fed did not even specify money growth rates for January/February and June/July 1979. The FOMC ranges for money fluctuated considerably across the monthly decision-making periods. Roles were significantly reversed after October 1979. The FOMC range for fed funds was widened to 4 percent. The Fed hardly deserves congratulations for hitting the funds target more or less continuously since it now was practicing the General Custer principle. The October 1979 and immediately subsequent meetings did not specify a *range* for money growth; growth rates "in the order of" a certain number were specified. By January 1980 a range, albeit smaller than previously stated, was again specified. Although the Fed did not hit the unique money targets during the October to December 1979 periods, the difference between target and actual values during the period was consistently less than the difference between mid-range and actual values prior to October. The Fed reduced the size of the money target *and* became more accurate, in total contradiction of the Custer principle.

Doubting Thomases, forced to convert, often become less devout with the passage of time. I believe this is true of the Fed and monetarism,

FIGURE 19–7
1979 Money Growth Rates, Actual and FOMC Target Range

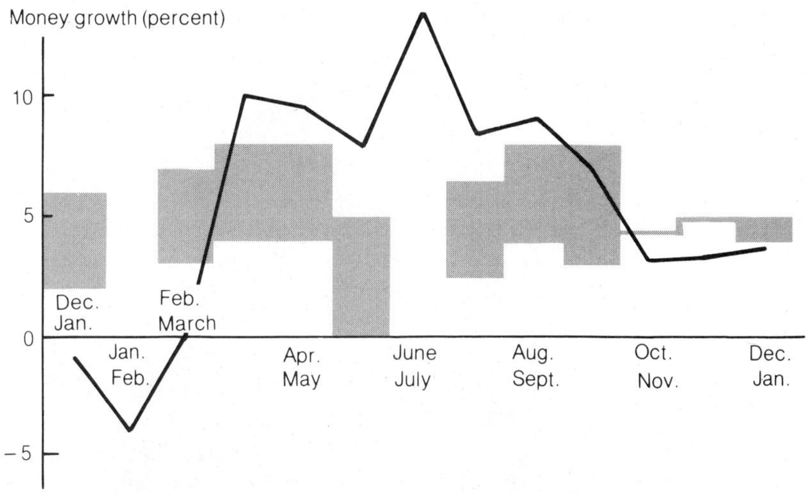

Note: Monetary targets were not specified for January/February and June/July. An implicit target range existed from October to December since the Fed specified growth rates "in the order of" some percentage.
Source: Federal Reserve Bank of St. Louis *Review*, March 1980, pp.4,11: and various Federal Reserve *Bulletins*.

while simultaneously recognizing that the 1975 contradictory statements of Samuelson, Modigliani, and Friedman suggest the impossibility of judging unambiguously the strength of the Fed's commitment to monetarism. Many interpret two facts as indicators of a less monetarist Fed. First, *in late 1982 the relationship between all money measures and income deteriorated due to financial innovation*, as we mentioned in our analysis of the money definitions. *The deterioration was so great for M-1 that the Fed switched from M-1 to M-2 and M-3.* Let's hear it in the Fed's own words.

> The Committee . . . continued the practice, begun in October, 1982, of placing principal weight on the broader monetary aggregates—M-2 and M-3—in the implementation of monetary policy. Because of difficulties in gauging the relation between transaction balances and economic activity, . . . less than customary weight would be assigned to M-1, at least until that aggregate had exhibited more regular and predictable behavior.[26]

If the choice of money aggregates is an indicator of the Fed's attachment to monetarism, the Fed is becoming a born again monetarist in mid-1984, though still not as good a one as it was in 1981. More weight is again being placed on M-1.

The reduction in interest rate volatility also beginning around late 1982 is the second signal of a less monetarist/more Keynesian Fed. Throughout 1978 and early 1979 the federal funds and Treasury bill rates rose *smoothly*. Short-run interest rate fluctuations then became pronounced following the historic October 1979 FOMC meeting. The 1980–1982 interest rate peaks and valleys were leveled by 1983. Look at Figure 19–8 to see how unstable short-term interest rates were during October 1979–82, the period of high monetarism at the Federal Reserve. Figure 19–8 also illustrates interest rate stability and the more Keynesian approach existing prior to October 1979 and again after October 1982.

No book can be absolutely current. For clues—only clues, there is no definitive answer—about the Fed's current viewpoint and major intermediate targets, see the monthly *Federal Reserve Bulletin*, its *Annual Report*, or a quality financial publication such as *The Wall Street Journal*.

Money or Interest Rates

We can no longer sidestep a very difficult issue. "The question is," said Humpty Dumpty, "which is to be master—that's all."[27] Which *should* be

---

[26]Federal Reserve, *Annual Report, 1983,* pp. 12 and 13.

[27]Lewis Carroll (Charles Dodgson), *Through the Looking Glass* (New York: Elsevier and Everyman's Library).

FIGURE 19–8
Unstable Short-Term Interest Rates, October 1979–1982

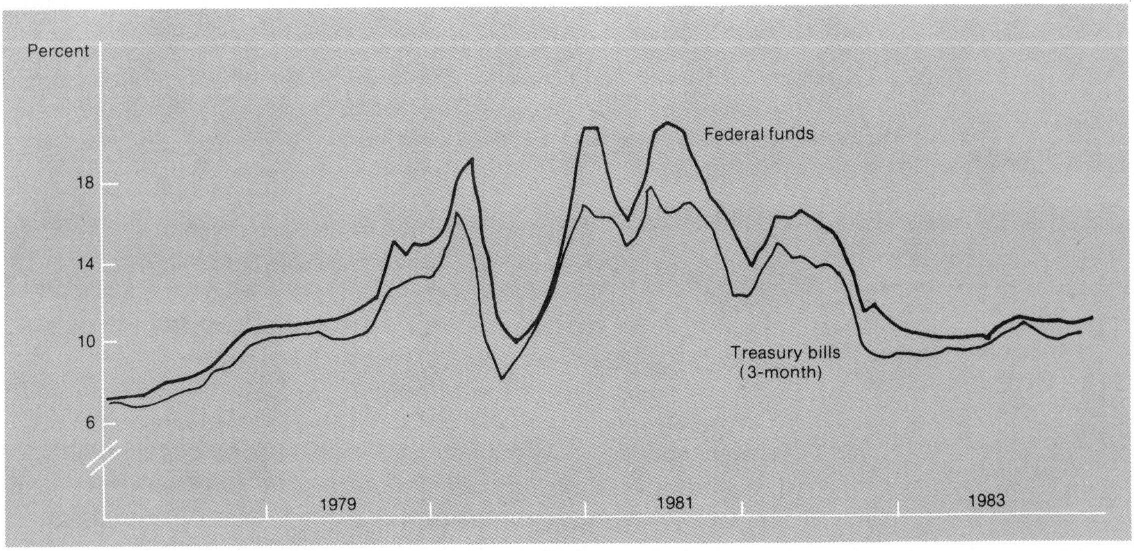

Source: Board of Governors of the Federal Reserve System, *70th Annual Report, 1983*, p. 14.

master, money or interest rates? For many years most academic economists favored an interest rate target. Advocates of a money target were a small, if vocal, minority. Their numbers grew rapidly and by 1979 they dominated the profession. This is not to say that so-called monetarists dominate the economics profession, and Keynesians are a minority. Monetarism and Keynesianism are convenient *multi*dimensional lables. *A money target instead of an interest rate target indeed is a cardinal tenet of monetarism.* Nevertheless, many supporters of a money target would be uncomfortable in the monetarist camp. The eclectic middle sides with the monetarists on this issue.

We sketch a scenario where the majority's position is the correct one.[28] Assume firms become pessimistic about the future sales outlook and respond by reducing investment spending today. The expectations pattern tends to be self-fulfilling. The reduced investment spending by firms causes producers of plant and equipment to lay off employees. With increased unemployment and lower incomes, the sales of all firms drop, just as had been expected. Since some investment spending is financed by borrowing,

[28]A formal proof using IS–LM analysis concludes Chapter 27.

lower investment spending reduces the demand for loans and interest rates fall. What happens to the money supply? It also falls slightly, other things being equal. According to Chapter 4, the money supply multiplier falls as the desired excess reserve ratio rises in response to lower interest rates. The base also falls as banks find it less profitable to borrow at the Fed. How should the Fed respond to high unemployment and low production levels? Clearly, the Fed should restore the previous level of aggregate demand by increasing the quantity of money and bank credit and, thereby, lowering interest rates further. If the money supply were the Fed's policy target, the appropriate response is sure to follow. Observing a fall in the money supply which is contrary to the desired policy, the Fed undertakes some combination of large open-market purchases, reserve requirement reductions, and discount rate reductions. However, if the rate of interest were the policy target, the Fed may well be lulled into sitting on its hands. Lower interest rates are necessary to restore full employment, but the decline in aggregate demand and high unemployment have simultaneously lowered interest rates. Observing that interest rates already have fallen, the Fed may believe its job has been done and fear an even greater reduction in interest rates—the appropriate policy to restore full employment—would simply be inflationary. *When variations in the demand for goods and services are the major economic disturbance, a money target is preferable to an interest rate target. Income fluctuations with a money stock policy are smaller in this case.*

Keynesian advocates of an interest rate target still exist because they are correct on occasion. Instead of a reduction in the demand for goods and services, assume greater uncertainty induces a shift in the demand for assets. Suppose individuals want more money and less illiquid bonds. As the public sells its bonds in the hope of acquiring cash, the interest rate tends to rise. If the interest rate were the Fed's target, then it immediately would purchase securities in the open market to prevent the higher interest rates. This is the appropriate policy in this case. Given society's constant outlook about goods and services, a constant interest rate is necessary to maintain output. Higher interest rates would have reduced spending and income. If the Fed had focused on the money supply, it would have remained largely idle because the sale of bonds mainly shuffles bonds and money among the public with little impact on the total. In this case, the higher interest rates would not be counteracted and would reduce spending and income.

If interest rate movements predominantly reflect changes in the demand for money as the last paragraph assumed, then interest rates would be good targets. On the other hand, if interest rates were influenced by a myriad of factors, then observation of their fluctuations tells us that something happened, but what? *The monetarist argument against interest rates states that money demand is stable and interest rates pick up too many signals, making interpretation of their fluctuations extremely difficult*. Monetarists stress the importance of inflationary expectations on interest rates. (Recall Chapter 6's analysis, which indicated that as a first approximation interest rates rise by the expected rate of inflation.) If, instead of the last paragraph's larger money demand, interest rates had risen due to higher inflationary expectations, and if the Fed had responded identically by *increasing* the money supply, then monetary policy fuels inflationary expectations. Resist the temptation to argue that the Fed would not act in this manner in this case. If the Fed knew what case it was, it would not need an intermediate target.

Reserves or Interest Rates as an Anterior Target

Advocates of a money target at first loudly applauded the second October 1979 change, namely, the shift from interest rates to reserves as a means of controlling money. In general, money and an anterior interest rate target are infeasible, largely for the same reasons that concurrent interest rate and money targets generally are infeasible. If nothing else, the federal funds rate and money do not have even the same dimensions. The Fed recognized the folly of its particular three-stage strategy and shifted to reserves as an anterior target.

> The principal reason advanced for shifting to an operating procedure aimed at controlling the supply of bank reserves more directly was that it would provide greater assurance that the Committee's objective for monetary growth could be achieved.[29]

No two targets, either synchronous or nonsynchronous, are perfectly compatible at all times unless they are identical, such as a short and long-run money supply target. Nevertheless, a dollar aggregate like reserves generally is far preferable to interest rates as an anterior target for money. In this case, however, a combination of very technical factors, including lagged reserve accounting prior to February 1984, did substantially reduce the advantages of reserves over interest rates as the anterior target. The next chapter shows that something even better than reserves exists. *The Fed should control the base.*

Open-Market Instructions: Vagueness versus Precision or Art versus Science

Whatever the intermediate variable may be, should its target value be specified precisely or vaguely? Recall that a shift towards greater precision is one of the major changes in open-market directives. Still, the directives generally specify fairly wide ranges. Why is the Fed so imprecise about

---

[29]*Federal Reserve Bulletin,* December 1979, p. 974.

its intermediate target? *First, policy vagueness facilitates reaching a consensus.* We said that policy disagreements stem from differences over (1) goals or ultimate targets, (2) forecasts of the state of the economy and the effect of nonpolicy variables, and (3) forecasts of the effect of the policy instruments on the goals. Yet policymakers rarely discuss such differences explicitly. Exposing the source of policy disagreements typically strengthens the disagreements and paralyzes decision making. Because precise policy proposals usually must be justified more rigorously, preciseness exposes sources of policy disagreement and reduces the likelihood of arriving at a consensus. If positions do not have to be justified, committee members may arrive at the same conclusion for different reasons. For example, someone who believes that a deep recession is imminent and that the policy instruments are very powerful will favor a "moderate" policy. But those who believe that a small stimulus is sufficient and that the policy instruments are relatively weak will also favor a "moderate" policy. Thus, two people come to the same conclusion for different reasons. Moreover, disagreement implies that compromises may be necessary. Compromises are more easily reached when committee members believe others are flexible. Precise targets suggest inflexibility and generate hostile reactions from other committee members. These ideas are partially confirmed by the greater number of dissenting opinions now that the directives are somewhat more precise.

Second, there is the General Custer principle: large targets make sharpshooters. Imprecise targets shield the Fed from the criticism that it does not hit its target. Moreover, the compatibility of vague intermediate targets with many goals not only facilitates decision making within the Fed but lessens outside criticism that the Fed is pursuing undersirable goals. It is much easier to deny charges when you admit nothing beforehand. As a result of frequent accusations of being overly concerned about inflation and paying too little attention to unemployment, the Fed feels constantly under siege. Vague responses are characteristic of any organization that feels threatened.

Finally, vague answers often are equated with expert answers to difficult questions, while precise answers allegedly are given to easy questions by those suffering from tunnel vision. *The need to maintain the aura that monetary policy cannot be reduced to a few simple rules and requires great breadth of vision is especially important to an independent Fed.* In other words, the long tenure of Fed Board members and other aspects of Federal Reserve independence, which will be discussed shortly, can be justified only if monetary policy is an art practiced by wise people above the political fray. The Fed has convinced others and, more important, itself that monetary policy is an art instead of a science.[30] Life is so

---

[30]Maisel, *Managing the Dollar,* p. 168.

Courtesy United Press International (UPI)

Arthur Burns, Chairman of the Federal Reserve Board, 1970–1978

complex that the FOMC demands the famous staff statistical summary and slide show before it begins deliberations. After a long pause and a deep draw on a pipe or cigar which fouls the air with curls of white smoke, your typical Fed officials begin their responses to senators' questions with, "Things are not so simple." While such an opening line might encourage follow-up questions—after all, no one should be embarrassed to ask questions about things that are not so simple—the opening line is designed to justify subsequent gobbledygook that unfortunately thoroughly intimidates most questioners and convinces them that Fed officials have the wisdom to deal with these not so simple issues.

Policy Indicators

The Fed cannot directly focus on the millions of market participants. There simply are too many. The Fed must infer the behavior of millions from a few prices and quantities. Individual economic units are luckier. Ignoring the Treasury's minor monetary powers, there is only one monetary authority. The effects of monetary policy on many large economic units are sufficiently strong yet uncertain and variable that it is profitable for them to search for indicators of monetary policy.[31] *Indicators of current policy are valuable because policy works with a lag and because it presages future policy, that is, policy also is serially correlated.* A combination of ease of observation, the profit motive, and just plain curiosity has produced thousands of Peeping Toms. What is the Fed up to? Defining terms formally, the *monetary policy indicator is the variable which best measures the effect of monetary policy on the goal variable.* Each economic unit here specifies its goal, which, in principle, could be virtually any variable. For example, a gold dealer wants to know the effect of Federal

Courtesy United Press International (UPI)

Paul Volcker, Chairman of the Federal Reserve Board, 1979–Present

---

[31]We accept Benjamin Friedman's minority viewpoint ("Targets, Instruments, and Indicators of Monetary Policy") that the *monetary authority* does not need an indicator. The *public* needs an indicator. Anterior targets and indicators are conceptually distinct although the same variable may fulfill both functions.

Reserve policies on the price of gold, which is his goal variable. The indicator literature invariably assumes, however, that some aggregate output or employment measure is the goal. These socially oriented goals are assumed because, as one might expect, the indicator problem has been discussed most extensively by academic economists, who seem motivated more by curiosity and a desire to heap blame or lavish praise than by profits.

While the Fed makes mere observation of its actions easy—it releases weekly data on its open-market operations and the base, and the discount rate and reserve ratios are known continuously—construction of an indicator which interprets and summarizes the Fed's actions is difficult. *A good indicator should possess two characteristics. First, the indicator should be dominated by the Fed's actions.* Thus, an indicator differs in an important way from the intermediate variable in a two-stage strategy, which should be influenced by the exogenous variables as well as the policy instruments. An indicator measures what the Fed is doing, while the intermediate target is *used by the Fed* to learn what to do. Because the Fed does focus on the intermediate variable, it partially, but only partially, reflects Fed action. *Second, the indicator should be closely related to the goal.* Unfortunately, there is no perfect indicator, in the sense that one cannot find a variable which changes only when the Fed acts and which has a one-to-one relationship with aggregate output. Second-best situations often are complex and indefinite, and this case is no exception. The most frequently suggested indicators are "adjusted" reserves; the "adjusted" monetary base; a short-term interest rate, particularly the federal funds rate; a long-term interest rate; and the money supply, where reserves or the base are adjusted for reserve requirement changes. For example, if reserve ratios are reduced by 10 percent, the adjusted base rises 10 percent.

In general, a trade-off exists between the two properties of a good indicator. The more strongly is a variable dominated by the Fed, the weaker typically is its relationship with the goal. This is so because short lags between policy instruments and indicators reduce the time that non-Fed variables can influence the indicator. However, this increases the number of non-Fed variables that can come between the indicator and goal, given any impact lag between Fed instruments and the goal.

A concrete example is helpful. The Fed's portfolio of securities, which measures net cumulative open-market operations, satisfies the first characteristic perfectly. The Fed, and only the Fed, is responsible for open-market operations. However, float has the same effect as open-market operations on banks' ability to lend and create deposits. Consequently, reserves or the base, which incorporate float, should be better related to the goal, but neither is perfectly controlled by the Fed. *There has been a tendency over time for the preferred indicator to shift closer toward*

Federal Reserve control and from interest rates to a monetary aggregate. Many who favored the money supply several years ago now prefer the adjusted base, thereby not attributing to the Fed any influence on the multiplier except through the reserve ratio. Proponents of long-term interest rates have largely shifted to short-term interest rates or adjusted reserves.

Should the Federal Reserve Be Independent?

Some hot topics become old hat so quickly that they burn less energy than some tepid issues which smolder year after year. The independence of the Fed has been one tepid issue from the moment of the Fed's existence until today. The independence of the Fed within the structure of the federal government is illustrated in several ways. First, *the tenure of Board members is 14 years, and they can be removed from office only for cause.* Board members cannot be removed from office simply because their views are unpopular or because they belong to the wrong party. The term of office is sufficiently long to minimize the threat of covert political pressure. *Moreover, the terms of office are staggered to prevent presidential "packing" of the Fed.* The President does not even get to appoint the Fed chair immediately.[32] *Second, Federal Reserve operations produce so much income that it is not dependent on congressional appropriations. Third, the Board reports and is accountable to Congress, not the executive. For many years the Board avoided virtually any contact with the administration.* The need for coordination has recently lead to the inclusion of the Fed chair in some meetings of main economic policymakers.

The independence of the Fed is far from absolute, particularly in the long run. Congress created the Fed and gave it the authority to execute the monetary responsibilities Congress has under the Constitution. At any time Congress may change the structure of the Fed or even abolish it. Aware of this, the Fed is sensitive to contemporary political opinion.

Defending the independence of the Federal Reserve at the 1976 commencement exercises at Bryant College, former Fed Chairman Arthur Burns said that *the major justification for an independent Fed is "the need for a strong monetary authority to discipline the inflationary tendencies inherent in modern economies."*[33] Decision makers prone to political pressure supposedly tolerate too high inflation rates in order to accomplish other goals.

---

[32]The chair's term of office is four years. If not reappointed to the chair, the person may continue serving the remaining portion of the 14-year term.

[33]Arthur Burns, "The Independence of the Federal Reserve System," *Challenge,* July 1976, p. 23. Reprinted with permission of publisher M. E. Sharpe, Inc., Armonk, New York, 10504.

> Under our scheme of governmental organization the Federal Reserve can make the hard decisions that might be avoided by decision makers subject to day to day pressures of political life.
>
> * * * * *
>
> Such a step [monetary policy lodged in the presidency] would create a potential for political mischief or abuse on a larger scale than we have yet seen. Certainly, if the spending propensities of federal officials were given freer rein, the inflationary tendency that weakened our economy over much of the past decade would in all likelihood be aggravated.[34]

There are three main arguments against the Fed's independence. First, an independent Fed is undemocratic. In a democratic society policy goals are formulated by elected officials. To the extent an appointed agency substitutes its goals for those of elected officials, a fourth branch of the Constitution has been indirectly created. *Second, even if everyone shared common goals, attainment of the goals requires coordinated policy, which independence largely precludes.*[35] *Third, an independent Fed is not much more likely to curtail inflation.* The same Chairman Burns, who while in office said that an independent Fed was absolutely essential in the battle against inflation, reflected with anguish after leaving office in 1979 that "viewed in the abstract, the Federal Reserve System had the power to abort the inflation at its incipient stage 15 years ago or at any later point, and it has the power to end it today. It did not do so because the Federal Reserve was itself caught up in the philosophic and political currents that were transforming American life and culture."[36]

Summary/Questions

Monetary policy in the postwar period has been characterized by relative constancy of goals but significant diversity in operating strategy. Prior to 1965 free reserves unquestionably were the intermediate target which the Fed sought to control in order to achieve its goals. A free reserves policy produces a procyclical monetary policy. Whenever aggregate demand increases, free reserves tend to fall. In order to maintain the target value of free reserves, the Fed purchases securities, causing interest rates to fall and the money supply to expand. Severe criticism finally dislodged the Fed's attachment to free reserves. The Fed then officially started wearing bifocals; its two proclaimed targets were interest rates and money. Just as one cannot simultaneously focus through both lenses of bifocals,

---

[34]Ibid., pp. 21 and 23.

[35]A formal proof of the need for policy coordination is presented in Chapter 29.

[36]Arthur F. Burns, "The Anguish of Central Banking," the 1979 Per Jacobsson Lecture, Belgrade, Yugoslavia, p. 14. Reprinted by the American Enterprise Institute.

the Fed generally cannot control both interest rates and money. Throughout the 1970s interest rates were the effective operating target, as Keynesians recommended. The relative ascendancy of monetarism and relative decline of Keynesianism is reflected in a shift from an effective interest rate policy to a money supply policy. Time is too short to tell how firmly rooted monetarism is at the Fed.

1. What conditions must exist in order for policymakers to achieve their ultimate goals?
2. What are the fundamental justifications for a two-stage policy strategy which focuses on an intermediate target?
3. Define free reserves. State the rationale for a free reserves target. When will free reserves be a poor intermediate target, that is, produce a procyclical monetary policy?
4. Demonstrate that the Fed generally cannot hit an interest rate and money target simultaneously.
5. Discuss the main features for Federal Reserve policy of Concurrent Resolution 133.
6. Define the forgiveness principle or base drift. Explain how different policy formulation and target evaluation periods encourage the forgiveness principle.
7. Compared to Concurrent Resolution 133, how did Humphrey-Hawkins strengthen the Fed's commitment to its long-run money supply target?
8. State in chronological order the main changes in the authorizations and operating instructions given to the manager of the system open-market account.
9. What two changes in the operating instructions of the October 6, 1979, FOMC meeting have led many people to claim that the meeting was historic?
10. Illustrate the importance of personalities in monetary policy by stating important changes in the open-market directive around the time Arthur Burns (1970) and Paul Volcker (1979) were each appointed Chairman.
11. What type of information is helpful in determining which of two stated intermediate targets is the effective intermediate target?
12. When is the money supply preferable to interest rates as an intermediate target? Are interest rates ever a better intermediate target than the money supply?
13. Whatever the intermediate target may be, why does the Fed specify a target range instead of a specific value?
14. What is meant by an indicator of monetary policy? What two characteristics should an ideal indicator possess?
15. In what ways is the Federal Reserve independent?
16. List the arguments for and against an independent Federal Reserve.

Can the Federal Reserve control the quantity of money?

20

The last chapter stated that the Fed cannot control money and interest rates simultaneously. We further claimed that the reason the Fed was quite wide of the short-run money mark was because it indeed chose to exercise some control over interest rates. There exists another possibility we did not consider: the Fed simply cannot control the money supply. This possibility should be analyzed because the money supply is the *only* long-run (annual) target, yet the Fed barely hit its big monetary target, as we indicated in the last chapter. Can the Federal Reserve control money? This is one of the basic questions of money and banking which must be answered affirmatively.

Control of the money supply by the Federal Reserve is the subject of unnecessary controversy because of (1) the linking of logically distinct but practically joint arguments, and (2) the failure to acknowledge unequivocably the existence of side constraints and costs. Two tenets of monetarism are: the Fed *should* control the money stock, and the Fed *can* control the money stock. The last chapter indicated that situations arise where the Fed should control interest rates instead of the money supply. While acknowledging this possibility, monetarists claim such situations are so infrequent that a monetary target is far superior to an interest rate target. The response to monetarists by most economists, particularly those within the Federal Reserve System, has verged on the illogical until quite recently. Most Fed officials preferred to claim lack of control rather than debate whether money or the rate of interest is the appropriate target. In other words, the Fed generally chose to link the monetarists' logically distinct propositions—the Fed can and should control money—and based its defense against the should-control proposition by denying the can-control proposition. Denial of the can-control proposition was largely based on the existence of many factors influencing the money supply. Presumably, the Fed cannot counteract these other factors.

In its more exact moments, the Fed acknowledges that the answer to the can-control issue is not clearly negative. The Fed then alleges only that the costs greatly exceed the benefits of monetary control, where the main costs are those associated with the interest rate fluctuations necessary to control money. Fluctuations in the rate of interest or other variables generally are imperfectly predicted, misallocate resources, and unquestionably increase the cost and difficulty of planning, particularly for financial institutions. However, neither the Fed nor anyone else has been able to measure the magnitude of the cost of variable interest rates. Without measurement, the cost-benefit argument against the should-control proposition must remain speculative. Perhaps because the cost-benefit argument is speculative, the Fed generally is careless in expressing its opposition to monetary control. It's much simpler to claim that money cannot be controlled. If the can-control question is negative, then the should-control question is moot.

Control, Time, and Uncertainty: The General Case

Whether the variable is an ultimate goal variable such as GNP or an intermediate variable such as money, the same two reasons explain the lack of perfect control, namely, the existence of lags or imperfect knowledge about the structure of the economy. The Fed can control interest rates exactly because they have no data lag, being continuously and instantaneously observed, and because they supposedly incur no impact lag, being immediately affected by the monetary policy tools. The money stock is observed with approximately a 10-day lag. Since we clearly lack perfect knowledge about the structure of the economy, the 10-day data lag implies that money cannot be controlled exactly. Is this a serious problem? Note well two fundamental principles about policymaking and control applicable to both fiscal and monetary policy. (1) Control must be discussed within some time frame of reference determined by the policymaker's ultimate goal and the structure of the economy. (2) In an uncertain world perfect control of an intermediate target (for example, the quantity of money) does *not* guarantee attainment of the ultimate goal (for example, some desired value of GNP). Consequently, perfect control is an unreasonable requirement. Control is said to exist when the actual value of the intermediate target approximately equals the desired value, given the ultimate goal.

Control and the Time Period

Fundamental principles surely are stated succinctly, so let us elaborate. Suppose that in view of the economic goals the Fed wants the money supply to remain constant. Suppose further that in spite of Federal Reserve efforts to keep the money supply constant, the various uncontrolled factors affecting the base and multiplier cause the money supply to follow an erratic path, which the Fed observes with a lag. The daily and even weekly money supply varies substantially, but the average money supply during calendar quarters remains constant. Does the Fed have control over the money supply in this case? Clearly the answer depends on the appropriate time interval of the analysis. No, the Fed does not control daily and weekly money balances, but it does control quarterly average balances. What is the appropriate time interval of analysis? If weekly fluctuations in the quantity of money had no effect on the goal variable, what matters being the quarterly average quantity of money, then the Fed does control money. Of course, if weekly fluctuations had significant effects on the goal, then the Fed does not control money. *The question of control is inseparable from the effect of the intermediate target on the goal;* the intermediate variable matters not in its own right but because of its effects on the goal. Economic policy is for practical people. Policymakers are judged on their ability to control variables which have a significant effect on the ultimate goal.

Control and Exogenous Factors

Regardless of the appropriate time period, policymakers never can hit the target value to the last decimal place. If there were an exact and predictable relationship between the intermediate variable and the goal, then lack of perfect control is the sole reason for not achieving the goal. For example, suppose the goal is a $3 trillion annual income (GNP), the full employment level of GNP. If income always were five times the money supply, then the money target is $600 billion, and actual income always differs from the goal by five times the difference between the actual and target money supply. No one seriously believes that the relationship between any intermediate target, monetary or otherwise, and the ultimate goal is exact and predictable. The monetary authority at best knows the average relationship between monetary policy and the goal. Strikes, oil embargoes, and government spending, which may be viewed as exogenous variables from the viewpoint of the monetary authority, have an effect on income. Income occasionally will be greater than $3 trillion because the exogenous forces are expansionary. Conversely, depressive exogenous forces cause income to fall short of the goal even when the money supply is $600 billion. Since perfect control over the intermediate variable does not guarantee achievement of the goal at all times, requiring perfect—to the last decimal—control is unreasonable. *Control, without any qualifying adjective, exists when the differences between the actual and target values of money are sufficiently small.* In such cases monetary errors explain only a small proportion of the discrepancy between the actual and goal values of GNP, the major discrepancy being due to exogenous forces.

The statement that monetary control exists when the difference between the actual and target values of the money supply is "sufficiently small" lacks precision. But that is exactly the point. *Control of a policy variable is not a matter of yes or no but of degree.* Barring the absolute, the existence of control cannot be proven but is the subject of agreement among reasonable people.

The Monetary Control Period

How are these general principles related to the question of control over the quantity of money? No one believes that reasonable (up to 2.5 percent) daily monetary fluctuations have any effect whatsoever on goal variables. (Of course, 2.5 percent daily is identical to over 900 percent annually, so we are talking about changes larger than typically observed.) Indeed, one is somewhat hard pressed to find individuals who believe that the observed fluctuations in the monthly average money supply have affected GNP. Money growth rates alternating monthly between 4 and 6 percent have virtually the same effect on GNP as a steady 5 percent growth per month. Discrepancies between the actual and targeted values of quarterly average money supply do cause GNP to deviate from its desired value, but the importance of even quarterly discrepancies should not be exaggerated. To be conservative and err on the side *against* monetary policy, and because the Fed has specified monthly growth ranges for money, assume months are the appropriate time period of analysis.[1]

An Operating Procedure to Control Money

Precisely what operating procedure should the Fed follow? Numerous operating procedures have been proposed, but we shall discuss only one which gives quite accurate results. As has been stressed, the money supply may be expressed as the product of the multiplier and the base, $M = m \cdot B$. Given some target money supply, the preferred operating procedure predicts the multiplier and, given this prediction, selects the

[1]Although the Fed often specifies a quarterly monetary growth target, the quarterly target is set *after* more than the first month has passed. This is identical to setting monthly targets. We return to the monthly targets in Chapter 29, where we discuss policy credibility and rational expectations.

value of the base consistent with the desired money supply. How the desired money supply value was selected is irrelevant for the can-control problem at hand. Under this regime the base becomes the intermediate target and the money supply is the goal.[2] With its prediction of the multiplier in hand, the FOMC operates on the base to attain some specified monthly average money supply. Intramonthly fluctuations in the base are tolerated; the FOMC focuses on the monthly average base. Monetary control requires both (1) hitting the monetary base target, and (2) predicting the multiplier relatively accurately. Expressing these ideas in terms of the general form of the money supply equation,

$$\text{Desired money supply} = \text{Predicted multiplier} \times \text{Target base}, \tag{20–1}$$

$$\text{Actual money supply} = \text{Actual multiplier} \times \text{Actual base}, \tag{20–2}$$

$$\frac{\text{Desired money supply}}{\text{Actual money supply}} = \frac{\text{Predicted multiplier}}{\text{Actual multiplier}} \times \frac{\text{Target base}}{\text{Actual base}} \tag{20–3}$$

The actual money supply approximately equals the target value when the actual base approximately equals the target value and the multiplier is predicted relatively accurately.[3]

Control of the Base

Could the Fed control money if it adopted the procedure outlined here? The answer nowadays is a loud yes, as the remainder of this section demonstrates. Consider first the Fed's ability to hit the *monthly average* monetary base target. As Chapter 17 said, uncontrolled accounts are pushing the base in one direction today and another tomorrow. Some of

---

[2]This is simpler than the equivalent notion of the base as anterior intermediate target and the money supply as posterior intermediate target.

[3]The reader may wonder why the opposite strategy is not proposed. That is, why not operate on the multiplier by changing reserve requirements and predict the base? From the viewpoint of monetary control, an important difference between the multiplier and base is the data lag. The Fed is virtually continuously aware of any changes in the base, which is a liability of the monetary authorities. At the beginning of each day the Fed and Treasury have balance sheet figures for the end of the previous day and, therefore, can compute the base. The Fed does not have to predict the base: it knows the value of the base. The multiplier includes ratios of items on banks' balance sheets, which are available to the authorities on a preliminary basis only after a time lag in some cases of several days, and highly accurate information may be available only after several months. For this reason and others, attempts to control the multiplier in the short run by frequently changing reserve requirements make little sense. This is not to deny that reserve requirement changes nearly always have a rapid effect on the multiplier, the possible exception being during a multiplier trap to be discussed shortly. The point, however, is that the resultant effects of reserve requirements changes are known accurately only after a lag.

the uncontrolled factors absorbing and supplying the base fluctuate significantly within a month but are more stable from month to month. Float is an example of such an account. Monthly fluctuations in other uncontrolled accounts, for example, Treasury deposits at the Fed, can be as large as intramonthly fluctuations. Nonetheless, *defensive and dynamic open-market operations can completely offset uncontrolled factors and hit a monthly base target.*[4] How can we be so definite? First, under this strategy the Fed knows just what has to be done. The (actual) monetary base is derived exclusively from the Fed and Treasury balance sheets, which are available daily. *The base has virtually no data lag.* While the Fed may well tolerate *intra*monthly variations of the monetary base, as the end of a month approaches the Fed knows virtually exactly the *monthly average* actual base, which is compared with the monthly average target base.[5] Second, the account manager can purchase or sell the appropriate amount of securities to close any gap between desired and actual values. Look again at the relative size of the accounts in the monetary base equation, Table 17–4, and the summary of Chapter 17. Fed holdings of U.S. government securities are ten times larger than any uncontrolled account. Moreover, the total trading volume of U.S. government securities is approximately $14 billion daily. A moderate annual rate of monetary growth (say, 6 percent) requires approximately a $0.5 billion monthly increase in the monetary base. Uncontrolled factors rarely change the base by more than $5 billion per month. Therefore, the maximum *monthly* volume of defensive and dynamic open-market operations, $5.5 billion, is less than half the *daily* trading volume of U.S. government securities. The base target can be hit precisely easily enough.

Predicting the Multiplier

Since the Fed can control the base, controlling the money supply then resolves on the Fed's ability to forecast the multiplier. Figure 20–1 shows the value of the money supply multiplier for an almost 20-year span. The multiplier varied considerably during this long period, hitting a high of 2.99 in 1965 and a low of 2.56 in 1982.[6] Is it reasonably stable over *short* periods? Chapter 4 indicated that the multiplier depends on income, interest rates, and numerous other variables. For purposes of short-run predictions, a much simpler relationship may yield sufficiently accurate

---

[4]Defensive and dynamic open-market operations were defined in Chapters 17 and 18.

[5]We are not suggesting that the account manager should take a vacation until the end of each month and ignore all beginning-of-month random forces. The text simply emphasizes that hitting a monthly average target is consistent with significant intramonthly variation.

[6]The multiplier in Figure 20–1 is the ratio of M-1 to the St. Louis Fed's adjusted (basically for reserve requirement changes) monetary base.

FIGURE 20–1
The Money Supply Multiplier

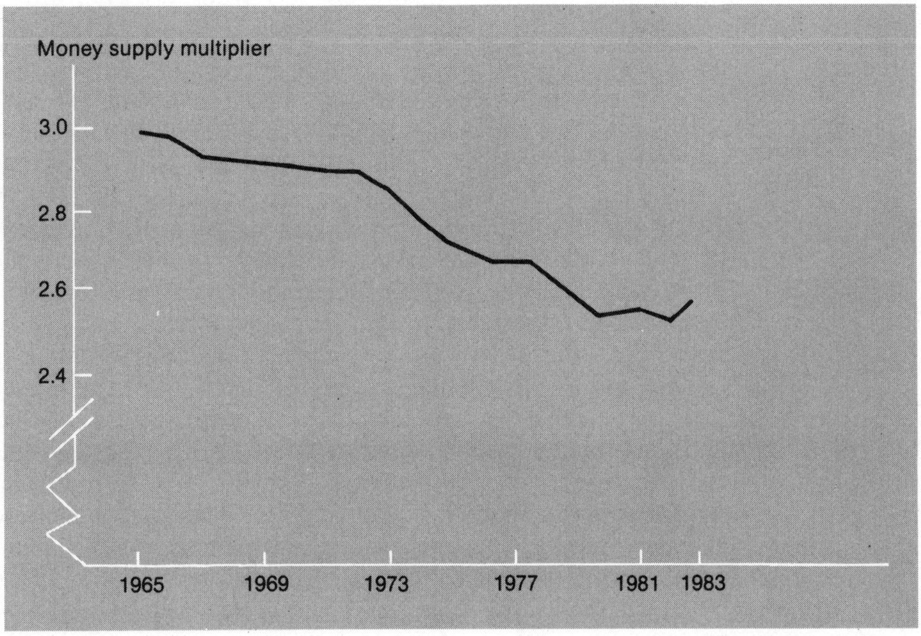

Source: St. Louis Fed, *Annual U.S. Economic Data, 1964–1983.*

forecasts of the multiplier. Albert Burger has proposed the following forecasting equation.[7]

(20–4)

Predicted money multiplier = 0.29 + 0.89 lagged money multiplier + 0.04 lagged Treasury bill rate percentage change

This forecasting equation takes as inputs variables that the Federal Reserve knows accurately. For example, to predict the December 1984 money multiplier with this equation, the Fed must know only the November 1984 multiplier and the Treasury bill rate in October and November. In essence,

[7]"Money Stock Control," in *Controlling Monetary Aggregates II: The Implementation* (Boston: Federal Reserve Bank of Boston, 1973). Equation (20–4) was constructed to forecast the old M-1 multiplier. Although old M-1 and new M-1 differ considerably, a similar equation with somewhat different coefficients should forecast the new M-1 multiplier reasonably accurately.

this is a very mechanical method that does not attempt to incorporate information the Fed might have about expected movements of such key factors as Treasury deposits in the forecast month. Surely this leads to prediction errors. While alternative forecasting equations should be able to perform as well as this simple, mechanical method, its virtue is precisely its simplicity, which facilitates implementation.[8] When the monthly forecasted multiplier given by Equation (20–4) is compared with the actual multiplier, *the forecasting errors are quite small.* The monthly average absolute forecasting percent error is about 0.5 percent.[9]

Since the money supply is the product of the multiplier and base, and since the monthly average value of the base can take any value the Fed wants, *the monthly average absolute difference between the desired and actual money supply would be about 0.5 percent when the Fed follows the outlined operating procedure.* Is this difference between desired and actual values sufficiently small that the Fed can claim control of the money supply? While recognizing that there is no definite answer, we would answer the question affirmatively. Yes, the Fed can control the money supply! GNP will differ from its goal value mainly because the Fed (like others) incorrectly estimates the target money supply, and only in small part because the Fed cannot hit the incorrectly estimated monetary target.

Qualifying Comments

We said several times in the last section that the Fed can control money *nowadays,* and we believe control will continue in the future. However, as Chapter 16 indicated, monetary control is a relatively recent phenomenon. Indeed, lack of control was one of the main reasons Congress passed the Federal Reserve Act in 1913. But a central bank is *not* a sufficient condition for monetary control. The operating strategy, laws and regulations, and the structure of the financial system all influence the degree of monetary control. For example, the Fed could not control money when its intermediate targets were free reserves and the federal funds rate.

---

[8]For an even simpler, more mechanistic but still relatively accurate (though not as accurate as Equation (20–4) method of forecasting the multiplier, see Anatol Balbach, "How Controllable is Money Growth?" Federal Reserve Bank of St. Louis *Review,* April 1981, pp. 3–12. James Johannes and Robert Rasche confirm the text in their important paper, "Predicting the Money Multiplier," *Journal of Monetary Economics,* July 1979, pp. 301–25. They construct a sophisticated Box-Jenkins ARIMA model of the multiplier which forecasts more accurately than Equation (20–4). However, its sophistication discourages its use by the average policymaker.

[9]The calculated errors are for the period 1964–71 and should be updated after the full effect of recent structural changes are felt. While the structural changes may have increased prediction errors, the 1964–71 period used to test the equation also was a difficult period for monetary control. Reserve requirements were changed seven times, and Reg Q ceilings caused the nonmoney/money deposit ratio to vary significantly.

A Reserve Target for Money

Assuming the Fed was unconcerned about interest rate fluctuations, can it control the money supply, given its current operating strategy of focusing on *reserves* instead of the base as the operating or anterior intermediate target? Our answer is a slightly qualified yes. We chose to express the money supply as the product of "the" multiplier times the base. The money supply may also be expressed as the product of any number of reserve measures and a multiplier m′, where the value of m′ depends on the specific reserve measure. For example, we show in the Appendix that if M = mB, where, as usual, M is the money supply, m is the (base) multiplier, and B is the base, then

$$M = \frac{(1 + k)m}{1 + k - mk}R = m'R \tag{20–5}$$

where R is total reserves, k is the currency/money deposit ratio and the other terms are as just defined. The Fed prefers Equation (20–5). Because it prefers Equation (20–5), the Fed's current strategy seeks the value of total reserves consistent with the given target value of the money and the predicted total reserve multiplier m′.[10] The Fed's current strategy is quite similar to our preferred strategy outlined in the last section, where the (base) multiplier is predicted, and the base is the operating target for the money supply. Although the two strategies are quite similar, the monetary base strategy is somewhat better. For reasons that are not obvious, *the base multiplier m is forecast better than the reserve multiplier.*[11] Precisely because the money stock is better controlled by focusing on the monetary base instead of total reserves, from the beginning we viewed money as the product of the (base) multiplier and the base although our equations in Chapter 4 are formally equivalent to Equation (20–5).

---

[10]Total reserves are the operating target across FOMC meetings but unborrowed reserves are the day-to-day target. "Under the approach adopted in October 1979, the FOMC sets short-run targets for monetary expansion. . . . A path for total reserves is calculated based on the expected relationship between reserves and the money stock—the so-called reserves-money multiplier. . . . A path for nonborrowed reserves then is calculated by making an allowance for the portion of total reserves expected to be provided through borrowings at the Federal Reserve Bank discount windows." Board of Governors of the Federal Reserve System, "Monetary Report to Congress Pursuant to the Full Employment and Balance Growth Act of 1978," February 25, 1981, p. 25.

[11]Burger, "Money Stock Control." The Fed, however, has recently claimed that there is no clear evidence that one multiplier is predicted more accurately than the other. "Monetary Policy Report to Congress," p. A29.

Money Supply Liquidity Trap

A money supply *liquidity trap* is the extreme case of lack of monetary control. The same term will be used in the discussion of money demand but the concepts are quite different.[12] A *money supply* liquidity trap refers to a situation where the Federal Reserve encounters great difficulties in changing the quantity of money *relatively rapidly.*[13] The control controversy concerns how closely the target can be hit; *the trap controversy concerns the possibility that* no *monetary change can be effected in the near future*. The discussion usually is phrased in terms of monetary increases because the possibility of a trap was first raised to excuse the Fed's conduct during the 1930s, when surely the appropriate policy was a large and rapid monetary expansion. Yet, the money supply fell by approximately one third during the Great Depression. By 1933 the economy slowly began climbing upward. Prices rose approximately 2.3 percent annually between 1933 and 1935, but they still were 20 percent lower than 1929 prices. Unemployment in 1936 was 16.9 percent. Only medicine men would have doubled reserve requirements, as the Fed did, in order to cure an "inflationary bias."[14] Apologists for the Fed argue that its misguided actions were of little consequence because any attempt at rapid monetary expansion was doomed to failure.[15]

To ascertain the validity of the apologists' claim, consider first how the Fed changes the money supply. The general instruments of monetary control are (1) open-market operations, (2) the discount rate, and (3) reserve requirements. The first two instruments affect the base, while the latter affects the money supply multiplier. A money supply trap exists if the Fed encounters difficulty changing (1) the multiplier through reserve

---

[12]A *money demand* liquidity trap occurs when monetary expansion, rapid or otherwise, has no effect on aggregate demand because additional money is hoarded.

[13]U.S. Congress, *Hearings on H.R. 5327* (Banking Act of 1935). 74th Congress, 1st Session, (Washington, D.C.: House Committee on Banking and Currency, 1935); George Horwich, "Effective Reserves, Credit, and Causality in the Banking System of the 'Thirties," in *Banking and Monetary Studies,* ed. Dean Carson (Homewood, Ill.: Richard D. Irwin, 1963); Karl Brunner and Allan H. Meltzer, "Liquidity Traps for Money, Bank Credit, and Interest Rates." *Journal of Political Economy,* January/February 1968. *Traps* can be defined differently, sometimes causing misunderstanding. Brunner and Meltzer's study is the most complete *comparative statics* study of traps. They largely ignore the question of the time involved in moving from one money supply to another. Here, the speed of adjustment rather than the ultimate effect determines whether or not a trap exists.

[14]In the late 1970s a woman finally was appointed to the Board of Governors of the Federal Reserve System. Reserve requirement policy in the 1930s was discussed in Chapter 4's section on excess reserves.

[15]The apologists allege even more frequently that a money demand liquidity trap existed so monetary expansion, even if successful, would have no effect on aggregate demand and output. The chapters on income theory consider this possibility.

requirement changes—a multiplier trap—*and* (2) the base through discounts and open-market operations—a base trap.[16]

A Money Supply Trap in 1929–1933

A multiplier trap clearly existed in the 1929–33 period due to legislation. The Fed did not have the authority to change reserve requirements! Did a base trap also exist? Whether or not the Fed could have prevented the sharp fall in the money supply during the Great Depression is debatable. At that time the Fed was subject to various "reserve" requirements in terms of gold and real bills. That is, *gold and real bills had to equal specified percentages of the Fed's currency in circulation and bank reserve deposits.* (All reserve requirements for the Fed were repealed by the late 1960s.) During the Great Depression commercial bank excess reserves were relatively low and discounts were still significant, though less than in the 1920s. Some economists claim that the Fed could not have engaged in massive open-market purchases because banks would have repaid their discounts, and the Fed would have failed to meet its required reserve ratios. While the *immediate* impact of open-market purchases on the base indeed is largely negated by repayment of discounts, *ceteris paribus,* the offset effect is relatively short lived. After an extensive analysis, Professor Milton Friedman concluded that the evidence does not support the existence of a liquidity trap in the early 1930s.[17] The Fed's excess "reserves" were sufficiently large, and the offset effect due to discounts was sufficiently short lived that massive open-market purchases were possible. Moreover, the *ceteris paribus* condition does not have to hold. The Fed could have lowered the discount rate.[18] The money supply could have increased in the Great Depression. Only a lack of determination prevented the Fed from increasing it.

A Money Supply Trap in the Late 1930s

By the late 1930s when the Fed incorrectly *increased* reserve requirements, banks were swollen with excess reserves, and discounts had fallen to an inconsequential amount. Whether a multiplier trap ever occurred

[16]We ignore the implausible case where a change in the base (multiplier) would induce an exactly countervailing change in the multiplier (base), keeping the money supply constant. There may be some interaction between the two determinants of money but, lacking perfect offset, the money supply responds to changes in either determinant. Our multiplier trap has also been called a bank credit trap.

[17]Milton Friedman and Anna Schwartz, *A Monetary History of the United States, 1867–1960* (Princeton: Princeton University Press, 1963). For a contrary view, see E. A. Goldenweiser, *American Monetary Policy* (New York: McGraw-Hill, 1951). Goldenweiser was the director of the Fed's Division of Research and Statistics.

[18]Recall that instead the Fed *raised* the discount rate for balance of payment purposes. See the section on discounts in Chapter 18.

when the Fed had the ability to change reserve requirements is debatable, but at no point in U.S. history were economic conditions more favorable for such an occurrence than during the late 1930s. Banks do have a desired excess reserve ratio, which implies that reserve requirement changes *in either direction* ultimately affect the money supply. However, we saw in Chapter 4 that banks reacted slowly to the reserve requirement increase. *If the Fed had instead lowered requirements, the additional excess reserves probably would have had little impact on the money supply in the short run*. Sometimes banks temporarily demand the extra excess reserves, and bank credit does not expand. When interest rates and the demand for loans are extremely low due to poor business conditions, as was true during the late 1930s, all credit-worthy borrowers have been satisfied. Finding additional borrowers takes time. Alternatively stated, an increase in actual excess reserves may initially raise the desired ratio because banks do not have ready borrowers. Ultimately, borrowers are found, the desired excess reserve ratio returns to its original level, and deposits increase to eliminate the undesired excess reserves. Because many banks are involved in the money supply process, completion of the expansion process takes time. Banks often ration credit during prosperous periods and, consequently, have a ready pool of credit-worthy borrowers that will make the expansion process faster during prosperous periods.

In the late 1930s the United States might have been in a multiplier trap. Higher reserve requirements between June and December 1936 were accompanied by a temporary monetary expansion rather than contraction. Reserve requirements fell between December 1937 and June 1938 but check deposits remained virtually unchanged.[19] *Temporarily* the money supply multiplier was more or less fixed, and lower required reserves were accompanied by a higher demand for excess reserves. However, to our knowledge *no one has claimed a base trap existed during the late 1930s*. Any claims about a base trap are limited to the Great Depression. Massive open-market purchases were possible and would *not* have resulted in a reserve deficiency for the Fed. The Fed held approximately only 7 percent of marketable U.S. government securities outstanding, which by 1938 was larger than the money supply.[20] The Fed also had more than an adequate amount of gold certificates by the late 1930s. Large open-market purchases were possible and would have increased the money supply.[21] *Mistakes rather than inability characterize Federal Reserve policy during the 1930s.*

---

[19]See Table 4–2.

[20]Board of Governors of the Federal Reserve System, *Banking and Monetary Statistics* (Washington, D.C.: National Capital Press, 1943), pp. 35, 512.

[21]Open-market purchases must increase the quantity of money provided at least some of the securities are sold by the public. If banks sell all the securities and demand the

Summary/Questions

This short chapter applies, extends, and summarizes many ideas expressed in earlier chapters. For example, Chapter 4 presented a history of the Federal Reserve's misguided reserve requirement policy and of the excess reserve situation in the late 1930s. The possibility of a slow adjustment process was mentioned then, and its full implications are drawn now. This pulling together of material is occasioned by the importance of the chapter's main topic: can the Federal Reserve control the quantity of money? Yes, the Fed can control money today. With an affirmative answer we are ready to explore monetary *policy,* and not simply monetary *disturbances*.

Although the total financial system was not one of this chapter's main topics, we should reemphasize at this time the importance of the financial system, which is the second main strand of thought running through the previous chapters. In the process of creating money, banks lend. Because the banking system is the major lender, the structure and performance of the banking industry were singled out for special attention. But banks are only one group of lenders. We expanded our sight to include nonbank intermediaries such as savings and loans, credit unions, life insurance companies, and retirement funds because as a group their loans exceed bank loans by approximately 50 percent. While a direct finance market where ultimate borrowers and lenders meet does exist, banks and nonbank intermediaries play a key role in a financial system which transfers funds and, ultimately, resources among economic units. A smoothly functioning financial system is absolutely essential to improve the allocation of resources, both among economic units and over time, and to reap the advantages of specialization.

1. Discuss the relationship between policy control, the time period, and policy goals.
2. What are the implications for policy control of exogenous factors influencing the goals?
3. What is the appropriate monetary control period?
4. Describe the preferred operating strategy for monetary control discussed in the text. How does it compare with the operating strategy outlined by the FOMC at the October 6, 1979, meeting?
5. Define a money supply liquidity trap, a base trap, and a multiplier trap. Which, if any, of these traps existed in 1929–33 and in the late 1930s?

additional reserves the multiplier falls sufficiently so that the money supply remains constant in spite of the increase in the base. However, banks never are the only sellers of securities. Sales by banks alone implies that they are indifferent between earning assets and reserves while the public is not.

Appendix: The Bank Reserves Multiplier

We expressed the money supply, M, as the product of "the" multiplier, m, and the base, B.

$$M = mB \tag{20A–1}$$

This appendix shows that the money supply may also be expressed as the product of a multiplier m′ and reserves, R, where m′ is given by Equation (20A–2),

$$M = m'R = \frac{(1 + k)m}{1 + k - mk}R, \tag{20A–2}$$

and k is the currency ratio, C/D

By definition, the base equals reserves plus currency, which may be expressed as the product of the currency ratio and deposits.

$$B = R + C = R + kD \tag{20A–3}$$

Making use of the money definition

$$M = D + C = (1 + k)D \tag{20A–4}$$

Substituting Equations (20A–3) and (20A–4) in (20A–1) gives

$$M = m(R + kD) = m\left(R + \frac{kM}{1 + k}\right) \tag{20A–5}$$

Rearranging Equation (20A–5) gives (20A–2). Q.E.D.

PART FIVE

Monetary Theory

21 An introduction to economic measurement and theory

> A billion seconds ago it was 1951. A billion minutes ago Jesus was alive and walking in Galilee. A billion hours ago no one walked on two feet on earth. And a billion dollars ago was 10.3 hours in Washington, D.C.
>
> *Alexander Trowbridge**

The basic questions of monetary economics are: (1) can the Federal Reserve control money and other financial variables, and (2) do money and finance affect real GNP, prices, and other important variables? Up to now we basically have been concerned with the first question. The following chapters on monetary theory answer the second question.

Prior to launching into monetary theory, however, let us examine the precise meaning of such terms as GNP, income, investment, and prices. The so-called national income and product accounts are the subject of the first part of this chapter. Just as we first had to know precisely what money is before analyzing the Fed's control of money, so we must know what GNP measures before explaining how money influences it. Presentation of GNP statistics fulfills a second major objective, illustrating the *actual* post-World War II performance of the U.S. economy. Since the purpose of the first section is simply to illustrate economic performance and provide necessary background material for the theoretical chapters that follow, we resisted the temptation to present a complete discussion of the national income and product accounts. Many technical items like the difference between net national product and national income are ignored when these differences are unimportant for our theoretical models. Because we will follow the aggregate expenditures equal income ap-

---

**Forbes,* August 27, 1984, p. 20.

proach, the alternative saving equals investment approach is relegated to an appendix. We describe the measurement of only those economic variables whose determinants will subsequently be analyzed.

Important as the material in the first half of the chapter is, the material in the second half is even more important. There we present the fundamental reasons for monetary disagreements and preview the developing neoclassical/Keynesian consensus. This gives clear order to a series of interrelated propositions developed over the next six chapters.

The Nature of Gross National Product

Gross national product, popularly known as GNP and represented in algebraic equations by Y, very simply measures production. More precisely, *GNP is the market value of all final goods and services produced by the nation during some stated period of time*. GNP is available on a quarterly basis and usually is expressed at an annual rate. That is, if GNP in January–March 1984 equals $900 billion, annualized GNP during this period is $3.6 trillion per year. GNP is not available for periods shorter than a quarter, but, of course, GNP for longer periods is readily computed by adding quarterly figures. The term *gross* indicates that the nation's entire output is measured, including that amount which simply replaces capital goods worn out during the period.

Table 21–1 presents data on GNP and related measures for selected years following World War II. Column (1) shows the annual *market* or nominal value of GNP (Y, for short), with quantity or output, y, valued at the level of prices, P, prevailing during the year. In symbols, $Y \equiv Py$. Changes in the market value of GNP reflect the behavior of both output and price, two variables with quite different welfare implications. Columns (2) and (3) break down nominal GNP into output and price; the product of column (2) and column (3), with the decimal shifted two places to the left, equals column (1). Column (2) shows the value of GNP for each year at constant (1972) prices. Since column (2) eliminates the effect of price changes from nominal GNP, it is an indicator of output and called real GNP. Column (3) is an index of prices of all goods and services included in GNP. It measures the general level of prices during the year as a percentage of prices in 1972. Columns (4) – (6) show the annual percentage change of columns (1) – (3). The percentage change of nominal GNP approximately equals the sum of the percentage changes of real GNP and prices. Annualized *quarterly* data for nominal (current dollar) GNP, real (1972 dollar) GNP, and the GNP price index are graphed in Figure 21–1.

The reader is encouraged to update Table 21–1 by looking at the secondary sources cited or the original *Survey of Current Business*. Do the updated data continue to support the following important observations about the post-World War II period?

TABLE 21–1
Nominal GNP, Real GNP, and the GNP Price Index, Annual Values and Percentage Changes (selected years between 1946 and 1984)

Year	(1) Y Nominal GNP ($ billions) $Y \equiv Py$	(2) y Real GNP at Constant 1972 prices ($ billions)	(3) P GNP Price Index (1972 = 100)	(4) Nominal GNP, Percentage Change	(5) Real GNP, Percentage Change	(6) GNP Price Index, Percentage Change
1946 . . .	209.8	478.3	43.8	—	—	—
1947 . . .	233.1	470.3	49.6	11.1	−1.7	12.9
1948 . . .	259.5	489.8	53.0	11.3	4.1	6.9
1949 . . .	258.3	492.2	52.5	−0.5	0.5	−0.9
1956 . . .	421.7	671.6	62.8	—	—	—
1957 . . .	444.0	683.8	64.9	5.3	1.8	3.4
1958 . . .	449.7	680.9	66.0	1.3	−0.4	1.7
1959 . . .	487.9	721.7	67.6	8.5	6.0	2.4
1966 . . .	756.0	984.8	76.8	—	—	—
1967 . . .	799.6	1011.4	79.1	5.8	2.7	3.0
1968 . . .	873.4	1058.1	82.5	9.2	4.6	4.4
1969 . . .	944.0	1087.6	86.8	8.1	2.8	5.1
1976 . . .	1718.0	1300.4	132.1	—	—	—
1977 . . .	1918.0	1371.7	139.8	11.6	5.5	5.8
1978 . . .	2156.1	1436.9	150.1	12.4	4.8	7.3
1979 . . .	2413.9	1483.0	162.8	12.0	3.2	8.5
1980 . . .	2627.4	1480.7	177.4	8.8	−0.2	9.0
1981 . . .	2954.1	1513.8	195.1	12.4	2.2	10.0
1982 . . .	3073.0	1485.4	206.9	4.0	−1.9	6.0
1983 . . .	3309.5	1534.8	215.6	7.7	3.3	4.2
1984 . . .	3664.2	1639.9	223.4	10.7	6.4	3.6

Source: *Economic Report of the President* and Federal Reserve *Bulletin*, various issues.

1. Nominal GNP has increased more or less continuously, the sole *annual* exception being 1949. Both higher prices and higher real GNP account for the growth of nominal GNP, with prices being somewhat more important. In 1984 real GNP and the price index were approximately 3.43 and 5.10 times, respectively, their levels in 1946. The few years of declining real GNP witnessed increases in nominal GNP as prices rose faster than output fell. The upward march of nominal GNP was interrupted in 1949, and prices fell that year.

2. The upward trend of real GNP—3.2 percent annually between 1946 and 1984—has been less consistent. Real GNP fell in eight years, *and five of those eight years have been after 1969*. The largest annual percentage decline of real GNP in the postwar period occurred in 1982, when it fell nearly 2 percent. Two successive years of declining GNP occurred in 1974–75. A three-year decline was narrowly averted by the GNP increase in 1981. Real GNP remained virtually constant during the four-year period 1979–82.

FIGURE 21–1
Gross National Product

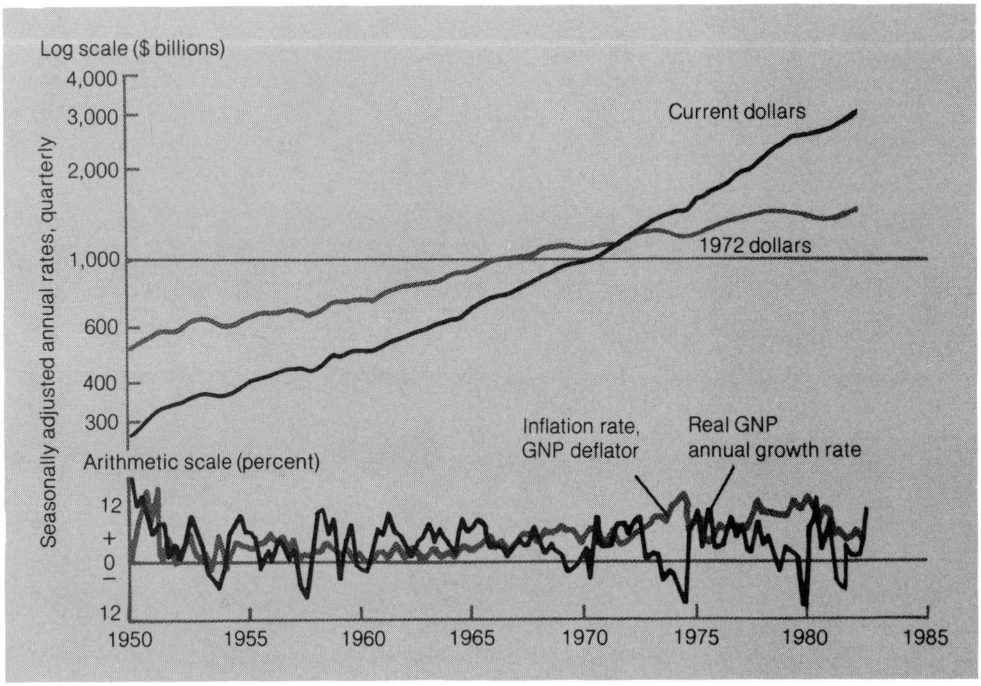

Source: Federal Reserve, *Historical Chart Book,* 1983.

Compared to the pre-war period, recent downturns have been shorter and more moderate. The average annual rate of decline of real GNP between 1929 and 1933 was approximately 8 percent, and output fell by 5.5 percent in 1938. Nowadays, "bad times" often are characterized by a failure of real GNP to grow fast enough rather than by a decline in GNP. Changes in GNP are reflected in the unemployment rate. While the 9.7 percent unemployment rate in 1982 was excessive, the average unemployment rate in 1930–33 was 18.3 percent.

3. In no other period in the history of the United States has inflation, measured by the percentage change in the GNP price index, been so persistent. Prices for a *full* year fell only once, in 1949. Moreover, the rate of inflation seems to be escalating. The average inflation rate was 2 percent between 1956–65, 5.7 percent in the following decade, and 7.7 between 1976–81. Between 1982 and 1984, however, the average annual

rate of inflation declined to 4.6 percent. Do more recent data confirm a permanent moderation of inflation?

Prior to the 1970s, there was a tendency to dismiss high rates of inflation as the inevitable consequences of unusual events, particularly wars. Prices rose sharply following World War II as price controls were phased out, during the height of the Korean conflict, 1951, and during the prolonged Vietnam War, 1965–70. However, the uncomfortably high rates of inflation in 1974–75 and 1978–80 cannot be explained by a war that requires low unemployment rates for the mobilization effort. The term *stagflation* was coined to describe 1974–75, years of declining or slowly growing GNP, high unemployment, and high inflation. The relationship between output and inflation is discussed in Chapter 28.

GNP as Expenditures for Product

All goods produced, as measured by GNP, must be acquired by someone. Defining expenditures to include all purchases, including the possibly involuntary additions to producers' inventories of goods not sold to non-producers, *GNP also is total expenditures on newly produced goods and services*. Algebraically,

$$E \equiv Y \equiv Py \tag{21–1}$$

where E represents total expenditures. The three-line identity symbol emphasizes that the expression is true by definition.

Total expenditures may be broken down in many ways. For example, total spending equals the spending of farmers, carpenters, and all others; spending of economic units east and west of the Mississippi River; and so on. If we were simply interested in definitions and measurement, every breakdown of total spending would be equally satisfactory. However, definitions and measurement are only a first step; we ultimately want to explain *desired* expenditures and the relationship between GNP and other goals. How much do people *want* to spend? What difference does it make for, say, the economic growth goal if one component of GNP increases and another decreases? Given our ultimate objectives, *breaking down total spending is useful only if the components react predictably to different factors or if their differential impact on other goals is important.* Classifying economic units as either east or west of the Mississippi is a waste of time since rivers have little, if any, effect on spending. However, if you believe that farmers and carpenters react predictably to different factors, or if their spending has an important effect on another goal, then this is the appropriate breakdown for you.

One classificatory scheme with a long history but made especially popular by Lord Keynes views GNP as the sum of spending by four major types of economic units, namely, households, firms, government, and foreigners. All economic units belong to one of the four classes, and terms are defined so the following is always true:

$$C + I + G + X - Z \equiv E \equiv Y \tag{21–2}$$

C = Consumption, household expenditures on current goods and services.
I = Gross private domestic investment, firms' current purchases to maintain and increase the capital stock.
G = Government expenditures on current goods and services.
X = Exports, foreign purchases of current goods and services.
Z = Imports, purchases by domestic units of foreign goods and services.

What are some examples of the various spending categories? Consumption includes three broad classes of purchases: consumer durables, nondurables, and services. Consumer durables include such things as new cars, stereos, and refrigerators. Nondurable goods include food, beverages, and clothing. Examples of consumer services are haircuts and admissions to rock concerts. Purchases of which of the following goods would be included in consumption: an ocean-view lot, a used car, and a Louis XIV antique desk? Not being *current* goods, none are included in consumption.

Gross private domestic investment, henceforth simply called investment, is the acquisition of current *commodities* that maintain and increase the capital stock, which includes houses and apartment buildings, producer's plant and equipment, and inventories. Because structures and producer's plant and equipment have a long life, purchases of these items are readily measured directly. Acquisition of inventories is measured by the change of inventories on hand during the period. Gross investment is the sum of depreciation, the expenditures necessary to maintain a capital stock that is used up during the production process, and net investment, increases in the stock of capital goods. The term *domestic* indicates that we include here purchases to maintain and increase the capital stock at home and not the capital abroad.

Most investment is made by economic units which everyone agrees are firms. However, households seemingly purchase new houses, so is it correct to say that investment is firms' current purchases to maintain and increase the capital stock? We attribute a schizophrenic personality to households, which become firms when they purchase a house. Why do we lump purchases of houses with business plant and equipment as investment? Because the factors which influence purchases of houses are quite similar to the determinants of business plant and equipment. Moreover, houses, like plant and equipment, are long lived and yield a stream of future services.

Business inventories are the buffer account which make total production equal sales. Suppose firms are producing more than the other economic units are purchasing. The "purchase" of the "unsold" goods by the producer is manifested in higher inventories and, therefore, investment. Inventories and investment fall when sales to households, government, and foreigners outstrip production. Suppose there is a sudden surge in new car sales. The surge was so sudden that car manufacturers do not have time to hire more workers and produce additional cars. How does this event affect GNP? Consumption increases and the inventory component of investment decreases by an equal amount leaving GNP unchanged, at least for the moment. Subsequently, GNP may increase as firms produce more to meet the enhanced demand.

Construction of houses, apartment buildings, shopping centers, office buildings, and factories is investment. Equipment increases when General Motors purchases a current computer, and inventories increase when IBM keeps the computer. In either case, investment occurs. Ask a person on the street for a good example of investment and he or she will probably mention General Motors and IBM common stock, a government bond, or a savings and loan deposit. Are these examples of investment? No. Investment is the acquisition of *commodities by firms* in order to maintain and increase the capital stock. Your purchase of IBM stock is not an example of investment for two reasons. First, only firms (including schizoid households acting like firms) invest; if an individual's spending is part of GNP, it is consumption. Second, IBM stock is a financial instrument and not a commodity. Even if a firm were to purchase IBM shares, it would not be investing in an economic sense. A firm invests when it purchases IBM computers instead of IBM stock. It is unfortunate that the term *investment* has a meaning in finance books and on the street different from its meaning in economics classrooms. *Investment* sometimes took its noneconomic meaning in the previous finance-oriented chapters, but that will *never* be the case henceforth. Our coining a new term for firms' acquisition of capital goods would only confuse matters more because the term *investment* has a long economic history.

Government expenditures on current goods and services are illustrated by purchases of armaments and the salaries of bureaucrats and teachers. Spending at all levels of government, local, state, and federal, are included. Transfer payments such as Social Security and welfare payments are *not* included in the expenditure side of GNP because the recipients, however deserving, do not provide the government with *goods and services* during the period. Private charitable contributions are not consumption, and collective contributions to the elderly and poor are not government expenditures.

Exports, which are foreign purchases of current goods and services, need little discussion. Wheat sales to Russia and the hotel expenses of foreign tourists are examples of exports. One may wonder why imports are subtracted to get GNP. Remember GNP is the output and expenditures for goods and services produced by a nation. The domestic sectors also purchase foreign goods, which are *already* included in consumption, investment, and government spending. Therefore, imports must be subtracted from exports in order to arrive at *national* product. For example, suppose you order a custom-made suit from Hong Kong. How does the purchase affect the GNP accounts? Consumption *and* imports increase, leaving GNP constant. If you had ordered a domestic suit instead, consumption and GNP increase. In principle, imports could be excluded from the other spending categories, thereby making it unnecessary to subtract them afterwards. Following such an approach would entail high data collection costs, however, because many imported goods are indistinguishable from domestic goods once they are off the docks.[1] Do you know if your shirt was made in the United States or abroad? Besides this very practical reason for including purchases of imported goods in the domestic spending categories (for example, consumption) and then subtracting total imports, one often wants a readily available summary of the net transactions with the rest of the world. Exports increase a nation's claims against the foreign sector. For example, sales by IBM of computers to a British firm might lead to larger IBM deposits in London banks. The larger deposits can be used to finance future purchases from British firms. Imports have the opposite effect; the claims of the rest of the world increase when we import. Net exports, exports minus imports, is a measure of foreign investment.[2] Just as investment is the acquisition of domestic capital goods which will yield services in the future, net exports give rise to claims against the rest of the world which can be used in the future to purchase goods and services.

Table 21–2 expresses the major expenditure components as a percentage of the total. The percentages have remained remarkably constant, with a few notable exceptions.

1. Consumption is by far the largest component of GNP. Households currently purchase approximately 65 percent of total production. The percentage fluctuates slightly with the business cycle but shows no long-run trend.

---

[1]Similarly, inspection of a domestically produced commodity does not necessarily suggest its expenditure category. True, all new homes are classified as investment, but a car could be included in any GNP component, depending on whether the purchaser is an individual, firm, governmental unit, or a foreigner.

[2]Net exports is not the only measure of foreign investment. Gifts, often called aid, from private citizens or the government to foreigners also increase the claims against a country. Net exports minus gifts to foreigners is traditionally called net foreign investment.

TABLE 21–2

GNP as Expenditures for Product, 1948–1984

Year	*Real GNP ($ billions)*	*Consumption (percent)*	*Investment (percent)*	*Government Expenditures (percent)*	*Exports (percent)*	*Imports (percent)*	*Net Exports (percent)*
1948	489.8	67.4	17.7	12.4	6.5	4.0	2.5
1950	534.8	67.1	18.8	13.5	4.9	4.2	0.7
1952	600.8	62.5	15.0	21.8	5.2	4.6	0.6
1954	616.1	64.4	14.4	20.7	4.9	4.4	0.5
1956	671.6	63.2	16.8	18.9	5.7	4.7	1.0
1958	680.9	64.5	13.8	21.2	5.2	4.6	0.6
1960	737.2	64.2	15.1	19.8	5.5	4.6	0.9
1962	800.3	62.9	15.1	20.9	5.4	4.5	0.9
1964	876.4	63.0	15.2	20.4	5.9	4.5	1.4
1966	984.8	61.7	16.5	21.7	5.7	5.0	0.7
1968	1058.1	61.7	15.1	22.9	5.7	5.5	0.2
1970	1085.6	63.0	14.3	22.3	6.4	6.0	0.4
1972	1185.9	62.6	16.1	21.6	6.2	6.5	−0.3
1974	1248.0	62.9	15.2	21.4	9.8	9.3	0.5
1976	1300.4	64.1	14.2	21.2	9.5	9.1	0.4
1978	1436.9	63.5	16.5	20.5	9.7	10.2	−0.5
1980	1480.7	63.6	15.0	20.4	13.0	11.9	1.1
1982	1485.4	64.8	13.5	21.1	11.3	10.7	0.6
1984	1639.9	63.9	17.4	20.4	10.0	11.7	−1.7

Source: *Economic Report of the President* and Federal Reserve *Bulletin,* various issues.

2. Investment as a proportion of GNP fell *slightly* in the postwar period. The decline is partially masked by its volatility. Investment is a small fraction of GNP, averaging approximately 15 percent, so any fall is a large proportional change. For example, if the investment/GNP ratio falls 2 percentage points from 15 to 13 percent, this is more than a 13 percent (2/15) decline in the relative importance of investment.

3. Following World War II government expenditures for goods and services fell precipitously, from approximately 39 percent of GNP in 1945 to 13 percent in 1946. The percentage remained at the low level until the Korean War (1952), when government expenditures rose to approximately 22 percent. While wars invariably increase government spending, a unique feature of the Korean War was the failure of total government spending to revert to its prewar level. The decline in the relative importance of defense expenditures was countered by other federal expenditures and especially state and local government spending, so total government spending on goods and services remained steady at 20 to 22 percent. The percentage did *not* decline during the Reagan administration. Because investment and government expenditures are small fractions of GNP, a

small decline in the investment share of GNP and an increase in the government share translate into a large change in the relative importance of these two expenditure categories. In the late 1940s government expenditures were less than investment, but government expenditures were approximately 35 percent larger than investment in the 1980s.

4. Imports and to a lesser extent exports increased sharply compared to GNP. Most developed economies were in shambles following World War II. As a result, imports to the United States were unusually low and exports by the United States were unusually large. Net exports in the late 1940s were approximately 2 to 3 percent of GNP. In the 1950s and 1960s exports more or less kept pace with GNP, imports grew somewhat faster, and net exports seldom exceeded 1 percent. *Foreign trade veritably exploded in the 1970s*. The export share of GNP nearly doubled, substantially surpassing the high percentage of exports following World War II. More and costlier oil is the most important factor behind the import rise. Wheat sales one year, an oil embargo the next year, and huge deficits another year have made *net exports more volatile, but there is little indication of a significant long-run change in the importance of net exports*. Net exports were negative in 1983 and are even more so today in 1984, but a couple of observations do not necessarily indicate a trend. Net exports also were negative in 1972 but then rebounded sharply. Table 21–2 shows a very significant foreign surplus in 1980.

We shall postpone analysis of the balance of payments and international finance until the very end. As a result, throughout much of the subsequent theoretical analysis, we refrain from *explicitly* analyzing exports and imports. Particularly in the Keynesian sections where investment is largely autonomous, investment plus exports are considered one component, and consumption minus imports are another component. At some places, however, exports and imports are analyzed explicitly, and then investment and consumption are not "adjusted."

GNP as Income

Expenditures on goods and services produced by a nation are the receipts of producers, which (*a*) pay households for supplying labor and other factors of production, (*b*) pay taxes, and (*c*) retain some receipts as profits. Since we are measuring *national* product, all the income accrues to the three domestic sectors. Households also pay taxes, which may be thought of as government income. Thus, the total amount spent is distributed and becomes income. Symmetry with the expenditure side suggests that GNP viewed as the distribution of receipts be expressed as the sum of household disposable income (household income minus taxes), business disposable income, and government income or, more simply, taxes. We then have income and expenditures of three domestic sectors. However, the subsequent theoretical models disregard the division of private income between households and business. Since we view the GNP accounts as an aid to the theoretical models, we immediately consolidate the household and business sectors when looking at GNP as the distribution of receipts. The division of income between the private sector and government is important.

$$Y \equiv Py \equiv Y_d + T \tag{21–3}$$

where Y_d is private disposable income, and T is taxes. Since *private disposable income is GNP minus taxes,* Equation (21–3) is true by definition. *Household* disposable income is approximately 85 percent of *private* disposable income; business income, which includes depreciation allowances, makes up the remainder. Subsequent exposition is simplified by talking as if disposable private income accrues entirely to the household sector.

Transfer payments, which are not included in government expenditures, are treated as negative taxes and subtracted from gross tax revenues to get net taxes. The effect of government on the private income stream is measured by net taxes. Taxes reduce private disposable income, and Social Security benefits, relief payments, and other transfers increase disposable income. The symbol T in Equation (21–3) represents net taxes.

Table 21–3 shows the income side of GNP. Column 1, private disposable income, plus column 2, net taxes, sum to 100. The private income

TABLE 21–3

GNP as Income from Production and Deficits, 1948–1984 (All as percent of GNP.)

Year	(1) Private Disposable Income	(2) Net Taxes	(3) Gross Taxes	(4) Transfer Payments	(5) Government Saving (−, deficit)
1948	84.4	15.6	22.2	6.6	3.2
1950	83.7	16.3	23.6	7.3	2.8
1952	79.3	20.7	26.0	5.3	−1.1
1954	78.6	21.4	27.2	5.8	−0.7
1956	79.9	20.1	26.1	6.0	1.2
1958	81.6	18.4	25.7	7.3	−2.8
1960	79.6	20.4	27.5	7.1	0.6
1962	79.7	20.3	27.8	7.5	−0.6
1964	80.0	20.0	27.3	7.3	−0.4
1966	78.8	21.2	28.2	7.0	−0.5
1968	77.8	22.2	30.3	8.1	−0.7
1970	78.6	21.4	30.9	9.5	−0.9
1972	78.7	21.3	31.4	10.1	−0.3
1974	78.8	21.2	32.2	11.0	−0.2
1976	80.9	19.1	31.4	12.3	−2.2
1978	79.5	20.5	32.3	11.8	0.0
1980	81.0	19.0	31.7	12.7	−1.4
1982	82.7	17.3	29.5	12.2	−3.8
1984	82.9	17.1	28.5	11.4	−3.3

Source: *Economic Report of the President* and Federal Reserve *Bulletin*, various issues.

share equaled about 84 percent during the late 1940s, fell to somewhat less than 80 percent by 1952, and remained at that level until the early 1980s, when recessions and the Reagan tax cuts brought it back almost to the level of the late 1940s. Of course, net taxes followed a converse pattern. Like the change in the investment and government relationship, the small absolute decline in disposable income translated into a large relative increase in net taxes, which may explain the loud uproar about taxes in the late 1970s. The net tax share of GNP increased by a quarter from approximately 16 to 20 percent between the late 1940s and 1970s. Moreover, government is redistributing a larger proportion of GNP. *Gross taxes and transfer payments as a proportion of GNP rose more sharply than net taxes.* See columns 3 and 4.

The last column shows total (federal and local) government saving, the difference between net taxes and expenditures on goods and services. The almost unbroken string of negative numbers since 1962 indicates that government is a perennial dissaver or, equivalently, usually runs a deficit. *The absolute and relative size of the 1980s deficit is unusual, however.* Deficits are absolutely larger than they ever were even during World War II and, in spite of economic growth, are a significantly larger fraction of GNP than in any other peacetime year. The *federal* deficit is even larger than the all-government deficit shown in column 5; state and local governments had a large surplus.

The large tax cuts of the early 1980s naturally reduced the gross taxes/GNP percentage.[3] Since we previously mentioned that the share of government expenditures on goods and services did *not* decline during the early 1980s (see Table 21–2), and Table 21–3 shows that the transfer payments percentage declined only slightly, a large absolute and relative deficit was inevitable.

Equilibrium Conditions

Stating truisms and definitions is not a waste of time if it provides some insight to the solution of a problem. Seemingly trite observations like peanuts sold equal peanuts bought and the price paid by buyers is the price received by sellers ultimately led to an important conclusion: supply of and demand for peanuts determine its quantity and price. Peanut quantity and price are at *equilibrium* when *desired* sales equal *desired* purchases. The same is true for GNP, which is nothing other than the sum of all commodities. Expressing GNP as spending and production emphasizes that actual GNP depends on the interaction of demand *and* supply

[3]We shall see in the next chapter that lower tax rates may increase dollar tax receipts even though the tax share of GNP falls. For additional data on the federal deficit, see Chapter 34.

for all commodities. With exports (X) and imports (Z) subsumed in investment and consumption, respectively, the equilibrium condition is

$$C + I + G = Y \tag{21–4}$$

Ignoring X and Z, Equations (21–2) and (21–4) look quite similar but they make entirely different statements. Equation (21–2) says that during any time period *actual* expenditures on current goods and services equal *actual* production. Equation (21–4) says that prices and output remain constant when *desired* spending equals *desired* production. Compact expression is the purpose of algebraic equations, but algebra is almost too compact in this case. We try to indicate the very different statements being made by Equations (21–2) and (21–4) by using the identity symbol (≡) when referring to actual magnitudes and the equality symbol (=) when referring to desired magnitudes. Many authors do not make even this distinction; then, actual and desired magnitudes are distinguished only by the verbal discussion surrounding the equations.

Does Equation (21–4) hold at all times? Is desired spending always equal to desired production? Of course not. If desired spending is greater than desired production, output and/or prices will increase. In subsequent chapters we analyze whether output, prices, or some combination of the two will increase. For the moment, assume prices are rigid and only output increases. Why does output increase when desired expenditures exceed desired production, and why do actual expenditures always equal actual production? For simplicity, assume no government or foreign sector. Suppose desired consumption is $80, and desired inventory accumulation investment is $30. Actual and desired production during the period is $100. Therefore, desired expenditures exceed production by $10. What happens? Firms stand ready to meet the demand of households, who succeed in purchasing commodities worth $80. Since production equaled $100 and consumption is $80, actual inventory investment is $20, which is $10 less than the desired amount. Actual expenditures equal actual production. Why did *firms* produce commodities worth $100 when *firms and households* wanted to purchase commodities worth $110? Economic units are unaware of the plans of other economic units. If firms knew that desired consumption was $80, they would have produced commodities worth $110 in order to invest $30. Presumably, firms thought desired consumption was $70. How do firms react to their underestimate of demand? They increase production; prices are rigid, by assumption. Since actual investment was $10 less than desired investment when production was $100, firms might produce commodities worth $110, anticipating that the previous $10 short-fall in investment will be corrected. This probably is not the end of the story as the higher production, employment, and household income could well cause consumption to rise above $80. Subsequent chapters discuss in full the so-called multiplier. For our purposes the story can end here; we simply wanted to show why production increases when it is less than desired spending. Summarizing this example.

$C + I + G > Y$	desired values
$80 + 30 + 0 > 100$	desired values
$80 + 20 + 0 \equiv 100$	actual values

Can the following inequality hold?

$$C + I + G < Y. \tag{21–5}$$

Certainly. Indeed, the unusual case is represented by Equation (21–4). Most of the time the economy is not in equilibrium; prices and/or output often are changing. The law of symmetry usually holds in economics. Reversing the argument in the preceding paragraph, prices and/or output fall when inequality (21–5) holds.

Reasons for Monetary Disagreements

What effects do money and finance have on real GNP, its components, and prices? Although economics is said to have been born in 1776 with the publication of Adam Smith's *The Wealth of Nations,* our discipline celebrated its bicentennial without final and conclusive answers to such a fundamental issue as the relationship between money and policy goals. Chapter 1 stated various *non*economic reasons for monetary disagreements. More interesting from our viewpoint are the "purely" economic reasons for disagreement. First, *economists, unlike chemists and some other natural scientists, cannot perform controlled experiments*. In a controlled experiment a chemist may raise temperature 25° or add 2 grams of sulfur while holding everything else constant. In this manner the effect of heat or sulfur is learned quite precisely. The monetary authority cannot hold everything else constant while changing the quantity of money. While the money supply is changing, OPEC is raising oil prices, a drought is reducing farm output by 5 percent, defense expenditures are increasing, and so on. Suppose output also changes during the period. Did money or the defense expenditures or something else cause the output variation? Economists attempt to answer such questions with statistics.

Data, Computers, and Statistics

Statistical tests are relatively few and recent because (*a*) economic data and (*b*) computational facilities were lacking for many years. *Due to a lack of data, economics in its first 160 years was unable to judge competing theories of the relationship between money, output, and other goals*. It was only in the 1930s that Simon Kuznets, with the aid of others, constructed GNP estimates, a pathfinding endeavor which subsequently earned him a Nobel prize. While for many purposes Adam Smith should retain his title to paternity of economics, empirical economics in general, and the evaluation of money-income theories in particular, might better be dated from the 1930s work of the relatively obscure Simon Kuznets. Empirical economics is a modern science which has had less than 50 years to evaluate complex issues.

Early empirical work was extremely crude by modern standards. Economists themselves were dissatisfied with their work. *Monetary relationships are complex, and economists realized they lacked the statistical techniques and computational tools necessary to analyze large masses of data*. For all intents and purposes, *the* computational tool—the Almighty Computer—was not born until approximately 1960. Moreover, old computers, like people, are quickly overpowered by the new generation. A large 1960 computer was little more powerful than a sophisticated modern electronic hand calculator! Bred in an environment where theories could not be evaluated until the 1930s, and then only simplistically until 1960, positions hardened and biases developed.

Two radically different schools of monetary-macroeconomists existed in 1960, classicists and Keynesians. Classicists trace their roots to Adam Smith, other founders of economics, and, more contemporaneously, the 1936 "orthodox" economists, whom Keynes labeled classicists. No other economics book has had the impact of John Maynard Keynes's 1936 book, *The General Theory of Employment, Interest, and Money*. It revolutionized economics and still is the inspirational book of Keynesianism. Until 1960 neither school could be proven wrong due to data and computational limitations, and both had equal chances of being right.

In some respects classical and Keynesian economics are competing *general* theories which analyze the relationships among *many* variables. Neither is a specific theory concerning only one relationship, say, the effect of interest rates on the demand for money. Keynesian and classical economics contain many elements. Originally, some of the elements of the two theories were diametrically contradictory. For example, classicists stated monetary expansion *always* causes proportional nominal income changes, and early Keynesians suggested money has no effect on either real income or prices. *The availability of data and computational tools in the early 1960s had a profound effect on economics: it produced empirical evidence which convincingly contradicted extreme positions*. In response, the theories have been modified to make them more similar. This was the appropriate response. *Theories are judged mainly on the basis of their explanatory and predictive powers*. The response prompted Milton Friedman, the leading modern exponent of classical ideas, to say, "In one sense, we are all Keynesians now; in another no one is a Keynesian any longer."[4] *Economists currently are both classicists and Keynesians in the sense that some of the diametrically contradictory elements of the two theories have been disavowed in light of better empirical evidence.* Everyone now concedes that money matters; the magnitude of monetary effects is the current issue between neoclassicists and Keynesians. In other words, economists have reached consensus on true and false questions but disagree on multiple choice questions regarding how much, how long, how often, and so on. The days of stock answers to difficult economic questions fortunately are gone.

The reader must largely accept on faith that the moderate, modified versions of classical economics, which thus became neoclassical economics, and the modern Keynesian economics presented in this book enjoy considerable empirical support. This book summarizes and evaluates only a few empirical studies of the relationship among economic variables. Our main objective is a critical evaluation of the assumptions and logical structure of the neoclassical and Keynesian models. We hope that such a critical evaluation may suggest how future empirical studies should proceed. Knowledge of assumptions and their correspondence to reality may well provide a clue about future definitive empirical results. Empirical economics not grounded in theory and history flourishes in a chaos congenial to its mentality.

Time and Economic Adjustments

Consensus on some issues and the cooling of passions have led to a better understanding of monetary economics in general and classical and Keynesian economics in particular. Hard as it is to believe, many monetary-macroeconomists of the 1940s and 1950s lost sight of the undeniable fact that *adjustments to any disturbance take place over time*. A change in the quantity of money or some other initial condition does not cause sharp, if perhaps somewhat delayed, once-and-for-all jumps in dependent variables such as income, prices, and the rate of interest. Instead, the dependent variables respond more or less continuously over time. An ideal theory *readily* predicts the exact time path of the economic variables. Our world is less than ideal in many respects. Dynamic theories describing motion are complex. Simplicity dictates some approximation to movement over time.

Economists like moviemakers attempt to capture movement over time by a series of snapshots—a movie is just a series of still pictures. Classical and Keynesian models are examples of snapshots focused faraway and nearby, respectively. Technically speaking, *classical economics is a long-*

---

[4]Milton Friedman, *Dollars and Deficits* (Englewood Cliffs, N.J.: Prentice Hall, 1968), p. 15.

run static model, while Keynesian economics is a short-run static model. Time and motion seemingly do not exist in static models. Given some set of assumptions, which vary by time period, supply and demand curves are constructed. The static, snapshot models then determine equilibrium values at one moment in time and compare alternative equilibria as the exogenous variables change. These models do not describe in detail how one moves from one equilibrium to another. Because time seemingly is absent from static models, some economists forgot that classical economics attempts to explain the long run and Keynesian economics the short run. These economists thought the two models were strictly competitive, both attempting to explain the same period. In this case different conclusions occur because one model is correct and the other is wrong.

Again, hard as it is to believe, *for many years economists thought that only one series of snapshots was necessary. We supposedly needed either the classical long run or the Keynesian short run.* This sometimes is the case but often is not. Look at Figure 21–2. At time zero, some "shock" (change in initial conditions) occurs and disturbs variables X and Z. The light dotted and dark dashed lines in Figure 21–2 show the time path of

FIGURE 21–2

The time path of X and Z changes measured from their initial values; (lines showing the difference between the values of X and Z over time and their initial values).

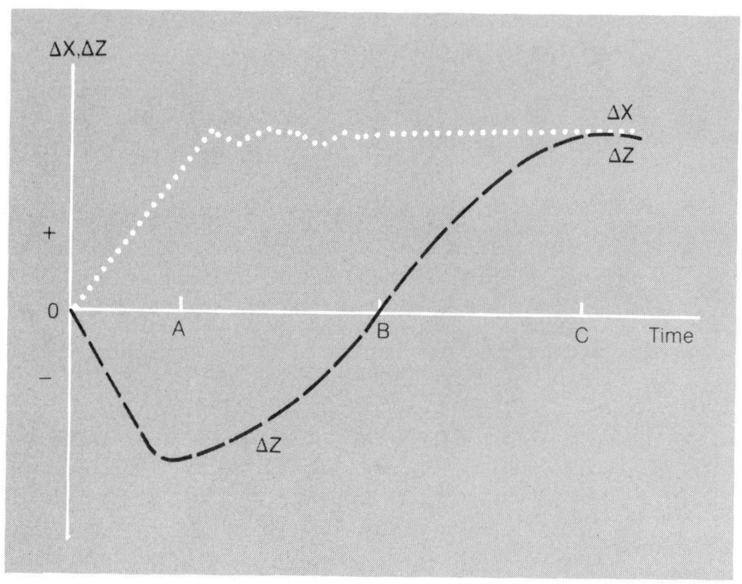

X and Z changes, respectively, measured from their initial values. In other words, the lines for X and Z show the differences between their current and initial values over time. The snapshot at some moment gives us one dot or dash while a movie films the entire dotted or dashed line.

Any single dot describes relatively accurately the position of the entire dotted line. One snapshot, static model, satisfactorily describes X changes. The same is *not* true of Z changes. One snapshot at time A, showing that the shock reduces Z, is deceiving since it ignores that the shock ultimately increases Z. One snapshot at time C is equally deceiving since one might well conclude the shock always causes Z to increase. We need at least two snapshots, at times A and C, to describe the time path of Z, and possibly three snapshots, at times A, B, and C. *Many economic variables have a time path like Z.*

The classical model is a *long-run* static model which takes a snapshot at time C. For 160 years, from 1776 to 1936, economists had only a long-run model taking its snapshot at time C. We owe Keynes a huge debt. The Keynesian model is a *short-run* model, taking its snapshot at time A. *The debate immediately following Keynes's pioneering study centered on which model, the long-run classical or short-run Keynesian, best described the average change over time.* Should we take *one* snapshot at time A or C? One had to choose sides; fence straddling was forbidden. *The debate was silly.* Fence straddling is now respectable. We are all Keynesians now, and no one is a Keynesian any longer for a second reason: *we now recognize that both neoclassical and modern Keynesian economics are necessary to describe changes over time.* While the two schools compete in some respects, they also are complementary, together approximating the changes that occur over time. When one recognizes the different time element implicit in the two models, they may *correctly* arrive at opposite conclusions. For variables like Z in Figure 21–2, Keynesians say policy is contractionary (in the short run) and classicists say it is expansionary (in the long run). Our economic film is still quite jerky. Two or three snapshots—a Keynesian short-run, a classical long-run and possibly an intermediate run linking the short and long—describe movement over time. Movies (economic dynamics, technically speaking) are too difficult to develop.

A concrete example close to home vividly illustrates how dependent answers are to the time period. Should you remain in college or immediately enter the labor market? Assume for simplicity that "culture" and other intangibles acquired at college are unimportant. The sole objective in going to college is to learn skills valued in the market and, thereby, increase one's lifetime earnings. Do the additional earnings of graduates justify the investment in a college education? What is the rate of return on a college education? Answers to these questions depend on the time horizon. Although data on earnings due to a college education are not

FIGURE 21–3
Relationship between the Rate of Return on a College Education and Years in the Labor Force

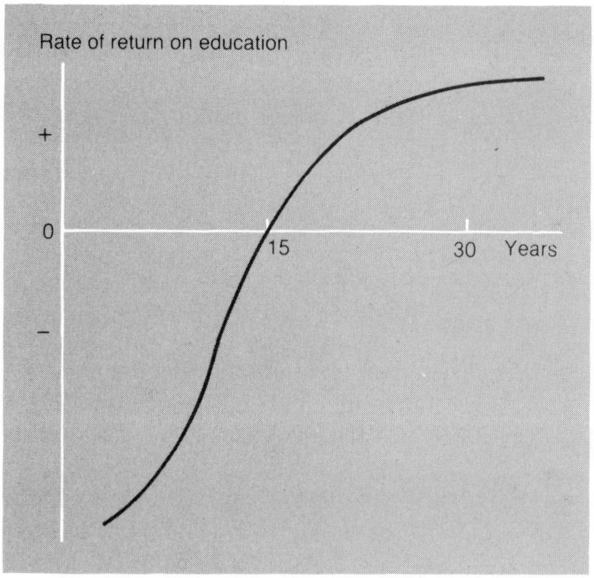

completely reliable, there is general agreement on the overall shape of the rate of return curve graphed in Figure 21–3. The policy tool in this example is a college education, and time begins at graduation and entrance into the labor market. A college education is an unwise venture for those who spend only a few years in the labor market. It takes about 15 years to recover all costs, the out-of-pocket cost for tuition and other items and the opportunity cost of earnings foregone while in college. The rate of return on a college education becomes positive beyond 15 years and exceeds the average rate of return on other investments when one remains in the labor market at least 30 years. The remain-in-college or enter-the-labor-market question is only one of many economic issues dependent on the time horizon.

A Preview of the Neoclassical/Keynesian Consensus

A complete presentation of modern classical and Keynesian economics is both long and difficult. To aid the reader, this very brief preview of the following six chapters states without any proof many essential features of the two schools. Those with less interest in economic theory should read this preview and a few chapters, perhaps those with conclusions difficult to accept without proof. While this preview may reduce the positive joy of discovery for those who plan to read all six chapters, it more often should reduce unpreparedness and the negative elements of surprise. Because Keynesian economics was wrapped in criticism of classical economics, we begin with the latter. Pride of place should not be misinterpreted as favoring classical economics. *Both* schools of thought are correct. While classical economics comes first, Keynesian economics is given more space.

Chapter 22 explains the two basic propositions of classical economics: Say's law and the quantity theory of money. An ordinary supply and demand graph for commodities helps focus quite sharply on many basic ideas in this preview. More informative but more complicated graphs will be developed in subsequent chapters. According to Say's law, the supply of commodities in the long run is perfectly inelastic (vertical) at full-employment output, given a *fixed* number of workers and technology. In terms of Figure 21–4, the relevant supply curve is S_L. With a perfectly vertical supply curve, demand fluctuations only influence prices. The quantity theory says that money is the only *policy* variable that influences demand and, therefore, prices. Different views concerning the determinants of supply are analyzed carefully since they distinguish from mainstream neoclassicists a splinter group, the so-called supply siders. This group's stock was greatly boosted by the election of President Reagan. Supply siders, but not mainstream neoclassicists, claim that tax reductions significantly increase output by shifting the supply curve rightward. Taxes are ineffective so long as they only influence demand.

Chapter 23 looks deeper at the quantity theory proposition that money has a strong and predictable effect on demand. In terms of Figure 21–4, Chapter 23 attempts to prove that monetary expansion always shifts the demand curve *far* rightward by the *same* amount. It also attempts to demonstrate why the demand curve intersects the supply curve at a feasible point so the supply-determined full-employment output is produced. (A demand curve that intersects S_L at a negative price is not a feasible solution.)

Chapter 24 is the first of four chapters on *Keynesian economics, where demand creates its own supply.* The supply curve in the Keynesian short run is the perfectly elastic (flat) S_S in Figure 21–4. After stating other fundamental assumptions of Keynesian economics, we review the "basic" $C + I + G = y$ Keynesian model. The model is "basic" because all demands, C, I, and G are either autonomous or dependent only on income, and this simple demand creates its own supply.

Review of the basic model facilitates understanding Chapter 25's advanced Keynesian model, which introduces the demand for and supply of money and interest rates effects on commodity demand. Chapter 25 discusses Keynes's money demand and modern extensions by William Baumol (inventory theoretic approach) and James Tobin (portfolio approach). The interaction between the commodities and financial markets

FIGURE 21–4
Aggregate Demand and Supply

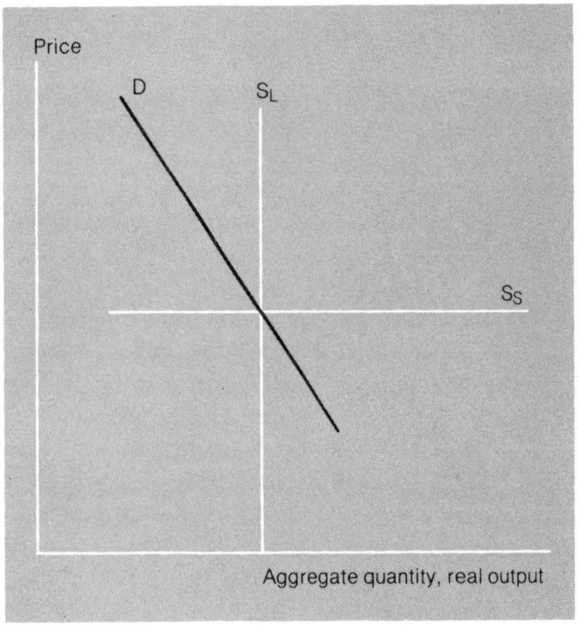

is explored using IS–LM machinery, a compact way of representing the advanced Keynesian model. Although its compactness makes understanding the IS–LM curves somewhat difficult, they are almost indispensable for analyzing more complex subsequent issues.

Chapter 26 examines within the IS–LM framework the determinants of the impact of monetary and fiscal policy on real GNP. We highlight the determinants that have differential impacts on monetary and fiscal policy. Keynesians place much less emphasis on monetary policy.

Chapter 27 analyzes some neoclassical/Keynesian differences, again within the IS–LM framework. We illustrate the extreme cases which so sharply divided the profession until 1960. We also show that recognition of the models' different time periods reconciles some apparent discrepancies. In particular, the Keynesian proposition that monetary expansion lowers interest rates and the classical proposition that permanent monetary expansion and inflation raise interest rates are consistent irrespective of the form of the demand for money. Monetary expansion lowers interest rates in the short run and raises them in the long run.

I suspect that many will want to sample both classical and Keynesian economics by reading Chapters 22 and 24–26, respectively. Others may prefer to concentrate on one school of thought and time period and just dabble in the other, e.g., read Chapters 22–24. *The only requirement is that both the classical and Keynesian sections be read in order.* For example, you can skip classical Chapter 23 and go directly to Keynesian Chapter 24, but do not attempt to read Keynesian Chapter 27 unless you read Keynesian Chapter 26.

Summary/Questions

During a given period of time the goods and services produced must be acquired by some group, possibly producers themselves. The GNP accounts tell us how much was produced and what group acquired the goods and services. Production in the United States more than tripled during the postwar period. The proportion of commodities acquired by household and businesses decreased while government expenditures increased its share of GNP. The GNP accounts do not tell us why production is one amount and not a different amount. They also do not tell us if GNP will be increasing or decreasing. Nevertheless, an understanding of the GNP accounts is a necessary first step. We must know where we are before analyzing why we are there and where we are going.

The following chapters examine the determinants of desired expenditures and production. What do desired expenditures equal? How can we change desired expenditures? These questions are of utmost importance because actual production and prices respond to desired values. If desired expenditures exceed actual expenditures and production, production and/or prices will increase as firms respond to the demand for commodities. When production ultimately equals desired expenditures, everyone can be satisfied and the price/output structure will be maintained.

Answers to the questions raised in the last paragraph are controversial today and, most probably, for all time. On the other hand, current disagreements are less intense today than 25 years ago. Empirical tests made possible by recently available data and computers have conclusively contradicted extreme positions on all fronts. Heightened awareness that economic policy works over time and that something true in the short run need not be true in the long run has also reduced economic disagreements and broadened the vision of economists. The issue no longer is the classical long run *or* the Keynesian short run. The issue is: are the classical long run *and* the Keynesian short run adequate? I think so, even though the two together still do not explain numerous economic events.

1. State the main trends in post-World War II nominal GNP, real GNP, and the GNP price index. How do the postwar trends compare with prewar trends?

2. What are the traditional components of total expenditures? What types of items are included in each component?
3. Which of the following items is an example of investment: (*a*) purchase of 19th-century gold coins, (*b*) construction of a vacation home, (*c*) purchase of land to build a vacation home, (*d*) purchase of oriental rugs, (*e*) purchase of common stock, (*f*) purchase of a new U.S.–made car by a car rental firm, and (*g*) purchase of a new car by a teacher?
4. What are the main trends in the relative importance of the GNP expenditure components?
5. What explains the differences in the trends of the government expenditures component of GNP and total government spending for whatever reason?
6. Can actual expenditures exceed actual production? Can desired expenditures exceed production? What adjustments occur when expenditures exceed production?
7. Discuss the trend in the government deficit.
8. What are the two main reasons for the small number of statistical studies prior to 1960 on the relationships among money, GNP, and other policy goals? What has been the impact of the recent statistical studies on monetary theory?
9. In what senses are we all Keynesians now, and in what senses is no one a Keynesian any longer?
10. Explain how classical and Keynesian economics are complementary *static* theories, jointly approximating a *dynamic* theory. What are the time frames of classical and Keynesian economics?
11. Is the effect of monetary policy on output and prices the same throughout time? Is even the qualitative effect, that is, positive or negative, of a policy dependent on the time period elapsed? If so, give several examples.

Fundamentals of neoclassical economics

22

Keynes so exaggerated J. B. Say's mistakes that if Say were alive, he would turn over in his grave.

Economists like other social scientists do not live in a vacuum. Theory, application, and politics interact. A laissez-faire philosophy and politics spawned the theory of comparative advantage and a free trade policy. Theories are constructed to explain current issues and policies, and current issues test the validity of theories. This principle explains the newer offerings of many economic departments, which include courses in computer models, pollution, and women's issues. Moreover, important developments in one area of economics influence the analysis in other areas. What were the most important economic events between 1776 and 1936? There is no correct answer but surely everyone would include the Industrial Revolution, growth of income in *selected* countries accompanied by stagnation in others, and increased international trade partially due to colonization. As the interaction of theory and application suggests, the early classical economists emphasized international economics and what is now called development economics. This emphasis influenced classical monetary analysis in the early as well as later period when interests widened. Indeed, classical monetary economics is incomprehensible without a digression on growth and development.

What were the causes of the Industrial Revolution and growth of income in selected European countries, Canada, and the United States? We do not expect a definitive answer to a much debated question. But before reading the next paragraph, pause at least a few minutes and list some important factors.

What sources of income growth did you list? Most classicists and modern development economists mention a larger capital stock generated by saving and, of course, investment. Capital is one of the factors of production. Its growth increases income. Capital accumulation takes the form of more factories, machines, and supporting transportation and communications systems. Growth of the labor force, another factor of production, is mentioned less frequently because it may cause divergent movements of income per capita and total income. A larger population and labor force may well reduce income per capita as additional workers tilling the same soil produce less than the average worker. Nevertheless, additional workers produce something, and GNP rises. Current total income would be much lower had the United States closed its borders in 1776. Growth requires not just more but better factors of production. Innovations and inventions, often called technological progress, increase the productivity of labor and capital goods. Education and technical and vocational training are other extremely important sources of income growth. The importance of a better educated and generally more skillful labor force is particularly obvious after a war, when seemingly devastated countries quickly return to their status as world powers. Primitive tools are more useful than the latest generation computers in unskilled hands. Entrepreneurship, a big word for a willingness to take risks and that little understood talent for management and organization, produces better mouse traps and economic growth. The so-called Protestant ethic which causes people to work hard is an additional cause of income growth.

We could expand the sources of growth but our purpose has been served. Since output and income is determined by the intersection of supply and demand, the sources of growth can be classified as supply factors or demand factors. Reread your and our lists of the sources of growth. Would you classify the overwhelming proportion of sources as supply or demand factors? Supply factors are dominant. A larger capital stock and labor force, technological progress, a better educated labor force, a stronger entrepreneurial spirit, better organization and management, and a continual willingness to work all increase supply. As stated, actual income and output is determined by the intersection of demand and supply. *The classicists thought demand was insatiable. Income increased mainly because the supply curve shifted outward and one moved along a demand curve.*

Income and output growth was hardly uniform in the classical period, like today. Most countries grew little if at all. Although early economic statistics are sketchy and not very reliable, it appears the distribution of income among countries was more skewed in 1936 than 1776. Why did some countries stagnate while others grew? Unfortunately, supply conditions prevented growth in most countries. Income stagnated in most countries in spite of an almost universal desire for consumer goods. True, income does not grow when demand is lacking and the population prefers to commune with nature and gambol through the woods wearing ashen cloth and eating wild berries. But this idyllic picture hardly represents underdeveloped countries, where labor typically works harder and longer but produces less because capital, skills, and entrepreneurship are scarce.

Essential Features of Classical Economics

Let's leave the past and come to the present. Suppose you are an economic advisor to an underdeveloped country. What growth policies would you prescribe? Would you recommend that the government encourage saving by creating government-sponsored financial intermediaries, build roads, support education and technical and vocational training, and dislodge bottlenecks hampering industry and agriculture? Alternatively, would you recommend a massive welfare program financed by additional money creation and a wide-ranging advertising campaign to whet appetites for luxuries? The choice of policies is obvious: prescribe the former and proscribe the latter. One set of policies stimulates aggregate supply while the latter stimulates demand. But aggregate demand is not deficient in underdeveloped countries. Supply constrains output. However desirable income redistribution may be, massive welfare payments which increase aggregate demand have little effect on output growth.

Say's Law

This fundamental classical belief that demand is insatiable is succinctly summarized by Say's Law: supply creates its own demand. Brevity often causes confusion. Adding a short phrase would make Say's Law less controversial. As just stated, the validity of many propositions depends on the time period of the analysis. History shows that supply creates its own demand *in the long run*. Look at Figure 22–1. The concept of full employment or maximum sustainable output is not precise. Nonetheless, examination of long historical records shows actual output paralleling the steady growth of full-employment output, with the former sometimes falling short and occasionally overshooting the latter. Classicists were optimistic that history would repeat itself. Demand will remain insatiable. The upward movement of productive capacity will drag demand along.

There is a business cycle, and recessions do occur.[1] No proof beyond recessions is necessary to establish that *supply does not create its own*

[1]Characterization of similar events varies over time. Economic downturns in classical times were crises and panics. Herbert Hoover thought this term too emotional and frightening. He said a *depression* accurately described economic conditions during his administration, 1929–33. The economy lacked vigor and spirits were low, but people were not hysterical and irrational. Following World War II, Herbert Hoover's calming depression became too alarming. The economy never was depressed, just recessed. By the 1970s recessions were outlawed by the political party in power. We now have rolling readjustments and growth pauses.

FIGURE 22–1
Actual and Full-Employment Trend GNP, 1900–1983

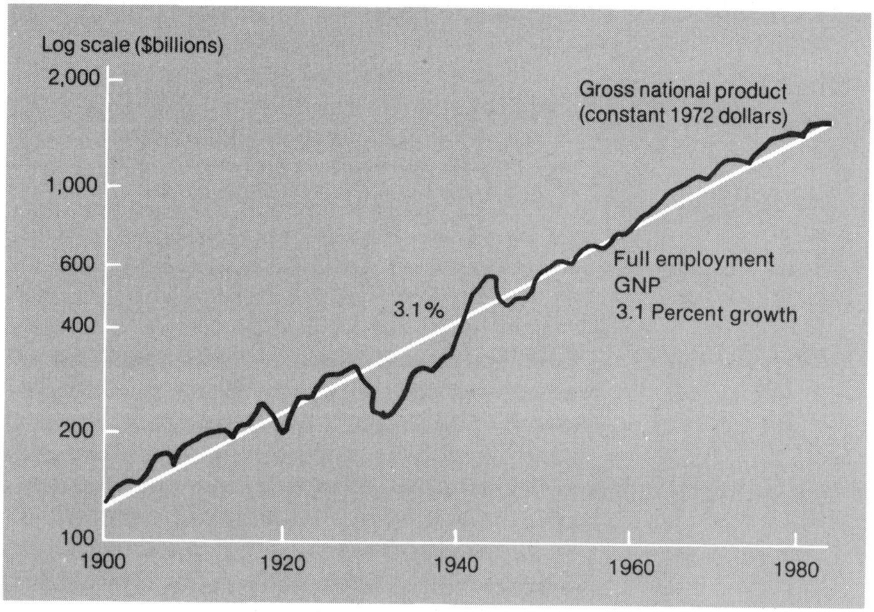

Source: Federal Reserve, *Historical Chart Book, 1983*.

demand in the short run. When methodological and philosophical divisions were keen among economists, quotation after quotation was dissected in an attempt to determine the time period implicit in Say's statement. True, one can find passages in J. B. Say's *Treatise* suggesting a *crude (and incorrect) version of Say's Law: supply creates its own demand at all times*. One can also find passages where Say recognizes that his law of markets is valid only in the long run. In any case, Say was not a great thinker and influential policymaker. He merits more than a toenote in history of economic thought textbooks precisely because Keynes rescued him from oblivion by attributing the crude version of Say's Law to all classicists. But were all classical economists dummies? Were they so oblivious to the real world that they alone failed to recognize recessions obvious to all? We think not. David Ricardo, the leading economist around 1800, certainly was a practical man. He made a fortune on the London Stock Exchange. John Stuart Mill was much more influential than Say; Mill was perhaps the most influential economist between 1830 and 1870. A child prodigy who suffered repeated bouts of psychological depression, Mill was not the most practical of men. Yet even he recognized the existence of economic depressions and the limitations of Say's Law in the short run.

> Although he who sells, really sells to buy, he need not buy at the same moment when he sells: and he does not therefore necessarily add to the *immediate* demand for one commodity when he adds to the supply of another. The buying and selling [in a monetary economy] being now separated, it may very well occur, that there may be, at some given time, a very general inclination to sell with as little delay as possible, accompanied with an equally general inclination to defer all purchases as long as possible . . . [W]hen there is a general anxiety to sell, and a general disinclination to buy, commodities of all kinds remain for a long time unsold, and those which find an immediate market, do so at a very low price. . . . It is true that this state can be only temporary, . . . and is generally followed by more than common briskness of demand.[2]

We believe the Mill passage correctly represents sometimes contradictory and unclear classical views. Some may think that we are overly generous to classical economists. At this late date, however, let us study classical theory for its truths and ignore any possible errors. This is not a book in the history of economic theory; classical theory, like every other theory, is worthy of detailed study only if it is accurate. *The classical model presented here assumes Say's Law does hold in the long run but not in the short run.*

Granting that classicists recognized that Say's Law holds only in the long run is not much of a concession. The important point is: how long is the long run? What *calendar* period of time corresponds with the *economic* concept of the long run? Classical economists unfortunately never answered the timing questions explicitly. The short and long periods mark off particular initial conditions (e.g., profit maximization), reactions, and adjustments such as market clearing and price flexibility. *Markets may not clear in the short run as prices are rigid. In the long run, however, markets clear as prices adjust.* The short period is chronologically shorter than the long period, and that is all classicists stated. (Fortunately, the periods were not reversed to really confuse matters.) The clock time of the short and long period is not a theoretical question. Empirical analysis—looking at the facts—is essential.

Although never stated explicitly, classical writings hint at the clock time of the short and long period.[3] Some classicists wrote as if Say's Law

---

[2] J. S. Mill, *Essays on Some Unsettled Questions of Political Economy* (London: John W. Parker, 1844), pp. 70–71. Italics in original.

[3] Failure to answer timing questions is not a uniquely classical sin and continues today. Recall your typical microeconomic principles course. Theories of the firm and industry emphasize the short and long run. The amount of capital and number of firms are fixed in the short run but vary in the long run. No principles or advanced theory text states the calendar time during which capital and the number of firms are fixed. The length of the short run might well depend on the specific industry. The short run probably is chronologically shorter in the garment industry than the steel industry, where efficient production requires larger and technologically more sophisticated plants. While the amount of capital and number of firms distinguish the short run from the long run in microeconomics, market clearing and flexible prices distinguish the short run from the long run in monetary economics.

held at all times. Why? As they interpreted the empirical evidence, the short run is chronologically short and matters little. One can ignore situations where Say's Law does not hold if the short run were, say, one month. Fleeting moments are not worth analyzing. On the other hand, Say's Law is irrelevant if the long run is a century. If we were pressed to estimate (guess?) the length of the short run for the *representative classicist*, our hesitant answer is one to two years. Within that time frame, output should *automatically* rebound to the maximum potential supply. Prices and interest rates should adjust quite rapidly to restore equilibrium. Recessions are temporary. In fact, the average duration of recessions has been 18 months. Classicists were shocked by the Great Depression, which began in 1929. By 1933 the economy definitely should have returned to full employment. Instead, the economy just hit bottom after a protracted decline. Full employment was another eight years away!

The Great Depression was too painful to be dismissed as a unique case. *Adjustment to full employment sometimes is very slow*. Nonetheless, extreme cases can be overemphasized. Even if the short run always were about 10 years, as was the case in 1929, can we ignore the long run? Can we ignore policies which have effects 10 years hence? Perhaps some, but not all. Our favorite education example of Chapter 21 illustrates your agreement that not all effects beyond 10 years can be ignored. The rate of return on education is negative for those with only a 10 year horizon.

Quantity Theory of Money

What role does money play in the long-run classical model? *Money determines prices. It does not affect long-run real output because monetary policy influences only the demand for commodities*. Aggregate supply is unrelated to the quantity of money.[4] Money, particularly the fiat variety, would be miraculous indeed if it had any appreciable effect on a nation's ability to produce. No nation would invest and sacrifice current consumption in order to increase future output if printing costless money could accomplish the same objective. Because the *demand for money is stable*, monetary expansion *consistently* increases aggregate demand, which ultimately influences prices alone. *The classical doctrine that the demand for money is stable and that monetary changes have a predictable effect on demand and,* ceteris paribus, *cause proportional price changes is called the quantity theory of money*. This is the second fundamental belief of classical economics.

Nominal income (and output) is the product of prices, P, and real income, y. *An alternative expression of the quantity theory of money is:*

---

[4]Some argue that money is a productive factor. The argument is correct but of the second order of smalls.

monetary changes consistently cause proportional nominal income changes but leave real income unchanged in the long run.

Neoclassical Economists

Many current economists accept the two fundamental theorems of classical economics: (1) Say's Law, that is, supply creates its own demand in the long run, and (2) the quantity theory of money, that is, money has a strong and predictable effect on demand and tends to cause proportional price changes. The modern economists who unfailingly accept the two fundamental propositions are called neoclassical economists. Until about 1970, neoclassical economists were sufficiently homogeneous in their beliefs that they typically were considered a single group and called monetarists. Since 1970, however, two splinter groups have arisen, supply-side economists and rational expectations economists. Thus, three groups now reside in the neoclassical camp: monetarists, supply siders, and rational expectationists.

The monetarists are not only the oldest but also the largest neoclassical group. As such, they form the standard against which the other two are measured. The leading monetarist clearly is Milton Friedman, a long-time professor at the University of Chicago and now at Stanford University's Hoover Institution of War, Peace, and Revolution. Although Friedman and monetarism are almost synonymous, other internationally respected monetarists include Philip Cagan of Columbia University, Karl Brunner of the University of Rochester, and Allan Meltzer of Carnegie-Mellon, to name a few. The Federal Reserve Bank of St. Louis is a long-time advocate of monetarism within the System.

The supply siders are the smallest neoclassical group but became highly influential with the election of President Ronald Reagan. The best known academic supply sider is Arthur Laffer of the University of Southern California. Many members of the Reagan administration are alleged to be supply siders. Contrary to monetarists, supply siders believe that relative prices and fiscal policy, particularly tax policy, can significantly influence real output through its effects on *supply*, hence their name. Note that supply siders are good bearers of the classical torch. Tax policy influences output because taxes affect supply, which creates its own demand. While taxes may also affect demand, this is only incidental and totally unnecessary according to supply siders. If taxes only influenced demand, then output would be unchanged. Monetarists deny that fiscal policy has an *appreciable* effect on either demand or supply and, therefore, output.

Among the leading members of the rational expectations school are Robert Lucas of the University of Chicago and Thomas Sargent and Neil Wallace of the University of Minnesota. The Federal Reserve System is not monolithic. The Federal Reserve Bank of Minneapolis advocates rational expectations as strongly as the St. Louis Fed advocates monetarism. The rational expectations approach is quite complex and cannot be summarized quickly without making it sound foolish. With our apologies then to the rational expectations school, whose views will be presented more fully in Chapters 28 and 29, rational expectations comes close to accepting the strong Keynesian interpretation of Say's Law, that is, supply creates its own demand at all times. Of course, rational expectations advocates recognize that output sometimes is below full employment. They claim that such situations occur because suppliers underestimate demand and produce too little, and not because demand is lacking. Markets clear at all times according to the rational expectations school. The school further claims that estimates of demand are unbiased; overestimates at some points are matched by underestimates at other points. Stated somewhat differently, expectations are rational when they are not systematically wrong. Therefore, while output below full employment for a *short* time is consistent with rational expectations, prolonged depressions or expansions indicate systematically incorrect estimates and contradict rational expectations. Compared to monetarists, the rational expectations school claims the economy is much more stable. Major recessions and booms contradict rational expectations but do not necessarily contradict monetarism.

Aggregate Supply

Unless stated otherwise, the composite neoclassical model presented in this and the next chapter is acceptable to all three groups. The remainder of this chapter takes a close look at supply, the piper which plays the tune in neoclassical economics. What determines supply in the long run? After answering that question, we extend somewhat our discussion of the quantity theory of money. However, the reader must await the next chapter for a complete presentation of the quantity theory and the adjustments which make demand equal supply. This chapter presents the basics.

The Production Function

Goods and services do not fall like manna from heaven. An often long and complicated production process transforms inputs, also called factors of production, into goods and services, or output. *The technological relationship between factors of production (inputs) and output is called the production function.* Land, capital, and labor are factors of production. For simplicity, however, assume homogeneous labor is the only variable factor and a standard commodity output, gizmos. Gizmos are extremely versatile. They are eaten (consumption), produce little gizmos (investment), and are hurled at the enemy (government expenditures). Figure

22–2 graphs a production function. Output, y, is on the vertical axis, and labor, L, is on the horizontal axis. The curve is upward sloping at first and then downward sloping. By definition, the curve's slope is the change in output, measured on the vertical axis, divided by the change in labor, measured on the horizontal axis. The slope, $\Delta y/\Delta L$, measures the marginal physical product of labor, MPP_L, the additional output produced by an additional worker. The line L^D in Figure 22–3 graphs the declining mar-

FIGURE 22–2
Production Function Relationship between Output and Input

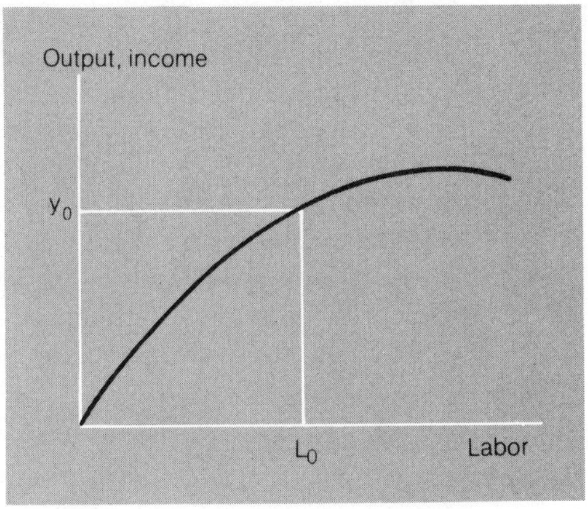

FIGURE 22–3
Supply and Demand for Labor as Functions of the Real Wage

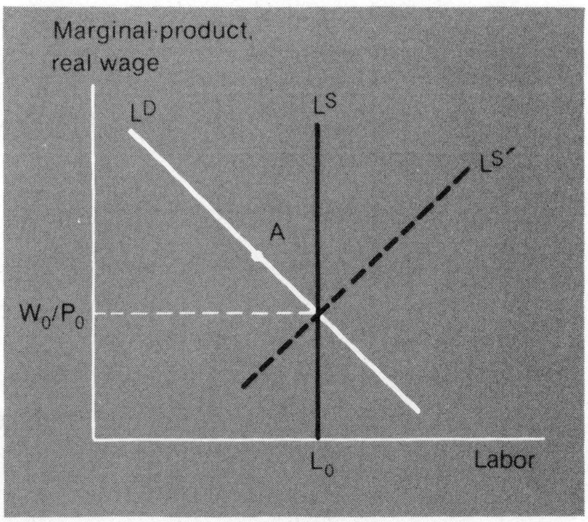

ginal physical product of labor implied by the production function which becomes flatter in Figure 22–2. The existence of fixed factors explains the declining marginal product of labor. As additional workers till the soil and are supervised less closely by a limited number of managers, each additional worker becomes less productive.[5] After employment becomes quite large, additional workers actually reduce output as congestion becomes severe and management of large numbers becomes chaotic. As economists, however, we can ignore the downward sloping portion of the production function and negative marginal products due to severe congestion. Profit-oriented firms will never hire that many workers.

The height of the production function depends positively on the quantity of capital, the quality of the labor force, and the degree of technological advancement and entrepreneurship. The production function shifts when the just enumerated factors change. For example, technological progress and a more skillful labor force shift the production function upward more or less smoothly and continuously over time. Dramatic changes in the annual or decadal rate of technological progress are common in selective industries but rare economywide. Analysis of these shifts is left to development and managerial economists. For simplicity, we ignore production function shifts.

The Demand for Labor

The demand and supply of labor determine the number of workers employed and, in conjunction with the production function, output. Consider first the demand for labor. What is the objective of firms? Why do firms produce?

Prior to World War II profit maximization was the only objective economists considered. Although most economic texts still assume profit maximization is the objective at all times, post-World War II economists have discussed other objectives, such as sales maximization (market share) subject to some minimum profit constraint. Herbert Simon won the 1978 Nobel prize in economics largely for his nonprofit-maximizing theories of the firm. The new theories were constructed to better describe the "real world," particularly in the short run. Attempts to maximize profits at every moment can be counterproductive. Suppose you owned a restaurant. Would you loudly announce a temporary 20 percent price surcharge whenever the waiting line was long, and parade in front of the restaurant with a sale sign whenever it was empty? Alternatively, would you purposely cut costs and food quality some days? Such actions may maximize

[5]Recalling Principles of Economics, what name is given to this fundamental law of production? The law of diminishing returns.

profits in the short run but are almost guaranteed to drive you out of business. Tomorrow's demand depends on a firm's behavior today. Consequently, characterization of firm's behavior and objectives depends on the time period. For now just accept that *in the long run the profit-maximization assumption is realistic*. Firms cannot ignore competitive pressure forever. Firms continually seeking objectives besides profit maximization eventually will be bankrupt as new and more profit-conscious firms enter an industry. Indeed, the desire "to make a buck" is so strong that entry in competitive industries tends to eliminate economic profit. In the long run firms earn only accounting profits equal to a normal rate of return on capital.

Assuming profit maximization, firms hire workers until the additional cost equals the additional revenue generated by workers.[6] In a competitive industry the additional cost of labor is the wage rate, W. Competitive firms can hire any amount at the existing wage rate. The revenue generated by an extra worker is the product of the commodity price, P, times the marginal physical product of labor. Expressing the profit-maximizing condition algebraically,

(22–1)

$$W = P \cdot MPP_L, \text{ or } MPP_L = \frac{W}{P}$$

Profit-maximizing firms equate the marginal physical product of labor and the real wage, W/P. Placing the real wage on the vertical axis in Figure 22–3 transforms the technologically determined marginal physical product of labor curve into the demand curve for labor by profit-maximizing firms. As stated earlier, the marginal physical product of labor declines as additional workers are hired. This implies that the real wage firms are willing to pay declines as additional workers are hired. Alternatively stated, as the real wage falls firms find it profitable to hire more, if less productive, workers. This certainly corresponds with common sense. When labor costs are high relative to the product price, that is, the real wage is high, firms will demand little labor.

The Supply of Labor

The neoclassical supply of labor reflects the maximization of a leisure/commodities preference (utility) curve. Individuals derive satisfaction from both leisure and commodities which are plotted on the first horizontal and vertical axes, respectively, of Figure 22–4. Most people would like 24 hours of leisure daily and an unlimited quantity of commodities, repre-

---

[6]Technically speaking, profit maximization equates the marginal cost of labor and its marginal revenue product.

FIGURE 22–4
Opportunity Locus

The real wage determines the commodities/leisure trade-off.

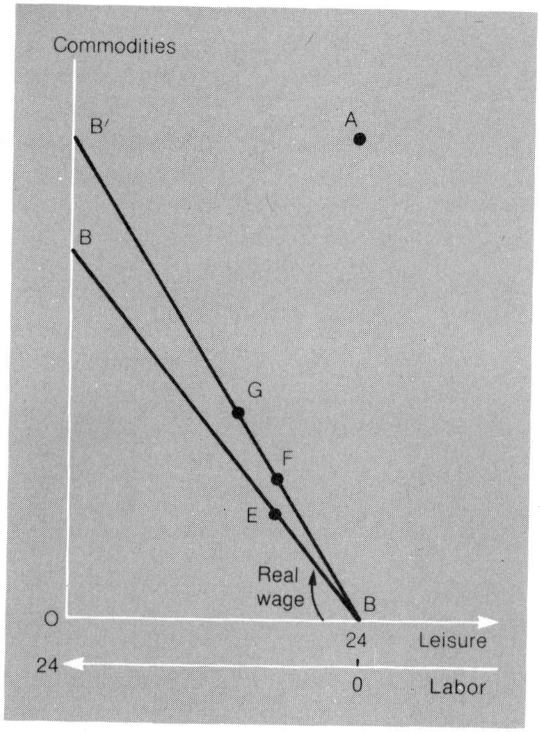

sented by point A in Figure 22–4. What people like and what they can achieve do not coincide. Economics, the study of scarcity, says individuals cannot enjoy unlimited amounts of both. All work and no play makes Jack a dull boy, and all play and no work makes Jack starve. The two horizontal axes in Figure 22–4 emphasize that every day has 24 hours which must be divided between leisure and labor (work effort). Jack foregoes some leisure and works in order to purchase commodities now and in the future. *The real wage measures the rate at which leisure can be transformed into commodities by working*. For example, if the wage rate is \$6 per hour and the price of commodities (gizmos) is \$4, work effort and the sacrifice of an hour's leisure allows Jack to purchase 1.5 gizmos. The \$6 nominal wage does not measure the rewards of work effort in terms of commodities. The real wage, and *only* the real wage, sets the opportunity locus (trade-off curve) between leisure and commodities given by line BB in Figure 22–4. Ignore line BB′ for the moment. In this example

Jack could loaf all day and be broke, enjoy 23 hours of leisure (work 1 hour) and be able to purchase 1.5 gizmos, enjoy 22 hours of leisure and be able to purchase 3 gizmos, and so on. The absolute value of the slope of the opportunity locus BB equals the real wage, 1.5 in our example. Workers select that leisure (and labor since leisure and labor must equal 24 hours per day) and commodities combination on the trade-off curve which maximizes their preferences. Without drawing indifference curves, assume utility maximization occurs at point E. *The work decision in the long-run neoclassical model is uniquely determined by the real wage which sets the trade-off curve, given workers' preferences for leisure and commodities.*

How do changes in the real wage affect the amount of labor supplied? Monetarists and supply siders differ on this question. All price changes have so-called *income and substitution effects*. Higher real wages allow one to enjoy more commodities (leisure) for any *given* quantity of leisure (commodities)—the income effect—and increase the cost of leisure in terms of commodities foregone—the substitution effect. In terms of Figure 22–4, a higher real wage rotates the opportunity locus upward to BB′, which illustrates that the higher real wage makes one better off. Aside from the intercept, every point on BB′ is above and to the right of BB. Since leisure is desirable, one tends to acquire more leisure (work less) when real wage rises—the income effect. However, the higher real wage has increased the cost of leisure in terms of commodities foregone. This tends to reduce the amount of leisure demanded and, therefore, increase labor supplied—the substitution effect. In terms of Figure 22–4, the opportunity locus has become steeper in moving upward. *Monetarists claim that the negative (positive) income effect on work effort (leisure) approximately equals the substitution effect so that labor supplied is virtually independent of the real wage.* Graphically, monetarists claim the typical worker selects a point on BB′ slightly to the left of F, which is directly above E. To make the monetarist/supply-sider distinction sharper, let the total independence point F represent the monetarist position. In Figure 22–3 this monetarist position is illustrated by the solid vertical supply curve. Supply siders on the other hand say that the substitution effect strongly dominates. Higher real wages induce *greater* (less) *work effort* (leisure). The supply-siders' position is illustrated by point G in Figure 22–4 and the dashed upward sloping supply curve in Figure 22–3.

Disagreement within the neoclassical camp about the slope of the labor supply curve sometimes obscures the fundamental similarity: *all neoclassicists claim that labor supply simply depends on the real wage.* For example, suppose wages were to double. Would *any* neoclassicist predict *unequivocally* that the amount of labor supplied will increase? No. What happened to prices? If prices also doubled so the real wage were unchanged, the opportunity locus remains fixed. The same work effort maximizes one's preference between leisure and commodities. *Thus, the supply of labor in classical monetary theory, like the supply and demand curves for all products in traditional microeconomics, is grounded on maximization principles.* Firms and consumers *ultimately* maximize profits or preferences, yielding supply and demand curves.

Preference maximization, just like profit maximization, is unrealistic in the short run. Contracts, custom, and misperception of wages and prices prevent short-run preference maximization. For example, employment contracts at a specified money wage are quite common. As prices and, therefore, the real wage change, many individuals are obligated by contracts to work the same number of hours. Fortunately, we no longer live in a slave society. Contracts elapse. In the long run contracts do not constrain preference maximization. Subsequent chapters analyze the short-run determinants of labor supply. The purpose of this brief paragraph is to warn against the uncritical application of a theory for all time and space. *Most long-run neoclassical assumptions are unrealistic in the short run.*

Labor Market Equilibrium and the Aggregate Supply Curve

Look at Figure 22–3. The demand and supply of labor uniquely determine a real wage and amount of labor effort. This is true regardless of the shape of the supply curve. Given the existing capital stock, quality of labor, and degree of entrepreneurship as represented by the production function, Figure 22–2, the level of output and income is determined. Note well what happens: *output is determined independently of consumer and other demands for commodities.* Firms' quest for profits and individuals' preferences for leisure and commodities determine output. By definition, *the aggregate supply curve shows how much firms want to produce at alternative prices, given consistency between their demand for and the supply of labor.* The classical case, where supply completely determines output, is illustrated by the vertical aggregate supply curve, AS, in Figure 22–5. The vertical line illustrates that the unique output is consistent with any price level, provided the nominal wage adjusts to keep the real wage constant.

The equilibrium employment naturally is a point on the labor supply curve and represents full employment, in the sense that society's work/leisure preferences are satisfied at the existing wage/price structure. Thus, the unique aggregate supply output in Figure 22–5 is full-employment output.[7]

---

[7]Full employment and related concepts are analyzed in greater detail in Chapter 28.

FIGURE 22–5
The Classical Aggregate Supply Curve

The quantity theory states that money, and only money, determines the equilibrium point on the aggregate supply curve and, therefore, prices.

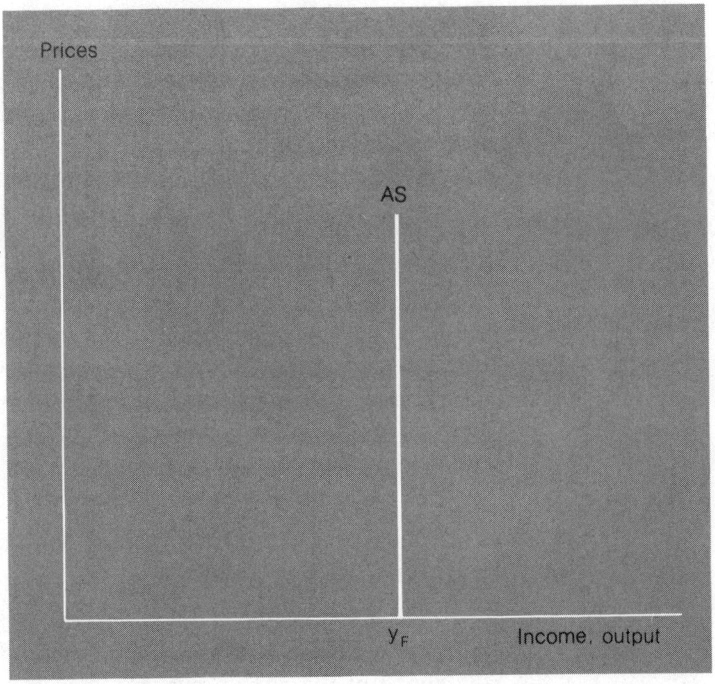

The Quantity Theory and Say's Law Again

Classical economists had a very simple money demand equation which neoclassicists no longer accept. However, within the context of the entire classical/neoclassical model where commodity supply is independent of commodity demand, the simple classical money demand equation and a more complex equation yield the same conclusions.[8] Since simplicity is desirable, let us accept the classical money demand equation. Classicists viewed money solely as a medium of exchange. In other words, they had only a transactions demand for money. The demand for money according to classicists is proportional to one's transactions and income. In symbols,

$$M = kPy \tag{22–2}$$

[8]The form of the money demand relationship is extremely important in Keynesian economics where aggregate supply is not fixed.

where P is prices, y is real income or output, and k is the factor of proportionality linking money (M) and nominal income (Py). Assuming a given money supply, Equation (22–2) also represents the equilibrium relationship in the money market because at equilibrium demand equals supply.

Equation (22–2) is called the cash balance or Cambridge k version of the quantity theory because economists from Cambridge University favored its use. Irving Fisher, America's most distinguished classicist, favored the velocity version of the quantity theory. Cambridge economists looked at money while it was being held in anticipation of spending. Fisher's velocity version, however, looks at money directly as it is being spent and changing hands. The average desired rate of turnover of money, that is, the average rate at which people want to spend money, is called desired velocity, V. Since money is used in all expenditures, money multiplied by its velocity determines the equilibrium *value* of total spending and income.

$$MV = Py \tag{22–3}$$

For example, suppose velocity is six per year. Then a $1 billion money supply can generate annual income payments of $6 billion because the average dollar is spent six times during the year. Clearly, V and k are reciprocals, $V = 1/k$ and $k = 1/V$. If the average dollar is spent six times per year, then the average dollar is held 1/6 of a year. Classicists thought that velocity or its reciprocal, the transaction coefficient k, could be treated *as if* it were a known constant. That is, the *the quantity theory says that k or V and, therefore, the demand for money, is stable, predictable, and independent of the quantity of money.*

What are the implications of the quantity theory proposition that money determines the equilibrium value of spending and income when output is fixed? *Money determines prices.* A given quantity of money which turns over a fixed number of times per period can finance a given volume of transactions. If the number of items which can be purchased rises, the price per item must fall. Money, and only money, determines the equilibrium point on the aggregate supply curve in Figure 22–5.

The quantity theory is often misinterpreted. The statement, "money is spent at a highly predictable rate," frequently is garbled to "*only* money influences expenditures." Classicists clearly recognized that the last phrase is false. Aggregate demand also depends directly on disposable income and inversely on the rate of interest according to classicists. The next chapters provide a rigorous justification for the last sentence. Most people accept it without proof. It is intuitively plausible that households and firms will buy more items such as food, autos, and houses when their incomes rise and the rate of interest falls. To be sure, classicists claimed that real money balances, M/P, also influence spending. By dividing the number of dollars by the price of goods and services, real money balances measures the purchasing power of money. A. C. Pigou, the leading classicist at the time of Keynes's *General Theory*, stressed that the purchasing power is *used consistently*. Thus, the real money balance effect on spending is also called the *Pigou effect*. Ignoring taxes so that disposable and total income coincide, this paragraph is summarized algebraically by

$$E = E(\underset{+}{y}, \underset{-}{r}, \underset{+}{M/P}), \tag{22–4}$$

where E is aggregate expenditures, r is the rate of interest, and the other terms are as previously defined. The sign under the variables indicates the direction of the variable's effect, positive (direct) or negative (inverse), on expenditures.

Figure 22–6 graphs aggregate expenditures, E, or, using more Keynesian notation, C+I+G, on the vertical axis and income, y, on the horizontal axis. The 45° line contains all the points equidistant to the axes, by definition. The aggregate expenditure curve slopes upward but its slope is less than one, that is, it is flatter than the 45° line. *Demand increases as income increases but not by the full amount. Lower interest rates or larger real money balances shift the aggregate demand curve upward.* The unique aggregate supply determined by the labor market is the solid vertical line labelled y_0. Temporarily ignore the broken demand and supply lines. Since the 45° line contains all the points equidistant to the axes, it is the equilibrium line. All along this line supply equals demand. In terms of Figure 22–6, *Say's Law states that the aggregate demand curve will intersect the 45° line at the same point it is intersected by the vertical supply line, without need of any government policy*. Figure 22–6 illustrates the neoclassical belief in Say's Law; the solid EE curve goes through point A. If demand *temporarily* fell below EE, interest rate or price declines *automatically* shift the curve back up. *Aggregate demand is very responsive to the rate of interest and price level*. Lower interest rates or lower prices which increase real money balances restore full employment.

The neoclassical belief in Say's Law within a growth setting claims that as supply shifts to the broken line y_1, the expenditure curve also shifts to maintain full employment. The supply increase by itself causes a less than equal increase in demand as the economy moves from point A to B, which is below D. However, automatic interest rate and price adjustments cause the expenditure curve to shift upward and intersect the 45° line at point D.

Monetary and Fiscal Policy

Suppose the quantity of money increases. How does the economy respond? People now have more money than they need for current trans-

FIGURE 22–6
Aggregate Expenditures and Output

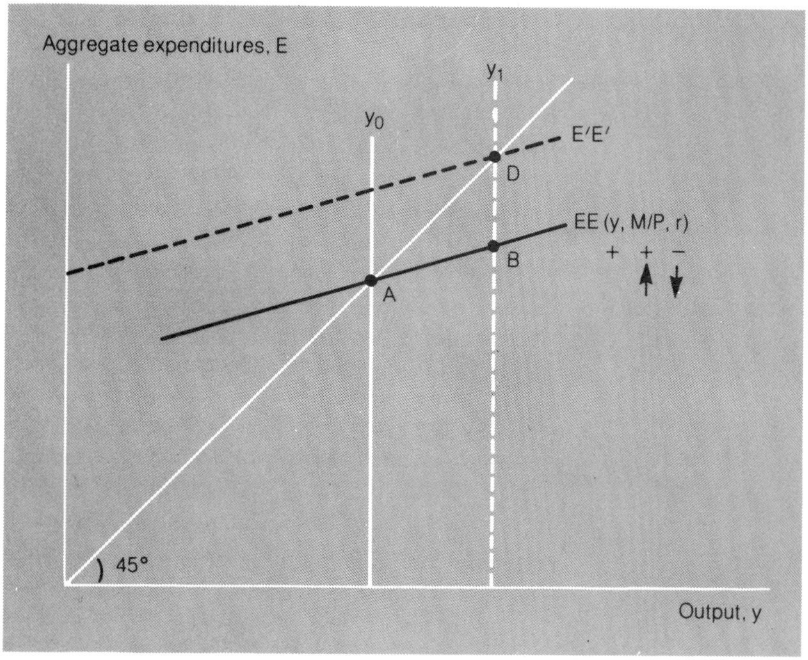

actions. Consequently, they spend the additional money balances. Since velocity and its reciprocal, k, are independent of the quantity of money, inspection of Equations (22–2) and (22–3) indicates that nominal income, Py, increases proportionally. Because the supply of commodities is independent of the quantity of money in the long run, higher prices explain *all* of the nominal income increase. *Monetary changes affect prices proportionally without affecting output.*

Money may not affect output in the long run, but does it influence other economic variables besides the price level? In particular, does the quantity of money have any *long-run* effect on the rate of interest? No. The demand for commodities depends on the rate of interest. Therefore, *if monetary expansion permanently lowered the rate of interest, the demand for commodities would permanently exceed the supply of commodities, which is independent of money. Such a situation is impossible; equilibrium eventually prevails. In the long run the rate of interest also is independent of the quantity of money.*[9]

[9]Note that the argument in the text is based on the rate of interest necessary to equate aggregate *expenditures* and output and is independent of the relationship between money demand and the rate of interest. If the money supply doubles, prices double, and the rate

Now assume fiscal policy instead of monetary policy is expansionary. More specifically, assume personal income tax rates are reduced, and the government issues bonds to finance the same level of expenditures. What is the long-run effect of the tax reduction? Neoclassicists agree that tax cuts have no effect on *aggregate demand*. When velocity can be treated as a constant, tax reductions which do not change the quantity of money cannot change nominal income (Py) and, therefore, do not shift the aggregate demand curve. To be sure, lower taxes increase *disposable income*, which tends to produce more spending and shift EE upward in Figure 22–6. However, the government sells additional bonds in order to raise the money necessary to pay for its expenditures. The additional bond sales drive up interest rates and reduce spending, shifting EE downward in Figure 22–6. *Because tax reductions and equal bond sales by the Treasury have no effect on money, the interest rate effect must exactly cancel the disposable income effect when velocity is constant.*

Do personal income tax reductions affect aggregate supply? To answer this question we must consider the effect of taxes on the production function and the demand and supply of labor, the relationships which underlie the aggregate supply curve. The production function is a *technological* relationship, and profit-maximizing firms hire workers until the *technologically* determined marginal physical product of labor equals the real wage. Consequently, taxes do not affect either the production function or the demand for labor.[10] Taxes may influence the supply of labor, however. *After-tax wages determine the commodities one can purchase by working*. Because of this, a reduction in tax rates has the same effect on the leisure-commodities opportunity locus as an increase in the pretax real wage. The monetarist's vertical labor supply curve, derived when we were implicitly ignoring taxes, claims that the amount of labor supplied is fixed irrespective of the pretax real wage. Therefore, *labor supply in the monetarist case is unaffected by taxes*. This is so because of the equivalence of pretax wage increases and tax cuts for the after-tax wage, which is the determinant of the leisure-commodities opportunity locus and labor supply. With labor supply unaffected by taxes, equilibrium employment and the aggregate supply curve also are unaffected by tax cuts.

Supply siders, however, claim that labor supply is highly responsive to the after-tax real wage. Let the vertical axis in Figure 22–4 measure

---

of interest remains constant, then real money demand equals the real supply whether or not money demand depends on the rate of interest.

[10]This is not entirely correct, particularly when capital and other factors are subsumed in the production function. In that case, taxes shift the production function if the inputs being held fixed are affected. We chose to ignore this possibility *for the moment*. The relationship between deficits, the capital stock, and output is reserved for Chapter 34.

the *pretax* real wage, which is the real wage relevant for the demand for labor. Because lower taxes and lower pretax wages have exactly opposite impacts on after-tax real wages and the commodities workers can purchase by working, tax cuts shift the supply of labor *plotted against the pretax real wage* downward according to supply siders.[11] In other words, any given amount of labor will be supplied at a lower pretax real wage because lower taxes raise the after-tax wage, the wage relevant to workers. Equilibrium employment increases, and the vertical aggregate supply shifts rightward. *Output increases only because aggregate supply increases. If tax cuts had shifted the aggregate demand curve upward, prices would rise but output would remain fixed so long as taxes do not shift aggregate supply.*

Extreme supply siders claim that output increases so much that (dollar) tax *receipts* actually increase when tax *rates* decrease. This viewpoint, which is illustrated by the Laffer curve, is relegated to the appendix because it is more in the order of ephemeral possibilities than real probabilities. Nevertheless, the Laffer curve's importance for understanding current policy suggests placement of the appendix immediately after the chapter questions. All subsequent appendixes are theoretical and appear at the end of the book.

Summary/Questions

Economic theory, policy, and history are interrelated. Theories are constructed to explain important economic events, and economic and social policy is strongly influenced by theory. As Keynes so eloquently stated, "Practical men, who believe themselves to be quite exempt from any intellectual influences, are usually the slaves of some defunct economist. Madmen in authority, who hear voices in the air, are distilling their frenzy from some academic scribbler of a few years back."[12] Keynes wrote *The General Theory* to free practical men from slavery to classical economics which, according to Keynes, "is misleading and disastrous if we attempt to apply it to the facts of experience."[13] While Keynes undoubtedly was the brightest mid-20th-century economist, his criticism of classical economics was too harsh. Classical economics may be incomplete and is incapable of analyzing every problem. However, it does explain many facts well, which justifies its study. Dispel any idea that the study of

[11]The monetarist's vertical supply curve cannot be shifted downward.

[12]*The General Theory*, p. 383. By permission of the Royal Economic Society and Macmillan, London and Baskingstoke.

[13]Ibid., p. 3.

classical theory is prompted by a sense of history or the desire to pay homage to our ancestors. To repeat, we study classical economics because it explains some aspects of the past and accurately predicts the future.

Keynes was more successful than even he had envisaged. *The General Theory* almost immediately made many practical people the slaves of Keynes, a testimonial to the ideas contained in the book. But slavish devotion to either Keynesian or neoclassical economics is wrong. *Both Keynesian economics with its emphasis on the short run and neoclassical economics with its emphasis on the long run are necessary to understand the unfolding over time of the effects of money and other policy variables.* Keynesian and neoclassical economics are competitive in some respects but, on balance, are better viewed as complementary, jointly providing an approximation to a dynamic theory.

The two basic propositions of classical economics which all current neoclassicists accept are (1) Say's Law, and (2) the quantity theory of money. We showed how supply factors alone determine output in the long run. Although money may have a predictable effect on aggregate demand, money can only affect prices when output is determined by supply. Subsequent chapters on Keynesian economics show that monetary and fiscal policy can influence output in the short run. In the long run, however, monetary policy influences prices alone, and fiscal policy without supply-side effects simply alters the composition of output. More government spending implies fewer private goods from a fixed supply.

1. Explain the two fundamental beliefs of classical economists.
2. What three groups of economists make up the neoclassical school? What are the main differences between the three groups?
3. Explain how neoclassicists derive output independently of demand. What are the fundamental assumptions underlying the neoclassical supply and demand for labor? What variable determines the amount of labor supplied and demanded?
4. Write the cash balance (Cambridge k) and velocity versions of the quantity theory equation. Define terms and indicate how they are related.
5. What is the effect of monetary changes in the long-run neoclassical model? What assumption is made about k(V)?
6. What is the long-run effect of lower taxes according to (1) monetarists, and (2) supply-side economists?

Appendix: Taxes and the Laffer Curve

Tax receipts equal the product of the tax rate and tax base. In the case of the income tax, the base is income, of course, so that

$$T = t \cdot Y \qquad \textbf{(22A–1)}$$

where T is tax receipts, t is the income tax rate, and Y, as usual, is nominal income. For simplicity, we are assuming proportional instead of progressive taxes. Clearly, if either the income tax rate or income is zero, tax receipts also are zero. Does the government get all the income if the tax rate were 100 percent? Yes, but in that case all the income is nothing. Aside from a few workaholics, a confiscatory 100 percent tax rate totally eliminates the incentive to work. Income in Equation (22A–1) cannot be considered a constant; it depends on the tax rate. Since tax receipts are zero when the tax rate is zero or 100 percent, and since we observe that the government does collect taxes when the tax rate is positive but less than confiscatory, the relationship between tax receipts and tax rates must first be positive and then negative, as is illustrated in Figure 22A–1. Tax receipts are maximized at some intermediate tax rate below 100 percent. The backward bending curves in Figure 22A–1 are Laffer curves. The Laffer curve typically is drawn as a semicircle or, at least, a nice smooth curve such as SS. However, the curve MM in Figure 22A–1 also satisfies the condition that tax receipts are positive except when the tax rate is zero or 100 percent.

All supply siders claim that tax rate reductions increase work effort and, therefore, income. In terms of Equation (22A–1), a smaller t allegedly increases Y. The more extreme supply siders claim tax receipts actually

FIGURE 22A–1
Laffer Curves

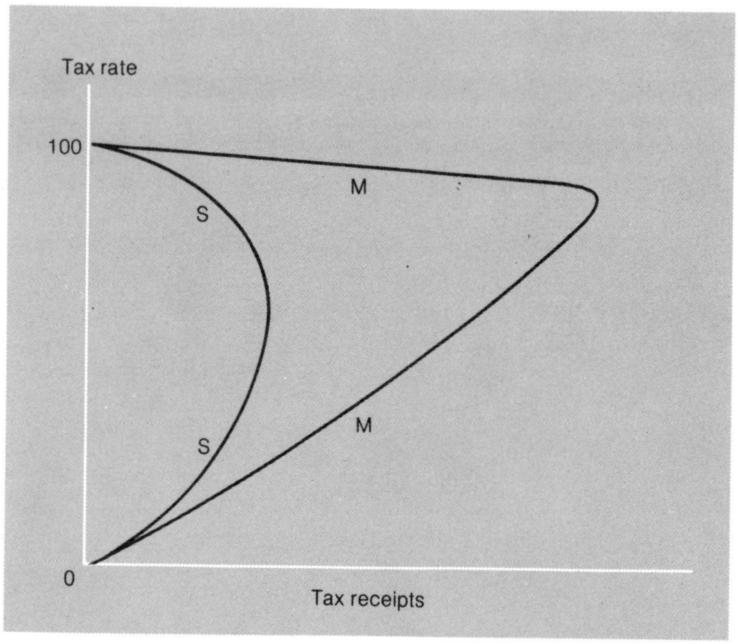

will increase because the percentage increase in income will exceed the percentage decrease in the tax rate. The economy supposedly is on the backward bending portion of the SS curve! Note that a positively sloped labor supply curve, so that tax cuts have a positive effect on labor supply, does not by itself guarantee this conclusion. The Reagan tax cuts and the ensuing deficits greatly depleted the ranks of extreme supply siders.

What type of labor supply curve in Figure 22–3 is implied by Laffer curve MM? Curve MM implies the labor supply curve is vertical until the real wage is extremely low. There is a proportional (straight line) relationship between tax receipts and tax rates until rates approach 100 percent because work effort and income are constant. Laffer curve MM represents the monetarist position; the labor supply curve is vertical about wage and tax rates likely to be observed. (No one should be forced to qualify every statement for fear of being interpreted too literally. What would happen if the wage rate were one mill is irrelevant.) Monetarists join their Keynesian colleagues in claiming that tax rate reductions tend to lower tax receipts.

23 Neoclassical economics: A detailed analysis

This chapter is for those from Missouri, the show-me state. (Non-Missourians uninterested in proof may proceed directly to Chapter 24 without loss of continuity.) With the aid of graphs we attempt to justify the major propositions of neoclassical economics outlined in the previous chapter while simultaneously illustrating secondary issues. We primarily will analyze:

1. The determinants of velocity, with emphasis being placed on the reasons for treating it as a constant.
2. Rate of interest and price adjustments which equate aggregate demand to a given full-employment income without need of monetary or fiscal policy.

The quantity theory of money hypothesis that prices tend to be proportional to the quantity of money hinges on velocity being exogenous. The last chapter, however, offered no rationale for treating velocity and the transactions coefficient as constants. Moreover, the last chapter stopped short of attempting to justify Say's Law. We did show that supply determines a unique level of output. We still must show how the desired expenditures of households and firms adjust in the long run to equal the supply-determined output, *without need for government intervention*. The automatic adjustment process may be so slow, however, that one may wish to supplement it with short-run discretionary policy. The concluding section evaluates the relationship between the effectiveness of short-run monetary and fiscal policy and the cause of temporary deficiencies in expenditures.

Appendix A contains a numerical example of the entire classical model. Instead of saving the appendix for dessert, some may prefer to turn to it after completing each section and compare piece by piece the graphic approach in the text and the numerical example in the appendix. Indeed, one can immediately turn to the first part of the appendix, which numerically derives the aggregate supply curve presented graphically in the previous chapter. Appendix A is found at the end of the book.

Commodity Theory of Money

Monetary expansion through the debasement of coins was a recurrent phenomenon during the Middle Ages. Since inflation invariably followed debasement and monetary expansion, the public quite naturally believed the two events were related. The precise relationship, however, was unclear for many years. *Commodity theorists* argued that money's value or purchasing power depended on the commodity value of the money substance itself. Debasement reduces the gold or other commodity content of coins, by definition. According to the commodity theorists this makes money less valuable by raising the general price level of commodities. The fact that the quantity of money increases was thought irrelevant. *The commodity theorists argued that replacing full-bodied gold coins with an equal amount of coins with less gold content or paper money would be highly inflationary.* Such a theory may sound incredibly naive to the modern reader long since accustomed to inconvertible paper money. But the commodity theory was difficult to disprove for many years as debasement was the principal means of monetary expansion. It probably still has a few adherents. Many supported the 1934 devaluation of the dollar (lowering the gold content of the dollar or raising the dollar price of gold) as a *direct* means of raising the depressed U.S. price level. Quantity theorists viewed debasement as incidental to monetary expansion. They claimed that monetary expansion, however achieved, caused inflation. The Spanish discovery of gold in the New World settled the controversy between commodity and quantity theorists. The influx of Spanish gold coins, which were not debased, raised prices throughout Europe as the quantity theorists predicted and contrary to the commodity theory.

Quantity Theory of Money

Although the quantity theory of money is one of the oldest and most widely publicized economic theories—it almost invariably is presented in principles texts—it also is one of the most misunderstood. Look at Figure 23–1, which graphs quarterly velocity between 1960 and 1983.[1] Velocity

---

[1]Velocity did not increase sharply through the 20th century. It rose moderately in the early decades and fell significantly between 1930 and 1945.

FIGURE 23–1
Income Velocity of Money, 1960–1983

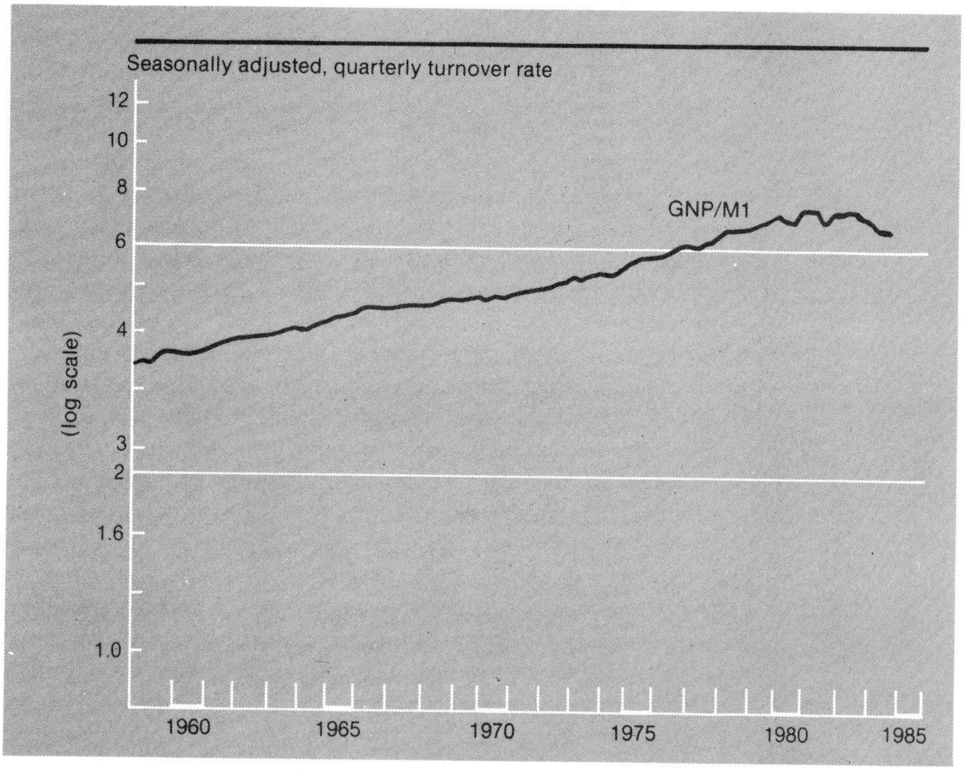

has been far from constant; it has a strong upward trend. Many people, economists included, claim that Figure 23–1 contradicts the quantity theory. In fact, the graph seemingly confirms one aspect of a properly understood quantity theory. Most quantity theorists, and certainly all the luminaries, claimed that policy effectiveness is the same whether velocity is constant or changed in its prescribed manner. In other words, *sophisticated quantity theorists claimed that for policy purposes the behavior of velocity was equivalent to being constant.* This special meaning of *constant* explains the more cumbersome, but also more accurate, sentences in the last chapter where we said, "Velocity may be treated *as if* it were a constant." Some modern economists forget the *as if* clause and attribute a naive quantity theory to all classicists. In fact, only a small minority were naive quantity theorists, claiming incorrectly, as Figure 23–1 shows, that velocity was constant in the sense of unchanging.

Why and how is velocity *as if* constant? In view of the confusion regarding the quantity theory and this chapter's admittedly Missourian orientation, we begin with basic principles and tolerate some slight repetition of the last chapter so that the full quantity theory is available in one place.

Equations of Exchange and Quantity Theory Equations

The quantity theory of money is mainly a theory of the price level. It also is a theory of money demand and of the effects and importance of money versus other factors. Thus, the quantity theory encompasses many elements. One thing the quantity theory is not: it is not a theory of money supply. It assumes the central bank has perfect control of the money supply, which can be set at any desired value.[2] We usually assume government fiat money, a simplification with little effect on the conclusions. The other financial asset besides money is a standard perpetual bond or consol whose yield is "the" interest rate.

The two versions of the quantity theory, Irving Fisher's velocity approach and the cash-balance approach associated with A. C. Pigou and other Cambridge University economists, differ more in appearance than substance. *All classical economists viewed money as the medium of exchange*. Any financial asset which is not a medium of exchange is a bond. Indeed, the essential difference between money and bonds is that the former is the medium of exchange. Classical economists virtually ignored any other function of money. They gave only lip service to money's role as a temporary abode of purchasing power (asset held for contingencies) and unit of account (asset with a fixed *dollar* value). Money is held to carry out some reasonably well-defined purchasing plan. Thus, classicists had a "pure" transactions demand for money.

The *starting* point of Fisher's velocity version of the quantity theory is the elementary observation that all transactions involve the exchange of a nonmoney commodity and money. During any given period of time, the value of money expenditures equals the value of all commodities sold. Alternatively stated, the value of all goods purchased and sold are equal, and money is used to purchase every good. Fisher's equation of exchange expresses this truism algebraically.

$$MV_T \equiv P_T T \tag{23–1}$$

[2]Wicksell's cumulative process analyzes the short-run interaction between aggregate demand and the money supply in an economy with a passive central bank which lets commercial banks dictate monetary policy. Thus, Wicksell should not be considered a quantity theorist with respect to the money supply.

where M is money, V_T is the transactions velocity or average rate of transactions turnover of money, P_T is the price index of all commodities sold, and T measures the quantities of all goods sold during the period. In one sense the equation of exchange is somewhat of a misnomer. It is an identity or truism and not the traditional equilibrium equation. To repeat, the equation of exchange simply says that observed money expenditures equal the value of all commodities sold. Such a truism may be the starting point of a theory, but is not a theory with predictive content. Nevertheless, let us examine the truism more carefully.

Fisher called the right-hand side of Equation (23–1) the sale-of-goods side. Each sale is regarded as the product of a price and quantity. As stated several times in the preceding paragraph, all sales are measured. Thus, P_TT includes the value of GNP as well as sales of second-hand commodities, bonds, and labor services. Money is exchanged in every transaction. Clearly P_T and T are rather special kinds of indexes of price and quantity, respectively. The left-hand or money side expresses total expenditures as the product of money times its velocity. In principle, velocity can be measured directly by attaching to every dollar bill a beeper, which would signal the central bank's computer every time the dollar bill changed hands. At the end of the time period, the computer would tally how many transactions were made with each dollar, that is, whether it turned over zero, one, two times, or more. The weighted average of these numbers of turnover is velocity. Principle may correspond with reality in the future. Today, actual velocity is computed residually by dividing total sales by money. Velocity is that number which makes the equation true. Suppose total transactions per year are $200 and the money stock is $25. What does velocity equal? The average rate of money turnover is eight per year.

The exchange truism is the foundation of the Fisherian quantity theory equation, which is an equilibrium equation. The equilibrium relationship was expressed by Fisher as

$$MV_T = P_TT \qquad \textbf{(23–2)}$$

The variables are similar to Equation (23–2) except that they represent *desired* instead of actual values. For example, V_T in Equation (23–2) is the possibly unobserved desired rate of turnover. Actual velocity, which is readily computed, need not equal desired velocity just as the quantity of bread purchased need not equal demand. To further distinguish the truism from the equilibrium statement, Equations (23–1) and (23–2) used the identity (≡) and equality (=) symbols, respectively. Equation (23–2) says algebraically that individuals are just satisfied with their money balances and the money market is in equilibrium when the rate people want to spend and, thereby, reduce their money balances—MV_T—equals the rate they add to their money balances through the sale of goods —$P_T T$. When desired subtractions equal desired additions the amount remains constant, a feature of equilibrium.

The ambiguities of the concepts of "total quantities" (T) and the "general price level" (P_T)—particularly those arising from the mixture of intermediate, final, and capital asset transactions—were never satisfactorily resolved. Nevertheless, the early classicists used total transactions because it could be approximated by bank debits (the value of all checks written). Reasonably accurate banking and financial statistics antedate most other statistical series. The more recent development of GNP statistics has stressed the importance of current production and income rather than total transactions. As a result, the quantity equation has more recently tended to be expressed in terms of GNP instead of transactions. Instead of Equation (23–1) we have

$$MV \equiv Py \tag{23–3}$$

where M represents, as before, money; V is income velocity, the average number of times during the period that money is used in making GNP expenditures; P is the GNP price index; and y is real GNP. A GNP version of the equilibrium Equation (23–3) may also be written.

$$MV = Py \tag{23–3a}$$

Equations (22–3) and (23–3a) are identical.

Fisher's equation looks at the means of payment in motion, moving from one person to another. Cambridge economists preferred to look at the means of payment at rest. Money is held for some period of time before it is spent on current goods and services. The quantity of money, M, can be expressed as the product of its average holding period for nominal GNP expenditures, k, times nominal GNP, or Py.

$$M \equiv kPy \tag{23–4}$$

Defining the Cambridge k as "the average time period that money is held" makes clear the reciprocal relationship with velocity, even when the algebraic equations are unwritten. If the average dollar is spent seven times during the year (V = 7), then 1/7 year measures the length of time the average dollar is held (k = 1/7).

Provided one recognizes the truisms expressed algebraically by Equations (23–3) and (23–4), V and k may be defined more mechanically without objection. Rearranging Equations (23–3) and (23–4),

$$V \equiv Py/M, \tag{23–3'}$$

$$k \equiv M/Py \tag{23–4'}$$

Velocity is the ratio of nominal income to money and k is the ratio of money to nominal income. These mechanical definitions will be used later. Remember, however, that the identities were not written merely to define k and V but rather to express the truism that money is held for some time interval and then spent. The Cambridge k, like velocity, could be measured independently by the beeper technique. Instead, it is derived residually from independently measured money and income data.

Just as the actual velocity equation of exchange, (23–1), provided the foundation for the desired velocity version of the quantity theory of money, (23–2), so (23–4) led to the Cambridge or cash-balance version of the quantity theory of money.

$$M = kPy \tag{23–5}$$

Equation (23–5) expresses the equilibrium relationship in the money market. The left-hand side is the exogenously determined money supply. The right-hand side is money demand, which is the product of the desired length of time people want to hold their money income multiplied by income. More simply, money demand is some desired proportion, k, of nominal income. The equality of demand and supply at equilibrium gives Equation (23–5).

Velocity versus the Cambridge k

Although Equations (23–3a) and (23–5) are mathematically equivalent, Pigou and his Cambridge cohorts insisted that their equation (23–5) was much clearer from an economic viewpoint than Fisher's equation (23–3a). Pigou preferred to view equilibrium as a position of balance between buyers and sellers for the *existing* quantity. He had a stock equilibrium concept. Like other equilibrium equations, (23–5) has demand on one side and supply on the other. The left-hand side of Equation (23–3a) has MV, which is neither money demand nor supply. Fisher, of course, disagreed with the Cambridge economists' assessment of the economic clarity of Equations (23–3a) and (23–5). He favored a flow equilibrium concept, which views equilibrium as occurring when desired money reductions (MV) equal desired money additions. Since both approaches are correct while emphasizing different elements, the use of both is convenient. Some problems are more easily analyzed by considering money in motion than at rest, and vice versa. Fisher's money-in-flight quantity theory equation does incorporate a basic neoclassical belief: money has an important effect on spending.

Prerequisites of a Theory

A theory must specify the determinants of the variables and describe their interrelationship. Simply noting that $MV = Py$ or $M = kPy$ at equilibrium tells us virtually nothing. Suppose the money supply doubled. The equation says that at the new equilibrium either velocity is cut in half (or, equivalently, k doubles), prices double, real output doubles, or some combination of velocity, prices, and output change. An endless number of combinations satisfies the equilibrium equation. The quantity theory is anything but wishy-washy. It analyzes the determinants of and interaction among the variables and yields definite predictions.

We already know the determinants of two variables in the quantity theory equation. The quantity of money is perfectly controlled by the Fed, at least as a first approximation. *Money is a causal factor and does not respond to any of the variables in the equation.* When the central bank changes the quantity of money, the other variables must respond. Equilibrium output and real income do not respond to monetary changes, however. Output is determined by the supply and demand for labor and the production function. Do monetary changes affect velocity, V, or its mathematical equivalent, the transactions coefficient, k? No. *In general, V and k are relatively stable and independent of the quantity of money.* The implication of an "as if" fixed transactions coefficient is that prices and money change proportionately, $M = \bar{k}P\bar{y}$, where the bars over k and y indicate these variables are independent of money. Double money and prices double.

Determinants of the Transactions Coefficient, Velocity, and Transactions Demand

Precisely what factors influence velocity, and why can it be considered a constant? In other words, the demand for money is proportional to income. What are the determinants of the proportionality factor, k, and why can it be considered a constant? Fisher and his followers often gave the impression that money is a hot potato. Households want to spend or lend their money holdings as soon as possible. Money per se has no utility, in contrast to commodities and bonds. Nevertheless, *velocity is not infinite, and money is held longer than a split second because of institutional and technological factors.* Thus, classicists had a very mechanical approach to the transactions coefficient, velocity, and money demand. *One technological factor limiting velocity is the speed of transportation and communications.* Trains in 1900 and now faster airplanes carry checks from New York to California. Even if money were spent immediately, transit time lags limit the rate of money turnover. For example, if all payments went through the mails which took a week for delivery, velocity could be no greater than 52 per year, and a dollar is "held" at least 1/52 of the year. *As transportation and communications improve through time, Fisher said velocity would rise and the transactions coefficient would fall.*

A second determinant of velocity is the degree of synchronization of receipts and expenditures. Households and business firms would hold little or no money if they were assured that a sufficient amount of money would flow to them just at the moment expenditures are anticipated. But receipts and expenditures are not perfectly synchronized. Households may be paid weekly or monthly. Paydays are a joyous occasion but not enough to spend everything immediately and starve the rest of the pay period. The holding period of money falls and velocity rises as receipts and expenditures are better synchronized. Imagine an author who receives $3,000 royalty checks each quarter and spends it all evenly during the quarter. Our author's money balances have the sawtooth pattern illustrated in Figures 23–2. The author begins the quarter with $3,000 and is penniless as the quarter ends. The process repeats itself each quarter, so annual income and expenditures are $12,000. Average money balances are $1,500, and annualized k is 1/8 ($1,500/$12,000). Some of the money is spent instantaneously, and some is held a full quarter. On average, money is held one and a half months or, equivalently, one eighth of a year. Velocity is eight times a year. Now suppose the author receives royalty checks monthly so receipts and expenditures are more closely synchronized. At the beginning of each month the author receives $1,000, which is spent evenly throughout the month. Annual income and expenditures remain $12,000. Our author's money holdings are now illustrated in Figure 23–2B. The average dollar is spent every half month. Annual velocity is 24, or k = 1/24.

Receipts and payments are more unsynchronized in farming than in nearly any other occupation. Consequently, according to Fisher, velocity would rise as the proportion of farmers falls and the economy becomes more industrialized.

Discussion of the total transactions version of the equation of exchange ($MV_T \equiv P_T T$) was not motivated alone by a desire to know the history of economic thought. It helps explain why *specialization or the degree of vertical integration is a determinant of the income velocity of money.* Money is used in all transactions, whether one purchases final goods and services or intermediate goods and financial assets. Less vertical integration increases intermediate goods transactions, by definition, as some firms produce raw materials and others manufacture final goods and services. A vertically integrated baking industry purchases wheat and sells bread, eliminating independent millers. As firms become more specialized and production becomes less vertically integrated, the volume of non-GNP transactions increases. Since money is held for GNP and non-GNP transactions, *greater specialization increases the money/income (GNP)*

FIGURES 23–2
Transactions Balances

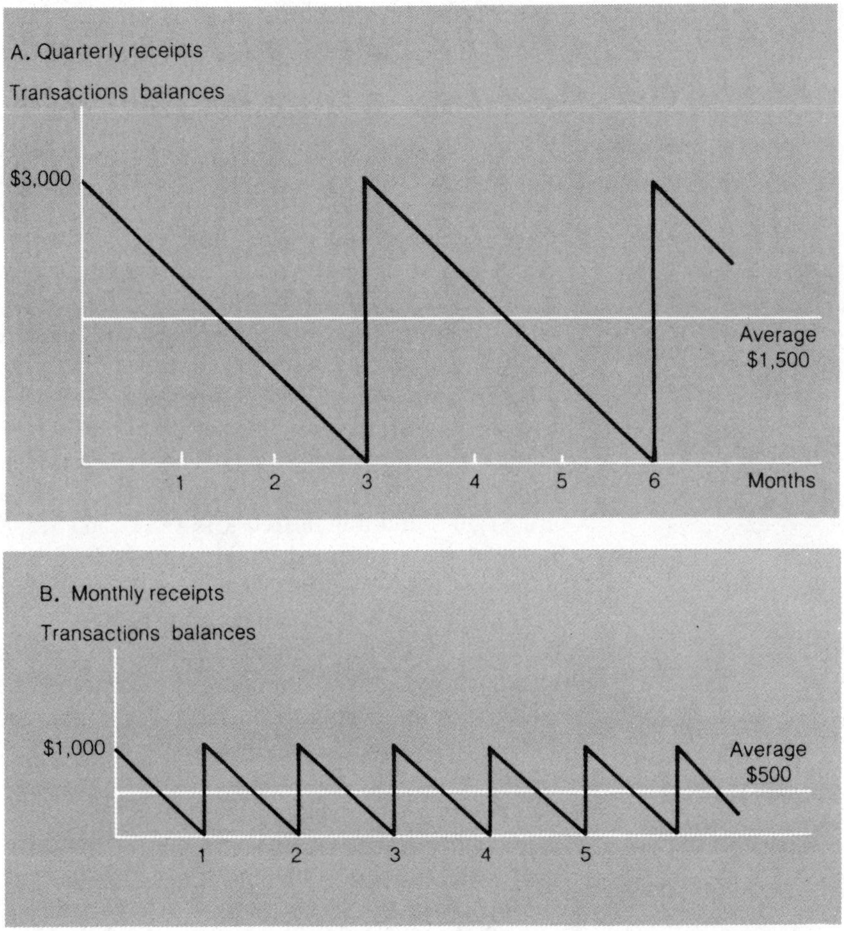

ratio k, because more money must be held for the non-GNP transactions. In other words, *transactions* velocity or the number of times the average dollar changes hands for *whatever* reason measures the "work" money performs. Specialization does not affect the total work money can perform but does decrease (increase) the amount of work money performs for GNP (non-GNP) purposes. Therefore, specialization reduces GNP velocity. For example, suppose all transactions initially are associated with GNP, and, on the average, money is spent weekly. Income (GNP) and transactions velocities both are 52 per year. Assume firms suddenly specialize and intermediate transactions are as large as GNP transactions.

Money should continue to change hands every week. However, only half the money is spent on final goods; the other half is spent on intermediate goods. Total transactions velocity remains at 52, but income velocity drops to 26 per year.[3]

Finally, Fisher recognized that velocity depends on the availability of credit. Many individuals during Fisher's time had accounts at grocery and general stores. They signed for groceries and paid the grocer on their paydays. Credit synchronizes receipts and payments more closely and increases money's rate of turnover, or reduces its average holding period. *The increasing availability and use of credit enters the quantity theory equation by raising velocity.*

Recognition of credit effects on velocity seemingly forces attention on the rate of interest, which may be viewed as the price of credit. However, Fisher and his velocity approach followers stopped short of considering the relationship between velocity and interest rates. Velocity and the demand for money were very mechanical in Fisher's hands. Slow trains and unsynchronized receipts and payments limited the rate of turnover of money. Fisher was blinded by concentrating on money in motion rather than at rest, or so others have suggested. Whatever may be the reason for Fisher's failure, the Cambridge economists, who preferred the cash-balance version of the quantity theory to Fisher's velocity version, *sometimes* recognized that the transactions coefficient, k, depends on the rate of interest. Of course, this implies velocity also depends on interest rates since $k = 1/V$. Consistency is the hobgoblin of little minds, and Marshall, Pigou, and other Cambridge economists had great minds. On their best days, Cambridge economists stated explicitly and clearly the negative relationship between desired money holdings and interest rates (positive relationship between velocity and interest rates).[4] On other days, and there were many, Cambridge economists overlooked the effect of interest rates on the money/income ratio. *On balance, classicists believed k and V and, therefore, the demand for money were independent of interest rates in the long run.*

In summary, a realization that k and V are not immutable constants prompted the classical analysis of their determinants. Fisher and other classicists thought that velocity would rise slightly over time due to (1) technological change and transportation improvements, (2) industrialization and more synchronized receipts and payments, and (3) wider financial markets and greater credit availability. These three factors should

---

[3]The decline in income velocity with real income constant implies that prices fall. Alternatively, prices fall when total transactions velocity remains constant and transactions increase.

[4]A. C. Pigov, "The Value of Money," *Quarterly Journal of Economics* 32 (November 1917): pp. 38–65.

outweigh velocity decreases due to greater specialization and less vertical integration.

The Modern Quantity Theory and Keynesian Transactions Demand

Virtually no one fully accepts every aspect of the classical quantity theory of money. Yet virtually everyone accepts some aspect of it, and virtually every aspect is accepted by someone. Keynesian economists believe that the classical money demand equation and the analysis of the determinants of velocity are important elements of total money demand. Keynes claimed, however, that classicists had only a transactions demand for money. He mentioned another element to money demand, as subsequent chapters will describe. Indeed, the Keynesian second element to total money demand prompted our mention in the last section of the possibility of interest rates influencing the demand for money. Current empirical evidence strongly supports the validity of the Keynesian second element or, at least, indicates that the *classicists erred in assuming money demand is independent of the rate of interest*. The demand for money certainly does depend on the rate of interest. *This does not deny, however, the usefulness of the classical quantity theory as a partial explanation of total money demand, as Keynes recognized.*

Neoclassical economists on the other hand totally repudiate the *specific* form of the classical money demand. *Neoclassicists do not emphasize that money is the medium of exchange*. In fact, they largely ignore the specific services performed by money. Neoclassicists look at money as simply one of many assets. This asset approach inevitably leads to the assumption that money demand depends on wealth or some proxy such as Friedman's permanent income, which is an exponentially declining, weighted average of current and lagged income. Moreover, with the possible exception of Professor Friedman, every neoclassicist includes an interest rate term in the demand for money.[5] As mentioned in the last chapter, however, *from the viewpoint of the entire neoclassical model the precise form of the money demand relationship is largely irrelevant*. Most quantity theory conclusions follow whether or not money demand depends on current income or wealth and the rate of interest, as we demonstrate rigorously in later chapters.[6] Since the form of the classical quantity theory

---

[5]Friedman's position on the interest elasticity of the demand for money is not altogether clear. Virtually everyone interpreted, correctly I believe, his "The Demand for Money: Some Theoretical and Empirical Results," *Journal of Political Economy,* August 1959, as saying that the demand for money is independent of the rate of interest. However, Friedman said, "We have been misinterpreted wrongly, I believe, as saying that (the Cambridge) k is completely independent of interest rates." ("A Theoretical Framework for Monetary Analysis," *Journal of Political Economy,* March–April 1970, p. 216.)

[6]This is not true for the Keynesian model. Within the Keynesian model the effects of monetary and fiscal policy do depend crucially on whether or not money demand depends on the rate of interest.

Equations (23–2) and (23–5) are particularly simple, let us attribute them to neoclassicists as well as classicists and proceed directly to the important quantity theory conclusions, which neoclassicists wholeheartedly embrace.

Quantity Theory Conclusions

The quantity theory says that velocity and the factor of proportionality, k, linking money demand and income depend on technological and institutional factors such as the transportation system. *These technological and institutional factors are exogenous; they influence variables within the system but are not influenced by the included variables, particularly the quantity of money. Moreover, these institutional factors are stable and predictable.* Because velocity is (1) independent of the quantity of money and (2) stable and predictable, it may be treated as a constant for monetary policy purposes. When both conditions are satisfied, any variation in velocity does not reduce the policymaker's control over the endogenous price level, as we show shortly.

First, however, a totally noneconomic example confirms that a particular type of movement and constancy are equivalent. Suppose Disney World initiates a new "show." With a class A ticket you can throw rotten tomatoes at Donald Duck. Under what conditions would you be likely to hit the old lecher? Ideally, Donald would remain still. Even if this were not the case, your chances of hitting him are equally good if he moves predictably—say, smoothly from one side of the stage to the other—and independently—Donald does not duck. You would be lucky indeed to hit him if he moved randomly and reacted to your toss.

Figure 23–3 graphs the cash balance version of the quantity theory, $M = kPy$. The price level is on the horizontal axis and money is on the vertical axis. The solid ray from the origin graphs the money demand curve, given the average money holding period, k, and real income. Ignore for the moment the dashed lines from the origin. The slope of the ray is ky or, equivalently, y/V. ($M^D = kPy$, and $\Delta M^D = ky\Delta P$. In words, the difference equation says that the change in money demand equals ky multiplied by the price change. $\Delta M^D = ky\Delta P$ is equivalent to $\Delta M^D/\Delta P = ky$, which is the slope of the ray since money and prices are on the vertical and horizontal axes, respectively. In terms of velocity, the slope of the ray is y/V since $k = 1/V$.) The solid horizontal line M^S_0 represents the initial money supply set by the central bank. Equilibrium as shown by the intersection of the two lines determines the price level, P_0.

Suppose velocity decreases. The demand curve rotates from B to A in Figure 23–3. The steeper curve indicates more money is demanded at every price level. Assuming a fixed money supply M^S_0, the price level falls to P_2. Can the central bank maintain the desired price level at P_0? Yes, indeed. *The technological and institutional determinants of velocity change smoothly, which makes velocity growth highly predictable.* With

FIGURE 23–3
The Quantity Theory: Money Demand and Supply

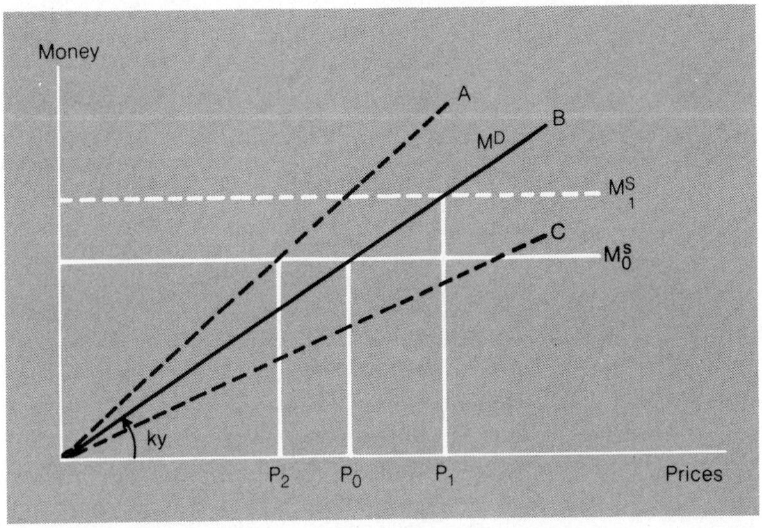

curve A predicted accurately, the central bank increases the money supply to M^S_1. Independence means that the money demand curve does *not* rotate further as supply increases; real income and the average holding period of money balances are independent of the quantity of money. The economy moves along money demand curve A and price level P_0 again prevails.

Look at Figure 23–1 again. It seemingly confirms the quantity theory assumptions that velocity is stable, changes smoothly over time, and is predictable. Velocity does not appear to jump randomly. Instead, the upward trend through 1981 is relatively smooth, so next quarter's velocity is reasonably well predicted by extrapolation. Velocity declined relatively predictively around 1982. We realize that the terms *seemingly confirms, relatively smooth,* and *reasonably well predicted* are imprecise, and someone may not accept our interpretation. At this point, however, more precise measures are too disruptive to the flow of thought. Remember neoclassical theory concerns the long run; velocity changes smoothly and predictably in the long run. A precise evaluation that concludes that *quarterly* velocity is unpredictable does not necessarily contradict the quantity theory. Such a precise evaluation simply implies the long run is longer than a quarter. Velocity per one, two, or five years could be stable and predictable even if quarterly velocity is not. The empirical Chapter 30 presents better evidence on the question of timing and other neoclassical/ Keynesian controversies. The imprecise evidence contained in Figure 23–1 is presented to dispel at an earlier stage the sometimes entrenched idea that neoclassical economics is a fairy tale in never-never land. The path of quarterly velocity is not perfectly smooth but not so random that the long run is the indefinite future.

Assumptions and conclusions of the quantity theory of money seem straightforward but must be interpreted carefully. First, the quantity theory says all prices, including the wage rate or price of labor services, respond proportionally to money. This follows from the assumption of a constant output. Employment and output remain constant only if the real wage is unchanged; commodity prices and wages change proportionally so that the real wage is unchanged. (See Figures 22–3 and 22–4.) Thus, the price effects of money should be interpreted broadly. Second, the quantity theory equation states *mathematically* that money, output, and velocity growth have equally powerful effects on prices. However, money *economically* "determines" prices in the long run because full-employment output and velocity change slowly and predictably, while money growth often is rapid and quite volatile. Figures 22–1 and 23–1 confirm the slow and steady growth of income and velocity. Prices would follow a steady course if the monetary authority maintained a steady policy. For example, suppose full-employment output outstrips any velocity increase. In symbols, y is rising faster than V. If the money stock remained constant, prices would fall steadily and gradually. On the other hand, rapid and uniform rates of monetary expansion would be associated with high and uniform rates of inflation. More likely, however, the monetary authority accelerates and decelerates monetary growth and inflation accelerates and decelerates. *Variations in the rate of inflation are almost exclusively due to variations in money growth.* Thereby, we can avoid the more accurate but cumbersome statement, "Monetary changes cause price changes proportional to what they otherwise would have equaled," and simply state, "Monetary changes cause proportional price changes."

The Commodities Market and Aggregate Expenditures

In terms of Figure 23–4, which is Figure 22–6 redrawn here for convenience, the crude version of Say's Law states that the aggregate expenditure curve coincides with the 45° line. In this case, supply by itself always creates its own demand. We argued, however, that classicists generally were too smart to subscribe to the crude version, which is contradicted by the facts. Recessions occur; supply does not create its own demand at all times. The classical analysis of the commodities market is designed to explain the valid version of Say's Law. Before discussing the difficult adjustment process, however, we methodically explain why aggregate demand depends on the rate of interest and real money balances. A thorough explanation of income effects on demand is unnecessary at this point

FIGURE 23–4
Aggregate Expenditures and Output

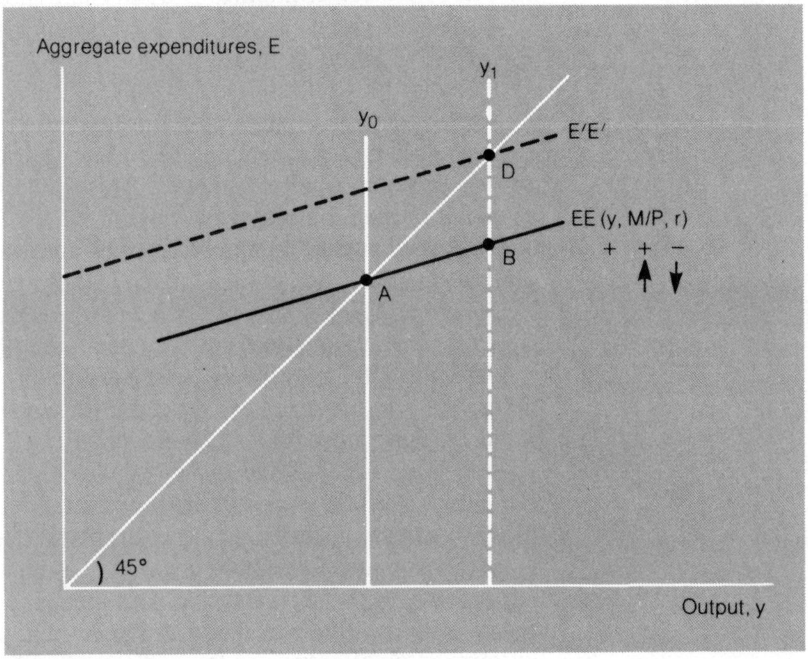

and is postponed until the chapters on Keynesian economics.[7] Full-employment income already is determined by supply conditions. We need understand only those determinants whose variations cause demand to equal a given supply.

The Rate of Interest and Investment

Classical economists presented several reasons for an inverse relationship between expenditures and the rate of interest. Let us first discuss the interest rate effect Keynes accepted, albeit half-heartedly. Investment is the acquisition of new capital goods such as machines that, when combined with other factors of production, produce a stream of commodities in the future. The investment decision entails two calculations: compute the rate of return on the investment and then compare it with the rate of interest. The rate of return on an investment and the yield on bonds are computed in a similar manner. Suppose the price of the capital good is K

[7]The consumption function, an important determinant of equilibrium income in the Keynesian model, incorporates income effects.

in general ($100 as a specific example) and the anticipated net revenue at the end of the year is R_1($110). Net revenue is the anticipated additional revenue from the sales of commodities produced with the machine minus all costs of production—labor and raw materials, for example—except the initial cost of the machine (depreciation) and interest. For simplicity assume the machine disintegrates at the end of the year. The rate of return on the investment—or the marginal efficiency of investment—is that rate of discount which equates the prices of capital goods and the present value of the net revenue.

$$\begin{aligned} K &= R_1/(1 + rr) \\ \$100 &= \$110/(1 + 0.1) \end{aligned} \tag{23–6}$$

In terms of Equation (23–6), the marginal efficiency of investment is rr, 0.1 stated as a decimal, or 10 percent, in our specific example.

Profit-maximizing firms compare the marginal efficiency of investment and the rate of interest. (Remember we are abstracting from the myriad of interest rates and assuming a homogeneous bond which yields "the" rate of interest.) If the marginal efficiency of investment, possibly adjusted downward for the riskiness of anticipated future sales, is greater than the rate of interest, the investment will be undertaken whether the firm must borrow or has sufficient money on hand. In this respect firms are no different from you and me. We would borrow at, say, 8 percent, when we can invest the proceeds at 10 percent. Firms with sufficient money on hand to finance the investment view the rate of interest as an opportunity return; it is the return that firms sacrifice by using the money themselves rather than lending it to someone else. Firms maximize profits by undertaking all investments yielding returns greater than the opportunity return. If the marginal efficiency of investment just equals the rate of interest, the investment is a matter of indifference; if the marginal efficiency of investment is less, the investment should not be undertaken.

The marginal efficiency of investment schedule, more simply called the investment schedule, shows the amount of desired investment at alternative interest rates, r. The downward-sloping line labeled I(r) in Figure 23–5 is such an investment schedule. Why is the investment schedule downward sloping? First, Keynes, or at least early Keynesians, stressed the projects approach to investment, where alternative investment projects are ranked by their rate of return. Few investment projects yield rates of returns greater than or equal to some arbitrarily high rate of interest and, therefore, investment by profit-maximizing firms is low. As the rate of interest falls, more investments yielding at least equal rates of return are undertaken. An additional, and in some respects preferable, explanation given by classicists for the negative relationship between investment and the rate of interest is based on the substitutability of factors of production. For example, one can mow a yard with an inexpensive

FIGURE 23–5
Investment Schedule

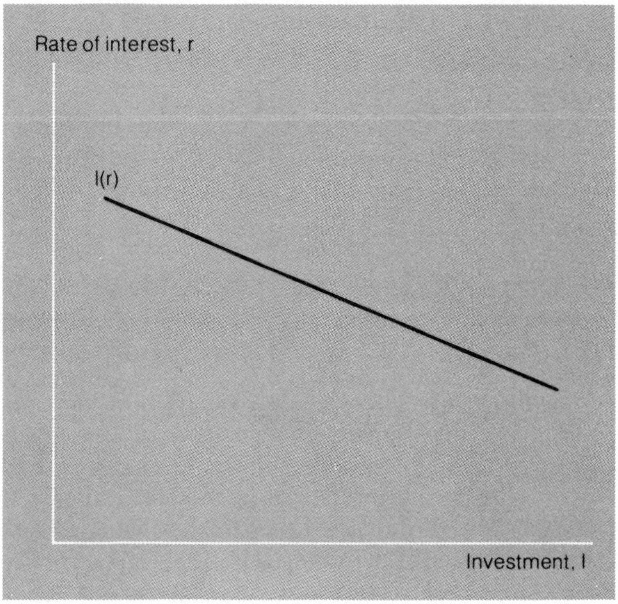

hand mower and substantial labor effort or with a capital intensive riding mower and less labor effort. The optimal capital stock associated with any given output is negatively related to the rate of interest, other things being equal. At low interest rates profit-maximizing firms substitute capital for labor until the rate of return on capital equals the rate of interest. Net investment is the additional capital stock during the period. As the rate of interest declines, firms undertake more investments and move towards the larger optimal capital stock.[8]

The investment curve becomes more elastic or flatter as one offers additional reasons for its downward slope. In contrast to Keynesians, who rely almost exclusively on the projects explanation for a downward sloping investment curve, *classicists claimed the investment curve is quite*

[8]An analogy may aid in differentiating between the ranking of alternative investment projects and optimal capital stock explanations for a downward-sloping investment schedule. Why is the aggregate demand curve for, say, tea downward sloping? Two explanations are possible. First, each person may demand a fixed quantity of tea but the price people are willing to pay varies. As the price of tea falls, more people buy tea. The ranking of alternative projects approach is analagous. It ignores the substitutability of capital and labor and assumes each new project is associated with a fixed capital stock. An alternative explanation says that as the price of tea (the rate of interest) falls, each person buys more tea (net investment expands) and substitutes tea (capital) for coffee (labor). Our emphasis on GNP and gross investment would add depreciation to this explanation for net investment.

elastic. Substantially larger net investment is undertaken in order to increase the capital stock sufficiently and equate the rate of return on capital with the lower interest rates.

In drawing the investment schedule or any other demand curve, we assume all other factors affecting demand are given and unchanged. The investment schedule shifts as firms' estimates of net revenue, R_1, vary. Looking at Equation (23–6), higher anticipated net revenue raises the rate of return on investment and shifts the investment schedule upward. The future is uncertain. Waves of excessive optimism and pessimism regarding future sales would dramatically shift the investment schedule. Our discussion of the quantity theory suggests that classicists discounted this possibility. The economy is basically stable. In the past firms usually have found ready buyers and they expect this pattern to continue. *Quite moderate shifts of the investment schedule are the rule according to neoclassicists and, anticipating future chapters, the exception according to Keynes.*

How are these properties of the investment schedule reflected in Figure 23–4's aggregate expenditure curve? The sensitivity of investment to the rate of interest causes slightly lower interest rates to shift the expenditure curve significantly upward. The relative stability of the investment curve says that expenditure curve shifts due to firms' behavior are quite moderate except when the rate of interest changes.

The Rate of Interest and Consumption

Keynes largely dismissed the claim of classical economics that two factors made consumption depend on the rate of interest. First, interest rates have a direct financial cost effect on consumption or, equivalently, a direct rate of return impact on saving. Some households who had been planning to borrow in order to finance a major expenditure will be deterred by high finance costs. Moreover, those households already planning to save will be encouraged to save more. Households refrain from current consumption and save in order to provide for the future. The rate of interest measures the tradeoff between current consumption and future consumption made possible by saving. For example, suppose the rate of interest is 8 percent (.08 written as a decimal) and gizmos cost \$1. By saving \$1 today one can purchase 1.08 next year.[9] As the rate of interest rises and current consumption can be substituted for more future consumption, the typical household consumes less and saves more. Second, interest rates indirectly influence consumption through their impact on wealth, as we show in the next section.

---

[9]We are assuming the rate of inflation is zero. The distinction between real and nominal interest rates was discussed in Chapter 6.

The Rate of Interest, Wealth, and the Pigou Effect

The final major determinant of expenditures is wealth or net worth. Wealth is a stock, while income and expenditures are flows. Wealth appears on a balance sheet constructed for a moment in time, while income is measured during some time interval. The real value of the capital stock and equity issues, K, real bond holdings, B/rP, and real money balances, M_0/P, comprise a single economic unit's wealth, W.

$$W = K + B/rP + M_0/P \tag{23-7}$$

In Equation (23–7), B is the number of perpetual bonds paying $1 each per period, so that their dollar value is B/r. To get the real value of anything, divide the dollar value by the price level.

How does wealth affect spending? Suppose you win the grand prize in the Maryland lottery and become an instant millionaire. Will you spend a different amount now that you are wealthier, other things being equal? Most people will spend more. *There is a positive wealth effect on consumption.*

Classicists claimed that as a first approximation the specific form in which wealth is held is irrelevant for expenditures. For example, the lottery winner's additional spending would be approximately the same whether Maryland officials paid out cash or IBM stock of equal value. Nevertheless, *classicists did emphasize the real money balance effect, also called the Pigou effect in honor of its popularizer.* Consider why bond and capital value effects generally were ignored. Bonds are the assets of creditors but the equal liability of debtors. *Assuming a closed economy and similar spending patterns for all citizens, from the viewpoint of society as a whole, net bond holdings are zero and have no effect on spending.* The greater expenditures by wealthy bond holders cancel lesser expenditures by poor bond issuers.[10]

The value of the capital stock owned directly and the equity issues of corporations do not wash out in the aggregate. Capital values and stock prices equal the discounted or capitalized value of their net revenue stream. Therefore, stock prices vary inversely with the rate of interest. Look at Equation (23–6) again. When the rate of interest rises, the price of capital and common stock, K, falls since the rate of return, rr, and interest rate

[10]We are implicitly assuming that all money is fiat money. Demand deposits are assets of depositors and liabilities of banks and not part of society's wealth. Therefore, society's wealth is less than its real money balances when demand deposits exist. In this case wealth equals the monetary base. Since the money supply equals the money supply multiplier times the base, $M = mB$, wealth equals the money supply divided by its multiplier. We are also assuming the public views any government bonds as their own and that they are simultaneously an asset and liability.

are equated at equilibrium.[11] *Recognition of wealth effects adds another dimension to the interest rate-expenditures relationship.* Assuming net revenue is approximately constant—the investment curve shifts little—capital stock values depend only on the rate of interest, which already has been listed as a determinant of spending. Because recognition of wealth effects usually introduces only real balances as an *additional* determinant of *aggregate* spending, the more general wealth effect often was equated with the *real balance or Pigou effect, which says that more money or a lower price level has a direct and positive effect on the demand for commodities.* As we shall see later, Keynes claimed that money at best has an indirect effect on spending. *It is wrong, however, to believe that the Pigou effect attributes to money some property different from any other asset.* An increase in wealth, however attained, increases spending. In subsequent chapters we will relax the assumption of zero net bond holdings and, thereby, make the aggregate wealth effect even more powerful.

The determinants of expenditures are shown explicitly in Figure 23–4. Although classicists believed that large government expenditures were unnecessary for full employment, they clearly recognized that it is a component of demand and has the *potential* for shifting the expenditure curve.

Long-Run Equilibrium

Having specified the determinants of expenditures, we now can attempt to explain how full-employment supply creates its own demand *without any government action.* Exposition of this difficult argument is facilitated by assuming full-employment output is produced at all times. The next section on short-run changes allows output to fall below full employment temporarily before rebounding back up to full employment. Take heed that our attempt to justify Say's Law is only partially successful. Neither the classicists nor anyone following them has been able to "prove" that demand will equal full-employment output in the long run. At best one can present a plausible explanation of the process by which demand adjusts toward supply. Whether demand will finally equal supply cannot be proven. While this may sound deficient, neither Keynes nor anyone else has "proven" the opposite, that is, demand will not equal full-employment output.

The adjustment process relies heavily on *Walras's Law, which places a restriction on demand and supply due to the budget constraint.* Demand and supply curves are not wishful-thinking curves; they do not indicate

---

[11]Although K was viewed as fixed when Equation (23–7) was first presented, it is in fact variable, as we now recognize.

the quantities requested from a fairy godmother. Demand and supply curves recognize that we live in a quid pro quo economy. If we demand more of one commodity, we must demand less of another or supply more of a third commodity in order to acquire the funds to make the purchase. For example, if we demand more apples we must demand fewer oranges, reduce our money holdings, or supply more bonds (borrow). Suppose there are n goods and services which include money, bonds, factors of production, and consumer items. *Formally stated, Walras's Law says that the sum of the demand and supply for all n goods and services are always equal*. Mathematically,

$$\sum_{i=1}^{n} P_iD_i \equiv \sum_{i=1}^{n} P_iS_i, \text{ or } \sum_{i=1}^{n} P_i(D_i - S_i) \equiv 0,$$

where D_i and S_i are demand and supply, respectively, and P_i is the price for the ith good. The ith market is in equilibrium when $D_i - S_i = 0$. An alternative statement of Walras's Law is: if $n - 1$ markets are in equilibrium, the nth market must also be in equilibrium. *Disequilibrium is never limited to a single market*.

Suppose the economy is at full-employment equilibrium as represented by the broken lines y_1 and E′E′ in Figure 23–4. Now assume firms' investment opportunities decline and consumers suddenly become bearish and save more. The investment schedule in Figure 23–5 shifts leftward and the aggregate expenditure curve in Figure 23–4 shifts downward, becoming the solid line EE. The unchanged full-employment output temporarily exceeds demand by BD. How is demand again equated to full-employment output? *According to Walras's Law, a decline in the demand for commodities cannot be the only change*. The firms and consumers who were previously purchasing commodities must be doing something with their funds. In our highly aggregated model the only alternatives to commodities are bonds and money. *Neoclassicists typically assume that lower investment demand will be accompanied by a reduction in the supply of bonds (less borrowing)*. When consumers become bearish and save more, they typically use their additional savings to demand bonds (lend more). Both the reduced supply of bonds by investors and the enhanced demand by savers lower the rate of interest, which shifts the aggregate expenditure curve back up to E′E′. A lower rate of interest generally is sufficient for full employment.

The second and more complicated case supposes firms and households hoard the funds previously spent on investment and consumption. In other words, the reduced demand for commodities manifests itself in a larger demand for real money balances. At any price and income level more money is demanded. The money demand curve in Figure 23–3 shifts from B to A and becomes steeper as the Cambridge k increased, or velocity decreased. At the initial price level P_0 the demand for money exceeds supply M^S_0 so individuals hoard income receipts and do not purchase commodities. There is no reason for the rate of interest to fall as the additional saving is not lent. Prices fall, however, as aggregate demand is less than output. The price decline from P_0 to P_2 in Figure 23–3 satisfies society's demand for additional real money balances. The same amount of *nominal* money balances is satisfactory at the lower price level. Hoarding stops. The nominal quantity of money demanded again equals the fixed nominal supply at P_2. Aggregate expenditures fell to EE because society wanted additional real money balances. When prices fall and society has its additional real balances, the expenditure curve shifts back to its initial position.[12]

We therefore have two alternative ways to maintain full employment: interest rate or price level movements. Which alternative is most likely? Interest rate movements. The demand curve for money is quite stable. It rarely shifts. *Spending shifts are typically associated with shifts in lending instead of the demand for money. The rate of interest typically adjusts expenditures and full-employment output, but sometimes price level variations are necessary.*

Short-Run Policy

Classicists and neoclassicists pay little attention to the short run because they believe the economy adjusts rapidly toward full employment. In his monumental 515-page book, *The Purchasing Power of Money,* Irving Fisher devoted just a 19-page chapter to the so-called transition period—the short run.[13] The economy may adjust rapidly but not instantaneously, however. What relationships exist in the short run before all adjustments have occurred? Again suppose that consumers save more (spend less) and lend the additional saving. The *equilibrium* interest rate falls. However, the *market* interest rate may not fall rapidly enough and may remain above the new equilibrium for some time. A "sticky" rate of interest causes demand to shift back to E′E′ in Figure 23–4 only *after* a long lag. Full-employment output will be greater than spending for some time. Were firms to continue producing full-employment output, undesired invento-

---

[12] We are implicitly assuming that the *real* demand and supply of loanable funds is independent of the price level. The *nominal* demand and supply of funds is proportional to the price level. If the loan market contains a real balance effect, the shifts in saving and money demand will lower both interest and prices. The truly interested student might read Don Patinkin, *Money, Interest, and Prices: An Integration of Monetary and Value Theory,* 2d ed (New York: Harper & Row, 1965), an encyclopedic text on neoclassical economics. In terms of Patinkin's graph, we are assuming the BB curve is flat. Appendix B discusses some quite advanced issues about saving, investment, the rate of interest, and Walras's Law.

[13] New York: Macmillan, 1926. Chapter 4.

ries would accumulate. *If the market rate of interest is sticky and does not fall rapidly enough, output will temporarily fall below full employment as firms attempt to reduce the accumulating undesired inventories.* Should the government pump up demand by undertaking additional expenditures financed by borrowing? Such a policy prevents the market interest rate from having to fall as the government borrows (sells bonds equal to) the additional amount the private sector is saving and lending. Larger government expenditures would shift the aggregate expenditure curve back to E′E′ and offset the downward private spending shift. *Classicists generally opposed government expenditures as a means of achieving full employment. First, classicists doubted the market interest rate was sticky and did not fall rapidly enough to restore full employment.* Second, even if interest rates were sticky, the appropriate policy is not greater government expenditures, which prevents the interest rate from having to fall. Classicists were harsh disciplinarians. If the rate of interest will not fall by itself, beat it down. How is this accomplished? By monetary expansion, which temporarily lowers the rate of interest. Monetary expansion increases further the already swollen supply of credit and dislodges the temporarily sticky interest rate. *Laissez-faire classicists spurned government expenditures because they thought most government expenditures were wasteful.* Society derived little benefits from the goods and services provided by the government. Full employment achieved by additional government-sponsored ditch digging and pyramid building is not preferable to unemployment according to classicists.

Regardless of their benefits, government expenditures are inappropriate when the additional saving is hoarded. In this case, society saves more because it wants additional real money balances. The money demand curve shifts upward from B to A in Figure 23–3. The interest rate is unchanged *not* because it is sticky but because the additional saving is hoarded, leaving the supply of credit constant. Sticky prices instead of interest rates cause problems. If prices do not fall rapidly enough to increase real balances and shift the demand curve back to E′E′ in Figure 23–4, output will decline as it is greater than demand at the constant rate of interest. Firms will not let inventories accumulate for long periods. The central bank can prevent a recession. *If society cannot "manufacture" the additional real balances demanded because prices are sticky, the central bank simply increases the nominal money supply.* In terms of Figure 23–3, the shift of the money demand curve is countered with an upward shift of the money supply. Society now has the additional money balance it wants, and the expenditure schedule shifts back and intersects the 45° line at full-employment output

Government expenditures cannot prevent recessions induced by hoarding and sticky prices. Government spending financed by bonds has no effect on the money supply and is hardly likely to dislodge a downwardly sticky price level. *Only larger real balances achieved through monetary expansion or deflation can restore equilibrium in this case.*[14] In terms of Figure 23–4, additional government spending does *tend* to shift the expenditure curve from EE up to E′E′. There is an important difference, however, between this sticky prices case and the previous sticky interest rate case. In the previous case, the government bond sales necessary to finance the expenditures did *not* raise interest rates, by definition of "sticky" interest rates. The curve remained at E′E′. In this case, however, the bond sales do raise interest rates. Prices, and not interest rates, are sticky. Higher interest rates shift the curve back down to EE. The negative financial effect of government spending offsets its positive direct effect. The net effect is an expenditure curve invariant to government spending.

Table 23–1 summarizes the classical analysis presented in this and the previous sections. *It illustrates the classical conclusion that monetary and fiscal actions are rarely necessary to restore full employment. The economy automatically reaches equilibrium, mainly through interest rate but sometimes through price adjustments.* Interest rates in particular are very flexible. This is good because additional saving normally is lent. When interest rates are sufficiently responsive to the additional lending, full-employment output will again be demanded. In those *rare* cases where interest rates are sticky, both expansionary monetary and fiscal policies

TABLE 23–1
Effects of Lower Expenditures

	Associated Disturbance	
	Lending	*Hoarding (increased money demand)*
Frequency	Often	Seldom
Automatic adjustment variable	Interest rate	Prices
Likelihood of short-run stickiness, which requires policy actions	Seldom	Occasionally
Effective policies	Monetary and Fiscal	Monetary only
Desirable policy	Monetary	Monetary

[14]In a passage totally out of keeping with the *General Theory,* Keynes accepts this very classical proposition. "Unemployment develops, that is to say, because people want the moon;—men cannot be employed when the object of desire (i.e., money) is something which cannot be produced and the demand for which cannot be readily choked off. There is *no* remedy but to persuade the public that green cheese is practically the same thing and to have a green cheese factory (i.e., a central bank) under public control." p. 235. [Italics added.]

are effective. Monetary policy will dislodge the sticky interest rates, besides increasing demand directly through the real balance effect. Government deficit spending financed by bonds increases total spending in this case because it does not raise *sticky* interest rates, by definition, and, therefore, does not reduce private spending. Even when effective, classicists opposed government spending because it absorbs scarce resources, which are better used by the private sector.

To be sure, prices are much less flexible downward than interest rates. But sticky prices are rarely troublesome. Flexible prices are necessary only when saving is hoarded due to an unstable money demand. The quantity theory says that money demand is stable, however. On those rare occasions when people save to acquire more real balances, M/P, the sometimes sticky prices are readily countered by increasing fiat money. Since *bond* financed government spending does not increase money, by definition, and will not dislodge the sticky prices, it is totally ineffective in this case. *If, by chance, the economy does not adjust rapidly enough, monetary policy always is the desirable policy.*

The viewpoints and conclusions in this section were attributed to classicists. Do neoclassicists accept these classical viewpoints? Totally.

Summary/Questions

Classicists believed that the demand for money was proportional to income. They analyzed the determinants of the factor of proportionality and concluded it could change over time. However, they also concluded that at any one time the proportionality factor or, equivalently, velocity, was predictable and independent of the quantity of money. Neoclassical economists can no longer accept every classical belief; the data flatly contradict some of them. However, some data presented later continue to support the fundamental classical belief that money has a predictable and independent effect on (nominal) income. Just because money has a predictable effect on income is not a sufficient condition for an active monetary policy. The economy is basically stable; interest rate and price adjustments normally bring the economy back to full employment quite rapidly. Discretionary policy usually is unnecessary. However, if discretionary policy is adopted, monetary policy is the appropriate choice.[15] While fiscal policy *usually* can do the job, it uses scarce resources. Moreover, when people are not spending because they want more ready pur-

[15]We shall discuss lags and the controversy between discretionary policy and a monetary rule after the Keynesian model has been presented.

chasing power (real balances), only the monetary authorities can satisfy the public's demand and restore full employment if prices are sticky.

1. Define the commodity theory of money. When was it widely advocated?
2. Explain the difference between the equation of exchange and the quantity theory of money equation.
3. In what sense is velocity, or the transactions coefficient k, a constant according to classicists and neoclassicists?
4. What are the main differences between the velocity and cash balance approaches to the quantity theory of money?
5. List the determinants of velocity according to classical economists and state their effect (positive or negative) on velocity.
6. State the main differences and similarities between the classical and modern quantity theories.
7. Draw two graphs. Place velocity and time on the axes of one graph and the change in velocity and the change in the quantity of money on the axes of the second graph. On each graph, draw two scatters of points, one which tends to confirm and another which contradicts the quantity theory of money.
8. Explain why investment is negatively related to the rate of interest. What is the neoclassical view concerning the shape and position of the investment schedule?
9. Define the Pigou effect and Walras's Law.
10. Assume aggregate expenditures decline. According to neoclassicists, what types of automatic adjustments restore full-employment equilibrium? Which adjustment is most likely, and why?
11. Assume some "stickiness," that is, the automatic adjustments are long delayed, so that output would tend to decline when demand falls. Under what conditions can *(a)* monetary and *(b)* fiscal policy maintain full employment? Considering resource costs and program benefits, which policy should be adopted according to neoclassicists?

Keynesian economics: Fundamental assumptions and the basic model

24

The methodological approach adopted in discussing classical economics is repeated here: fundamental assumptions of Keynesian economics are stated before getting down to nuts and bolts. There is altogether too much emphasis in economics on the nuts and bolts of curve shifting and intersection points without any appreciation of fundamental assumptions, which often yield clues regarding the generality and predictive content of the model. For example, the intersection of the neoclassical curves says that output and unemployment are independent of the rate of monetary expansion, which solely influences the price level. Nevertheless, a central bank aware of the assumptions of neoclassical theory would *not* slam the brakes on the money supply if it were unwilling to sustain some temporary unemployment. The neoclassical curves are not appropriate at all times, only in the long run. Do not get me wrong, the nuts and bolts are important, but only *after* the fundamental assumptions are well understood. If, contrary to my expectation, you have time to read only part of this chapter, by all means read the first section on fundamental assumptions. The nuts and bolts tend to be forgotten sooner—though let us hope not before the final exam—and are less important in understanding the basic policy issues which divide economists and politicians.

The second section builds the basic C + I + G = y Keynesian model. Although recent empirical evidence suggests the basic model explains facts relatively poorly, it is pedagogically useful to begin with a basic model which reviews your Principles course, and then add more nuts and bolts to construct the advanced Keynesian model of the next chapters.

Moreover, the basic model was "the" Keynesian model, or at least a good approximation of it, until the mid-1950s, and a small but dying breed of staunch Keynesians still believe the evidence supports the basic model. (The advanced model has much stronger empirical support in our mind.) In any case, the same fundamental assumptions underlie this chapter's basic Keynesian model and next chapter's advanced model.

Fundamental Assumptions

John Maynard Keynes was a man of many talents. He was the leading British academic economist of the 1930s, editor of the scholarly *Economic Journal,* advisor to British governments, and still found time to systematically spend part of each day making money. No, his talents were not that diverse; he was neither a forger nor banker and did not "create" currency or demand deposits. He made money in the street sense of the word. In the Roaring 20s he lost every penny of his small inheritance by speculating on the German mark. But Keynes, always the contrarian, made it up 100 times in the 1930s. As his business success might suggest, Keynes the first-rate theorist was not given to wasting his talents on minor issues or economically optimal but politically unacceptable policies. He was a practical man who tackled the big issues. Of course, the big issue in the early 1930s was the Great Depression. Keynes's contemporaries, the classicists, were a patient lot who preached caution. The economy adjusts rapidly, and prosperity was around the corner. Keynes thought otherwise. His famous dictum—in the long run we are all dead—expresses his belief that *the economy adjusts very slowly,* the ultimate effect of some disturbance being realized many decades from now. *Given this belief, Keynes naturally emphasized the short run and ignored the long run.*

Keynes's Law

What determines output and real income in the short run? Classicists gave but passing attention to this vital question, so Keynes had to answer it virtually "from scratch." If Say's Law summarizes classical economics, *Keynes's Law is: demand creates its own supply. Say's Law is correct in the long run, and Keynes's Law is essentially correct in the short run.* You may not be able to squeeze blood out of a turnip, but our economy is not a turnip. It is more like a restaurant, extending an analogy used earlier. Suppose a restaurant which traditionally has been half full suddenly receives a three-star rating from the premiere food critic. Crowds storm the restaurant to discover what they had been missing. Some of the new patrons will be seated immediately and their demands are met. Others form a queue. Management spots the queue and tells the waiters to discourage customers from lingering after dinner so the latecomers can be served. Water glasses are not refilled, and ashtrays are not cleaned. The restaurant traditionally stays open to midnight to serve the after-theater set and the few Spaniards unable to adapt to the "barbaric" custom of eating dinner before 11:00 P.M. However, a skeleton crew usually is sufficient to satisfy this meager demand, and most workers leave at 10:00 P.M. Our critic's review upset normal operations. If the waiters were unable to prevent lingering and the queue still exists at 10:00 P.M., the staff is asked to work overtime. Management does everything possible to justify the food critic's review. Demand creates its own supply in the short run. Firms do not attempt to maximize profits in the short run but instead strive to maintain or even increase their market share by meeting demand.

Homey examples of general principles are often eschewed by professionals because counterexamples are likely. After turnips are harvested, no amount of demand, however large, will increase supply until the following season.[1] True, the quantity of *every* product may not be determined by demand in the short run, but Keynes's Law applies to a sufficiently large number of industries as to characterize reasonably well the entire economy. Moreover, *the statistical evidence tends to support the proposition that demand creates its own supply in the short run.* But statistics is such an arcane science beset by difficulties that the inability to construct homey examples supporting the statistical "evidence" is a sign that something is definitely amiss.

You often will find Say's Law listed in the index of money and banking or history of economic thought books. As far as we know, you will never find Keynes's Law. We dubbed the assumption that demand creates its own supply Keynes's Law because it underlies all Keynesian models. With exports and imports subsumed, the commodities market is in equilibrium when desired expenditures, E, the sum of consumption, investment, and government expenditures, equal desired production. In symbols, the equilibrium condition is

$$E = C + I + G = y$$

Keynesian economics concentrates exclusively on specifying the determinants of the expenditure components. Then the equilibrium equation is used. Absolutely no attention is given to the determinants of desired production.[2] Why? One must simply specify desired expenditures because demand creates its own supply.

---

[1]We shall accept this as a counterexample to Keynes's Law although it implicitly assumes, perhaps unrealistically, that the short run is less than one year.

[2]Chapter 28 presents a model with an aggregate supply curve derived by assuming that labor demand is a function of the real wage but labor supply depends on nominal wages. This intermediate model is neither neoclassical nor Keynesian in our mind. Of course, if one prefers to call the intermediate model a very sophisticated Keynesian model, then the text accurately describes only the simple C + I + G and advanced IS–LM Keynesian models.

In terms of Figure 24–1, a graph we used previously to illustrate Say's Law, Keynesian economics analyzes the aggregate expenditure curve, EE. Aggregate expenditure is measured on the vertical axis, and output is on the horizontal axis. The upward-sloping aggregate expenditure curve illustrates the dependence of demand on output. After specifying the position of the EE curve, one looks where it crosses the 45° line to ascertain the equilibrium level of income since along the 45° line demand equals output. An aggregate output or supply curve is ignored; it is assumed that such a curve will intersect the 45° line whenever the expenditure curve does.

An alternative statement of Keynes's Law is: supply is perfectly elastic in the short run so prices are independent of demand. The horizontal SS line in Figure 24–2 is the perfectly elastic supply curve at a price P_0. Temporarily ignore the dashed line S′S′. The demand curve DD has the usual shape; more output is demanded at lower prices. As demand increases from DD to D′D′, more is produced—demand creates its own supply—but prices remain constant. Our restaurant keeps prices fixed while it attempts to justify the food critic's review. As we argued, Keynes's Law is essentially correct, and the virtually continuous upward march in the price level does not necessarily contradict it. The observed price level depends on the interaction of demand and supply. Prices rise because the horizontal supply curve shifts upward to S′S′ and not because demand

FIGURE 24–1

Fundamental Keynesian Graph, Unspecified Supply Adjusts to Demand

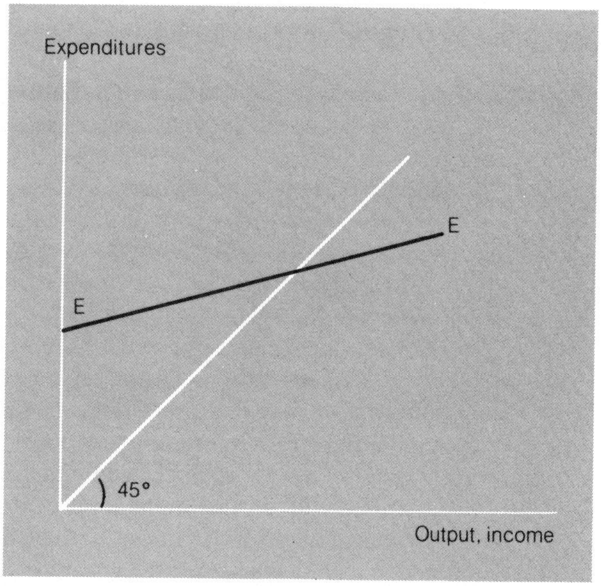

FIGURE 24–2
Keynesian Aggregate Demand and Supply

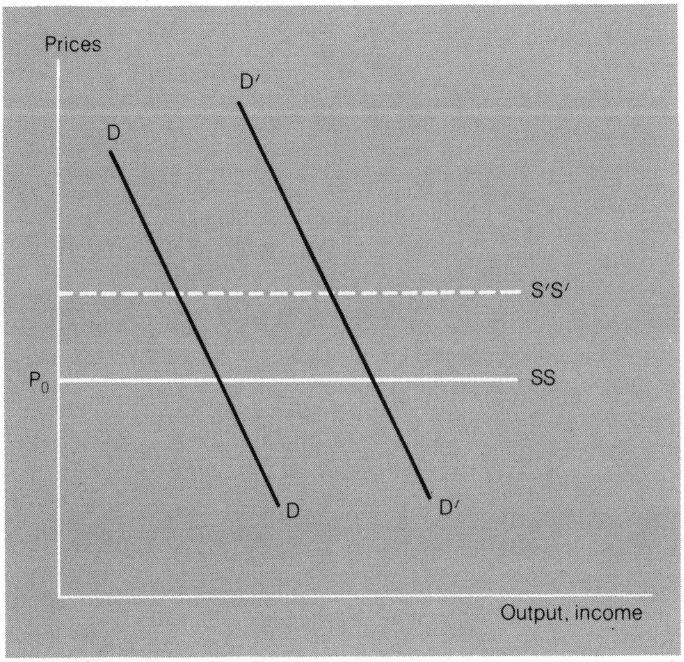

increases. Keynesian economics is silent about the position and shifts of the supply curve. If pressed, a Keynesian might state briefly and quickly that *past* wage contracts and possibly *past* demand may affect the *present* supply curve. However, the past is a given in the present, so the *supply curve is exogenous*. To simplify the analysis, shifts of the exogenous supply curve are never considered and, therefore, prices are assumed to be fixed. Keynesian economics analyzes the demand curve. What determines its position, and how do various policies shift the demand curve? A flat supply curve does not imply that Keynes's answer to these questions is incorrect.

The Keynesian perfectly elastic supply, fixed-price assumption is unrealistic. Prices do rise as everyone is aware. We cannot even allege the assumption is correct after the lapse of sufficient time; the Keynesian model describes short-run reactions. In Keynes's defense, however, no model is entirely realistic and general. Specifying the determinants of a marginally upward-sloping supply curve adds somewhat greater realism, but complicates the analysis significantly since the interaction of supply and demand could not be ignored. *Keynes thought, and the empirical evidence confirms, that aggregate price adjustments lag behind aggregate quantity adjustments.*[3] As a first approximation, Keynes let only quantity adjust.

Recession Prone Economies

What calendar period corresponds with the short run during which demand creates its own supply and prices are independent of demand, or approximately so? How long do price adjustments lag behind quantity adjustments? Keynes clearly realized that *the calendar length of the short run depends on the initial conditions, the most important being the rate of unemployment.* At high rates of unemployment, demand has a long-lasting effect on output. At low rates of unemployment, however, an increase in desired expenditures has a short-lived effect on output. Prices rise soon after. Full employment, a slippery economic concept described in detail in Chapter 28, is not some technological minimum level of unemployment and maximum output. No one defines full employment as zero unemployment. Actual output has occasionally been greater than full-employment output, particularly during wars. There *always* is some slack in the economy—not everyone is working seven days a week—and Keynes's Law is always correct, if only for a short calendar period when the economy is at "full employment."

Now Keynes was a practical man. Why did he analyze the short run during which demand creates its own supply and prices are independent of demand? *According to Keynes, the short run was much more than a fleeting moment and worthy of analysis because aggregate demand is chronically deficient. Recessions and depressions punctuated by an occasional boom are the norm.* If this were *not* the case, the Keynesian analysis of the responsiveness of aggregate demand to fiscal and monetary policy would be largely a matter of curiosity with little practical significance. If the unemployment rate typically was low and output was high, then changes in aggregate demand induced by fiscal or monetary policy would have short-lived effects on output. In this case, the effects of price changes, which would occur soon after demand shifts, should not be ignored. The world in 1936 was ripe for Keynesian economics. Although the economy touched bottom in 1933, unemployment still equaled ap-

---

[3]Following Marshall, traditional *microeconomics* correctly assumes that the microeconomic short-run supply curve is steeper than the long-run curve. However, the converse is true in the aggregate. The firm or industry analyzed in microeconomics adjusts quantity in the short run by employing different quantities of a few variable factors of production. In the long run all factors are variable, new firms enter the industry, and resources are drawn from other firms and industries, making the microeconomic supply curve flatter. From the viewpoint of the entire economy, however, resources are fixed; there are no "other" firms and industries which the aggregate economy can utilize. The aggregate economy is more elastic in the short run when misperceptions, contracts, custom, and other such factors impede profit and utility maximization.

proximately 17 percent in 1936. Prices between 1933 and 1936 were more or less stable, albeit at a low level. Policies stressing demand expansion were bound to gain wide currency.

The L-Shaped Supply Curve

Complex ideas are difficult to state succinctly and even more difficult to represent graphically. The Keynesian aggregate supply curve is often drawn as a reverse L.

FIGURE 24–3 Modified Keynesian Aggregate Supply

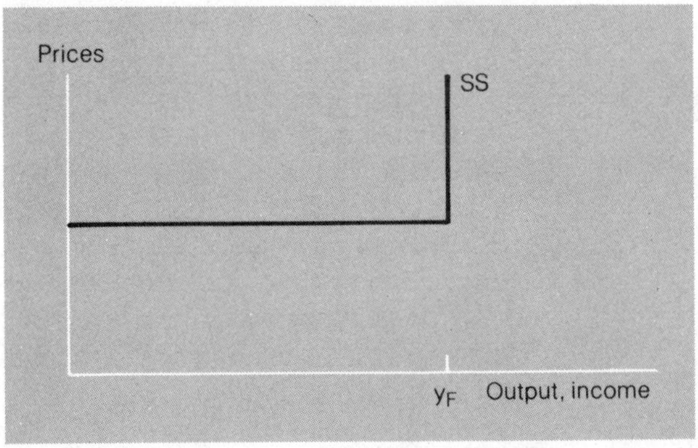

In some respects Figure 24–3 does capture Keynes's ideas. Recall that Keynes said that (1) quantity always responds first to changes in demand, and (2) the lagged price response, if any, depends on the existing level of output. According to Figure 24–3, increases in demand up to some point, labeled y_F for full-employment income, cause output to increase but have no effect on price. When output already is y_F, further increases in demand simply raise prices. While there certainly is a strong semblance between Keynesian thought and Figure 24–3, the latter does not capture Keynesian thought perfectly. In particular, Figure 24–3 denies the valid proposition that quantity always responds to changes in demand, if only for a short calendar period of time. The flat aggregate supply curve in Figure 24–2 does show this valid Keynesian proposition. However, the flat aggregate supply curve fails to illustrate the lagged price response when output is quite high. Indeed, it is precisely this failure which leads many Keynesians to draw a reverse L-shaped supply curve. For the moment we prefer to view the supply curve as perfectly flat throughout. This seems best, provided one realizes the length of time the curve remains flat and does not shift upward is a function of where one is on the curve. Figure 24–3 may be viewed as mixing elements of both classical and Keynesian economics, which may not be objectionable if only one model is to be used for all time and space. It resembles the now old-fashioned view that there is a permanent trade-off between inflation and unemployment, as discussed in Chapter 28. Our approach with two sharply different time periods and models facilitates understanding the modern view that the unemployment-inflation relationship shifts over time.

Keynesian economics assumes that monetary policy and interest rates are of secondary importance. Indeed, monetary policy might be useless as a means of stimulating the economy out of a deep depression. *Fiscal policy in the form of government expenditures and taxes is the key policy for controlling aggregate demand.* This fundamental Keynesian assumption shines through in the manner desired expenditures are expressed: the sum of government expenditures and other items. Money is not highlighted because it has an indirect and secondary effect on aggregate demand.[4] This Keynesian assumption is debatable; some empirical studies confirm and some deny it. At least the advanced Keynesian model in the next chapter is sufficiently general that this assumption can be relaxed by changing the slopes of various curves.

In summary, Keynesian economics describes short-run adjustments. It assumes:

1. Demand creates its own supply.
2. Prices are exogenous.
3. The economy is basically recession prone with an occasional boom pulling the economy out of its normally lethargic state.
4. Monetary policy is of secondary importance. Fiscal policy is the key policy for controlling aggregate demand.

Assumptions 1 and 2 are not independent; either one largely implies the other. While assumption 3 is not an integral component of the Keynesian *theoretical models,* it provides the foundation for many Keynesian *policy*

---

[4]Recall that Fisher and other classicists expressed desired expenditures as the product of money and velocity. Might you prefer the Fisherian expression if you interpreted the empirical evidence as confirming the importance of money?

prescriptions. Assumption 4 is unrelated to the other assumptions. While the advanced Keynesian model can be purged of assumption 4, doing so violates Keynes's thought and a widely accepted, easy way of labeling economists as Keynesians or monetarists. Economists who interpret the diverse and sometimes contradictory empirical evidence as supporting assumption 4 are often called Keynesian, whatever their other beliefs.

The Basic Keynesian Model: Determinants of Spending

The introductory section argued for presentation of the basic Keynesian or C + I + G = y model on pedagogical and policy grounds. The pedagogical objective is best met by presenting the basic Keynesian model in a manner different from that in virtually every Principles course, where nuts and bolts are varied repeatedly, but the feature distinguishing the basic and advanced Keynesian models is left unclear. Since this admittedly is a review, let's focus immediately on the distinguishing feature of the *basic* Keynesian model.

The basic Keynesian model solves the equilibrium level of income with the aid of only one equilibrium equation, $C + I + G = y$. Graphically, only one figure is necessary. *Only one equation or graph is necessary because all desired spending, $C + I + G$, is either autonomous or induced, that is, dependent on income*. Induced spending in a *basic* Keynesian model should depend on income in a simple way: let induced spending be proportional to income. Therefore, the general form of C + I + G becomes A + Ry, where A is autonomous spending and Ry is induced spending. *The proportionality factor, R, is more technically called the marginal propensity to respend national income*. When desired spending takes this form, we can set spending equal to output and get a unique equilibrium value of y.

$$A + Ry = y$$

$$y = \frac{A}{1 - R}$$

What name do we give to the reciprocal of 1 − R? The multiplier. R, the marginal propensity to respend, lies between zero and one. Therefore, the reciprocal of 1 − R is greater than one and called the multiplier. *Income is the product of autonomous spending and the multiplier*. If spending depended on the rate of interest or any other endogenous variable, the equilibrium equation would contain two variables and generally not yield a unique solution for income.

We will present several versions of the basic Keynesian model in the process of analyzing various policy issues. The versions differ in many ways but they all have a common element as versions of the basic Keynesian model: all spending is either autonomous or induced.

Government Spending

In which spending category, autonomous or induced, does government spending belong? Although Keynesian economics emphasizes fiscal policy, the most basic Keynesian model is totally silent about the determinants of government expenditures. It is an entirely autonomous variable. Government spending influences income and, in the advanced IS–LM model of the next chapter, the rate of interest, but government spending itself is not influenced by income and the rate of interest. The causation goes from government expenditures to income, and not vice versa. Only fiscal policymakers can change government spending. Autonomous variables and parameters are denoted by lower-case letters or capital letters with a subscript zero. As a particular example assume government spending equals 200.

$$G = G_0 = 200 \tag{24–1}$$

Assuming prices are fixed, nominal and real values coincide as the price index equals unity.

The Investment Schedule

Keynes accepted the classical/neoclassical formal analysis of investment but reversed the importance of anticipated net revenue and the rate of interest.[5] Recall that the rate of return on an investment is that rate of discount which equates the cost of the investment and the present value of the anticipated net revenue stream. Profit-maximizing firms undertake all investments with rates of return greater than or equal to the market rate of interest. Neoclassicists claim that investment is quite sensitive to the rate of interest because the net revenue stream declines gradually as firms invest more and the capital stock grows. Keynes questioned this. He thought investment opportunities were quite limited and the rate of return dropped sharply during any period of time. Keynes's main quarrel with the classicists, however, was their lack of attention to the uncertainty of the future net revenue stream generated by investments. Many investment projects have a long life. Estimates of net revenue 5, 20, and 40 years hence are necessary to calculate the rate of return on an investment. According to Keynes, these distant estimates of net revenue are so uncertain that they are unduly influenced by a mob psychology. "In estimating the prospects of investment we must have regard, there-

---

[5]Those who skipped Chapter 23 can read just the section on investment, which stands by itself.

fore, to the nerves and hysteria and even the digestions and reactions to the weather of these upon whose spontaneous activity it largely depends.''[6] The ''state of confidence'' is alternately euphoric and melancholic, and anticipated net revenues and the rates of return on investment rise and fall. The state of confidence becomes the primary and the rate of interest is a decidedly secondary determinant of investment. Figure 24–4 summarizes Keynes's thought. *The investment schedule is very steep—the rate of return on investment drops sharply during any time period—and over time shifts from A to B to C with changes in the state of confidence. In contrast, the neoclassicists claim the investment schedule is relatively flat and stable.*

The state of confidence that is so important to investment may be measured indirectly or by surveying firms, but we do not know its determinants. Thus, it becomes an exogenous variable in the model. *The state of confidence is the cancer of the economic system:* whether or not

FIGURE 24–4

Investment Relatively Unresponsive to the Rate of Interest Shifts with Changes in the State of Confidence

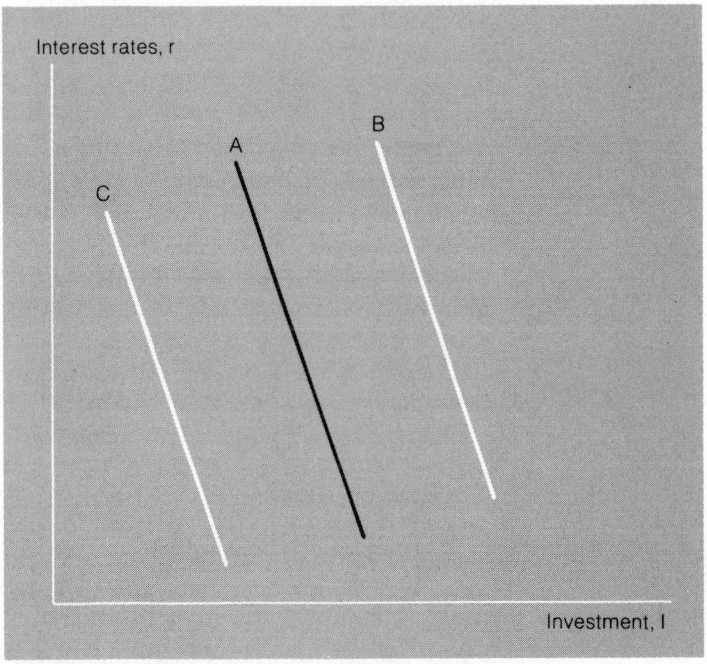

[6]J. M. Keynes, *The General Theory of Employment, Interest, and Money,* (New York: Harcourt Brace Jovanovich, 1936), p. 162.

you have it is extremely important; you can tell whether you have it; we are uncertain of its causes. Keynes thought the exogenous state of confidence was so important compared to the rate of interest that expressing investment as a function of the rate of interest might be misleading. Look at Figure 24–4 again. What explains changes over time in the amount of investment? Variations in the state of confidence, which shift the investment schedule, are much more important than interest rate variations causing movements along an investment schedule. All economic models are simplifications, and basic models are only first approximations. *The basic Keynesian model ignores the effect of interest rates on investment; investment depends solely on the state of confidence.*

Another interpretation of the simple Keynesian model says investment also depends on the rate of interest, but the rate of interest is fixed. Whichever interpretation one prefers—investment depends solely on the state of confidence or investment depends on the state of confidence and a fixed rate of interest—investment is an autonomous variable. As a specific example assume desired investment equals 150.

(24–2)

$$I = I_0 = I(r_0) = 150$$

The Consumption Function

According to Keynes, current disposable income, total income minus taxes, definitely is the most powerful determinant of desired consumption and private saving. The Keynesian consumption function in general and as a specific example is

(24–3)

$$\begin{aligned} C &= a + b(y - T) \\ &= 140 + 0.75(y - T) \end{aligned}$$

The parameter a (140) is the level of consumption independent of *disposable* income. The parameter b (0.75) measures the change in consumption per unit change in disposable income and is called the marginal propensity to consume disposable income, $MPC(y_d)$.

$$MPC(y_d) = \frac{\Delta C}{\Delta y_d} = b = 0.75$$

Keynes accepted the classical assumption, which has since been repeatedly confirmed by the data, that households consume only a fraction of incremental disposable income. As income increases, households consume and save more. The parameter b lies between zero and one, $0 < b < 1$.

Keynes disagreed with his classical teachers about the effects on desired consumption of interest rates and wealth measured by real money balances. Keynes thought that interest rates and wealth effects on consumption were sufficiently small that they could be ignored altogether or consolidated with other factors and considered to be exogenous. Current statistical estimates of interest rate and wealth effects are more mixed than the estimates of other economic hypotheses. However, even those who have estimated significant interest rate and wealth effects probably agree that disposable income is the most important determinant of short-run consumption.[7] Regardless of the outcome of the statistical debate, Equation (24–3) does represent the beliefs of Keynes.

In the most basic Keynesian model all taxes are autonomous. Property, estate and inheritance, and transfer taxes are examples of autonomous taxes. (Don't worry, the autonomous tax assumption will be relaxed shortly.) The tax equation is

$$\begin{aligned} T &= T_0 \\ &= 120 \end{aligned} \tag{24–4}$$

Substituting the tax equation in the consumption function gives

$$\begin{aligned} C &= a - bT_0 + by \\ &= 140 - 0.75(120) + 0.75y \end{aligned} \tag{24–3'}$$

While a(140) is the value of consumption independent of *disposable* income, $a - bT_o = 50$ is the value of *autonomous* consumption independent of total *national* output and income, y. Autonomous consumption may be interpreted as the minimum consumption necessary to maintain body and soul. Induced consumption is by. *In this most basic Keynesian model, only consumption has an induced component.* With taxes fixed, the marginal propensities to consume disposable and national income are equal, eg., b.

Figure 24–5 graphs the consumption function, labeled C. Consumption is on the vertical axis and the horizontal axis measures national income

---

[7]This statement certainly is true when wealth is approximated by real money balances. Some economists employ more comprehensive measures of nonhuman wealth which include the capital stock. Even when allowance is made for the fact that wealth is greater than quarterly or annual income, the wealth coefficient typically is smaller and less significant. Professor Friedman and others have related consumption to permanent income, which represents the return on total human and nonhuman wealth and is measured empirically by a weighted average of current and past incomes. When consumption depends on permanent income, the validity of the statement in the text depends on the rate of decline of the weights attached to past incomes in computing permanent income, the calendar length of the Keynesian short-run and other economic and semantic issues—for example, consumption here measures all household expenditures rather than Friedman's flow of services from durable goods—beyond the scope of a money and banking book.

FIGURE 24–5
Aggregate Expenditures and Income

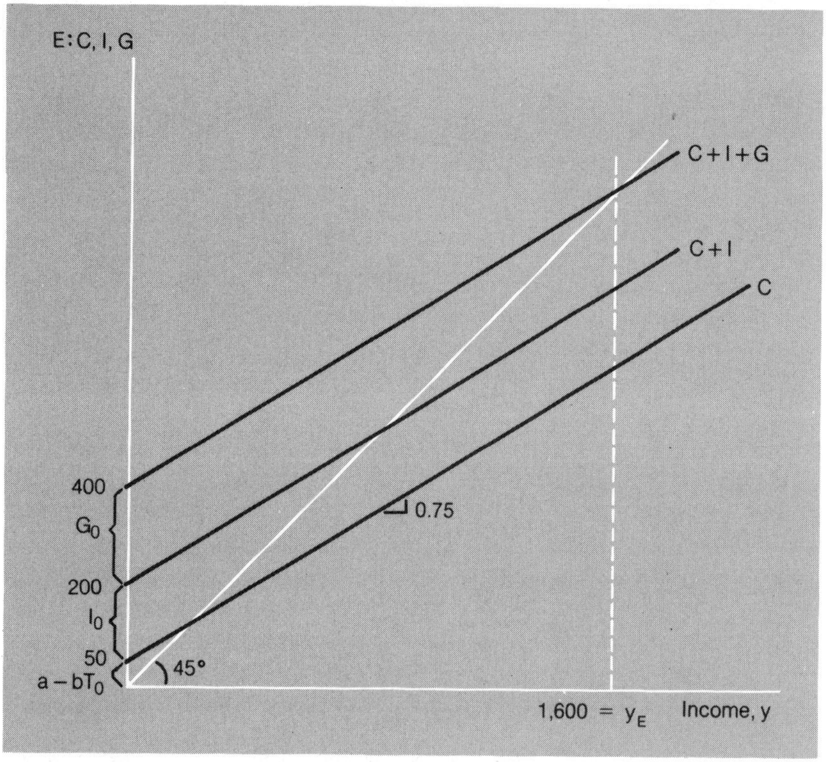

and output since this is the variable to be solved. We are interested in national income instead of disposable income. Temporarily ignore the other lines. The intercept of the consumption line C measures autonomous consumption, $50 = a - bT_0$, and the slope of the line is 0.75, the marginal propensity to consume national income.

Equilibrium Relationships

Having specified that the three components of spending are autonomous or depend only on income, we can now determine algebraically the equilibrium level of output and real income because demand creates its own supply. Setting aggregate demand equal to income and making use of Equations (24–1)—(24–4), we solve for income in terms of the parameters and exogenous variables.

$$
\begin{aligned}
C + I + G &= y \\
a - bT_0 + by + I_0 + G_0 &= y \\
y &= \frac{1}{1-b}(a - bT_0 + I_0 + G_0) \\
&= \frac{1}{1-0.75}(140 - 0.75(120) + 150 + 200) \\
&= 1{,}600
\end{aligned} \tag{24–5}
$$

The terms in parentheses in the third line of Equation (24–5) are total exogenous or autonomous spending. (Look at Equations (24–1)—(24–4) and calculate desired total spending when $y = 0$.) Equilibrium real—and nominal with the price level fixed at unity—income equals autonomous spending times a multiplier, which in this case is the inverse of one minus the marginal propensity to consume. The respending propensity here corresponds with the marginal propensity to consume since only consumers spend more as income increases. Investment and government expenditures are completely autonomous.

Figure 24–5 graphs the spending relationships. Autonomous investment and government expenditures are added to consumption by shifting the curve upward to C + I and C + I + G. The intercept of the total expenditures curve, $E = C + I + G$, is total autonomous spending, $400 = a - bT_0 + I_0 + G_0$, and its slope is $0.75 = b$, the marginal propensity to consume national income. All the points equidistant to the axes lie along the 45° (degree) line, by definition. The total expenditures curve intersects the 45° line at income $y_E = 1{,}600 = (a - bT_0 + I_0 + G_0)/1 - b$, making this the equilibrium level of income. Consider why any other level of income and output is not an equilibrium. Suppose income were below y_E. At income levels below the equilibrium, aggregate expenditures exceed supply. The C + I + G curve is above the 45° line. Assuming firms satisfy the demand of households and government, actual investment is less than desired. Inventories are declining, or not increasing as fast as desired. Firms respond by increasing production and national income. Demand creates its own supply. Conversely, when income is greater than y_E, demand is less than supply. Firms' inventories are increasing at an undesired high rate, and output is curtailed.

One should be aware of the rationale for the algebraic and geometric solutions. Equilibrium output cannot be zero because autonomous spending is positive. *Autonomous spending is the force driving the economy.* It creates a gap between aggregate demand and zero output. As output increases by one unit, the gap is reduced by less than one unit because demand responds to output. *Provision of the autonomous spending induces respending.* In our example, as output increases by 1, demand increases by $0.75 = b$, so the gap between demand and output is reduced by 0.25 = 1 − b, which is the difference between the slopes of the 45° line and the expenditure curve. Thus, the multiplier, 4.0 = 1/1 − 0.25 = 1/(1 − b), measures the number of units of output necessary to close the *gap* by 1 unit. At equilibrium the gap must be closed. Equilibrium output is the product of the multiplier (gap closing factor) and autonomous expenditures (gap).

The Multiplier, Fiscal Policy, and Fine Tuning

Income y_E may be the short-run equilibrium level of income, but is it the full-employment level of income? Keynes thought not. Generally, income would be substantially below full employment. Investment opportunities are strictly limited, and households are not spendthrifts. When income equals y_E the *private* sector is stuck. Of course, if the private sector were not stuck, y_E would not be an equilibrium. Prices are assumed fixed but even if they were to fall, demand would not increase. Look at the Keynesian spending equation again. Does C, I, or G depend on the price level? No. Moreover, interest rate adjustments do not bring the economy to full employment. Interest rates are fixed or have no effect on spending. How does one get out of this depressing situation? One could hope and pray for a return of entrepreneurial spirits. A more effective way is available according to Keynes. Look at Equation (24–5) again. *I, G_0, and T_0 appear side-by-side. Moreover, all three are autonomous. This suggested to Keynes that fiscal policy could readily offset investment variations.*

Let's first illustrate the mechanics of fiscal policy and then explain its economic rationale and various implementation problems. Inspection of equilibrium Equation (24–5) confirms that when investment, government expenditures, or taxes change, other things being equal, income changes in the following manner.

(24–6)

$$\begin{aligned}\Delta y/\Delta I &= 1/(1-b) = 1/0.25 = 4\\ \Delta y/\Delta G_o &= 1/(1-b) = 1/0.25 = 4\\ \Delta y/\Delta T_o &= -b/(1-b) = -0.75/0.25 = -3\end{aligned}$$

Since b, the marginal propensity to consume, lies between zero and one, the first equation in (24–6) confirms that investment variations have a magnified effect on aggregate economic instability. The investment multiplier is defined as the change in income per unit change in investment, $\Delta y/\Delta I$. The investment multiplier equals the term multiplying total autonomous expenditures in equilibrium Equation (24–5).[8]

---

[8]Similar modes of expression should not be confused with similar economic relationships. The money supply and government spending multipliers depend on entirely different factors and are economically unrelated, just as the same is true for the monetary base and autonomous spending.

The second equation in (24–6) shows that government expenditures multiplier, $\Delta y/\Delta G_0$, exactly equals the investment multiplier. Government only needs to nudge the economy in order to maintain full employment. For example, suppose the gap between equilibrium and full-employment income is 100. How much additional government spending is necessary to close the full-employment gap in our example? Just 25 in our example since the marginal propensity to consume is 0.75, and the multiplier is 4.0. *The necessity of fine tuning, that is, active fiscal demand management, is one of Keynes's key messages. Government spending should be high on average and flexible in order to offset the economy's natural tendency toward recessions and the mercurial state of investor confidence.*

The negative sign of the tax multiplier is readily understandable since higher taxes reduce disposable income and consumption. However, why is the autonomous tax multiplier absolutely smaller than the government spending multiplier? It is smaller because taxes do not have a dollar-for-dollar effect on autonomous spending. Higher autonomous taxes reduce disposable income dollar for dollar, but the change in autonomous consumption is only $-b$. Therefore, $-bT_0$ appears as the autonomous spending term in Equation (24–5). The lower autonomous consumption due to taxes, $-b$, is multiplied by the same number to get the autonomous tax multiplier, i.e., $\Delta y/\Delta T_0 = -b/(1 - b)$. Additional government spending is more expansionary than an equal tax cut. In terms of Figure 24–5, the expenditure curve is shifted upward more by government spending than an equal tax cut. This is *one* reason why Keynesians advocate fine tuning by means of government spending instead of taxes.

Mechanical answers often are a convenient starting point, but one must go beyond mechanics and understand the economic rationale for the multiplier, which plays a central role in Keynesian economics. *The fundamental reason for the multiplier is the dependence of spending on income.* The exposition is more easily followed with the aid of Table 24–1 and Figure 24–6, an enlargement of Figure 24–5 around the equilibrium. The

TABLE 24–1
The Multiplier: An Illustration

Time Period	*Desired Spending*				*Output*	*Actual*
	C	*I*	*G*	*C + I + G*	*y*	*I*
0	1,250	150	200	1,600	1,600	150.0
1	1,250	150	201	1,601	1,600	149.0
2	1,250.75	150	201	1,601.75	1,601	149.25
3	1,251.31	150	201	1,602.31	1,601.75	149.44
4					1,602.31	
.						
.						
.						
∞	1,253	150	201	1,604	1,604	150.0

initial equilibrium values at time period 0 are shown in the first row of Table 24–1 and are represented by the line C + I + G in Figure 24–6. In period 1 the government spends $1 more, shifting the aggregate demand curve upward to C + I + G + $1. Output, however, remains constant at $1,600. Firms' failure to anticipate government and other demands makes current output depend on prior demand, as the downward-pointing arrows in Table 24–1 indicate. The row for time period 1 in Table 24–1

FIGURE 24–6
Aggregate Expenditures and Income

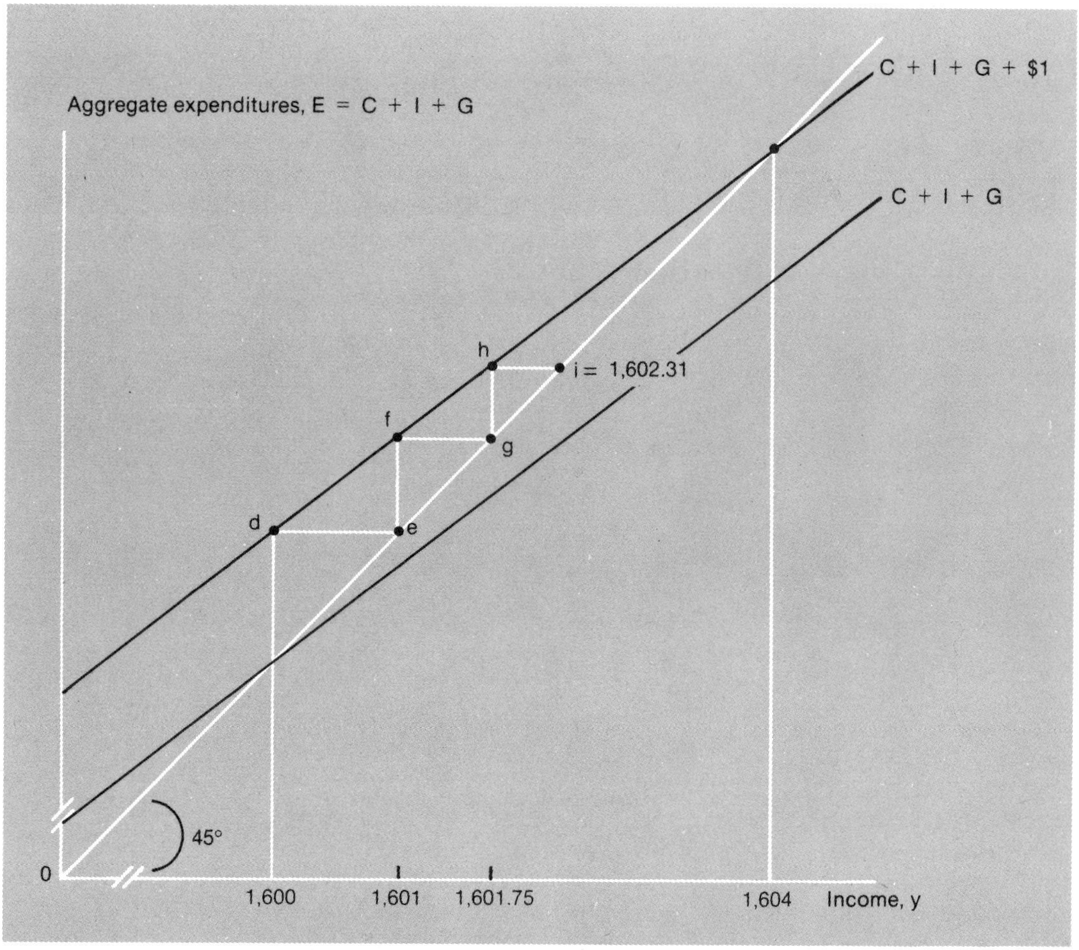

corresponds with point d in Figure 24–6. Desired spending at point d exceeds output as firms' actual inventory investment is \$1 below the desired level.

In the next period, firms hire additional workers to meet the additional government demand and possibly pay larger dividends if the government purchase enhances firms' earnings. In any case, output and income increase \$1.00 to \$1,601 in period 2, and we move to point e in Figure 24–6. If the private sector did not respond to higher incomes, this would end the story. But the private sector does respond. Households spend $b = 0.75$ times their larger disposable income. Consumption in period 2 increases from 1,250 to 1,250.75. The induced consumption spending is represented graphically by sliding along the curve from point d to f in Figure 24–6. At point f demand again exceeds output. In period 3, firms hire yet more workers to meet this newly induced household demand, and output and income increase further. Successive rounds of additional income and induced spending follow with each successive round of additional income getting smaller and smaller as b is less than one. Eventually, the additional government expenditures increase income by $1/(1-b)$. The argument is symmetric; lower government spending reduces income by the multiplier.[9]

Fiscal Policy as an Automatic Stabilizer

Fine tuning is easy in principle. Neoclassicists claim that, in fact, various policy implementation problems make fine tuning virtually impossible. Government expenditures are not a spigot which can be turned on and off readily. The government does not have projects waiting to be implemented as soon as investment falls. Moreover, when investment recovers, curtailment of government expenditures currently underway may be extremely difficult. Should a road be left unfinished and lead to nowhere just because investment increases? We shall explore in depth the issue of lags in subsequent policy chapters. For the moment, let's make the case against fiscal policy as strong as possible. Assume fine tuning just will not work. Does this imply that fiscal policy does not stabilize the economy? No. According to Keynesians the mere *existence* of income taxes stabilizes the economy, in the sense that *income taxes reduce the multiplier associated with volatile investment*. The remainder of the section proves this.

Since it is painfully clear that income taxes do exist, let us relax the assumption built in Equation (24–4) that all taxes are autonomous. The new tax equation is

---

[9]This successive rounds explanation of the multiplier is formally called period analysis. After n rounds or periods, $\Delta y = \Delta G + b\,\Delta G + (b)^2\,\Delta G + \ldots + (b)^{n-2}\Delta G$. At the limit the sum of this geometric series is $\Delta G/(1 - b)$.

(24–4′)

$$T = T_0 + ty,$$
$$= 120 + 0.2y,$$

where T_0 still is autonomous taxes and t is the (constant) marginal tax rate, 20 percent in our example. All taxes, autonomous as well as income, influence disposable income and consumption. Rewriting the general consumption function (24–3) for convenience and then substituting tax equation (24–4′) gives Equation (24–3″).

(24–3)

$$C = a + b(y - T),$$

(24–3″)

$$= a - bT_o + b(1 - t)y$$

With income taxes, the marginal propensities to consume *national* and *disposable* income no longer coincide. According to Equation (24–3), the marginal propensity to consume *disposable* income (y − T) is b. However, when national income increases by $1, taxes increase by t, and disposable income increases by only (1 − t), of which b is spent. Therefore, the marginal propensity to consume *national* income is b(1 − t), which is the term multiplying y in Equation (24–3″).[10] Graphically, income taxes make the consumption function in Figure 24–5 flatter.

The income tax is an example of an *automatic stabilizer: any policy whose mere (constant) existence reduces the national income respending propensity (induced spending) and, thereby, reduces the autonomous spending multiplier.* For example, suppose national output and income increase $1 in response to larger desired investment. A multiplier effect is now set in motion as the newly hired workers respond by spending more. If income taxes did not exist, the $1 additional national income translates into $1 additional disposable income, and in this round consumption increases by $b. With a tax rate of t, however, disposable income increases by $1 − t. Since consumers continue to spend the same fraction of their *disposable* income, consumption increases by $b(1 − t) in this case. The changes in disposable income and consumption are smaller in each spending round when taxes exist. The marginal propensity to consume *national* income and the investment multiplier are negatively related to the income tax rate.

How much do income taxes reduce the multiplier? Setting the new consumption function C (Equation (24–3″)) + I (Equation (24–2)) + G (Equation (24–1)) = y and rearranging, the equilibrium level of income expressed algebraically now is[11]

---

[10]The term b(1 − t) also multiplies y in Equation (24–3), though this may not appear to be true because Equation (24–3) does not explicitly show that T is a function of y.

[11]If you cannot get (24–5′), refer back to (24–5). Replace consumption function (24–3′) with (24–3″) and follow the same steps.

$$y = \frac{1}{1-b(1-t)}(a - bT_0 + I_0 + G_0) \tag{24–5'}$$

First, note that Equation (24–5′) is an example of the basic Keynesian equation $y = (1/(1 - R))A$. In this case the respending propensity R is $b(1 - t)$. Only consumers spend $b(1 - t)$ as national income changes. The four terms in parentheses are autonomous spending. Inspection of Equation (24–5′) shows the investment and government spending multipliers are $1/1 - b(1 - t)$ when income taxes exist. Look at Equation (24–6). Without income taxes the multipliers are larger, $1/1 - b$. In our example with $b = 0.75$, a 20 percent income tax reduces the multiplier from 4 to 2.5. While anything less than confiscatory taxes ($t = 1$) does not altogether prevent *magnified* income fluctuations due to investment, high income taxes make the volatile animal spirits of investors much less troublesome.

Case study: A basic Keynesian interpretation of the Great Depression[12]

The reactions of government to the Great Depression, interpreted according to the basic model in Table 24–2, illustrate the novelty of Keynes's message that fiscal policy is a tool to manage aggregate demand. Between 1929 and 1933 real GNP fell approximately 30 percent, or $62.1 billion in 1958 prices. The unemployment rate rose from approximately 3 to 25 percent. The problem was a lack of demand,

TABLE 24–2 Real (1958 prices) and Percentage Changes of GNP and Autonomous Spending between 1929–1933 and Average Values of Parameters

	Real Change (Billions)	*Percentage Change*	*Average Values*
GNP	−62.1	−30.5	—
Investment	−36.6	−87.5	—
Autonomous consumption: a	0.0	0.0	—
Autonomous consumption: −bT	+0.5	+5.9	—
Government spending	+1.3	+5.9	—
Income tax rate	—	—	0.028
Multiplier, $1/(1 - b(1 - t))$	—	—	1.78

[12]This section accepts the parameter estimates of Robert J. Gordon, *Macroeconomics* (Boston: Little, Brown, 1981), pp. 84–87.

which is understated by the figures just mentioned. Between 1929 and 1933 the labor force grew, technology improved, and full-employment output rose. Therefore, the gap between full-employment and actual GNP widened by more than the 30 percent decline in real GNP. Table 24–2 supports the Keynesian belief that a volatile investment is a major cause of business cycles. Investment virtually collapsed during the Great Depression, falling approximately 87 percent, or $36.6 billion in 1958 prices.[13] The second component of private autonomous spending, consumption independent of *disposable* income and represented by the parameter a, is assumed to have remained constant.

Although Keynes's book, which spelled out in detail the rationale for fiscal policy, was published after the Great Depression, Keynesian ideas were sufficiently well developed during the Depression that some economists and bankers advocated an expansionary fiscal policy. However, the government was non-Keynesian and did little to counteract the collapse of investment. Income tax rates were so low, approximately 3 percent, that they contributed little automatic stability.[14] Real autonomous tax collections declined $1.2 billion and augmented autonomous consumption by $0.5 billion since tax reductions increase disposable income. Even this minor contribution to demand was largely fortuitous. Tax rates on property and other nonincome variables were raised significantly. Indeed, tax rates were raised in 1932 more than in any previous peacetime year. The value of property and other autonomous variables fell so much that autonomous tax receipts fell in spite of rate increases. Government spending was only slightly more expansionary, increasing $1.3 billion. The total contribution of fiscal policy to autonomous demand, that is, the sum of government spending and the consumption effect of autonomous taxes, was $1.8 billion, or about 5 percent of the decline in investment. Government stood by idly; fine tuning was not attempted in the Great Depression. Total autonomous spending fell $34.8 billion, $36.6 minus $1.8 billion. Fortu-

[13]Investment includes net exports. We are assuming actual and desired values coincide.

[14]Seventy percent of net taxes in 1929 were estimated to be autonomous. The income tax rate was estimated by dividing 30 percent of net taxes by GNP.

nately, the marginal propensity to consume private disposable income, b, was not that high and the multiplier effect of autonomous spending on income was relatively low.[15] The multiplier was 1.78, so GNP declined by \$62.1 billion, \$34.8 billion times 1.78.

How did the government rationalize its actions, or lack of them, in terms of the basic model? Policymakers alleged that the state of confidence of investors was negatively related to the government deficit. If additional government spending and larger deficits so impaired the state of confidence as to lead to an equal reduction in investment, then government spending would have no effect on income. Such a situation seems extremely doubtful but cannot be ruled out. When one considers an enigma like the state of confidence, virtually anything is possible. One could argue that additional government expenditures will be interpreted as a sign of determination to combat depressions and thereby enhance the state of confidence. Keynes took a middle-of-the-road position, assuming investment is independent of government expenditures. In this case government expenditures can counteract variations in the private demand for commodities.

Fiscal Policy: An Automatic Destabilizer?

Some neoclassicists will concede nothing to fiscal policy. Assume government spending is only partially autonomous, G_0. It also has an induced component, gy,

$$G = G_0 + gy \tag{24–1'}$$
$$G = 200 + 0.15y$$

where g (0.15) is government's marginal propensity to spend. What is the justification for assuming that government spending is partially induced? A mere glance at the historical data presented in Chapter 21 is sufficient justification; government spending has paralleled the upward trend of income. Even those totally unaware of the historical record would expect government spending to be positively related to income. We can consider

---

[15]Table 24–2 implies that the marginal propensity to consume total private, both household *and* business, disposable income is about 0.45. This is much lower than the propensity to consume household disposable income, which is greater than 90 percent. As stated in Chapter 21, the models presented here do not segregate private income.

two extreme types of government: (1) it is totally unresponsive to the wants of the public and simply attempts to enlarge itself, or (2) it represents perfectly the wants of the public. If the former were the case, government spending would be positively related to income because the income tax system provides government the wherewithal to spend. The government may well believe there is an upper limit to its spending which can be financed by bond sales and money creation. Spending beyond the limit must be financed by taxes. As income rises, the government earns a *fiscal dividend, that is, tax receipts rise with income even though tax rates are unchanged.* What happens to the fiscal dividend? It is spent, however foolishly, by officials seeking reelection and determined to enlarge government. High marginal tax rates without any propensity to spend by government imply budget surpluses much larger than ever witnessed.

Now consider the other extreme. Suppose government represented perfectly the wants of the public. Would the fiscal dividend also be spent in this case? At least partially. The consumption function says that as incomes rise, households want more sporting equipment, books, cars, and other consumer goods. The same should be true of goods and services provided by government. As incomes rise households should want more and better parks, schools, highways, and defense. While many may wish that the government not spend the entire fiscal dividend, virtually everyone wants some additional government goods and services, making g, government's marginal propensity to spend, positive.[16] Most governments are a blend of the two extremes and, therefore, government spending is positively related to income.

How does this modification of government's behavior change our results? The equilibrium level of income is still given by setting aggregate expenditures equal to income. Using Equations (24–1′), (24–2) and (24–3″), equilibrium income in terms of the parameters and exogenous variables is:

(24–5″)

$$C + I + G = y$$
$$a - bT_0 + b(1 - t)y + I_0 + G_0 + gy = y$$
$$y = \frac{1}{1 - b(1 - t) - g}(a - bT_0 + I_0 + G_0)$$
$$y = \frac{1}{1 - 0.75(1 - 0.2) - 0.15}(60 - 0.75(20) + 150 + 200)$$
$$= 1{,}600$$

[16]To be sure, some government expenditures decrease with income. However, the classic example, unemployment compensation payments, is not even an expenditure for goods and services but is a transfer payment (negative tax). On balance, the many positively related government expenditure programs dominate, perhaps not quarterly but quite probably an-

As expected, equilibrium income in this modified basic Keynesian model has the form (1/1 − R) A. The terms in parentheses in the third line of Equation (24–5″) are total autonomous spending, A. The multiplier equals 1/1 − b(1 − t) − g. The previous model with income taxes assumed only one sector, households, have a marginal propensity, b(1 − t), to spend national income. The modification adds government's respending propensity, g. Since we are retaining the assumption that investment is independent of income, the total, household plus government, respending propensity, R, is b(1 − t) + g. *The multiplier always is the inverse of one minus the total respending propensity.*

When government expenditures depend on income, the fiscal system need no longer be an automatic stabilizer.[17] From Equations (24–5), (24–5′), and (24–5″) we get the following relationships.

$$\Delta y / \Delta I_0 = \frac{1}{1-b}$$ when there is no fiscal system or only autonomous taxes.

$$\Delta y / \Delta I_0 = \frac{1}{1-b\,(1-t)}$$ when income taxes are collected but not spent.

$$\Delta y / \Delta I_0 = \frac{1}{1-b(1-t)-g}$$ when income taxes are collected and government spends.

Income taxes reduce the autonomous spending multiplier, but government's marginal propensity to spend increases it. Whether or not the fiscal system is an automatic stabilizer depends on the values of the marginal propensity to consume disposable income, b, the tax rate, t, and the government spending rate, g. In good Swiss tradition our numerical example yields a neutral position: fiscal policy is neither an automatic stabilizer nor destabilizer. Note that *neutrality requires a tax rate larger than the government respending propensity because the marginal propensity*

---

nually. We recognize that the time period is the crucial issue. Anticipated income and tax receipts this *week* certainly do not induce this *week's* government expenditures. Congress's clear and strong recognition of the fiscal dividend, which is one reason the Reagan administration successfully pushed tax indexation, suggests, however, that *annual* income and taxes influence *annual* expenditures. Inflation is the major reason for indexation, as we explain in Chapter 28.

[17]Those who claim that the fiscal system still is an *automatic* stabilizer because additional government spending typically requires legislation or some other positive action will want the word "automatic" deleted from the sentence in the text. While I have no desire to get drawn into a semantic debate, a policy which occurs regularly and mechanically, even if it requires some positive Pavlovian action, can be considered automatic. I am just as comfortable with or without "automatic".

to consume is less than one. The same principle explains why the tax multiplier is less than the government spending multiplier. See Equation (24–6).

Summary/Questions

Each spending category in the basic model has an autonomous component: $a - bT_0$ for consumption, I_0 for investment, and G_0 for government expenditures. The standard basic model assumes only one sector, households, have a marginal propensity to spend national income, b. The equilibrium level of income is

$$y = \frac{A}{1 - R} = \frac{a - bT_0 + I_0 + G_0}{1 - b}$$

The standard basic model can readily be modified by adding income taxes and an induced component to government spending and investment and by introducing exports and imports explicitly. This changes the specific form of the multiplier and autonomous spending without altering the fundamental structure of the model and the multiplier concept. What cannot be added without abandoning the single equation solution is another variable influencing spending.

The investment component of autonomous spending is the engine of magnified income variations which Keynesians claim can be neutralized by varying government spending counter to investment. Fiscal policy rules the roost. It is *the* stabilization tool. What role does money play in the basic Keynesian model? Absolutely none. Money is not a type of autonomous spending and has no direct effect on spending. Money may influence interest rates and other variables but, by definition, this has no effect on *autonomous* spending.

The advanced Keynesian model developed in the next chapters assigns money a minor supporting role, not surprisingly. Basic models are recognized to be first approximations which give the flavor of advanced models. It would hardly make sense to have a basic Keynesian model where money does not matter at all and an advanced Keynesian model where only money matters. The advanced model is very flexible, however. While Keynesians do assume the shapes of the curves in their advanced model are such that money has little effect on income, the shapes of the curves can be changed easily enough to radically change this conclusion. Even if one interprets the evidence as indicating that money matters a great deal and, accordingly, changes the shapes of the Keynesian curves in the advanced model, knowledge of the basic Keynesian model is important because it dominates the thought of some policymakers and so forcefully emphasizes the importance of demand in the short run.

Our analysis of the theoretical structure of the basic Keynesian model was guided by various policy issues. A difficult policy issue was saved for you to solve. In 1982–84, when this was written, GNP was substantially below full employment and the government budget showed an extremely large deficit. According to the *basic* Keynesian model, only what type of policy will *simultaneously* increase GNP and reduce the deficit?[18]

1. State the basic assumptions of Keynesian economics.
2. Define (*a*) Keynes's Law, (*b*) the marginal propensity to consume national income, (*c*) fiscal dividend, (*d*) automatic stabilizer, (*e*) respending propensity, (*f*) autonomous spending, and (*g*) fine tuning.
3. How do neoclassical and Keynesian views about investment differ?
4. Assume the following spending equations.

$$C = 30 + 0.75y$$
$$I = 100$$
$$G = 150$$

   a. What does autonomous spending equal?
   b. What is the value of the marginal propensity to consume national income? What is the value of the multiplier?
   c. What is the equilibrium level of income?
5. Some have modified the standard basic Keynesian model by including an induced spending component to investment and government spending. That is, the investment and government expenditure relationships are

$$G = G_0 + gy \tag{24–1'}$$

$$I = I_0 + vy \tag{24–2'}$$

   where g and v are the marginal propensities to spend by government and firms, respectively. The consumption relationship *with income taxes* is

$$C = a - bT_0 + b(1 - t)y. \tag{24–3''}$$

   a. Determine equilibrium income in terms of autonomous spending and the parameters.
   b. What is the value of the autonomous spending multiplier?
   c. State the economic rationale for the multiplier and, in so doing, explain why the multiplier in this case with induced investment

[18]Hint: look at Equation (24–6) and answer Question 6.

and government spending differs from the multiplier shown in Equation (24–5″)

d. Why may government expenditures and investment depend on income?

6. Assume the standard basic model with completely autonomous investment and government expenditures so that equilibrium income is

$$y = \frac{1}{1-b}(a - bT_0 + I_0 + G_0)$$

a. The balanced budget multiplier says that equal increases in taxes and government spending, so that government's budget remains balanced (unaffected), increases income by the same amount. Prove the balanced budget multiplier for the standard basic Keynesian model.

b. Assume income taxes exist so equilibrium income is given by Equation (24–5′). Let *autonomous* taxes and government spending increase the same amount. Will income change, and if so, how much? What is the change in *total* taxes? What is the effect on the government budget? What increase in *autonomous* taxes is necessary for the balanced budget multiplier?

7. How does recognition that government spending depends positively on income affect the automatic stabilizer properties of the fiscal system?

Keynesian money demand and an introduction to the IS–LM model

25

The advanced Keynesian model, called IS–LM for reasons explained shortly, extends the basic model by incorporating interest rate effects. While Keynes did not abandon the importance of the state of confidence as a determinant of investment, he met the classicists halfway in his advanced model by including the rate of interest. Output and income still are determined by investment and the other components of aggregate demand, which now depend on the rate of interest in addition to income and autonomous elements. Monetary policy can now play an indirect role. *If monetary policy can change the rate of interest, and if investment is responsive to the rate of interest, then monetary policy can affect GNP.* As stated earlier, Keynes thought monetary policy was relatively insignificant compared to fiscal policy.

With the aid of graphs the next section elaborates on the aggregate demand, rate of interest, and income interrelationship. We then consider the demand and supply of money, which determine the rate of interest. Reviewers of *The General Theory* proclaimed that Keynes's theory of the demand for money was a milestone marking the death of an incomplete and inadequate classical transactions theory and the birth of the asset approach. With the passage of time, quick reviews were superseded by scholarly tomes, and praise of Keynes's *specific* money demand theory became fainter, if not totally absent. Nevertheless, Keynes's specific theory is presented in considerable detail. Some knowledge of the history of economic thought is desirable, and whose theory should we know if not that of the most influential 20th century economist? Moreover, knowledge of the admittedly somewhat erroneous *specific* money demand theory is essential to understand numerous Keynesian policy proposals. Note well that only the *specific* Keynesian explanation is flawed; the originally revolutionary *general* Keynesian belief that money demand depends on the rate of interest is now almost universally accepted. The final section integrates the commodities and money market relationships and determines the general equilibrium values of income and the rate of interest.

Aggregate Expenditures and the Rate of Interest

To highlight the differences between the basic and advanced Keynesian model, let us ignore any possible modifications of the basic model. In particular, let us assume consumption depends only on disposable income, and taxes and government expenditures are entirely autonomous. Equations (25–1) and (25–2) state the general forms along with specific examples of the consumption function and government expenditures.

(25–1)

$$\begin{aligned} C &= a + b(y - T_0) = a - bT_0 + by \\ &= 140 + 0.75(y - 120) = 50 + 0.75y \end{aligned}$$

(25–2)

$$\begin{aligned} G &= G_0 \\ &= 200 \end{aligned}$$

At this point the notation for Equations (25–1) and (25–2) needs no explanation. The consumption function, C, is graphed first in Figure 25–1A and then government expenditure is added, shifting the curve upward to C + G. *A fundamental difference between the basic and advanced Keynesian models is the investment relationship. Keynes accepted the classical explanations for a negative relationship between investment and the rate of intere...* For example, as stated in Chapter 23, the downward-sloping investment curve may be viewed as an ordering of investment projects by its rate of return, which is equated to the rate of interest, r, by firms. As the rate of interest falls, firms find it profitable to undertake additional investments that yield lower rates of return. The general form of the investment relationship and a specific example are given by Equation (25–3).

(25–3)

$$\begin{aligned} I &= I_0 - er \\ &= 190 - 5r \end{aligned}$$

I_0 is autonomous investment which may still be viewed as a measure of firms' state of confidence. The parameter e(5) measures the responsiveness of investment to the rate of interest, that is, $\Delta I/\Delta r = -e$. *The basic model, a first approximation, says* $e = 0$*; the advanced Keynesian model says e is small, relative to autonomous investment, but not zero.*

Figure 25–1B graphs the investment function, I.[1] Temporarily ignore dashed curve I′. Given Equation (25–3), a mathematician would have investment on the vertical axis and the rate of interest on the horizontal axis. Economists, however, traditionally reverse the axes.[2] This makes somewhat more difficult the achievement of an important objective of this book: development of equal proficiency in the algebraic and graphical approaches and, therefore, employment of both interchangeably. How are the parameters represented graphically? The investment curve intersects the horizontal axis at $I = I_0 = 190$. (Look at Equation (25–3) When $r = 0$, as is true by definition along the horizontal axis, $I = I_0 = 190$.) Since the rate of interest and investment are on the vertical and horizontal axes, respectively, the slope of the investment curve, $\Delta r/\Delta I$, is $-1/e$. (Look at Equation (25–3) again. The change in investment per unit change in the rate of interest, $\Delta I/\Delta r$, equals $-e$. Taking the inverse, $\Delta r/\Delta I$ is $-1/e$.) Thus, the inverse of the algebraic measure of the sensitivity of investment to the rate of interest corresponds with the slope in the graphical approach. When investment is very responsive to the rate of interest so that e is large, then the investment curve is flat (the absolute value of the slope is small). Although slope and elasticity are not identical concepts, they often are equated in monetary/macroeconomics.[3] A flat

---

[1]The slope of Figure 25–1B does not correspond with our numerical example, which was selected so that the equilibrium interest rate is much smaller than the equilibrium income. We believe this gives the numerical example a greater semblance of reality although, of course, if one interpreted investment and the other components of aggregate demand as being measured in trillions of dollars and the interest rate in percentage points, then the reverse would be true. Correspondence of measurement units between the numerical example and the graph would make the latter less helpful.

[2]To help explain the workings of the economy, Leon Walras used algebra and hardly any graphs, while Alfred Marshall used graphs and hardly any algebra. The influence of these two economists was so strong that economists who offered both algebraic and graphical examples adopted Marshall's graphs and Walras's algebra even though the two economists reversed variables. Walras focused on quantities demanded and supplied at a given price or rate of interest, while Marshall theorized in terms of the demand and supply price or rate of interest for a given quantity. For example, Walras focused on the amount of investment that would occur at a rate of interest. In his algebraic examples, investment is on the left-hand side and the rate of interest is on the right. If he did have graphs, which he did not, Walras surely would have had investment on the vertical axis and the rate of interest on the horizontal. Marshall had the rate of interest on the vertical axis and investment on the horizontal axis because he focused on the rate of interest necessary to induce some given amount of investment. If Marshall had used equations, he surely would have placed the rate of interest on the left-hand side.

[3]The slope is the ratio of changes, that is, $\Delta y/\Delta x$, while the elasticity is the ratio of *percentage* changes, that is, $\Delta y/y \div \Delta x/x$, or $x\Delta y/y\Delta x$. Slope and elasticity clearly are not equal. A straight line has a constant slope but its elasticity is variable. Two parallel lines have identical slopes but different elasticities. Nevertheless, monetary/macroeconomists typically equate slope and elasticity because they usually compare two lines at the point of intersection. At such a point, the flatter line is more elastic and vice versa.

FIGURE 25–1

Aggregate Expenditures and the Rate of Interest

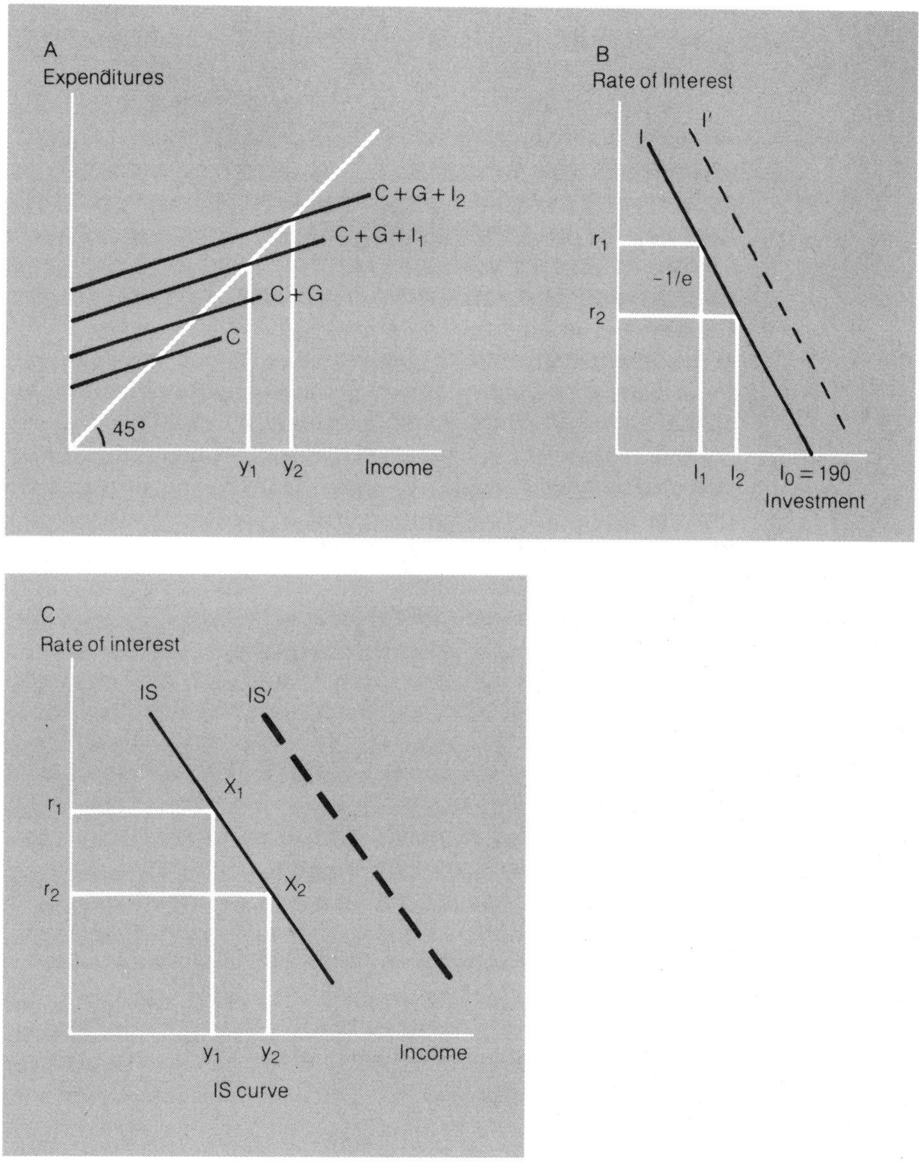

(steep) curve is said to be elastic (inelastic). According to our new terminology, the investment curve is elastic when investment is sensitive to the rate of interest. Figure 25–1B is drawn relatively steep (inelastic) because it is assumed investment is *not* very responsive to the rate of interest. If the rate of interest influenced investment more strongly, then the investment curve would be flatter (more elastic).

The rate of interest is not a parameter in the advanced Keynesian model; it is an endogenous variable to be determined by the economic system. As a result, equality of aggregate expenditures and income does not yield a unique equilibrium level of income. Investment and aggregate expenditures and, therefore, the equilibrium level of income take many values, depending on the rate of interest. Look at Figures 25–1A and 25–1B. Assume the rate of interest is r_1 percent so investment is I_1. Shifting the C + G curve upward by I_1, the aggregate expenditure curve $C + G + I_1$ corresponding to rate of interest r_1 intersects the 45° line at y_1.[4] Point X_1 in panel C of Figure 25–1 shows the equilibrium income, interest rate combination (y_1, r_1). Suppose the rate of interest falls to r_2 percent. According to Figure 25–1B, firms invest more, which shifts the expenditure curve in Figure 25–1A to $C + G + I_2$. Aggregate expenditures and, therefore, equilibrium income are negatively related to the rate of interest. Point X_2 in Figure 25–1C shows the equilibrium income, y_2, when the rate of interest is r_2.

The IS Curve: Aggregate Expenditures Equal Income

Proceeding in the above manner for all possible interest rates, one gets the solid IS curve in Figure 25–1C. Temporarily ignore the dashed IS′ curve. *The IS curve is a downward sloping curve showing all the interest rate-income combinations which equate aggregate expenditures and income.*[5] The IS curve in panel C consolidates the consumption, government, and investment relationships graphed in panels A and B.

Nearly all downward sloping curves are demand curves. Consequently, is the IS curve a demand curve? No, and it is not a supply curve either. *The IS curve is an equilibrium curve.* Equality of aggregate expenditures and income is the equilibrium condition in the commodities market. The IS curve is downward sloping because lower interest rates increase the investment component of aggregate expenditures, and at equilibrium aggregate expenditures equal income.

---

[4]Although investment and income are measured in the same units, viz., dollars, the scale differs between Figures 25–1A and 25–1B so both figures can be approximately the same size even though investment is a small component of income.

[5]The IS equation is derived algebraically in Appendix A of Chapter 26.

The IS curve derives its name from the saving-investment approach to income determination. The commodities market is in equilibrium when expenditures equal income or, equivalently, when investment equals saving, hence IS. As stated in appendixes, we think the expenditures-income approach is easier and more insightful.

In the basic model, the IS curve is a vertical line at the unique income level because investment is totally unresponsive to the rate of interest, i.e., the parameter e is zero. In this case where e is nonzero, we must know the rate of interest to determine equilibrium income.

The Demand and Supply of Money

Keynes looked at the money market to determine the rate of interest. He assumed decisions are made sequentially. Households first decide on the basis of their disposable income how much to consume and save. Having made this decision, households then allocate their saving between financial assets. To simplify the analysis, Keynes assumed there were only two assets, money and long-term bonds. The private sector and government issue long-term bonds but all bonds are viewed as identical. *Sequential decision making suggested to Keynes that the specific asset market to be analyzed in order to determine the rate of interest is a matter of indifference.* For example, suppose money demand exceeds supply. How can the Keynesian household acquire additional money balances? The Keynesian household must borrow; it does not consume less and save more because this decision depends simply on disposable income. The excess demand for money and additional borrowing cause higher interest rates. Compared to classicists, Keynes restricted the scope of economic behavior. The classicists admitted that consumers may save more and hoard because an excess demand for money exists. Excess supply situations even more strongly illustrate according to Keynes that either asset market may be analyzed. Suppose that the money supply increases so that supply now exceeds money demand. The excess supply normally will be directly and immediately associated with additional lending and lower interest rates. This is so because in most economies the money supply expands through open-market purchases and bank loan and check deposit expansion. Clearly, this will be associated with falling interest rates, at least initially. Even if the government expands supply by printing additional fiat money, the same result occurs according to Keynes. Having previously decided how much to consume and save, households buy bonds or, equivalently, lend the additional money. Keynes preferred to analyze the supply and demand for money instead of bonds.

Keynes was much less certain than classical economists that the monetary authorities could control the money supply, partly because he emphasized the short run while they emphasized the long run. The Keynesian money *supply* liquidity trap says that the monetary authorities sometimes cannot rapidly change the quantity of money. Nevertheless, in his complete economic model Keynes ignores the money supply trap and assumes that the monetary authorities attempt and, in fact, do control the quantity of money. The classical money supply hypothesis was adopted in order to reduce the sources of different classical and Keynesian conclusions. The money supply, M^S, is an exogenous variable, M_0.

Transactions and Precautionary Demands for Money

Any misgivings Keynes may have had about the money supply equation were minor compared to his criticism of the classical demand for money. Recall that the classicists viewed money strictly as a medium of exchange and had only a transactions demand for money. Keynes accused them of major sins of omission instead of commission. He wholeheartedly endorsed the classical transactions demand for money but castigated them for overlooking other important elements of money demand. In addition to being a medium of exchange, money also is a temporary abode of purchasing power and unit of account. The three functions or services performed by money suggest that *total money demand is the sum of three components: the transactions demand, the precautionary demand, and the speculative demand for money.*

More recent research shows that Keynes should have embraced the classical transactions demand somewhat less warmly. After recognizing that money is the medium of exchange, the classicists immediately leaped to the conclusion that money demand is proportional to income, a proxy for transactions, where the factor of proportionality depends on such factors as the regularity and frequency of payment, the rapidity of communications and transportation, and the degree of vertical integration.[6] The demand for the medium of exchange certainly should be related to income but why should it be proportional to income instead of depending on the square root of income or income squared? The classicists and Keynes offer no justification for the proportionality assumption.

William Baumol's and James Tobin's inventory theoretic approach to the transactions demand, which is summarized in Appendix A, states that the transactions demand depends on the square root of income. More important, *according to Baumol and Tobin the demand for money for transactions purposes also depends positively on brokerage costs and negatively on the interest rate*. The dependence of money demand on the interest rate is a major Keynesian conclusion repeatedly confirmed empirically but denied by classicists. The intuitive rationale for including

---

[6]The classical transactions demand for money was presented in Chapter 23.

brokerage costs and the rate of interest parallels the discussion of these two variables as determinants of desired excess reserve.[7] Suppose our author is paid $3,000 quarterly and spends the entire amount evenly during the quarter. The sawtooth pattern A in Figure 25–2 need not represent the individual's cash balances, as the classicists implicity assumed.[8] Although money is received, the author could buy and sell bonds and not hold money for any significant period of time. Sawtooth pattern B represents the cash balances of an individual who used half, $1,500, of the quarterly salary to buy bonds and then sells the bonds at midquarter. What bond purchase strategy would make transactions balances follow sawtooth pattern C? An immediate $2,000 bond purchase followed by a $1,000 sale one month hence, and another $1,000 sale two months hence, yields pattern C. Note that the same cash pattern occurs when the individual is paid monthly and does not enter the bond market. Which of these three, or possibly other, cash patterns is selected? The Baumol-Tobin inventory theoretic approach assumes profit maximization.[9] Pattern B is preferred to A when the brokerage cost of buying and selling bonds worth $1,500 is less than the interest earned on the bonds during the first half of the quarter. Lower brokerage costs and higher interest rates encourage individuals to buy and sell bonds more frequently and economize on average transactions balances. At sufficiently high interest rates the individual would select pattern C, where average cash balances are only $500.

The studies by Baumol and Tobin notwithstanding, we shall assume as did Keynes and the classicists that the transactions demand for money, M_T^D, is proportional to income and independent of the rate of interest.

(25–4)

$$\frac{M_T^D}{P} = k'y \qquad \text{or } M_T^D = Pk'y$$

$$M_T^D = .2y$$

To emphasize that Keynes, unlike the classicists, viewed the transactions demand as only one component of total money demand, the factor of proportionality is k′ instead of the Cambridge k. Although the price level is assumed fixed, the effect of relaxing this assumption in later chapters is more easily understood when the price level appears explicitly in the algebraic versions of Equation (25–4). The price level is 1 in our numerical example, and k′ = .2. Why is the simple proportionality assumption

---

[7]Cf. Chapter 4.

[8]See Figure 23–2 and the surrounding discussion on the determinants of velocity.

[9]The Baumol-Tobin analysis is described as inventory theoretic because it is based on the principles underlying optimal inventory control. Inventories are held to bridge gaps between production and sales. Money is held to bridge gaps between receipts and expenditures.

FIGURE 25–2

Transactions Balances under Different Assumptions about Bond Purchases and Sales

(A) Transactions balances when $3,000 are received at the beginning of each quarter and spent at a constant rate. No bonds are purchased or sold.
(B) Transactions balances when $3,000 are received at the beginning of each quarter and $1,500 are immediately used to buy bonds, which are sold at midquarter. Spending occurs at a constant rate.
(C) Transactions balances when $3,000 are received at the beginning of each quarter and an immediate $2,000 bond purchase is followed by a $1,000 bond sale in month 1 and another sale in month 2. Spending occurs at a constant rate.

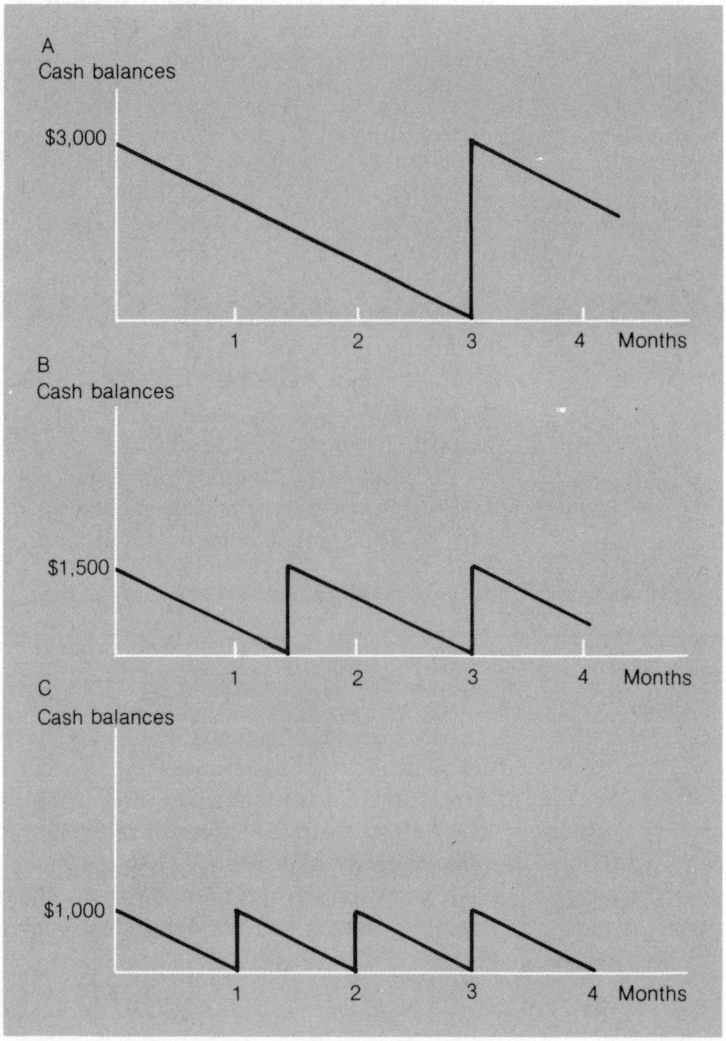

substituted for the more complicated Baumol-Tobin square root formula? Simplicity is desirable, provided no serious errors are introduced. Substituting income for its square root is no serious error.[10] Omitting the rate of interest could be a serious error. However, as we shall see shortly, Keynes introduced the rate of interest in his speculative demand. Given that the interest rate appears in the speculative demand, nothing is gained by adding an interest rate term in the transactions demand, and the analytic convenience of attaching a different motive to each variable would be lost.[11]

The precautionary demand is typically mentioned for the sake of completeness and then is often dismissed because, like the rate of interest in the transactions demand, its effects are captured elsewhere. We shall follow this traditional approach. *The demand for money for precautionary purposes emphasizes that money is a temporary abode of purchasing power which is particularly useful because general uncertainty about the future is the rule.* Let us divide uncertainty into two classes: uncertainty about interest rates (bond prices), and uncertainty about any other factor, called general uncertainty. General uncertainty includes uncertainty about such things as one's job, salary, health; the availability of specific commodities; and the value of total expenditures. A serious illness could drastically reduce one's income and simultaneously increase total expenditures. The house or car of your dreams may suddenly come on the market and require quick purchase. The precautionary motive for money demand says that individuals faced with general uncertainty will hold a temporary abode of purchasing power in order to protect themselves against unfavorable events and take advantage of favorable events. What variables determine the amount of precautionary balances demanded? One obvious variable, the degree of general uncertainty, is extremely difficult to measure. Keynes said income is the main determinant that can be measured.

The precautionary demand depends positively on income because for any degree of uncertainty the rich have more to lose from unfavorable events and also have more favorable opportunities. Mr. Rich and I may feel equally uncertain about our jobs, but he suffers a greater loss if he is fired. The possible sale of a $1 million mansion excites Mr. Rich but is totally immaterial to me; my precautionary balances are designed to

---

[10]Postwar data suggests the square root model is only marginally more accurate than the classical proportionality model. The square root and proportionality models imply the income elasticity of money demand is 0.5 and 1.0, respectively. Goldfeld's postwar study estimates the income elasticity is 0.68, and most longer run studies have estimates close to unity. S. Goldfeld, "The Demand for Money Revisited," *Brookings Papers on Economic Activity*, no. 3 (1973).

[11]Of course, no one actually segregates dollar bills by the motive for holding them.

take advantage of a possible hamburger sale at the supermarket. While we could add another income term in the money demand expression in order to capture the precautionary motive, this only complicates matters and adds nothing new. The transactions motive already suggests that money demand is positively related to income. Think of k′ in Equation (25–4) as capturing both transactions and precautionary factors.

Speculative Demand and Liquidity Preference

Two of Keynes's major hypotheses were: (1) there exists a speculative demand for money whereby households will demand money instead of the alternative asset, a perpetuity, even if they do not foresee any likelihood of near-term expenditures, and (2) the speculative demand for money depends negatively on the rate of interest. The speculative demand is also called the asset demand, and the graph of the speculative money demand is traditionally called the liquidity preference curve. Figure 25–3 graphs several downward-sloping liquidity preference curves. *The speculative demand was crucial to Keynes because it implies that monetary policy* may *be totally ineffective*. Consider the converse. Suppose there is no speculative demand. In this case with only a transactions and precautionary demand, no one holds more money than dictated by planned

FIGURE 25–3
Liquidity Preference Curves

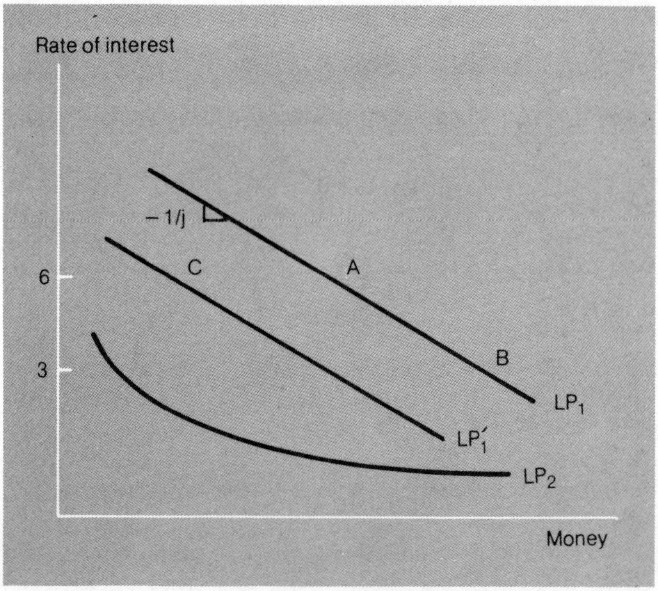

expenditures and an allowance for uncertain expenditures. Suppose further that the authorities increase the quantity of money. In this case the money balances will be spent. Transactions and spending must increase if money demand is to again equal money supply. If a speculative demand exists, then monetary equilibrium could be achieved by less than proportional transactions and income changes. Indeed, if the entire monetary expansion is absorbed as additional speculative balances, then monetary policy has no effect on spending. *Policy is effective to the extent that money market equilibrium is achieved through adjustments in transactions demand instead of speculative demand.*

Two explanations for speculative money demand are popular: Keynes's expected return explanation and Tobin's portfolio risk explanation. The two explanations stem from the relaxation of different crucial assumptions which led classicists to omit the speculative demand. Both explanations emphasize the unit of account property of money and deduce the negatively sloped liquidity preference curve. The Keynesian explanation additionally deduces two other properties of speculative demand which have important policy implications. For this reason, and because of Keynes's unique place in the history of economics, the Keynesian explanation is presented here while Tobin's explanation is relegated to Appendix B.

After deciding how much money to hold for planned and probable expenditures, assume an economic unit has sufficient wealth to acquire a portfolio of additional money and perpetual bonds. *Classicists assumed economic units were strict profit maximizers.* The money-bonds portfolio decision is based solely on the expected total return, which is the sum of the interest (coupon) and capital returns. That asset with the highest expected total return is selected. Currency earns no interest. While the interest return on other types of money, for example, check deposits, is positive in some countries and in some time periods, let us assume for simplicity that interest on all types of money is zero. This guarantees that the interest return is less on money than bonds, as indeed is normally the case. The second component of total yield is the capital yield, the difference between future and current dollar values. *Being the unit of account, the capital yield on money must be zero.* A $20 bill today is still a $20 bill a year hence; it may purchase fewer commodities because the dollar value of other commodities rises while the value of a $20 bill remains constant.[12] Bonds are not the unit of account. Holders of either bonds or money suffer real purchasing power losses as the prices of commodities rise, and bond holders incur additional nominal capital losses when in-

[12]While the unit of account function is served by many interest paying accounts such as savings deposits and leads to the broad M = 3 definition of money, Keynes's argument does not depend on the assumption that the return on money is zero. The essential feature of the unit of account is certainty of return, if any, and capital value.

terest rates rise. Assuming the perpetuity pays $1 per period, the expected total *dollar* return on bonds, R_T, during the period is

(25–5)

$$\text{Expected total dollar return} = \text{Coupon} + \text{Expected capital return}$$

$$R_T = 1 + (1/r_E - 1/r_0),$$

where $1/r_E$ is the expected end-of-period price of bonds, and $1/r_0$ is the current bond price. (Equation (25–5) makes use of the inverse relationship between bond prices and interest rates. That is, r_E is the expected rate, and $1/r_E$ is the expected bond price.)

Classicists recognized the uncertainty of interest rates and bond prices but assumed that the expected or average capital yield was zero. In other words, they assumed the expected future rate of interest always equaled the current rate. Lack of a speculative demand is the inevitable *correct* conclusion from these classical assumptions. Expected profit (and return) maximizers do not hold any speculative money balances in this case because money offers no return while the expected total return on bonds equals the coupon. *The crucial assumptions which led classicists to reject the existence of a speculative demand for money are: (1) economic units are expected profit maximizers, and (2) expected future and current interest rates are equal,* so that the expected capital yield on bonds is zero. *Drop either of these two assumptions and the unit-of-account property of money can imply an aggregate speculative demand that is negatively related to the rate of interest.*

Keynes denied the second classical assumption and let the expected future interest rate diverge from the current rate. The classical long-run time period almost requires the equality of actual and expected interest rates and bond prices. A divergence between the current and expected future value tends to narrow over time. In a long-run equilibrium, which by definition precludes any narrowing or other changes, current and future values will coincide. For example, suppose the current rate of interest is 8 percent and the expected future interest rate is 10 percent. While such a time situation certainly could exist for a short period of time, interest rates surely are not always overestimated. Individuals learn; eventually expectations will be revised downward if the current rate remains at 8 percent. The revised expectations cause other behavioral changes, for example, lower expected interest rates may induce greater investment. Revisions stop and constancy occurs when the actual and expected interest rates are equal. In the long run the expected total return on bonds coincides with the coupon yield as the expected capital yield vanishes. In the Keynesian short run, however, the expected total return on bonds may well be negative. *Speculative money balances are held by those economic units expecting future interest rates sufficiently above the cur-*

rent rate that the expected capital loss is greater than the interest yield, making the total return on bonds negative. Continuing our example, when the current interest on consols paying \$1 per period is 8 percent, their price is \$12.50. A profit-maximizing individual who expects the rate of interest to rise to 10 percent, and bond prices to fall to \$10, will hold money because the \$2.50 capital loss exceeds the \$1 coupon. Money may not bear interest and as the unit of account cannot offer a capital yield, but this is preferable to expected losses on bonds. When the rate of interest is very high, nearly everyone will be expecting lower interest rates and capital gains from higher bond prices. Therefore, nearly everyone prefers bonds at high interest rates, and the speculative demand for money is very small. As the rate of interest falls, the expected rate of more and more households will exceed the current rate of interest. These households sell their bonds to avoid the expected capital losses and hold speculative money balances. At very low interest rates nearly everyone is expecting higher rates, and speculative money balances are large. *Given society's set of expectations, speculative money demand is negatively related to the rate of interest.*

Properties of the Keynesian Liquidity Preference Curve

Keynes's explanation of the speculative demand in terms of discrepancies between current and normal interest rates further suggests that *the liquidity preference schedule is unstable and ultimately becomes flat. Each of these properties of the liquidity preference schedule has important policy implications*. Consider first why the schedule is unstable. The Keynesian explanation assumes a given aggregate set of expected future interest rates. Test your knowledge of the importance of the given expected rate by answering the following: how, if at all, will the liquidity preference LP_1 curve in Figure 25–3 be affected if everyone suddenly revises their expectation, and when are revisions likely? The liquidity preference curve shifts in the same direction as the revision in the expected rate. Lower expected rates shift LP_1 downward to LP'_1. Temporarily ignore the curve labeled LP_2. Lower expected rates and higher expected bond prices tend to raise the return on bonds, given any current rate of interest, and reduce the amount of money demanded. To counteract this tendency and induce households to demand the same amount of money, the current interest rate (bond price) must be lower (higher). Instead of considering the rate of interest necessary to induce the same amount of money demanded—the vertical shift of the LP_1 curve—analyze the problem in terms of the amount of money demanded at every interest rate—the horizontal shift of the LP_1 curve. When lower future interest rates and larger capital gains are expected, at every current rate of interest and price of bonds some holders of speculative money balances will now expect a positive return on bonds and switch from money to bonds. The liquidity preference curve shifts leftward from A to C.[13]

When is the expected rate of interest likely to change and shift the liquidity preference curve? Households' expected rate of interest and the position of the liquidity preference curve is based in large part on past and current experience, as suggested by our discussion of the equivalence of expected and actual values in the long run. This implies that *moving along a liquidity preference curve causes it to shift*. For example, suppose the rate of interest had been 6 percent in the past so most households are expecting the rate of interest to be approximately 6 percent in the future. This expectation gives LP_1. Suppose the rate of interest falls from 6 to 3 percent, a rate of interest most households consider abnormally low. One moves from point A to point B on LP_1 in Figure 25–3 as households demand more money to avoid the expected loss on bonds when the rate of interest rebounds upward. If the rate of interest is maintained at 3 percent, however, it will no longer seem abnormally low. The normal interest rate will be revised downward, and the liquidity preference curve shifts to LP'_1. Movements in the current rate of interest are not the only source of variation in the normal rate, which plays a role analogous to entrepreneurs' state of confidence in the investment schedule. Keynes thought households' normal rate of interest is little understood and highly variable, causing a continually shifting, unstable liquidity preference curve.

Abstracting from instability and assuming the normal rate of interest is fixed, the Keynesian explanation of liquidity preference says that the liquidity preference curve eventually becomes flat. Technically speaking, *at some low rate of interest the liquidity preference curve becomes perfectly elastic, and a money demand liquidity trap exists. The liquidity trap, illustrated by LP_2 in Figure 25–3, sets a floor on the rate of interest.*[14] At some sufficiently low interest rate the economy enters a liquidity trap because everyone expects higher interest rates and avoids capital losses by holding only money. The demand for money becomes absolute. If the monetary authority were to increase the money supply, *the additional money balances would be willingly held. In a liquidity trap money does not influence spending and, therefore, income.* The liquidity trap is a dilemma the monetary authorities want to avoid.

The post-Keynesian portfolio explanation of liquidity preference in terms of interest being the reward for risk is silent about the stability and slope of the schedule. It is compatible with the linear liquidity preference relationships in Figure 25–3. Let us assume this is the case and consider

---

[13]The two equivalent ways of viewing the shift are presented for the reader's convenience. Select the approach you find easier.

[14]The term *liquidity trap* without qualifying adjectives henceforth always is a money *demand* liquidity trap.

instability and the liquidity trap later as special cases. The algebraic form and a specific example of a linear total money demand function is

(25–6)

$$\frac{M^D}{P_0} = k'y + h - jr$$

$$M^D = P_0(k'y + h - jr)$$
$$M^D = .2y + 116 - 2r$$

The first term, k′y, is the transactions demand, and h − jr represents the linear downward-sloping liquidity preference. The parameter j measures the responsiveness of speculative demand to the rate of interest. The price level again is set at 1.

The LM Curve: Money Demand Equals Money Supply

Economists are excellent matchmakers: a downward-sloping curve is invariably united with an upward-sloping curve to produce a unique point. Our discussion of the Keynesian money demand has prepared us to maintain the tradition. *The LM or money market equilibrium curve yields a positive relationship between income and the rate of interest.* Let's see why. Figure 25–4A graphs the Keynesian money demand, given by Equation (25–6), and a totally exogenous money supply, which is the solid vertical line M^S_0 in the figure. Temporarily ignore the broken vertical line M^S_1. Since Figure 25–4 has the rate of interest on the vertical axis and money on the horizontal axis, the slope of a liquidity preference curve, $\Delta r/\Delta M^D$, is $-1/j$. If j is large, the slope of any linear liquidity preference curve in Figure 25–4 is small (flat), indicating that a small change in the rate of interest leads to a large change in liquidity preference. The position of a liquidity preference curve depends on the level of income. Higher incomes increase the amount of money demand for transactions purposes and shift the liquidity preference curve rightward. The extent of the rightward shift depends positively on k′. Inspection of Figure 25–4A shows that as income increases the rate of interest which equilibrates the money market rises. The solid LM curve in Figure 25–4B graphs the money market equilibrium relationship, given the solid vertical supply. (Again ignore the broken LM_1.)

The LM curve is an upward-sloping curve containing all the income and interest rate combinations that equate money demand and a given money supply. It is upward sloping because as income increases, the amount of money demanded for transactions increases. In order to maintain equilibrium in the money market, the amount demanded for speculative purposes must fall. This happens when the rate of interest rises.

FIGURE 25–4

Construction of the LM Curve

The LM curve is an upward sloping curve showing all the interest rate-income combinations which equate money demand and supply.

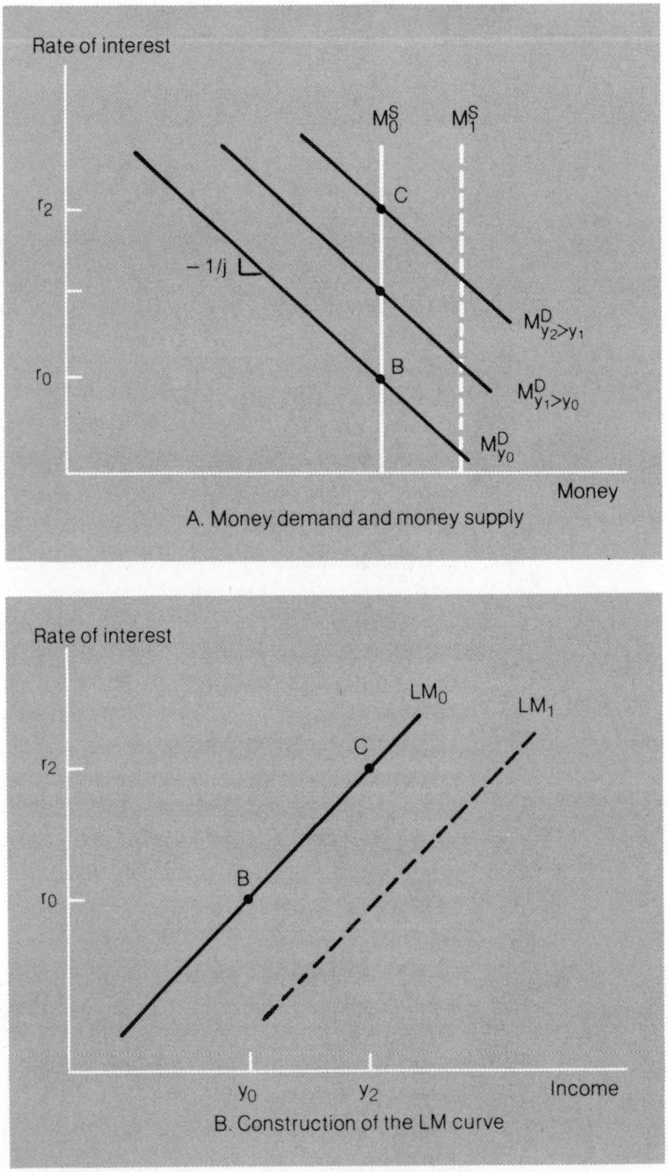

The LM curve is so-called because money demand originally was written as L (for liquidity) instead of M^D. At equilibrium, money demand, L equals money supply, M.

IS and LM: General Equilibrium

The IS curve is the commodities market equilibrium curve. Along the entire IS curve aggregate expenditures equal income. Given the appropriate rate of interest, expenditures can equal virtually every level of income. The LM curve is the money market equilibrium curve. Along the entire LM curve money demand equals supply. The demand for and supply of money are equal at virtually every interest rate, given the appropriate income level. *The intersection of the IS and LM curves in Figure 25–5 represents general equilibrium. A unique interest rate and income com-*

FIGURE 25–5

IS and LM: General Equilibrium

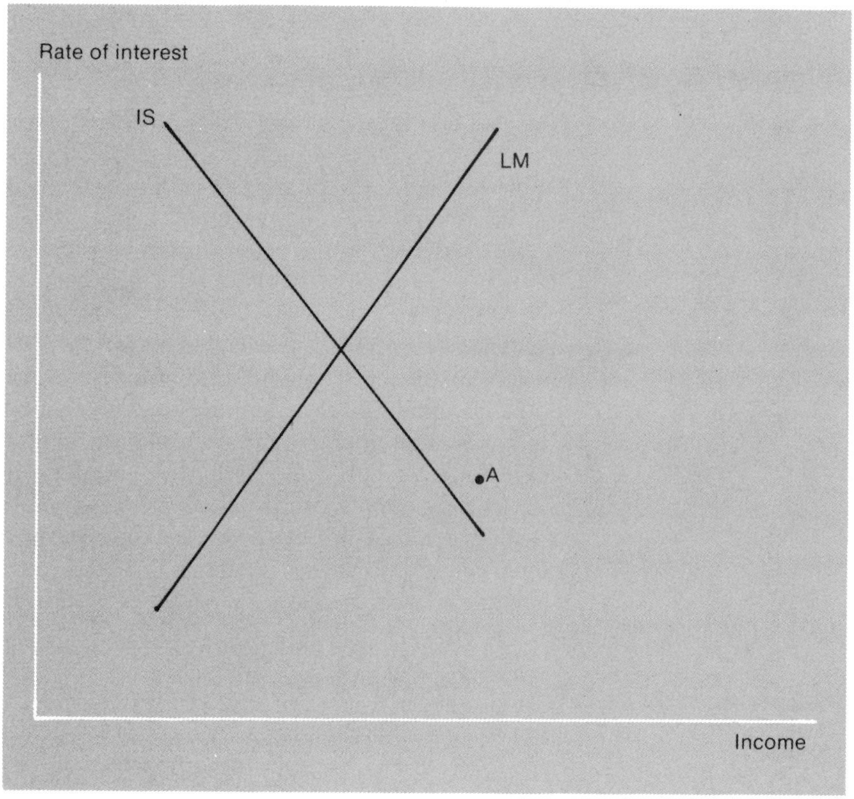

bination equates both aggregate expenditures and income and the demand for and supply of money. The algebraic and numerical solutions for the general equilibrium income and rate of interest are found in Appendix A of Chapter 26.

Since the economy rarely is at equilibrium, one should analyze the adjustment process or sequence of events leading to equilibrium. For example, suppose the current (nonequilibrium) interest rate and income is represented by point A in Figure 25–5. Precisely what changes occur over time before equilibrium is reached? Because the supply and demand equations cannot pinpoint the precise adjustment path, the analysis is relegated to Appendix C. The appendix presents several adjustment paths, some of which are consistent with the cyclical fluctuations which characterize developed economies. In the process of adjusting to a *single* shock, the economy undergoes peaks and troughs before equilibrium is reached. The business cycle need *not* be produced by a series of expansionary and contractionary shocks.

Summary/Questions

The rate of interest, which is ignored in the basic Keynesian model, links the real and financial sectors in the IS-LM model. The rate of interest enters the real sector in a neoclassically-oriented investment function. At low interest rates more investment projects are profitable. While the role Keynes assigned to the rate of interest in the real sector was quite standard, the speculative motive and dependence of money demand on the rate of interest is a *crucial* Keynesian contribution. Keynes explained the existence of speculative balances in terms of a divergence between the current and future expected rate of interest. As interest rates rise, more profit-maximizing economic units avoid speculative money balances and prefer the high appreciation potential of bonds. If there were no speculative holdings so that money demand is independent of the rate of interest, then money supply, transactions, and income would be rigidly tied. If money were held simply for transactions purposes, only income changes could equilibrate money demand to exogenous money supply changes. Conversely, only monetary changes could produce income variations.

1. What are the main differences between the basic and advanced Keynesian models?
2. Suppose the investment equation is $I = I_0 - er$. How is the slope of the investment schedule related to "e"?
3. Derive graphically and define the IS curve. Carefully explain why it is downward sloping.

4. How, if at all, do the Keynesian transactions money demand and the classical (total) money demand differ?
5. Explain intuitively why the transactions demand for money should depend on brokerage costs and the rate of interest.
6. Discuss the precautionary demand for money. What function or service performed by money does it stress? What variables influence the amount of money demanded for precautionary purposes?
7. What is meant by the speculative or asset demand for money? What are the implications for monetary policy of the speculative demand for money?
8. Discuss Keynes's derivation of the speculative demand for money. What assumptions led classical economists to deny the existence of the speculative demand for money? Which assumption did Keynes drop? As explained by Keynes, is the speculative demand a short- or long-run phenomenon? Explain.
9. What are the two main properties of the downward-sloping *Keynesian* liquidity preference curve?
10. Define a (money demand) liquidity trap. When may it tend to occur? What is the relationship between the current and expected rate of interest in a liquidity trap?
11. Derive and define the LM curve. Carefully explain why it is upward sloping.
12. What is meant by the *general* equilibrium rate of interest and income? Are there many equilibrium levels of income? Are there many equilibrium rates of interest?

Monetary and fiscal multipliers within the IS–LM model

26

Monetarists have reservations about any analysis based on the IS–LM model and about the need for any short-run stabilization policy. Nevertheless, they have used the IS–LM model, which remains the most popular short-run monetary-macroeconomic model, to compare the sizes of the monetary and fiscal policy multipliers. Keynesians also like to engage in comparative policy evaluation. Indeed, because both like comparisons so much but come to diametrically opposite conclusions, the relative size of the monetary and fiscal policy multipliers has become one of the most divisive issues. This divisive, and important, issue merits a complete chapter.

In contrast to the basic Keynesian model where money is completely ineffective, in the IS–LM model money *may* affect income through the interest rate. If monetary policy changes the rate of interest, and if investment is responsive to the rate of interest, then monetary policy affects GNP. While recognition of interest rate effects opens a crack for monetary policy, it could foreclose the use of fiscal policy as a stabilization tool. Fiscal policy has an indirect negative effect on investment. For example, suppose a recession exists and government spends more and cuts taxes in order to stimulate the economy. The expansionary fiscal policy probably has no direct effect on investment. However, the expansionary fiscal policy creates a budget deficit that must be financed. Assuming the Federal Reserve maintains a neutral policy and does not accommodate the Treasury by open-market purchases and monetary expansion, bond sales to the public are the only means of financing the deficit. The sale of bonds by the Treasury or anyone else tends to lower bond prices, or, equivalently, raise the rate of interest. In this manner fiscal policy has an indirect negative effect on investment. *The higher interest rates associated with budget deficits could reduce investment by an amount equal to the increase in government expenditures, in which case fiscal policy has no effect on aggregate demand.* Keynes recognized this possibility but discounted it. As he interpreted the economic data, the negative indirect effect of fiscal policy on investment was quite small.

Monetarists disagree with Keynes. As they interpret the data, money has a strong positive, if indirect, effect on aggregate demand, while fiscal policy has such a strong negative indirect effect on investment as to render it virtually useless. Perhaps because measurement of indirect effects is the issue, the Keynesian-monetarist controversy may remain unresolved longer than other economic controversies. Under the circumstances, knowledge of alternative outcomes and the circumstances under which they occur is highly desirable.

The first section shows the effects of monetary and fiscal expansion on income, the three major spending components, and the rate of interest. These conclusions and others are proven in the algebraic Appendix A. The next section analyzes the common set of four factors which influence the size of the monetary and fiscal multipliers. We then illustrate with IS–LM curves the importance of all four factors for each multiplier. The text, however, tackles only the easier cases, leaving the more difficult ones for Appendixes B and C. The final section briefly indicates why monetarists and Keynesians can steadfastly maintain totally contradictory positions about the monetary and fiscal multipliers. All three appendixes are at the end of the book.

An Introduction to Monetary and Fiscal Policy

Suppose equilibrium income is below full-employment income as Keynes assumed to be the typical case. The Fed correctly increases the quantity of money. What are the effects of the monetary expansion? Looking at the expansion from the viewpoint of the money suppliers, the Fed generally must bid up bond prices and, thereby, lower interest rates in order to acquire bonds. Similarly, commercial banks with additional (excess) reserves expand loans and deposits by reducing the loan rate. Lower interest rates generate the second step in the expansion process: investment increases. Output and income increase as firms hire more workers to produce machinery and other investment goods. The newly hired workers respond by consuming more, which increases income even further. Ultimately, however, equilibrium prevails. *Monetary expansion increases equilibrium income and decreases the equilibrium rate of interest. Both components of private spending, consumption and invest-*

ment, increase.[1] *Monetary policy is symmetric. A monetary contraction reduces income and raises the rate of interest.*

Suppose instead that expansionary fiscal policy had been initiated. To draw a sharp distinction between monetary and fiscal policy, we *always* assume that greater government spending or lower taxes, which creates a budget deficit, is financed by the sale of bonds. When the private sector purchases the bonds, private deposits and the money supply, which is defined to exclude government deposits, decline. As the government spends the proceeds of the bond sale, the money supply returns to its original quantity. Abstracting from these very short-run effects—the government typically sells bonds and acquires funds immediately prior to its expansionary fiscal program—additional government spending increases demand directly, or lower taxes directly increase disposable income and consumption. In either case, firms' inventories are initially depleted. They respond by hiring more workers to restock their inventories and meet the fiscally induced demand. Production and income increase directly. This sets in motion an adjustment process which may make the immediate and ultimate effects radically different.

The first step is favorable to fiscal policy. Consumption by the recently hired workers triggers a multiplier effect. However, the higher level of income increases the amount of money demanded for transactions purposes. Since the money supply is fixed, the larger money demand raises the rate of interest, which in turn reduces investment as some projects are no longer profitable. *The curtailment of investments by expansionary fiscal policy distinguishes the IS–LM model from the basic Keynesian model and reduces the fiscal multiplier.* The negative feedback effect

TABLE 26–1

Effects of Monetary and Fiscal Expansion on Major Variables (+, increase; –, decrease; 0, no change)

		Fiscal	
	Monetary Increase	*Spending Increase*	*Tax Cut*
Income	+	+	+
Rate of interest	–	+	+
Consumption	+	+	+
Investment	+	–	–
Government spending	0	+	0

[1]We shall consider exports and imports later.

generally does not completely offset the positive direct effect. *Government spending or lower taxes raises equilibrium income and the rate of interest. Consumption increases but investment decreases. Fiscal policy also is symmetric. Income and the rate of interest fall when government spends less or taxes more.* Table 26–1 summarizes the effects of expansionary monetary and fiscal policy on income, the rate of interest, and the spending components.

Figure 26–1 illustrates the effects of monetary and fiscal policy in terms of IS and LM curves. For monetary policy ignore the dashed IS curve. Monetary expansion shifts the LM downward and rightward but has no effect on the IS curve since aggregate expenditures do not depend *directly* on the quantity of money. The rate of interest falls from r_o to r_m, and income increases to y_m. Go back to Figure 25–4, where the larger money supply is represented by the broken vertical line. The graph readily shows that for any given income and liquidity preference curve, a lower rate of interest equates money demand and supply. The larger money supply gives the dashed LM curve. *Monetary expansion shifts the LM curve downward and rightward. The converse is true: monetary contraction shifts the LM curve upward and leftward.* At this point we should no longer need graphical aids for the converse case and can proceed directly to the economic rationale. The LM curve is the money market equilibrium curve. When the money supply is curtailed, less must be demanded if equilibrium again recurs. Given any income level (horizontal coordinate) and transactions demand, the equilibrium amount demanded for speculative purposes must fall, which occurs when the interest rate rises. The LM curve shifts upward. We can also view monetary contraction as shifting the LM curve leftward. Given any interest rate (vertical coordinate) and speculative demand, the equilibrium amount demanded for transactions purposes must fall, which occurs when income decreases.

Additional government spending or a tax cut shifts the IS rightward to IS′ in Figure 26–1 but has no effect on the LM curve. Therefore, both income and interest rates rise. The IS curve summarizes much information. It incorporates the C, I, and G curves. *Any shift in these underlying curves causes the IS curve to shift.* The solid IS curve in Figure 25–1C corresponds with the solid investment line in Figure 25–1B. Now assume investment increases; a technological breakthrough or heightened expectations cause firms to invest more at every rate of interest. The dashed I′ line in Figure 25–1B represents the new investment relationship. At every rate of interest a larger amount would be added to C + G in Figure 25–1A, so the C + G + I total expenditure curve intersects the 45° line at a higher point. The dashed investment line gives the dashed IS′ line. Clearly, either consumption or government spending shifts have the same effect on the total expenditure curve as the investment shift. *Greater*

FIGURE 26–1

Monetary Expansion Shifts the LM Rightward, and Fiscal Expansion Shifts the IS Rightward

Monetary expansion lowers the rate of interest to r_m, and fiscal expansion raises the rate of interest to r_g. Income effects are assumed equal.

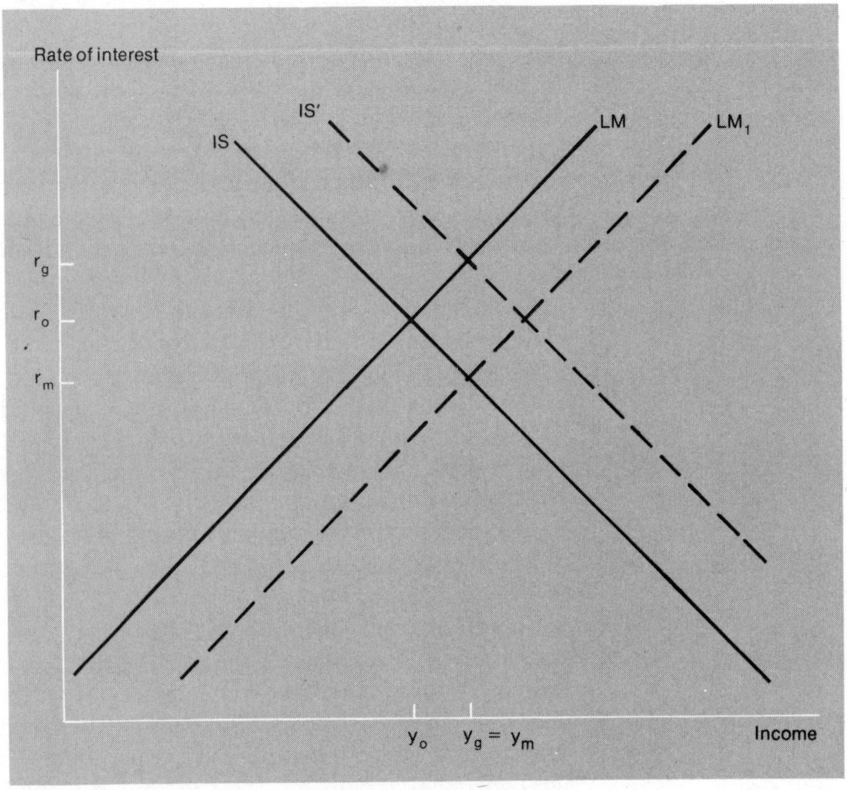

investment or government spending or an autonomous tax cut which increases consumption shifts the IS curve upward and rightward.[2]

Although not shown graphically the converse is true. Less investment or government spending shifts the IS curve downward and leftward. Going beyond graphics, the economic rationale for the IS shift readily follows from its definition. The IS curve shows all the interest rate-income combinations where income equals aggregate demand. When the latter decreases at every rate of interest, the equality will be maintained only if

[2]Government spending shifts the IS more than an equal tax cut because the latter has a smaller immediate impact on demand due to a fractional marginal propensity to consume. This is analogous to the greater impact of government spending on the C + I + G curve in Figure 25–1A.

income falls—the IS curve shifts leftward. One could equally well view the curve shifting downward. At every income level, the rate of interest must be lower in order to keep expenditures constant.[3]

Although not associated with either monetary or fiscal policy, now is the most convenient time to note that money demand and supply shifts have opposite effects on the LM curve. This is in accord with ordinary supply and demand, where equal but opposite shifts have the same effect on price. For example, an increase in demand has the same effect on price as an equal decrease in supply. The analog of price in the LM analysis is an income-interest rate combination. *A reduction in money demand has the same effect on the LM curve as monetary expansion. A decrease (increase) in money demand shifts the LM downward (upward) and rightward (leftward).* While not illustrated in Figure 25–4A in order to prevent excessive clutter, visualize each liquidity preference curve shifting leftward the same distance the money supply was shifted rightward. The new demand curves and initial (solid) money supply also produce the dashed LM curve. When money demand falls, lower interest rates, which increase the amount demanded for speculative purposes, or higher levels of income, which increase the amount demanded for transactions purposes, are necessary if the amount demanded again equals the constant money supply.[4]

Determinants of the Money and Fiscal Multipliers

Figure 26–1 assumed that monetary and fiscal expansion have the same effect on income. This hardly needs to be true. Let us first analyze the determinants of the money multiplier, which henceforth is defined as the ratio of the income change to the money change, $\Delta y/\Delta M$. (Do not confuse this multiplier with the money *supply* multiplier analyzed in Chapters 3 and 4. The two multipliers are not related in any way.) What conditions

---

[3]This and most of the chapter's other conclusions are proven algebraically in Appendix A. The mathematically oriented who intend to use the appendix are encouraged to do so *right now*. However, do *not* devour the entire appendix in one sitting. Alternate between equivalent sections in the text and appendix.

[4]Those who forget the important distinction between demand and the quantity demanded sometimes *incorrectly* believe that the argument in the text and Figure 25–4 imply that fiscal policy shifts the LM curve upward. Because expansionary fiscal policy increases income, the amount *demanded* for transactions purposes increases. The economy moves to a higher liquidity preference curve in Figure 25–4A, and the rate of interest rises. However, this represents a movement along an LM curve, and not a shift of the curve, since the axes of the LM curve like the IS curve measure income and the rate of interest. The LM curve shifts when the amount of money demanded at any *given* income changes. Similarly, monetary policy produces a movement along a *fixed* IS curve because it affects the amount spent, but not the spending functions (25–1) to (25–3). This will change when we introduce a real balance effect.

must exist for the money multiplier to be large? When is it small? The answers to these questions proceed from the adjustment process sketched in the last section. Since monetary policy "works" because interest rates affect spending, the money multiplier is large, *ceteris paribus,* when (1) monetary expansion produces a sharply lower interest rate, and (2) investment spending responds strongly to the lower interest rate. In terms of the structural equations, *the money multiplier is large,* ceteris paribus, *when (1) liquidity preference is not responsive to the rate of interest, and its slope (−1/j) is absolutely large and steep, and (2) the investment function is responsive to the rate of interest, and its slope (−1/e) is absolutely small and flat.*

Figure 26–2a draws steep and flat liquidity preference (lp) curves and money supply curves. Concentrate on the solid lp curves and temporarily ignore the dashed ones. Inspection of Figure 26–2a shows that monetary

FIGURE 26–2 The Effect of the Slopes of the Liquidity Preference and Investment Schedules on the Multipliers

The money (fiscal) multiplier is large when the liquidity preference curve is steep (flat) and the investment schedule is flat (steep).

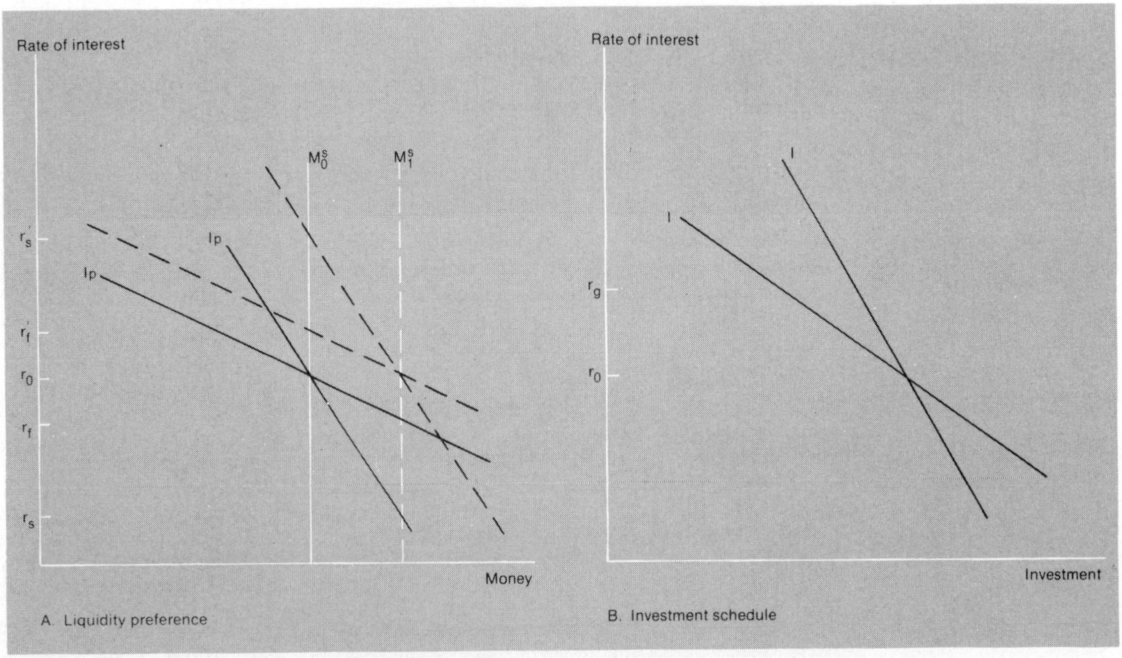

expansion, which shifts the solid vertical M_0^S to the dashed M_1^S, reduces the rate of interest less when the lp curve is flat, $r_f > r_s$. Because the steep curve signifies that money *demand* is not responsive to the rate of interest, the latter must fall more to make the former equal the exogenous money supply. Given any degree of interest rate responsiveness by investors, income increases more when the lp curve is steep.

Of course, the responsiveness of investment to the rate of interest should not be considered a "given." Figure 26–2b draws flat and steep investment (I) curves. When I is very responsive to the rate of interest so that the curve is flat, then any reduction in the rate of interest leads to larger increases in investment and income.

The fiscal policy multiplier also depends on the slopes of the lp and I curves, but in a manner precisely *opposite* to monetary policy multiplier. *The fiscal multiplier is large, ceteris paribus, when (1) lp is responsive to the rate of interest, and its slope* $(-1/j)$ *is absolutely small and flat, and (2) the I function is not responsive to the rate of interest, and its slope* $(-1/e)$ *is absolutely large and steep.*

When fiscal policy increases income, additional transactions (money) balances are demanded. In terms of Figure 26–2a, the lp curves shift rightward to the dashed position. Since the money supply is constant in this case, the rate of interest rises in order to reduce the amount demanded for speculative purposes and again equate total money demand with the constant supply. When speculative money demand is very responsive to the rate of interest so that the lp curve is quite flat, then only slightly higher interest rates (namely, r_f') reduce speculative balances and provide the necessary transactions balances. Compare r_f' and r_s' in Figure 26–2a. Since higher interest rates reduce investment and income, fiscal policy is more expansionary the flatter the lp curve.

The opposite effect on the two multipliers of the slope of the I curve is seen quite readily. Additional government spending or lower taxes increases the rate of interest (to r_g in Figure 26–2b) and reduces investment. For the fiscal multiplier to be large, the reduction in investment must be small, which is the case when the I curve is steep. As just stated, the money multiplier is large when the I curve is flat. Monetary policy is very expansionary when a movement *down* the I curve *increases* investment significantly, while fiscal policy is very expansionary when a movement *up* the I curve *decreases* investment insignificantly.

Both the money and fiscal multipliers also depend in the *same* way on the marginal propensity to consume (MPC) and the money demand transactions coefficient (k′). *The money and fiscal multipliers are directly related to the MPC.* The MPC, the only determinant of the fiscal multiplier in the standard basic Keynesian model, clearly continues to play a role in the IS–LM model. The distinguishing feature of the IS–LM model is the recognition of financial markets, not the induced spending concept.

Additional government spending increases income, which still induces extra consumption, and yet more income. Similarly, the investment generated by monetary expansion increases income, which induces extra consumption, and still more income. In either case, income increases more if the MPC and induced consumption are greater.

Both multipliers are inversely related to the transactions coefficient, k'. The relationship is clearer for monetary policy since a low k' means that velocity is high. When k' is small, the additional money is turned over more frequently and yields a higher income. Alternatively stated, the smaller the amount of money demanded *per* transaction, the more *total* transactions and income must increase in order to equate money demand with the larger supply. Similar reasoning suggests the same inverse relationship for fiscal policy. When the economy needs little money *per* transaction, fiscal policy increases total transactions and income more. In terms of Figure 26–2a, the magnitude of the rightward shift of the lp curves depends directly on k'. When k' is small so that fiscal expansion increases the demand for transactions balances only slightly, the lp curves shift slightly, and, *ceteris paribus*, the interest rate rise and investment cutback are small.

The Slopes of IS–LM and the Multipliers*

In some economic circles it is chic to knock IS–LM analysis. I agree, IS–LM is *not* the best analytical tool to tackle several problems. Nevertheless, there are many good reasons why IS–LM remains the most popular monetary-macroeconomic analytical tool. It is taught even in some Principles courses, and advanced graduate students routinely use it. Like it or not, those who plan to take other economics courses and especially economics majors and potential graduate students will want to master IS–LM. The first step in mastering IS–LM is knowledge of the relationships among the four determinants of the policy multipliers and the *slopes* of the IS and LM curves. We take the first step here but relegate to Appendixes B and C the second and third steps, analyses of the relationship among the four multiplier determinants and the magnitude of IS and LM *shifts* due to unitary changes in policy.

Since monetary expansion shifts the LM curve but *not* the IS curve, *the money multiplier is larger the flatter the IS curve*. Inspection of Figure 26–3 confirms this. For the flat IS', income increases to y'_1, which is greater than y_1 for the steeper IS. What determines the slope of the IS? Which of the four determinants mentioned in the section produces a flat IS curve and, therefore, a large money multiplier? First, the properties

*The nontheoretical reader may proceed directly to the next section on "crowding out."

FIGURE 26–3

Monetary Expansion Shifts the LM Curve Rightward

Monetary expansion increases income and lowers the rate of interest. Income increases more when the IS curve is elastic (flat).

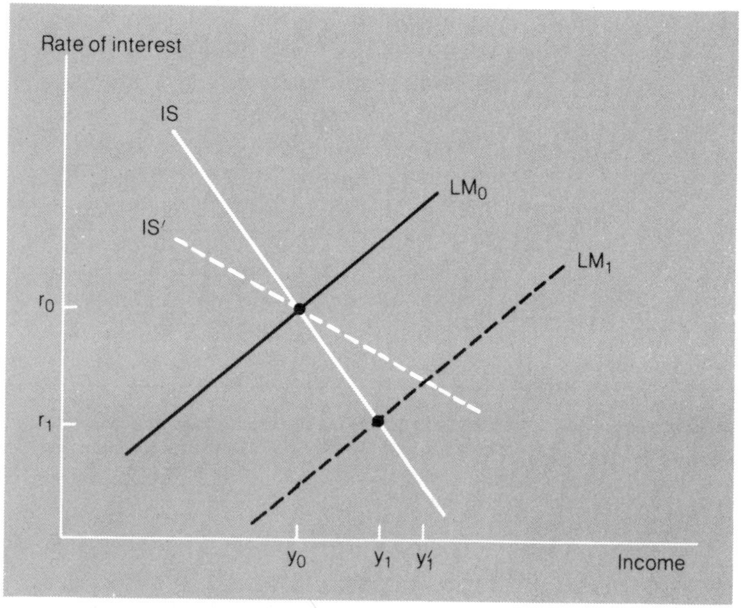

of *money* demand and supply cannot influence the IS curve since it is the *commodities* market equilibrium curve. The slope of IS, just as its position, depends on the underlying investment *and* consumption function. *The IS curve is flat when* (1) investment is quite responsive to the rate of interest so that *the investment schedule is flat, and* (2) *the marginal propensity to consume is large* so that the consumption function is steep. Symmetry again prevails; opposite conditions produce a steep IS curve. (Henceforth, always assume symmetry unless specifically stated otherwise.)

The economic rationale for this follows from the definition of the IS curve: all interest-rate/income points where aggregate demand equals income. When the investment component of aggregate demand is responsive to the rate of interest, then small interest rate changes lead to large expenditure and income changes and a flat IS curve, other things being equal. The last explanation implicitly considered the income change necessary to maintain equilibrium when the rate of interest changes. Now consider the opposite situation. An increase in income produces an excess supply in the commodities market because the marginal propensity to consume is less than unity. The larger is the MPC, the smaller is the excess supply. Consequently, a small decline in the rate of interest is sufficient, other things being equal, to eliminate the excess supply of commodities when the MPC is large. Perhaps more simply, the IS curve tends to be flat when the MPC is high because the income multiplier of any interest rate induced aggregate expenditure change is large.

Since *fiscal* policy shifts the IS curve but *not* the LM curve, *the government spending multiplier is larger the flatter the LM curve*. Inspection of Figure 26–4 confirms this. For the flat LM′, income increases to y'_1, which is greater than y_1 for the steeper LM. What determines the slope of the LM? First, the properties of the *expenditure* relationships cannot influence the LM curve, which is the money market equilibrium curve. The slope of LM, just as its position, depends on the underlying money

FIGURE 26–4
Government Spending Shifts the IS Curve Rightward

Additional government expenditures increases income and the rate of interest. Income increases more when the LM curve is elastic (flat). The distance $y_B - y_1$ represents crowding out, which is the income expansion curtailed by the financial consequences of a budget deficit.

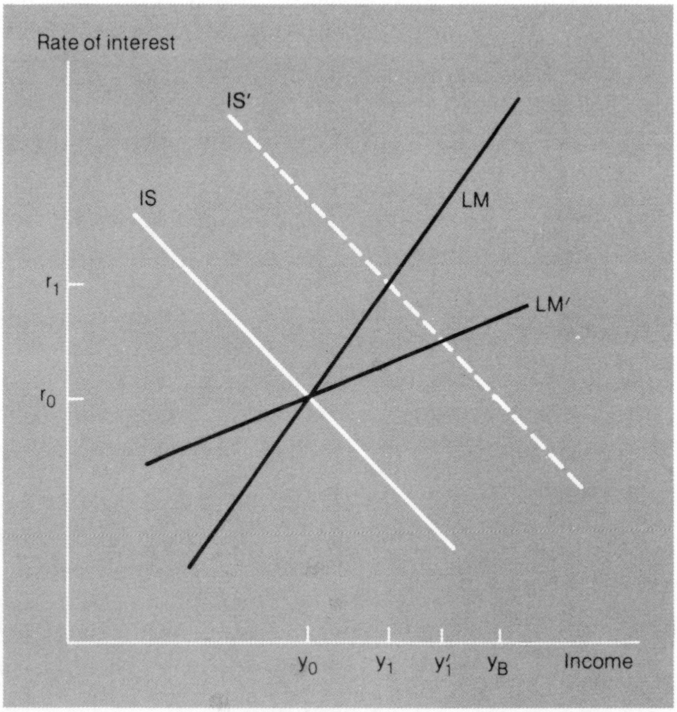

demand and supply. With an exogenous money supply, *the LM curve is flat when* (1) speculative money demand is quite responsive to the rate of interest so that *the liquidity preference curve is flat, and* (2) *the transactions coefficient k′ is small.* (All this should sound very familiar, with LM and IS switching places in this and the previous paragraphs.)

The economic rationale for this follows from the definition of the LM curve: all interest rate-income points where money demand equals supply. As we move up the LM curve the amount of money demanded for transactions purposes increases, and the amount demanded for speculative purposes decreases so the sum of the two equals the fixed money supply. When the liquidity preference curve is relatively flat so that a higher interest rate causes a large reduction in the amount demanded for speculative purposes, then, *ceteris paribus,* a large increase in income and transactions is necessary to equilibriate the money market. Therefore, the LM, with income on the horizontal axis is flat. The *ceteris paribus* restriction is dropped by introducing the transactions coefficient k′, the second determinant of the slope of LM. A small transactions coefficient means that income must change a large amount to produce any given change in the amount demanded for transactions purposes. Consequently, for any *given* change in the rate of interest and the amount demanded for speculative purposes, the LM curve, with income on the horizontal axis, is flatter when the transactions coefficient is small.

Fiscal Policy, the LM Curve, and Crowding Out

The advanced Keynesian (IS–LM) government spending multiplier is smaller than the basic Keynesian multiplier because the basic model, by ignoring financial effects, implicitly assumes that either investment is independent of the rate of interest or the rate of interest is constant. Graphically, horizontal shifts of the IS curve hold the rate of interest constant. *The magnitude of the horizontal shift of the IS curve equals the autonomous spending change times the basic Keynesian multiplier.* In other words, the horizontal shift of the IS curve per unit change in government spending equals the basic multiplier. According to the basic model, income increases to y_B in Figure 26–4. The higher interest rates in the IS–LM model reduce investment and the multiplier. Assuming the steep LM curve is appropriate so equilibrium income is y_1, the distance $y_B - y_1$ in Figure 26–4 measures the so-called "*crowding out*" *effect, the offsetting reduction in investment and income that follows expansionary fiscal policy due to money market repercussions and higher interest rates.* The sale of government bonds to finance government expenditures reduces the funds available to private firms. As drawn in Figure 26–4, the direct effect of government expenditures does not crowd out an equal amount of private spending so, on balance, government spending still has a positive effect on income.

Monetarists and Keynesians on the Slopes of the Investment and Liquidity Preference Curves and the Size of the Money and Government Expenditure Multipliers

Table 26–2 summarizes the relationship between monetary and fiscal multipliers and their determinants. Both multipliers are positively related to the marginal propensity to consume and negatively related to the money transactions coefficient. Perhaps because these two determinants have the same general effect on both multipliers, empirical estimates of the marginal propensity to consume and the money transactions coefficient are not that controversial. Let us concentrate on the two controversial determinants, the elasticities of the investment and liquidity preference schedules. *Monetarists, like their classical predecessors, claim the investment schedule is relatively elastic and the liquidity preference schedule is inelastic, if it exists at all.* Although monetarists emphasize the long run where demand affects prices but not output, they accept the Keynesian proposition that output responds to demand in the short run. *Monetarists' beliefs about the elasticities have prompted them to allege, as Table 26–2 indicates, that the money multiplier is large and the government spending multiplier is small. This is one of the major tenets of monetarism. Keynes turned matters upside down. He said the investment schedule was relatively inelastic, and the liquidity preference curve was elastic. Money then has little effect on demand and output.* The authorities should rely on fiscal policy to manage demand and output.

Is the money multiplier, in fact, large or small? Who is correct, the monetarists or the Keynesians? While understanding the logical structure of Keynesian economics is facilitated by an uninterrupted analysis of theoretical issues before evaluating the empirical studies, these questions are so important that at least a brief answer now is appropriate. A more

TABLE 26–2

Relationship between Multipliers and Their Determinants

	Size of money multiplier		*Size of government spending multiplier*
Investment schedule			
Elastic	Large	Monetarist	Small
Inelastic	Small	Keynesian	Large
Liquidity preference			
Elastic	Small	Keynesian	Large
Inelastic	Large	Monetarist	Small
Large MPC	Large		Large
Small transactions coefficient	Large		Large

detailed summary of the empirical literature is presented in Chapter 30. The evidence on the size of the multipliers is inconclusive, largely because two research strategies are followed. Keynesians estimate large scale structural models, that is, postulate many demand and supply equations and estimate them statistically. The Keynesian econometric models are like our IS–LM only more complicated. For example, instead of one consumption equation, there are equations for durables, nondurables, and services, which depend on somewhat different variables. After each equation is estimated statistically, the model is thrown into a computer to simulate the response of the economy. The computer grinds out predictions based on the many estimated equations and their interactions. The large-scale models generally find that the investment schedule is quite inelastic and liquidity preference sufficiently elastic that the government spending multiplier is considerably larger than the money multiplier. Monetarists do not attempt to estimate supply and demand equations. They get to the "bottom line" and relate income directly to money and government spending. These bottom line or reduced form studies show that the money multiplier is large, and the government spending multiplier is virtually zero. Monetarists and Keynesians coexist because we do not know why two reasonable research strategies should yield diametrically different answers.

Questions

1. What factors cause shifts in the (*a*) LM and (*b*) IS curves?
2. What is the effect of monetary *contraction* on GNP, consumption, investment, and the rate of interest?
3. List the four parameters which determine the size of the money multiplier. What is the economic rationale for the direction of the relationship between each parameter and the multiplier?
4. Explain the relationship between the size of the money multiplier and the slope of the IS curve.
5. Answer questions similar to Questions 2–4 for government spending instead of the quantity of money.
6. Define and illustrate "crowding out."
7. In which model, the basic or advanced Keynesian model, is the government spending multiplier larger? In which model, the quantity theory or the advanced Keynesian model, is the nominal income/money multiplier larger? Explain your answer. (In explaining your answer, assume that any non-zero parameter that appears in two models has the same value.)

Selected neoclassical/ Keynesian controversies

27

This chapter uses the IS–LM machinery to analyze selected theoretical and policy controversies. We begin with the extreme cases popular in the 1950s, when divisions between neoclassicists and Keynesians were very sharp. The controversies are analyzed in order of difficulty, from the easiest to the most difficult. The reader is warned that the last section in particular is a real challenge. Some may prefer to read a few sections, skip to the next chapter and later, if at all, return to this chapter. Too much IS–LM at one sitting has been known to cause indigestion.

Extreme Cases: Constant Velocity, Liquidity Trap, and a Vertical Investment Schedule

The classical assumption that velocity is fixed because money demand has only a transactions component implies the vertical LM curve illustrated in Figure 27–1. Algebraically, the Cambridge version of the classical model states

$$M = kPy \tag{27–1}$$

In the classical long run, k and y were considered fixed, and the money supply determined the price level. In the Keynesian short run, k and P are considered fixed, in which case the money Equation (27–1) uniquely determines real income. Of course, this is precisely what a vertical LM curve illustrates; the vertical LM has only one value of income. The rate

FIGURE 27–1
Classical Money Demand or Constant Velocity

The classical transactions demand produces a vertical LM curve and makes fiscal policy totally ineffective.

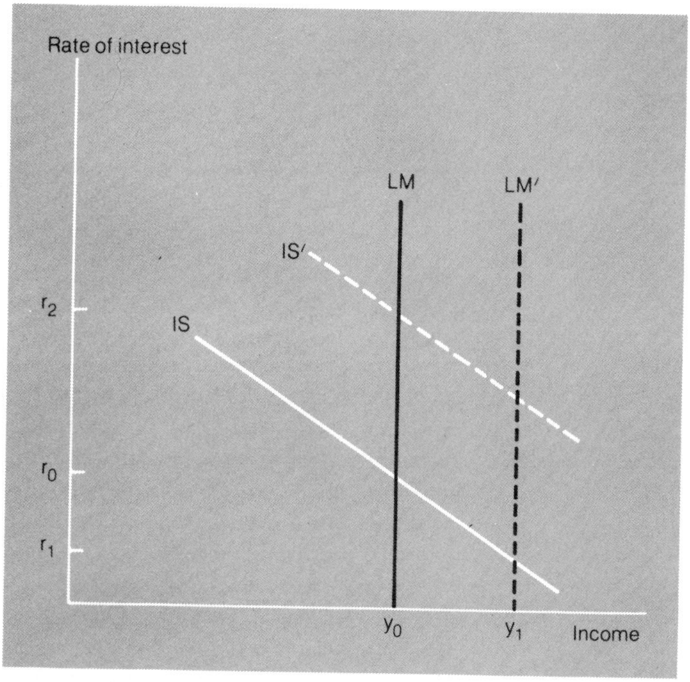

of interest does not appear in Equation (27–1) and, thereby, is irrelevant, which again is precisely what a vertical LM curve implies. Suppose the government spends more and finances its expenditures by selling bonds. As we learned in the previous chapter, the IS curve shifts out to IS′ but the LM curve remains fixed. Equilibrium income also remains fixed at y_0, and the interest rate rises to r_2. In order to finance a larger volume of transactions, the money supply must increase or some speculative balances must be transferred into transactions balances. Government spending does not affect the money supply. *In the normal Keynesian case, fiscal policy is effective because it raises the rate of interest and thereby transfers money from speculative to transactions purposes. When money is held simply for transactions and there are no speculative balances that can be transferred, additional government expenditures raise the interest rate but only succeed in reducing investment and private spending by an equal amount. The "crowding out" effect is complete.*

Restating some of these arguments in terms of velocity, velocity is variable along a normal upward-sloping LM curve. The LM curve is constructed for a fixed money supply. As one moves up the LM curve and income increases, velocity also increases. In the normal case, government expenditures influence income because the economy lands on a point higher up the LM curve where velocity is greater. The vertical LM illustrates constant velocity. When the money supply and velocity are constant, government spending has no effect on demand and income. Algebraically, velocity and the inverse of the Cambridge k in the normal *Keynesian* case are

$$V = \frac{1}{k} = \frac{Py}{M} = \frac{y}{(M/P)} = \frac{y}{k'y + h - jr} = \frac{1}{k' + \dfrac{h - jr}{y}} \tag{27–2}$$

where, using earlier notation, the real demand for money, M/P, is $k'y + h - jr$. Expansionary fiscal policy reduces the term $(h - jr)/y$—the numerator becomes smaller and the denominator larger. According to Equation (27–2), this increases velocity and, equivalently, reduces the Cambridge k, which is not a constant equal to the transactions coefficient k′.

Monetary policy is effective in the classical case. Expansionary monetary policy shifts the LM outward, and the new equilibrium income increases, $y_1 > y_0$. The rate of interest falls from r_0 to r_1. Knowing the reason for the interest rate decline readily explains why, contrary to the situation being considered, monetary policy will be completely ineffective at certain times. In the classical money demand case, the rate of interest does *not* fall in order for speculative demand to absorb the larger supply. The rate of interest has no direct effect on money demand. The rate of interest falls because this is the only way in the IS–LM model that aggregate demand and income can increase and, thereby, absorb the additional money supply into transactions balances. The interest rate is the only channel of monetary policy, that is, the only link between the real and monetary sectors. Given this, *monetary policy is totally ineffective when either (1) the rate of interest does not respond to monetary policy, or (2) aggregate demand and income are independent of the rate of interest*. These cases are essentially the basic Keynesian model, which may be viewed as a special case of the more general IS–LM model.

The rate of interest does not respond to monetary policy when the economy is in a liquidity trap because, by definition, the rate of interest is already at its minimum. Any increase in the quantity of money is hoarded. Figure 27–2A illustrates liquidity preference curves subject to a liquidity trap, and Figure 27–2B graphs corresponding LM curves. Liquidity preference curves become perfectly elastic at the minimum interest rate r_{LT}. Given a low level of income relative to the quantity of money,

FIGURE 27–2

The Extreme Keynesian Cases

Money demand is perfectly elastic in a liquidity trap.

A liquidity trap or a vertical IS curve makes monetary policy totally ineffective.

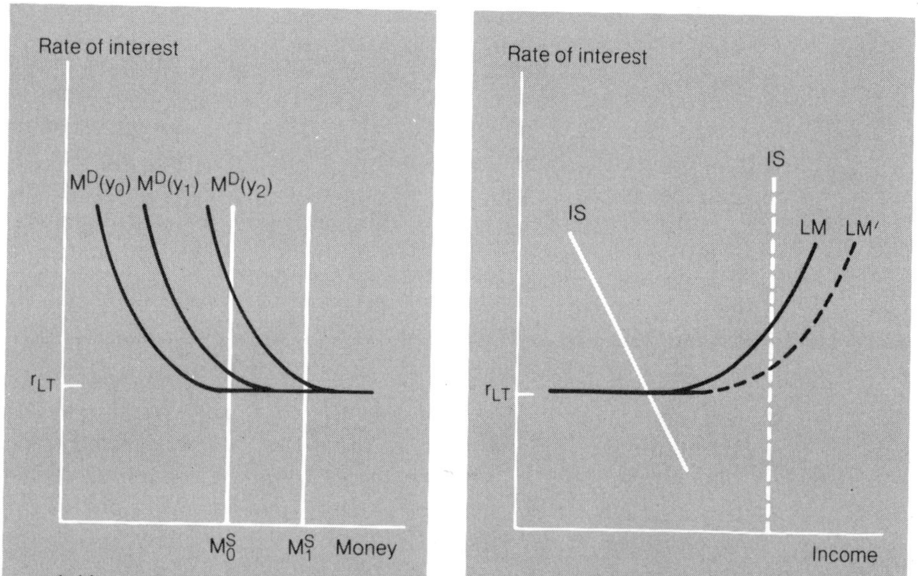

A. Money demand and the liquidity trap

B. A liquidity trap and a vertical IS curve: The curses of monetary policy

the economy will be in a liquidity trap. Looking at Figure 27–2A, at income y_0 the transactions demand is so low compared to the money supply M_0^S that the resultant large quantity of speculative balances drives the rate of interest to its minimum value. As income and the transactions demand increase, the liquidity preference curve shifts rightward and intersects the M_0^S above r_{LT}. Correspondingly, the LM curve is flat at r_{LT} for a stretch, but eventually slopes upward. Assuming the solid IS curve in Figure 27–2B so the economy is in a liquidity trap, increasing the money supply from M_0^S to M_1^S in Figure 27–2A simply makes money more redundant. Monetary expansion extends the flat portion of the LM curve without influencing the rate of interest. While Keynes viewed the liquidity trap as a theoretical possibility of little practical importance, many of his followers thought the economy would often be mired in a liquidity trap, thereby making monetary policy completely ineffective.

The liquidity trap is the total denial of the quantity theory, which says that velocity is independent of the quantity of money. When the economy is in a liquidity trap, velocity is entirely dependent on the quantity of money. If the trap exists and nominal income, Py, is independent of the quantity of money, the quantity theory equation MV = Py is satisfied only if velocity is perfectly flexible. Double the money supply and velocity is cut in half.

Figure 27–2B also illustrates the second case when monetary policy is totally ineffective. The dashed vertical IS curve occurs when investment is independent of the rate of interest, as the basic Keynesian model alleges. Assuming the economy is not in a liquidity trap, monetary expansion reduces the rate of interest but demand and income do not respond. The rate of interest falls enough to absorb into speculative balances all the additional money.

An Interest Responsive Money Supply

In view of our prior discussion of the influences of the private and banking sectors on the money supply in the short run, we should relax the assumption that the Fed controls the money supply perfectly. *In the highly aggregated IS–LM model we can capture to some extent the nonpolicy induced effects on the money supply by adding a positive interest rate term to the money supply equation.*

(27–3)

$$M^S = M_0 + j'r$$

The money supply now is the sum of two components, an exogenous term measuring the Fed's influence, M_0, and an endogenous term measuring interest rate effects on the money supply. The money supply depends positively on the rate because higher interest rates cause a reduction in the nonmoney deposit and excess reserve ratios and induce banks to borrow more at the discount window. The upward-sloping money supply line in Figure 27–3A graphs Equation (27–3). In this case, "an increase in the money supply" means an increase in the exogenous component, which shifts the money supply line rightward.

Even if a perfectly inelastic classical money demand curve exists, inspection of Figure 27–3 shows that the LM curve is positively sloped when the money supply is partially endogenous. In particular, look at points D and E in Figures 27–3A and 27–3B. The private sector no longer need have speculative balances in order for income to increase in the presence of an uncooperative monetary authority. Higher incomes and transactions can now be financed by the *private* expansion of the money supply. The LM curve is positively sloped when either (1) money demand

FIGURE 27–3
Money Supply Responsive to the Rate of Interest

An interest responsive money supply produces an upward sloping LM curve even if money is held only for transactions purposes.

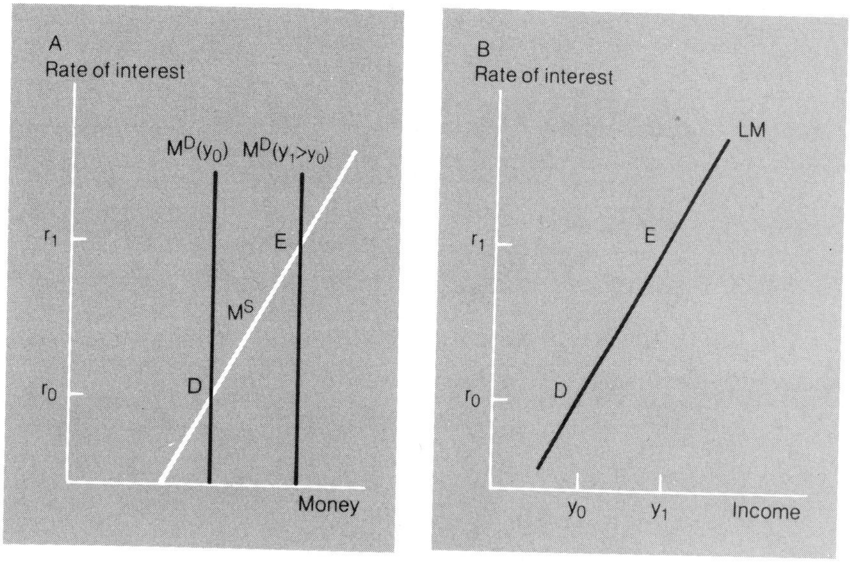

and interest rates are negatively related, or (2) money supply and interest rates are positively related.

An interest responsive money supply relationship has important implications for fiscal and monetary policy. First, a classical money demand does not necessarily make fiscal policy totally ineffective. With the Fed inactive on the sidelines, deficit spending raises the rate of interest and induces banks to provide the necessary transactions balances. Second, the money multiplier is reduced by the interest responsiveness of the money supply. In the previous chapter we indicated that the money multiplier decreases as money demand becomes more interest responsive. Introducing a positive money supply relationship is analytically equivalent to making the negative money demand relationship more elastic. What matters is the responsiveness of the money *market* to the rate of interest; whether the amount of money supplied increases or the amount of money demanded decreases as the rate of interest rises is irrelevant. Note that the exogenous and endogenous money components move in different directions. *Total monetary expansion is less than the exogenous expansion induced by the Fed because the Fed's expansionary policy reduces the rate of interest, which causes the private sector to contract the money supply*. This is why the monetary *policy* multiplier, defined as the change in income divided by the *exogenous* money supply change, is smaller when the money supply contains an endogenous component. Only the exogenous money supply reflects policy. Expansionary monetary policy in this case is partially offset by contractionary monetary reactions.

Money and the Rate of Interest at Full Employment

The IS–LM model is quite flexible. It can be used to analyze the effect of various events under different assumptions. For example, we just saw that the effect of monetary and fiscal policy in the Keynesian short run depends crucially on the form of the money demand function and the resultant LM curve. We illustrate the flexibility of the IS–LM model by analyzing the effect of money on the rate of interest, an effect which may be puzzling the reader because at various points in this book we have espoused virtually every position. In Chapter 6 we indicated that a sufficiently strong and *prolonged monetary expansion raises the nominal rate of interest* because individuals who anticipate inflation and a declining purchasing power of the dollar attempt to maintain their real return. The chapters on *neoclassical economics stressed that a* solitary *monetary injection simply raises prices and wages, without influencing the rate of interest*. A few chapters later we discovered that *according to Keynes monetary expansion reduces the rate of interest*. At each point we emphasized the validity of the different positions, and we are not going to retract anything now. Consider first why neoclassicists and Keynesians disagree about the effect on the rate of interest of a solitary monetary injection and then consider the effect of a sustained monetary expansion.

The neoclassical and Keynesian conclusions follow logically from their assumptions. Which assumption is crucial, causing the different conclusions? The assumptions of neoclassical and Keynesian economics differ in several respects. *The IS–LM model shows that the crucial assumption is the length of the time period and, consequently, the current level of income relative to full-employment income. In Chapter 23 we asserted, and now we have the tools to prove rigorously, the neoclassical conclusion that the rate of interest does not depend on the quantity of money in the long run even if money demand depends on the rate of interest.*

Figure 27–4 graphs the now familiar IS and LM curves. A new wrinkle is the dashed vertical line at y_F, full-employment income. We begin by assuming the economy is at a long-run equilibrium where the current level of *real* income given by the intersection of the solid IS and LM curves equals full-employment income. As we indicated earlier, full employment is not the technological maximum output. Actual output sometimes exceeds full employment. At *least* 3 percent unemployment—and quite probably considerably more—and "only" a 40-hour work week now are

FIGURE 27–4

Money and the Rate of Interest at Full Employment

A solitary monetary injection and a temporary inflation have no long-run effect on the rate of interest even if the demand for money depends on the rate of interest. Permanent inflation raises the rate of interest.

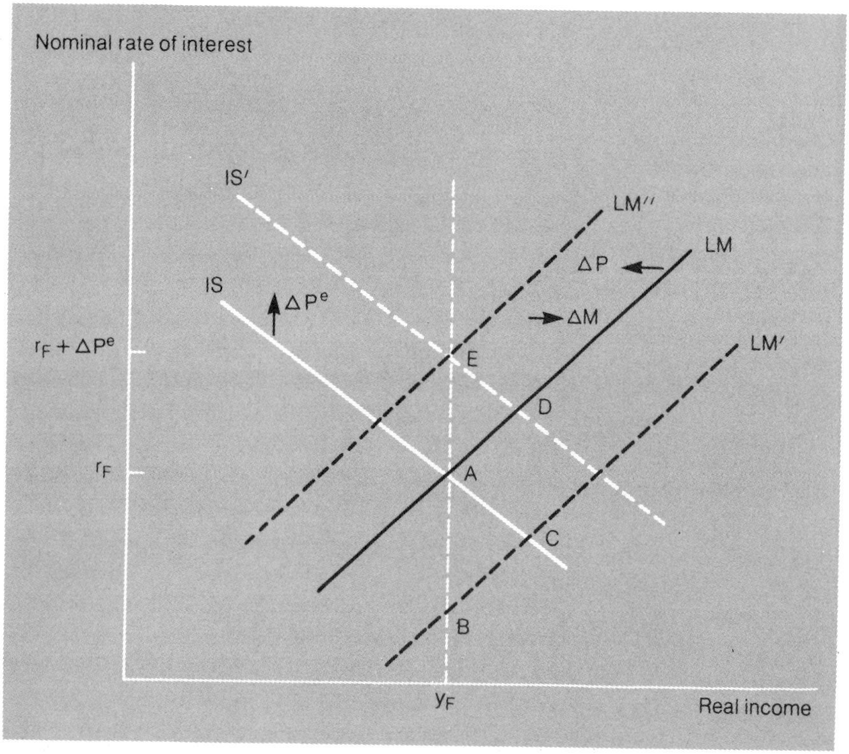

consistent with full-employment output. If most people worked longer hours, as they did for many generations, output would rise above full employment. *Full employment is best viewed as the long-run economically sustainable output.* Actual output may be both greater than and less than full employment in the short run.

Suppose the Fed mistakenly increases the quantity of money. What happens? The short-run general equilibrium income-rate of interest combination now is given by point C, the intersection of IS and LM′ in Figure 27–4. How does the economy reach the short-run equilibrium? Assume the "special" adjustment process outlined in Appendix C of Chapter 25. (All appendixes are optional; those who skipped Appendix C need not return to it now.) The rate of interest *first falls precipitously* from A to B. *This is the liquidity effect, where the entire monetary expansion is temporarily absorbed into speculative money balances through an interest rate decline*. Spending does not adjust immediately to interest rates. With the passage of time, however, the depressed interest rate does stimulate investment demand and rebounds somewhat as output adjusts to the higher level of demand. Let's assume for simplicity that the economy moves directly from B to short-run general equilibrium point C, where labor is working overtime and output exceeds full employment. Firms meet the demand *at existing prices* without regard for current profits, which may actually decline somewhat as overtime pay raises wage costs.

Prices and the LM Curve

Point C is only a short-run equilibrium; current output exceeds full employment. Workers who initially accept overtime eagerly now desire a return to their typical work schedule. Firms note that the monetary expansion and higher demand is permanent and attempt to restore their profit margins by raising prices. Allowing sufficient time to elapse for prices to rise makes it incumbent to distinguish between nominal (dollar) income and real (fixed price) income, where the latter is measured on the horizontal axis. *Higher prices* and nominal income, given any real income, *shift the LM curve upward and leftward*. In order to stress this important fact, we draw Figure 27–4A and rewrite the money market equilibrium equations.

$$M = P(k'y + h - jr) \tag{27–4N}$$

$$\frac{M}{P} = k'y + h - jr \tag{27–4R}$$

Money performs various services and is held for various reasons. Equation (27–4N) for the *nominal* money market indicates that the number of dollars needed is proportional to the price level. For example, an individual may hold money in order to buy one gizmo. The amount of money needed to buy one gizmo clearly depends on the price of gizmos. At any real income and output level, more money will be necessary for transactions purposes when prices are higher. Higher prices increase the nominal demand for money—the right-hand side of Equation (27–4N)—but have no direct effect on nominal supply—the left-hand side of Equation (27–4N). Equation (27–4R) for the real money market indicates that higher prices reduce the real supply of money without affecting real demand. Whichever version, nominal or real, one prefers, higher prices create an excess demand for money, which shifts the LM curve up.

Four variables appear in Equation (27–4N) or its equivalent, (27–4R). Graphs, however, have only two axes. With the (nominal) rate of interest

FIGURE 27–4A

Money Supply and Price Changes Shift the LM in Different Directions

A larger quantity of money shifts the LM downward, but higher prices shift the LM upward.

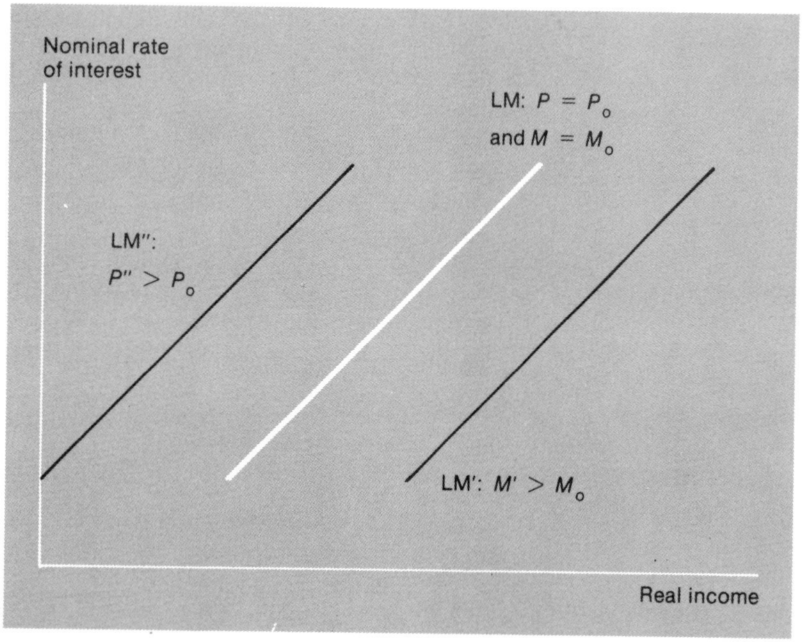

and real income on the axes of the graph, *there is a separate LM curve for each nominal money supply and price level*. A larger quantity of money shifts the LM downward and rightward to LM′ in Figure 27–4A. A higher price level shifts the LM upward and leftward to LM″. Inspection of Equations (27–4N) and (27–4R) shows that proportional changes in money and prices leave the LM unchanged. So long as prices do not rise in proportion to the solitary monetary expansion, the LM curve is below its initial position because the rightward shift of the LM due to monetary expansion exceeds its leftward shift due to higher prices.

Returning to Figure 27–4, assume that prices have not yet risen proportionally so that the LM continues to intersect the IS curve at an interest rate below r_F. The inflationary pressure pushing the LM up persists so long as the rate of interest remains below r_F, the rate consistent with full employment. The rate of interest and LM curve return to their initial positions only when the price increase is proportional to the monetary expansion. At that point the quantity of real money balances equals its initial value, and the *temporary* inflation stops. The same real income and rate of interest equilibrate the economy when the real quantity of money, M/P, is unchanged.

In Figure 27–4 the economy moves from point C back to A. Although money *demand* depends on the rate of interest, as illustrated by the upward-sloping LM curves, the long-run equilibrium rate of interest does not depend on the *quantity* of money. Aggregate expenditures at long-run equilibrium equal full-employment output. Since money does not affect full-employment output, it cannot ultimately affect the rate of interest, which is a determinant of aggregate expenditures. The upward movement of the rate of interest from B to C and from C to A is called the *real income* and *actual price effect*, respectively, of the monetary expansion. The sum of the real income and actual price effects is the *nominal income effect*. William Gibson estimated the liquidity effect lasts approximately two months, after which interest rates start to rise. Interest rates fully rebound to their initial level and the (nominal) income effect is complete well within a year.[1]

Real Balances and the Rate of Interest during Inflations

Suppose the expansion was not an isolated event; the Fed persistently pursues an expansionary policy. Inflation no longer is a temporary phenomenon. Inflation persists and society comes to expect it. In this case the adjustment process no longer ends with the actual price and nominal income effects. The rate of interest rises above the initial equilibrium, with the economy settling at point E instead of A in Figure 27–4. This occurs because expected inflation shifts the investment schedule and IS curve upward. Investment involves the purchase of plant and equipment to produce future goods. By definition, inflation raises the price of future goods relative to current goods and, therefore, increases the rate of return on investment. For example, assume a $100 machine, which for simplicity is the only factor of production, yields 105 gizmos one year hence. In a stable environment the gizmos are expected to fetch $1 each, making the rate of return on the machine 5 percent. Inflation is a monetary phenomenon and does not influence the machine's real rate of return. It continues to produce 105 gizmos. However, the price of gizmos next year is higher in an inflationary environment. Assuming firms expect a 5 percent inflation so the gizmos will sell for $1.05 instead of $1, the nominal rate of return rises to approximately 10 percent. Abstracting from progressive taxes and other complications, as a first approximation *the IS curve shifts upward*

---

[1]William Gibson, "Interest Rates and Monetary Policy," *Journal of Political Economy*, June 1970, pp. 431–54; and "Price Expectations Effects on Interest Rates," *Journal of Finance*, March 1970, pp. 19–34. Other researchers have estimated a substantially longer liquidity effect.

by the expected rate of inflation, and the real rate of interest remains constant. This rise in the nominal rate of interest from A to E is called the *inflationary expectations* or *Fisher effect.*

If the price increase were proportional to the monetary expansion so the real quantity of money remained constant and the initial LM curve prevailed—the outward movement of the LM due to the monetary expansion being just counteracted by the inward movement due to inflation—the higher IS curve would intersect the LM at point D beyond full employment. This cannot be the permanent solution. Outputs greater than full employment are temporary. *For some time period inflation will outpace the monetary expansion, real money balances will fall, and the LM curve rises above its initial position* to LM″ in Figure 27–4. *Inflation is characterized by high nominal interest rates and tight money in a real sense. There are more dollars around—indeed, this is the cause of the inflation—but there are fewer dollars relative to the prices of commodities.* While this conclusion may seem paradoxical, further reflection suggests its reasonableness. The purchasing power of money sinks during an inflation. Like passengers on the Titanic, money holders attempt to jump ship, preferring commodities to money. This further sinks the purchasing power of money. Society economizes on their real money holdings because their cost is high. Eventually, however, the rate of inflation just equals the rate of monetary expansion, and the LM curve is stabilized at its higher position.[2] *A solitary monetary injection permanently raises prices proportionally but has no permanent effect on the rate of inflation, which is temporarily positive as prices adjust upward. Similarly, continued monetary growth eventually raises the rate of inflation equally, but temporarily inflation exceeds its permanent rate.* While inflation induces people to reduce their command over commodities held in the form of money, the reduction of real balances is not continual.

Figure 27–5 highlights the information embedded in Figure 27–4 and summarizes this and the previous section. It illustrates explicitly the *general* time path of several variables in response to continuous monetary expansion starting from a full-employment position. The top panel shows the rate of inflation (the period-to-period percentage rate of change of prices), while the bottom panel shows the percentage change, measured from the *initial* equilibrium, in real money balances and the nominal interest rate. The permanent rate of monetary expansion is illustrated by the horizontal line above the time axis in both panels. The figure confirms the often heard claims of consumers and firms during the high-inflation period around 1980 that finance was *not* widely available. Inflation pro-

[2] In terms of Equation (27–4R), inflation reduces h. As a result, M/P falls and r rises at $y = y_F$.

FIGURE 27–5
Percentage Change over Time of Prices, Real Money Balances, and Nominal Interest Rates in Response to a Monetary Expansion Starting from a Position of Full Employment

The rate of inflation first is less than and then is greater than the rate of monetary expansion. In the long run the rates of monetary expansion and inflation are equal.

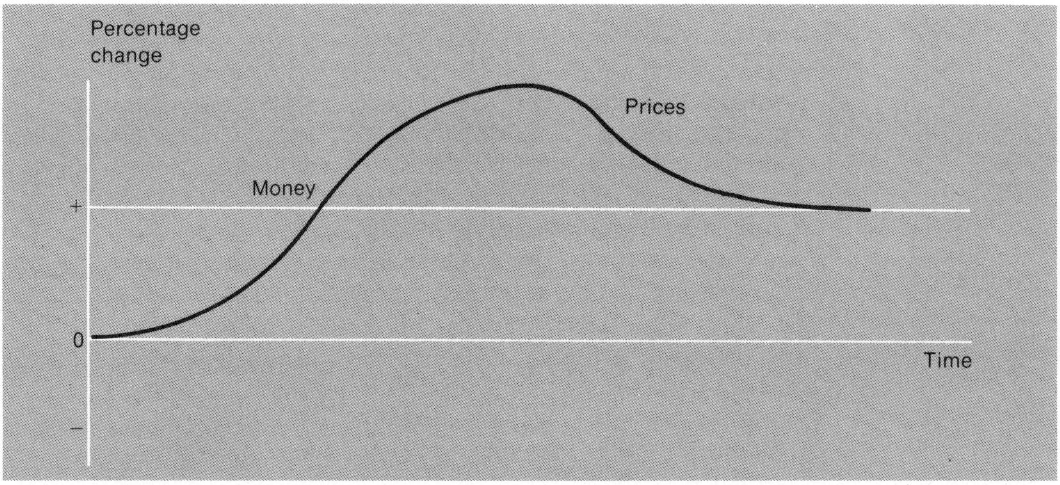

Monetary expansion and inflation first lower and then raise the rate of interest. Monetary expansion and inflation first raise and then lower the quantity of real money balances.

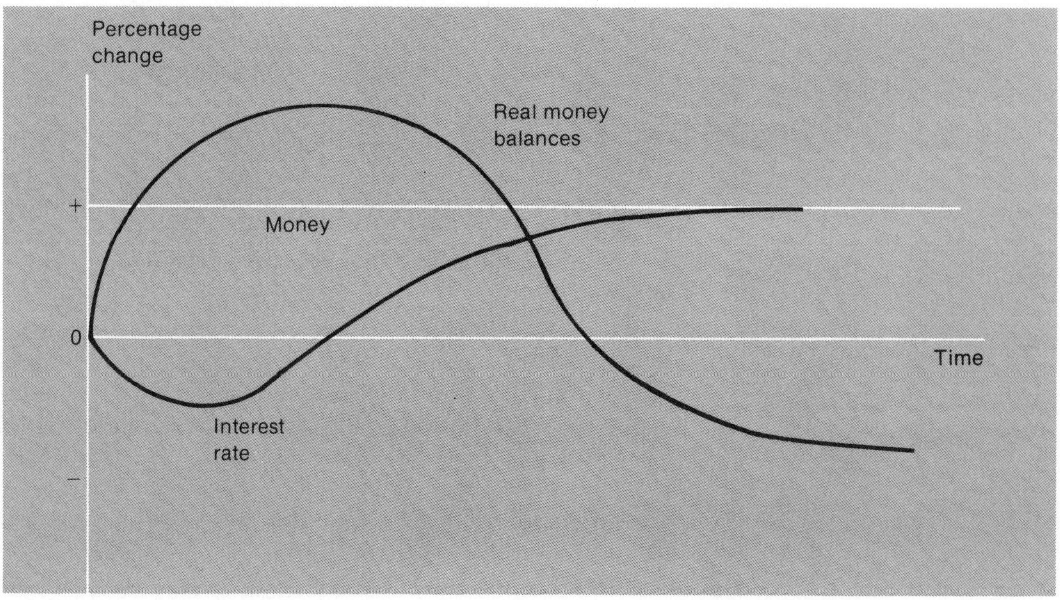

duced by expanding the nominal money supply reduces the real money supply and raises its price as measured by the nominal rate of interest.

The Real Balance Effect and the Neoclassical Adjustment Process

Neoclassicists believe that the economy will not be stuck below full employment permanently. Natural forces propel the economy toward full employment. The neoclassical adjustment process of Chapter 23 is now presented within the IS–LM framework. Assume the economy is at full employment and, for simplicity, let money demand take the classical form. Given the quantity of money and the transactions coefficient, the price level has adjusted so that the classical LM equation $M_0 = kPy$, is satisfied at full-employment income y_F. The vertical line in Figure 27–6 is the classical LM curve. Suppose this happy state of affairs is disturbed by a reduction in aggregate demand. The IS curve shifts inward to IS′. The classicists assumed, and Keynes concurred, that individuals typically would buy bonds with the funds previously being spent. Since neither money demand nor supply shifts, the LM curve remains fixed.[3] (Ignore the dashed LM curve.) Looking at Figure 27–6, it appears that a downward movement in the rate of interest to r'_F is sufficient to maintain full employment. The IS is quite elastic according to neoclassicists because as the rate of interest falls (1) firms undertake newly profitable investment projects, (2) methods of producing already profitable projects become more capital intensive, and (3) consumers spend more directly and also indirectly due to the impact of interest rates on capital and common stock values in particular and, more generally, on total wealth.[4] With interest rates quite flexible in both directions, full employment is restored automatically without any government intervention.

At this point Keynes parted company with his classical mentors. First, Keynes stressed the unit of account function of money and the speculative demand for money, in which case the LM is upward sloping but not vertical. Clearly, an IS curve shifted downward would intersect a positively sloped LM curve at an income below y_F. *Interest rate adjustments are insufficient to maintain full employment when society holds speculative money balances*. Some other adjustment is necessary. Second, even if money is held for transactions purposes only and the LM curve is vertical, Keynes thought aggregate demand was so limited and unresponsive to the rate of interest that the full-employment rate of interest

---

[3]A bond market equilibrium curve, similar to the commodities (IS) and money (LM) market equilibrium curves, exists and shifts along with the IS curve because the demand for bonds also changed. We can ignore the bond market equilibrium curve because the intersection of the IS and LM curves is sufficient to determine the equilibrium interest rate and income. The bond market curve passes through the IS–LM intersection point by Walras's Law.

[4]Cf., "The Commodities Market and Aggregate Expenditures" in Chapter 23.

FIGURE 27–6
The Real Balance Effect and Adjustments toward Equilibrium

The real balance effect shifts the IS curve rightward, guaranteeing that monetary policy can produce full employment.

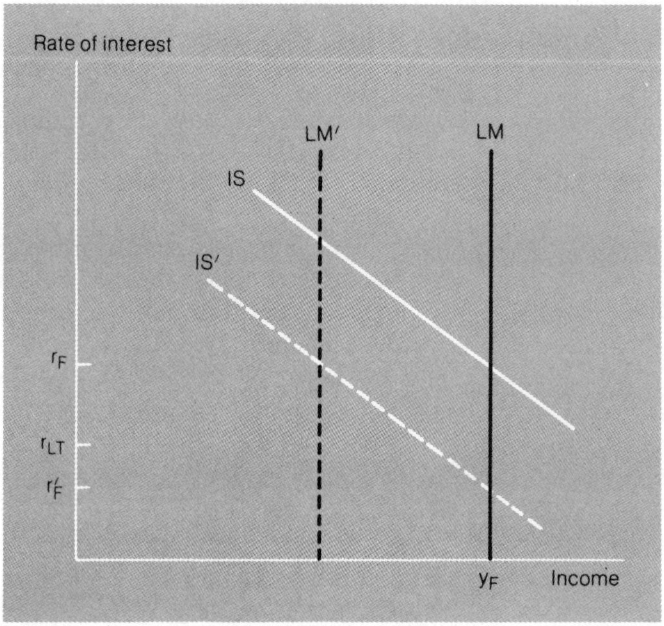

was infeasible. Keynes dismissed the second and third reasons given in the last paragraph for interest rate effects on spending. A negative rate of interest would be necessary if the IS curve shifted inward so much or was so unresponsive to the rate of interest that it crossed y_F below the horizontal axis. If demand were so limited, interest rate adjustments would be insufficient to maintain full employment. Negative interest rates never have and never will be observed. Why lend and be paid back less when one can hold money? The rate of interest must be above some minimum positive value—the liquidity trap rate of interest r_{LT}. In his less pessimistic moments Keynes thought the full-employment rate of interest was positive, though below the liquidity trap rate of interest. Whichever is the case, Keynes thought the economy would be mired at underemployment equilibrium unless the government undertook expansionary fiscal policies.

The situation would be worse if consumers hoarded the funds previously spent on commodities instead of buying bonds. The decreased demand for commodities now is associated with an equal increased demand for money. Recalling that an increase in the demand for money has the same effect as a decrease in supply, in this case both the IS and LM shift inward by the same amount. The dashed curves in Figure 27–6 are applicable. The equilibrium rate of interest stays constant while income falls below full employment. The issue here is not whether interest rate adjustments are sufficient; the rate of interest has no reason whatsoever to adjust. While neoclassicists play down the likelihood of this hoarding case, they do *not* feel that it occasionally violates the basic proposition that the economy contains endogenous forces driving the economy toward full employment. If full employment is the amount that firms and workers want and are willing to produce, and if current output is less than that amount, then neoclassicists say that eventually—certainly not immediately—wages and prices will fall. If workers *never* are willing to lower their wage demands, are they really unemployed and willing to work? Neoclassicists think not. The amount of unemployment that the rate of interest cannot reduce at first will ultimately be eliminated by a decline in the price level. Lower prices shift the LM curve outward. A given quantity of money can finance more transactions when the price of each transaction is lower. The LM curve returns to its initial position, restoring full employment.

Figure 27–6 may make it appear that the rate of interest must fall along with prices. Is the magnitude of the interest rate decline feasible, or are we just back at a previous case Keynes thought likely? As drawn in Figure 27–6 the solid LM curve and broken IS curve intersect at a rate of interest below the liquidity trap rate, r_{LT}. Is the economy doomed to underemployment even if prices decline? Neoclassicists say no. Professor Pigou in particular thought, and modern empirical studies confirm, that consumption depends on wealth in addition to current income. While it is true that money is only one component of wealth in virtually every society, let us ignore other assets and equate wealth with money. Abstracting from interest rate effects, the Pigovian consumption function is:

$$C = a + b(y - T) + b'(M/P)$$

where b' measures the real balance (wealth) or Pigou effect. Real money balances now have a *direct* effect on consumption and aggregate demand. The real balance effect says that as prices fall and real money balances increase the IS curve shifts outward. The outward shift of *both* the IS and LM curves as prices decline eliminates the need for interest rate adjustments.

The importance of the real balance effect as an *endogenous* propeller toward equilibrium may well be academic. Over time prices have become less flexible downward. Monetary authorities may be unwilling to rely on the quite possibly long delayed automatic price adjustments. This does not diminish the importance of the real balance effect as an *exogenous* propeller toward equilibrium. If the price level is sticky and fails to produce additional real money balances, the Fed should intervene. Either lower endogenous prices or more exogenous money increases real balances and aggregate demand even in a liquidity trap. Money no longer exclusively affects aggregate demand indirectly via the rate of interest. *The real balance effect says consumption depends directly on money so that monetary expansion shifts the IS curve outward.* The real balance effect brings money to the forefront. It denies that monetary policy is ever totally impotent. *With a real balance effect directly influencing spending and shifting the IS curve outward, monetary policy is effective even if the economy is in a liquidity trap and interest rates cannot fall further.*

Money Supply versus Interest Rates: Instability of IS–LM

For many problems it is convenient to ignore lags and uncertainty and assume an omniscient policymaker. However, the neoclassical/Keynesian controversy regarding the money supply versus interest rates as the intermediate target of monetary policy, a controversy we discussed intuitively in Chapter 19, can be analyzed rigorously only if lags and uncertainty are introduced explicitly within the IS–LM framework.[5] To simplify somewhat an analysis which still is quite involved, ignore any real balance effect. Assume the Fed can control perfectly the rate of interest or money supply so the financial variables may be viewed as policy tools as well as intermediate targets. Let full-employment income, represented by y_F in Figure 27–7, be the ultimate goal which the policymaker attempts to achieve by selecting the money supply or rate of interest. No particular interest rate or money supply is desirable in itself. For simplicity, assume that incomes on either side of full employment are equally undesirable. Society foregoes commodities when income is less than full employment, and incomes above full employment cause inflation. The goal is y_F. The dispersion of actual income about y_F measures failure to achieve the goal. The further is income from y_F, the less successful is the policymaker. Of course, complete success (zero failure) occurs when income always is y_F, that is, the dispersion is zero.

We first show that *the choice between the money supply and rate of interest as intermediate targets may be decided on the basis of personal prejudice or the toss of a coin when certainty exists. In this case attainment of full employment is independent of the intermediate target.* When certainty exists, aggregate expenditures and money demand are known because there are no unknown random forces causing deviations from

---

[5]This section is based on William Poole's pathfinding "Optimal Choice of Monetary Policy Instruments in a Simple Stochastic Model," *Quarterly Journal of Economics,* May 1970, pp. 197–216.

FIGURE 27–7
Unstable Aggregate Demand

When aggregate demand is uncertain and the IS curve is unstable, a money supply policy is superior to an interest rate policy.

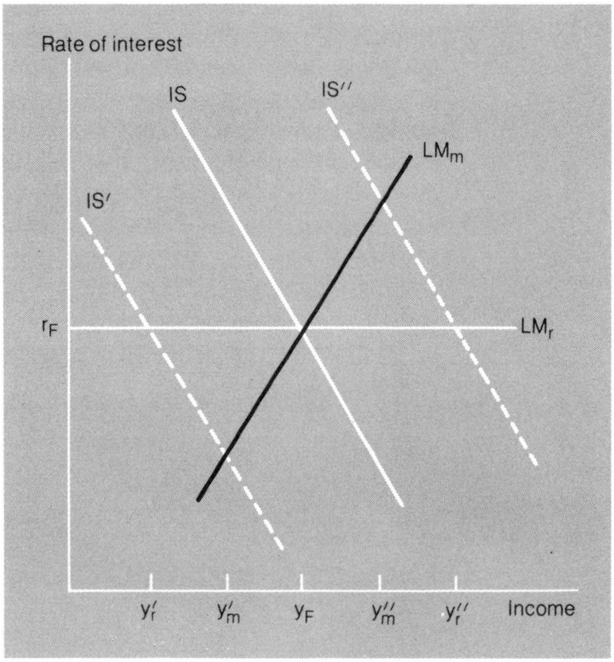

the average. Stated somewhat differently, in a certain world the predicted demands are always realized. In terms of the IS–LM graph, certainty exists when we always know exactly the shape and position of the IS curve and, given the money supply selected, the LM. Suppose the certain aggregate demand yields the solid IS curve in Figure 27–7. The central banker who prefers an interest rate policy would peg it at r_F, confident that the resultant income would then be y_F. Those who prefer a money supply policy would select a money supply M_F that in conjunction with the certain money demand would produce an LM curve that intersects the certain IS curve at y_F. (See LM_m in Figure 27–7.) The policymaker generally cannot control both the rate of interest and money supply. Certainty implies, however, that the relationship between the two is known and constant. If the authorities peg the interest rate at r_F, the resultant money supply must be M_F. If the money supply is M_F, the interest rate must be r_F. Which variable the authority cares to emphasize is irrelevant.

Most policymakers are no dumber than the rest of us. The goals are not attained at all times because we live in an uncertain world. We simply do not know all the factors which influence aggregate and money demands, much less their precise effects. Lags are a complicating factor. Today's interest rate and money supply influence aggregate demand in the future, making accurate prediction of the future values of the other determinants of aggregate demand necessary if the goal is to be achieved. Even if interest rates and money had an immediate effect on aggregate demand, the inability to monitor demand continuously produces deviations from the goal. This quarter's GNP is uncertain until next quarter. Current money demand also is uncertain. We do not know where we are until we have left. Although the policymaker is uncertain about (1) the current state of the economy, (2) future behavior of the economy, and (3) the structure of the economy and the effects of policy, some decision must be made now. It is hardly surprising that the goal often eludes the policymaker.

Let's give the policymaker a break. Assume money demand is known, and the authorities are uncertain about only aggregate demand. *Average* aggregate demand and its dispersion are known, but the average value may not be realized at any one time. For example, the policymaker may know that aggregate demand averages 100 but at any one time could be between 80 and 120. We may view the IS as a band instead of a line. This is represented graphically by an unstable average IS curve shifting outward and inward. Average aggregate demand produces the solid IS. Firms and consumers at times are especially bullish for unknown reasons—that elusive state of confidence again. The high aggregate expenditures produces IS″ instead of the normal IS. At other times, low expenditures yield IS′. *The band formed by IS′ and IS″ measures the instability of aggregate demand and the uncertainty the policymaker faces. In such a "real world" setting the authorities are unable to maintain the economy at full employment.* While complete success is unattainable, the policymaker chooses a course of action which is correct on the average. The specific course of action selected now matters.

Suppose a money supply policy is selected. Given the solid average IS and a known money demand, the authorities optimally select the money supply which produces LM_m, as was true when total certainty existed. The policymaker awaits the outcome of his action. He can confidently predict the position of the LM curve since money demand is known with certainty, by assumption. Aggregate demand and the position of the IS curve are uncertain but finally manifest themselves. Income averages y_F but is not constant. Given the optimal money supply, the inflationary income y''_m occurs when aggregate demand is above normal, and the recessionary income y'_m occurs when aggregate demand is below normal. The distance between y'_m and y''_m measures the failure of a money supply policy.[6] Interest rates are allowed to vary when the authorities select a money supply policy.

Suppose an interest rate policy is adopted instead. The interest rate is set at r_F, which is correct on average. *The flat LM_r in Figure 27–7 is not a traditional LM curve. It is a money market equilibrium curve, but the money supply is not being held constant.* Indeed, as we move out along LM_r, the money supply is increasing in order to maintain the rate of interest constant in spite of higher income and transactions requirements. Figure 27–7 shows that an interest rate policy lets income fluctuate from y'_r to y''_r, which is wider than the fluctuations which occur under a money supply policy. *When aggregate demand is uncertain and the IS curve is unstable, a money supply policy is superior to an interest rate policy.* The interest rate policy effectively creates a liquidity trap and the basic Keynesian multiplier. The central banker with a firm grip on the money supply inevitably lets the rate of interest fluctuate. These interest rate fluctuations moderate aggregate demand. The central banker determined to maintain a rate of interest provides no moderating influence and must let the money supply follow aggregate demand.

The opposite case is represented by Figure 27–8. Aggregate demand now is certain, and money demand is uncertain. In this case the IS curve is fixed. A money supply policy leads to LM fluctuations from LM′ to LM″. The optimal money supply and average money demand generate LM, which intersects the IS at y_F. A money demand larger (smaller) than expected generates LM′ (LM″), given the fixed money supply. A money supply policy lets income fluctuate from y'_m to y''_m in Figure 27–8. *When aggregate demand is certain and the IS curve is stable, an interest rate policy is superior to a money supply policy.* Indeed, an interest rate policy maintains income precisely on target. An interest rate policy still loses control of the money supply. In this case, however, lack of monetary control is desirable. *By concentrating on the rate of interest and ignoring the money supply, the latter dutifully trails money demand and exactly neutralizes its fluctuations.* Money supply increases (decreases) equal money demand increases (decreases).

Uncertainty is not limited to one area. Both the real and monetary relationships are uncertain. Which policy is superior in this case? As one might have surmised, the relative degree of uncertainty and instability of IS and LM determine the superior policy. *If money demand is known with*

---

[6]If it appears that a superior money supply policy exists, you probably are implicitly trying to create a certain world. True, y_F could be maintained indefinitely by counteracting any movement of the IS by an opposite movement of the LM. But this is exactly the certainty case just considered where the policymaker knows the IS and then positions the LM to achieve full employment. The essential aspect of uncertainty is decision making *before* some outcome is known.

FIGURE 27–8
Unstable Money Demand

When money demand is uncertain and the LM curve is unstable, an interest rate policy is superior to a money supply policy.

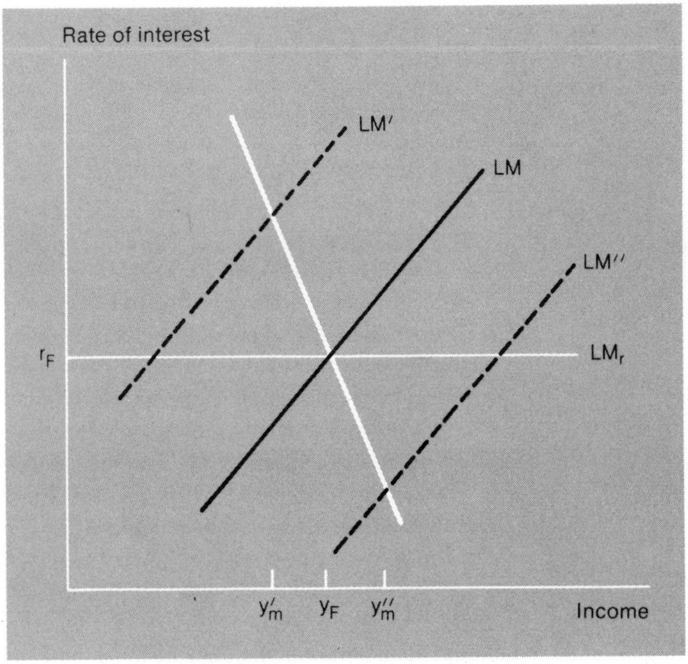

greater certainty than aggregate demand so the LM is more stable than the IS, then a money supply policy is superior to an interest rate policy, and conversely. This is illustrated in Figure 27–9, where the LM shifts less than the IS. When a money supply policy is followed, income fluctuates from y'_m to y''_m, which is less than the y'_r to y''_r income fluctuations which occur when an interest rate policy is adopted.

Monetarists advocate a money supply policy while Keynesians advocate an interest rate policy. Are these policy prescriptions in accord with the remainder of monetarist and Keynesian theory? We have emphasized that compared to their Keynesian colleagues, monetarists interpret the economic data as indicating that the *entire* economic system is quite stable. That is, monetarists expect the IS *and* LM curves to remain within a narrow band while Keynesians expect wide fluctuations. Our emphasis on this disagreement between monetarists and Keynesians is not misguided and explains other policy differences. It is important to note, however, that *overall* economic stability is not an issue in the money

FIGURE 27–9
Unstable Aggregate Demand and Money Demand

When money demand is more certain than aggregate demand and the LM curve is more stable than the IS curve, income fluctuations are minimized by stabilizing the money supply instead of the rate of interest.

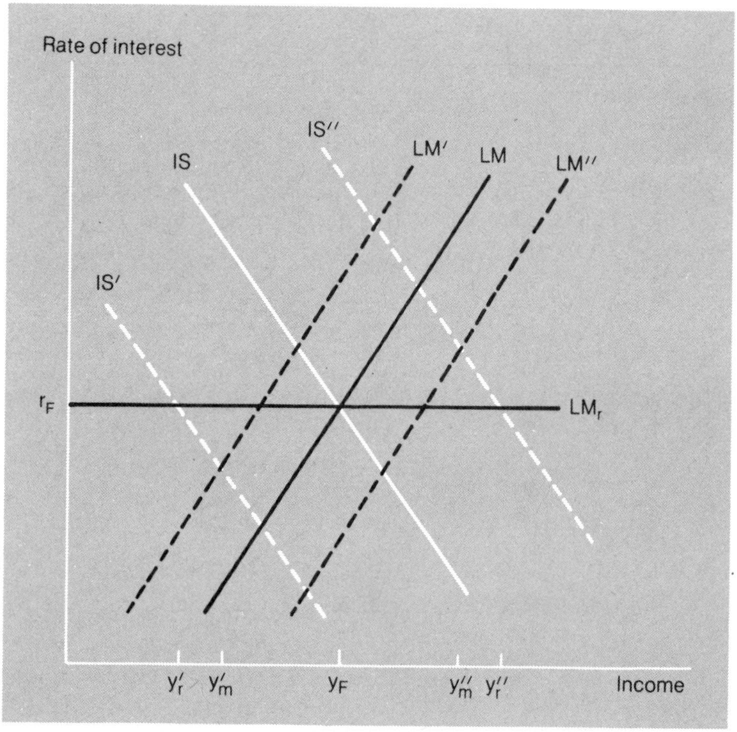

supply versus rate of interest debate. At issue here is the *relative* stability of aggregate demand versus money demand. *Classicists and their modern disciples have long emphasized that velocity and money demand is one of the most stable economic relationships, more stable than aggregate demand. Their preference for a money supply target is consistent with their view about velocity.* The basic Keynesian model stressed the volatility of investment, which at first glance would seem inconsistent with an interest rate policy. Those familiar with Keynes's explanation of the speculative demand realize that his theory and policy prescriptions are not *necessarily* contradictory. According to Keynes, money demand also is unstable. The expected future rate of interest is a critical variable in Keynes's explanation of the speculative money demand. Keynes was uncertain how expectations of the future are formed. Even if expectations of the future depend solely on current and past values, any change in the current rate of interest then affects the expected future rate. This causes the liquidity preference and LM curves to shift.[7] The monetary authority may as well select an interest rate policy if the LM is as unstable as the IS.

Questions

1. When is the (*a*) money multiplier and (*b*) government spending multiplier zero? Give economic explanations for your answers and illustrate them with IS–LM graphs.
2. Define a (money demand) liquidity trap. Draw liquidity preference and LM curves which illustrate a liquidity trap.
3. How does recognition of a positive relationship between the rate of interest and the amount of money supplied influence (*a*) the slope of the LM curve, (*b*) the size of the government spending multiplier, and (*c*) the size of the (exogenous) money multiplier?
4. Discuss the pattern of interest rates over time when the rate of monetary growth *decelerates*.
5. With the aid of an IS–LM graph, illustrate the liquidity, real income, actual price, and expected price effects on the rate of interest of monetary *contraction*.
6. Too much easy money makes it tight. Explain. Pay particular attention to the difference between nominal and real values.
7. Illustrate with IS–LM curves the real balance effect of a monetary *contraction*. Discuss the significance of the real balance effect for monetary policy.
8. Since prices rarely fall, the real balance effect is a theoretical nicety of no practical significance. Critically evaluate the statement.
9. Carefully explain and illustrate with IS–LM graphs the relationship between uncertainty about aggregate expenditures and money demand on the one hand and interest rates or money supply intermediate targets on the other hand.
10. How do monetarists and Keynesians justify their preferred operating target?

---

[7]See Appendix B for Chapter 25.

PART SIX

Domestic and International Policy Issues

28 The inflation-unemployment relationship

There is no subtler, no surer means of overturning the existing basis of Society than to debauch the currency. The process engages all the hidden forces of economic law on the side of destruction, and does it in a manner which not one man in a million is able to diagnose.

*John Maynard Keynes**

The famous microeconomic trade-off curve between guns and butter was eclipsed in popularity in the early 1960s by another trade-off curve, the so-called Phillips curve. Named after the late British economist A. W. Phillips, the curve purports to show a *permanent* trade-off between the rate of inflation and the rate of unemployment.[1] That is, Phillips stated that the rate of unemployment could be permanently lowered at the cost of a higher rate of inflation. Phillips's 1958 study was perhaps the single most influential economic study since Keynes's *General Theory*. It dominated the thinking of academics and policymakers for a decade. The influence of the Phillips curve was relatively short lived, however. In his 1968 American Economic Association presidential address, Professor Milton Friedman questioned the existence of a *permanent* trade-off.[2] He stated that there is only a short-run or *temporary* trade-off between inflation and unemployment. The strength and speed of the impact of Friedman's critique rival Phillips's original study. What seemed like an immutable

---

**Essays in Persuasion* (New York: W. W. Norton, 1963), p. 78.

[1] A. W. Phillips, "The Relationship between Unemployment and the Rate of Change of Money Wage Rates in the United-Kingdom, 1861–1957," *Economica*, November 1958, pp. 282–99.

[2] Milton Friedman, "The Role of Monetary Policy," *American Economic Review*, March 1968, pp. 1–7.

truth in 1958 was questioned in 1968 and repudiated by 1978. Virtually no one now believes there is a permanent trade-off of any great consequence between inflation and unemployment, given probable inflation rates. (The trade-off during hyperinflations and major deflations is highly speculative due to the limited number of observations.) Indeed, by the late 1970s the rational expectations school that we met briefly in Chapter 22 went beyond Friedman and claimed that there is neither a temporary nor permanent inflation-unemployment trade-off. The first and major part of this chapter looks at the rise and fall of the Phillips curve and other theories about the inflation-unemployment relationship. The latter part looks at the cost of inflation since everyone agrees that money is the major cause of any rapid and prolonged inflation and the sole cause of hyperinflation.

Neoclassical and Keynesian Supply and Demand

Let's begin, quite naturally, with "our own" theory of inflation and unemployment, which very simply integrates the neoclassical long-run and the Keynesian short-run ideas about the price-output relationship into a unified theory of inflation and unemployment. Since the transformation from price-output to inflation-unemployment is relatively straightforward, this section mainly reviews the neoclassical and Keynesian price-output relationship. A brief review of the assumptions behind the alternative price-output relationships is important in its own right and facilitates subsequent construction of an intermediate case that contains elements of both neoclassical and Keynesian economics.

The price and quantity of a single commodity is determined by its demand and supply. Similar analysis may be applied to commodities in general. *The aggregate demand curve shows the relationship between (aggregate) output and the (general) price level when all the nonlabor markets are in equilibrium, given the money supply, fiscal policy, and other exogenous variables*. Reread the last sentence carefully. Note that the aggregate demand curve is *not* an ordinary demand curve; it is a special *equilibrium* curve called the aggregate demand curve simply because price and quantity are on the axes. We will demonstrate immediately the validity of a downward-sloping aggregate demand curve, as illustrated in Figure 28–1. Aggregate demand increases, that is, the curve shifts from AD to AD′, when the quantity of money increases or when government spending increases, assuming the demand for money does depend on the rate of interest.

Aggregate Demand

The validity of the last paragraph is seen quite readily with the aid of the now familiar IS–LM graph. The money *and* commodities markets are the nonlabor markets which yield the aggregate demand (henceforth, AD)

FIGURE 28–1
Aggregate Demand and Aggregate Supply

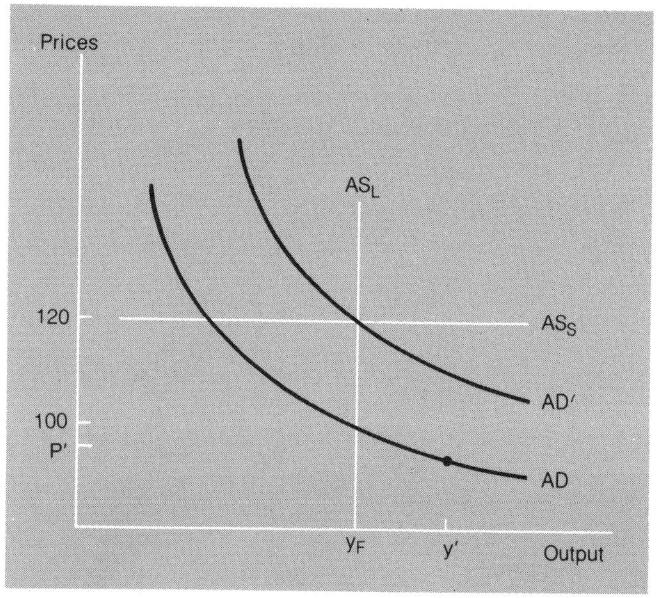

curve. When prices are variable, there is a separate LM curve for each price level, as we indicated in Chapter 27. For a *given* money supply and real income, higher prices increase the amount of money demanded and shift the LM upward in Figure 28–2. Higher prices increase the transactions balances required by any real income and, therefore, the rate of interest, given the money supply. A higher price level produces LM″ rather than LM′. Ignoring any real balance effect so that prices do not have a direct effect on expenditures, there is a single IS curve independent of the price level. Figure 28–2 shows that LM curves associated with lower prices intersect the IS at higher levels of output. The intersection of IS and LM′ in Figure 28–2 gives the point (y′, P′) on the AD curve in Figure 28–1. The AD curve, like microeconomic demand curves with price and output (quantity) on the axes, is downward sloping. Along AD, however, the rate of interest varies. Figures 28–1 and 28–2 indicate that lower interest rates occur along points further down the AD curve. Because lower prices reduce the amount of money demanded, the interest rate falls, which in turn increases output.

In general, both monetary and fiscal policy shift the AD curve. Visualize expansionary fiscal policy shifting the IS curve rightward in Figure 28–2. The new, rightward IS curve will intersect any LM curve, with its given price level, at a higher level of output. Thus, expansionary fiscal policy shifts both the IS and AD curves rightward. Now visualize that

FIGURE 28–2
IS, LM, and Prices: Higher Prices Shift the LM Upward

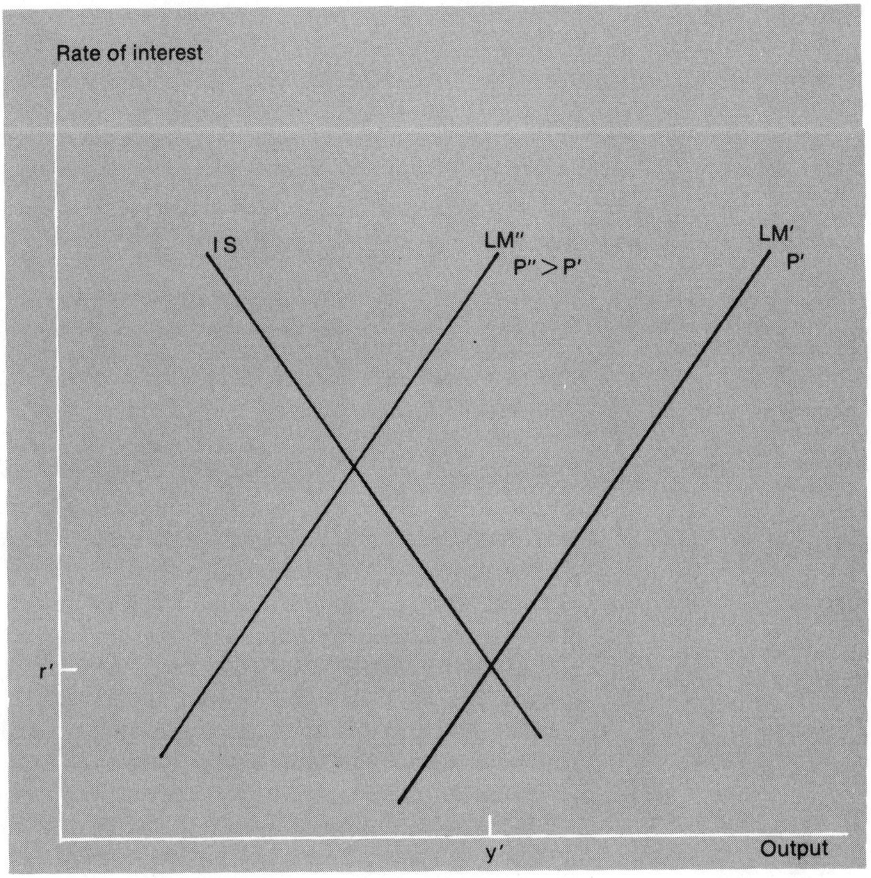

the entire set of LM curves shifts rightward due to expansionary monetary policy. The LM curve for any given price level is further rightward due to the monetary expansion and, therefore, intersects the IS further rightward. Expansionary monetary policy shifts both the set of LM and AD curves.

A classical money demand and liquidity trap are special cases. As we stated in Chapter 22, in the classical case where the demand for money is independent of the rate of interest, fiscal policy has no effect on the AD curve. In this case, the AD curve coincides with the quantity theory equation.

$$M_o = Pk'y \qquad \textbf{(28–1A)}$$

With M_o and k′ given, Equation (28–1A) is sufficient to specify the non-labor market curve linking P and y.[3] In the general case, however, there is an additional variable, the rate of interest.

$$M_o = P(k'y + h - jr) \tag{28–1B}$$

Because government spending raises interest rates and reduces speculative money balances, it also shifts the aggregate demand curve upward. In other words, with a higher r and constant M_o, some combination of higher P and y is again necessary to satisfy Equation (28–1B). Monetary policy on the other hand does not shift the AD curve when the economy is in a liquidity trap.[4] Let's ignore liquidity traps; they occur too infrequently, if at all. Indeed, let us assume for simplicity that all variations in AD are due to monetary policy. For most purposes of this chapter, the source of AD variations is irrelevant.

Neoclassical Aggregate Supply and Full Employment

By definition, *the aggregate supply curve shows the relationship between (aggregate) output and the (general) price level implied by the production function and equilibrium in the labor market*. For simplicity, assume the production function and labor force are fixed. This assumption keeps constant the aggregate supply curve, whatever its shape. In this case, changes in price and output are due exclusively to the variability of demand, which traces out aggregate supply.[5] That is, all the observed price and output combinations are assumed to lie on a single aggregate supply curve. (We shall indicate later the modifications necessary when supply is also allowed to vary.)

The vertical line AS_L in Figure 28–1 is the aggregate supply curve in the *long run*. We derived it rigorously at the end of Chapter 22. In the long run, which is the domain of neoclassical economics, firms maximize profits and households maximize utility. This produces labor demand and supply curves which depend *solely* on the real wage. Prices and wages eventually adjust to reach the *unique* equilibrium real wage and employment because disequilibrium represents a situation where all gains have

---

[3]True, additional government spending *always directly* increases commodity demand, by definition. However, the AD curve takes into account induced relationships. Government spending does not shift the AD curve when money demand takes the classical form because crowding out is complete.

[4]The linear Equation (28–1B) rules out a liquidity trap.

[5]The analog in a growth economy is supply and demand curves which shift at constant and variable rates, respectively. We shall assume throughout the remainder of this chapter that the economy is initially in equilibrium but shall later drop the implicit assumption that labor is the only factor of production.

not been exploited. Economic agents seeking to improve their lot eventually attain their maximum. Thus, classicists attribute optimality to full employment. *According to classicists, full employment is the unique, optimal level of employment and output attained in the long run by maximizing households and firms.*

Aggregate supply and demand have the price level and output on the axes. Inflation is the rate of change of prices. What is the impact on inflation and unemployment of variations in AD when the aggregate supply (henceforth, AS) curve is vertical? If demand remains constant at AD or AD′ in Figure 28–1, the price level remains constant at 100 or 120, respectively. Of course, constant prices are zero inflation. In Figure 28–3, the economy lands at the zero inflation/full-employment point, or the bliss point. Increases (decreases) in aggregate demand move the economy up (down) the vertical inflation-unemployment curve, I-U_L. *Increases in aggregate demand generate inflation but have no effect on unemployment in the long run.*

Full employment generally does not mean zero unemployment. The degree of heterogeneity and lack of information determine the positive unemployment rate corresponding to full-employment output, U_F in Figure 28–3. If there were a homogeneous product (our gizmo), a homoge-

FIGURE 28–3
Inflation-Unemployment Relationship

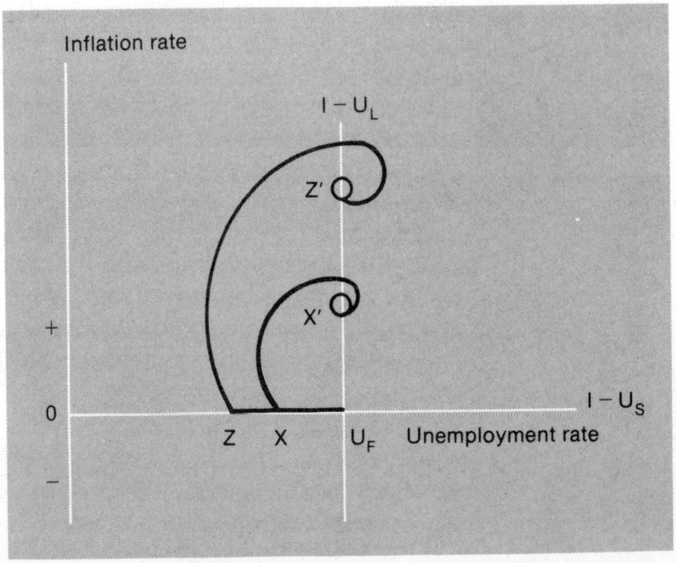

neous labor force, and homogeneous jobs, as we assumed in Chapter 22 for simplicity, then the full-employment rate of unemployment is zero. When all jobs are exactly alike and all workers are exactly alike, a general lack of jobs is the only reason for unemployment. What other justification could there be for the existence of people who are *willing and able* to hold *the* job but do not have one?

However convenient the assumption of homogeneity may be on occasion, it clearly is unrealistic. The problems due to heterogeneity are compounded by a lack of information and an inability to assess differences quickly and inexpensively. Neoclassical economists realize that in a heterogeneous economy it is absurd to require zero unemployment for full employment and labor market equilibrium. Go behind equilibrium to supply and demand. Neoclassicists derived the demand for labor assuming that firms maximize profits. The supply of labor assumes that households are maximizing utility in terms of leisure and consumption. When workers are heterogeneous and employers lack information so that differences among workers cannot be assessed immediately, then profit maximization does *not* require that every job be filled instantly. Although it may be profitable to hire a worker, which worker should be hired? The first person to apply for a job rarely will be the best suited. Profits typically are increased by keeping the job temporarily unfilled. Similarly, when workers lack information about jobs, then utility maximization does *not* require that every worker accept the first job. Although one may want to work in general, remaining unemployed until one finds the specific job for which one is well suited will increase earnings and utility.

Keynesian Aggregate Supply

In the short run, which is the domain of Keynesian economics, demand creates its own supply. The Keynesian AS curve in Figure 28–1 is AS_S, a perfectly flat curve at some "sticky" price level. In Chapter 24 we appealed to (1) labor market contracts which explicitly or implicitly give employers the option to hire any number of workers at a predetermined nominal wage, and (2) firms' desire to maintain product market shares as sources of a flat short-run nonprofit-maximizing aggregate supply curve. Exhibit 1 presents a somewhat more thorough explanation for sticky short-run wages and prices. Similar reasoning to that used earlier allows us to transform the flat AS curve into a flat inflation-unemployment curve in Figure 28–3. For convenience, always start the analysis from the bliss point of short- and long-run equilibrium. The line $I\text{-}U_S$ shows the inflation-unemployment values produced in the short run by different rates of change in aggregate demand. Expanding demand moves the economy leftward along $I\text{-}U_S$ in the short run.

The Transition from the Short to the Long Run

Assume demand increases at some given rate. Beginning from the bliss point, the economy initially moves along I-U_S to, say, point X but ultimately moves to point X′ on I-U_L. This necessarily implies that during the interim increases in aggregate demand reduce unemployment *and* are inflationary. Although the analysis does not pinpoint exact time paths, the curve linking X and X′ outlines the general response of inflation and unemployment *over time* to a constant rate of increase in demand. As drawn, overshooting occurs. For a while, the rates of inflation and unemployment exceed their long-run values although initially both were below equilibrium. Suppose the curve XX′ was generated by a 5 percent annual increase in the rate of monetary expansion and aggregate demand. How would the economy have responded to a 10 percent rate of increase? The greater increase in demand produces the curve ZZ′.

The reader should keep firmly in mind what is held constant and is allowed to vary along these curves. *Along I-U_S and I-U_L the time period is held constant. The curves are generated by different rates of changes of demand. The curve XX′ measures the response of the economy at different times to a constant increase in demand.*

EXHIBIT 28–1

Why Prices and Wages are Sticky in the Short Run

Explicit or implicit contracts, fair pricing, and other sources of inertia are fundamental assumptions underlying the short-run supply and demand curves for labor and commodities. Continuous wage settlements would be too time consuming and economically and psychologically disruptive. As a result, labor and management execute wage contracts which last several periods. While more wage contracts are containing cost of living adjustment (COLA) clauses, they still are the exception, and the adjustment for inflation rarely is complete. Besides stipulating wages, many labor contracts explicitly give, and the remainder implicitly give, the employer the right to require overtime, albeit at a higher wage. Thus, the employer is readily able to change output in response to demand. And firms do initially respond to demand by changing production. Some firms have granted buyers options to purchase goods and must respond to demand. Although such legally mandated responses to demand are relatively rare, many firms and consumers have entered into *implicit contracts* whereby firms are expected to satisfy automatically the demand of favored customers who purchase goods frequently and ignore an occasional better deal elsewhere. Few managers will use the term *implicit contracts*, but the often expressed objective of maintaining market share is tantamount to confirming their existence.

Implicit contracts exist between labor and management as well. Labor wants management not to lay off workers at the first sign of a weakening in product demand. The firm is supposed to produce for inventories, make postponed repairs, and, at worse, just slow down the assembly line. Firms behave in this manner; productivity, the ratio of output to employment, falls during the early phase of a recession. Firms are not expected to maintain the labor force indefinitely. At some point layoffs begin. And what do firms and laid-off workers expect from each other? Firms expect workers to wait around some reasonable length of time before even looking for another job. This is illustrated by the terms used when workers are "let go." A person is fired for incompetence but laid off when demand falls. Firms prefer to rehire laid-off workers instead of new workers when demand rebounds because they avoid training costs. Workers who endure layoffs can expect them to become less frequent in the future. Layoffs are largely allocated on the basis of seniority. The low-seniority workers who are laid off first can acquire the security of senior workers only by waiting to be recalled. Most do so. About 80 percent of laid-off workers return to the same job with the same employer.

The increasing complexity of products and the growing importance of the service sector has reduced the proportion of aggregate output which can be evaluated qualitatively very easily. This has strengthened the need for confidence between firms/professionals and their customers. How can a firm instill confidence about itself in its customers? One way confidence is instilled is by adopting the medieval philosopher's "fair price" instead of the modern economist's "equilibrium price" determined by demand and supply. Economists have so highly extolled the virtues of supply and demand pricing as a rationing device that few publicly admit their belief in fair pricing. However, the very persistent and widespread attachment to the fair price has only been sublimated. It periodically surfaces with a vengeance. During calamities, pricing according to supply and demand is called profiteering and is severely punished. How does one price fairly? Ignore demand; price on the basis of cost or supply exclusively. If costs rise, it is only "fair" to pass the higher costs along in terms of a higher price. Failure to do so lowers profits. Raising price in response to demand increases profits. If a firm does this, will it also cut quality, which is not readily ascertained, in order to raise profits? The combination of fair pricing, which ties price to cost, and contracts, which fix costs, is an explanation for the legacy Keynes gave us: a flat short-run aggregate supply curve. To be sure, more work remains to be done. "After three decades, the major intellectual problem continues to be the fact that so little (short-run) response to demand shifts comes through prices and wages" (William Nordhaus, "Inflation Theory and Policy," *American Economic Review*, May 1976, p. 62.)

The Intermediate Case

If the previous section is correct, then variations in demand should produce a downward-sloping inflation-unemployment curve in the intermediate run characterized by a combination of the assumptions underlying the short and long run. This indeed is the case. The term of most union negotiated labor contracts is two to three years. The typical implicit contract between firms and their customers to price fairly and meet demand is considerably shorter. Define the intermediate run as a time period long enough for firms to maximize profits but short enough to prevent workers bound by contracts from maximizing their preference. The intermediate run is illustrated in Figure 28–4. Contracts which constrain workers produce the flat labor supply curve. Since the demand for labor by profit-maximizing firms depends negatively on the real wage but the nominal wage is on the axis, there exists a demand curve for each price level. A higher price level lowers the real wage and shifts the demand curve rightward. Employment and outpout increase as labor is committed by contracts to work as much as employers demand. Although not illustrated, the aggregated supply curve clearly is upward sloping in the intermediate run. Higher prices induce firms to produce more.

Figure 28–5 graphs the intermediate-run inflation-unemployment relationship, I-U_I, implied by Figure 28–4. *In the intermediate run there is a trade-off between the goals of price stability and low unemployment.* The greater is the increase in aggregate demand, the higher is the rate of inflation and employment and, consequently, the lower is unemployment. Mr. Phillips anticipated the shape of our intermediate-run curve. There is an important difference, however, between our intermediate-run curve and the traditional Phillips curve. Mr. Phillips and his supporters claim

FIGURE 28–4

Labor Demand and Supply in the Intermediate Run

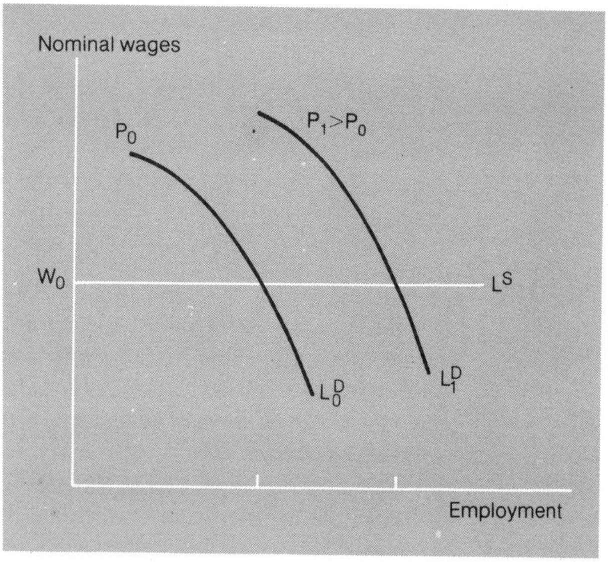

FIGURE 28–5

Inflation-Unemployment Relationship by Time Period

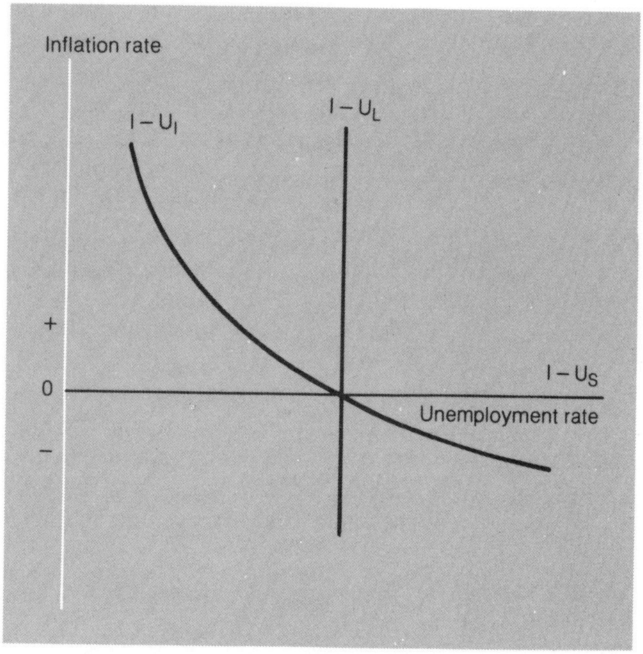

there is a *permanent* trade-off between inflation and unemployment. We claim the trade-off is only *temporary*. Precisely because we reject permanency, which is an integral part of the Phillips curve analysis, we avoided the term in the previous section and drew three curves in Figure 28–5. Henceforth, we will use the term Phillips curve—it is simpler than the inflation-unemployment relationship—but qualifying time period adjectives usually will be attached.

The Phillips Curve

As this chapter's introductory section noted, belief in a stable Phillips curve thoroughly dominated professional economic analysis in the early 1960s. In view of this, we should demonstrate the fallacies of the Phillips curve and not dismiss it cavalierly as contrary to our viewpoint.

Phillips initially analyzed the relationship between the rate of change of *wages* and the unemployment rate in Great Britain between 1861 and 1913. While all the wage change/unemployment points did not fall along a smooth curve like $I\text{-}U_I$, there certainly was a tight negative relationship between the variables prior to World War I. To test whether this was a true empirical regularity or a sampling fluke, Phillips also plotted the data for 1948–57. They were just as close to the curve as the original points!

Virtually immediately after publication of Phillips's study, economists feverishly rushed to test the relationship for other countries and other times. The rate of inflation, a variable much more in the public consciousness, was almost invariably substituted for the rate of change of wages without affecting the general conclusion.[6] For country after country the data suggested the existence of a trade-off between inflation and the rate of unemployment. In the euphoria of participating in the confirmation of a veritable empirical regularity, most researchers failed to notice that the most recent study typically illustrated a weaker trade-off than earlier studies showed. Economists became more and more convinced about the trade-off as study after study showed it was becoming weaker and weaker.

Phillips and his many early imitators were more concerned about finding the curve than explaining it. This made some wag say that the Phillips curve was an empirical fact in search of a theory. Richard Lipsey took up the challenge of rationalizing the Phillips curve.[7] Lipsey observed that the rate of change of a commodity's price depends on its excess demand. The same should be true for a factor of production like labor. Lipsey reasoned that the unemployment rate was a good proxy for the excess

---

[6]We shall see shortly that the substitution influences the height but not the shape of the trade-off curve.

[7]Richard Lipsey, "The Relation between Unemployment and the Rate of Change of Money Wage Rates in the United Kingdom, 1862–1957: A Further Analysis" *Economica*, February 1960, pp. 1–31.

demand for labor. The price of labor is the wage rate. Consequently, when unemployment is low, there should be a large excess demand for labor, and wage increases should be large. In order to maintain their income share, firms must pass forward any wage increase in excess of productivity gains.[8] Therefore, when unemployment is low, inflation is high. There is a negative relationship between the rates of unemployment and inflation. Although many niceties have been ignored, we captured the basic explanation for the Phillips curve.

Read the last paragraph again. Read it a third time. The explanation for the Phillips curve is straightforward and totally convincing, or at least it convinced nearly all economists for several years. Did you spot the flaw? Before explaining the flaw, we adopt the philosophy of the Phillips curve to show that a flaw does exist. Look at Figure 28–6 which graphs unemployment and inflation rates for the United States. The proof of the pudding is in the eating. *There simply is no overall Phillips curve*, so that the explanation for it cannot be totally accurate. Yet the explanation for the Phillips curve cannot be totally inaccurate and simultaneously so convincing. A closer look at Figure 28–6 reveals vestiges of Phillips curves. When the inflational-unemployment points are connected chronologically, as Figure 28–6 does, there appear to be numerous Phillips curves which have shifted upward over time. *For several years there is a trade-off between inflation and unemployment, but after many years the trade-off vanishes.*

The Friedman-Phelps Natural Rate Hypothesis

Milton Friedman first pricked the Phillips balloon and Edmund Phelps totally deflated it.[9] The two main flaws in the Phillips curve argument are the implicit assumptions that (1) wages and prices are well known to

---

[8]Labor's share of income, Py, is WL/Py, where W is the wage rate, and L is employment. For our purposes, the expression is best rearranged and written as (W/P)/(y/L), the ratio of the real wage to labor productivity, y/L. The last expression indicates that labor's share and, therefore, the share of the remaining factors are constant when real wages and productivity change by the same rate or, equivalently, when the growth of nominal wages exceeds the rate of inflation by the growth of productivity. Since shares have remained approximately constant and productivity growth is positive, the inflation-unemployment and wage change-unemployment curves have the same general shape but the former lies below the latter by the rate of productivity growth.

Expressing the text mathematically,

$$\Delta W = f(L^D - L^S), f' > 0,$$
$$U = g(L^D - L^S), g' < 0,$$
$$\Delta P = h(\Delta W) \qquad h' > 0,$$

where U, L^D, L^S, and P are the unemployment rate, labor demand, labor supply, and price level, respectively. Primes signify derivatives. These equations imply

$$\Delta P = \Theta(U) \qquad \Theta' < 0,$$

The inflation rate, ΔP, is negatively related to the rate of unemployment.

[9]Milton Friedman, "The Role of Monetary Policy," and Edmund Phelps, *Inflation Policy and Unemployment Theory* (New York: W. W. Norton, 1973).

FIGURE 28–6
U.S. Unemployment and Inflation Rates, 1953–1984

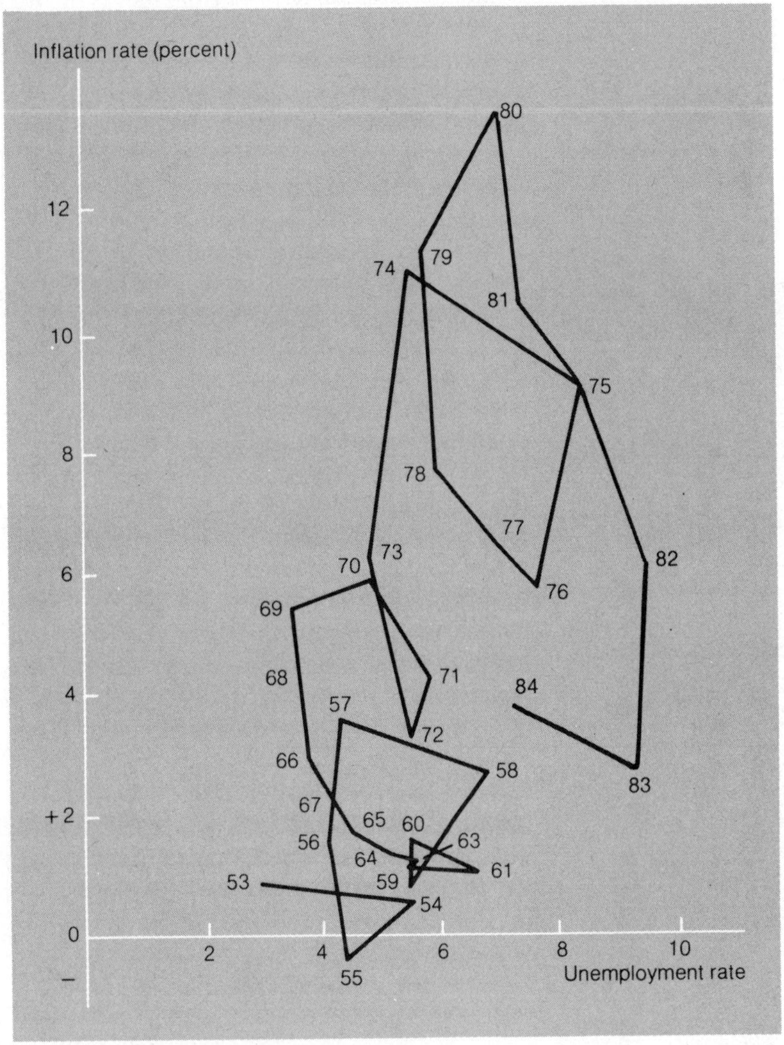

Source: *Economic Report of the President, 1984.*

everyone, and (2) contracts which create future commitments do not exist. Friedman and Phelps strongly emphasize incorrect wage and price perceptions. The complexity of their argument has caused many to lose the forest for the trees. Since the implications of contracts and wage and price misperceptions are similar, we first offer a glimpse of our final destination using an easier approach combining both elements. We then travel the Friedman-Phelps road of price misperceptions exclusively.

When contracts exist, current wage settlements do not reflect current excess demand exclusively, but also reflect expected inflation and future demand. The natural rate of unemployment occurs when profit-maximizing firms and utility-maximizing workers correctly estimate the level and (given heterogeneity) structure of future wages and prices. The natural rate is the *optimal* rate of unemployment since it occurs when *maximization* plans are realized, and expected and actual values are equal. The natural rate is equivalent to the neoclassical full-employment rate of unemployment—a horrible term if ever there was one—in the sense that both claim optimality and inevitability. People eventually adjust, and expectations are realized. The very definition of the natural rate suggests why it may diverge from the actual rate. *Incorrect estimates of inflation and wages cause the actual rate of unemployment to diverge from the natural rate.* The divergence persists while contracts exist. In contrast, the neoclassical concept of full employment as labor market equilibrium is silent about the causes of divergence from full employment. The natural rate is represented in Figure 28–7 by u_N. The vertical line at u_N illustrates that the natural rate is consistent with any rate of inflation, provided it is anticipated.

Although both sides are ultimately interested in the real wage, assume labor market participants strike nominal wage bargains. Continuous wage bargains are too costly. Define the intermediate run as the average duration of labor contracts. Because of contracts, current wage settlements reflect not only the current rate of unemployment as Phillips claimed but also the expected rate of inflation during the intermediate run. Begin the analysis from a position of zero anticipated inflation. On the basis of this anticipation and other factors, a wage settlement is reached. When aggregated demand is such that the actual rate of inflation is zero, neither side is disappointed by the outcome and feels it made a mistake. The plans of both sides of the market are realized when the actual and expected inflation rates coincide, and the unemployment rate equals the natural rate, by definition. The economy is at point A in Figure 28–7.

Suppose aggregate demand suddenly accelerates. The public underestimates the rate of inflation, which turns out to be 5 percent instead of zero. In this case the unemployment rate will fall. Firms find the unanticipated inflation has reduced the real wage and respond by hiring more workers, who have committed themselves by contracts. *The unemployment rate is below (above) the natural rate when the actual rate of inflation is greater (less) than the anticipated rate.* The curve through points A and B is the Phillips curve when the expected rate of inflation is zero, $\pi^e = 0$.

The expectation formation process clearly is a key element in this theory. *An integral component of the Friedman-Phelps theory is the assumption that the expected rate of inflation depends entirely on past rates.* As a first approximation, let the expected rate equal last period's inflation

FIGURE 28–7
Phillips Curves Shifted by the Expected Inflation Rate

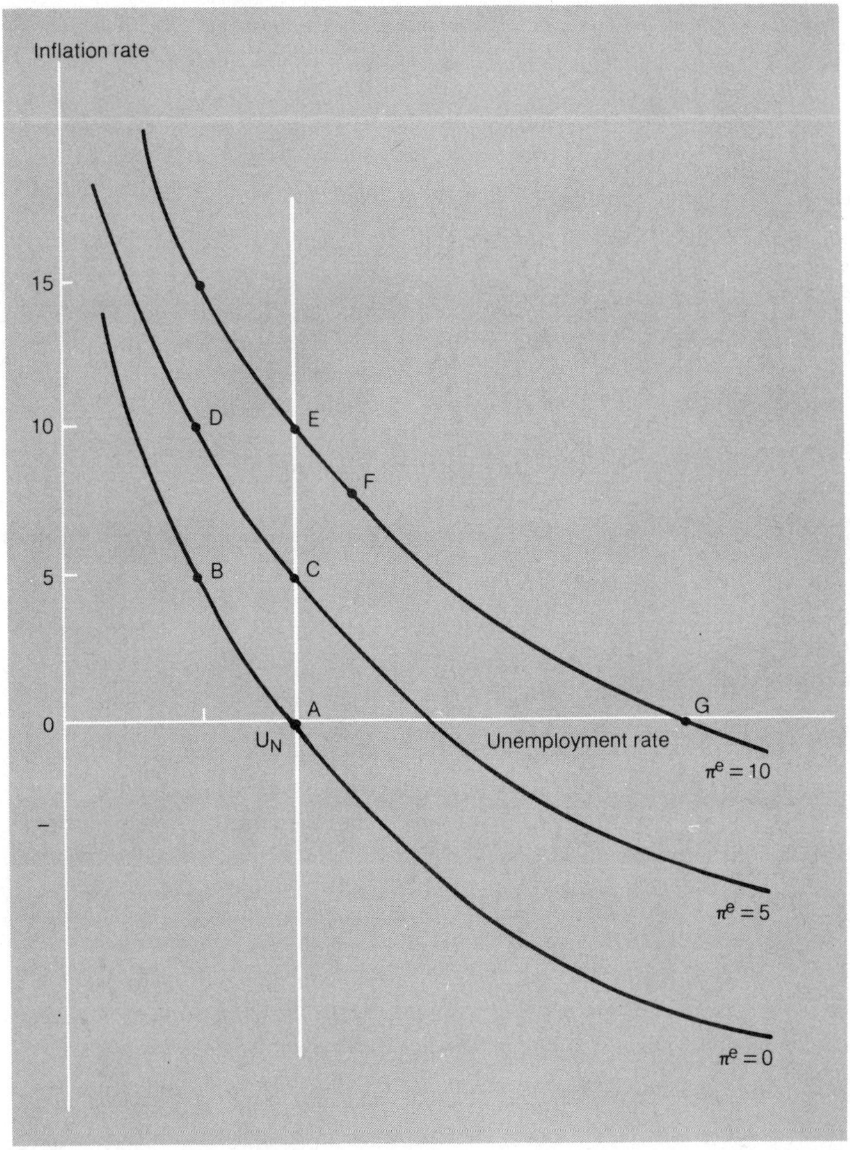

rate, or 5 percent in our example. How does the shift to a higher expected rate of inflation influence behavior? Wage settlements at the next bargaining round will equal the old wage settlement adjusted upward by the expected rate of inflation because firms and workers are ultimately interested in real magnitudes. For example, if the bargaining process led to a 2 percent wage increase when inflation was not expected, then the same bargaining process produces 7 percent wage increase when a 5 percent inflation rate is expected. If aggregate demand and the rate of inflation continue to rise at the same 5 percent rate, the economy moves back to the natural rate at 5 percent inflation, point C. Just as at point A, neither side is disappointed at C; plans are realized; and anticipated and actual real wages coincide. Nominal variables were correctly escalated upward at C in order to keep real variables constant. The shape of a curve formed by ABC clearly resembles our inflation-unemployment curves over time in Figure 28–3.

What inflation rate is necessary to maintain the unemployment rate at the level of point B? The inflation rate must rise to 10 percent. The movement from point A to B was caused by a real wage 5 percent less than anticipated. With the 5 percent higher inflationary expectations and wage settlement, the same 5 percent real wage reduction requires a 10 percent rate of inflation. The economy moves from point B to D. Thus, the Phillips curve is shifted upward by the expected rate of inflation.

The natural rate hypothesis says that there is a trade-off between inflation and unemployment in the intermediate run when contracts made on the basis of a *given* expected rate of inflation are binding. However, because expectations are based on the past, movement up (down) an intermediate-run Phillips curve increases (decreases) the expected rate of inflation and future contractual wages, which shifts the curve upward (downward). What inflation rate is necessary in order to permanently maintain unemployment below the natural rate? Inflation must be *accelerating* so that the actual rate always exceeds the expected rate. What previously required a 5 percent rate of inflation now requires a 10 percent rate, then a 15 percent rate, and so on. For this reason, *the Friedman-Phelps hypothesis is also called the accelerationist hypothesis. Accelerating (decelerating), and not simply high (low), inflation rates are necessary in order to maintain the unemployment rate below (above) the natural rate.*[10]

---

[10]The fundamental equation summarizing the natural rate hypothesis is

$$u_{n,t} - u_t = \alpha(\pi_t - \pi^e_t),$$

where the subscript t is any time period, α is a positive parameter, and the other terms are as previously defined. With the very simple forecasting equation $\pi^e_t = \pi_{t-1}$, the fundamental equation becomes

$$u_{n,t} - u_t = (\pi_t - \pi_{t-1}).$$

Rising, and not just high, rates of inflation are necessary to lower the unemployment rate below the natural.

Diversity, Misperceptions, and Information

Friedman and Phelps emphasize temporary misperceptions about diverse wages and prices and information costs as the sources of shifting Phillips curves. Let the natural rate concept include correct wage and price estimates both *across* jobs and commodities and over time. In terms of the variables of greatest interest, the natural rate occurs when individuals correctly estimate the *distribution* of salaries and rates of inflation. Begin the analysis again at point A, where constant price and wage distributions produce the natural rate because constancy was anticipated. Now suppose aggregate demand increases by 5 percent. Because the acquisition of information is costly, some time may elapse before firms realize that aggregate demand increased. Suppose our firm then raises its prices 5 percent although it remains uncertain about the precise aggregate demand increase and the reaction of other firms. At this point the firm knows with certainty that *its* real wage has fallen. The real wage for a firm is the ratio of *its* wage rate to the price of *its* product alone. *The* real wage is very different for each heterogeneous producer. The firm's lack of information about the prices of other products is irrelevant for its labor market decisions.

Suppose firms react to their lower real wage by raising the nominal wage somewhat in the hopes of hiring more workers. Will firms be successful? Yes. Just as firms were not immediately aware of the aggregate demand increase and responded with a lag, so the unemployed will not immediately realize that salaries in general have risen. They will accept what they believe are especially good paying jobs. Moreover, from the viewpoint of workers, the relevant real wage is their nominal wage divided by some *general* price index. Workers consume a broad basket of goods, not just their employer's products. Because workers need more information than firms do, and because information spreads slowly, unexpected inflation is associated with a decline in unemployment. The economy moves from point A to B. Provided aggregate demand, prices, and the salary distribution continue to increase at a constant rate, they all become anticipated correctly and the economy moves to C. What can keep unemployment below the natural rate? People must be fooled again. Demand must rise further. Firms recognize the expansion more quickly than workers. They raise wages somewhat and prices even more. Workers do not accurately perceive the higher inflation. They incorrectly believe the higher nominal wages increase real wages. In fact, real wages fall, which is why firms hire additional workers. *People will be fooled by accelerating inflation according to Friedman-Phelps because forecasts are based on some average of past inflation rates.*

Rational Expectations and the Phillips Curve

From the viewpoint of the inflation-unemployment relationship, the distinguishing characteristic of the rational expectations school, that we met briefly in Chapter 22, is their belief that *market participants use all relevant information efficiently*. Because they do so, their forecasts are optimal. *Rational expectations are unbiased and not systematically wrong. Expectations are rational when any difference between realized and expected values are a random variable*. Perfect foresight is a *special* case of rational expectations, where information has been used so efficiently that there are no forecasting errors, by definition. The efficient use of information and rational expectations, however, only require that forecasting errors be random and not systematically wrong. If rational expectations required perfect forecasting, no one would take it seriously.

The rational expectations school denies that there is a Phillips curve *which can be exploited by the authorities*, even in the short run. That is, *the school says that there is no temporary, much less permanent, trade-off between inflation and unemployment*. A vertical line best measures the relationship between inflation and unemployment irrespective of the time period. Rational expectationalists are not ostriches with their heads in the sand; they do realize unemployment has not always equaled the natural rate. Rational expectations accept the Friedman-Phelps propositions that mistakes cause unemployment to diverge from the natural rate. For example, unemployment is below the natural rate whenever the actual rate of inflation exceeds the expected rate. Rational expectations say that mistakes are not systematic. That is, individuals do *not* underestimate the actual rate of inflation for a significant period of time. An underestimate this period is just as likely to be followed by an overestimate as by another underestimate. The distribution of mistakes is random about zero. Consequently, the rational expectations school says the inflation and unemployment points ordered chronologically should be distributed randomly about the vertical long-run Phillips curve.

Expressing the last paragraph differently, the rational expectations school denies the natural rate/accelerationist hypothesis that you can fool people *permanently*. Suppose the economy is at the bliss point A in Figure 28–7, and the Fed unexpectedly increases the rate of growth of money by 5 percent. The economy moves to point B. Economic units now ask themselves, "What is the Fed up to?" *If there was any calculated reason for the Fed's action, the public will soon discover it*. Suppose the Fed's new objective is the lower than natural rate of unemployment associated with point B. When expectations are based exclusively on past rates of inflation, the Fed's objective is attained by accelerating monetary expansion to 10 percent. The rational expectations school says that individuals look beyond the past for their expectations of the future. Individuals use all relevant information and soon discover the Fed's systematic strategy of accelerating inflation. A 10 percent rate of inflation becomes expected, and the economy bypasses point D and moves directly from B to E. Suppose the Fed learned that individuals were expecting a 10 percent rate of inflation. Could it maintain the low unemployment rate by increasing the money supply by 15 percent? No, according to the rational expectations school. As soon as the public realizes that the Fed is committed to maintaining the low unemployment, no inflation rate will necessarily surprise them. Ever faster rates of inflation become expected.

Winding Down Inflation

Suppose policymakers decide to wind down inflation after reaching point D in Figure 28–7. We look at what must be done, first according to the natural rate/accelerationist hypothesis and then according to rational expectations. The 10 percent rate of inflation associated with point D becomes expected in the next bargaining round. The relevant intermediate-run Phillips curve is labeled $\pi^e = 10$. In order to reduce the rate of inflation, unemployment must rise above the natural rate. Policymakers have two options. First, they could adopt a *gradualist policy*. The gradualist policy is illustrated by the stagflation point F, where inflation has fallen and unemployment has risen moderately. However, inflation and unemployment still remain high, at least compared to point B. Inflation declines slowly, causing the downward shift of each period's Phillips curve to be gradual. The disadvantage of the gradualist policy is the length of time needed to wind down inflation. The alternative according to the natural rate hypothesis is the ''bite the bullet'' policy illustrated by point G. Aggregate demand is cut so drastically that the rate of inflation plummets, squeezing dry inflationary expectations. Next period's intermediate-run Phillips curve is $\pi^e = 0$. The disadvantage of this policy is the extremely high unemployment rate endured for a short period of time. The better policy, gradualist or bite the bullet, clearly depends on the precise shape of the intermediate run Phillips curve and on the cost of inflation and unemployment.

The rational expectations school holds out the possibility that inflation may be brought to a screeching halt without having to endure a high unemployment rate. In order to accomplish this, policymakers must convince the public that they are totally committed to ending inflation and will bear whatever cost is necessary, including massive unemployment. But the public will be convinced only if the commitment is truly genuine. Pious hosannas to the goal of price stability are not sufficient. *The credibility of policymakers is the key element*. In terms of Figure 28–7, the hope that rational expectations holds out is that although the economy may be at point E, policymakers who convince the public of their willingness to drag the economy to G can adopt policies that instead move the economy directly to A. If a 10 percent rate of inflation has existed and is expected to continue, at the next wage bargain labor asks for, say, a 12 percent wage increase. After the traditional protests about the exorbitant demands of labor, management quickly settles, since it believes that the government will rescue it by expanding the money supply and engineering an inflation which eats up the wage increase. If the government does not expand the money supply, the 12 percent wage settlement will be exorbitant, and unemployment will skyrocket.

Neither management nor labor benefits from massive unemployment. The same policy of not expanding the money supply would have entirely different effects if it had been correctly anticipated. Management never would have agreed to a 12 percent wage increase if it had known that demand was going to be curtailed so drastically that prices would remain constant. Indeed, labor never would have asked for a 12 percent wage increase. The parties would instead have settled for a 2 percent wage increase, which firms could afford without laying off workers.

While rational expectations say that the mere thought of having to take bad-tasting medicine may induce spontaneous remission, it also says that the medicine may not cure. Suppose the actual and expected rates of inflation are 10 percent. The government then timidly reduces the rate of growth of money below the expected value. Inflation moderates somewhat, but unemployment rises. The economy moves from point E to F in Figure 28–7. *If the public believes that policymakers are unwilling to tolerate the higher unemployment rate and will quickly reverse themselves, then the expected rate of inflation and short-run Phillips curve will not shift down.* Indeed, the short-run curve could shift up if the public believes the government in the following period will attempt to compensate for its "mistaken" policy by increasing the money supply even faster than previously.

Credibility, Expectations Formation, and Balance of Payments

The rational expectations school says that in order to gain credibility and realize the small side benefits of unemployment, policymakers should never proclaim targets which they cannot or do not intend to meet. Reconsider the issue of specifying money supply targets, which we discussed in Chapter 19 and 20. At open-market meetings the committee specifies a target range of monetary growth for the next month. We stated that no one seriously believes that monthly fluctuations in the rate of growth of money have any effect on ultimate goals such as unemployment and inflation. The effect of even quarterly monetary fluctuations is small; the goals depend on the "underlying," that is, semiannual or longer, rates of monetary growth. After saying that, we proceeded to examine the Fed's ability to control monthly growth. What was the purpose of the examination? Why worry whether the Fed can control the money supply month-by-month when monthly monetary fluctuations are irrelevant in terms of goals? The justification given in Chapter 20 was that the demonstration of monthly control guaranteed control over whatever longer period may be relevant. We now can give a second and more important justification. *Monthly monetary targets should be hit simply because they are an-*

nounced. The Fed's credibility would otherwise be undermined. How should the public interpret Federal Reserve statements that it failed to hit the proclaimed monetary target because the costs of interest rate variability are too high? If the costs of interest rate variability are so high, how will the Fed react to the very real costs of unemployment above the natural rate? The public might be led to believe that the Fed will not persevere in any anti-inflation program.

The expectations generating mechanism of both the natural rate/accelerationist and rational expectations theories are partially confirmed and partially contradicted by the data. Look at Figure 28–6 again. There definitely are intermediate-run Phillips curves, which contradict the rational expectations hypothesis that prediction errors are random. In particular, look at the points for 1961–69. The unemployment rate continuously fell, which according to *both* theories occurs when underestimates of inflation become larger, that is, the spread between the actual and expected rates of inflation widens. A decade is long enough that such errors should be considered systematic, in contradiction to the rational expectations hypothesis.[11]

A single Phillips curve fits the British data for 1861–1913 reasonably well. This implies that for more than 50 years the expected rate of inflation was relatively constant even though the actual rate varied significantly. In contrast, the intermediate-run American Phillips curves in the approximately 30 years since 1953 are extremely unstable. For example, the 1973 boom shifted the Phillips curve up; the 1974–75 recession shifted it down; the 1976–78 expansion shifted the 1979 curve up so that it closely coincided with the 1974–75 curve. The very steep slide down the 1980–82 curve shifted the 1983 point far inward. The difference in the stability of the pre-World War I and post-World War II Phillips curves is difficult to reconcile with the accelerationist hypothesis that expectations depend simply and consistently on past inflation rates. However, the stability difference is easily reconciled with the rational expectations hypothesis that past inflation rates *and* all other relevant information, including the policymaker's objectives, determine expectations.

To the extent governments had any conscious economic goals prior to World War I, they were exchange rate and price stability. Pre-World War I was the heyday of the classical gold standard, where each nation's commitment to keep the price of gold constant in terms of its currency

---

[11]Virtually everyone correctly states that the data for the 1930s contradict the rational expectations hypothesis. We present the 1960s data instead because of our previously stated objection to letting the 1930s be a sample of one. Moreover, we suspect that many are unaware that the 1960s contradict the rational expectations hypothesis, which was formulated in the late 1960s and early 1970s. Our suspicion is based on the almost universally accepted proposition that new theories are developed when existing theories cannot explain the recent past. Certainly, this was the Keynesian case. The rational expectations hypothesis is the exception that disproves the rule. It was formulated and gained fairly wide acceptance although it was contradicted by the recent past.

bound them together in a fixed exchange rate system. A country's inflation rate cannot materially exceed the inflation rate of its trading partners in a fixed exchange rate system because different inflation rates change the relative price of foreign and domestic commodities and lead to balance of payments effects. For example, high inflation rates in a fixed exchange rate system cause imports (exports) to increase (decrease) as they become inexpensive (expensive) compared to domestic (foreign) commodities. This in turn leads to a balance of payments deficit, which must be corrected if the exchange rate is to remain fixed in a country with limited gold reserves.[12] The solution to the balance of payments problem is simple: stop the inflation which caused it. The discipline of the gold standard stabilized inflationary expectations. A sudden surge in the inflation rate was not interpreted as the beginning of a long-run trend.

In the early post-World War II period the United States was on a modified gold standard. Gold did not circulate, and the money supply was not directly tied to gold. Moreover, the exchange rate was an "adjustable peg," in contrast to the "pegged pegged" exchange rates under the gold standard. That is, in the postwar period it was understood that exchange rates would be adjusted, if necessary, in order to accommodate other goals, while in the pre-World War I period no other goal dominated exchange rate stability. The Full Employment Act of 1946 specified various goals, but the act's name reflects the major goal. People came to the reasonable conclusion that exchange rate depreciation and inflation would be tolerated if they reduced the unemployment rate. In 1971 the United States formally erased any vestige of the gold standard as the dollar was no longer convertible into gold at a fixed price. Exchange rates and the price of gold became flexible. Without the discipline of fixed exchange rates, the Fed can, in principle, inflate at will. The exchange rate automatically fluctuates in accordance with inflation. Under these circumstances a sudden surge in the 1970s inflation rate could be interpreted as the beginning of a long-run trend. So long as policymakers were unaware of or did not intend to use the short-run Phillip curve, it remained stable. *When the public realized in the postwar period that policymakers intended to climb up the Phillips curve, it immediately started to shift.*

The Costs of Inflation

Without a credible monetary authority which squeezes dry inflationary expectations by mere threats of engineering a depression, the cost of winding down inflation is unemployment exceeding the natural rate. Are the costs of inflation sufficiently high to warrant suffering the temporary

---

[12]Chapter 17's section on gold discussed the effect of gold purchases and sales and the evolution of the gold standard. Chapter 32 analyzes more comprehensively the international economy.

unemployment and lower output, or should we learn to live with inflation? If Keynes's estimate in this chapter's lead quotation is correct, fewer than 250 Americans are able to answer the question. We make no claims of belonging to that select group. Nevertheless, we cannot shy away from analyzing the costs of inflation. For our purposes we distinguish between (perfectly) anticipated and unanticipated inflation caused by the excessive growth of money and, therefore, aggregate demand. We will ignore inflations caused by reductions in aggregate supply due to droughts, higher prices for imported oil, and so on. Supply induced inflations are temporary, provided policymakers are willing to accept the lower output.

Anticipated Inflation

Economists have traditionally constructed a scenario where the costs of anticipated inflation are trivial. Suppose everyone expects a continuation of the rate of inflation, say, 10 percent, that has been occurring for a very long period of time. In such an economy all private contracts which involve the future delivery of money or goods will take the inflation into account, given no legal impediments. For example, we saw in Chapter 6 that during anticipated inflations borrowers and lenders agree that more dollars should be repaid since each dollar is worth less. Nominal interest rates are adjusted upward for anticipated inflation in order to keep the real rate of interest constant in economies without usury laws or other legal restrictions. Long-term wage contracts and leases also would be escalated for inflation. Suppose further that the transfer and tax system is perfectly indexed so that all government receipts and payments depend on real magnitudes alone. Real aftertax income is independent of the rate of inflation in a perfectly indexed system. *According to traditional economic analysis, anticipated inflation produces only two minor costs in such an economy.*

First, any inflation, anticipated or not, creates "menu" costs. That is, resources must be spent marking up prices on menus and catalogues and changing vending machines' coin slots.

Second, anticipated inflation produces so-called shoe leather costs. Assume for simplicity that fiat currency is the only type of money. The mechanics of interest payments on currency are so difficult that it is invariably assumed that currency would continue to pay zero interest irrespective of the rate of inflation. Assuming that the interest rate on all other assets adjusts upward for the expected rate of inflation, the interest opportunity cost of holding money rises. Therefore, the demand for money falls, and velocity rises. Individuals economize on money, which is produced at zero cost, and use more real resources to make their transactions and better synchronize their receipts and expenditures. For example, in order to be fully invested and earn the high interest rates, individuals wear out shoe leather running to their broker's office on paydays and then running back to sell the bonds and get the cash needed to buy a can of tuna. Even if we recognize the additional opportunity cost of employing more brokers, the costs of anticipated inflation in such an economy are so trivial that they do not justify the unemployment necessary to eliminate inflation.

Before leaving that rarefied world of perfect indexation, we note two features ignored by the traditional analysis just presented. First, the monetary expansion necessary to increase aggregate demand permanently yields the government resources. If the distribution of goods between the public and government sectors is constant, "normal" taxes must be cut in order to satisfy the government budget constraint. Since some costs are always associated with the collection of any tax, the cost saving due to lower "normal" tax collections makes the net costs of monetary expansion and anticipated inflation even less than the menu and shoe leather costs.[13] When money creation is viewed as a source of government revenue, the nature of menu and shoe leather costs should be clear. They are the collection costs to the public of the inflationary tax on money. As Benjamin Franklin realized, a 10 percent inflation and a 10 percent tax on money with prices constant reduce money holders' purchasing power equally. When money creation takes the place of income taxes, we stop running to our accountants and lawyers and instead run to our broker to avoid the tax on money.

The traditional analysis also ignores the psychological costs of inflation. Even if prices, wages, and nominal wealth all changed proportionally so that no one was hurt in real terms, most people would feel cheated by inflation. Workers attribute a large proportion of the increase in their nominal wages to their own merit or luck rather than to inflation, which, even if anticipated, is seen as being caused by the unreasonable action of others. Inflation is viewed as an unwarranted reduction in the real wage that otherwise would have been earned. *"A significant real cost of inflation is thus what it does to morale, to social coherence, and to people's attitudes towards each other."*[14]

Adjustment Problems and Imperfect Indexation

The perfectly indexed economy where, apart from psychological costs, anticipated inflation is virtually costless is a useful abstraction, but only

---

[13]Lump sum taxes do not create an excess burden, by definition, but are costly to collect. The poll tax collector of old was a very real person who could have been producing some good or service.

[14]Gardner Ackley, "The Cost of Inflation," *American Economic Review*, May 1978, p. 151. Ackley is one of the few economists who we believe correctly assigns a heavy weight to the psychological costs of inflation.

that. First, there is the adjustment problem. Bonds and mortgages with an initial term to maturity of 30 years and more are quite common. Some real estate leases are equally long term. Therefore, even if all new contracts suddenly reflect anticipated inflation perfectly, it takes at least 30 years before anticipated inflation has no effect on the economy. Those who issued 30-year bonds just prior to a rise in anticipated inflation enjoy a real gain at the expense of lenders for the full period.

Our economy hardly is perfectly indexed. Consequently, even anticipated inflation redistributes income and wealth and misallocates resources beyond the adjustment period. Legal restrictions are a source of imperfect indexation. For example, resources are diverted away from borrowers when usury laws prevent them from paying the necessary inflation premium. Financial institutions prohibited by Regulation Q from paying any interest on demand deposits and competitive interest on time deposits shrank in size in the late 1970s compared to money market mutual funds which were unrestricted. While it is true that usury laws and Reg Q are being abolished precisely because the high inflation rate of the late 1970s made them a real burden, new legal restrictions always seem to replace old ones.

The tax system produces perhaps the major distortions during anticipated inflation. Tax rates in a progressive tax system rise with income brackets. As a simple but totally adequate example, suppose the tax rate is 20 percent on incomes up to $10,000 and 30 percent on anything above $10,000. Suppose a person's income is $10,000 so that his or her aftertax income is $8,000. What happens when this person's nominal income just keeps pace with a 100 percent inflation? He or she becomes a victim of "bracket creep" and finds real aftertax income reduced. In our example, the tax bill rises to $5,000 (20 percent of the first $10,000 and 30 percent of the next $10,000); nominal aftertax income is $15,000; and real aftertax income—the income that matters most—falls to $7,500. *The government gains twice from inflation*. First, the money creation which produces the inflation gives it the wherewithal to acquire commodities. Second, inflation shoves people into higher tax brackets and increases tax collections.

One obvious solution to the bracket creep problem is to tie income tax brackets to the inflation rate. Indexed brackets effectively set tax rates on real wages instead of nominal wages. President Reagan did index tax brackets beginning in 1985. However, indexed tax brackets do *not* produce a system where real tax collections are independent of inflation because *other sources of income exist besides wages*. In particular, consider the effect of inflation and taxes on the interest income of lenders. Suppose that the rate of interest was 5 percent when prices were stable and the tax rate was 50 percent. The real aftertax rate of interest was 2.5 percent. What happens when a 7 percent rate of inflation is anticipated, and the nominal interest rate rises to 12 percent? Nominal aftertax interest is 6 percent, and real aftertax interest is negative, −1.0 percent! The impoverishment of the lender in this example has nothing to do with bracket creep; we assumed a constant 50 percent tax rate. The lender is worse off because he or she is taxed on the 7 percent inflation premium necessary to keep real wealth constant.[15]

We have just scratched the surface of the accounting and tax problems in an inflationary economy. In principle, one could devise a tax system which avoids bracket creep, does not tax inflation premiums, allows real depreciation, taxes real but not nominal capital gains, and so on. In reality, no such tax system has ever existed, and it will exist only in one's flight of fancy.

Unanticipated Inflation

Just as an economy where all contracts and the fiscal system are perfectly indexed for inflation is a useful abstraction, so the very idea of anticipated inflation, as used in the last section and in the literature generally, is a useful abstraction, but only that. Anticipated inflation occurs when everyone correctly knows *with certainty* the future inflation rate. Anticipated inflation clearly is quite different from the real world situation where people with varying degrees of uncertainty construct different and possibly incorrect estimates of future inflation. In fact, *all inflations have been unanticipated.* Of course, the degree of unanticipated inflation varies. At one extreme, expectations are held with little confidence, vary widely among people, and are wrong on average, that is, irrational. At the other extreme, expectations are homogeneous, correct on average (rational), and firmly held, although not with certainty. The cost of inflation, as measured by the income and wealth redistribution and resource misallocation that occurs because the economy is imperfectly indexed, depends directly on the degree of unanticipated inflation.

There is much evidence that the variability of inflation increases with its average level.[16] Since the variability of inflation or any other factor tends to produce less accurate, less firmly held, and less homogeneous expectations, the costs of inflation are positively related to its average

---

[15]The 50 percent tax on the 7 percent inflation premium is 3.5 percent, which equals the reduction in the real aftertax return from 2.5 to −1.0 percent.

[16]Benjamin Klein, "The Social Cost of the Recent Inflation: The Mirage of Steady 'Anticipated' Inflation," *Journal of Monetary Economics*, supplement series, 1976, pp. 185–212; Dennis Logue and Thomas Willet, "A Note on the Relation between the Rate and Variability of Inflation," *Economica*, May 1976, pp. 151–58; Arthur Okun, "The Mirage of Steady Inflation," *Brookings Papers* 3 (1971):485–98. Note that there is no mechanical reason why inflation rates must fluctuate more when their average rate is high. For example, the inflation rate could fluctuate between 0 and 4 percent on the one hand and, between 8 and 12 on the other, so that variability is independent of the average level. What could and what does happen are different.

rate. *High inflation rates are to be avoided because they are more likely to be unanticipated.*

Who are the main beneficiaries of the redistribution caused by unanticipated inflation? For simplicity, assume inflation is completely unanticipated. Consider wealth redistribution first. Neither nominal interest rates nor anything else is adjusted for (totally) unanticipated inflation, by definition, so that the real wealth of holders of dollar denominated assets such as bonds falls. Conversely, bond issuers gain as the principal received exceeds the principal repaid in terms of purchasing power. What groups are net debtors whose wealth rises with unanticipated inflation? Are they the poor, professionals, farmers, and so on? Surprisingly perhaps, the wealth position of the poor is not improved by inflation. The poor simply are unable to borrow much, and they tend to hold dollar-denominated assets such as savings accounts. Households on balance are net creditors, and corporations are net debtors, so that the former lose and the latter gain from unanticipated inflation. However, because corporations are owned by households, this redistribution is robbing Peter to pay Paul. Although we sometimes talk about "our government," ownership is less immediate in this case. Given the huge national debt, *unanticipated inflation transfers wealth from the private to the government sector.* Within the private sector, the principal class of wealth losers are retired persons, who have a larger than normal proportion of dollar-denominated assets. The main gainers are young homeowners who have large mortgages compared to their dollar assets. Contrary to the beliefs in the 1960s, inflation does not benefit common stock holders.

Besides its wealth gain, the government gains real income from inflation due to imperfect indexation. Within the private sector, what groups' relative incomes rise during inflation? There is a strong feeling in some circles that inflation has a major impact on relative income. In particular, some claim that capitalists gain at the expense of workers because prices rise before wages. Others go so far as to claim that inflation is caused by attempts of labor unions and other organized groups to raise their relative income. However, the evidence indicates that inflation has little *systematic* effect on the relative income of broad social and economic groups. Inflation does *not* systematically change the relative income of capitalists versus workers, union workers versus nonunion workers, or the rich versus the poor.[17] The retired do lose somewhat from inflation, but much less so now that Social Security is indexed.

The misallocation of resources is the second main cost of inflation. Because long-term contracts of all kinds are riskier during inflations and

---

[17]G. Leland Bach, "Inflation: Who Gains and Who Loses," *Challenge*, July 1974, pp. 48–55; and G. Leland Bach and Albert Ando, "The Redistributional Effects of Inflation," *Review of Economics and Statistics*, February 1957, pp. 1–13.

because most households and firms are risk averse, *long-term contracts generally, and long-term credit markets especially, tend to dry up*. For example, suppose the real rate of interest was 5 percent when prices were stable, and the rate of inflation now is expected to be 7 percent. The expectation is not held with certainty; it could be more or less than 7 percent. In this case, neither risk-averse borrowers nor lenders find a 12 percent nominal loan rate as attractive as a certain 5 percent real rate. Loan rates *higher* than 12 percent are necessary to compensate risk-averse lenders for the risk that the rate of inflation could be more than 7 percent. Loan rates *lower* than 12 are necessary to compensate risk-averse borrowers for the risk that the rate of inflation could be less than 7 percent. If 5 percent was the maximum (minimum) real rate the borrower (lender) would pay (accept), then a loan cannot be effected in an inflationary environment. Output falls as large-scale, long-term projects that characterize the most industrialized economies can no longer be financed because savers now purchase real estate or collectibles such as gold instead of lending.

Summary/Questions

Can we lower our unemployment rate by increasing aggregate demand? The Phillips curve approach optimistically says that we can *permanently* lower our unemployment rate by enduring a *permanently* mild rate of inflation. The more modern natural rate/accelerationist approach claims that a *permanent* inflation only *temporarily* lowers our unemployment rate. A *permanently* lower than natural rate of unemployment can be achieved only by ever *increasing* rates of inflation, which are unanticipated. The yet more modern rational expectations approach says that a permanently lower than natural rate of unemployment can*not* be achieved by any *demand* policy, including accelerating inflation. In order to permanently lower the rate of unemployment, policymakers must engineer a systematic policy, such as accelerating inflation. However, any systematic *demand* policy would soon be discovered by the public, who would act in a manner to thwart it because the natural rate of unemployment is optimal. Yes, the unemployment rate can be too low, as well as too high, of course. *Supply* policies which create a more skilled and better informed labor force are necessary in order to permanently lower the natural rate of unemployment.

Inflation ranks very high on the national worry list. Nevertheless, economists have had little success in pinpointing the broad economic and social groups whose relative position is lowered by inflation. One beneficiary is clear: the government. There also is general agreement that anticipated inflation is much less costly than *un*anticipated inflation. Since permanent inflation becomes anticipated, the Phillips curve said in the early 1960s that the low costs of anticipated inflation yield the benefits of low unemployment. The Friedman-Phelps natural rate hypothesis stated in the early 1970s that the high costs of unanticipated inflation yield low unemployment. All inflations are a more serious problem according to the rational expectations approach. It says in the 1980s that costly anticipated inflation yields no benefits, and unanticipated inflation cannot be consistently engineered. Over time, economists are seeing less benefits and more costs to inflation. They are joining the public in placing inflation higher on the national worry list.

1. Derive and define the aggregate demand curve. Draw and define aggregate supply curves for the classical long run and Keynesian short run. Discuss, with the aid of aggregate demand and supply graphs, the inflation-unemployment relationship implied by an integration of the Keynesian and classical models.
2. For an intermediate run which contains elements of the Keynesian short run and classical long run, derive an inflation-unemployment curve showing a trade-off.
3. Define the Phillips curve. Give the theoretical justification for the Phillips curve. What are the main flaws in the theoretical justification of the Phillips curve?
4. Explain carefully the Friedman-Phelps natural rate or accelerationist hypothesis. What is the main difference between it and the Phillips curve?
5. Explain the rational expectations view about the Phillips curve.
6. The expectations generating process is crucial to any theory. Discuss (*a*) the expectations generating mechanism of the natural rate and rational expectations hypotheses, (*b*) the data which contradict each hypothesis, and (*c*) the importance of credibility to the rational expectations school.
7. What are the costs of anticipated inflation in an economy which is perfectly indexed?
8. Do you believe the last question is important or unimportant? Explain.
9. What are the main costs of unanticipated inflation? What demographic groups and product sectors are the main gainers and losers from inflation?

Issues in domestic monetary policy

29

This chapter discusses selected issues in domestic monetary policy. Each section is more or less independent of the others. We make no pretense of being encyclopedic, and some may even quarrel with our selection of issues to be covered. Some issues such as leads and lags cannot be easily handled in the static neoclassical and Keynesian models and are presented here for the first time. We also expand on certain topics mentioned briefly earlier. All theories are simplifications; the world is too complex to attempt to explain everything. In this "second pass" some simplifying assumptions are dropped to broaden the applicability of the analysis.

Rules versus Discretion

The so-called rules versus discretion debate concerning the conduct of monetary policy might be labeled laissez-faire versus fine tuning. This is a debate between the two flanks of the economics profession. Professor Friedman and other staunch monetarists support a rules policy. Indeed, they more than support it; a rules policy is near the top of any list of the tenets of monetarism. *A rules policy has the money supply grow at a constant rate dictated by long-run objectives. Therefore, monetary changes are independent of the past and near future predicted values of goal variables such as GNP.* All prescribed policies are not rules, as here defined. For example, policymakers who *methodically* and *automatically* reduce the rate of growth of money by some fraction of last period's rate of growth of GNP would *not* be following a rules policy because the rate of growth of money would be variable and dependent on past GNP. Constancy alone does not qualify as a rule. A constant *interest rate* policy also is not a rules policy. The opposite of rules, discretionary policy, was advocated especially strongly by the economic advisors of the Kennedy and Johnson administrations. *Discretionary policy is characterized by frequent changes dependent on past and near future predicted values of the goal variables.*

Proponents of a monetary rule advocate a fiscal policy consistent with the philosophy underlying their approach to monetary policy. A rules approach to fiscal policy sets tax *rates* and spending *programs* that do not vary in response to the business cycle. Tax receipts and the number of people who qualify for such spending programs as unemployment compensation would automatically vary during the cycle. *The budget would swing from a surplus during the expansion to a deficit during the contraction but balance over the business cycle.* Discretionary fiscal policy would vary tax rates and spending programs so the budgetary swings over the business cycle would be substantially greater. Moreover, advocates of discretionary fiscal policy deny the desirability of balancing the budget over the business cycles. Perpetual deficits varying in size according to the state of the economy are acceptable. Because many of the same points are at issue whether the policy being debated is monetary or fiscal, we prefer the more general laissez-faire versus fine tuning to rules versus discretion, where the latter is almost exclusively associated with the monetary policy debate.

The money supply can grow at many constant rates—10 percent, 5 percent, 0 percent (in which case the money supply remains fixed), −5 percent, and so on. What should the specific rate of monetary growth be? What long-run objective governs the specific rate? In the final analysis the rate of monetary growth simply affects the long-run rate of inflation. Proponents of a monetary rule invariably oppose high rates of inflation; price stability or even a mild deflation is preferable. Given these desired rates of inflation, a straightforward application of the quantity theory equation says the money supply should grow at approximately 4 percent. For small changes, the percentage form of the quantity theory equation is

$$\frac{\Delta M}{M} + \frac{\Delta V}{V} = \frac{\Delta P}{P} + \frac{\Delta y}{y}$$

The equation says that the sum of the percentage change of money and velocity—the left-hand side—equals the sum of the rate of inflation and real income growth—the right-hand side. For example, if there are 5 percent more dollars and each dollar is spent 2 percent faster the price and/or quantity of commodities rises 7 percent. Assuming velocity remains constant and real output grows 4 percent annually on average, long-run price stability requires a 4 percent rate of monetary expansion. Suppose our assumptions are incorrect: velocity increases by 1 percent, and real output grows 3 percent annually on average. In this case the same 4 percent rate of monetary expansion would generate an underlying 2 percent rate of inflation. Monetarists would not be upset by this outcome; the economic differences between a long-run mild deflation, price stability, and mild inflation are minor. The main thing is not to change the rate of monetary expansion and the corresponding long-run rate of inflation, which should be relatively low at most. With 4 percent being perhaps the preferred rate of monetary growth, any *constant* growth rate between 1 and 7 percent is acceptable, given the likely changes in velocity and real output. Monetary growth outside this range is likely to generate too much deflation or inflation.

Justifications for a Rules Policy

Why do Professor Friedman and others favor rules? On what basis do they prefer rules over discretion? Rules are advocated on several grounds. First, an obvious point which, nevertheless, bears stating. *Advocates of a monetary rule believe that money matters in the sense that it has an important effect on aggregate demand.* While the precise moderate (between 1 and 7 percent) rate of monetary growth may be unimportant because aggregate demand only affects the rate of inflation in the long run, a monetary policy which influences aggregate demand causes real output fluctuations in the short run. If money did not matter and had little effect on aggregate demand and output in the short run, the way monetary policy was conducted would be irrelevant. Those who believe money does not matter do not take the rules versus discretion debate seriously. The belief that money matters is a necessary but not sufficient condition to advocate a rules policy. Other arguments in favor of a rules policy must be marshalled.

The second justification says that a monetary rule is the only way to make the Fed consider the money supply. The only good Fed is a shackled Fed. The Fed frequently employed a target or intermediate variable other than the money supply. For example, the Fed often attempted to stabilize interest rates. As we demonstrated in Chapter 27, a policy of stabilizing interest rates magnifies business cycles caused by shifts in aggregate demand. An increase in aggregate demand which tends to overheat the economy also raises the rate of interest as borrowing and the demand for money increase. The higher interest rates reduce some of the expansionary pressure. If the Fed stabilizes interest rates, the moderating influence on the economy of higher interest rates during the boom is lost, by definition.

The Fed's attention has not been riveted on interest rates exclusively. Taking a longer look backward than in Chapter 19, during the late 1920s the Fed was alarmed by stock market speculation fueled in large part by low margin bank loans. Lacking the power to single out loans for stock purchases, a determined Fed embarked on a general contractionary policy which reduced total bank loans and the money supply, along with stock market loans. The general contractionary policy did indeed have the desired negative effect on the stock market, and much more. To cleanse the stock market from the speculative influences of the late 1920s, the money supply fell and helped precipitate the Great Depression of the 1930s. The cure was worse than the disease. Monetarists are pessimistic that the Fed will learn from history. The economy is doomed to more booms and busts as the rate of interest, stock market, and other target variables continue to blind the Fed from watching the money supply. Even if discretionary *monetary* policy were preferable to a rule, the Fed would quickly abandon *monetary* policy and practice an interest rate or some other policy. The Fed's October 1979 resolve to pay greater (but not total) attention to the money supply may not be long lasting. A rule forces the Fed to consider only the money supply.

Even if the unlikely occurred and the Fed learned from history to focus on money, *rules are preferable to discretionary policy because (a) the economy is basically stable, and (b) policy lags are long and variable.* Conditions (*a*) and (*b*) imply that a discretionary policy will magnify the business cycle. At this point a graph is helpful. Figure 29–1 abstracts from the upward trend and assumes full-employment income remains constant at Y_F. The solid sine curve intersecting Y_F represents the path of income assuming a monetary rule. We assume for simplicity that the real income path is independent of the specific rule rate of monetary growth, which influences only the long-run rate of inflation. A monetary rule is a neutral policy which neither magnifies nor dampens the normal expansions and contractions of the economy. In a stable economy the expansions and contractions are mild and short. In terms of Figure 29–1, the maximum vertical distance between the solid curve and Y_F measures the amplitude of the business cycle, and the horizontal distance between alternate intersections of Y_F measures the length of the cycle. Since the "mild" and "short" cycles which characterize stable economies are relative concepts, the solid sine curve by itself is at most suggestive of stability. The curve representing income under a neutral policy must be compared with policy lags and the income pattern discretionary policy generates.[1]

---

[1]In other words, *(a)* the economy is basically stable, and *(b)* policy lags are long and variables are not independent statements. Recessions in an unregulated economy are mild *relative* to the havoc monetary mismanagement could cause; the policy lags are long *relative* to the time it takes a temporarily depressed economy to bounce back unassisted.

FIGURE 29–1

Output with Discretionary and Rules Policies in a Basically Stable Economy

Discretionary policy represented by the dashed curve magnifies instability. The rules policy represented by the solid curve is preferred because the economy is basically stable and policy lags are long and variable.

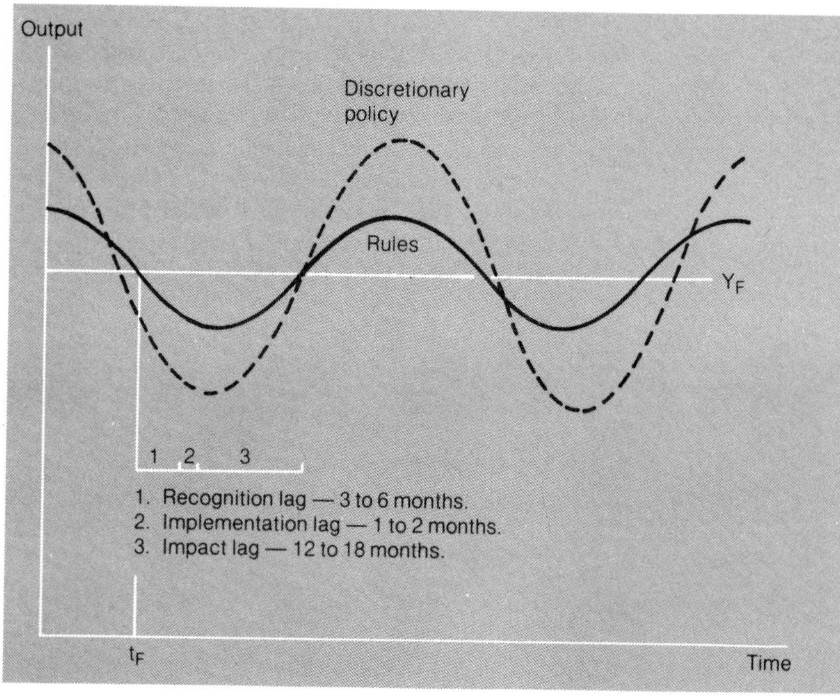

Monetary Policy Lags

The total policy lag may usefully be divided into three components which vary in length by type of policy and degree of economic knowledge.

1. Recognition lag. The recognition lag is the time interval between the need for policy action and its recognition by policymakers.
2. Implementation lag. The implementation lag is the time interval between the recognition that policy action is necessary and its implementation.
3. Impact lag. The impact lag is the time interval between the implementation of policy and its impact on the economy.[2]

[2]Sometimes the recognition and implementation lags are consolidated and called the inside lag, and the impact lag is called the outside lag. The inside lag then is the time interval between the need for policy action and its implementation.

Ideally, the recognition lag would be a lead; the policymaker should anticipate the need for policy action so there is sufficient time for the implementation and impact of policy. A recognition lead is extremely unlikely for two reasons. First, policymakers, like most individuals, are risk averse. *It simply is too risky politically and financially for them to base their actions on predictions instead of on facts or data,* which, at best, become available instantaneously or, at worse, after a long lag. Even though expansionary policy may be appropriate during a boom because the impact lag is so long that the policy will not take hold until the subsequent recession, such policy timing is likely to earn one ridicule because either the impact lag is often ignored or the projected recession does not occur. Policymakers must first observe the goals decline before expansionary policy can be safely contemplated.

If there were a single, well defined goal, as we assumed for simplicity in Chapter 19, then the data lag would be the sole reason for the recognition lag. Policymakers clearly have multiple goals, however. The time necessary to analyze and interpret the data for multiple goals, some of which are expansionary while others are contractionary, is a second reason for the recognition lag.

Assuming monetary and fiscal policy have the same ultimate goals, the length of the recognition lag is independent of the type of policy. Neither policymaker has a systematic advantage in collecting and analyzing data. *The recognition lag now typically is between three and six months.* It has declined over time and may be shortened somewhat more as the collection of data and their analysis improve. However, a recognition lag of one to two months is the absolute minimum.

The implementation lag which follows the recognition lag is largely institutionally determined. For this reason we ignored the implementation lag in Chapter 19. The monetary policy implementation lag was shortened significantly with the creation of the Federal Reserve and an elastic money supply. *In the United States the implementation lag for monetary policy currently is approximately one to two months.* Monetary policy can be initiated virtually immediately after the need is recognized by means of telephone conferences revising the instructions given to the account manager at the last Open Market Committee meeting. In any case, the committee meets approximately monthly in Washington. Nevertheless, it may take up to two months to fully implement the policy change in order to minimize the short-run perceived and actual disruptive effects of money on the rate of interest and other financial variables.

If the implementation lag for monetary policy is short and predictable, the lag for fiscal policy is the precise opposite, long and variable. Distributional and stabilization issues become inexorably intermeshed when tax and spending programs are proposed. For example, when a tax cut is necessary to stimulate the economy, each group views itself as fighting simply to restore its rightful income share while simultaneously viewing other groups as intent on further enriching themselves at its expense. When each group perceives that an increase in its income share is necessary in order to compensate for previous injustices, even an across-the-board tax cut is considered unfair and discriminatory. It takes time for coalitions to form and resolve the distributional impact of a tax cut needed for stabilization purposes. In a parliamentary system like Great Britain, where the executive branch is the leadership of the party controlling the legislature and votes by party line are the rule, the fiscal policy implementation lag is quite short. In the United States, however, where the separation of powers is a fundamental concept underlying the Constitution and votes by party line are the exception, the implementation lag can be so long that countercyclical fiscal policy should be attempted only when its desirability is utterly obvious. During a crisis, coalitions are formed more rapidly and the implementation lag is shorter. While everyone recognizes that the implementation lag in the United States is excessively long and variable, attempts to shorten the lag have been unsuccessful. The Democratic Kennedy and Johnson administrations requested from the Democratic Congress the authority to impose across-the-board tax changes. Party ties not withstanding, Congress balked, ever zealous of safeguarding its powers.

The impact lag is perhaps the most controversial. After analyzing the data, Professor Friedman concludes that the monetary policy impact lag is long—about 12 to 18 months—and quite variable. Other monetarists, however, find that the impact lag is considerably shorter. For example, the St. Louis Fed, whose model is described in detail in the next chapter, finds that money has a significant impact on GNP virtually instantaneously, and the impact grows monotonically throughout a year. On the other hand, some large-scale Keynesian structural models find that it takes a full year before monetary policy has any effect, and the full effect is not realized until four years afterwards. Detailed estimates of the impact lag of monetary and fiscal policy are presented in the next chapter. For now, suffice it to say that the estimates are quite diverse.

The various monetary policy lags as estimated by Professor Friedman are graphed in Figure 29–1. Although income is falling before time t_F, an expansionary policy is undesirable since resources are more than fully employed before t_F and inflation threatens. An expansionary policy should bolster aggregate demand at time t_F when the economy naturally starts to fall below full employment. However, the need to bolster aggregate demand is recognized approximately three to six months later. It takes the Fed about a month or two to increase the money supply, and aggregate demand responds about 15 months later. The total lag—the time interval between the start of a recession and the expansionary effect of monetary policy on aggregate demand—averages about two years but is quite variable. *The economy is stable in the sense that the average length of time it takes an unassisted economy to rebound to full employment approximately equals the total lag of monetary policy*. The effects of the expansionary monetary policy normally are felt precisely when they are unnecessary. The ex-ante countercyclical policy becomes an ex-post procyclical policy. Instcad of dampening the business cycle, discretionary monetary policy tends to magnify it. The dashed sine curve illustrates the time path of real income when discretionary policy is pursued.

As the average length of the monetary policy lag decreases, discretionary policy is more likely to dampen business cycles, *ceteris paribus*. Compared to Professor Friedman, the St. Louis Fed and other monetarists assert the monetary policy lag is considerably shorter. Nevertheless, *monetarists are united in opposing discretionary policy. The likelihood that monetary policy will dampen business cycles depends on the variability of the policy lag in addition to its average value*. Monetarists believe that the variability is sufficiently large that discretionary policy is undesirable even if the average lag is relatively short. A graph like Figure 29–1 cannot illustrate the variability of the lags; only the average values of the time paths and lags can be portrayed. While Figure 29–1 illustrates Professor Friedman's view that monetary policy is misdirected on average—the dashed average discretionary curve and the solid average rule curve are in phase but the amplitude of the former is greater—neither Professor Friedman nor anyone else believes monetary policy is *always* destabilizing. Indeed, the case against discretion does not require monetary policy to be destabilizing even most of the time. In other words, discretionary policy in an uncertain and variable world is undesirable even if it is neutral on average. Discretionary policy is advantageous only if it is countercyclical more often than it is procyclical. This is so because the loss from not achieving the goal is typically measured by the square of the difference between the actual value of the variable and the goal value. For example, assume the goal is a \$100 GNP while actual GNP is \$95. The loss from not achieving the goal is $25 = 5^2$ (the loss units are not dollars). Now suppose discretionary policy is implemented. Because the policy lag is unpredictable, GNP fluctuates between \$90 and \$100 instead of always equaling \$100. The average effect of the policy is zero; half the time it successfully attains the goal but the other half it decreases GNP by \$5 and makes matters worse. Nevertheless, discretionary policy is inferior to a neutral policy. One period there is no loss as GNP equals \$100, but the loss the next period is $100 = 10^2$ as GNP equals 90. The mean loss under a discretionary policy is 50, more than the 25 loss under a neutral policy.

Finally, monetarists offer various philosophical/political arguments in favor of rules. The late Professor Henry Simon virtually alleged that discretion would enslave us and rules would set us free.

> There is imminent danger, however, that actual governmental policies will undermine irreparably the kind of economic and political life which most of us prefer to the possible alternatives. This danger manifests itself . . . in measures and policies which involves delegation of legislative powers and the setting-up of *authorities instead of rules*.
>
> It is this danger of substituting authorities for rules which especially deserves attention among students of money. An enterprise system cannot function effectively in the face of extreme uncertainty as to the action of monetary authorities or, for that matter, as to monetary legislation. . . . We seem largely to have lost sight of the essential point, namely, that definite, stable, legislative rules of the game as to money are of paramount importance to the survival of a system based on freedom of enterprise.[3]

Behind all the philosophical/political arguments is the belief that rules minimize the likelihood of high rates of inflation. While monetarists believe that the effects of moderate (say, up to 5 percent) inflation are not that significant, they believe that high rates of inflation at least fray the social and political fabric of society, and more probably tear it asunder. For example, any comprehensive attempt to explain the rise of the Third Reich cannot ignore the inflation of the early 1920s, which left many Germans feeling betrayed. High rates of inflation have occurred only when discretionary policy prevailed. A government is unlikely to announce that it *permanently* will increase the money supply by, say, 100 percent and hope to achieve approximately the same rate of inflation. Even when governments have announced such high rates of monetary growth, they invariably are seen as temporary and often are reductions from even higher rates of monetary expansion. While it seems plausible that rules effectively will end hyperinflation, there is little historical evidence to support this proposition since no country has adopted a rules policy.

Considering polar cases is useful as it focuses attention on basic issues. We must point out, however, that many economists and politicians favor an intermediate policy which allows officials discretion when there is a relatively large deviation from the goal. For example, an intermediate policy might specify that the money supply should grow at 4 percent provided the rate of unemployment is within 2 percentage points of the full-employment rate. When the unemployment rate deviates from the full-employment rate by more than 2 percent, officials should do whatever necessary to ensure a speedy return to full employment. Such an intermediate policy is thought to raise significantly the likelihood that discretionary policy will, in fact, be countercyclical because the length of time it takes the economy to close any gap between the actual and target values

---

[3]Henry Simons, "Rules versus Authorities in Monetary Policy," *Journal of Political Economy*, February 1936. Reprinted by permission of The University of Chicago Press.

of a variable is positively related to the size of the gap. Attempts to smooth every little wiggle are likely to be counterproductive. Thus, the intermediate policy is a call for benign neglect except when a clear and present danger exists.

The Rational Expectations Challenge

The rational expectations hypothesis, which we discussed briefly in Chapters 22 (see "Neoclassical Economists") and 28, claims that a monetary rule, as defined in the last section, simply is an example of systematic, perfectly predictable policies, *all* of which are equivalent and superior to discretionary policy as a means of achieving full employment. For example, according to rational expectations, unemployment would be the same whether the *prescribed* policy had the money supply increase at a 4 percent constant rate, alternate quarterly between 4 and 20 percent, or increase at a prespecified constantly accelerating rate. All have the same effect on employment because all are systematic, perfectly predictable policies. Indeed, pegging the rate of interest at 8 percent, also a systematic policy, has the same effect on employment as any of the money growth policies. (Of course, these systematic policies will have different effects on inflation and possibly other goal variables.) *The average unemployment rate is independent of the systematic policy adopted.* The discretionary, unsystematic policies of well meaning economic tinkers who keep their decisions secret only increase the variability of unemployment without affecting its average value.

The fundamental and startling rational expectations conclusion that any unpredictable, discretionary policy aggravates unemployment follows from the assumptions that utility- and profit-maximizing households and firms (1) know the structure of the economy except for random errors, (2) forecast (form an expectation about) economic nonpolicy *and* policy variables and, (3) act partially on the basis of these forecasts. Rational expectations say that systematic policy may *potentially* have a large impact on employment but *actually* has no impact because it induces compensating action by *maximizing* households and firms. In other words, maximizing households and firms take into account *all* systematic events, including policy actions, in their decision making process. If the private sector knows that government will set policy variables at low levels, then wage settlements and other private contracts will be low in order to maximize utility and profits. Because the private sector has well defined and constant maximizing objectives and knows the structure of the economy except for random shocks, only random shocks due to exogenous factors and unsystematic policy prevent firms and households from achieving their objectives. While random shocks would occur even if government did not exist, government can only *add* to them. Neither government nor anyone else can reduce the private random shocks; if anyone could, the shocks would not be random.

Rational expectations advocates implore policymakers not to doubt the validity of the last two sentences even if highly significant statistical relationships exist. They claim that knowledge of the past does not justify current actions. In particular, the so-called Lucas critique, an integral element of rational expectations, says that *the implementation of a new policy may induce a structural shift, and not simply a movement to a different position on the same structure.*[4] Suppose Figure 29–2 shows the observed relationship between economic variables x and y. A government policy that attempts to exploit the historical curve and move the economy from point A to point B may cause the whole curve to shift and, therefore,

FIGURE 29–2

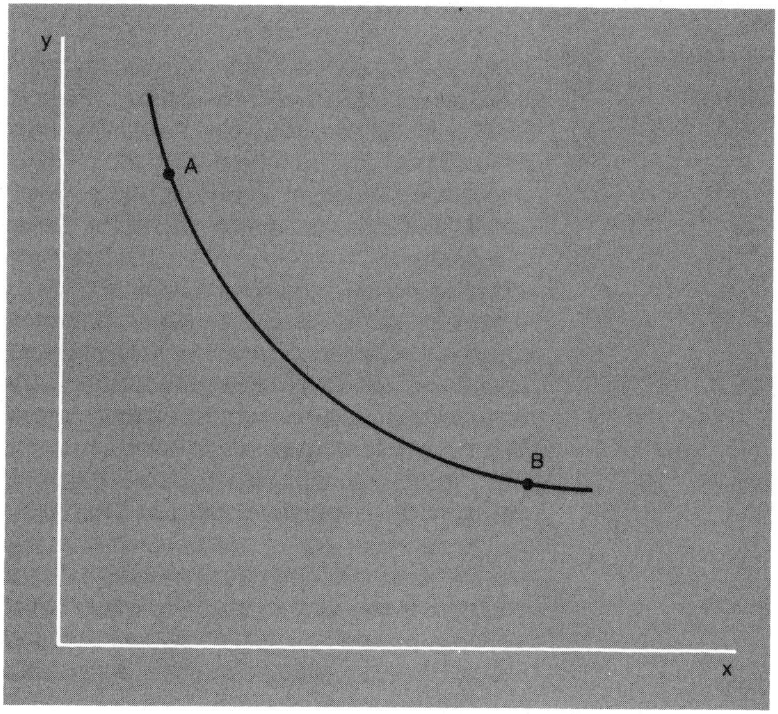

[4]Robert Lucas, "Econometric Policy Evaluation: A Critique," in Karl Brunner and Alan Meltzer, eds., *The Phillips Curve and Labor Markets,* Carnegie-Rochester Conference Series on Public Policy, vol. 1 (Amsterdam: North-Holland, 1976), pp. 19–46.

make policy ineffective.[5] The likelihood of a structural shift depends on the extent of the attempted policy change. The greater is the distance between points A and B in Figure 29–2, the more likely that policy will shift the curve. In very nontechnical terms, large policy changes cause people to believe that the ball game will now be played under an entirely different set of rules. People adjust their behavioral pattern, and *the statistical curve derived from the previous behavioral pattern no longer holds.* Observed economic relationships depend on government policy. Consequently, changes in government policy make historical economic relationships unreliable guides for the future.

The first paragraph of this section said that all systematic policies have identical effects on output, according to rational expectations advocates. Thus, they must have cringed on reading Chapter 27's final section, which claimed that a systematic money supply policy and a systematic interest rate policy have different impacts on output when the structure of the economy is uncertain and aggregate expenditure and money demand shocks exist. How does one reconcile the analysis in Chapter 27 with rational expectations? Chapter 27 assumed that the shocks and shifts in the IS and LM curves were independent of the policy followed. As the last paragraph suggests, rational expectations deny this. IS and LM shifts due to nonpolicy variables depend on the policy adopted. *When government shifts from a systematic money supply policy to a systematic interest rate policy, the structure of the economy will change to keep income fluctuations constant.*

Rational expectations have been oversold by its advocates and underbought by its opponents. Consider just a few criticisms of rational expectations. First, rational expectations implicitly assume that full employment is society's only goal, which clearly is not the case. Rational expectations recognize that different systematic policies may have different effects on inflation and other economic variables besides employment. The belief that *all* systematic policies are equivalent for employment purposes and *never* induce a trade-off between employment and other economic variables implies that the other, nonemployment variables are inconsequential to society. Second, distributional effects and private bargaining and transactions costs sometimes prevent the private sector from reaching the maximum. For example, perfect competitors are not necessarily less profit oriented than monopolists. Industries remain competitive because it is too costly to organize. Government with its power to compel and coordinate may help the private sector achieve higher em-

---

[5]The very careful reader noted that Figures 1–1 and 29–2 are identical. According to the rational expectations hypothesis, the division between politics and economics is not perfectly clear cut.

ployment rates and, more generally, greater utility.[6] Finally, rational expectations assume that all economic agents know precisely how the economy operates, except for the random shocks. This clearly is not the case. If government were better informed than the private sector, then discretionary policy could be beneficial.

In spite of some serious limitations, rational expectations have made some valuable contributions. Rational expectations correctly stress that the private sector constantly is trying to maximize. If it fails to do so, can policymakers be expected to succeed? Neither private problems nor good intentions are a sufficient condition for public policy. Recognition by rational expectations that observed behavior is largely based on *unobserved* expectations, which may be correct on average but quite wide of the mark at any one time, explains why economic analysis can be fraught with difficulty and controversy, as the following example shows. Suppose firms expect the Fed to adopt a tight money policy and, in anticipation, curtail output. Suppose further that firms forecast incorrectly; the Fed adopts an easy money policy. One then observes a recession and easy money although tight money, which had been expected, causes recessions. Now, forecasts will not be systematically wrong in the same direction. Sometimes expected monetary policy will be even more expansionary than realized. The importance of money will appear exaggerated in this case. Firms greatly increase production in anticipation of the very expansionary monetary policy but realized policy is only modestly expansionary. If *expectations could be measured directly, expectational errors would not obscure economic relationships. However, neither direct nor consistently accurate indirect measures of expectations exist.* Expectations at best are unbiased; forecasts may be correct on average, sometimes overestimating and other times underestimating. Systematic relationships in this case can be detected, but the existence of forecast errors makes it difficult. Moreover, the observed systematic relationships may not hold in the future when the authority changes its operating regime. Fortunately for chemists, molecules do not form expectations about electric charges and jump on the basis of the discrepancy between the expected and actual charge. If molecules behaved in this fashion, chemistry would be as inexact as economics.

Channels of Monetary Policy

What are the channels of monetary policy? What are the transmission mechanisms linking monetary policy and income? Before answering the questions, we should note that all disciplines develop a vocabulary which

[6]We are *not* advocating government sponsored monopolies.

occasionally seems designed to confuse the uninitiated. Economists' *investment* is one example, and *channels of monetary policy* is another. On first hearing the term, nearly everyone *incorrectly* associates the channels of monetary policy with the instruments of monetary policy, for example, open-market operations. Those who hope to earn their union card in economics cannot, however, avoid such confusing terms. You will never be considered a master economist unless you talk like one. *The channels of monetary policy refers to the linkages between money and income or the means by which monetary changes cause aggregate expenditure changes. Empirical research has confirmed three channels of monetary policy: (1) interest rates, (2) credit rationing, and (3) wealth.*

In the Keynesian models, the rate of interest is the only channel of monetary policy. In particular, money affects income because money influences the rate of interest, which in turn influences firms' investment. Early researchers attempted to quantify this channel by interviewing business executives, who stated the rate of interest had only a minor effect on investment. What one says and what one does often do not coincide, and interviews can be biased. In any case, subsequent statistical analysis has assigned to the rate of interest a greater importance on firms' plant and equipment decisions. The *immediate* effect of the rate of interest on investment is small indeed as the interviews suggested, but the effect grows over time. For example, the rate of interest has a delayed effect on the desired capital stock of steel companies. Then the investment necessary to acquire the desired capital stock is lagged in order to lower costs. Stretching the construction period of a steel mill from one to three years substantially reduces costs. Considerably more responsive than plant and equipment, however, is the housing component of investment. The government's attempts to insulate the housing industry from the roller coaster pattern of interest rates in recent years have been only marginally successful. The rate of interest remains an important determinant of housing. Finally, the interest rate channel is more pervasive than Keynes indicated. Econometric studies find that durable consumption and state and local government spending also are somewhat responsive to interest rates. Professor Friedman goes even further. He alleges that interest rates influence all types of spending including nondurables and services. The diversity of interest rates coupled with their all pervasive effects has led Professor Friedman to the somewhat paradoxical position of favoring the rate of growth of money over any one interest rate as a measure of "the" rate of interest channel.

Credit Rationing

The rate of interest is only one term or provision in any loan contract. The amount of the loan, term to maturity, and collateral are a few other terms. Neoclassical and Keynesian models assume a standard loan with terms which remain constant over time except for a rate of interest, which adjusts in response to the demand and supply for money and credit. In other words, the rate of interest is assumed to be the sole means of allocating the available money and credit. The simplification is reasonably accurate most of the time but occasionally is wide of the truth. *Credit rationing occurs when the rate of interest remains fixed and the other terms of a loan are adjusted to allocate the supply of money and credit.* Credit rationing may preclude one from receiving credit regardless of how high an interest rate one is willing to pay. There is no denying the existence of credit rationing. One sometimes hears that banks and other depository institutions are not making loans. While the statement never is literally correct—loans are maturing continuously and being renewed—it quickly conveys to the potential borrower the fact that credit is being rationed. The previous relationship between the borrower and the bank, the size of the borrower, the color of the borrower's skin, or some other factor is paramount in determining whether a loan is granted in such cases. *By changing the magnitude of credit rationing, monetary policy affects aggregate demand while the rate of interest remains constant.*

While the extent of credit rationing at any one time is difficult to measure, a consensus states that *credit rationing is positively related to the level and change in the rate of interest and will decline significantly in the 1980s.* Since interest rates typically are high and rising during a boom, credit rationing is procyclical, being prevalent during booms and virtually nonexistent during depressions. Usury laws, Regulation Q ceilings on deposits, and other institutional factors explain the positive relationship between credit rationing and interest rates. Consumer loans and mortgages typically were subject to usury laws, which were adopted by most states because of an alleged need to protect naive consumers from sophisticated lenders. After protecting the individual consumer, many states sought to protect the collective whole by extending usury laws to state and local borrowing. The usury laws probably harmed consumers individually and collectively more than they helped them. When the rate of interest hit the usury law maximum, state and local governments were forced to postpone expenditures, and consumer credit and mortgages were rationed as these interest rates could not rise further, by definition. Consumers willing to pay higher rates saw credit flowing to firms instead. Many state legislatures throughout the 1960s and 1970s raised the maximum rate shortly after it became binding, apparently cognizant of the value (lessness?) of usury laws. By 1980, Congress passed legislation which virtually abolished state usury laws on mortgages. This complemented the gradual dismantlement of Regulation Q mentioned earlier. Henceforth, savings and loan associations in particular will be able to pay depositors and charge homeowners whatever interest rate is necessary.

Credit rationing is not altogether a thing of the past. At times the Fed wants to lessen the visibility of a program severely restraining the economy and specifically asks bankers to refrain from raising their loan rates. Asked not to use the rate of interest as an allocation device, bankers ration credit. Bankers need not be cajoled to ration credit. They are mindful that poll after poll shows that low interest rates are an ultimate goal for most individuals, and not simply a means of achieving some desired GNP or other goal. When market interest rates rise, banks temporarily maintain their loan rates at the expense of higher profits. Too sharp and rapid an increase in loan rates is sure to incur the wrath of Congress and may produce lower long-run profits. Banks bide their time and ration credit. A higher Federal Reserve discount rate can reduce the time period that credit is rationed since bankers can rightfully claim that they are just copying the Fed.

Wealth Effects

The third channel of monetary policy is the wealth effect. As we indicated earlier, consumption depends on wealth, so that money influences aggregate demand if it affects wealth. Does money affect wealth? When money is fiat money exclusively and is injected into the economic system by transfer payments instead of open-market purchases, then monetary expansion clearly increases society's wealth as someone has additional assets and no one incurred a liability or lost assets. These assumptions were implicit in our discussion of the real balance of Pigou effect. However convenient the assumptions may be, they certainly are unrealistic for an economy like the United States where open-market purchases are the main monetary policy instrument. Some economists have argued that monetary expansion effected by open-market purchases does not generate a wealth effect. At first glance the argument seems plausible. Look at matters from the viewpoint of the seller of the bond. He has additional money but his holdings of government bonds decrease by an equal amount. The composition of the seller's assets changes but his total assets and wealth remain constant. *Those who argue that monetary expansion effected by open-market purchases does not generate a wealth effect err because they concentrate on the wealth of the bond seller alone and ignore how the purchase affects the wealth of the rest of society. We will show that an open-market purchase directly increases society's net wealth and, in addition, may do so indirectly by lowering the rate of interest and increasing the value of common stocks.*

Common stocks are the ownership claims on firms' plant and equipment and other assets. Being ownership claims, common stocks do not cancel in an aggregate balance sheet and are one component of society's wealth. Higher stock prices enrich stockholders without impoverishing anyone. As a first approximation, the price of common stock equals the capitalized or present value of the firm's earnings stream. Recalling our earlier analysis of interest rates and present values, lower (higher) interest rates raise (reduce) stock prices. The negative relationship between stock prices and the rate of interest is not based exclusively on the premise that stock prices equal the present value of earning streams. Stocks and bonds are substitutes. When interest rates fall and bond prices rise, common stocks appear cheap at current prices, and their dividend yield seems high. Individuals purchase stocks and raise their prices sufficiently so that they no longer are cheap. Therefore, if monetary expansion lowers the rate of interest, then wealth and, subsequently, consumption and income increase.

While it is useful to distinguish the interest rate induced wealth effect from the direct interest rate effect, neither channel is operative when the economy is in a liquidity trap and interest rates are fixed. Moreover, the procyclical nature of credit rationing suggests that rationing is virtually nonexistent in a liquidity trap and, as such, less rationing is an ineffective channel of aggregate demand expansion. It is the banks which seek creditworthy customers during a liquidity trap. Nevertheless, an open-market purchase directly creates an aggregate net wealth effect, which renders monetary policy effective even during a liquidity trap. True, an open-market purchase does not increase the wealth of the seller who receives, say, \$100 cash for a \$100 bond. The rest of society is the beneficiary. The government bond is worth \$100 because its owner is promised future payments. The open-market purchase frees the rest of society from having to make those payments. The net wealth of the rest of society increases as its liabilities fall. The rest of society is better off and spends more.

Aggregate net wealth may not increase directly by an amount equal to the open-market purchase. We previously argued that private bonds are *not* net wealth from the viewpoint of society as a whole. Private bonds are assets to their owners, but they also are the equal liabilities of specific issuers. Government bonds are the liabilities of society as a whole. *Ceteris paribus,* higher taxes will be levied in order to pay bondholders. Therefore, a \$1 government bond does not represent net wealth of \$1.[7] On the other hand, the rest of society may partially ignore the tax liabilities implied by government bonds outstanding. The tax liabilities associated with government bonds are less direct and more uncertain than private debt.[8] Let \$k equal the net wealth of a \$1 government bond, where $0<k<1$. Money itself does not create a contingent tax liability and increases net wealth by \$1. However, an open-market purchase increases aggregate net

[7]If a \$1 government bond did contribute \$1 toward net wealth, then an open-market purchase would not directly increase aggregate net wealth.

[8]In technical terms, the rest of society may use a higher interest rate than bondholders to discount the stream of bond payments. See Don Patinkin, *Money, Interest, and Prices: An Integration of Monetary and Value Theory,* 2d ed (New York: Harper & Row, 1965), pp. 288–94.

wealth by only \$1-k because the reduction in bonds outstanding reduces wealth by \$k.

Cooperative Monetary and Fiscal Policy: Multiple Goals and Policy Uncertainty

So far we largely have viewed monetary and fiscal policy as substitutes. One group says the money multiplier is large and predictable while the fiscal multiplier is small and variable, and another group says the opposite. One group says policymakers should rely on monetary policy, while another group advocates fiscal policy. Is there ever a need for monetary *and* fiscal policy? Are the two policies ever complements instead of substitutes? Must policy be coordinated because only a unique combination of monetary and fiscal policy will achieve the goals? The answer to all three questions is yes. *Both monetary and fiscal policy are necessary when either (1) the use of policy is subject to a constraint, (2) society has multiple goals, or (3) policy effects are uncertain.*

We have been implicitly assuming so far that society has a single goal such as full-employment income, and that the effects of policy are known. In such a case, monetary and fiscal policy can be substitutes. If income is below full employment, the income goal generally can be attained by either additional money or government spending. Even "extreme" cases such as a money demand or investment schedule entirely unresponsive to the rate of interest do not require both monetary and fiscal policy. In these extreme cases one policy is completely ineffective, and reliance must be placed exclusively on the other. *Given the single-mindedness and perfect-knowledge assumptions, monetary and fiscal policy are complementary only if there exists some constraint to the use of policy.* For example, suppose private autonomous expenditures fell by \$30 but the institutional structure limits the government spending increase to no more than \$10. Suppose further the maximum monetary expansion increases aggregate demand by \$20. In this case both monetary and fiscal policy are necessary.

Even if we can ignore constraints and lack of knowledge of the structure of the economy, both monetary and fiscal policy are necessary because society has multiple goals. The assumption that full-employment income is the only goal is unrealistic. As we mentioned earlier, economists traditionally allege society's goals also encompass economic growth, price stability, and exchange rate stability. Many polls indicate a low rate of interest is an independent goal of the general populace. Let us assume the rate of interest is the second goal in order to be able later to illustrate the argument with IS–LM curves. Whatever its merits as an independent goal, the rate of interest does influence significantly the widely accepted goals of economic growth and exchange rate stability. Low rates of interest stimulate economic growth by increasing investment but lower the exchange rate and worsen the balance of payments.

Suppose the interest rate already is sufficiently low that the goals are a higher income and constant rate of interest. (Further reductions in the rate of interest are undesirable because of its impact on the balance of payments.) In this case neither monetary nor fiscal policy alone can achieve both goals. Expansionary monetary policy increases income *and* lowers interest rates. Expansionary fiscal policy increases income *and* raises interest rates. For income to increase while the rate of interest remains constant, both monetary and fiscal policy must be expansionary. Look at Figure 29–3. The solid IS and LM curves representing the initial position of the economy show income is y_0 and the rate of interest is r_0. Suppose the objective is y_F while any rate of interest is acceptable. This is illus-

FIGURE 29–3
Complementary Monetary and Fiscal Policy

Both monetary and fiscal policy are necessary to achieve a specific income/rate of interest combination such as (y_F,r_O). In general, the number of policy instruments must equal the number of goals.

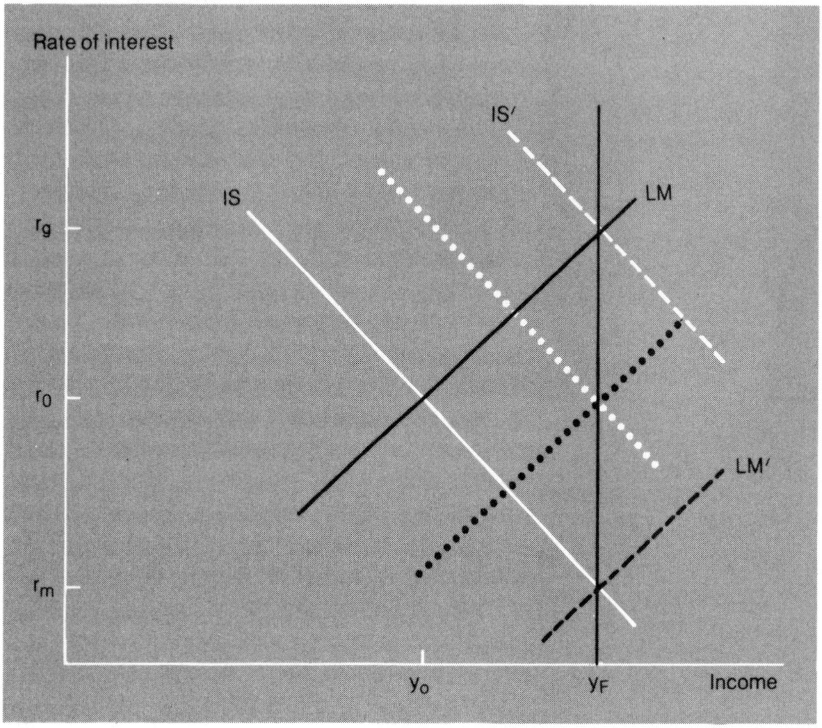

trated by the vertical line, any point on which is equally desirable. Either expansionary monetary policy which shifts the LM curve from the solid to the dashed position or expansionary fiscal policy which shifts the IS curve to the dashed position is sufficient. Now assume an interest rate goal so only one point on the y_F line is acceptable. Barring the fortuitous where either r_g or r_m is the interest rate goal, *neither monetary nor fiscal policy alone is sufficient*. If the multiple goal is r_0 and y_F, expansionary monetary and fiscal policy are necessary as indicated by the dotted IS and LM curves. *The attainment of multiple policy goals requires cooperation. Only one pair of IS and LM curves goes through any one point.*

The last paragraph is illustrative of an important economic principle: the number of independent policy instruments generally must equal the number of goals.[9] If we have three goals, we need three instruments; four goals, four instruments; and so on. While proving this principle is difficult, the reader familiar with a somewhat similar principle in mathematics may be more willing to accept this economic principle. Generally, how many equations are needed to solve for two variables? Two. Many values of the variables x and y satisfy the equation $x + 2y = 5$. If $x = 0$, then $y = 2.5 = (5/2)$ satisfies the equation, and if $y = 0$, then $x = 5$ satisfies the equation. *Letting one variable equal zero is the analog of using only one policy to achieve the goal.* The two equations $x + 2y = 5$ and $x + 3y = 7$ have a unique non-zero solution: $x = 1$ and $y = 2$. *The number of equations and variables are the analogs of goals and instruments, respectively.* Both instruments (variables) x and y must be "used," that is, cannot equal zero, in order to solve the two equations (goals). No values of x and y satisfy the three equations $x + 2y = 5$, $x + 3y = 7$, and $x + 4y = 8$. Two instruments cannot satisfy three goals.

The Need for Cooperation*

Attainment of multiple goals may require seemingly perverse and foolish actions by one policymaker. This is best demonstrated by an algebraic/numerical example. Since the principle to be illustrated here is not particular to monetary or fiscal policy, we use general notation. Let the goal variables be y_1 and y_2. Given the current values of the variables, the desired changes in y_1 and y_2 are 3 and 6, respectively. Algebraically

$$\Delta y_1^d = 3 \quad \text{and} \quad \Delta y_2^d = 6 \tag{29–1}$$

where the superscript represents "desired."

[9]Nobel Prize winner Jan Tinbergen first elucidated this principle in *On the Theory of Economic Policy* (Amsterdam, 1952).

*The reader may skip this *difficult* section without loss of continuity.

There also are two policy tools, x_1 and x_2. The effects of the tools on the goals, which we assume are known with certainty, are shown below.

$$\Delta y_1 = \Delta x_1 \quad \text{and} \quad \Delta y_2 = \Delta x_1, \qquad \textbf{(29–2)}$$
$$\Delta y_1 = 3\Delta x_2 \quad \text{and} \quad \Delta y_2 = 5\Delta x_2.$$

The equations above are multipliers, although written somewhat differently than usual. For example, the x_2 multiplier on y_1 is 3. Both x_1 and x_2 have positive effects on y_1 and y_2, and society wants both y_1 and y_2 to increase. Given this, one's "gut" reaction is that both policy tools should increase. However, neither policy tool can accomplish both goals simultaneously. Looking at Equations (29–1) and (29–2), x_1 has the same effect on goals y_1 and y_2, but society wants the change in y_2 to be twice the change y_1. If $\Delta x_1 = 3$ so $\Delta y_1 = 3$ and the first goal is satisfied, then $\Delta y_2 = 3$, which is only 50 percent of Δy_2^d. A unitary increase in x_2 fulfills the y_1 goal but leaves the y_2 goal a unit short; $\Delta y_2 = 5$ instead of 6. The tool x_2 does come close to achieving both goals, but close is not good enough. It appears both x_1 and x_2 should increase. How much should the two tools be increased in order to fulfill the goals exactly?

The reader has been given a difficult *technical* problem. However, we have assumed the even more difficult *political* and *economic* problems were solved. The political problem is the achievement of a consensus on specific goals given here by Equation (29–1). For example, everyone favors full employment but what specifically is full employment? Is it 4 percent unemployment, 6 percent, or some other number? Policies proposed when unemployment is, say, 5 percent clearly depend on one's estimate of full employment. A consensus on many economic policies is difficult because they are zero sum games, that is, the benefits to our group or in one area are offset by equal losses elsewhere. After a consensus finally has been reached the effect of the instruments on the goals must be ascertained. Economists spend a lifetime estimating imperfectly the type of information assumed to be known with certainty in Equation (29–2). Having been given the outcome of the political process, Equation (29–1), and of economic investigations, Equation (29–2), the technician sets the dials at appropriate levels.

What answer did you get? By how much must x_1 and x_2 change to achieve the goal? The answer is the solution to the equations

$$3 = \Delta x_1 + 3\Delta x_2 \qquad \textbf{(29–3)}$$
$$6 = \Delta x_1 + 5\Delta x_2$$

Equations (29–3) are derived from Equations (29–1) and (29–2). The goal or desired change, the left-hand side of (29–3), is set equal to the sum of the changes due to x_1 and x_2, the right-hand side. Solving Equation (29–3),

$$\Delta x_1 = -1.5 \quad \text{and} \quad \Delta x_2 = 1.5$$

When one looks in isolation at the policymaker responsible for x_1, he appears to be doing the wrong thing. One wants variables y_1 and y_2 to increase, and x_1 causes both variables to increase. Yet the policymaker decreases x_1. Policymaker x_1 is acting correctly, however. Simultaneous achievement of the goals requires reducing x_1. Policymakers should not be judged in isolation.

Policy Uncertainty

The estimates of the government spending and money multipliers are numerous and diverse. No policymaker should assume that he has a pipeline to the Truth making his estimates perfectly accurate. Even if there were a single goal, the use of both monetary and fiscal policy is desirable because the effects of policy are uncertain.[10] The joint use of monetary and fiscal policy does not guarantee the goal will be fulfilled, but it does reduce the likelihood of large errors. Consider the following example. Suppose the goal is to increase y by 8 so that $\Delta y^d = 8$. For simplicity, assume the relationships between the goal and two tools, x_1 and x_2, are similar. The expected x_1 and x_2 multipliers are 4 but the actual values in each case are uncertain. The probabilities are one third that the x_1 and x_2 multipliers will be 2, 4, or 6. Mathematically,

$$E(\Delta y/\Delta x_1) = E(\Delta y/\Delta x_2) = 4$$

$$Pr(\Delta y/\Delta x_1 = 2) = Pr(\Delta y/\Delta x_1 = 4) = Pr(\Delta y/\Delta x_1 = 6) = 1/3$$

$$Pr(\Delta y/\Delta x_2 = 2) = Pr(\Delta y/\Delta x_2 = 4) = Pr(\Delta y/\Delta x_2 = 6) = 1/3$$

If *either* x_1 or x_2 is used, the policymakers increase the tool by 2 units so the expected change in y equals the desired change. The probabilities are one third the actual change may be either 4, 8, or 12.

$$\text{Given } \Delta x_1 \textit{ or } \Delta x_2 = 2, \quad E(\Delta y) = 8, \text{ and}$$
$$Pr(\Delta y = 4) = Pr(\Delta y = 8) = Pr(\Delta y = 12) = 1/3 \tag{29–4}$$

---

[10]The uncertainty considered here differs from the uncertainty present in the analysis of the money supply versus interest rate controversy. The earlier uncertainty was about the state of the economy as represented by aggregate expenditures and money demand. The uncertainty currently considered deals with the effects of policy. In terms of the IS–LM curve, we previously were uncertain about the position of the IS and LM curves. We now consider uncertainty regarding the magnitude of the shifts of the curves in response to government spending and monetary policy.

Now assume the policymakers increase *both* x_1 *and* x_2 by one unit so the expected change also equals 8.

(29–5)

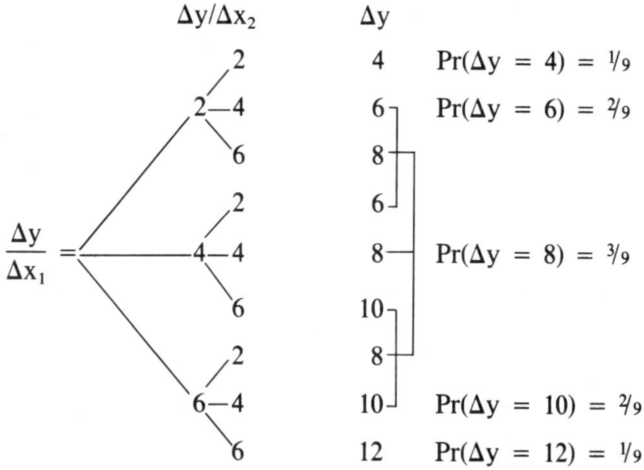

Regardless of the value of $\Delta y/\Delta x_1$, each of the three possible values of $\Delta y/\Delta x_2$ is assumed equally likely.[11] The probability that $\Delta y = 4$ is $1/3$ when either x_1 or x_2 is employed. When both policies are used, the probability that $\Delta y = 4$ is reduced to $1/9$, where the latter is the product of the equal $1/3$ probabilities that $\Delta y/\Delta x_1 = 2$ and $\Delta y/\Delta x_2 = 2$. A comparison of Equations (29–4) and (29–5) shows that reliance on both policies instead of one alone reduces the likelihood of large errors and the variability of the goal.

While probably not immediately apparent, Equations (29–4) and (29–5) are another illustration of the advantages of portfolio diversification. The policy tools correspond with assets in this case. Neither an investor nor a policymaker in an uncertain world should place all his eggs in one basket. The use of both policies spreads the risk and minimizes the likelihood of unfavorable outcomes.

Characteristics of Effective Policy

What are the criteria for evaluating policy effectiveness? What characteristics must a policy instrument, monetary or otherwise, possess in order to be efficient? The characteristic most often listed first by others and implicitly stressed by us so far is the size of the GNP multiplier, or, more generally, the average impact of the instrument on the goal. While a large

[11]Our assumption that policies x_1 and x_2 are independent simplifies the analysis but is not crucial. The use of both policies reduces variability provided the policies are not perfectly positively correlated.

multiplier is not always desirable, *the effectiveness of a policy generally is positively related to its multiplier*. Why is policy effectiveness positively related to its multiplier? Clearly, policy is totally worthless if the multiplier is zero. Provided the multiplier is positive, however small, it is less clear that a large multiplier enhances the policy's effectiveness. Suppose the money multiplier equals 50 in economy A and 2 in economy B, and income is $100 below the full-employment level in both economies. Is monetary policy more effective in economy A? In economies A and B the monetary authorities would increase the money supply by $2 and $50, respectively, and achieve the goal. Why is policy more effective in A because the money supply must increase by only $2 instead of $50? Monetary expansion during any time period may be constrained for various reasons. *The existence of constraints on policy changes implies that a large multiplier enhances policy effectiveness*. In our example, if the constraint limiting the money supply change were $30, the goal could be achieved in economy A but not in economy B.

The Resource Cost and Direct Benefits of Monetary and Fiscal Policy

Any policy uses resources. Because of this fact, the size of the multiplier is an important criterion of policy effectiveness. Policies differ in the amount of resources used. Any type of spending, private or government, uses resources equal to the amount spent. In contrast to the dollar-for-dollar relationship between government spending and resource cost, there is virtually no resource cost to tax and monetary policy. The resource cost of tax policy includes the time spent in reaching a consensus on the specific tax provisions, the cost of printing new forms, the time spent by taxpayers familiarizing themselves with new tax laws, and so on. These costs typically are a small percentage of tax receipts. Similarly, the annual cost of monetary changes is small and may be ignored as a first approximation.[12] Additional government spending next year is much more costly in terms of resources than equal tax cuts or monetary in-

---

[12]We are not contradicting our earlier assertion that currency is fiat money but checkable deposits are full-bodied money. The present value of the cost of checkable deposits maintained forever equals the amount of the deposits. However, the text here considers the annual cost of deposits. Annual banking costs and revenues are a small fraction of their assets and deposits.

Money and government spending have different dimensions; the former is a stock while the latter is a flow. This makes a meaningful comparison of costs difficult. The dollar-for-dollar relationship between government spending and resource cost is independent of the time period. For example, whether the government spends $1 during a calendar quarter or decelerates its spending rate to spend the same amount during a year, resources worth $1 are used. On the other hand, the cost of maintaining money in existence clearly depends on the time period. The cost of a larger money supply for a calendar quarter is one fourth the cost of a larger money supply for a full year. Should we compare $1 government spending with the cost of maintaining an additional dollar in circulation for a quarter, a year, or

creases. Government spending, however, also yields society *direct* benefits. Society values the police and fire protection, schools, roads, and other goods and services provided by government. The *direct* benefits of tax and monetary policy are small and, like their cost, may be ignored. The benefits from tax cuts are derived from the additional commodity and asset purchases made possible, and not from the tax cut per se.

What are the implications for stabilization policy of the different resource costs and benefits of the various policies? In an ideal world, government spending would *not* be used for stabilization purposes, so fiscal policy would be limited to tax policy. Stabilization policy would rely on monetary policy or tax policy exclusively, if attempted at all. Government would spend for allocation purposes exclusively, that is, in order to provide society with goods that the private sector cannot produce, for example, defense. Resources are allocated correctly when the marginal benefit of government spending equals marginal cost. In an ideal world, government spending programs would be expanded to the point where the benefit from an additional dollar spent equals unity, which is the marginal resource cost. Once the appropriate allocation of resources and goods and services between the private and government sectors has been determined, the government selects that monetary and tax policy combination which will pay for its expenditures and promote full employment with price stability. If aggregate expenditures fall and discretionary policy is advisable, the government should cut taxes or increase the quantity of money in order to stabilize the economy. The benefits from expanding government spending beyond the current *optimum* do not justify the cost, by definition. While this argument appears to be a powerful weapon for opponents of government spending, the sword cuts both ways. Government programs which have been selected appropriately must not be cut during inflationary periods. We must not let national defense and our schools deteriorate during inflation, just as we must recognize the folly of a public works project to build pyramids when we and our neighbors are unemployed.[13]

The Direct Benefits and Effectiveness of Government Spending

We do not and will not live in an ideal world. Countercyclical government spending has been and will continue to be employed. Considering

---

forever? While a full answer is beyond the scope of this book, the answer depends in part on the goal and the time pattern and ultimate size of the multiplier between policy and goal. By comparing annual costs, we are implicitly assuming that within a year money and government spending have roughly the same effect on income, which is the goal and has the dimension of a flow.

[13]Technically speaking, the opportunity cost of government spending is zero only if unemployment exists *and* it cannot be reduced by monetary or tax policy.

the cost and benefits of government spending, is a large or small government spending multiplier desirable? The answer clearly depends on how one evaluates government spending, but the precise relationship between one's evaluation of government spending and the size of the multiplier of effective policy is contrary to the initial reaction of many. Because tastes and opinions differ, government is spending the correct amount and *aggregate* marginal benefits equal cost even though some believe government is wasteful and others denounce it for penny pinching. *Government spending is considered effective when the size of the multiplier is negatively related to one's evaluation of the benefits from government spending.*[14] For those who believe that the direct benefits of government programs are small and spending is at a point where marginal benefits are far below costs, a *large* multiplier enhances the effectiveness of government spending because the resource cost of achieving full employment is low. For example, if income is $100 below full employment and government builds pyramids or otherwise spends foolishly to lift the economy out of a recession, government would waste and the private sector would forego $10 if the multiplier were 10. Government waste rises to $50 if the multiplier were 2. On the other hand, if your analysis of the data indicates the government spending multiplier is small and you consider government spending beneficial, then you should grade government spending highly. In this case the government can provide society with parks, clean air, and other worthwhile products because the private sector's respending propensity and the multiplier are small, which is all to the good because the private sector would have acquired electric toothbrushes, gas guzzlers, and other silly products.

Although there is no logical connection between one's evaluation of the benefits of government spending and one's empirical estimate of the government spending multiplier, the two are *positively* related. Conservatives like Professor Milton Friedman believe much government spending is wasteful, and the government spending multiplier is small. Liberals like Professor John Kenneth Galbraith believe the benefits of government spending far outweigh the cost, and the government spending multiplier is large. Therefore, both conservatives and liberals believe that government spending is inefficient, at least in its resource effects. Everyone feels frustrated by government spending. Conservatives who oppose government spending would like the government multiplier to be large so that only a little "wasteful" spending would push the economy to full employment. The desired and estimated values of the multiplier do not coincide. While conservatives would like a large government spending

[14]We are implicitly assuming the economy is more prone to recessions than overemployment.

multiplier, they estimate the multiplier to be small. Precisely because it is small, we must tolerate significant government waste in our quest for economic stability. On the other hand, liberals who support government spending would like the government multiplier to be small so that we could reap substantial benefits from government spending before being constrained by full employment. The desired and estimated values of the multiplier do not coincide. Liberals would like a small government spending multiplier, but their estimates indicate it is large. Precisely because it is large, we must forsake significant government benefits in our quest for economic stability.

The big-bang-for-a-buck philosophy was made most explicit by the Defense Department in the 1950s. A weapons system which could cheaply kill all our enemies 100 times over was an efficient system. We prepared for global warfare and discounted local skirmishes. This bang-for-buck philosophy is so deeply enrooted that those whose empirical studies estimate a large government spending multiplier often uncritically allege government spending is effective. A large multiplier definitely enhances policy effectiveness when the maximum policy change is constrained. Reflecting on the resource cost and direct benefit of government spending indicates, however, that a large multiplier enhances policy effectiveness only if one believes that the benefits of government spending are quite small so the amount of low benefit/high cost government programs cannot expand much. Moreover, a large multiplier definitely is undesirable when the policy is uncontrolled. Suppose the money multiplier were one trillion so that extremely small monetary changes would rock the economy from severe depressions to galloping inflations. In this case the danger to livelihoods due to float and other uncontrolled sources of the monetary base would rival the danger to life due to accidental nuclear warfare. If the arguments against a large multiplier are almost as persuasive as the pro arguments, why did we stress the multiplier in earlier chapters? As we shall see shortly, the size of the multiplier is positively associated with most other policy characteristics which unquestionably enhance effectiveness. It is for this reason that the multiplier was stressed in the first pass at difficult problems where some simplification was essential. *The multiplier is not unimportant in its own right but its main importance stems from its positive relationship with other effectiveness characteristics.*

Policy Reliability

In an uncertain, unpredictable world THE multiplier is the AVERAGE multiplier. A policy will not have the same effect at all times; the effect of any policy will be variable. *To be effective and have a high likelihood of attaining the goal, the variability of policy must be small relative to its average effect*. In other words, policy reliability is directly related to its t-ratio, which equals the average multiplier estimate divided by its standard deviation, a measure of variability. Algebraically,

$$\text{Policy reliability (t–ratio)} = \frac{\text{average multiplier estimate}}{\text{standard deviation}}$$

Thus, the bang-for-a-buck or (average) size of multiplier criterion is positively related to a policy's reliability.

Table 29–1 illustrates that deviations from the goal will be small and policy is reliable when the t-ratio is large. The table assumes there are three policy instruments, A, B, and C, none of which has a perfectly predictable multiplier effect on the goal. Each policy yields three equally likely (probability = ⅓) multipliers. For example, one third of the time the multiplier of policy A is 2, one third of the time it is 3, and one third of the time it is 4. The information in the first three rows is summarized by row 4, which shows the average or expected multiplier divided by its standard deviation.[15] Policy B has a larger average multiplier than either policy A or C. The standard deviation of policies A and B are equal and smaller than the variability of policy C. (The range, a more easily computed but inferior measure of variability, also shows that C is more variable than either A or B, which are equally variable.) Therefore, B, A, and C is the ranking of the policies ordered by the t-ratio, a measure of reliability. Assuming the goal variable y is 15 units below the desired

TABLE 29–1

Policy Is Effective When the Variability of the Multiplier Is Small Relative to Its Average Value

	Possible Multiplier Values		
Probability	$\Delta y/\Delta A$	$\Delta y/\Delta B$	$\Delta y/\Delta C$
1/3	2	4	1
1/3	3	5	3
1/3	4	6	5
	t = Average multiplier/variability (standard deviation)		
	$3/\sqrt{2/3}$	$5/\sqrt{2/3}$	$3/\sqrt{8/3}$
	Possible values of Δy given current shortfall of 15		
	ΔA = 5	ΔB = 3	ΔC = 5
1/3	10	12	5
1/3	15	15	15
1/3	20	18	25

[15]See any statistics book for formulas to compute the standard deviation.

value, the last three rows of Table 29–1 indicate the possible outcomes when policy is adjusted to be correct on average. For example, $\Delta A = 5$ because the average A multiplier is 3, and the y shortfall is 15. The rankings ordered by the t-ratios and closeness to the goal of $\Delta y = 15$ coincide. Policy B is most reliable; its average multiplier is large relative to its variability.[16]

A third criterion of policy effectiveness is short time lags, the importance of which was emphasized in the rules versus discretion debate. As a first approximation, the recognition lag is identical for all policies. *Effective policies have short implementation and impact lags.*[17]

Policies often are not coordinated even though coordination is essential to the achievement of multiple goals. When policy is uncoordinated, a policymaker with one instrument cannot attain multiple goals and may not even attempt to achieve the highest ranking goal because of the policy's undesirable side effects on secondary goals. *Effective policy in an uncoordinated environment is free of undesirable side effects.*

The brevity of the last two paragraphs should be not interpreted as indicating that short time lags and the lack of undesirable side effects are relatively unimportant. The brevity is due to their prior analysis.

Summary/Questions

The basic Keynesian model's portrayal of the simplicity of implementing policies that continuously maintain full employment contrasts sharply with reality. Policymakers encounter numerous difficult problems. The first thing any policymaker must do is determine the goals. Precisely what is he or she attempting to accomplish? Monetary and fiscal policymakers have often disagreed on goals. In the 1940s a strong Treasury brought the Fed under its complete control, while in the 1960s the Fed and Treasury acted as coequals when they disagreed and cooperated when they shared common goals.

Cooperation is essential to achieve multiple goals. Cooperation also is essential when the effects of the policies themselves are uncertain. The next chapter illustrates this uncertainty by presenting a small sample of the diverse estimates of the monetary and fiscal policy multipliers. The

---

[16]We are not suggesting that a policymaker should rely on policy B exclusively. A previous section stated that multiple policies should be employed when their effects are uncertain. The greater reliability of B implies the policymaker will prescribe larger doses of B than A and C. The substitution for B of an independent distribution identical to either A or C reduces aggregate reliability.

[17]Sometimes the lengths of the two lags are listed as separate criteria, in which case a short implementation lag is called policy reversibility.

use of multiple policies when uncertainty exists reduces the likelihood of large deviations from the goal, just as a diversified portfolio reduces the likelihood of large losses.

Professor Friedman and most monetarists believe that the variability in the magnitude and timing of monetary policy, in combination with an average lag of one to one and a half years, precludes the effective use of monetary policy as a stabilization tool. No one is questioning the Fed's motives or *relative* ability. Monetarists just claim that effective stabilization policy is beyond the ability of any group and, consequently, a rules policy should be adopted.

1. Distinguish between monetary policy conducted according to (*a*) rules and (*b*) discretion. Contrast the proposed fiscal policy of the advocates of (*a*) rules and (*b*) discretionary policy.
2. According to monetarists, what should the rate of growth of money equal? Why?
3. Explain why monetarists prefer a rules policy.
4. List and define the three lags that occur when using discretionary policy.
5. Carefully justify the rational expectations conclusion that from the viewpoint of output all systematic, predictable policies are equivalent and superior to any unsystematic, discretionary policy.
6. Define the "Lucas critique." What are its implications for the value of empirical work?
7. State some arguments for and against rational expectations.
8. List the three channels or transmission mechanisms of monetary policy. Which channel operates in Keynesian models?
9. What is credit rationing? In what portion of the business cycle is it more prevalent?
10. When does monetary expansion increase society's wealth?
11. What is the basis for the contention that the wealth effect occurs even when the monetary base increases by an open-market purchase?
12. How many instruments are needed to attain a set of goals? Illustrate your answer with an IS–LM graph, given the goal is a lower interest rate and constant income.
13. In an uncertain world, what is the benefit of using both monetary and fiscal policy?
14. If you believe that the benefits of government spending are extremely small, would you prefer a large or a small government spending multiplier? Explain.
15. What are the criteria by which one judges the effectiveness of monetary or fiscal policy?

An empirical summary of the money-income relationship

30

Economic theory does not pin down the monetary and fiscal policy multipliers. It is time we look at the empirical evidence. The evidence is inconclusive largely because two a priori reasonable research strategies yield different results. *One research strategy estimates large-scale structural models, that is, postulates many demand and supply equations and estimates them statistically.* The large-scale econometric models are like our IS–LM, only more complicated. Our IS–LM model has a total of eight equations, six demand and supply equations—consumption, investment, government spending, taxes, money demand, and money supply—and two equilibrium equations—IS and LM. Some large-scale structural models have more than 900 equations. Instead of one consumption equation, there are equations for durables, nondurables, and services, each of which is influenced by somewhat different variables. We might expect the rate of interest to have a greater effect on durables, such as automobiles, than on services. The really large models further disaggregate durables, nondurables, and services. After all the equations are estimated statistically, the model is thrown into a computer to simulate the estimated response of the economy to the autonomous variables, particularly monetary and fiscal policy variables. The computer grinds out predictions based on the many estimated equations and their interaction.

The second research strategy cuts through the thicket of supply and demand equations and gets to the bottom line immediately. *Reduced form models relate income directly to monetary and fiscal policy variables and, occasionally, other exogenous variables such as labor strikes*. The simplicity of reduced form models makes possible their presentation.

$$\Delta Y_t = a_0 + \sum_{i=0}^{n} b_i \Delta M_{t-i} + \sum_{i=0}^{n} c_i \Delta G_{t-i} + \sum_{i=0}^{n} d_i \Delta T_{t-i} \tag{30–1}$$

The reduced form Equation (30–1) relates the change in income in any time period t to current and lagged changes in money, government spending, and taxes.[1] (A 900-equation structural model must for now remain a figment of the imagination.) Equation (30–1) may be viewed as a modified version of Equation (26A–3), which expresses the equilibrium value of income after solving simultaneously the IS–LM equations. The modifications to Equation (26A–3) include (1) expressing the variables as first differences (changes) instead of levels, (2) introducing lagged terms, and (3) dropping the nonpolicy exogenous variables, such as autonomous consumption, in order to focus on the policy variables. (Statistically speaking, the nonpolicy exogenous variables are included in the error term, which makes the R^2 of the estimated equation less than unity.) By not estimating any supply and demand equations, reduced form models make no attempt to answer "how" and "why" questions, but focus exclusively on "what." The builders of reduced form models realize that the policy variables affect many endogenous variables besides income, and that the effect on income may not be direct. Nevertheless, they believe that better answers are acquired by concentrating on one issue—the what question.

There are pros and cons to the two types of models. From a purely methodological and statistical viewpoint, however, there is no reason to believe that either type of model would produce biased estimates of the effects of monetary and fiscal policy. That is, *a theoretical statistician would predict that the two research methodologies yield similar answers*. Why should structural models per se systematically estimate a larger or smaller money multiplier than reduced form models? They should not, yet they do. And largely because they do, we have our two main schools of economists, monetarists and Keynesians.

1. Compared to structural models, reduced form models typically find that monetary policy has a larger multiplier and that fiscal policy has a smaller multiplier. Indeed, some reduced form models find that within a year fiscal policy has no effect on income.
2. Compared to structural models, both monetary and fiscal policy have shorter lags in reduced form models. The full impact of both policies occurs within a year in some reduced form models while structural models have up to four year lags.

---

[1]We encountered a similar equation in Chapter 2. One empirical test of the definition of money selects the money measure that performs best in the equation.

Different Empirical Estimates: A Mystery or Tale of Torture?

The admonition "seek and ye shall find" is nowhere more true than in empirical work. Economists who believed a priori that money matters constructed reduced form models and discovered strong empirical evidence for their position. Similarly, most structural models were estimated by fiscalists whose a priori beliefs were confirmed. A nasty thought inevitably comes to mind: are the different results from the structural and reduced form models a real economic mystery or have some clever people tortured the data until they confessed? The data have been tortured; much experimentation preceded the reported results. This *partially* explains the different results. However, the remaining difference is sufficiently large that we appear to have a real economic mystery.

Before presenting evidence supporting the mystery viewpoint, we must point out that empirical work is not for the squeamish. Empirical studies *must* torture the data to some extent. Empirical studies begin with a hypothesis which is to be confirmed or denied; they do not seek illustrations of known facts. Because empirical studies are *searches* for *possible* explanations that have no natural tendency to reveal themselves, some experimentation is necessary. For example, our hypothesis may state that variables X and Y are related, other things being equal. Empirical studies then attempt to ascertain the type of relationship, if any. Is the relationship linear, quadratic, logarithmic, or yet some other form? Is the relationship between current values alone or should lagged values be included? What are the other things that must be held constant in order to ascertain the relationship between variables X and Y? Even if, by chance, we initially postulate the best answers to these questions, how would we know they were the best unless we subsequently found worse answers? The question is not should we torture the data, but did we torture them enough or too much? Because the data finally confess what we want to hear does not necessarily imply excessive torture. True, seek and ye shall find. We are also exhorted to leave no stone unturned.

There are two main reasons for believing that a mystery exists. First, the single equation reduced form model can be relatively easily examined for signs of excessive torture and, quite predictably, was so examined by Keynesians who found the initial results contrary to their a priori beliefs. The model was tested and retested in order to ascertain whether it satisfied the canons of proper statistical methods and whether the results were sensitive to the calendar time period of the analysis. We shall mention some of the less abstruse statistical arguments shortly. The statistical retesting discovered some contusions but no signs of gross torture. The upshot was a narrowing of the difference between the two types of models. However, no amount of retesting has been able to close the gap fully.

Second, monetarists' preference for reduced form models and Keynesians' preference for large-scale structural models are consistent with their philosophical viewpoint and general outlook about the structure of the economy expressed long *before* any empirical studies. For example, monetarists Henry Simon in 1936 and Milton Friedman in 1953 came out for monetary rules largely because they thought the economy was too complex and uncertain for discretionary policy.[2] When computational and statistical advances made empirical work feasible in the 1960s, in accord with their earlier statements monetarists spurned large scale models because they require more knowledge than available. Empirical studies answer the questions asked; they do not pose questions or make suggestions. No data series has ever whispered, "Hey, bunkie, include me in your explanation of the demand for variable X." Monetarists say that the (incorrect) exclusion of variables due to lack of knowledge makes the estimates of the included variables highly suspect.[3] Keynesians, on the other hand, are more confident about their ability to ask good questions and to include the appropriate variables. Moreover, their perceived need for regulation and intervention in many areas necessitates large scale structural models.

The St. Louis Model*

Milton Friedman and David Meiselman constructed the first reduced form model.[4] Pathfinders in any area rarely have the last word. They are no exception. Numerous critics were quick to point out several flaws in their study which, if corrected, invalidated their conclusion that the results were "strikingly one-sided" in support of monetary policy and against the Keynesian government spending multiplier, and, more generally, any autonomous spending multiplier.[5] Just as the dust was settling, Leonall

---

[2]Henry Simons, "Rules versus Authorities in Monetary Policy," *Journal of Political Economy,* February 1936, pp. 1–30; and Milton Friedman, "The Effects of a Full-Employment Policy on Economic Stability: A Formal Analysis," in *Essays in Positive Economics* (Chicago: University of Chicago Press, 1953), pp. 117–32. Variable (uncertain) lags is one reason for a monetary rule.

[3]Technically speaking, omitted variables lead to biased estimates when they are correlated with the included variables, which is quite likely to be the case with the time series data used by structural models.

*First warning: proceed directly to Chapter 31 if you did not read the Appendix to Chapter 2.

[4]"The Relative Stability of Monetary Velocity and the Investment Multiplier in the United States," in Commission on Money and Credit, *Stabilization Policies* (Englewood Cliffs, N.J.: Prentice-Hall, 1963), pp. 165–268.

[5]Ibid., p. 166. Some of the more important critiques were Donald Hester, "Keynes and the Quantity Theory: A Comment on the Friedman-Meiselman CMC Paper," *Review of Economics and Statistics,* November 1964; Albert Ando and Franco Modigliani, "Velocity and the Investment Multiplier," and Michael de Prano and Thomas Mayer, "Autonomous

Andersen and Jerry Jordan from the St. Louis Federal Reserve Bank published a reduced form equation free of many of the flaws the critics were harping about but which was even more "strikingly one-sided."[6] Andersen then teamed up with his St. Louis colleague Keith Carlson and expanded the reduced form approach to other variables besides income.[7] Equation (30–1) is the St. Louis Fed reduced form equation for nominal GNP. The regression estimate of this equation using quarterly data is presented in Table 30–1. Tax variables initially were included, but the estimated coefficients were very small and statistically insignificant. The lag structure, namely the value of n in Equation (30–1), is an empirical question estimated here to equal 4. GNP this quarter depends on monetary and fiscal policy in the current and four prior calendar quarters and on the unspecified exogenous factors. *The full effect of both policies is felt in 5 quarters*. The numbers *not* in parenthesis across the ΔM row are the estimates of the b_i coefficients for money in Equation (30–1), and similarly for government spending. The numbers in parenthesis are explained shortly.

The dimension of the variables is the change (first difference), so the coefficients are estimates of the money and government spending multipliers.[8] Because regression coefficients show the effect of one variable

TABLE 30–1
Regression Coefficients and t-Values in Parentheses of Quarterly Nominal GNP Changes on Money and Government Spending Changes.*

Lag/time Period	*0/t*	*1/t − 1*	*2/t − 2*	*3/t − 3*	*4/t − 4*	*Sum*
ΔM	1.22	1.80	1.62	0.87	0.06	5.57
	(2.73)	(7.34)	(4.25)	(3.65)	(0.12)	(8.06)
ΔG	0.56	0.45	0.01	−0.43	−0.54	0.05
	(2.57)	(3.43)	(0.08)	(−3.18)	(−2.47)	(0.17)
$R^2 = 0.66$						

*Regression coefficients are impact multipliers.
Source: L. Andersen and K. Carlson, "A Monetarist Model for Economic Stabilization," Federal Reserve Bank of St. Louis *Review*, April 1970, p. 11. The money supply is old M-1, and government spending is measured assuming full employment. The estimate of the constant term is 2.67.

Expenditures and Money," *American Economic Review*, September 1965. Replies by Friedman and Meiselman and rejoinders also appear in the journal cited. One of the main flaws of the Friedman-Meiselman study was the use of *actual* spending and taxes. This reduces the measured impact of fiscal policy due to the "reverse causation" argument, which will be discussed shortly.

[6]"Monetary and Fiscal Actions: A Test of Their Relative Importance in Economic Stabilization," Federal Reserve Bank of St. Louis *Review*, November 1968, pp. 11–24.

[7]L. Andersen and K. Carlson, "A Monetarist Model for Economic Stabilization," Federal Reserve Bank of St. Louis *Review*, April 1970, pp. 7–25.

[8]The estimates in Table 30–1 are based on data from 1953 to 1969. Benjamin Friedman published updated (through 1976) estimates of the St. Louis equation. His conclusion, and the article's title, was "Even the St. Louis Model Now Believes in Fiscal Policy," *Journal*

holding the other variables constant, and because money and taxes (although not shown here) initially were included, the government budget constraint implies that these are estimates of *deficit financed* government spending multipliers. The coefficients are impact or short-run multipliers. For example, the coefficient for ΔM in the middle column says that, other things being equal, the GNP change this quarter is 1.62 times the money change lagged two quarters, or, equivalently, the GNP change two quarters hence equals 1.62 times the current monetary change.

Table 30–2 is derived from Table 30–1 to highlight the *cumulative* (sometimes also called long-run) *multipliers, which equal the sum of the impact multipliers to that date*. For example, suppose the quantity of money increases $1 this quarter, everything else remaining constant. Nominal GNP increases $1.22 the same period and $1.80 the next period, so the cumulative increase by next period is $3.02. An easily remembered *approximation* to Table 30–2 is available. A $1 increase in the quantity of money causes nominal GNP to increase approximately $1.5 this quarter and in each of the two subsequent quarters. *The money multiplier attains its long-run value of approximately 5.50 in a year*. GNP increases by approximately the amount of government spending within six months, remains at the same level for another quarter, and then falls during the next six months. By the end of 15 months GNP virtually reverts to its original value. *Government spending crowds out an almost equal amount of private spending in slightly more than a year. The St. Louis equation*

TABLE 30–2

St. Louis Model's Money and Government Spending Multipliers

Quarters Elapsed	*0*	*1*	*2*	*3*	*4*	*5+*
Money multiplier:						
Impact	1.22	1.80	1.62	0.87	0.06	0.00
Cumulative	1.22	3.02	4.64	5.51	5.57	5.57
Government multiplier:						
Impact	0.56	0.45	0.01	−0.43	−0.54	0.00
Cumulative	0.56	1.01	1.02	0.59	0.05	0.05

of Money, Credit, and Banking, May 1977, pp. 365–67. The long-run government spending multiplier is approximately 1.5 according to Benjamin Friedman. However, extension of the sample period makes the first difference form violate the least squares assumption of homoscedasticity. When all variables are expressed in their percentage change instead of change (first difference) so that the estimated coefficients are elasticities instead of multipliers, the least squares assumption of homoscedasticity seems to be satisfied, and the estimates are very similar to those presented in Table 30–1. (See Keith Carlson, "Does the St. Louis Equation Now Believe in Fiscal Policy?" Federal Reserve Bank of St. Louis *Review,* February 1978, pp. 13–19.) Because the "old" results created such a stir when first published, and because multipliers are much more commonly used than elasticities, we present the old results instead of the equivalent new results.

says that government spending changes the composition of output but not the total.

The last chapter stated that magnitude or multiplier effects per se are not the be all and end all of policy. Which policy is more predictable and reliable? Reliability is measured by the t values shown in parentheses. (Recall that the t value is the ratio of the regression coefficient [average measure] to its standard deviation [variability measure].) Except for the fourth quarter after the monetary expansion, at which time an equilibrium has been reached for all practical purposes, Table 30–1 indicates that quarter-by-quarter monetary policy is more reliable than fiscal policy. The difference in the reliability of the two policies is most dramatic when viewed over the entire year. See the t-ratios for the column labeled Sum in Table 30–1. In summary, the St. Louis equation finds that, relative to fiscal policy, monetary policy is much (1) stronger, (2) faster, and (3) more reliable.[9]

Large-Scale Structural Models

Some of the better known large-scale structural models and the number of their equations are: BEA (Bureau of Economic Analysis), 346; DRI (Data Resource, Inc.), 1,009; Wharton, 937; and MPS (MIT-Penn-Social Science Research Council, which formerly was called the Fed-MIT-Penn model). [10] Figures 30–1 and 30–2 show the cumulative or long-run money and government spending multipliers, respectively, given by these large scale models and, for comparison purposes, by the St. Louis model.[11] While in their more conciliatory moments Keynesians claim that everyone now believes that "money matters," surely the builders and users of the BEA model must be nonbelievers. According to the BEA model, money affects *neither* prices *nor* output since nominal GNP multipliers are being estimated. The BEA model says there *is* a liquidity trap.

---

[9]The St. Louis equation only measures the impact lag. However, everyone agrees that the implementation lag is much shorter for monetary policy.

[10]Harry Kelegian and Bruce Vavrichek, "An Evaluation of the Forecasting Properties of Macro Economic Models, with Special Emphasis on Model Size," in Jan Kmenta and James Ramsey, eds., *Large-Scale Macro-economic Models* (Amsterdam: North Holland, 1981). The numbers, which include the exogenous variables, are only meant to be suggestive. These models are revised relatively frequently.

[11]Gary Fromm and Lawrence R. Klein, "The NBER/NSF Model Comparison Seminar: An Analysis of Results," in *Econometric Model Performance: Comparative Simulation Studies of the U.S. Economy,* ed. L. Klein and E. Burmeister (Philadelphia: University of Pennsylvania Press, 1976), pp. 402, 405. Except for the St. Louis multiplier, the results presented on their p. 405 are unborrowed reserves multipliers. Money is an endogenous variable in the large scale models. For comparability, the cumulative unborrowed reserve multipliers for each period have been multiplied by 0.135, the ratio of unborrowed reserves to the money supply in 1970. While the adjustment factor could be allowed to vary over time due to lags in the money supply response to Fed action, the fundamental patterns in Figures 30–1 and 30–2 are unaltered by such refinements.

FIGURE 30–1
Cumulative Nominal GNP/Money Multipliers Predicted by Various Models, by Quarters Elapsed from Date on Monetary Change

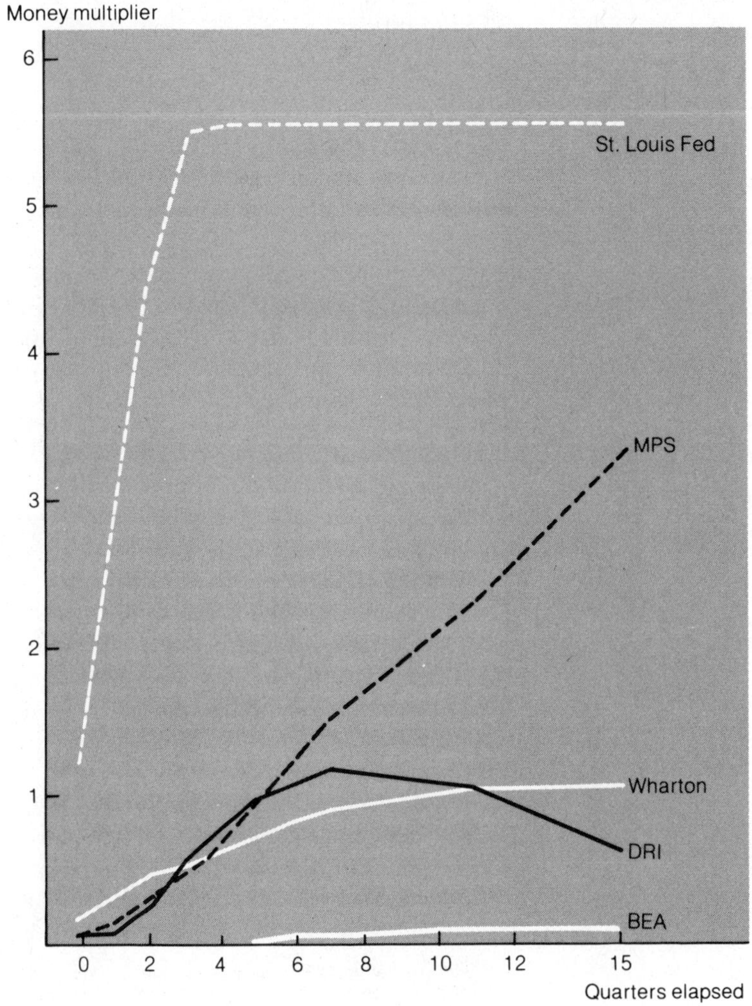

Source: Gary Fromm and Lawrence Klein, "The NBER/NSF Model Comparison Seminar: An Analysis of Results," in *Econometric Model Performance: Comparative Simulation Studies of the U.S. Economy*, ed. L. Klein and E. Burmeister (Philadelphia: University of Pennsylvania Press, 1976), p. 405. All results except St. Louis' have been multiplied by 0.135 to convert unborrowed reserves to money. The St. Louis estimates are from L. Andersen and K. Carlson, "A 'Monetarist Model' for Economic Stabilization," Federal Reserve Bank of St. Louis *Review*, April 1970. See our Table 30–2.

The DRI, MPS, and Wharton model estimates of the one-year cumulative money multiplier are a remarkably similar 0.5, and the two-year cumulative multipliers are about 1.25. At this point the three models part company. Monetary policy is gaining steam according to the MPS and Wharton models. However, the DRI model says monetary policy is pe-

FIGURE 30–2
Cumulative Nominal GNP/Government Spending Multipliers Predicted by Various Models, by Quarters Elapsed from Date of Spending Change

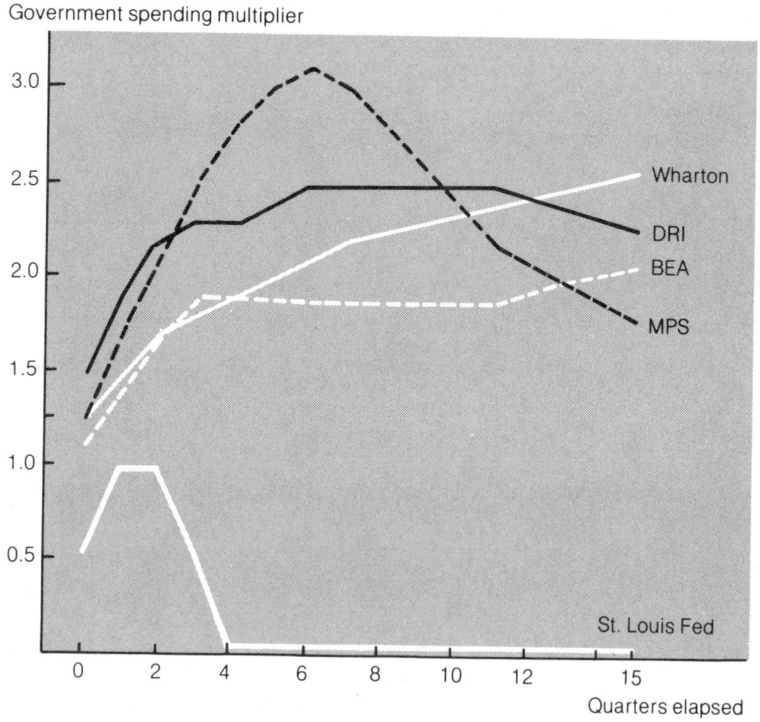

Source: Gary Fromm and Lawrence Klein, "The NBER/NSF Model Comparison Seminar: An Analysis of Results," in *Econometric Model Performance: Comparative Simulation Studies of the U.S. Economy*, ed. L. Klein and E. Burmeister (Philadelphia: University of Pennsylvania Press, 1976), p. 402. The St. Louis estimates are from our Table 30–2.

tering out, with the nominal GNP/money multiplier falling to approximately two thirds. The money multiplier in the MPS model climbs to approximately 3.5 at the end of four years.[12] The Wharton money multiplier gains steam so slowly that it still is hovering somewhat above unity at the end of four years. Given the difficulty of knowing even the direction, expansionary or contractionary, of appropriate policy a year hence, much less four years hence, the model builders—who have time for little else—and the users— who pay significant sums for the models' forecasts—might believe that money matters but, if so, money matters *very* little indeed to them.

The structural model estimates of fiscal policy are somewhat more uniform. First, the contemporaneous government spending multiplier of

[12]Figure 30–1 does not show multipliers beyond four years. However, we should note that given a sufficiently long time, the MPS money multiplier rivals St. Louis's. The five-year forward MPS multiplier is nearly five.

all the structural models is marginally greater than unity. Firms fully meet the government's demand in the quarter, and some spending is induced. In contrast, the St. Louis model says that within the initial quarter firms partially meet government spending out of inventories and expand somewhat—the contemporaneous government spending multiplier is positive but less than 1.0. Second, structural models estimate the government spending multiplier is approximately 2 at the end of the year. Third, the government spending multiplier beyond a year wanders more or less aimlessly, with the average estimate remaining at approximately 2 after four years. Even the structural models claim that the early Keynesian textbook examples of a marginal propensity to consume out of GNP of 0.75 and government spending multiplier of 4.0 are way too high.

One of the main problems of large-scale models is their failure to yield estimates of policy reliability. After all the equations are estimated statistically, multipliers are calculated by changing a policy variable and throwing the model into a computer, which calculates the predictions based on *all* the estimated equations *and* their interaction. Because monetary and fiscal policy interact with so many other variables that then influence GNP, measures of the standard deviation of the multipliers are meaningless.[13] Without a measure of variability, t-values or other measures of policy reliability cannot be constructed.

A Reconciliation of Structural and Reduced Form Results**

Empirical studies of the demand for money, which we shall not present, unanimously (Friedman notwithstanding) confirm that the demand for money does depend on the rate of interest. At the same time, the studies show that the demand for money is not very sensitive to the rate of interest. More important, there is virtually no evidence that the demand for money becomes more elastic at lower rates of interest and eventually approaches a liquidity trap.[14] The empirical money demand studies in conjunction with the advanced Keynesian IS–LM model, which remains the most popular theoretical model, imply that *the St. Louis estimates of the government spending multiplier and the structural model estimates*

---

[13]Standard deviations could be computed but they would be so large that every t-ratio would be insignificant, and comparisons of policy reliability would be meaningless.

**Second warning: proceed directly to Chapter 31 if you do not have a strong statistical background.

[14]For an excellent summary of the empirical money literature, see chapters 6–8 of David Laidler, *The Demand for Money: Theories and Evidence,* 2nd ed. (New York: Dun-Donnelly, 1977). Goldfeld apparently also was thoroughly convinced that there is no liquidity trap. He methodically analyzed every unsettled issue about money demand in 1973 and 1976 and did not explore the possibility of a trap. Stephen Goldfeld, "The Demand for Money Revisited," *Brookings Papers on Economic Activity* 3(1973): 577–638, and "The Case of the Missing Money," *Brookings Papers on Economic Activity* 3(1976): 683–730.

of the money multiplier are implausibly low. How can one reconcile the empirical money demand and multiplier estimates?

Before attempting such a reconciliation, let us convince any doubting Thomases that a reconciliation is necessary. The easier case is the inconsistency of an interest sensitive money demand and a virtually zero government spending multiplier. Government spending, like any other spending financed by bond sales, drives up interest rates. When higher interest rates reduce the amount of money demanded, the same money stock can finance more transactions and a higher GNP. The government spending multiplier should be positive. In terms of IS–LM curves, when the demand for money depends on interest rates, the LM curve is positively sloped, and not vertical. An increase in government purchases, which shifts the IS curve outward, produces a higher output.

Now consider why the typical structural model estimate of a 1.25 money multiplier after two years is implausibly low. Velocity, being the ratio of nominal GNP to money, measures the rate at which *average* money balances are spent. It equaled 4.56 in 1970. The money multiplier, being the ratio of nominal GNP changes to money changes, measures the rate at which *marginal* money balances are spent. *Actual* velocity and the structural model *estimates* of the multiplier imply that money is becoming less productive in terms of expenditures, that is, the marginal product of money is less than the average product. How would a declining productivity of money be reflected in its demand? The demand for money must exhibit either (1) diseconomies of scale, or (2) a liquidity preference curve which becomes much more elastic at low interest rates, so that larger proportions of money end up as idle speculative balances. Diseconomies of scale mean that (transactions) money demand increases more than proportionally with expenditures, which would be necessary if money is becoming less productive. Alternatively, a liquidity trap must be close at hand for velocity to greatly exceed the multiplier. In a liquidity trap the multiplier is zero, by definition, but velocity is positive—some output is produced even in a great depression. Empirical money demand studies confirm neither of these two conditions. *The demand for money exhibits neither diseconomies of scale nor increasing interest elasticity at low rates.*[15]

The St. Louis Fed says its fiscal policy multiplier estimates are consistent with an interest elastic money demand provided the IS–LM frame-

---

[15]Again, Friedman notwithstanding. Friedman's finding that money is a luxury, that is, the "income" elasticity of money demand exceeds unity, does imply that long-run marginal velocity is less than the average. However, because his income measure is permanent income, which changes by a fraction of nominal income changes in the short run when permanent and nominal incomes do not coincide, marginal velocity can exceed the average. The St. Louis money multiplier estimate is consistent with constant or slightly increasing economies of scale, which is the result most money demand studies find. Milton Friedman, "The Demand for Money: Some Theoretical and Empirical Results," *Journal of Political Economy,* June 1959, pp. 327–51.

work is expanded to include (1) interest rate induced wealth effects, and (2) portfolio diversification effects. Because higher interest rates reduce common stock values, which along with other components of wealth influence consumption positively, the higher interest rates produced by government expenditures curtail consumption in addition to investment. Moreover, a *permanent* increase in government spending necessitates a *perpetual* stream of government bonds. This causes a portfolio imbalance. To diversify portfolios, the demand for money increases at any given interest rate.[16] In terms of the IS–LM graph, additional government spending shifts the IS outward, but recognition of portfolio diversification effects means that the LM will continually shift inward. The increased demand for money and inward LM shift curtails GNP considerably because the IS curve is relatively flat due to the interest rate induced wealth effect.

Surprisingly, advocates of large-scale models have not attempted to reconcile their typical money multiplier estimates and empirical money demand studies. Instead, they have focused on the so-called reverse causation argument, which says that money and GNP are related because GNP changes cause monetary changes, the reverse of the causation pattern normally alleged. There certainly is an element of truth to the reverse causation argument. We saw in Chapter 19 that the Fed often attempts to stabilize interest rates. When an autonomous increase in demand raises GNP and interest rates, the Fed must expand the money supply to moderate the interest rate rise. If reduced form models for the postwar United States were the sole evidence for a money/income relationship, then the reverse causation argument would carry great weight. However, there is strong evidence of a money/income relationship long before the Fed existed and in many other countries.

The reverse causation argument can be extended. If the significant statistical relationship between money and income does not necessarily mean that money influences GNP, then the insignificant statistical relationship between fiscal policy and GNP is consistent with fiscal policy influencing GNP. For example, suppose firms' "animal spirits" are low, and investment and GNP tend to fall. Suppose further that fiscal policy becomes expansionary and *does* counteract the exogenous change in demand. GNP and fiscal policy would be statistically unrelated. GNP would be constant period after period while fiscal policy would be extremely variable. However, in this case it would be wrong to conclude that the lack of statistical relationship means that fiscal policy is impotent. GNP

---

[16]We are not attributing the higher money demand to a wealth effect because monetarists argue that government bonds, like private bonds, are not net wealth because society capitalizes completely the future tax liabilities generated by the required bond interest payments. Moreover, attributing wealth effects to government bonds would cut both ways; it would increase money demand and consumption. We previously argued that government bonds are partially ($0<k<1$)net wealth.

remains constant only because fiscal policy does influence it and compensates for the exogenous factors. *The paradox is: the better a policy stabilizes the economy by counteracting the effect of exogenous factors, the more worthless the policy appears statistically.* While this may explain to some extent the small fiscal policy coefficient in the reduced form models, it cannot be the whole explanation. The implementation lag of fiscal policy is just too long for one seriously to believe that it offsets a major amount of exogenous GNP variations. Moreover, this extension of the reverse causation argument also suggests that the monetary coefficients could be too low. After 1951, which precedes the starting date for all the models, the Fed pegged interest rates only in the short run. Interest rates do rise, albeit with some lag, in an expansion, and monetary policy is countercyclical.

Prediction Errors

Let us take another tack to the question: which model gives the best multiplier estimates? There simply is no definitive answer. Nevertheless, the model's *overall predictive performance* in the post-model-building period provides one *tentative* answer.[17] We shall accept the multiplier estimates of the model which best predicts income. For example, suppose a model is estimated in late 1975. Beginning with the first quarter of 1976, the actual values of exogenous variables and the actual initial values of lagged endogenous variables are substituted in the model, which is run forward to predict nominal GNP one, two, three, or more quarters in the future. The process is repeated for the second quarter of 1976, and so on. Figure 30–3 shows the prediction errors by the number of quarters ahead forecasted.[18] Errors for the DRI and MPS models could not be computed. The figure indicates that bigger does not necessarily mean better. The BEA and Wharton forecasts one quarter ahead were significantly more accurate than the St. Louis forecast. The errors of the large-scale models were approximately only 50 percent the initial St. Louis error. However, the forecasts of the large models, particularly the Wharton model, deteriorate badly as the forecast period lengthens. The five quarter ahead forecast errors of the BEA and Wharton models were approximately two and three times, respectively, as large as the St. Louis error. On balance,

[17]"Testing a model by means of a test period that occurs after the model was built is the only way to discriminate between the (inferior) models that have been chosen to fit primarily the random and non-enduring features of the premodel-building data, and the (superior) models that have been chosen to fit primarily the systematic and enduring features of the economy." (Carl Christ, "Judging the Performance of Econometric Models of the U.S. Economy," in Klein and Burmeister, *Econometric Model Performance,* p. 324). Parenthesis in original.

[18]Error here refers to the root mean square error of the dynamic simulation.

FIGURE 30–3

Nominal GNP Prediction Errors of Various Models, by Number of Quarters Ahead Forecasted

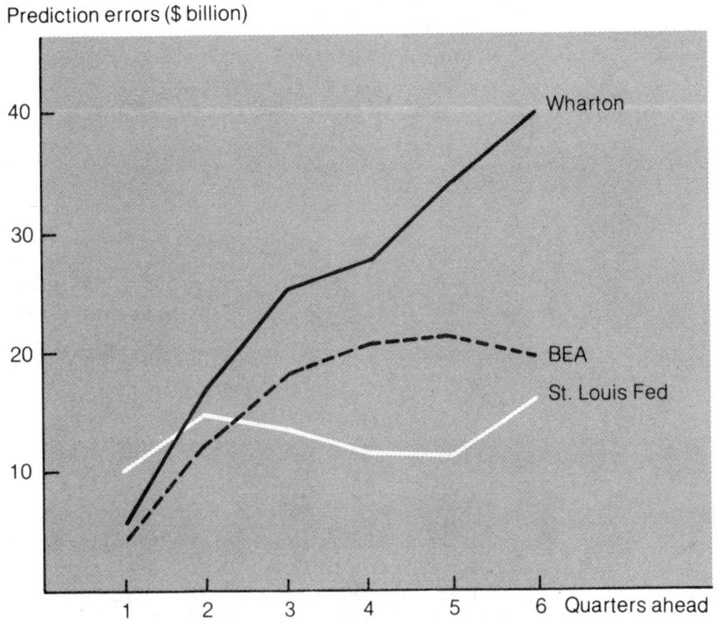

Source: Gary Fromm and Lawrence Klein, "The NBER/NSF Model Comparison Seminar: An Analysis of Results," in *Econometric Performance: Comparative Simulation Studies of the U.S. Economy,* ed. L. Klein and E. Burmeister (Philadelphia: University of Pennsylvania Press, 1976), p. 387. Prediction errors are the root mean square error.

the St. Louis model is the qualified winner in the nominal GNP forecasting sweepstakes. If for no other reason, the qualification is necessary because relative prediction errors may well depend on the forecast period.[19] The St. Louis model could predict accurately five years ago and inaccurately today. Even if there were unqualified proof that the St. Louis model always was the overall best forecasting model, the model's multiplier estimates need not be the most accurate. GNP could be forecasted accurately because overestimates of the effects of one policy are being compensated

[19]This indeed seems to be the case. The errors shown in Figure 30–3 generally are for the late 1960s and early 1970s. The paper by Kelejian and Vavrichek, "An Evaluation of the Forecasting Performance of Macro Economic Models," shows that between 1976 and mid 1978 the prediction errors of the St. Louis Fed model approximately equaled the average error of seven large scale models. Among the large scale models, bigger is not necessarily better. Kelejian and Vavrichek recognize that the sample number of predictions for any one model was quite small, which makes their conclusions tentative. One effect of the small sample size is a decidedly nonmonotonic relationship between forecast errors and the length of the forecast period. The theoretical section of their paper illustrates that superior forecasting does not necessarily imply superior structural specification. Model validation and forecasting performance are separable issues.

by underestimates of another policy. While we may never know the size of the money multiplier, the St. Louis estimate at least deserves serious consideration.

Sectoral Detail in the MPS Model

Let us make some use of the main benefit provided by large models and take a quick glance at sectoral detail. We scrutinize only the MPS (MIT-Penn-Social Science Research Council) model because it develops the financial sector more fully than the other large models do. The MPS model includes the three channels of monetary policy mentioned in Chapter 29: (1) interest rate (per se) effect, (2) wealth effect induced by interest rates, and (3) credit rationing.[20] Figure 30–4 and Table 30–3 show the *direct* effect, by channel, on four major aggregate demand components of a $1 billion increase in unborrowed reserves. Direct effect here means that induced spending/multiplier repercussions and feedbacks from GNP to the financial sector are purposely not measured. Figure 30–4 shows that interest rates (per se) have a minor effect on consumption, mainly through automobile purchases and other durables. However, about 40 percent of the impact of monetary policy occurs through interest rate induced wealth effects on consumption. Monetary policy influences interest rates, which influence stock prices, which in turn influence consumption. Assigning a separate channel to this indirect interest rate effect emphasizes its strength and indirectly castigates those who neglected it for many years.

Table 30–3 shows that while housing contributes nearly half of the early impact of monetary policy, its importance gradually declines over time. This pattern is attributed largely to the rationing channel and to the more rapid effect of interest rates on housing than on plant and equipment. In periods immediately following the policy change, market interest rates fall relative to the sluggish deposit rates of financial intermediaries. Deposit flows are stimulated, and financial intermediaries awash with deposits reduce credit rationing. As time goes on, the normal relation between market and deposit rates and between mortgage rates and other loan terms are restored. As this happens, the rationing effect diminishes. In fact, by the end of four years the rationing effect changes direction. The delayed increase in demand by the other sectors puts pressure on the direct finance market, reduces deposit flows, and increases credit rationing. This reduces housing construction. The more rapid effect of interest rates on housing than plant and equipment may be explained by the shorter construction

---

[20]The (direct) interest rate effect usually is called the cost of capital effect. The latter may be viewed as a refined version of the former made necessary by "real world" complications, primarily taxes, investment tax credit, depreciation, relative price changes, and inflation.

FIGURE 30–4

Direct Effect on Final Demand of a $1 Billion Increase in Unborrowed Reserves

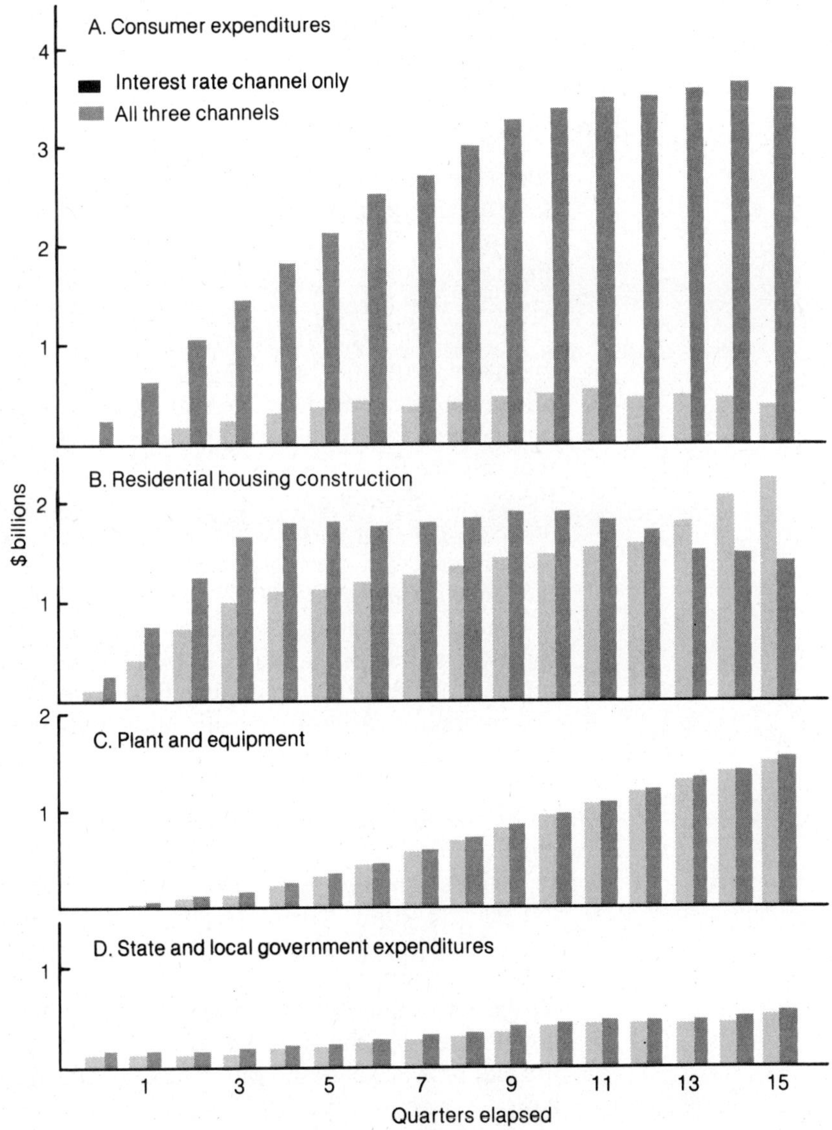

Source: Frank deLeeuw and Edward Gramlich, "The Channels of Monetary Policy," Federal Reserve *Bulletin*, June 1969.

TABLE 30–3
MPS Model Percentages of Total Direct Effect of Monetary Policy on GNP, by Sectors, Policy Channel, and Calendar Quarters after Policy Implementation

	Consumption Expenditure			*Investment*			
				Housing Construction			*Plant and Equipment,*
Quarter	*Interest Rate*	*Wealth*	*Total*	*Interest Rate*	*Credit Rationing*	*Total*	*Interest Rate*
4	8.6	34.3	42.9	28.6	17.1	45.7	5.7
8	7.4	42.6	50.0	24.1	9.3	33.4	11.1
12	7.4	44.1	51.5	22.1	4.4	26.5	16.2
16	5.7	45.7	51.4	31.4	−11.4	20.0	21.4

	Local Government, Interest Rate	*Total*			
Quarter		*Interest Rate*	*Wealth*	*Credit Rationing*	*Total**
4	5.7	48.6	34.3	17.1	100.0
8	5.6	48.2	42.6	9.3	100.0
12	5.8	51.5	44.1	4.4	100.0
16	7.1	65.6	45.7	−11.4	100.0

*May not sum due to rounding.
Source: Frank deLeeuw and Edward Gramlich, "The Channels of Monetary Policy," *Federal Reserve Bulletin*, June 1969.

period of the former. By the end of four years monetary policy has the same impact on both types of investment.

Construction expenditures of state and local governments like consumer expenditures are influenced somewhat by the rate of interest. Only the federal government is totally insensitive to the rate of interest.

Summary/Questions

The questions "How much do monetary and fiscal policy matter?" and "In what ways do monetary and fiscal policy matter?" are central issues underlying many specific problems in the private and public sectors. Because the questions are so important, the answers deserve careful scrutiny. It is discouraging to report that virtually every empirical study has an implausible element. For example, we suggested that the wealth effect induced by interest rate might explain the virtually zero fiscal policy multipliers in the St. Louis model. The MPS model does indeed find strong evidence for a wealth effect. However, it also finds that the fiscal policy multiplier is positive. The large-scale structural model estimates of the money multiplier are inconsistent with the huge body of empirical money demand studies. If the studies summarized here contain an implausible element, they also are methodologically reasonable and contain many plausible elements. There is no need to be disheartened. A discipline is vibrant and controversial only if it is in a mild state of disarray. Besides, every new answer only brings a new question.

1. Briefly describe and compare the methodological approach of large-scale structural models and reduced form or bottom line models.

2. Outline the conclusions of large-scale structural and reduced form models concerning the magnitude and speed of the impact of monetary and fiscal policy.

3. Which research approach, large-scale structural or reduced form models, is favored by *(a)* monetarists and *(b)* Keynesians?

4. State two reasons for believing that the difference in the results of large-scale structural and reduced form models are not simply due to the excessive manipulation of the data in order to confirm preconceived beliefs.

5.* Summarize the findings of the St. Louis Fed model concerning the *(a)* strength, *(b)* speed, and *(c)* reliability of monetary and fiscal policy.

6.* Answer the last question for the average large-scale structural model.

7.** Carefully explain why the St. Louis estimates of the government spending multiplier and the structural model estimates of the money multiplier are implausibly low, given the value of actual velocity and the typical estimate of the demand for money.

8.** Define reverse causation. Explain the extension of the reverse causation argument which states that effective stabilization tools tend to be statistically insignificant.

9.** Compare the prediction errors of the St. Louis model on the one hand and the average structural model on the other.

10.** State the findings of the MPS model concerning the relative importance of the channels of monetary policy and the sectors affected by monetary policy.

International banking

31

Throughout much of this book we have ignored the foreign sector and implicitly assumed a closed economy. At various points, however, we did stress the openness of our economy, where domestic events produce repercussions abroad, and vice versa. For example, we analyzed the Eurodollar market almost at the very beginning of the book (in Chapter 2) and again in Chapter 8, the gold standard in Chapter 17, and the relationship between the Phillips curve and exchange rate policies in Chapter 28. The distinguishing feature of this and the next two chapters is the *sustained* emphasis on international economics.

Following the institutions first/theory second organization of the book, this chapter considers the implications of openness for monetary control and the performance of the U.S. banking industry. Chapter 33 shows how the money, output, and price relationship is affected by the degree of openness and the foreign exchange system, that is, the system for exchanging one nation's money for another. The transitional Chapter 32 explains the essential features of alternative foreign exchange systems. In every country large commercial banks and the central bank play a key role in the foreign exchange system.

The Seeds of International Banking

Prior to World War II the United States had an almost strictly domestic banking system. Only six large U.S. banks had foreign offices, and these offices were few in number and small in terms of deposits. Foreign transactions typically involved a domestic bank and foreign correspondent bank. As our earlier analysis of the Eurodollar market indicated, large domestic banks sought to become giant international banks in the 1950s and 1960s mainly (1) to avoid stricter domestic banking regulations, e.g., Regulation Q and reserve requirements, and (2) to support the growth of U.S. foreign trade and the transformation of the Fortune 500 from national to multinational corporations. By 1970, U.S. banks had offices in most industrialized nations and large less developed countries, e.g., Brazil. Deposits of U.S. banks abroad totaled $50 billion by 1970, much of it denominated in U.S. dollars but a significant amount denominated in *local* currencies, hence, non-Eurodollars. International banking became a significant factor by 1970, more significant than the Eurodollar market.

The Federal Reserve realized almost immediately that variations in Eurodollars, which are nonmoney from the viewpoint of M-1, could, nevertheless, affect M-1 through their impact on the money supply multiplier. The expansion of Eurodollars or any other nonmoney requiring reserves reduces M-1 but increases credit outstanding. However, as the Fed paid little attention to the money supply prior to 1970, it tolerated, and at times even encouraged, the growth of the Eurodollar market and the internationalization of U.S. banks for two reasons. First, the Fed thought that international banking and foreign borrowing abroad rather than within the United States would relieve pressure on the U.S. balance of payments, as will be explained shortly. Second, the Fed feared that the large U.S. banks might leave the Federal Reserve System, as they had the right to do in 1970. It let foreign branches of U.S. banks operate under the more permissive foreign regulations to appease the parent banks.

The invasion by U.S. giant banks had a strong negative impact on foreign banks' profits. Although U.S. banks went abroad to service their blood relatives, the Fortune 500 multinational corporations, once abroad they made loans to and accepted deposits from nationals of the host countries. With their own offices abroad, U.S. banks reduced their correspondent relationships with foreign banks. Quite naturally, foreign banks responded by attempting to stop the internationalization of U.S. banks. Some were successful. Mexico, for example, banned offices of U.S. banks. Such policies were loudly decried in the United States. So long as internationalization was strictly a one-way street from the United States to other countries, as was largely true until approximately 1970, U.S. firms and banks were among the strongest supporters of free trade and capital movements. Indeed, banks and the Fed could afford to be outright magnanimous in 1970. The very few foreign banks in the U.S. were allowed to operate under *their* countries' regulations instead of the generally much stricter U.S. banking regulations.

Foreign Banks Discover the United States

World War II destroyed much of the rest of the industrialized world. By 1970, however, other nations had fully recovered and were ready to challenge the United States. Foreign exports (U.S. imports) grew; foreign industrial firms established offices in the United States and purchased American firms; foreign tourists and recent immigrants were more numerous. Just as 10 to 20 years earlier U.S. banks followed U.S. industrial firms and citizens abroad, so foreign banks in the 1970s followed Toyota, Nissan, Nestle, Phillips NV, and other foreign firms. The internationalization of banking became a two-way proposition.

In 1972, 60 foreign banks operated in the United States. During 1978 alone, 90 foreign banks opened offices in the United States.[1] By 1979 foreign banks were not only opening offices but buying large U.S. banks. For example, Standard Chartered Bank of London bought Union Bank of Los Angeles, America's 25th largest bank. The Hong Kong and Shanghai Bank took control of Marine Midland (New York), which at the time ranked 12th among American banks, with assets of $14.3 billion. Between 1972 and 1980 the assets of foreign banks in the United States grew nearly 600 percent to $172 billion.[2] Foreign banks held over 10 percent of banking assets in the United States by 1980.

Domestic banks claimed in the late 1970s that foreign banks were capturing a larger share of the United States banking market because the latter enjoyed the unfair advantage of operating under permissive foreign regulations rather than strict U.S. regulations. Contrary to the United States, *in most other countries banks can operate nationwide, have no (or very low) cash reserve requirements, and engage in many investment banking operations*. When England's Barclays Bank came to America, it opened a branch in New York. Being accustomed to nationwide banking in England, Barclays requested and was dutifully granted permission to expand to 14 (non New York State) cities! By 1978, 27 foreign banks operated branches in more than one state. Some states went to extremes to attract foreign banks. For example, Illinois, a unit banking state, allowed foreign banks to operate multiple branches while poor Continental Illinois and other Illinois banks were limited to one office. What amount of cash, *nonearning* reserves was Barclays required to hold against its deposits? None. As an English bank it had to meet England's liquidity ratios, that is, interest-*earning* liquid assets had to at least equal specified

---

[1]Eric N. Compton, *Inside Commercial Banking*, 2d ed. (New York: John Wiley & Sons, 1983), pp. 195ff.

[2]"Which Have the Edge: U.S. Banks Abroad or Foreign Banks Here?" *ABA Banking Journal*, August 1981, p. 80.

ratios. It was exempt from the Fed's reserve requirements and even from the less strict state requirements. With high interest-earning reserves, foreign banks could pay higher deposit rates and charge lower loan rates, thereby taking business away from U.S. banks.

Before evaluating the charge that foreign banks have an unfair advantage in the United States over domestic banks, note that foreign banks still are playing catch-up in the international banking arena. U.S. banks generally prefer to operate overseas through branches which are legally integral parts of the parent bank. The assets of foreign branches of U.S. banks equaled about $315 billion in 1982. To this sum one should add another $85 billion, the assets of foreign *subsidiaries* of U.S. banks. Some banking activities overseas are more effectively conducted by separately incorporated subsidiaries.[3] Thus, the direct and indirect assets of U.S. banks overseas equaled about $400 billion, which is nearly twice the assets of foreign banks in the United States.

The Edge Act and International Banking Act

Lack of reserve requirements and investment banking powers did give foreign banks a strong advantage in the United States. However, U.S. banks overstated the advantage that foreign banks derived by effective nationwide branch banking. First, most foreign banks are *wholesale banks* servicing a selective clientele of large foreign or American firms, and *not retail banks* servicing American consumers and "ma and pa" companies. Just as proximity to customers is much less important for wholesale merchants than retail stores, so also different capabilities and types of transactions make proximity much less important for customers of wholesale banks than retail banks. Second, for many years *the Edge Act granted U.S. banks something resembling nationwide branching for international purposes*. In particular, the Edge Act, passed by Congress in 1919 as an amendment to the Federal Reserve Act, allows banks to create subsidiary corporations which, in turn, can establish specialized offices across state lines that deal *exclusively* with either foreign or domestic firms engaged in international trade. For example, California's Bank of America per se does not have a branch in New York. However, its Edge subsidiary in New York accepted deposits and lent over $6 billion, *all* of which the bank and its customers affirm is associated with the financing of international trade. Since the branches of foreign banks can finance international *and* purely domestic trade, Edge corporations restricted to

---

[3]James Houpt, "Performance and Characteristics of Edge Corporations," Federal Reserve Board of Governors, processed, January 1981 and updated 1984, and James Houpt and Michael G. Martinson, "Foreign Subsidiaries of U.S. Banking Organizations," Federal Reserve Staff Studies No. 120.

international trade do not place foreign and American banks on equal footing across the United States. Nevertheless, U.S. banks took advantage of the Edge Act in the 1970s and opened numerous Edge subsidiaries in New York, Chicago, Miami, Los Angeles, and other cities with a large volume of foreign trade.

After much lobbying by American banks for competitive equality among all banks in the United States, Congress passed in 1978 the International Banking Act (IBA). The IBA endorsed a "national treatment" policy, which gives foreign banks the same powers *and limitations* as their domestic counterparts. As suggested earlier, the IBA had to institute three major changes in order to implement the national treatment principle of parity. First, interstate expansion by foreign banks was prohibited.[4] A foreign bank with offices in more than one state was required to elect one of those states as its home state and was prohibited from establishing *new* branches outside its home state. Branches in existence in 1978, when IBA was enacted, were "grandfathered." Second, the Fed was authorized to treat foreign banks as member banks and levy federal reserve requirements. Third, foreign banks became subject to the Fed's prohibitions on nonbanking activities.

International Banking in the 1980s

The Fed had a change of heart in 1981. After having contributed greatly to the growth of the Eurodollar market—a $600 billion market by 1981—due to its restrictive regulatory practices at home, the Fed beckoned home to America the Eurodollars owned by foreigners. To accomplish this the Fed permitted U.S. banks in December 1981 to establish international banking facilities (IBFs), which conduct a deposit and loan business with *foreign* firms without being subject to reserve requirements or Reg Q interest rate ceilings. "As a result, banking offices located in the United States can, through their IBFs, conduct transactions with foreign residents in a regulatory environment broadly similar to that of the Eurocurrency market without having to use an offshore facility."[5] To help assure that (1) IBFs are simply doing at home what U.S. branches abroad would be doing with their foreign customers, and (2) IBF accounts are not being substituted for transactions accounts in M-1 and thereby complicating domestic monetary policy, IBFs have limited powers. For example, IBFs can only lend and accept deposits from foreigners *who will use the funds*

---

[4]Foreign banks like domestic banks can create Edge subsidiaries which cross state lines. Sydney Key and James Brady, "Implementation of the International Banking Act," *Federal Reserve Bulletin* (October 1979), 785–96; James Houpt, "Performance and Characteristics"; Sydney Key, "International Banking Facilities," *Federal Reserve Bulletin, October 1982, 565–77.*

[5]Key, "International Banking Facilities," p. 565.

abroad. The minimum transaction is $100,000. Nevertheless, IBFs have grown very rapidly. Their assets equaled $160 billion after being in business for only nine months.

Loans to firms and especially governments in less developed countries (LDCs) are the aspect of international banking that has attracted the most attention from the popular press in the 1980s. There is no denying that some banks have seriously overexposed themselves in countries from Argentina to Zaire. U.S. banking regulation generally limits the loan to any one borrower to 10 percent of a bank's net worth. This is true irrespective of the credit worthiness of the borrower. However, with its foreign branches free from such U.S. regulations and with a home office which naively treated each Argentinean government agency as a separate borrower, one large New York bank succeeded in lending Argentina over 50 percent of its net worth. Of course, banks' overexposure would have gone largely unnoticed had LDCs promptly met all their loan payments. This has not been the case, however. Critics claim that many LDCs were entrapped to live beyond their means by overly optimistic bankers all too eager to lend. Even Mexico, the fourth largest oil producer following its discoveries in the late 1970s, was on the verge of default. A consortium of U.S. and foreign banks agreed to "reschedule" Mexico's loans. Rescheduling loans, i.e., extending their maturity so that no *principal* payments are due in the near future, has become a widely used stopgap measure. When the limits of creative accounting would have been stretched too far by rescheduling *interest* payments as well as *principal,* the banks persuaded the U.S. Treasury, Fed, and international organizations to lend Mexico the interest payments in order for Mexico to remain current with the banks.

Is good taxpayer money being thrown out to save bad bank loans? Only time will tell. True, with the benefit of hindsight many bank dealings with LDCs illustrate excessive optimism and a naivete bordering on sheer stupidity. But can banks really be blamed for lacking foresight about oil prices, the cause of much of their borrowers' problems? Unlike Mexico, most LDCs deeply in debt to the banks lack oil. The quantum jump in oil prices initiated by OPEC countries in 1973 and 1979 effectively required a massive redistribution of wealth from oil importing to oil exporting countries. Any redistribution is painful, particularly if it must occur quickly. By lending to oil importing LDCs, banks have been delaying and, therefore, making easier the redistribution that LDCs must make. The danger is that LDCs will claim that they have already made enough of a sacrifice. They may use the loans not simply to delay but to avoid redistribution by defaulting on the banks. In this case, bank stockholders through their losses will effectively be the ones who pay the higher oil prices and redistribute wealth to OPEC.

Summary/Questions

The U.S. banking industry will never be strictly domestic again; the internationalization of U.S. banks has gone on too long and makes too much economic sense. Between 1977 and 1981 the 10 largest U.S. banks earned 50 percent of their profits abroad. However, recent experience with the LDCs has decidely slowed, if not altogether stopped, the expansion of international banking. In 1982, U.S. bank loans to foreigners increased approximately $100 billion. The increase was only $30 billion in 1983, and in the first few months of 1984 a small decrease was recorded. Moreover, a greater proportion of new foreign loans are "traditional" collateralized loans financing trade or a specific project.

1. Discuss the pattern of international banking before and after 1970. Why did the Fed tolerate, or even encourage, the internationalization of U.S. banks?
2. Why did the Fed originally permit foreign banks to operate under the rules of their country? What were the main advantages to foreign banks of freedom from Federal Reserve regulations?
3. State the main features of the Edge Act, the International Banking Act (IBA), and international banking facilities (IBFs).
4. What explains the large proportion of "problem" loans to foreign countries? How have bank operations changed as a result?

Foreign exchange and the balance of payments

32

The money of all countries is *generally* acceptable only within the country. For example, every restaurant in Spain accepts pesetas, but a Spaniard with only pesetas in Kansas is likely to go hungry. Discussion of Eurodollars should not obscure the fact that even the U.S. dollar, which plays a special role in international trade, can be used abroad only for selective types of transactions. Californians in London cannot use their U.S. dollars at McDonald's. When that quintessential American restaurant goes to London, it demands a (British) pound for a Quarter Pounder. Thus, there is a market for *foreign exchange,* the term for any type of foreign money. Nationals of different countries exchange monies in foreign exchange markets.

Foreign exchange markets sound mysterious, but they are not. The next section briefly explains how foreign exchange transactions are made. Foreign exchange markets, like most other markets, are determined by supply and demand. Anything that increases the demand for foreign exchange also tends to raise its price. The second section lists the main sources of demand for and supply of foreign exchange. We do not directly observe either demand or supply, however. We observe quantities, which are influenced by supply and demand but do not necessarily equal either one. This leads us to the balance of payments, which records the quantities associated with the supply and demand for foreign exchange. In other words, the balance of payments shows all the transactions between the residents of one country and foreigners. The final and far-and-away longest section concerns exchange rate regimes or the role of the government in the foreign exchange market. At one extreme, the government withdraws completely, in which case private equals total demand and supply. At the other extreme, government attempts to completely dominate private demand and supply; its first priority is a permanently fixed price of foreign exchange. The latter extreme is the gold standard, which a few are attempting to revive.

Foreign Exchange Markets

The (foreign) *exchange rate* is the price of one money in terms of another. For example, if one pays $1.40 to get £1 (£ is the symbol for the British pound sterling), the price of pounds is $1.40 or, equivalently, the price of dollars is £0.71. Were the exchange rate to change to $1.25 = £1, the dollar is said to *appreciate* as it takes fewer dollars to buy pounds. British goods with a given pound price cost less in U.S. dollars when the dollar appreciates. In our example the pound *depreciated* as the price of the dollar rose to £0.80 (= 1/1.25), and pounds buy fewer dollars. For simplicity, we henceforth shall assume only one foreign currency, pounds.

For major trading countries such as the United States and Britain, there is a foreign exchange market for each money component. For example, at major airports (and train stations abroad) money exchange dealers swap dollar bills for pound notes at the prevailing exchange rate. At American Express offices in the United States you can buy with U.S. dollars traveler's checks denominated in British pounds. Alternatively, you can buy dollar-denominated traveler's checks and exchange them for pound notes or pound traveler's checks after you arrive in Britain. While consumers/tourists make predominantly these types of foreign exchange transactions, most foreign exchange transactions involve bank deposits.

The largest banks and a few nonbanks are foreign exchange dealers, standing ready to buy and sell deposits in foreign countries throughout the world. For example, a New York importer who needs pounds to pay a British manufacturer will go to her bank. The bank will debit her dollar account in New York and immediately communicate electronically with its London correspondent (which may be its own branch) by means of special Burroughs-Texas Instrument terminals linked to SWIFT (Society of Worldwide Interbank Financial Telecommunications) or CHIPS (New York Clearing House Interbank Payment System) computers. Our New York importer is credited an equivalent amount in pounds in London. Assuming £1 = $1.25, Figure 32–1 shows the effect of this transaction on the balance sheet of all three parties. The reader should be able to show that the dollar deposits in New York of London banks decrease when American exporters demanding dollars present them with pound checks issued by British importers. Although few U.S. banks are foreign exchange *dealers* owning foreign-denominated deposits, virtually all banks

FIGURE 32–1

New York Importer Buys British Pound Deposits in London from a New York Bank

New York Bank

Deposits in London	−£100 (=$125)	Importer's deposits	−$125

New York Importer

		Deposits at NY Bank	−$125
		Deposits at London Bank	+£100 (= $125)

London Bank

Deposits of NY Bank	−£100		
Deposits of NY importer	+£100		

can arrange foreign exchange transactions by contacting the large New York banks. The mechanics do become more complicated as there are four parties, Importer, Small U.S. Bank, Large U.S. Bank, and London Bank. Total foreign exchange transactions in all currencies exceed $100 billion *daily*, a staggering amount considering that *annual* U.S. exports are about $300 billion.

Foreign Exchange Demand and Supply

The exchange rate for pounds, like the prices our New York importer pays for most other commodities, is determined by supply and demand. For the moment let us assume that the government is totally inactive in the foreign exchange market; only private demand and supply exist. There are two equivalent ways of looking at the exchange rate—the price of pounds in terms of dollars or the price of dollars in terms of pounds—because we may look at the foreign exchange market in either of two ways, as a market for dollars or as a market for pounds. In other words, because one money is exchanged for another on the foreign exchange market, one demands (buys) dollars by supplying (offering) pounds, and one supplies (offers) dollars in order to demand (buy) pounds. Let us concentrate on the demand and supply of dollars and the price of dollars quoted in pounds, as illustrated in Figure 32–2. Since dollars are American money, in our two-country world Americans supply dollars and Britons demand dollars.[1] The dollar *appreciates* as one moves up the vertical axis in Figure 32–2.

[1]Since for our purposes a negative demand is equivalent to a positive supply, it is convenient to view one nationality as always being on one side of the market. For example, when Britons reduce their dollar holdings, we view demand as decreasing instead of supply increasing.

FIGURE 32–2
The Foreign Exchange Market

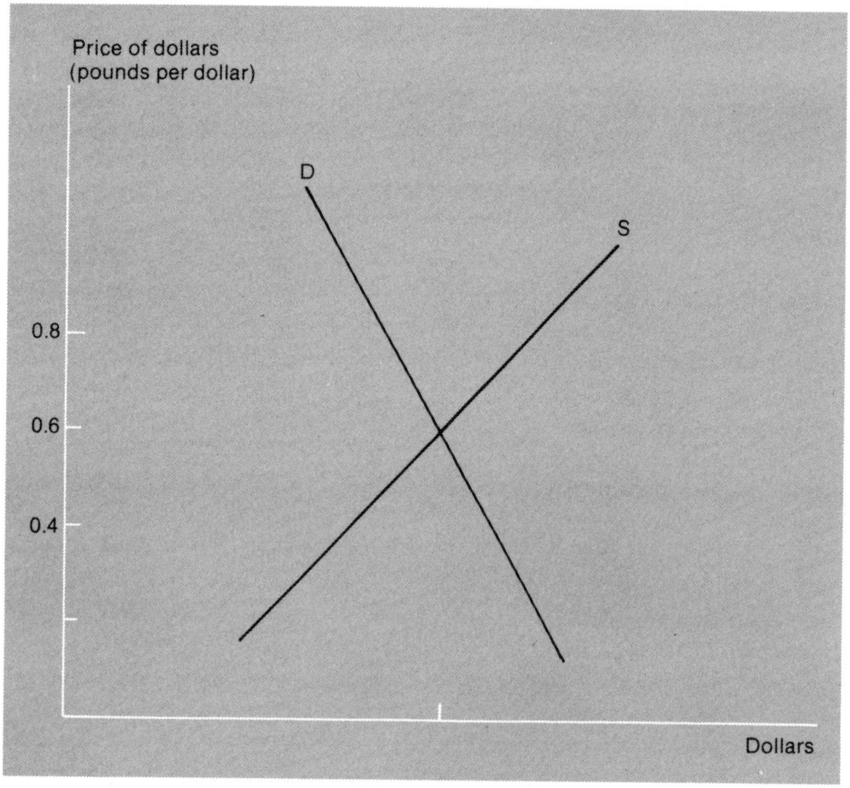

The British demand for dollars arises from three main sources: (1) British imports (American exports) of goods and services, (2) British capital outflows, that is, British purchases of U.S. securities and physical assets such as real estate, and (3) the international media of exchange properties of the dollar. Analysis of the factors which influence these three sources of demand suggests that the demand curve is downward sloping and shifts outward when either (1) British incomes increase, (2) British prices rise *relative* to U.S. prices, (3) U.S. interest rates rise *relative* to British interest rates, or (4) the dollar is expected to appreciate.

Consider the demand due to British purchases of American exports. If the dollar *appreciates* from, say, £0.6 = \$1 to £0.8 = \$1, the pound price of American exports rises, *ceteris paribus,* Britons will import less of the more expensive U.S. goods and will demand fewer dollars for this purpose. Thus the demand curve is downward sloping. Higher British incomes and higher British prices relative to U.S. prices shift the demand curve outward as Britons purchase additional foreign goods. In other words, British imports as well as British domestic consumption depend on British income. An increase in British prices relative to U.S. prices makes U.S. goods more attractive to Britons at any *given* exchange rate, thereby shifting the demand curve outward. Inflation in the United States is consistent with an increase in the relative British price level. Provided the United States inflation rate is less than the inflation rate abroad, foreign prices rise relatively, and the demand for dollars increases.

Capital flows out of Britain when Britons import (buy) foreign securities, by definition. Whether Britons import U.S. Treasury bonds or American computers, they need dollars first. We distinguish between British imports of goods and services and British capital outflows because the two sources of demand have different determinants. Our British cousins like ourselves compare interest rates on alternative securities. When U.S. interest rates rise relative to British interest rates, the British demand for dollars shifts outward in order to buy (import) the now more attractive U.S. securities.[2] Conversely, lower interest rates in the United States, *ceteris paribus,* shift the demand curve inward and tend to depreciate the dollar.

A few currencies, the U.S. dollar being the best example by far, are international media of exchange. Just as nationals of one country adopted domestic media of exchange as the number of trades increased, the international community adopted universal media of exchange to facilitate some trades. While some Filipino sugar producers will accept pesetas from Spanish confectioners and then swap the pesetas for Norwegian krone in order to pay sardine canners, all concerned often find it more convenient to use a common means of payment. Of course, the international means of payment will be the currencies of economically and politically stable and powerful countries. Instability in many small countries induces a massive flight to the dollar and other international means of payment.

The expected future exchange rate is the final important determinant of all three sources of demand. If the dollar is expected to appreciate, the demand for dollars increases as Britons accelerate their imports of goods and services while American products at the existing exchange still are cheap in terms of pounds. Expected exchange rates have an even more important impact on capital flows. Everyone wants assets that are expected to appreciate. Capital flows out of Britain and the demand for dollars increases when the dollar is expected to appreciate. Conversely, expectation of the dollar's depreciation (pound's appreciation) shifts demand inward.

---

[2]We are emphasizing the short run, where portfolio adjustments occur. In the long run, portfolios balance and capital flows cease. Thus, relative returns have little effect on the long-run demand for foreign exchange. Both the short-run and long-run demand and, ultimately, the exchange rate depend to some extent on the absolute level of prices and interest rates. However, relative values are more important in the short run.

Since the supply of dollars is equivalent to the demand for pounds by Americans, symmetry with the previous paragraphs suggests that the supply of dollars is upward sloping. For example, we stated that when the dollar appreciates from, say, £0.6 = $1 to £0.8 = $1, American exports (British imports) fall because American goods become more expensive in Britain. The appreciation from the American side makes British goods cost less, and American imports rise. More dollars are supplied to buy imports as the exchange rate appreciates.[3] Again, recognition of the symmetrical nature of foreign exchange markets suggests that the supply curve shifts outward when (1) U.S. incomes rise, (2) U.S. prices rise relative to foreign prices, (3) foreign interest rates rise relative to U.S. interest rates, or (4) the dollar (pound) is expected to depreciate (appreciate). The Fed further thought that institutional changes such as the growth of the Eurodollar market would reduce the supply of U.S. dollars. A Eurodollar market encourages foreigners to borrow abroad. Were foreigners to borrow in the United States instead, the United States would export capital and supply dollars to lend (buy foreign securities).

In a competitive foreign exchange market without any government intervention, the equilibrium exchange rate will equate private supply and demand. Since higher foreign incomes shift the demand curve outward and higher domestic incomes shift the supply curve outward, it follows that an increase in foreign income relative to U.S. income tends to appreciate the dollar.[4] This is so because the relative income effect causes U.S. exports (foreign imports) to increase relative to U.S. imports (foreign exports). Moreover, the reader should be able to show that an increase in the relative U.S. interest rate and a decrease in the relative U.S. price level also tend to appreciate the dollar against foreign currencies. Expected appreciation or depreciation tends to be self-fulfilling. Institutional changes such as the Eurodollar market affect the equilibrium exchange rate by shifting demand or supply.

A Glimpse at the Balance of Payments

The balance-of-payments accounts record all transactions between the residents of one country and foreigners. In many respects the balance of

---

[3]We are implicitly assuming that the demand for imports is elastic. In this case, the quantity of imports increases more than their dollar price decreases, and the dollar amount spent on imports rises. None of the following arguments require an elastic demand for imports and upward-sloping supply of foreign exchange. We only require that the supply curve, if downward sloping, be steeper than the demand curve. This is more or less equivalent to the Marshall-Lerner condition that the sum of the absolute value of the import and export price elasticities exceed unity.

[4]The statement is true so long as demand depends simply on income and the two countries' import propensities remain constant, whatever their value. The level of the exchange rate does depend on the value of the import propensities. However, the statement in the text concerns the *appreciation* of the currency.

TABLE 32–1

U.S. Balance of Payments, 1983 ($ Billions)

Current Account:		
Merchandise exports	+200	
Merchandise imports	−261	
Merchandise or trade balance		−61
Net service exports, U.S. income from investments abroad, and unilateral transfers	+ 19	
Current balance		−42
Private Capital Account:		
Foreign private net purchases of U.S. assets	+ 86	
U.S. private net purchases of foreign assets	− 48	
Capital account balance		+38
Current and capital account balance		− 4
Government/Official Reserve Account:		
Foreign government purchase of U.S. assets	+ 5	
U.S. government purchase of official assets (increase, −)	− 1	
Net balance on official account		+ 4
Overall balance of payments	Always zero	

payments is an ex-post, realized version of the ex-ante, desired demand and supply of foreign exchange. Table 32–1 shows the U.S. balance-of-payments accounts for 1983 with the many different types of transactions aggregated into a few small classes to reflect some sources of the demand for and supply of dollars listed in the previous section. *Transactions which require a payment by foreigners to Americans and create a use of dollars are recorded as a credit* (+). U.S. merchandise exports is a credit item in the U.S. balance of payments. *Transactions which require a payment by Americans to foreigners are recorded as a debit* (−). U.S. merchandise imports is a debit item.

Because the various transactions depend on different variables and respond to different policies, various "balances" are computed. The merchandise (such as cars, steel, and oil) balance depends on incomes, the ratio of U.S. to foreign prices, and the exchange rate. It shows a deficit (−), indicating that the U.S. imported more merchandise than it exported. Service exports include tourist expenditures, insurance payments, transportation charges, and payments for other things that cannot be touched. Because total U.S. investments abroad were much larger than foreign investments in the United States—remember the U.S. multinational corporation—net U.S. income from investments abroad was highly positive. Net service exports, U.S. income from investments abroad, and unilateral transfers are added to the merchandise balance to get the *current account balance*. This showed a deficit of $−42 billion.

The private foreign sector in 1983 purchased dollar assets worth $86 billion. These assets were acquired both for "investment" and "means of payment" purposes, but it is impossible to state precisely which assets serve which purpose. New investments abroad by U.S. citizens were substantially less, only $48 billion, giving a capital account surplus of $38 billion. Such a surplus is not necessarily good. If it continues, the United States eventually will become a net-debtor country, with its liabilities to foreigners exceeding its foreign assets. When this occurs, the investment income mentioned in the last paragraph might reverse its current positive effect.

When one hears about a balance of payments surplus or deficit without a qualifying adjective, the speaker typically has in mind the current and capital account balance. This showed a deficit of $-4 billion in 1983. If governments did not participate in the foreign exchange market, then this "balance" would always balance, *never* showing either a deficit or surplus. The dollars provided (sold) by U.S. private citizens must necessarily equal the dollars used (bought) by foreign private citizens if governments do not exist. *Governments must finance a current and capital account surplus or deficit. They do this by buying or selling official assets, which are gold, "reserve" deposits at the International Monetary Fund (IMF), and other countries' currencies.* (We shall describe the functions of the IMF shortly.) In 1983 official dollar assets of foreign governments increased $5 billion. Thus, the total, private and government, foreign use of dollars exceeded the amount provided by U.S. private citizens by $1 billion. This amount was provided by the U.S. government when it purchased official assets. U.S. government holdings of foreign currency and its (reserve) deposits at the IMF were the official assets that increased; the U.S. government's gold stock remained constant. The overall, private and government, balance of payments always equals zero. Dollars that the U.S. private and government sectors provide to all, private and government, foreigners necessarily equal the dollars used by all foreigners.

Exchange Rate Regimes

When government directly and indirectly withdraws from the foreign exchange market, a *perfectly flexible exchange rate regime* exists. A "clean float" characterizes exchange rate fluctuations which automatically adjust private supply and demand for foreign exchange. Since 1973 there has been a strong worldwide movement toward flexible exchange rates, but no government has yet irrevocably renounced all exchange rate intervention. Even the United States, which has a long history of participating much less actively than other countries in foreign exchange markets under the earlier adjustable-peg Bretton Woods regime to be described shortly, does not have a perfectly clean float. U.S. authorities have occasionally intervened in foreign exchange markets since 1973, and not simply to prop up some LDC currency on the verge of collapse. As we just saw, in 1983 U.S. authorities offered $1 billion to purchase official assets. A "dirty float" with "managed flexibility" characterizes the exchange rate in the United States, Canada, Japan, and the European community.[5] Intervention, that is, changes in a country's official asset holdings, occurs *infrequently* in a dirty float and is designed to smooth *short-term* disorderly conditions. Intervention in this case is *not* directed at maintaining a non-equilibrium exchange rate for any appreciable period of time. The U.S. has one of the cleanest dirty floats. Exchange rate fluctuations were reported almost daily by the popular press during autumn 1984 as U.S. authorities repeatedly permitted the dollar to touch new highs against most foreign currencies.

Government follows a *strict* policy of benign neglect toward the exchange rate in a perfectly flexible exchange-rate system, or one approaching it. It not only withdraws from direct participation in the foreign exchange market but it adopts policies irrespective of their indirect effect on the exchange rate through private supply and demand. In particular, government does not manipulate interest rates with a view toward their exchange rate consequences. The exchange rate in a perfectly flexible system is extremely important to the private sector but irrelevant to public officials, who focus on other objectives.

The Gold Standard

Most countries were on the gold standard prior to World War I and during the early part of the interlude between the two world wars. The gold standard encompasses many elements. Even when we largely assumed a closed economy in Chapter 17, pages 312–17, we had to mention the gold standard because purchases and sales of gold influence the monetary base and domestic money supply. The reader may want to review those pages. We now discuss the more strongly internationally oriented, open-economy elements of the gold standard.

Recall that countries on a gold standard fix the value of their currencies in terms of gold. Indeed, gold coins circulate freely with paper money in countries on a strict gold standard. Because currencies were tied to a common commodity, gold, exchange rates among currencies were fixed. *An essential feature of the gold standard is a resolute determination to maintain the gold value of currencies and, therefore, stable exchange*

[5]A number of European countries established the European Monetary System in 1979 to stabilize exchange rates among their currencies while simultaneously permitting a joint float against non-European currencies. Many smaller countries peg their currency to one of the major currencies, and then float with the major currency.

rates at virtually any cost.[6] In this respect the gold standard is the antithesis of perfectly flexible exchange rates.

How can governments maintain the fixed exchange rate when private demand and supply for foreign exchange and, therefore, the competitive equilibrium rate continuously shift? Under the gold standard each country held gold as its official asset and bought (sold) gold in order to increase (decrease) the private supply of its currency in the foreign exchange market. Look at Figure 32–2 again. Suppose the fixed exchange rate is £0.8 = $1 but the private market equilibrium rate now is £0.6 = $1. The U.S. authorities can maintain the *overvalued* fixed exchange rate by selling gold, thereby reducing the private supply of dollars provided to buy pounds.[7] In other words, the dollar will *not* depreciate when American importers pay British exporters with gold. *Gold flows out of countries attempting to maintain an overvalued currency.* Conversely, gold flows into a country attempting to maintain an undervalued exchange rate such as £0.4 = $1 in Figure 32–2. The Treasury in this case would have to supplement the private supply of dollars by buying gold from foreigners.

Because every country's gold stock was limited, gold outflows were only a *temporary* solution for an *overvalued* currency. *All* countries were supposed to adhere to certain "rules of the game" which were thought to assure a rapid *permanent* solution. First, countries were *not* supposed to sterilize either gold inflows or outflows by open-market operations or other means. *The money supply should be proportional to the gold stock. The money supply would rise (fall) in countries with an undervalued (overvalued) exchange rate as the central bank bought (sold) gold flowing in (out). Second, money supply changes were supposed to induce proportional price changes in the same diretion according to the quantity theory.* Thus, prices fall (rise) in countries with overvalued (undervalued) currencies. In terms of Figure 32–2, prices fall when the exchange rate is set at £0.8 = $1. Third, the relative and absolute price decline in countries with overvalued currencies increases the foreign demand for their products and currencies and decreases the foreign exchange supply as imports become less attractive. In this manner the equilibrium exchange rate adjusts toward the exchange rate fixed by the gold standard.

---

[6]Market exchange rates fluctuated slightly about the gold standard mint parities because of transportation costs. The mint parity plus or minus transportation costs equal the so-called gold points, which are the upper and lower bounds to exchange rate fluctuations. For example, suppose the mint parity was £1 = $4, and transportation costs between London and New York were one-half percent. In this case, gold flows by arbitrageurs keeps the exchange rate within the gold-points range of £1 = $3.98 and £1 = $4.02. Gold worth £1 in London will bring only $3.98 in New York after transportation costs. Gold worth $4.02 in New York will bring only £1 in London.

[7]Clearly, one could equally correctly view gold sales as increasing the demand for dollars.

The gold standard adjustment mechanism works reasonably well provided prices are sufficiently flexible. Even so, the adjustment process is somewhat painful for countries with overvalued currencies because *monetary changes influence real income first and prices subsequently,* as we stressed in previous chapters. A country which curtails its money supply must endure a temporary recession. The less flexible are prices, the longer is the recession. Painful income effects are substituted during recessions for relatively painless price effects as an adjustment mechanism. In our example, lower incomes in the United States shift imports and the supply of dollars inward, thereby raising the equilibrium rate toward the fixed rate. Since inflation is hardly popular, there was a strong tendency for countries with undervalued currencies to ignore the rules of the game and keep their money supply and price level constant. Countries accumulating gold which do not play by the rules force all adjustment on countries losing gold, where prices ultimately must fall more and where recessions must be more severe.

The Adjustable-Peg Bretton Woods System, 1945–1973

Exchange rate regimes illustrate well that economic systems typically change gradually. The adjustable-peg Bretton Woods system of 1945–73 chronologically and economically straddles the old gold standard and the modern flexible exchange-rate regime.

Most countries financed at least part of World War I through money creation and inflation. With the price of other goods rising, gold at the price fixed by the gold standard became cheap. When their citizens' demand for gold greatly depleted their central bank's gold stock, most countries were forced off the gold standard. Inflation was not the only reason for abandoning the gold standard. During great wars and other extraordinary periods, trade patterns are disrupted, and massive capital flows search erratically for safe havens. As a result, competitive exchange rates will deviate significantly from the gold standard rate fixed during normal times. The adjustment costs of maintaining the fixed rate are so high during periods of great upheaval that the gold standard is abandoned.

The return of normalcy in the allied countries and LDCs shortly after World War I was accompanied by a resumption of the gold standard. Normalcy did not last long, however. Nazism shattered political normalcy in Europe. The Great Depression shattered economic normalcy worldwide. With unemployment rates already at 20 percent, few countries were willing to incur the large adjustment costs required by the gold standard during any extraordinary period where competitive and fixed exchange rates differ significantly. Experimentation and diversity characterize the exchange rate system of the late 1930s. A few countries stuck with the gold standard; others flirted with floating rates. A combination of uncertainty about exchange rate systems and higher tariffs worldwide reduced international trade and capital flows.

Before a solution to the problems of the 1930s could be found, the world fought another war. As the allied powers sensed victory was close at hand in 1944, their high-ranking financial officials met in the resort town of Bretton Woods, New Hampshire, to design the postwar international financial system. *The Bretton Woods system was an adjustable-peg, gold-exchange standard with the U.S. dollar playing a special role in supplementing gold as an international reserve asset.* The adjustable-peg feature meant that each country was required to keep the exchange rate within 1 percent of its par or official value so long as a *fundamental* disequilibrium did not exist.[8] Countries were obligated to buy and sell gold and other international reserve assets. They were required, if necessary, to undertake domestic stabilization policies such as tax increases and money supply reductions in order to keep the exchange rate within the par range in spite of *temporary* disequilibriums, that is, short-run differences between the par and competitive exchange rates. A *fundamental* disequilibrium was said to exist, and a country was allowed to appreciate or depreciate its currency, only when a strongly deflationary or inflationary program would have been necessary to close a long-term and large gap between the par and competitive exchange rates. Very simply, revaluations and devaluations were supposed to be the policy of last resort.

The Bretton Woods conference created the International Monetary Fund (IMF). Each country contributed gold to the IMF and agreed to provide it with a prespecified amount of its currency. The IMF in turn lent gold and foreign currencies at market interest rates to help countries finance temporary disequilibriums. Each country's account (often called reserve deposits) at the IMF was credited by the amount of its gold contribution and the amount of its currency that other countries borrowed. For example, when Britain borrowed U.S. dollars through the IMF, the latter credited the U.S. account. Loans typically were conditional on a change in the domestic policies which had created the disequilibrium. Moreover, the IMF was consulted over proposed appreciations and depreciations; determination of a fundamental disequilibrium was not the unilateral decision of a central bank. Fundamental disequilibriums were not found to exist very often; exchange rates remained remarkably stable. France lowered, and Germany raised, the par value of its currency twice during 1950–70. No other major industrialized country changed the par value of its currency more than once, and the United States, Switzerland, Japan, and Italy kept par values fixed throughout the period.

The United States expressed the par value of the dollar in terms of gold. More precisely, $1 = 1/35 oz. of gold. The United States held a huge

---

[8]The 1 percent is the analog of gold points during the gold standard era

stockpile of gold. Many countries had a deep faith in the United States's commitment and ability to "defend the dollar". They thought that dollar assets were as good as gold in all respects and better than gold in one important respect, namely, dollar assets can yield current income. As a result, the official assets of many countries consisted of small quantities of gold and credits at the IMF and large quantities of dollar assets such as U.S. Treasury bills, which could be exchanged for gold to maintain the currency's par value. Given this faith in the U.S. dollar and the composition of official assets, many countries expressed the par values of their currencies in terms of the U.S. dollar. For example, the Philippine peso was defined as being equal to U.S. $0.50. *A gold-exchange standard economizes on the use of gold.* In this case, many currencies were only indirectly convertible to gold as the official assets of many countries consisted primarily of dollars.

Which country or countries were responsible for maintaining exchange rates when temporary disequilibriums existed? The different manner of expressing exchange rates and the different composition of official assets between the United States on the one hand and other countries suggested a natural division of labor. The United States was responsible for maintaining convertibility of the dollar at $1 = $\frac{1}{35}$ oz. gold, and all other countries were responsible for maintaining convertibility of their currencies into dollars. For example, if the British pound tended to depreciate in terms of the U.S. dollar, Britain *alone* was required to sell gold and dollars and, if necessary, initiate contractionary domestic policies. This would reduce the private demand for dollars and stem the pound's depreciation.

Like many bureaucratically created "standards," the Bretton Woods-IMF standard had numerous flaws, as evidenced by its relatively short existence. First, the distinction between temporary and fundamental disequilibrium was never defined by the IMF. This created uncertainty in the public's mind about the stability of exchange rates, and uncertainty in the authorities' minds about the policies that should be adopted. Failure to provide definitions in no way implies that IMF bureaucrats were stupid or lazy. Indeed, the IMF could *not* define fundamental disequilibrium without inviting its occurrence and unstable exchange rates, which the IMF wanted to avoid. British speculators who anticipate that the pound will depreciate from, say, £0.6 = $1 to £0.8 = $1 expect to earn 33 percent profit by first buying dollars at £0.6 and then reselling them at £0.8. If "fundamental disequilibrium" were well defined so that profit-seeking speculators knew when a devaluation of the pound was imminent, speculators would dump the pound, bringing about the devaluation they expected. Exchange rate uncertainty, which tends to reduce trade and capital flows, is an essential feature of an adjustable-peg system.

The second and major flaw of the Bretton Woods system was a reduction in the confidence in the U.S. dollar, which was *inevitable* under a gold-exchange system. Because international trade grew very rapidly, foreign central banks needed increasing quantities of dollar assets in order to keep a constant ratio of official assets to trade flows. In terms of Figure 32–2, the supply of dollars had to exceed the private demand in order for foreign central banks to acquire dollars as an international means of payment. The need by foreign governments for U.S. dollars was not matched by equal increases in the United States's gold holdings because worldwide gold production lagged. As a result, the ratio of foreign central bank dollar assets to U.S. gold was bound to grow and eventually cast doubt on the ability of the United States to maintain gold convertibility.

The Bretton Woods system collapsed even sooner than some expected because of the U.S. inflation in the late 1960s. According to our earlier analysis of the foreign exchange market, U.S. inflation (relative to other countries) decreases the private demand for and increases the supply of dollars. Foreign central banks were required to buy dollars to prevent their currencies from appreciating. This increased further the ratio of foreign dollar holdings to U.S. gold. When the irascible General Charles de Gaulle told the French central bank, "À bas le dollar américain, prenons l'or" (enough with the U.S. dollar, let's go for the gold), the Bretton Woods system, like Humpty Dumpty, had a great fall. Try as they may, the IMF and others could not put Bretton Woods together again. The IMF itself survived, however. It is an important source of international reserves for countries that float dirty.

Summary/Questions

A strong asymmetry exists in a fixed exchange rate system such as the gold standard. Because every country's gold stock is limited, gold can only temporarily finance a balance of payments deficit (on current and capital account) and an overvalued exchange rate. Ultimately, countries with overvalued currencies and gold outflows *must* adopt contractionary domestic policies in order to remain on the gold standard. On the other hand, countries with undervalued currencies and gold inflows need not adjust. There might be no limit to the amount of gold these countries are willing to accumulate and sterilize. The rules of the gold standard game are readily broken by one set of players.

The Bretton Woods system institutionalized another important asymmetry when it created an international gold exchange/dollar standard. All other countries had to make wholehearted efforts to maintain the fixed exchange rate, while the United States could ignore exchange rates and the balance of payments. True, Bretton Woods allowed exchange rates adjustments, but only *after* often painful domestic monetary and fiscal policies failed to correct a fundamental disequilibrium. The United States, however, could go its merry way. It could, and often did, ignore the impact of its policies on international monetary relationships. Other countries adjusted their policies to compensate for the impact of U.S. policies on international monetary relationships. This asymmetry existed especially in the early years of Bretton Woods because the United States dollar became an official asset. Countries believed that any amount of dollars, however large, could be exchanged for gold. The dollar was as good as gold, and better. Dollar assets earn interest, while gold does not. The United States had an infinite supply of official assets when the dollar was an official asset acceptable by everyone worldwide. In other words, the citizens and government of the United States can create an infinite amount of dollar-denominated assets. So long as foreigners are willing to hold such assets, the U.S. dollar could remain overvalued, and a balance of payments deficits could persist. This is precisely what occurred for many years. When people lost faith in the dollar, as they inevitably would of anything overvalued, Bretton Woods and the gold exchange/dollar system collapsed.

1. Define exchange rate, appreciation, depreciation, and balance of payments.
2. List the main determinants of the demand for and supply of foreign exchange. Assuming no intervention by governments, would the dollar appreciate or depreciate against the pound when (*a*) U.S. (British) income rises, (*b*) U.S. interest rates rise relative to British rates, (*c*) U.S. prices rise relative to British prices, (*d*) international uncertainty increases the desirability of the dollar, and (*e*) the pound is expected to depreciate in the future?
3. Does the balance of payments balance? What types of items create debits and credits in the balance of payments? Give examples of "balances," debit items, and credit items.
4. Define and compare flexible exchange rates, the gold standard, and the adjustable-peg Bretton Woods exchange rate regime.
5. There exists an asymmetry in the adjustments required of different countries in the (*a*) gold standard, and (*b*) Bretton Woods system. Explain.
6. What is the difference between a clean and a dirty float? How do the objectives of governments differ when they intervene in fixed versus flexible exchange rate systems?

Monetary and fiscal policy with fixed and flexible exchange rates

33

Today's problems reflect yesterday's solutions.

How would our earlier conclusions about monetary and fiscal policy be altered by the openness of economies? The precise answer to this question depends on the exchange rate regime, the degree of openness, and the size of the local economy relative to the rest of the world. For simplicity, we will ignore the outdated, intermediate Bretton Woods regime and consider only pure (extreme?) regimes, the gold standard and perfectly flexible exchange rates. Throughout much of the chapter the gold standard simply means that maintenance of the fixed exchange rate is the authorities' first priority. Everything is secondary to the fixed exchange rate. We will at times consider other elements of the gold standard besides fixed exchange rates. Arguments supporting these other elements are often based on syllogistic reasoning. But are all attempts to resurrect the gold standard misguided? Are yesterday's solutions still the answer to today's problems?

Short-Run Policy in Open Economies

First, note a general conclusion true irrespective of exchange rate regimes. *Openness tends to reduce the short-run impact on GNP of both monetary and fiscal policy.* This is so because some of the induced spending will be for imports, thereby dampening the growth of *national* product. In terms of the previous IS–LM model, which remains appropriate for short-run analysis, the smaller MPC for national product in open economies makes the IS curve steeper. IS_o (''o'' for open) is steeper than IS_c (''c'' for closed) in Figure 33–1. Inspection of the figure shows that national output increases less in the open economy when monetary expansion shifts the LM to LM′.

Ignoring the possibility of capital flows, the *reduction* in the policy multipliers compared to the closed economy case tends to be less under flexible exchange rates than under the gold standard. This is so because the higher imports depreciate the currency with flexible exchange rates, which tends to dampen the import expansion and increase exports. Within open economies, the MPC for national product is higher in countries with flexible exchange rates. The IS curve is flatter when exchange rates are flexible instead of fixed, which makes the money multiplier larger. In summary, when we ignore capital flows, (1) closed economies, (2) open

FIGURE 33–1

Imports Reduce the Impact of Monetary and Fiscal Policy on GNP

The MPC for national product is less in open economies due to imports. This makes the IS steeper in open economies and reduces both the monetary and fiscal policy multipliers.

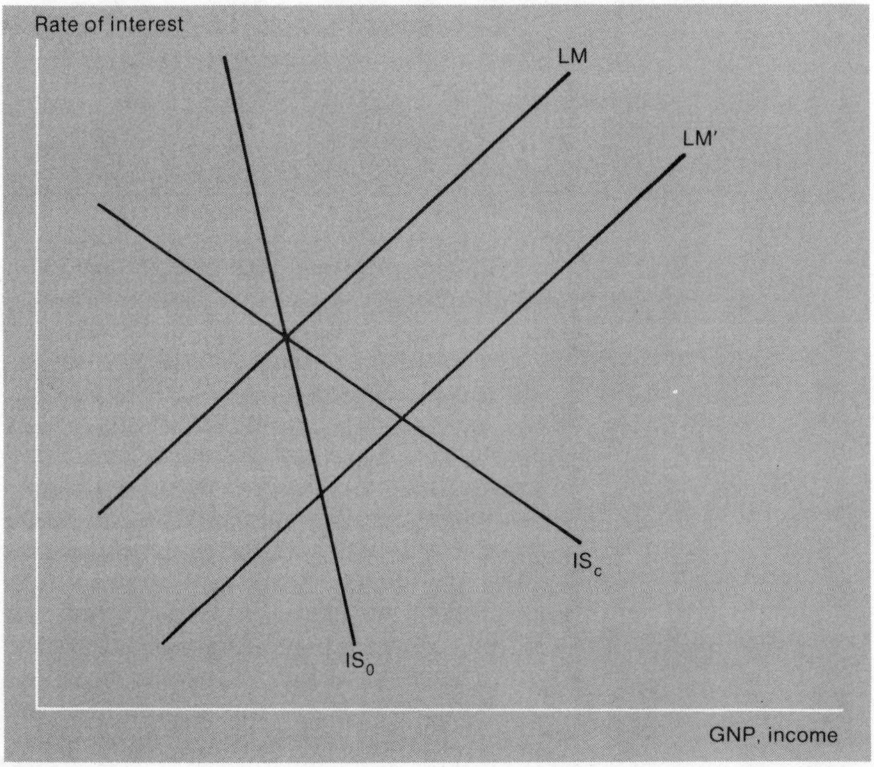

economies with flexible exchange rates, and (3) open economies on a gold standard order regimes according to the short-run effectiveness of both monetary and fiscal policy.

Short-Run Policy and Capital Flows

Let's continue to focus on the short run with fixed domestic prices, but now let capital flows exist. Indeed, *assume the extreme case of perfect capital mobility, which implies that interest rates are equalized worldwide.*[1] Capitalists seek the highest returns. Perfectly mobile capital continuously flows into any country where the interest rate is high. The capital flows stop only when interest rates are equalized. For small countries, the worldwide interest rate is a parameter; nothing a small country can do will influence the worldwide interest rate. *Given perfect capital mobility, short-run monetary policy in a small country is entirely ineffective under the gold standard.*

Let us illustrate the validity of the last sentence for an open-market purchase and monetary expansion. This *tends* to lower the interest rate. But we just saw that the interest rate ultimately cannot fall in this case. The *tendency* for the interest rate to fall induces capital outflows as citizens seek higher returns abroad. The capital outflows in turn tend to depreciate the currency. To prevent the depreciation and maintain fixed exchange rates under the gold standard, the central bank will have to sell gold. This reduces the monetary base and money supply and raises the interest rate back to the initial level.

Look at what happens to the money supply. It too is fixed, in the sense that *the equilibrium money stock cannot be changed by the monetary authorities*. Monetary policy does not exist. Temporary monetary expansion subsequently triggers an exactly equal monetary contraction. Suppose this were *not* the case; suppose the monetary expansion is permanent. This requires a larger money demand at equilibrium. Our analysis of money demand indicates that the interest rate must fall and/or income must rise. However, the interest rate is fixed when capital is perfectly mobile, by definition. Aggregate expenditures and income are also fixed because the rate of interest is fixed *and* because exchange rates, which

---

[1]Perfect capital mobility does not imply interest rate equalization in dynamic models and in models with forward markets. In a dynamic model where expected exchange rates do not necessarily equal current exchange rates, perfect capital mobility and risk neutrality imply that positive interest rate differentials equal the expected exchange rate depreciation. This is the Fisher proposition or open interest rate arbitrage. Alternatively, we could assume forward-exchange markets and (closed) interest rate arbitrage. This produces the interest rate parity theorem, which says that an interest rate differential equals the spot-exchange/forward-exchange differential. Since uniform interest rates and a constant interest rate differential have similar policy implications, we assume the simpler, uniform case.

influence imports and exports, are fixed under the gold standard.[2] Because the amount of money demanded is fixed, the money supply cannot be changed permanently.

The next-to-last sentence suggests why an independent monetary policy is viable under flexible exchange rates. Monetary expansion "works" because it depreciates the currency. Monetary expansion creates the same initial *tendency* for interest rates to fall and consequent capital outflow, which is allowed to depreciate the currency when exchange rates are flexible. The depreciation lowers imports and raises exports and, therefore, increases GNP. The money supply can be increased. Monetary expansion is entirely absorbed by the *transactions* demand for money because net exports and GNP depend on the depreciated exchange rate. Monetary policy in an open economy with flexible exchange rates is effective even if interest rates are fixed.[3]

Restating the last two paragraphs graphically and algebraically, the horizontal line at r_w in Figure 33–2 is the worldwide, fixed interest rate. The general form of the IS equation in an *open economy* is:

$$E(y, r, e) = y, \tag{33–1}$$

where the new term e is the foreign exchange rate. Since an IS–LM graph has only two axes, income, y, and the rate of interest, r, changes in e shift the IS curve. In particular, a depreciation which reduces imports and increases exports shifts the IS rightward in Figure 33–2.

Assume the initial curves are IS and LM. Monetary expansion then shifts the LM to LM′. The interest rate falls to r_m in a closed economy. In an open economy with perfect capital mobility, however, the rate of interest cannot fall. Lenders will not lend domestically at an interest rate below the worldwide rate. As lenders supply the local currency on the foreign market in order to buy the higher-yielding foreign assets, the currency tends to depreciate. The tendency becomes reality in a flexible exchange-rate system, and the IS curve shifts rightward to IS′ in Figure 33–2. Monetary expansion is possible and increases income with flexible exchange rates. In a fixed exchange-rate system, however, the tendency toward depreciation must be nullified, by definition. Monetary policy is not allowed to shift the IS rightward.[4] Since the interest rate must remain

---

[2]We are ignoring any real balance effects. Interest rates and the exchange rate are the sole links or channels between the financial and real sectors.

[3]It is tempting but *wrong* to say that a liquidity trap no longer makes monetary policy ineffective. A liquidity trap is a stronger assumption than interest rate constancy. Without wealth or credit rationing effects, a liquidity trap makes monetary policy ineffective even in open economies with flexible exchange rates. Note that we implicitly assumed a liquidity trap did *not* exist. That is why the speculative demand could not absorb the monetary expansion at the fixed interest rate, and the transactions demand had to increase.

[4]Again, we are ignoring a real balance effect.

FIGURE 33–2
Capital Mobility and Monetary Policy

Fixed exchange rates together with perfect capital mobility preclude the use of monetary policy in small countries. Monetary policy is feasible when the exchange rate is flexible.

The domestic interest rate and foreign exchange rate are the links between money and GNP in open economies. When capital is perfectly mobile, the domestic interest rate is determined by the foreign interest rate. The links are fixed when the exchange rate is fixed, which makes permanent changes in the money supply impossible. Flexible exchange rates, which shift the IS curve, opens a link for monetary policy.

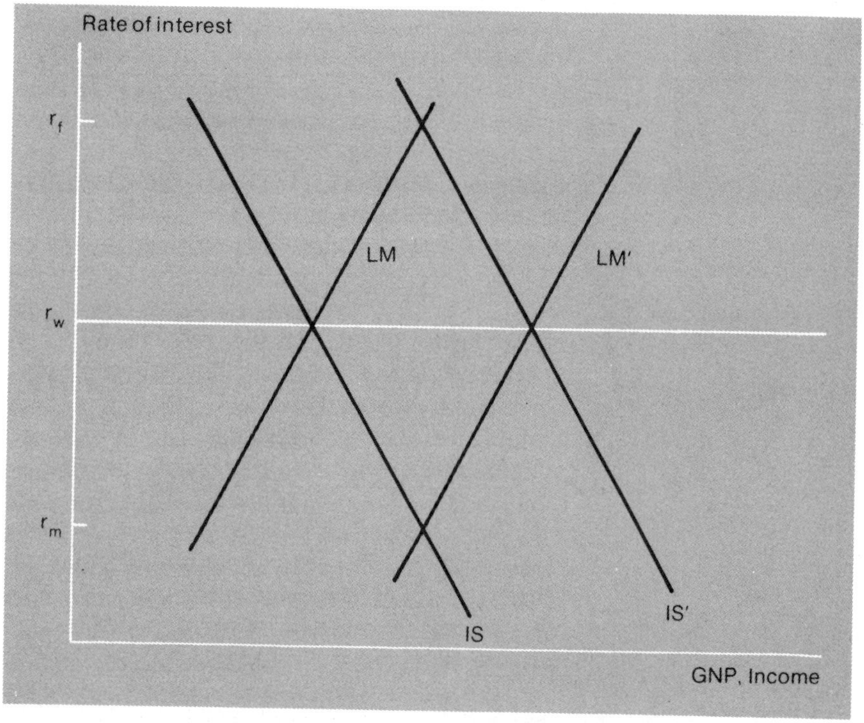

Capital Mobility and Fiscal Policy

When exchange rates are fixed and capital is perfectly mobile, fiscal policy is effective only because it induces accommodating monetary policy. An independent monetary policy is feasible and precludes the use of fiscal policy when exchange rates are flexible.

In order to maintain the fixed exchange rate in spite of capital flows induced by fiscal policy, monetary policy must parallel fiscal policy. Fiscal policy variations produce completely offsetting exchange rate variations in a flexible system with an independent monetary policy.

at r_w, the LM must shift back to its initial position. The tendency toward depreciation is nullified by a monetary contraction exactly offsetting the initial expansion.

We discovered several examples where extreme changes in an economic variable turn monetary and fiscal policy on their heads. For example, fiscal policy is ineffective when the liquidity preference is perfectly inelastic. Make the liquidity preference curve perfectly elastic—the liquidity trap—and monetary policy becomes ineffective. We have yet another example of policy reversals. When exchange rates change from flexible to fixed in small countries with perfect capital mobility, it is *pure* fiscal policy that becomes infeasible, where pure fiscal policy is government deficits financed by bond sales with the money supply remaining constant. Recall that additional government spending and deficits shift the IS to IS′ in Figure 33–2. Captions above and below Figure 33–2 emphasize that it illustrates two separate cases. The fiscal expansion raises income and the rate of interest to r_f in a closed economy. In an open economy the *potentially* higher interest rates induce capital inflows and increase the foreign demand for the local currency. In order to keep exchange rates fixed, the central bank must provide foreigners with the currency that they will use to buy local bonds. The central bank buys the gold or official assets that foreigners are offering.[5] This increases the money supply and prevents the interest rate from rising. Shifting the IS to IS′ generates a money supply increase which shifts the LM to LM′ in countries with fixed exchange rates. See Figure 33–2.

Expressing the above argument entirely in terms of the supply and demand for money, additional government spending increases GNP and the amount of money demanded for transactions purposes. The transactions increase cannot be accommodated by a reduction in the amount demanded for speculative purposes because the interest rate is fixed. The only alternative is an increase in the money supply.

Pure fiscal policy is possible but becomes totally ineffective when exchange rates are flexible. Expansionary fiscal policy again initially tends to raise interest rates and induces capital inflows. Authorities committed to a clean float and a constant monetary policy let the currency appreciate. This shifts IS′ back down in Figure 33–2 as appreciation decreases net exports. *The net export contraction must exactly equal the fiscal expansion, leaving GNP unchanged.* Why is this so? A constant money supply implies a constant money demand at equilibrium. With the rate of interest constant, the amount of money demanded for speculative purposes remains fixed. Pure fiscal policy cannot increase GNP because the speculative demand cannot be depressed to provide the necessary money balances for transaction purposes. In order to intersect the given LM at r_w in Figure 33–2, the IS must shift back to its initial position.

The reader may want to test his or her mastery of this section by applying the above arguments to the case of monetary and fiscal contraction.

---

[5]Alternatively, the central bank could engage in an ''ordinary'' open-market purchase so that the private domestic sector can satisfy the foreign demand. The important point is that the money supply increases in either case.

Relaxation of either the small country or perfect capital mobility assumption changes the conclusions of this section in the direction of those for closed economies. This occurs because the relaxation of either assumption lets monetary and fiscal policy affect the rate of interest. The policies of large countries such as the United States influence to some extent rates of interest worldwide. Capital is not perfectly mobile; any country's domestic policies do change the domestic and foreign interest rate differential. Consequently, while this section is not entirely applicable to the United States today, the growth of both the world economy and capital mobility will increase this section's applicability.

The Long Run, Tradable Commodities, and the Price Level

Let us now abstract from capital flows and focus on the long run, where prices are flexible.[6] If goods were identical and readily transportable worldwide, then, *according to the purchasing power parity (PPP) theorem, the ratio of domestic prices in any two countries will equal their exchange rate in the long run.* This equalizes the purchasing power of a currency at home and abroad or, equivalently, equalizes prices worldwide. For example, suppose the exchange rate is £1 = $2, but gizmos cost $1.50 in the United States and £1 in Britain. The dollar buys more at home than in Britain. This cannot persist; if it did, the United States would export its total output. U.S. exporters would buy gizmos at $1.50, sell them in Britain for £1, and convert this sum to $2, making a $0.50 profit per gizmo. This action by traders leads to the PPP theorem when markets are free. The U.S. exports tends to appreciate the dollar. Moreover, the reduction in U.S. gizmos at home raises their dollar price, and the flood of U.S. gizmos in Britain lowers their price in pounds.

The PPP theorem is expressed algebraically as

$$e = P_D/P_F \tag{33–2}$$

where e is the exchange rate expressed as the price in domestic currency of a unit of foreign exchange, P_D is the price of domestic commodities, and P_F is the price of foreign commodities. For example, £1 will cost $2 when the dollar price of gizmos is twice the pound price. A country which is small compared to the rest of the world cannot influence foreign prices. First assume exchange rates are fixed. *According to the PPP theorem,*

---

[6]Capital flows are a short-run phenomenon. They are the means of achieving a long-run equilibrium in the international stock of assets and liabilities. For example, higher foreign interest rates increase the demand for foreign assets. Capital outflows occur only so long as the stock demand is unsatisfied.

the domestic price level is determined by the foreign price level, given the fixed exchange rate. In terms of Equation (33–2), when e is fixed, P_D varies according to P_F. The quantity theory, however, states that the (domestic) money supply determines (domestic) prices in the long run. The inevitable conclusion that follows from these assumptions is that *monetary authorities adhering to the fixed exchange rate cannot control the money supply in the long run*. Ignore output effects and skip directly to the long run where prices are variable. If the money supply were to increase, domestic prices would rise. Exports would fall and imports would rise. The currency tends to depreciate in the foreign exchange market. The authorities permit the depreciation and the adjustment process ends here when exchange rates are flexible. The depreciation satisfies the PPP theorem and restores net exports so that income does not fall. With a fixed exchange rate, however, the currency is not allowed to depreciate. The authorities sell gold or other official assets, which reduces the money supply. This reduction must exactly equal the initial expansion. If not, the money supply and domestic price level would change, and the PPP theorem would not be satisfied at the fixed exchange rate.

Of course, countries produce different products, and many similar products are not tradable. For example, one cannot ship haircuts from New York to London. Consequently, the price of haircuts in terms of the same currency may differ across countries. What are the implications of product differences and nontradables for the PPP theorem and fixed exchange rates? If tastes, technology, and the competitive structure of markets remain constant, then the ratio of foreign to domestic prices may differ from the price of foreign exchange by a *constant* amount according to the PPP theorem. Because the wedge between prices and exchange rates is determined by tastes, technology, and market structure, monetary authorities in small countries adhering to pegged exchange rates still cannot change the money supply and domestic price level in the *long run*.

The Gold Standard

A fixed exchange rate is only one, albeit important, element of the gold standard. Do the other elements suggest the desirability of letting foreign prices determine domestic prices? Definitely yes, provided foreigners are playing by the rules of the game and some plausible assumptions are approximately satisfied. Assume worldwide gold production increases at the same rate as worldwide total output. According to the gold standard rules, the worldwide money supply then will increase at the same rate as worldwide total GNP. Assuming velocity is constant, the quantity theory states that worldwide prices are constant in the long run. Long-run, worldwide inflation is feasible only when countries violate the canons of the gold standard, barring major gold discoveries.

Pegged exchange rates tie prices worldwide according to the PPP theorem. If exchange rates are pegged but other countries are not on the gold standard, then there is no constraint on the worldwide price level. Small countries still cannot pursue an independent monetary policy, but there is no guarantee that this is desirable. If the rest of the world can and does adopt inflationary policies, then a small country must follow suit. Large countries can pursue an independent monetary policy because they influence prices in other countries. In other words, *countries must export inflation in order to produce it domestically when exchange rates are pegged.*

An Evaluation of Pegged and Flexible Exchange Rates

What are the major advantages and disadvantages of pegged versus flexible exchange rates? First, international trade and capital flows are stimulated by the greater certainty about the prices of foreign goods induced by pegged exchange rates. The uncertainties under flexible exchange rates are reduced by the creation of forward exchange markets, where one enters into contracts today for the future sale or purchase of foreign exchange. However, forward markets are never complete across all currencies and over all time periods. Moreover, forward markets and hedging are costly operations.

The second and, for our purposes, main difference between pegged and flexible exchange rates is that *pegged exchange rates inhibit an independent monetary policy, that is, a monetary policy directed at domestic policy goals.* Alternatively stated, the authorities cannot change the money supply at will; monetary changes must be consistent with pegged exchange rates.[7] When is the restriction on monetary changes particularly undesirable? Consider first the short run. We saw that monetary policy is entirely infeasible in the extreme case of perfect capital mobility. Maintenance of the pegged exchange rate prevents any attention to domestic issues. This clearly is undesirable. In the more realistic case of less than perfect capital mobility, at least some domestic interest rate and money supply variations are possible.[8] Monetary changes then move aggregate demand and GNP

---

[7]In terms of Chapter 29's discussion on the number of policy instruments and goals, pegged exchange rates set another goal but do not offer another instrument. Assuming that monetary policy is the sole instrument or, equivalently, that the number of instruments just equaled the number of domestic goals, the total number of goals exceeds the number of instruments with pegged exchange rates. When the exchange rate has priority, the domestic goals generally are not attainable.

[8]The large size of the United States economy probably is as important as imperfect capital mobility in explaining domestic interest rate and money supply variations in the 1950s under Bretton Woods. In any case, capital mobility undoubtedly has increased.

in the same direction but tend to move the balance of payments and exchange rate in the opposite direction. For example, monetary expansion increases income but tends to depreciate the currency and produce a payments deficit because both imports rise and capital flows out in search of higher returns abroad. Consequently, *any disturbance which creates a recession (boom) and balance of payments deficit (surplus) severely restricts monetary authorities adhering to a pegged exchange-rate system.* To eliminate the payments deficit (surplus) the monetary authority must sell (buy) assets and decrease (increase) the money supply, which aggravates the recession (boom).

What are examples of disturbances that severely inhibit an independent, domestically-oriented policy, and are such disturbances likely? Changes in tastes or technology which reduce the demand for our exports or increase our demand for imports cause a recession and balance of payments deficit. A monetary authority determined to fight the payments deficit and prevent a depreciation on the foreign exchange market must adopt a contractionary monetary policy. Alternatively, the authorities cannot dampen a domestic investment boom which attracts sufficient foreign capital inflows to produce a balance of payments surplus. Indeed, in order to curtail the payments surplus the authorities must purchase official assets and increase the money supply, thereby adding fuel to the investment boom. Pegged exchange rates do not severely inhibit an independent short-run monetary policy only when disturbances simultaneously produce a recession (boom) and a balance of payments surplus (deficit). Such disturbances exist but are relatively infrequent.

The Gold Standard Again

The edge that flexible exchange rates have over pegged rates is less strong in the long run, particularly when countries are on the gold standard. Flexible exchange rates let national authorities determine the domestic price level and rate of inflation. Authorities *who act responsibly* should be granted this power. They are able to guarantee long-run price stability, something that authorities constrained by the gold standard cannot do. The long-run rate of inflation equals the rate of growth of velocity plus the difference between the growth of money and output. The "rules" of the gold standard made money growth depend on the gold stock. Therefore, with velocity constant, inflation and the rate that money growth exceeds output growth under the gold standard is determined by the extent of discoveries or technological improvements which cause gold production to outstrip other production. Gold production lagged and prices fell worldwide between 1870 and 1890. The South African gold discoveries of the 1890s caused a worldwide inflation. Because technological progress and discoveries do not occur at constant rates, and because velocity changes, though predictably so, the gold standard cannot guarantee price stability. Nevertheless, deflations and inflations during the gold standard era were quite mild compared to the price instability witnessed since countries adopted flexible exchange rates. A properly managed money supply and price stability are hopes which, in fact, typically have not been realized with flexible exchange rates. Authorities often act irresponsibly.

Summary/Questions

The gold standard disciplines irresponsible authorities and achieves greater price stability by incurring high mining costs. The desire to avoid resource implementation costs has led to calls for a worldwide system of pegged exchange rates *not* tied to any commodity such as gold. The whole world would be tied together and set adrift without a gold anchor. Such a system, which has some similarities with Bretton Woods, may appear to be intermediate in terms of price stability between flexible exchange rates and a strict gold standard. This need not be the case, however. Large countries have little to choose between flexible and fixed rates not tied to gold. Their authorities would determine domestic prices in either case. Compared to flexible exchange rates, *prices are less stable worldwide if authorities are less responsible in large countries than in small countries.* The responsible authorities in small countries could not swim against the tide set by large countries when exchange rates are pegged. Flexible rates are less inflationary than pegged rates in small countries with authorities less irresponsible than the authorities in large countries.

1. How does recognition of the economy's openness affect the short-run impact of monetary and fiscal policy on GNP, ignoring capital flows? Which regime, pegged or flexible exchange rates, produces larger policy multipliers, again ignoring capital flows?
2. Define perfect capital mobility and the purchasing power parity (PPP) theorem.
3. Explain why the equilibrium money stock cannot be changed in a small country adhering to pegged exchange rates when either capital is perfectly mobile or the PPP theorem holds.
4. Explain why pure fiscal policy, that is, a deficit financed entirely by bonds, is not feasible in a small country adhering to pegged exchange rates, assuming capital is perfectly mobile.
5. How does exchange rate flexibility influence the impact on GNP of monetary and fiscal policy when capital is mobile?

6. If gold production and total production grow at approximately the same rate, and if velocity is approximately constant, then prices must fluctuate little under the gold standard. Explain.
7. What types of disturbances greatly impede the attainment of short-run domestic goals when a country pegs exchange rates?
8. Who or what determines the worldwide price level in the long run when countries *(a)* are on the gold standard, and *(b)* peg exchange rates but do not tie them to gold or any other commodity.

Budget deficits, monetary policy, and exchange rates

34

And that is why this enormous national debt engineered by this [Reagan] administration is harming these [Latin American] countries and fueling this [illegal] immigration.

*Walter Mondale**

Well, my rebuttal is I've heard the national debt blamed for a lot of things but not for illegal immigration.

*Ronald Reagan**

The budget deficit of the federal government was a central economic issue in the 1984 presidential debates. At the most elementary level the budget deficit exists because taxes fall short of expenditures. At this elementary level the deficit is strictly a fiscal issue and need not be discussed in a money and banking book. However, the deficit and monetary policy strongly interact in both cause and effect directions. Monetary policy influences deficits through its effect on income and, therefore, tax receipts, given the tax rates. The deficits in turn cause the Federal Reserve to adopt a different monetary policy. Fed Chairman Paul Volcker has been a particularly vocal critic of the deficits.[1] The relationships between deficits and monetary policy render appropriate, perhaps even imperative, a brief analysis of the deficits. The analysis applies several points made in previous chapters and is a good summary.

---

*Second Reagan-Mondale Debate, Kansas City, October 21, 1984.

[1] See Volcker's testimony before Congress as reported in virtually any 1984 issue of the *Federal Reserve Bulletin*.

The Size of the Deficits

The deficits are controversial. Some dismiss them as being inconsequential. Most worry deeply about the deficits. Those who worry about the deficits often do so for different and contradictory reasons. Whatever may be their consequences, at least everyone agrees the deficits are very large. Or are they? Table 34–1 shows various measures of the deficit from 1970 to 1984. Column 2 of the table shows the absolute nominal or dollar size of the deficit. From a 1984 viewpoint, there definitely is an upward trend in the absolute size of the deficit. Note that this was *not* the case from a 1979 viewpoint. The deficit rose sharply between 1974 and 1975 but then declined, reaching a value at the end of the decade about equal to its initial value. The absolute size of the deficits is strictly a 1980s "problem" when the starting point is 1970. Of course, moving the starting point backward to 1950 makes the whole period since 1970 a "problem."

The deficits have grown but so has the economy. Column 3 represents a relative measure of the deficits, namely, the deficits as a percent of GNP. The relative deficits do show an upward trend from 1970 to 1984, but the upward trend is less pronounced for the relative than for the absolute deficits. The relative deficits were approximately the same in 1971 and 1981, and the same was true in the deep recession years of 1975 and 1982. If the starting point is moved forward from 1970 to 1975, the upward trend in the relative deficits virtually vanishes. A sharp five-year drop beginning in 1975 is followed by an only somewhat sharper rise.

TABLE 34–1
Federal Deficits and Unemployment, 1970–1984

Year	*Deficits, $ Billions*	*Deficits/ GNP, Percent*	*Unemployment Rate, Percent*	*Cyclically-adjusted Deficits, Percent*
1970	12.1	1.23	4.9	2.33
1971	22.0	2.06	5.9	2.16
1972	17.3	1.47	5.6	1.87
1973	6.7	0.51	4.9	1.61
1974	10.7	0.76	5.6	1.16
1975	70.6	4.62	8.5	2.12
1976	53.8	3.16	7.7	1.46
1977	48.1	2.55	7.0	1.55
1978	29.4	1.40	6.0	1.40
1979	16.1	0.66	5.8	0.86
1980	61.4	2.33	7.1	1.23
1981	62.2	2.04	7.6	0.44
1982	147.1	4.79	9.7	1.07
1983	182.9	5.53	9.6	1.93
1984	175.2	4.78	7.5	3.28

The relative deficits are affected by the business cycle, which is proxied by the unemployment rate in column 4. Absolute government expenditures are little affected by the business cycle. Consequently, relative expenditures rise during recessions and fall during expansions. With a progressive tax system, relative taxes fall during a recession, by definition. This behavior by taxes and expenditures implies that the deficit automatically rises as the economy slides from a business cycle peak to a recession. Column 5 calculates a cyclically-adjusted or, similarly, full-employment budget deficit by subtracting from the relative deficit (column 3) the difference between the unemployment rate (column 4) and 6 percent, which is taken as the constant natural rate of unemployment. For a *given* relative deficit (column 3), the cyclically-adjusted deficit decreases as unemployment increases. Cyclically-adjusted deficits are less than relative deficits whenever unemployment exceeds 6 percent.

Fiscal policy is traditionally measured by the size of the cyclically-adjusted or full-employment budget deficit. While more sophisticated methods of calculating a cyclically-adjusted deficit exist, all show essentially the same conclusions.[2] When adjusted for the business cycle, *fiscal policy was extremely contractionary in 1981*. The second smallest cyclically-adjusted deficit, in 1979, was nearly twice as large as the 1981 deficit. The cyclically-adjusted deficit did increase very significantly beginning in 1982 due to the three-stage income tax rate cuts of the Reagan administration. (The composition of adjusted relative expenditures shifted from social to defense programs, but the total changed little.) Nevertheless, the 1982 figure was the third lowest, and the 1983 figure was in line with the figures for the early 1970s. Only by 1984 did the cyclically-adjusted deficits of the Reagan administration begin to exceed the historical standard.

Most economists and politicians in late 1984 are forecasting as large or larger *adjusted* deficits due to such factors as interest payments on a larger national debt and the indexation of tax brackets beginning in 1985. Readers should update Table 34–1. Were the forecasters correct? If not, did the forecasters simply miscalculate the behavior of the fiscal system and economy, or did Congress pass new, important tax and expenditure legislation? Note that a continuation of the cyclical expansion or another recession cannot explain the cyclically-adjusted deficit, by definition. Henceforth, "deficits" without qualifying adjectives mean the cyclically-adjusted federal deficit, which measures fiscal policy.[3]

---

[2]See U.S. Department of Commerce, Survey of Current Business (December 1983), 25–34. For other measures of fiscal policy see, Alan Blinder and Robert Solow, "Analytical Foundations of Fiscal Policy," in *The Economics of Public Finance* (Washington, D.C.: Brookings Institution, 1974) and Robert Eisner and Paul Pieper, "A New View of the Federal Debt and Budget Deficits," *American Economic Review* (March 1984), pp. 11–29.

[3]We follow the lead of political analysts and focus here on the federal deficit. Chapter 21 presented data for total (federal, state and local) government expenditures and taxes,

The Demand Side Consequences of the Deficit

For the moment let all variations in the deficit arise from tax rate changes which do not have any *direct* impact on supply. Thus, the deficit is assumed to be strictly a demand phenomenon which does not require a subjective, "noneconomic" evaluation of the cost and benefit of government expenditures, which are remaining fixed. Government expenditures here are independent of tax receipts. Given these assumptions, many of the alleged consequences of the deficit can be effectively analyzed with the IS–LM model. We must ignore some alleged consequences that would require much more sophisticated models or are very hypothetical, for example, the effect of deficits on immigration.

The Short Run: Output, Interest Rates, and Growth

Lower tax rates and larger deficit directly increase disposable income and consumption. In the short run, output responds to the higher demand, and the rate of interest rises as government finances its deficit by selling bonds. Recalling Chapter 26's discussion, lower taxes shift the IS curve outward to IS′ and the LM remains fixed. See Figure 34–1 but ignore LM′. *Deficits raise current output but could lower future output because investment and the future capital stock is crowded out by government bonds and higher interest rates.* Deficits inhibit growth *to the extent that investment varies inversely with the rate of interest.*

Chapter 29 stated that one policy instrument generally cannot achieve two goals. The multiple goal of current output and economic growth is an important explanation for opposition to deficits. Many feel that the "pure" deficits policy necessary to achieve the current output goal results in an interest rate that is too high, and future capital stocks and output growth rates that are too low. Some want a pure monetary policy; the LM shifts to LM′ in Figure 34–1, and the IS remains fixed. A pure monetary policy has the greatest effect on future income by lowering interest rates. Note, however, that expansionary fiscal policy need not necessarily reduce investment when investment also depends positively on income. Fiscal policy only is *less* growth oriented than monetary policy. The majority are not all that growth oriented and prefer a combination policy: expansionary monetary and fiscal policy. Both the IS and LM curves should shift rightward somewhat to intersect at full employment, y_f.

---

from which the total deficit can be calculated. Substituting total for federal deficits changes magnitudes but not general conclusions. For example, the total government budget shows a significant deficit, though less than the federal deficit in recent years, as state and local governments are running budget surpluses.

FIGURE 34–1

Larger deficits and expansionary fiscal policy raise the rate of interest and inhibit economic growth, at least relative to monetary policy. Expansionary monetary policy lowers the rate of interest and stimulates investment.

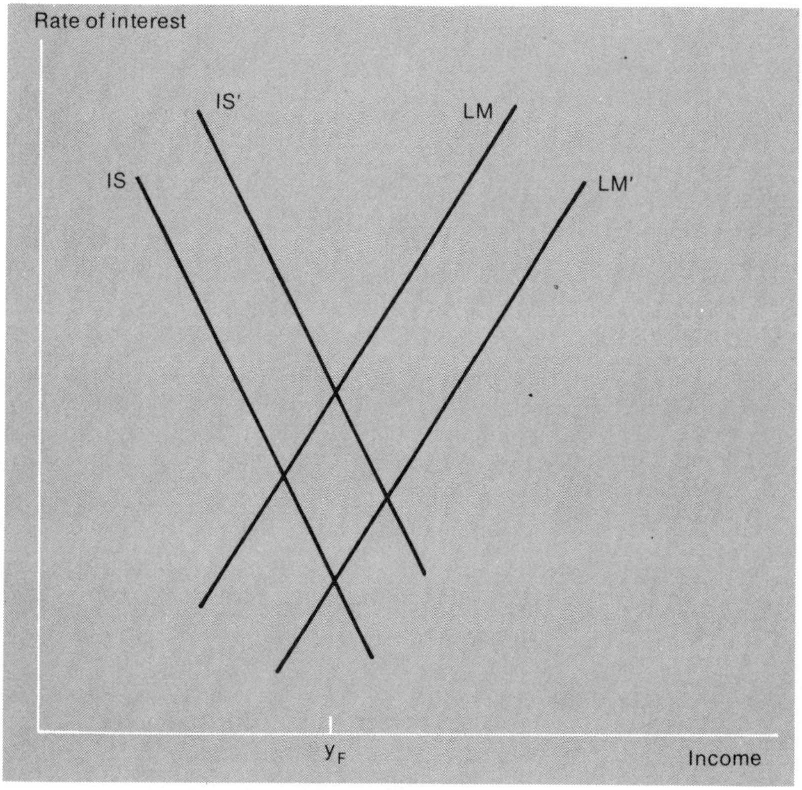

The Short Run: Interest Rates, the Exchange Rate, and Net Exports

The multiple goal of current income and positive net exports (surpluses on the current account of the balance of payments) is another explanation for opposition to the deficits in an economy with flexible exchange rates and substantial capital mobility. According to the last chapter, authorities of *small* countries cannot influence the domestic rate of interest when capital flows are perfectly mobile internationally. Clearly, the assumptions are not valid for the United States, where interest rates do vary independently. Capital is not perfectly mobile. The "small country" assumption also is not valid for the United States. Foreign investors have neither the resources nor inclination to snap up all the bonds the Treasury issues to finance the deficit. Because they do not, deficits do raise United States interest rates. However, foreigners purchase a significant proportion of the high-yielding U.S. bonds. Capital is mobile, though not perfectly so. *Foreign capital flows into the United States cause the U.S. dollar to appreciate when exchange rates are flexible*. The appreciation of the dollar reduces exports and increases imports. *Small or negative net exports are a consequence of the high interest rates created by the deficit.*

The bond purchases by foreigners and capital inflows, which cause the dollar to appreciate and produce small or negative net exports, do have the desirable *short-run* effect of lessening the interest rate increase associated with budget deficits. Because interest rates do not rise as much, any reduction in domestic investment will not be as great. Domestic investment is *not* crowded out by the federal deficit to the extent that the latter is financed by foreigners. Financial investment by foreigners facilitates economic (plant and equipment) investment domestically. The problem, however is that net foreign investment in the United States may not continue to be positive in the long run. In any case, current investment by foreigners requires future interest and principal payments to foreigners.

The Long Run: Deficits, Inflation, and Neutral Monetary Policy

Let us now focus on the long run, where full employment is presumed to exist. Are deficits and expansionary fiscal policy, like expansionary monetary policy, inflationary at full-employment? Yes, according to much of the popular press and many politicians. Economists of all stripes, however, have been much more reluctant than journalists and politicians to claim that the deficit per se is the source of our inflation. Professor Milton Friedman goes further than some economists. He categorically denies that fiscal policy causes inflation. His well-known opposition to fiscal policy is based on other reasons. Friedman said, "Inflation is always and everywhere a monetary phenomenon."[4] Who is correct, Friedman or the journalists and politicians?

We stated in Chapter 23 that Milton Friedman's position on the effect of interest rates on the demand for money is not altogether clear.[5] Nevertheless, virtually everyone has interpreted him as stating that the demand for money does not depend on the rate of interest. Although Friedman

---

[4]Milton Friedman, *Dollars and Deficits* (Englewood Cliffs, N.J.: Prentice-Hall, 1968), p. 39.

[5]See footnote 5, Chapter 23.

rejects the classical transactions approach to money and favors the asset approach, which views money simply as one of many assets, within the IS–LM model his denial of interest rate effects is equivalent to acceptance of the classical transactions demand, M = kPy. That is, according to Friedman, the LM curve is the dashed vertical line in Figure 34–2 at y_F. (The price level associated with the money supply cannot be illustrated in this graph with the rate of interest and real income on the axes.) A tax cut which shifts the IS curve to IS′ only raises the rate of interest in this special case. Interest sensitive spending is curtailed by the amount of additional spending due to higher disposable incomes. Real output is ul-

FIGURE 34–2 Deficits are a temporary source of inflation. Accommodative monetary policy accentuates the inflationary impact of deficit.

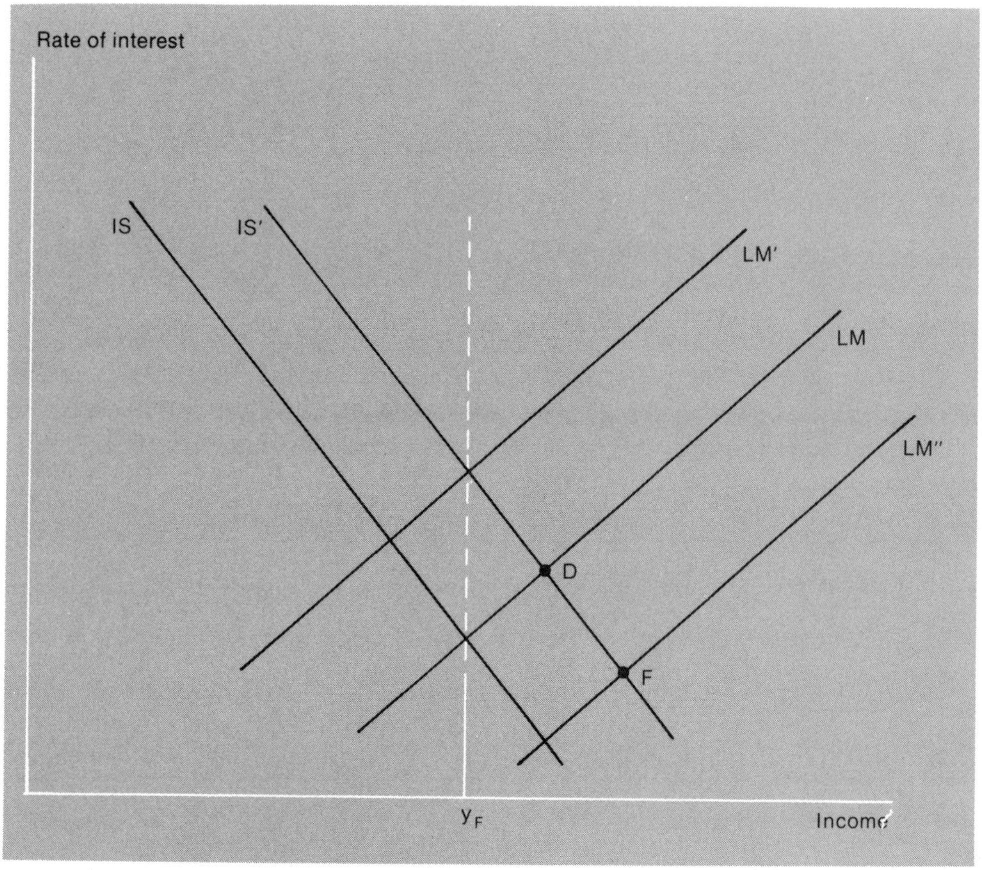

timately constant at full employment, and so is the price level because the constant velocity implies a rigid link between the value of expenditures and money. Given Friedman's assumptions, inflation is strictly a monetary phenomenon.

Perhaps, as Friedman claims, his position on the interest rate elasticity of the demand for money has been almost universally misinterpreted because, although he and monetarism are virtually synonymous, nearly every other monetarist includes an interest rate term in the demand for money. Consequently, let's draw upward-sloping LM curves. When the LM curve is upward sloping, tax cuts and budget deficits induce higher prices. Deficits financed by bonds shift the IS curve to IS′ while the solid LM curve remains fixed, assuming the Fed follows a hands-off policy. Point D in Figure 34–2 cannot be a permanent equilibrium. While firms temporarily meet the government induced demand and move to point D, they subsequently revert to their previous production plans and raise prices, causing the LM curve to shift upward to LM′. Because the higher interest rate necessary to reduce demand to its pretax-cut level also reduces the amount of money demanded for speculative purposes in this case, prices rise and transactions money demand increases enough to equate total money demand and the fixed supply. Deficits increase velocity and prices in the long run, given a Keynesian (non-Friedman monetarist) money demand.

While the Keynesian money demand does allow the deficit to be a source of inflation, it is not a likely major source. In Figure 34–2, full-employment output is held fixed so that the larger absolute deficit coincides with a *larger* deficit as a percentage of GNP. It is *increasing* relative deficits, rather than *large* absolute or even relative deficits, that cause inflation. Additional absolute deficits which just keep pace with a rising full-employment are no more inflationary than additional money which parallels income growth. In terms of Figure 34–2, tax cuts and a larger deficit which shift the IS curve out are not inflationary when the full-employment and LM lines shift out equally. IS and the y_F line shifted rightward by the same distance continue to intersect at the same interest rate. While the cyclically-adjusted relative deficit may increase for several years, and while a then large relative deficit may not be reduced, the relative deficit simply cannot increase continuously. In order to continuously shift the IS curve relative to full employment, the tax share of income must continuously fall or the government expenditure share of output must continuously rise, which is inconceivable. Thus, deficits are a *temporary* source of inflation; deficits are inflationary only when they increase faster than full employment GNP. Adding the word "sustained" makes Friedman absolutely correct; sustained inflation is always and everywhere a monetary phenomenon.

The Long Run: Deficits, Inflation, and Accommodative Monetary Policy

Why do many journalists and politicians claim that deficits are a major, sustained source of inflation? Are they just plain wrong? Not exactly. We analyzed the effects of changes in the deficit per se. In the "real world," however, many variables change simultaneously, and it is extremely difficult to disentangle their separate effects. Nonspecialists often attribute to the deficit the effects of other variables which usually move together with it. What variables usually increase when the deficit increases? One variable is the money supply. We saw in Chapters 19 and 20 that until quite recently money market conditions and interest rates were the Fed's operating target. The money supply fluctuated willy-nilly while interest rates were kept fixed, at least in the short run. Although the Fed is paying much more attention to the money supply today, it certainly has not altogether abandoned its fixation on interest rates. As a result, monetary policy tends to accommodate fiscal policy. To prevent the higher interest rates associated with larger deficits, the Fed increases the money supply.

While the Treasury is selling bonds to finance deficits, the Fed is conducting open-market purchases. For a short time at least, the Fed successfully keeps interest rates down. In terms of Figure 34–2, expansionary fiscal policy alone pushes the economy to point D. The accommodative monetary policy pushes the economy out further to point F. Point F is beyond full employment and cannot be a position of long-run equilibrium. Prices rise, which increases the amount of money demanded and shifts the LM″ curve upward. Assuming the Fed accepts the inevitability of higher interest rates and does not expand the money supply further, the temporarily accommodative monetary policy makes fiscal policy more inflationary than it would otherwise be. Prices must rise more to shift up to LM′ the accommodative policy LM″ instead of the constant policy LM.

Opposition to Deficits Based on the Benefits and Determinants of Government Expenditures

The 1984 election did focus greater attention on the federal budget. However, politicians and others had been concerned about the deficit for many years. The 1976 victorious Democratic presidential candidate, Jimmy Carter, promised to balance the federal budget by 1980. The promise went unkept. The 1980 victorious Republican presidential candidate, Ronald Reagan, promised to balance the federal budget by 1984. The promise went unkept. By 1984, 32 state legislatures had called for a constitutional convention to propose a balanced budget amendment and, thereby, prohibit deficits. The early concern about the deficit (when it was not much of an economic problem) and the recent derailment of the balanced budget amendment (when the deficits are an important economic problem at least by historical standards) suggest that the deficits are not entirely an economic issue. Noneconomic factors are essential to explain the puzzle of protracted deficits in spite of very broad political opposition to deficits. In 1978 Harvard's Benjamin Friedman said, "The left now raises the specter of enlarged deficits in opposition to the increasingly audible calls for tax reduction, while the right continues to cite the same threat against new government spending initiatives."[6] Let us explore Benjamin Friedman's suggestion that opposition to deficits partially reflects different estimates of (1) the benefits of government expenditures, and (2) the dynamic relationship between taxes and expenditures.

Government expenditures are hardly homogeneous. They include nuclear weapon systems and toxic waste clean-ups. Nevertheless, the right is united in opposition to government expenditures in general. In other words, holding the composition of government expenditures constant, the optimal level of expenditures is lower for the right than the left. *The old right opposes deficits because it feels they lead to greater government expenditures, whose costs exceed benefits*. The old right views taxes as more painful than debt. According to this viewpoint, increasing the pain of paying for government expenditures reduces their level. Elimination of the deficit by raising taxes alone would be too painful. Higher taxes and fiscal discipline are associated with less government spending.

The new right opposes government expenditures even more than the old right but tends to worry much less about the deficit for three reasons. First, the new right believes that deficits *brought about by tax cuts* have strong supply side or incentive effects which increase output. Indeed, extreme supply siders claim the economy is on the backward-bending portion of the Laffer Curve, so that lower tax rates ultimately increase tax receipts.[7] The creed of supply siders states that deficits are temporary phenomena that are cured by economic growth. When income responds fully to lower tax rates, the deficit will vanish. Second, the new right believes that society to a great extent anticipates higher future taxes in order to repay the current national debt and reacts by implicitly taxing itself today through voluntarily lower consumption (higher saving). According to this line of argument, debt-financed expenditures are *not* much less painful than tax-financed expenditures. People see through the government debt and view it as their own. Third, the new right believes others are driven by a philosophy described in the 1984 election as tax-and-spend and spend-and-tax. Government spends whatever additional

---

[6]Benjamin Friedman, "Crowding Out or Crowding In? Economic Consequences of Financing Government Deficits," *Brookings Papers on Economic Activity* (3: 1978), p. 593.

[7]See the appendix to Chapter 22.

tax receipts it gets. For some not well specified reason, the new right believes the maximum feasible deficit is limited in size. If taxes are cut so that the current deficit temporarily exceeds the maximum, government spending will be reduced. Similarly, higher taxes only lead to greater spending, thereby defeating the initial attempt to reduce the deficit below the maximum feasible. The second argument for ignoring deficits says that they do not encourage much additional government expenditures because they are almost as painful as taxes. The third argument goes further. Deficits actually discourage spending because of the existence of a maximum feasible deficit and the tax-and-spend philosophy.

Mr. Mondale's and the left's response to the deficits in the 1984 election lent some credence to the new right's tax-and-spend allegation. Mr. Mondale deplored the deficits in the strongest terms. He proposed significantly higher taxes to reduce the deficit. Yet, he also proposed somewhat higher overall expenditures. (True, the composition of expenditures was the major proposed change on the expenditure side.) If deficits per se are bad, why spend even a little more and make matters worse? Perhaps deficits are bad only because they constrain additional, highly beneficial government expenditures.[8]

Summary/Questions

The recent deficits are controversial because some of their alleged consequences are not readily visible or have been overstated by their opponents. For example, column 3 of Table 34–2 shows that the ratio of fixed investment (total investment excluding the change in inventories) to GNP held up quite well in 1981–83 despite a deep recession and large deficits. Investment was substantially greater in 1981–83 than in 1975, another deep recession year. Of course, this does not prove that deficits have little effect on investment. Some strongly positive factor totally unrelated to the deficits could fortuitously have been counteracting the strongly negative effect of deficits during the 1980s. On the other hand, those unalarmed by deficits *due to lower taxes* look at the data as a confirmation of their belief that opponents of deficits incorrectly ignore the direct, positive effect of lower taxes and higher deficits on the after-tax rate of return on investment and firms' retained earnings. All deficits raise interest rates, which tends to reduce investment. However, this tendency is counteracted by higher after-tax returns and larger retained

[8]See Chapter 29's "The Direct Benefit and Effectiveness of Government Spending" for the relationships among the size of the policy multiplier, policy effectiveness, and the estimated direct benefits of government expenditures.

TABLE 34–2
Deficits, Investment, Foreign Exchange Rate, and Net Exports, 1970–1984

Year	*Cyclically-adjusted Deficits, Percent*	*Fixed Investment/GNP, Percent*	*Exchange Rate Index, March 1973 = 100*	*Net Exports/ GNP, Percent*
1970	2.33	13.9	n.a.	+0.13
1971	2.16	14.4	n.a.	−0.05
1972	1.87	15.2	n.a.	−0.29
1973	1.61	15.4	99.2	+0.61
1974	1.16	14.4	101.4	+1.30
1975	2.12	12.6	98.3	+1.88
1976	1.46	13.1	105.6	+1.21
1977	1.55	14.0	103.3	+0.71
1978	1.40	14.4	92.4	+0.62
1979	0.86	16.9	88.1	+0.54
1980	1.23	15.6	87.4	+0.96
1981	0.44	15.4	102.9	+0.89
1982	1.07	14.3	116.6	+0.56
1983	1.93	14.4	125.3	−0.32
1984	3.28	15.8	138.2	−1.71

n.a. = not applicable.

earnings when deficits occur due to a *general*, personal *and* business, tax reduction.

Table 34–2 seemingly confirms that deficits appreciate the currency and reduce net exports. Column 4 presents a weighted-average index of the exchange value of the U.S. dollar against 10 major currencies. The index covers the flexible exchange-rate period, with March 1973 = 100. Higher index numbers note a sharp appreciation of the dollar between 1981–84. Column 5 shows that the net exports (exports minus imports)/ GNP ratio turned from positive to negative between 1981–84, the years the cyclically adjusted deficit rose to a new peak. Those unalarmed by deficits claim that the effects of deficits on the exchange rate have been grossly exaggerated. True, the higher interest rates associated with deficits do tend to appreciate the dollar. However, they also point out that the higher U.S income and temporary inflation associated with deficits tend to depreciate the dollar.[9] On balance, deficits may even depreciate the currency. Those unalarmed by deficits view the appreciation of the dollar as too strong to be caused by deficits; deficits are being blamed for some unknown factors influencing the exchange rate.

1. What are the advantages and disadvantages of the following measures of "the" deficit: the absolute or dollar amount, the relative (to GNP) amount, and a cyclically adjusted amount?

[9]Cf., Chapter 32. If deficits strongly appreciate the exchange rate and reduce the dollar price of imports, one could encounter the paradoxical situation where deficits are deflationary.

2. State the major trends in the alternative deficit measures. Have the trends been consistent during the entire period, or do subperiods show different trends?
3. Concentrating on the fact that deficits raise the rate of interest, state the effect of deficits on (1) investment and economic growth and (2) the exchange rate and net exports.
4. Deficits often induce significant inflation, but deficits themselves are at most temporarily inflationary. Explain carefully.
5. Consider three groups: the old right, the new right, and the left. For each group indicate how its viewpoint about deficits, which are the *difference* between government expenditures and taxes, in fact reflects its viewpoint about the desirable *level* of government expenditures and taxes and the dynamic relationship between the two.
6. Explain why a deficit produced by tax cuts could stimulate investment and depreciate the exchange rate when one ignores interest rate effects.

APPENDIXES

Appendix to Chapter 14: Regression Equations and Antitrust Policy

Lyle Gramley collected cross-section and time-series data for unit banks. Regression or least squares analysis was used to test the economies of scale hypothesis. Gramley's estimated regression equation is[1]

$$\begin{aligned} \text{Average cost} = {} & 1.37 - .39 \log \text{total assets} + .016x_2 \\ & + .022x_3 - .013x_4 + .016x_5 \\ & + .008x_6, \qquad R^2 = 0.78, \end{aligned} \tag{14A–1}$$

where average cost = total cost divided by total assets (output)

x_2 = Ratio of time to total deposits,
x_3 = Ratio of total loans to total assets,
x_4 = Ratio of non-Treasury securities to total assets,
x_5 = Ratio of consumer to total loans,
x_6 = Percent growth of assets.

Assets were measured in millions, and all ratios are expressed as percentages. While the equation is written to highlight the relationship being tested, in the estimation process the log of total assets and the variables standardizing for product mix, $x_2 - x_6$, are treated identically. The reader is encouraged to be aware of the specific standardizing variables and justify

[1]Lyle Gramley, *A Study of Scale Economies in Banking,* Federal Reserve Bank of Kansas City, 1962, p. 18.

the sign of their regression coefficients.[2] *The equation indicates economies of scale do exist:* the coefficient of log total assets is negative. Keeping product mix constant, average cost on balance changes by −0.39 when the log of total assets increases by one unit. The author did not report the t statistics but stated that all were greater than 2. Thus there is at least a 95 percent chance that one may rely on the relationship. Asset size and the standardizing variables explain 78 percent of the variation in average cost, that is, $R^2 = .78$.

The relationship between average cost and *log* total assets is linear so that the relationship between average cost and total assets is the nonlinear curve graphed in Figure 14–3. This means economies are not uniform. Economies of scale are significant when banks are small but rapidly diminish as bank size increases. For example, when assets, measured in millions, increase from 1 to 10 so the *log* increases by one unit—from 0 to 1—then average costs decrease 0.39, which is the coefficient of log total assets in Equation (14A–1). For average costs to decrease another 0.39, size would have to increase to 100 (million).

Loan Rates and Local Bank Structure. In 1955 the Federal Reserve conducted a relatively detailed nationwide survey of loans to small firms (assets under $1 million) in SMAs. The data were averaged by SMA. We want to test the relationship between loan rates and banking structure. Using a cross-section of SMAs, the following regression equation was estimated[3]

$$\begin{aligned}\text{Loan rate} = 7.032 &+ \underset{(2.41)}{.007}\ \text{Concentration} - \underset{(-1.91)}{.006}\ \text{Bank size} \\ &+ \underset{(2.27)}{2.7(10^{-5})}\ \text{Bank size squared} \\ &- \underset{(-13.28)}{.56X_4} + \underset{(3.55)}{.009X_5} + \underset{(2.20)}{.009X_6},\ R^2 = 0.73\end{aligned} \quad \textbf{(14A–2)}$$

where

X_4 = Log of average loan size (in $1,000s),
X_5 = Percentage of loans with maturities greater than one year,
X_6 = Percentage change in nonagricultural wage and salary employment, 1950–55.

---

[2]Total cost includes interest payments, hence the time to total deposits variable. For purposes of testing the operating efficiency hypothesis, the best measure of cost would exclude interest payments, but such a measure was not constructed by Gramley. However, the relationship between average wages and salaries and log total assets is very similar to that shown. Wages and salaries are too narrow a measure of cost; it ignores capital costs. Since the too broad and the too narrow measures give similar results, the lack of a proper measure probably is unimportant.

[3]Paul A. Meyer, "Price Discrimination, Regional Loan Rates, and the Structure of the Banking Industry," *Journal of Finance,* March 1967, pp. 37–48.

The regression equation again is written to highlight the relationship of particular interest. The numbers in parenthesis are t statistics. Variable X_6 is a proxy for loan demand, and loan size and maturity are "standardizing" variables. Lack of data or constancy across SMAs explains the omission of other determinants of cross-sectional interest rates listed in Chapter 6.

The regression coefficient of concentration is positive, as expected. The t statistic greater than 2 strongly suggests the relationship is systematic. The *absolute* value of the concentration coefficient is small (.007) because the survey data were collected years ago when interest rates were low. However, market power explained a significant portion of the *difference* in loan rates to small and large borrowers in 1955, and we may expect the same today. We indicated that large borrowers deal in a virtually competitive national market. Average concentration was 73 percent in the SMAs whose small borrower rates were analyzed. Therefore, rate discrimination against small borrowers due to the different types of markets in which small and large firms deal was approximately 0.50 percentage points (.007 × 73). The difference between loan rates to small and large borrowers was 1.80 percent in 1955. Consequently, bank monopoly power explains more than one fourth (0.50/1.80) of the difference in rates to small and large firms.

Average bank size, measured in millions of deposits, is the second market structure determinant of loan rates in SMAs. The coefficient of bank size is negative, while the coefficient for size squared is positive. This implies a parabola that opens upward, as drawn in Figure 14–4. Familiarity with calculus is essential to determine the average bank size which minimizes small borrower loan rates. Set the derivative of the loan rate with respect to bank size equal to zero and solve for bank size. That is, $d(\text{loan rate})/d(\text{bank size}) = -.006 + 5.4(10^{-5})\text{ bank size} = 0$, or bank size $= 6/5.4(10^{-2}) \cong 110$. The t statistics are just significant at conventional levels, which suggests that the relationship is systematic.

Bank Merger Policy. The results of the last section are not altogether surprising; many industries have monopolistic elements. What is surprising is that for many years antitrust laws, the traditional remedy against monopolies, were applicable to nonbanks alone. Until 1961 the Department of Justice alleged that commercial banks were exempt from the major antitrust laws, the Sherman and Clayton Acts. This is not to say that every proposed merger was consummated. Some bank regulatory agency always has had to approve any merger, which necessarily reduces the number of banks and increases average bank size. While approval of the most blatantly anticompetitive mergers was not forthcoming, the legal immunity of banking from the Clayton Act tended to encourage regulatory laxity. If the Department of Justice did not take action against monopoly in banking, why should the regulatory agencies take a tough stance? Congress provided an answer. The Bank Merger Act of 1960 forced regulators to adopt a more restrictive merger policy. The truly rude shock occurred the following year when the Department of Justice reversed its earlier position and filed a civil antitrust action against the approved merger of the Philadelphia National Bank and Girard Corn Exchange Bank, two large banks in Philadelphia. In 1963 the Supreme Court upheld the Justice Department's position that banks were subject to the Sherman and Clayton Acts, which were more restrictive than the Merger Act of 1960. In 1966 Congress joined the Court in implicitly criticizing bank regulators by strengthening the Bank Merger Act of 1960. A detailed analysis of recent antitrust banking law and court cases is beyond the scope of this book.[4] The important point is: there no longer is any doubt that the Justice Department working within the legal system and bank regulatory agencies by administrative determination may block any proposed merger that would result in a monopoly or substantially lessen competition in any section of the country.

---

[4]See Douglas V. Austin, "The Line of Commerce and the Relevant Geographic Market in Banking: What Fifteen Years of Trials and Tribulations Has Taught Us and Not Taught Us About the Measure of Banking Structure," in Federal Reserve Bank of Chicago, *Proceedings of a Conference on Bank Structure and Competition, 1977.*

Appendix to Chapter 21: The Saving-Investment Relationship

The saving-investment identity emphasizes that GNP is both spending and income and that households and government must refrain from acquiring commodities if firms are to maintain and increase the capital stock. Combining Equations (21–2) and (21–3) with exports (X) and imports (Z) subsumed in investment (I), and consumption (C), respectively, we express GNP as both spending and income.

(21A–1)

$$C + I + G \equiv Y \equiv Y_d + T$$

The production process gives rise to a circular flow of receipts. Firms pay households for labor services and other factors of production used to produce commodities. In addition, firms and households pay taxes. Firms do not run out of funds and the process continues because households and government use their income to acquire commodities. Households typically do not consume their entire income because they derive utility from current *and* future consumption. Households save in order to provide for the future. Private saving, S_p, is defined as disposable income minus consumption.

(21A–2)

$$\begin{aligned} S_p &\equiv Y_d - C \\ &\equiv Y - T - C \end{aligned}$$

Saving is often called a *leakage* because it equals the amount that does not flow back to the business sectors from households. Private saving measures the household sector's accumulation of financial assets, including money, which must inevitably occur when income and expenditures are not equal.

Look at Equations (21A–1) and (21A–2). Subtracting C from both sides of (21A–1) and substituting (21A–2) in (21A–1), one gets

(21A–3)

$$I + G \equiv S_P + T$$

In words, the purchases of current commodities by firms and government (I + G) must equal the commodities households do not purchase because they save and are taxed ($S_p + T$).

If there were no government so that $G \equiv T \equiv 0$ and private saving equaled total saving, then inspection of Equation (21A–3) shows that investment equals saving. The same is true when government exists, provided we recognize that government saving is an element of total saving. Analogous to households, the difference between government receipts and expenditures is called government saving, S_G.

(21A–4)

$$S_G \equiv T - G$$

It sometimes is convenient to have distinct terms for negative and positive government saving. Negative government saving is called a deficit, and positive government saving is a surplus. Total saving, S, is the sum of private and government saving.

(21A–5)

$$S \equiv S_p + S_G$$

Equations (21A–3) through (21A–5) readily imply that

(21A–6)

$$I \equiv S$$

Since Equations (21A–3) and (21A–6) follow from text Equation (21–2), the following statements are identical: during any given period of time (*a*) spending on current goods and services equals income, (*b*) total saving equals *private* investment, and (*c*) private saving plus taxes equal *private* investment plus government expenditures.

Call Equation (21A–6) the pure saving-investment equation, and let Equation (21A–3) be the modified saving-investment equation. Equation (21A–6) has a real and a financial interpretation. First, the real interpretation says that firms acquire those current goods which are not purchased by households and government. Second, households and government jointly acquire the financial claims issued by firms. (Of course, the government may incur a deficit, so that households also acquire government debt.) Since different groups save and invest, financial instruments must be associated with the saving-investment process.

The pure version of the saving-investment identity, Equation (21A–6), was preferred years ago to the modified version. Government was viewed as providing society with goods and services which are currently used up. For example, government expenditures include payments for the police protection society receives during the period. Consumption goods are also exhausted during the period. Total saving then corresponds to currently produced commodities not exhausted and available for the future.

The traditional view about government expenditures is not altogether accurate. Highways and bombers, which have long, useful lives, also are examples of government expenditures. Therefore, *private* investment or, equivalently, *total* saving may underestimate the provision for future needs. For this reason and because the analysis of fiscal policy is easier when taxes and government expenditures appear explicitly rather than being subsumed in total saving, Equation (21A–3) has gained in popularity. Equation (21A–3) views government expenditures and investment as contributing equally to economic growth.

Just as the actual expenditures-production identity is equivalent to the actual saving-investment identity, the *equilibrium* condition can be expressed by the equality of desired spending and production or by the equality of *desired saving and desired investment.* When desired saving and investment are equal, price and real output remain constant. We do not bother to prove this as one only need interpret Equations (21A–1)–(21A–6) as representing desired magnitudes. However, we do derive the relationship between desired saving and investment when desired spending is greater than income. Suppose

$$C + I + G > Y = Y_d + T \tag{21A–7}$$

Rearranging (21–12)

$$\begin{aligned} I &> Y_d - C + T - G = S_p + S_G = S, \text{ or} \\ I + G &> Y_d - C + T = S_p + T \end{aligned} \tag{21A–8}$$

In words, when desired spending is greater than income, then desired (private) investment exceeds *total* desired saving, or, equivalently, desired investment plus government expenditures exceed private saving plus taxes. Again the law of symmetry applies. Reverse the inequality in (21A–7) and what is the relationship between desired saving and investment? Desired saving exceeds investment when expenditure demand is less than supply.

How does one characterize a situation where price and output are decreasing? Is aggregate demand less than production, does desired total saving exceed investment, or does desired private saving plus taxes exceed investment plus government expenditures? All three approaches are correct and formally equivalent although they do emphasize different factors. *Prior to the 1930s aggregate demand and production were believed to be in balance most of the time, and government spending and taxes were quite low. Economists in those days emphasized the effect of policy on the composition of goods satisfying current and future needs. Therefore, the equilibrium relationship was expressed almost exclusively by the equality of desired saving and investment.* While many continue to express the equilibrium condition in the same manner, the aggregate demand-production approach is more popular today. Keynes in the 1930s stressed the likelihood of deficient aggregate demand. Restoring full employment was the primary policy objective; how policy affected the composition of output was of secondary importance. This led to expressing equilibrium as the equality of aggregate demand and production. While we think Keynes exaggerated the possibility of chronically deficient aggregate demand and unemployment, *we favor the aggregate demand-production approach because of its similarity with microeconomics*. Everyone knows that the price and/or quantity of peanuts or any other commodity fall when supply exceeds demand. You probably realized before reading this chapter that the same principle applies to commodities in general. Ask what happens when saving exceeds investment and you will get a correct answer less often. Microeconomics did not prepare us to think about equilibrium as the lack of expenditures by households being made up by business and government expenditures. Moreover, the expenditures approach does not necessarily ignore distributional effects. At several points we will emphasize the differential impact of policy on investment. While the saving- investment approach may have financial institutions lurking in the background because of its emphasis on sectoral income and expenditure imbalances, the saving-investment approach does not necessarily bring them to center stage, as we shall see later. We recognize, however, that some will disagree. For that reason we have another saving-investment appendix in Chapter 24.

Appendixes to Chapter 23

A: A Numerical Example

A numerical example of the classical model is offered here. Suppose the production function is

$$y = 25L - 0.1L^2 \qquad \text{production function} \tag{23A–1}$$

where y is output or real income, and L is labor. The derivative of the production function is the marginal physical product of labor, which is defined as the change in output per unit change of labor.

$$\Delta y/\Delta L = 25 - 0.2L \quad \text{marginal product of labor} \tag{23A–2}$$

(Those unfamiliar with calculus and unwilling to accept Equation (23A–2) on faith should read footnote 1.[1] Since calculus is not a prerequisite for this book, we use difference rather than differential notation.) Graphically, the marginal product is the slope of the production function. The slope becomes flatter and the marginal product falls as more workers are

[1]Suppose the quantity of labor changes. The new quantity of labor may be expressed as the old quantity plus the change, $L+\Delta L$, and similarly for output. Substituting $y+\Delta y$ and $L+\Delta L$ for y and L in Equation (23A–1), we get $y+\Delta y=25(L+\Delta L)-0.1(L+\Delta L)^2=25(L+\Delta L)-0.1(L^2+2L\Delta L+\Delta L^2)$. Substracting Equation (23A–1) from the last equation and dividing by ΔL gives $\Delta y/\Delta L=25-0.2L-0.1\Delta L$. As ΔL becomes small so we are at the margin, the ratio $\Delta y/\Delta L$ approaches $25-0.2L$.

hired. For example, at L = 50 Equation (23A–2) shows that the marginal product is 15; at L = 100 it is 5. (Ignore values of L greater than 125. Firms never hire so many workers that they trip over each other and have negative marginal products.) Profit-maximizing firms hire workers until the marginal product equals the real wage. Setting (23A–2) equal to the real wage and rearranging gives the demand for labor.

(23A–3) labor demand

$$25 - 0.2L^D = W/P$$
$$L^D = 125 - 5\ W/P$$

The demand for labor is negatively related to the real wage. Assume labor supply is positively related to the real wage.

(23A–4) labor supply

$$L^S = 94 + 1.2\ W/P$$

The equilibrium condition in the labor market gives the quantity of labor and real wage.

(23A–5) labor equilibrium

$$L^D = L^S$$
$$L^D = 125 - 5W/P = 94 + 1.2\ W/P = L^S$$
$$W/P = 5;\ L^D = L^S = 100$$

Substituting the equilibrium quantity of labor in the production function gives a unique full-employment output.

(23A–1′)

$$y = 25(100) - 0.1(100)^2 = 1{,}500$$

Output is derived independently of the demand for commodities.

Let us now turn to the quantity theory of money. Suppose money balances are held on the average for 0.40 of the period (k = 0.40). Money demand, M^D, is

(23A–6) money demand

$$M^D = kPy = 0.40P(1{,}500),$$

or if one prefers the Fisher "money demand" relationship,

(23A–6′)

$$M^DV = Py;\ M^D(2.5) = P(1{,}500),$$

where (23A–6) and (23A–6′) make use of the fact that y = 1,500. Suppose the money supply, M^S, is 1,200.

(23A–7) money supply

$$M^S = 1{,}200$$

Setting money demand and supply equal

(23A–8)
money equilibrium

$$M^D = M^S$$
$$M^D = 0.40P(1{,}500) = 1{,}200 = M^S$$
$$P = 2:\ M^S = M^D = 1{,}200$$

The quantity theory equation determines prices, which are proportional to the money supply. Consequently, real money balances are independent of the money supply. Real balances are 600 (1,200/2). The nominal wage is 10 since the real wage is 5. See Equation (23A–5).

Suppose aggregate expenditures are

(23A–9)

$$E = 625 + 0.6y + 0.1M/P - 17r$$ aggregate expenditures

Setting expenditures, E, equal to output, y,

(23A–10)

$$625 + 0.6y + 0.1M/P - 17r = y$$ commodities equilibrium

But the equilibrium values of real income (1,500) and real money balances (600) were determined earlier. On substituting these values in Equation (23A–10) and rearranging, the equilibrium condition in the commodities market gives the rate of interest.

(23A–10′)

$$625 + 0.60(1{,}500) + 0.1(600) - 17r = 1{,}500$$
$$r = 5$$

There is a supply and demand for bonds which can be ignored. According to Walras's Law, the bond market is in equilibrium when the labor, money, and commodities markets are in equilibrium.

Suppose the money supply doubles so that $M^S = 2{,}400$. What are the new equilibrium values of the variables? Money does not enter until Equation (23A–6). Therefore, the equilibrium output, real wage, and labor demanded and supplied are unaffected. Solving Equations (23A–6) through (23A–8), prices double, $P = 4$. Real balances still equal 600, or 2400/4. Since output and real balances are unaffected by the monetary expansion, inspection of Equation (23A–10) shows that the interest rate also is unaffected. Monetary changes only influence prices (including nominal wages).

Suppose instead that the aggregate expenditure curve shifts down so that it now equals $608 + 0.6y + 0.1M/P - 17r$. (Retain the original money supply assumption, that is, $M^S = 1{,}200$.) What are the new equilibrium values of the variables? In essence, the supposition changes Equation

(23A–9) and those that follow. Since Equations (23A–1) through (23A–8) determine income and real balances, the shift only changes the equilibrium interest rate, which now equals 4(!) percent. (This numerical exercise was constructed a *long* time ago!) Walras's Law states that some other demand of supply also changed. Presumably, the unspecified supply and demand for loanable funds (bonds) also changed.

Finally, assume that instead of the initial relationship, the money demand relationship is, $M^D = 0.5Py$, *and* the aggregate expenditure relationship is, $E = 610 + 0.6y - 0.1(M/P) - 17r$. What are the new equilibrium values of the variables? The reader who has followed the example this far knows the general approach to the problem but still wants his or her answer confirmed. In this case, only prices/wages change.[2] The new price (wage) level is 1.6 (8). This is the hoarding case. The public spends less because the demand for money balances increased.

B: Saving, Investment, and the Rate of Interest

Viewed in isolation, it appears that many interest rates could equilibrate the commodities market since aggregate demand is a function of output and real money balances in addition to the rate of interest. For example, the specific commodities market equilibrium equation used in Appendix A was

$$625 + 0.6y + 0.1M/P - 17r = y.$$

The set $y=1,500$, $M/P=600$, and $r=5$ satisfies the equation but so does $y=2,000$, $M/P=2,260$ and $r=3$, and so on. Within the context of the entire neoclassical model, however, only one rate of interest equates expenditures and output. The order of the markets analyzed in the text was not selected at random. The labor market determines real output. Given real output and velocity, the quantity theory equation yields the price level and real money balances. In the mechanical equation-solving sense, expenditures and output determine the rate of interest because the equilibrium values of the other determinants of aggregate demand are estimated elsewhere or exogenous, and the rate of interest is the remaining variable to be solved.[3] Indeed, the rate of interest does not appear in the

[2]The reader is warned that every possible mechanical modification of money demand and aggregate expenditures does not change the solution for the price level alone. Modification of two or more demand and supply relationships is a necessary but not sufficient condition for Walras's Law, which must be satisfied at all times.

[3]Restating the textual discussion somewhat more technically, in a truly general equilibrium static model where every price is an argument in all the excess demand functions one cannot say that any one market determines a price. However, the neoclassical model is not a truly general equilibrium system but can be solved recursively. "Aggregate expenditures and output determine the rate of interest" is a shorthand statement for a particular recursive structure where the noncommodity market equilibrium equations yield solutions for all the variables except the rate of interest. One then solves the commodities market equilibrium condition for the rate of interest.

labor and money market equations. It is assumed that the equilibrium interest rate is economically feasible. (Negative interest rates are not economically feasible.)

The fact that the equilibrium rate of interest in neoclassical economics can be ascertained by looking at the commodities market equilibrium relationship has baffled many modern economists. In some respects the neoclassical mode of expression has contributed toward misunderstanding neoclassical thought. Until quite recently, neoclassicists preferred to express the commodities market equilibrium relation as the equality of saving and investment instead of the equivalent equality of aggregate demand and output. The saving and investment approach highlights the fact that aggregate equilibrium does not require each economic unit to be in equilibrium, and that borrowing and lending is occurring in the background. For example, the aggregate economy is in equilibrium provided the excess commodities supply of savers, whose income exceeds spending by definition, equals the excess commodities demand of investors, who spend more than their income. After recognizing that every economic unit is not spending an amount exactly equal to its income, the logical next step is to inquire what households do with their saving and how firms acquire funds to invest. *One possibility* has savers demand bonds (lend) and investors supply bonds (borrow). Clearly, this demand and supply of bonds affect the rate of interest. Many have incorrectly concluded from the last two sentences that savers must *always* demand bonds and investors *always* supply bonds if the equilibrium rate of interest can be ascertained by the commodities market as well as the bond market. Since savers can hoard instead of demanding bonds, many claim the neoclassical model is absurd. This invalid criticism of neoclassical economics stems from a failure to recognize restrictions placed on *equilibrium* relations by Walras's Law.

When the economy is in *equilibrium,* the rate of interest determined by saving and investment also equates bond supply and demand. For simplicity, assume the government's budget balances; it neither borrows nor lends. Also assume savers and investors are distinct groups so savers do not invest, and conversely. Suppose a typical household's money balances at the beginning of the period are $1,500. Income during the period is $1,000 and consumption is $800. What happens to the household's $200 saving? In our simplified aggregate model with standard bonds (loans) and money, the household has two alternatives: it can demand bonds or it can hoard. Hoarding occurs when the demand for money is greater than the supply. The household hoards in this example when the demand for money is $1,700, $200 more than the household has.

$$\text{Saving} = \text{Bond demand} + \text{Hoarding}$$

Firms must finance their investments by either supplying bonds or dishoarding, i.e., running down their money balances.

$$\text{Investment} = \text{Bond supply} + \text{Dishoarding}$$

Inspection of the two equations above indicates that, in general, saving does not equal bond demand, and equality of saving and investment does *not* imply equality of bond supply and demand. Hoarding generally does not equal dishoarding. However, equilibrium, hardly the general case, implies certain restrictions. Given an aggregate money supply, money market equilibrium implies that hoarding, if any, just equals dishoarding. To the extent that one group is trying to build up its money balances, another group must be running them down if total money demand is to equal a fixed total supply. Therefore, when the money market is in equilibrium, the rate of interest which equates saving and investment also equates bond supply and demand. Look at the last two equations again. This is an illustration of Walras's Law. If the money and commodities markets are in equilibrium, then the last market, the bond market, must also be in equilibrium.

Appendix to Chapter 24: The Saving-Investment Approach

We presented the basic Keynesian model in order to provide the reader with a convenient review. In spite of our preference for the expenditure approach, we offer this appendix so that the chapter serves its intended purpose for those who were taught the saving-investment approach. Warning: The material in subsequent chapters is considered to be new, so that the saving-investment approach appears for the last time.

Let us derive the expression for equilibrium income in terms of the parameters and exogenous variables given in the text. As stated in Chapter 21, at equilibrium private saving plus taxes equal investment plus government spending.

(24A–1)

$$S_p + T = I + G$$

The right-hand side simply is the sum of two exogenous variables. What does the left-hand side equal? After paying taxes, income is consumed or saved. That is, private saving is disposable income minus consumption.

(24A–2)

$$S_p = y_d - C = y - T - C$$

Call private saving plus taxes modified saving, S_M, because it would equal saving if government did not exist, as Equation (24A–2) readily confirms.

(24A–3)

$$S_M = S_p + T = (y - T - C) + T = y - C$$

Modified saving is the leakage from the spending stream. Substituting the consumption Equation (24–3) given in the text,

(24A–4)

$$\begin{aligned} S_M &= y - a + bT_0 - by \\ &= -a + bT_0 + (1 - b)y \\ &= -140 + 0.75(120) + (1 - 0.75)y \quad = -50 + 0.25y \end{aligned}$$

The autonomous component of modified saving is the negative of autonomous consumption, and the sum of the marginal propensities to consume and save (modified) equal unity. As national income increases by a unit, saving increases by 1 − b, or 0.25 in our example. The S line in Figure 24A–1 graphs the saving relationship.

The injections to the spending stream are desired investment plus government expenditures, represented by a horizontal line I + G since they are independent of income. At equilibrium, leakages or the output not purchased by households equals the injections from firms and government. Setting the modified saving Equation (24A–4) equal to investment plus government expenditures, we get

FIGURE 24A–1
Saving Equals Investment plus Government Expenditures

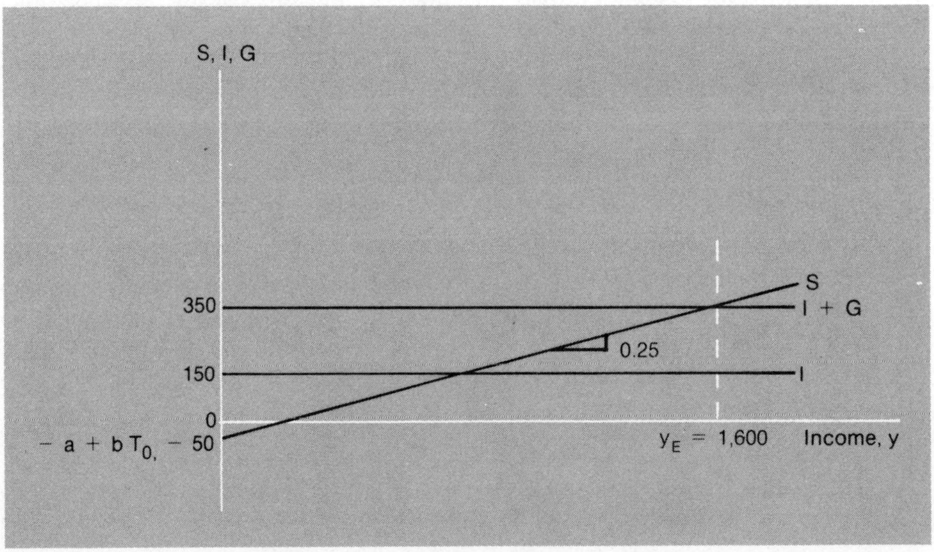

$$I_0 + G_0 = S_M$$
$$I_0 + G_0 = -a + bT_0 + (1 - b)y$$
$$y = \frac{1}{1 - b}(a - bT_0 + I_0 + G_0) = 1{,}600 \tag{24A–5}$$

In words, Equation (24A–5) says that income equals the multiplier, which is the inverse of the marginal propensity to save national income, times autonomous spending. Equations (24–5) and (24A–5) are identical, and their graphical representations, Figures 24–5 and 24A–1, are more or less complements showing the same equilibrium income. The gap between the $I + G$ and S_M curves is 400 when income is zero. The slope of the S_M curve and the rate at which the gap between the two curves is being closed are $0.25 = 1 - b = 1 - 0.75$.

Appendixes to Chapter 25

A: Inventory Theoretic Approach to the Transactions Demand for Money

Money is a medium of exchange. Ignore any other services money may perform; assume it is held only for transactions purposes. For simplicity, let all transactions be included in national income. Given these assumptions, how much money will an economic unit demand? The classicists *assumed* the average amount of money held would be proportional to income, where the proportionality factor k depended on such factors as the degree of synchronization of receipts and expenditures. The assumption seemed reasonable and had been made for so long that even Keynes accepted it unquestioningly. William Baumol and James Tobin are the doubting Thomases of monetary economics.[1] They were unwilling to assume that money demand is proportional to income. The demand for all other goods is derived from maximization or minimization principles. Why treat money differently? Extending cost minimization behavior to money demand, Baumol and Tobin found that money demand increases less than proportionally with income. In particular, money demand depends on the square root of income. More important, transactions demand depends

[1]William Baumol, "The Transaction Demand for Cash: An Inventory Theoretic Approach," *Quarterly Journal of Economics,*November 1952, pp. 545–56; and James Tobin, "The Interest Elasticity of Transactions Demand for Cash," *Review of Economics and Statistics,* August 1956, pp. 241–47.

negatively on the rate of interest. The remainder of the appendix proves the last two sentences.

Assume an individual will spend the amount y at an even rate during the time period. Our individual begins the period without any money and does not receive any income. To acquire money and spend y, the individual either sells bonds previously purchased or borrows. Assuming uniform and constant interest rates during the period, a cost minimizer is indifferent between the two ways of acquiring cash. We suppose bonds (assets) are sold. While a total of y bonds must be sold sometime during the time period, the cost minimizer decides when and how many bonds should be sold each time. For example, all y bonds could be sold at the beginning of the period, or y/2 bonds could be sold at the beginning and halfway through the period, or y/3 bonds could be sold at the beginning of each third, and so on. Express the number of times bonds are sold as y/X, where X equals the amount of bonds sold each time, called the lot size. For example, if you spend \$100 during the period (y = 100) and sold \$20 bonds each time (X = 20), then you sold bonds five times during the period.

The two components of total cost, brokerage cost and interest opportunity cost, are related to the lot size in opposite ways. Each bond purchase or sale entails a brokerage cost, b, which is the sum of commission payments to brokers and the opportunity cost of one's time spent making the bond transaction. Assuming for simplicity that the brokerage cost is independent of the the amount sold, total brokerage costs are by/X, the product of the cost per sale, b, times the number of sales, y/X. Total brokerage costs clearly are reduced by selling less frequently and increasing the lot size. Brokerage costs are minimized by selling bonds worth y at the beginning of the period. Algebraically, by/X decreases when X increases and is minimized when y = X, given that $y \geqslant X$.

Minimizing brokerage cost maximizes interest opportunity cost, however. When all the bonds are sold immediately and initial cash holdings equal the amount spent during the period, one completely foregoes interest income. By selling bonds more frequently and holding less cash and more bonds, interest opportunity cost is reduced. Since the cash acquired by selling X bonds periodically is expended at constant rate, average cash balances are X/2. Interest opportunity cost is rX/2, the product of the rate of interest, r, and average cash balances. Letting W represent total cost,

(25A–1)

$$\text{Total cost} = \text{Brokerage cost} + \text{Interest opportunity cost}$$

$$W = \frac{by}{X} + \frac{rX}{2}$$

Equation (25A–1) shows that brokerage cost is negatively and interest opportunity cost is positively related to the lot size of bond sales, X.

The decision variable is lot size. Costs are minimized by setting the derivative with respect to X equal to zero.

(25A–2)

$$\frac{dW}{dX} = -\frac{by}{X^2} + \frac{r}{2} = 0$$

Those unfamiliar with the calculus will have to accept without proof that Equation (25A–2) holds when costs are minimized. Solving Equation (25A–2) for the average cash balance, X/2, which, by definition, is the transactions demand for money, M_T^D,

(25A–3)

$$M_T^D = \frac{X}{2} = \sqrt{\frac{by}{2r}}$$

The transactions demand depends on the square root of brokerage cost and income and is negatively related to the rate of interest.

If the justification for the name *inventory theoretic* is unclear, consider the following example. A retailer sells commodities worth $1,000 at a constant rate during the period. The retailer buys a batch of commodities from the wholesaler and maintains an inventory due to acquisition costs (such as the cost of writing orders, inspecting the commodities on arrival, and paying the wholesaler's bill). Many of these acquisition costs are fixed. For example, the bookkeeping costs of paying a $30 and $300 bill are identical. Suppose acquisition costs per purchase are $12.50. The placement of large orders does tie up one's funds in large sterile inventories instead of interest earning securities. The interest opportunity cost of large inventories must be balanced against low acquisition costs. Suppose the rate of interest is 10 percent, or 0.1 written in decimal form. What is the optimal order size and, therefore, average inventory? Although some names have been changed—brokerage costs become acquisition costs—the retailer clearly faces the same problem as the person minimizing the cost of transactions balances. Substituting the numbers in this example in Equation (25A–3)

(25A–4)

$$\frac{X}{2} = 250 = \sqrt{\frac{12.50\ (1{,}000)}{2\ (0.1)}}$$

The order size X is 500, and the average inventory is 250.

B: Liquidity Preference, Risk, and Portfolio Theory

Keynes's explanation of liquidity preference has been criticized on two main grounds: (1) it is invalid in the long run, and (2) it implies only one asset is held while we observe portfolio diversification. James Tobin's explanation of liquidity preference is free of these criticisms while still stressing that money is a unit of account whose dollar price in the future is certain. Money is a risk-free asset.

Keynesian Liquidity Preference

Let us review Keynes's explanation given in the text. Assume expected *profit-maximizing* households have wealth which will not be spent during the period. They must decide which asset, money or bonds, to hold. Since the bond coupon payment always is greater than any interest payment on money, assume for simplicity that money earns no interest. The dollar value of money is fixed, but bond prices can vary. A profit maximizer will hold speculative money balances only if interest rates are expected to rise enough so that the capital loss on bonds exceeds the coupon payment. At any moment in time the expected future rate may exceed the current rate, and speculative balances may be positive. In the long run, however, the current and expected future rate coincide, invalidating Keynes's explanation for speculative balances. Constancy of the rate of interest and other economic variables characterizes long-run equilibrium, by definition. Those holding speculative balances in long-run equilibria because they incorrectly expect higher future rates of interest forego income. A profit maximizer will not suffer opportunity losses forever. Mistakes are eventually corrected; the expected rate eventually coincides with the constant long-run rate of interest, in which case profit maximizers hold bonds exclusively. While it is true that other features of the Keynesian model stress the short run, economists wanted a general explanation for liquidity preference instead of one valid only in the short run.

Even in the short run where interest rates may diverge, the Keynesian explanation implies behavior contradicted by observation. Rewriting the text's Equation (25–5) for your convenience,

(25B–1)

$$\begin{array}{cccccc} \text{Expected total dollar return} & = & \text{Coupon} & + & \text{Expected capital return} \\ R_T & = & 1 & + & (1/r_E - 1/r_0) \end{array}$$

where r_E and r_0 are the expected and current rates of interest, respectively. A profit maximizer will prefer bonds (money) when Equation (25B–1) is positive (negative). A unique switching point exists when the expected total return on bonds equals zero, the return on money. Setting Equation (25B–1) equal to zero,

$$R_T = 1 + (1/r_E - 1/r_C) = 0, \tag{25B–2}$$

where r_0 became r_C to signify the critical current rate which makes a profit maximizer indifferent between money and bonds, given the expectation of the future. Solving Equation (25B–2) for the critical rate,

$$r_C = r_E/(1 + r_E). \tag{25B–2′}$$

The critical rate, r_C, is always less than the expected interest rate. (The denominator in Equation (25B–2′) is greater than unity.) To be indifferent between money and bonds, the current interest rate must be less than the expected future rate, that is, interest rates must be expected to rise. For example, if $r_E = 0.1$, then the critical rate is approximately 0.09. An expected interest rate increase from approximately 9 percent to 10 percent causes a capital loss equal to the coupon payment.

Equation (25B–2) is rarely satisfied, and normally the household is not indifferent to money and bonds. Looking at Equations (25B–1) and (25B–2), we see that the return on bonds is positive and no speculative balances are held when the rate of interest is above the critical rate. Only money is held below the critical rate. The lines ABCD and AEFG in Figure 25B–1A graph the liquidity preference curves of persons R and S, respectively. Who expects higher interest rates, and who is wealthier? Person S expects higher future rates than person R and has a higher critical rate. Because person S expects higher rates and *lower* bond prices, person S holds sterile money balances at interest rates where person R still holds bonds. Person R is wealthier and can demand more money; BC is longer than EF. If expectations were uniform, each individual liquidity preference curve would be kinked at the same point, and the aggregate curve would have the same shape. Expectations are not uniform, however. The aggregate liquidity preference in Figure 25B–1B is a downward sloping curve precisely because expectations differ. According to Keynes, the aggregate curve is *not* downward sloping because each person holds more money as the interest rate falls. Instead, more people are supposed to sell all their bonds and hold only money. We do not observe this pattern of assets. Nearly everyone holds a diversified portfolio whose composition is relatively constant. Households do not put all their eggs in one basket.

Risk and Return Analysis

In search of a justification for speculative money demand in the long run and for portfolio diversification, James Tobin assumed that individuals calculate a probability distribution of future interest rates where the av-

FIGURE 25B–1
Liquidity Preference Curves: (A) Personal Curves and (B) Aggregate Curve

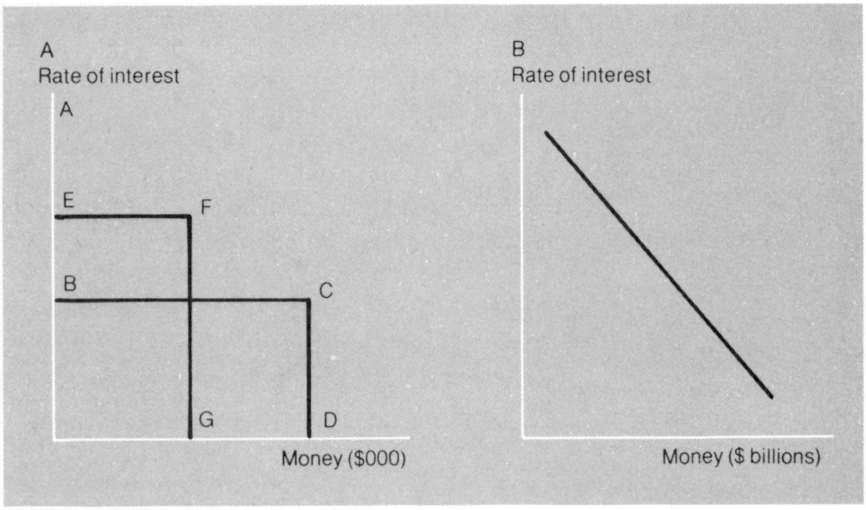

erage or expected future rate is assumed equal to the current rate.[2] Since neither a capital gain nor loss is anticipated, the expected total return on bonds equals the coupon payment, which is greater than the zero return on money. *Individuals need not hold bonds exclusively because they maximize a utility function which depends on two variables, expected return (income) and risk.* Expected return increases utility but risk decreases utility. The typical household is risk averse. It prefers a guaranteed $1 million to 50 percent chances of receiving nothing or $2 million. Although the expected return is $1 million in either case, the second case is risky. The household requires a higher expected return, perhaps $1.2 million achieved by increasing to 60 percent the probability of receiving $2 million, to be indifferent between the guaranteed and risky cases. Money does not yield a return but, being the unit of account, its return and price are certain. Bonds are risky. Although one may expect the future interest rate to equal the current rate, the expectation may not be realized. Contrary to expectations, the interest rate may rise (fall), causing capital losses (gains). Individuals normally hold both assets to earn some return and avoid some risk. The rate of interest may be viewed as the reward bondholders earn for bearing risk. Given their preferences for return and risk, households hold fewer risky bonds and more safe money as the rate of

[2]James Tobin, "Liquidity Preference as Behavior Towards Risks," *Review of Economic Studies*, February 1958, pp. 65–86. Tobin won the 1981 Nobel Prize largely on the basis of this article and his work on portfolio theory.

interest and reward for bearing risk fall. Alternatively stated, the rate of interest is the opportunity cost of holding a safe asset like money. As the rate of interest and opportunity cost of safety fall, households demand additional safe money balances. The remainder of this appendix uses graphs and algebra to prove the assertions made here and extends the analysis beyond liquidity preference proper to portfolio theory. Warning: Difficult material ahead. Proceed slowly.

The individual's basic problem is selecting the asset combination which maximizes a utility function dependent on the expected return and risk of the asset portfolio. The asset portfolio's expected return, E, is on the vertical axis of the top portion of Figure 25B–2. Risk, as measured by the standard deviation of returns, is on the horizontal axis. Indifference or constant utility curves are labeled U_i. In traditional microeconomics indifference curves are downward sloping because the two axes measure

FIGURE 25B–2
Portfolio Expected Return, Risk, and the Speculative Demand for Money

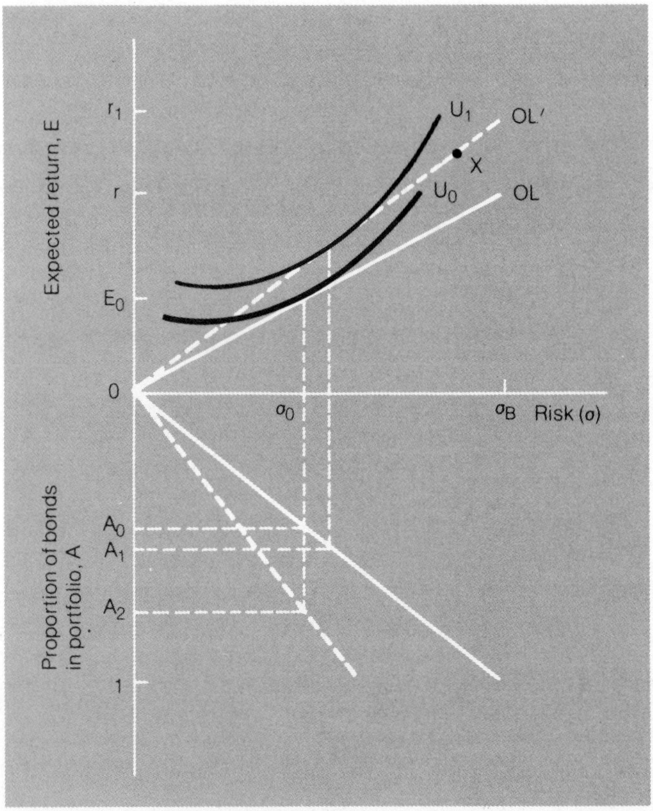

"goods" providing positive utility. In this case, however, a "bad," risk, is on one axis. To maintain constant utility, additional risk must be compensated by additional return. The indifference curves of risk averters are upward sloping.[3] A larger number subscript signifies greater utility. An individual would like to be at the far northwest portion of the graph. The opportunity locus, which here is the equivalent of the budget constraint in traditional microeconomics, limits the level of utility attainable. Let A be the proportion invested in bonds. For those anticipating that interest rates and the capital value of bonds will be constant, the expected total return on bonds equals the current rate of interest, r. The asset portfolio's expected return, E, depends on the proportion of bonds held.

(25B–3)

$$E = Ar$$

Since the zero yield on money is certain, portfolio risk, σ, also depends only on the proportion of bonds.

(25B–4)

$$\sigma = A\sigma_B,$$

where σ_B is the riskiness of bonds. The solid line in the bottom portion of Figure 25B–2 graphs Equation (25B–4) for a given σ_B. The maximum portfolio return and risk, which occur when the portfolio is fully invested in bonds, that is, $A = 1$, are r and σ_B, respectively. Solving Equations (25B–3) and (25B–4) for A, the solid opportunity locus labeled OL in Figure 25B–2 is

(25B–5)

$$E = (r/\sigma_B)\sigma.$$

The locus shows the asset portfolio's return and risk as the proportions of bonds and money vary, where the proportions can be ascertained from the bottom figure. The slope, $\Delta E/\Delta\sigma$, of the opportunity locus is r/σ_B because bonds increase portfolio return by r but also increase risk by σ_B. Maximum attainable utility occurs when the indifference curve is tangent to the opportunity locus. The utility maximizing portfolio return and risk are E_0, and σ_0, respectively, and the proportion of bonds in the portfolio is A_0. (The proportion of money is $1 - A_0$ since we are assuming two assets.)

Now assume the rate of interest rises from r to r_1. The increase is viewed as permanent and does not affect the riskiness of bonds. The solid bond proportion/portfolio risk line in the lower portion remains applicable but the opportunity locus rotates counterclockwise to OL′ as its slope

---

[3]What is the shape of the indifference curves for a Keynesian risk-neutral person who attempts to maximize return? The indifference curves would be horizontal.

steepens to r_1/σ_B. As illustrated in Figure 25B–2, the highest attainable indifference curve now is U_1. The proportion of bonds increases from A_0 to A_1 and, therefore, the proportion of money decreases as the rate of interest rises. The speculative demand and rate of interest are negatively related.

Consider some secondary and specialized issues. Suppose the government levies a proportional tax with full loss offset. That is, any loss is fully deductible against other income or a proportion of the loss is refunded. Possible gains are reduced but so are possible losses. This type of tax reduces the riskiness of bonds by the tax rate. Assuming a 20 percent tax rate, the bond proportion/portfolio risk line in the bottom portion of Figure 25B–2 rotates clockwise by the tax rate and becomes the broken line. The expected return also is lower by the tax rate. Therefore, the solid opportunity locus is unaffected by the tax. Equation (25B–5) and the slope of the locus depend on the interest rate/risk ratio, which is constant when both terms fall proportionally. Since the tax affects neither the indifference curves nor the opportunity locus, the utility maximizing *after-tax* return and risk remain constant at E_0 and σ_0, respectively. To achieve this result, the individual increases the proportion of bonds from A_0 to A_2, given the new risk curve. The tax system effectively makes the government and citizen partners. The government shares the return and risk. To maintain the preferred position after taxes, the citizen increases the pretax portfolio return and risk by holding more bonds and less money. The United States' tax system is progressive rather than proportional. Loss offset exists but, depending on the specific case, may not be complete. Therefore, the assumptions of the model are not entirely realistic for the U.S. Nevertheless, the model still may help explain the increasing demand for high risk "tax shelters."

Portfolio Theory

Let us now drop the assumption that there is one risky asset, and that expected future and current rates of interest coincide. In the single risky asset case, the asset is labeled a bond. When multiple risky assets are assumed, standard terminology differs for some reason now forgotten, and the risky assets are called stocks. Each person forms a probability distribution of rates of return for each stock and then calculates the expected (average) return and risk (dispersion) of return. A person may expect capital gains and losses, causing the expected total return to diverge from the current return. The utility maximizer first selects his optimum stock portfolio and then the optimum combination of money and the stock portfolio. What are some characteristics of the optimum stock portfolio? The expected return/risk ratio of the stock portfolio determines the slope of the opportunity locus. Looking at Figure 25B–2, a steeper opportunity locus allows one to reach a higher indifference curve. Therefore the optimum stock portfolio is that one stock or combination of stocks which has the highest estimated ratio of expected return to risk, because this ratio equals the slope of the opportunity locus. Suppose investing 70 percent of total stocks in stock G and 30 percent in stock H gives the largest return/risk ratio and generates the broken opportunity locus in Figure 25B–2.

The optimum stock portfolio typically will differ from person to person because stocks are appraised differently. Those who expect a +50 percent return on IBM stock will be buying IBM from those who expect a −50 percent return. A different appraisal is the *only* reason stock portfolios will differ. Your optimum stock portfolio, which gives the steepest opportunity locus and makes possible the highest indifference curve, depends simply on your estimates of expected return and risk. It is independent of the utility function. A very risk-averse pin-stripe banker and a mildly risk-averse nurse with identical estimates of stock performance will select the same stock portfolio, 70 percent G and 30 percent stock H in our example. Preferences for expected return and risk determine the specific point selected on the opportunity locus and, thereby, the proportion of the stock portfolio and money. For example, suppose the indifference curves drawn in Figure 25B–2 belong to our banker, who maximizes utility by holding A_1 (say, 40) percent of total assets in stock and $1 - A_1$ (say, 60) percent money. The unillustrated indifference curve for the less risk-averse nurse would be much flatter and tangent to the opportunity locus at a point such as X, where the proportion invested in stock is higher, say, 80 percent. (A vertical line from X will intersect the solid portfolio composition/risk line in the bottom portion at a point below A_1.) The conservative banker holds fewer stocks. The nurse who prefers more risk does *not* pick riskier stocks—the stocks of both the nurse and banker are divided between G and H in the same 70 versus 30 percent proportion. The nurse simply buys more of the optimum stock portfolio. A gambler borrows to buy the stock portfolio, in which case we can view his or her money holding as being negative. The optimum stock portfolio is leveraged up or down to attain the preferred return/risk combination.

Mark Twain said, "Put all your eggs in one basket and—WATCH THAT BASKET." Most people would disagree. They have many obligations and cannot spend their entire day searching for THE stock. Even those whose job is finding undervalue stocks admit that their evaluations may be wrong. Mutual funds and trust officers select widely diversified stock portfolios. While it is well known that diversification reduces risk, some are unaware that the risk reduction can be achieved *without* any sacrifice of expected return. Look at Table 25B–1. The first column shows the two equally likely rates of return, − 5 and +15 percent, earned on stock V and its expected return. The return on stocks V and W are identical, and V and

TABLE 25B–1
Diversification Reduces Risk without Changing Expected Return

	Returns on Stock V, 50 Percent Likelihood Each Outcome	*Returns on Stock W, 50 Percent Likelihood Each Outcome*	*Returns on Equal Holdings of Stocks V and W, 25 Percent Likelihood Each Outcome*
	−5	−5	−5
		+15	+5
	+15	−5	+5
		+15	+15
Expected return	+5	+5	+5

W are independent. The top portion of column 2 has four entries but only two are different. Column 3 shows that diversification reduces risk as returns are more closely centered about the expected value. Equal investments in stocks V and W reduce from 50 to 25 the likelihood of −5 and +15 percent rates of return. The expected return remains 5 percent. If portfolio diversification reduced both risk and return, it would be far less prevalent.

C: Equilibrium Adjustment Process

The intersection of the IS and LM curves forms four quadrants, labeled I, II, III, and IV in Figure 25C–1. Quadrant I is upward and rightward of the IS curve and simultaneously downward and rightward of the LM curve. The adjustments that occur when the economy is out of equilibrium are summarized by the arrows in Figure 25C–1. The arrows indicate that in quadrant I income, which is on the horizontal axis, falls (the horizontal arrow points left), and the rate of interest rises (the vertical arrow points up).

Consider first why income is falling at point A or any other point in quadrant I. To predict income changes we must compare the current situation relative to the *equilibrium* alternatives given by the IS line. A vertical line through point A intersects the IS line at a point below A. At the low point on the *equilibrium* IS line, aggregate demand equals income, by definition. Since the rate of interest is higher at point A, expenditures must be less than income, and income will be falling as shown by the horizontal arrow. *The IS curve is important because it separates the income-interest rate combinations where income will be rising from those where income will be falling.*

For reinforcement purposes, this time compare point A and the *horizontal* point on the IS line, where, by definition, income equals expen-

FIGURE 25C–1
IS and LM: Adjustments toward General Equilibrium

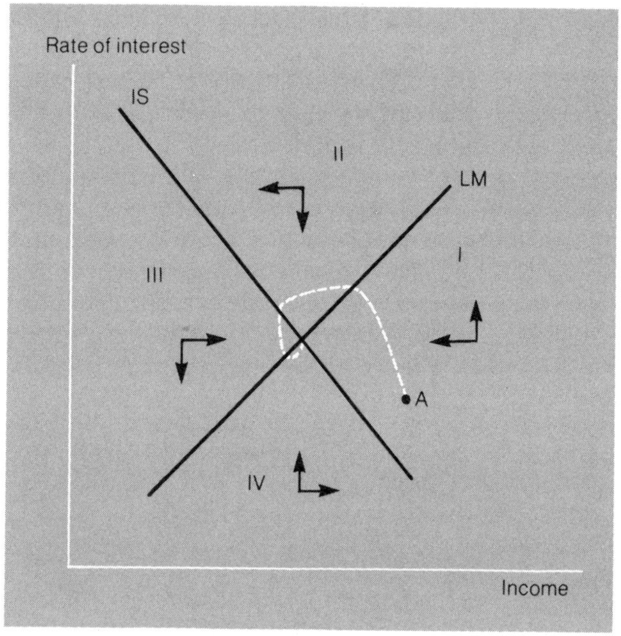

ditures. Income is greater at point A and, because the marginal propensity to consume is positive, expenditures also are greater. However, a consumption propensity less than unity implies that expenditures increase less than income. Income exceeds aggregate expenditures at point A. Unintended inventory accumulation occurs, and output falls.

Point A is one arbitrary point. The identical analysis is applicable to any other point above and to the right of the IS curve. *For any interest rate-income combination above and to the right of the IS curve, income will be falling.* Applying the same type of argument, the reader should verify that *for any interest rate-income combination below and to the left of the IS curve, income will be rising. Of course, when the economy is on the IS line, income is constant, a requirement for equilibrium.* The IS line, the product market equilibrium line, cannot be used to predict the behavior of interest rates; it solely predicts product and income changes.

Interest rate adjustments depend on the current position of the economy relative to the LM curve. For example, imagine a vertical line in Figure 25C–1 connecting point A and the LM curve, where the money supply just satisfies the transactions and speculative demand. By construction, income and the transactions demand for money are equal at the two points. The rate of interest is lower, and the amount of speculative demand is higher, at point A. Since money demand and supply are equal on the LM curve, money demand exceeds supply at point A. In the Keynesian analysis the excess demand for money leads people to borrow or, equivalently, sell bonds. The rate of interest rises. Indeed, the higher interest rate eventually induces people to be satisfied with the temporarily deficient money supply.[4]

Point A is an arbitrary point. The same argument is valid for any other point below and to the right of the LM line. *All income-interest rate combinations below and to the right of the LM line represent situations where the demand for money exceeds the supply, and the rate of interest rises*. The converse is true. *All income-interest rate combinations above and to the left of the LM line represent situations where money demand is less than supply, so the rate of interest falls. Once on the LM line there is no tendency for the rate of interest to change because the demand for and supply of money are equal*. The reader is strongly urged to pause and explain the direction of the horizontal and vertical arrows in all four quadrants.

Note the pattern of the arrows. Rotating the arrows counterclockwise 90° gives the arrows in the next quadrant. (A helpful if abhorrent reminder to the pattern formed by the arrows—linking the arrows forms a reverse swastika.) *The pattern of the arrows suggests that the economy swirls around but is inexorably propelled toward the equilibrium or resting point*. Equilibrium is the center of a whirlpool.[5] For example, suppose the economy is temporarily at point A in Figure 25C–1. The dotted curve is *one possible* equilibrium adjustment path which conforms with the pattern of the arrows. The theory does not specify the precise adjustment path. We could move directly and rapidly from A to the equilibrium without circling it.

Two "special" adjustment processes consistent with the general process just outlined are often mentioned. First, the money market does adjust more rapidly than the commodities market. At the extreme, let the money market adjust virtually instantaneously. This is represented graphically by assuming that whenever the economy is off the LM curve, it rapidly moves up or down vertically until it is back on the LM curve. It then slides along the LM until it reaches the IS–LM intersection point. A second adjustment process is represented by a series of vertical and horizontal lines which form a cobweb pattern. That is, the rate of interest and income might change sequentially instead of simultaneously. While

---

[4]As an exercise, analyze the situation by comparing point A and the point on the LM curve *horizontal* to A.

[5]Those who enjoy games can draw the IS–LM curves so that the economy is unstable and equilibrium acts as a center of centrifugal force. While such games may be fun, they do not help us understand our economy.

such a path is often assumed because of the pedagogical convenience of allowing only one variable to change at a time, the adjustment path illustrated here is more realistic. About point A the rising interest rate is simultaneously reducing the excess demand for money and investment, which causes income to fall. *At all times at least one of the variables adjusts toward equilibrium, and sometimes both variables move toward equilibrium.* For example, at every point in quadrant I income is approaching its equilibrium value. The rate of interest adjusts toward equilibrium only sometimes in this case. Some points in quadrant I, where interest rates rise, are below the equilibrium rate of interest. However, some points in quadrant I are *above* the equilibrium rate of interest, yet interest rates continue to rise. The broken equilibrium path curve illustrates the possibility of *over-shooting, where a variable is below equilibrium but rises above equilibrium*, and *undershooting, where a variable is above equilibrium and falls below equilibrium before reaching it.* The rate of interest and income may overshoot in quadrants I and IV, respectively, and the rate of interest and income may undershoot in quadrants III and II, respectively. The economy may follow upward and downward paths before settling down at equilibrium. *The more or less rhythmical short-run fluctuations which characterize industrial economies may be the result of overshooting and undershooting during the adjustment process instead of continually shifting equilibria.*

Appendixes to Chapter 26

A: IS–LM in Algebra and Numbers

This appendix first expresses Chapter 25 algebraically and numerically. In particular, we derive the IS and LM curves and the general equilibrium values of the variables. We then cover algebraically this chapter's topics in the precise order found in the text. To facilitate the suggested piecemeal use of the appendix, section headings after the first are identical to this chapter's. You will see that algebra is an extremely powerful tool; this appendix is much shorter than the chapter but covers basically all the material.

A Restatement of Chapter 25

We first derive algebraically and numerically the IS equation and then the LM equation. The two equations are subsequently combined to get the general equilibrium level of income and rate of interest.

The IS Equation. Chapter 25's three expenditure equations, consumption (25–1), government spending (25–2), and investment (25–3), are rewritten here for convenience.

(25–1)

$$\begin{aligned} C &= a + b(y - T_o) &&= a - bT_o + by \\ &= 140 + 0.75(y - 120) &&= 50 + 0.75y \end{aligned}$$

$$G = G_0 \\ = 200 \tag{25-2}$$

$$I = I_0 - er \\ = 190 - 5r \tag{25-3}$$

These three equations give the IS equation, (26A–1).

$$\begin{aligned} y &= \frac{a - bT_0 + I_0 + G_0}{1 - b} - \frac{er}{1 - b} \\ &= \frac{50 + 190 + 200}{1 - 0.75} - \frac{5r}{1 - 0.75} \\ &= 1{,}760 - 20r \end{aligned} \tag{26A-1}$$

Wait! How did we get Equation (26A–1)? The IS equation is the commodities market equilibrium equation, by definition. Therefore, set the sum of Equations (25–1), (25–2) and (25–3), which is C + I + G or aggregate expenditures, equal to y. Then rearrange, and one gets Equation (26A–1). The term b is the marginal propensity to consume national income and, in this case, the total respending propensity, ignoring interest rate effects. Investment and government spending are assumed to be independent of income. The inverse of 1 – b is the familiar multiplier. According to the IS equation (26A–1), income is (1) autonomous spending times the multiplier minus (2) the investment curtailed by the rate of interest, er, also multiplied upward. The second component distinguishes the basic and IS–LM Keynesian models; in the IS–LM model the equilibrium level of income depends on the rate of interest. In the basic model the IS curve is a vertical line at the *unique* income level because investment is totally unresponsive to the rate of interest, that is, the parameter e is zero.

The LM Equation. The LM equation indicates the equality of money demand and supply.

$$\begin{aligned} M^S &= M_0 = 300 && \text{supply} \\ \frac{M^D}{P_0} &= k'y + h - jr && \text{demand} \\ M^D &= 0.2y + 116 - 2r \end{aligned} \tag{25-6}$$

(26A–2)

$$\frac{M_0}{P_0} = k'y + h - jr, \text{ or,} \qquad \text{equilibrium, LM algebraic}$$

$$r = \frac{h - (M_0/P_0) + k'y}{j}$$

$$300 = 0.2y + 116 - 2r \qquad \text{equilibrium, LM numerical}$$

$$r = -92 + 0.1y$$

Briefly recapping these equations, the first equation assumes the money supply is totally exogenous, an assumption that will be dropped later. Total money demand, Chapter 25's Equation (25–6), has two components, transactions, $k'y$, and speculative, $h - jr$, money demand. In the numerical example the price level is set at unity. Setting supply equal to demand gives the money market equilibrium equation (26A–2) or, more simply, the LM equation.

Equilibrium Income and Rate of Interest. The general (money and commodities market) equilibrium solution, which is represented graphically by the intersection of the IS and LM curves, is determined algebraically by solving Equations (26A–1) and (26A–2) simultaneously.

(26A–3)

$$y = \frac{a - bT_0 + I_0 + G_0 - e(h - M_0/P_0)/j}{(1 - b) + (ek'/j)} = 1{,}200$$

$$r = \frac{k'(a - bT_0 + I_0 + G_0) + (1 - b)(h - M_0/P_0)}{j(1 - b) + ek'} = 28$$

We certainly do not expect anyone to memorize the general equilibrium income formula. Nevertheless, the rationale for Equation (26A–3) parallels the rationale for the much simpler income formula of the basic Keynesian model. Look at Equation (26A–2) again. If income were zero, the rate of interest would equal $(h - M_0/P_0)/j$. Investment, Equation (25–3), would then equal $I_0 - e(h - M_0/P_0)/j$. Therefore, what does the numerator of Equation (26A–3) measure? The numerator is total "autonomous" spending, the spending which would occur if income were zero. But income is not zero because firms respond to spending. The income generated by meeting the initial autonomous spending induces additional spending, and more rounds of income and spending. How much additional spending is induced per additional dollar of national income? The induced effect on consumption is the positive marginal propensity to consume, b, but the induced effect on investment is negative. As income increases by a dollar, the transactions demand for money increases by k'. To maintain equilibrium in the money market, the rate of interest must rise by k'/j. (Look at Equation (26A–2). What is the slope of the LM curve?) This reduces investment by ek'/j. The respending propensity in this case is b − (ek′/j). The denominator of Equation (26A–3) is precisely one minus the respending propensity. Just as in the basic Keynesian model, the IS–LM equilibrium level of income is autonomous spending times the multiplier, which is the inverse of one minus the respending propensity. The IS–LM income formula is more complicated because autonomous and induced spending include interest rate effects.

An Introduction to Monetary and Fiscal Policy

Suppose equilibrium income is below full-employment income. What is the effect of monetary expansion and government spending on income and the rate of interest? Differencing the general equilibrium equations (26A–3) with respect to money, M_0, and government spending, G_0, gives

$$\frac{\Delta y}{\Delta M_0} = \frac{e/P_0 j}{(1 - b) + (ek'/j)} = \frac{e/P_0}{j(1 - b) + ek'} \qquad \textbf{(26A–4)}$$

$$\frac{\Delta y}{\Delta G_0} = \frac{1}{(1 - b) + (ek'/j)} = \frac{j}{j(1 - b) + ek'} \qquad \textbf{(26A–5)}$$

$$\frac{\Delta r}{\Delta M} = \frac{-(1 - b)/P_0}{j(1 - b) + ek'} \qquad \textbf{(26A–6)}$$

$$\frac{\Delta r}{\Delta G_0} = \frac{k'}{j(1 - b) + ek'} \qquad \textbf{(26A–7)}$$

Since b lies between zero and one and all the other parameters are strictly positive and finite, both Equations (26A–4) and (26A–5) are positive—money and government spending have a positive effect on income. Equation (26A–6) is negative—monetary expansion reduces the rate of interest—and Equation (26A–7) is positive—government spending increases the rate of interest.

Determinants of the Money and Fiscal Multipliers

Inspection of Equation (26A–4) confirms that the money multiplier is large when:

1a. j is small. (Referring back to Equation (25–6), page 525, j is $\Delta M^D/\Delta r$, so that a small j means the *liquidity preference schedule is steep*.)

1b. e is large. (Referring back to Equation (25–3), page 511, e is $\Delta I/\Delta r$, so that a large e means the *investment schedule is flat*.)

1c. b is large. (b is the marginal propensity to consume.)
1d. k′ is small. (k′ is the money demand transactions coefficient.)

It follows from **1a** that the money multiplier is largest in the classical/quantity theory case where j is zero—there is no speculative demand.

Inspection of Equation (26A–5) indicates that the government spending multiplier is smaller in the IS–LM model than in the basic model since (ek′/j) is positive. The government spending multiplier tends to be large when

2a. j is large.
2b. e is small.
2c. b is large.
2d. k′ is small.

After **1a–1d**, the economic interpretation of **2a–2d** should be clear.

The Slopes of IS–LM and the Multipliers

What factors determine the slope of the IS curve? The algebraic approach readily yields the answer. Assuming the autonomous components in Equation (26A–1) are constant, first calculate the income change when the rate of interest changes.

(26A–8)

$$\Delta y = \frac{-e\Delta r}{1-b}$$

The IS curve plots the rate of interest on the vertical axis and income on the horizontal axis. Therefore, the slope of the IS curve is $\Delta r/\Delta y$, which according to Equation (26A–8) is

(26A–8′)

$$\left.\frac{\Delta r}{\Delta y}\right|_{IS} = \frac{-(1-b)}{e}$$

The slope of the IS curve depends on both the MPC and the slope of the investment schedule. Since the slope of a flat curve is (absolutely) small, by definition, a comparison of conditions **1b** and **1c** and Equation (26A–8′) indicates that as either the MPC (b) increases or the investment curve becomes flatter (e increases), the IS becomes flatter and, simultaneously, the money multiplier becomes larger. A flat IS curve unambiguously increases the money multiplier.

Differencing LM equation (26A–2) for a *given* quantity of real balances gives the slope of the LM curve.

(26A–9)

$$\left.\frac{\Delta r}{\Delta y}\right|_{LM} = \frac{k'}{j}$$

The slope of the LM curve depends on the transactions coefficient k′ and the slope of the liquidity preference curve, $(-1/j)$. A comparison of conditions **2b** and **2c** and Equation (26A–9) indicates that as either the transactions coefficient k′ decreases or the liquidity preference curve becomes flatter (j increases), the LM becomes flatter and, simultaneously, the government spending multiplier becomes larger.

B: Shifting IS–LM and the Slopes of the Liquidity Preference and Investment Curves

This appendix and C are *only* for the theoretically oriented who want to truly master the IS–LM machinery. These appendixes are very difficult because they analyze the effect of a parameter on the way a curve is shifted. The text in contrast analyzed the effect of parameters on curves which remained fixed. For example, the text's analysis of monetary policy, which shifts the LM, was limited to the determinants of the fixed IS. These appendixes indicate how the determinants of the slope of the LM also influence the direction and magnitude of the LM shift per unit change in the money supply.

For you bravehearted souls who ignored my warning, assume two economies, A and B, which are alike in *every* respect *except* for the liquidity preference relationship illustrated in Figure 26B–1A. Money demand is less responsive to the rate of interest in economy A. What shapes do the IS and LM curves take in economies A and B, and how do they respond to monetary changes? The answers are illustrated in Figure 26B–1B. Since economies A and B are assumed identical in *every* respect *except* for the liquidity preference curve, the IS curves for the two economies coincide because, by assumption, the aggregate expenditure curve is identical. The LM curves, which summarize the money demand-supply relationship, do not coincide. Recalling our earlier discussion, the slope of the LM curve partially reflects the slope of the liquidity preference schedule. The demand for speculative money balances is quite responsive to the rate of interest in economy B, and its LM curve is quite flat. In economy B any given increase in the rate of interest (vertical axis) causes a large reduction in the speculative demand, so income (horizontal axis) must increase significantly in order to generate a large compensatory change in transactions demand. The speculative demand and LM curves are inelastic in economy A. Assuming the unique IS curve intersects the two LM curves at their common point, the initial equilibrium income and rate of interest, y_0 and r_0, are the same in the two economies.

Let output be less than full employment. The monetary authorities in both economies respond by increasing the quantity of money by the same amount. The shift of the LM curve in economy B is illustrated by LM'_B in Figure 26B–1B. Income in B increases to y'_B. What is the new position of the LM curve in A, given the same monetary expansion, and where

FIGURE 26B–1

The Money Multiplier Increases When Liquidity Preference Becomes Inelastic (steep)

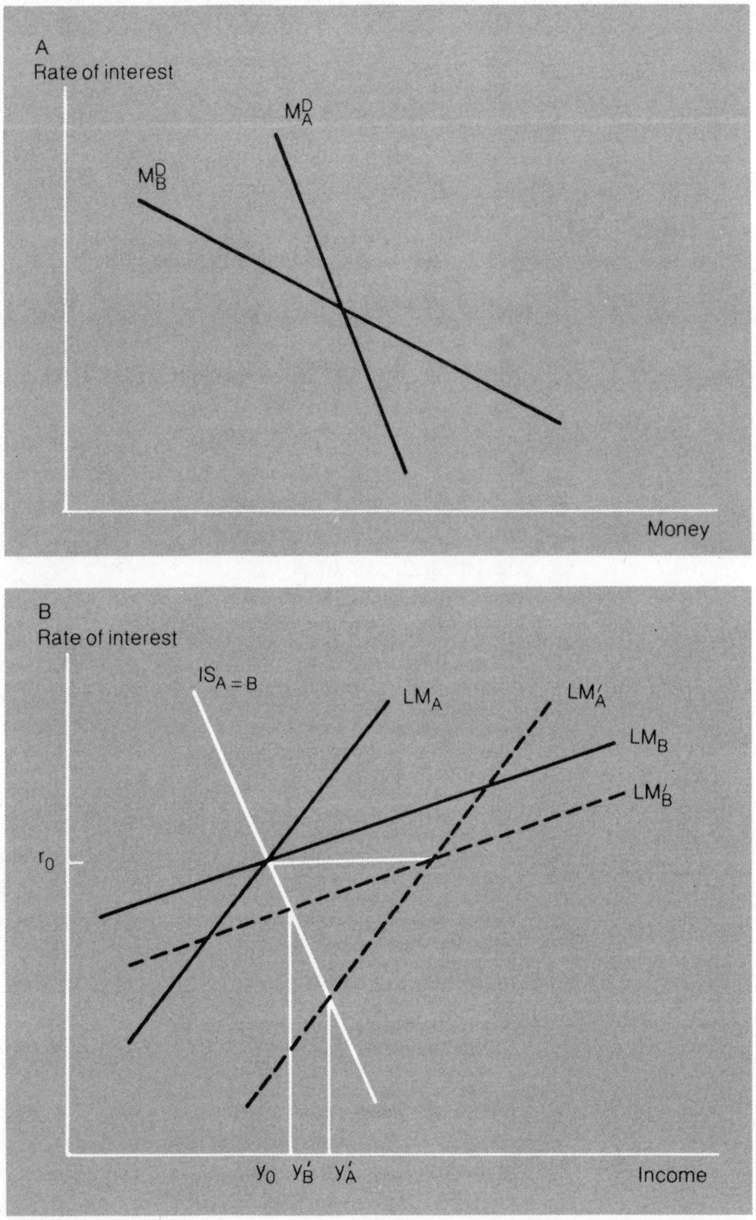

will it intersect IS? The almost universal immediate response says the LM curve in A shifts downward and intersects the IS at the same point, y'_B. Incomes in both economies were equal and increase equally. If this was your immediate reaction, check yourself. Why was Figure 26B–1 constructed? We are trying to show graphically that the money multiplier depends on the slope of the liquidity preference schedule. The new LM curve in A does not intersect the IS curve at y'_B; if it did, the money multiplier would *not* depend on the slope of the liquidity preference schedule.

When economies differ only in the responsiveness of money demand to the rate of interest, then monetary expansion shifts the LM curves by the same *horizontal* distance, as illustrated in Figure 26B–1B. Why does monetary expansion shift the LM curves by the same horizontal distance in this case? Given any monetary expansion, the total amount of money demanded must increase when the economy reaches a new equilibrium. The increase could occur because only transactions demand, only asset (speculative) demand, or some combination of the two components increases. Algebraically,

$$\Delta M^S = \Delta M^D_T + \Delta M^D_A,$$

where the terms are as previously defined. Consider our economy's demand for money at two points along a horizontal line. By virtue of being along a horizontal line where the rate of interest is constant, the speculative demand at the two points is identical, that is, $\Delta M^D_A = 0$. The transactions demand differs, however. Given any horizontal distance (income difference) between the points, the magnitude of the transactions demand difference depends on the transactions coefficient k′. In our economies A and B the transactions coefficients are identical; by assumption, only the slope of the liquidity preference differs. Therefore, the same horizontal distance produces the same change in money demand. *Because income is on the horizontal axis and has the same effect on money demand in our two economies, the LM curves shift by the same horizontal distance.* Looking at Figure 26B–1B, *the money multiplier is large when speculative money demand and, thereby, the LM curves are steep.*

We now examine the effect of the elasticity of the investment schedule on the size of the government spending multiplier. Continuing our partial equilibrium approach, let the elasticity of the investment schedule be the only difference between our hypothetical economies A and B. Figure 26B–2 draws the same LM curve for A and B. Let the investment schedule be less elastic in A than B. In economy A any given interest rate change leads to a smaller change in investment demand and, at equilibrium, income. The elasticity of the IS curves mirrors the investment schedules. Government spending financed by bonds shifts the IS curve outward. The extent of the horizontal shift is the same in both economies, as Figure

FIGURE 26B–2
The Government Spending Multiplier Is Large When the IS Curve Becomes Steep Due to an Inelastic Investment Schedule

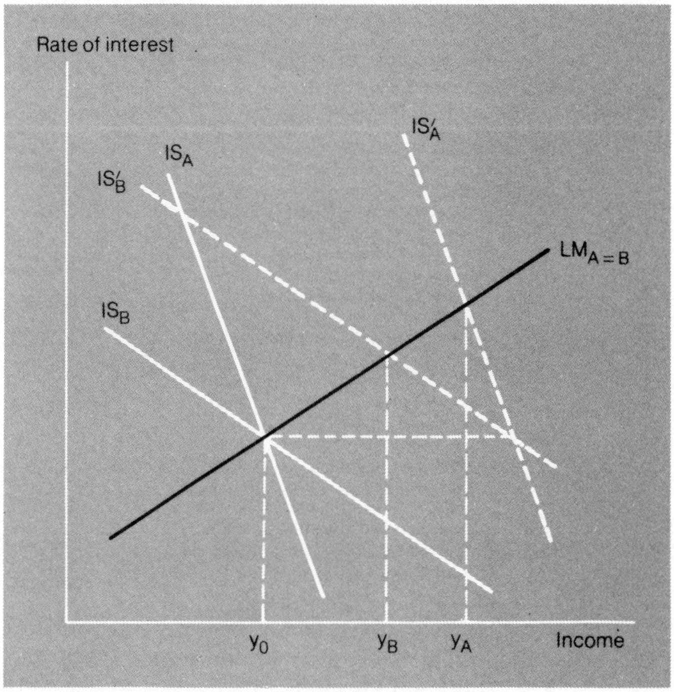

26B–2 illustrates. *The magnitude of the horizontal shift depends only on the marginal propensity to consume, which is assumed equal in both economies, because along a horizontal line the rate of interest and its effects are being held constant.* Income increases more in economy A, where the investment and IS curves are relatively inelastic.

C: Shifting IS–LM, the Transactions Coefficient, and the Marginal Propensity to Consume

The careful reader recalls that the slope of the LM also depends on the transactions coefficient k′. In particular, the LM curve is flat (steep) when k′ is small (large), *ceteris paribus*. According to Table 26–2, the money multiplier is large when k′ is small. Therefore, *the money multiplier is large when the LM curve is flat due to a small transactions coefficient*. We just demonstrated that *the money multiplier is large when speculative money demand and, thereby, the LM curve are steep*. The last two italicized sentences imply that *there is no consistent relationship between the slope of the LM curve and the money multiplier*. The money multiplier is large when the

LM is (1) steep due to an inelastic speculative money demand, or (2) flat due to a small transactions demand coefficient. The money multiplier is small when the LM curve is steep due to a large transactions demand coefficient. One has to know why the LM is steep before one can state whether the multiplier will be large or small.

We first examine the effect of the money transactions coefficient k' on the IS–LM curves. Assume two economies, A and B, which are alike in every respect except that the transactions coefficient is greater in economy B, $k'_B > k'_A$. What are the shapes of the IS–LM curves in the two economies, and how do they shift when monetary policy changes? The answers are illustrated in Figure 26C–1. The IS curves for the two economies coincide; the IS curve is independent of money demand, the sole difference between A and B. The LM curve is steeper in economy B. For a unit increase in income (horizontal axis), the amount demanded for transactions increases more in economy B, by assumption. To maintain equilibrium the speculative demand must decrease more in B and, therefore, the interest rate (vertical axis) must rise more since the speculative demand is assumed equally responsive to the rate of interest. Assume the unique IS

FIGURE 26C–1

The Money Multiplier Is Large When the LM Curve Is Flat Due to a Small Transactions Coefficient

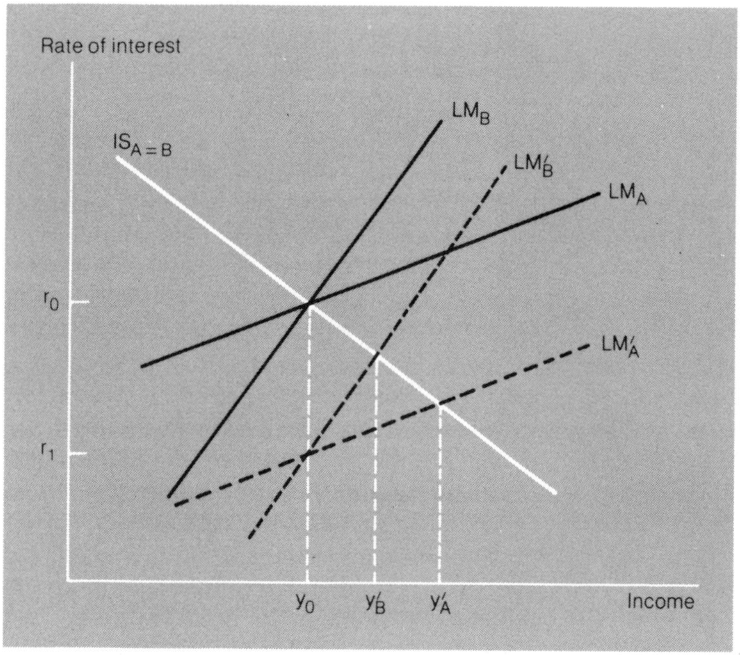

curve intersects the two LM curves at their common point.[1] Monetary expansion in economy B shifts its LM curve to LM'_B, and income increases to y'_B. Given the same monetary expansion in A, where is its new LM curve located? If we can ascertain one point on the new LM curve we can draw the entire curve because monetary expansion causes parallel shifts. The LM curves of the two economies shift *vertically* the same distance. The point (y_0,r_1) is on LM'_B and LM'_A. *The rate of interest is on the vertical axis. The extent of the vertical shift of the LM curve depends on the responsiveness of money demand to the rate of interest, as measured by the slope of the liquidity preference curve.* If the liquidity preference curve is steep, then the LM shifts down more because the interest rate has to fall more to produce a given change in the amount of money demanded. The same responsiveness of money demand to the interest rate is illustrated graphically by equal vertical shifts of the LM curve. The vertical shift is independent of the transactions coefficient because along a vertical line the transactions demand and income are constant, by construction. The same vertical shift implies that the LM_A curve shifts horizontally a greater distance. Looking at Figure 26C–1, the flat LM curve intersects the IS curve further to the right, that is, $y'_A > y'_B$. When the LM curve is flat because the transactions coefficient is small, the money multiplier is large.

A similar "paradox" is true for fiscal policy and the IS curve. *There is no consistent relationship between the slope of the IS curve and the government spending multiplier.* Test your supreme mastery of IS–LM analysis by carefully explaining and illustrating the following propositions:

1. The IS curve is very flat (steep) when the marginal propensity to consume (MPC) approaches one (zero).
2. The magnitude of the *horizontal* shift of the IS is directly related to the MPC.
3. Assume two economies, A and B, are alike in every respect except that the MPC is greater in economy B. Government spending in this case shifts the IS curves upward the same *vertical* distance, and income increases more in economy B, where the IS curve is flat.

Proposition 3 and Appendix B imply that one must know why the IS is steep before one can state whether the government spending multiplier will be large or small. Because of the monetarist-Keynesian disagreement about the investment schedule, it is typically assumed that the slope of the IS reflects *only* the slope of the investment curve. In *this* case a steep IS does imply a large fiscal multiplier. In *general*, however, a steep IS does *not* imply a large fiscal multiplier. If the IS curve is steep because the MPC is small, the fiscal multiplier also is small.

---

[1] We are also assuming a fixed element to transactions demand so that the LM curves intersect.

Index

C

F

N

T

W

Y–Z

This book has been set Compugraphic, in 10 and 9 point Times Roman, leaded 2 points. Part and chapter numbers are 30 point and 36 point Helvetica Bold; part and chapter titles are 24 point Helvetica Bold. The size of the type page is 36 by 47 picas.